Communications in Computer and Information Science 875

Commenced Publication in 2007
Founding and Former Series Editors:
Phoebe Chen, Alfredo Cuzzocrea, Xiaoyong Du, Orhun Kara, Ting Liu,
Dominik Ślęzak, and Xiaokang Yang

More information about this series at http://www.springer.com/series/7899

Yongtian Wang · Zhiguo Jiang
Yuxin Peng (Eds.)

Image and Graphics Technologies and Applications

13th Conference on Image and Graphics Technologies
and Applications, IGTA 2018
Beijing, China, April 8–10, 2018
Revised Selected Papers

Editors
Yongtian Wang
Beijing Institute of Technology
Beijing
China

Yuxin Peng
Peking University
Beijing
China

Zhiguo Jiang
Beihang University
Beijing
China

ISSN 1865-0929   ISSN 1865-0937 (electronic)
Communications in Computer and Information Science
ISBN 978-981-13-1701-9   ISBN 978-981-13-1702-6 (eBook)
https://doi.org/10.1007/978-981-13-1702-6

Library of Congress Control Number: 2018950528

This Springer imprint is published by the registered company Springer Nature Singapore Pte Ltd.
The registered company address is: 152 Beach Road, #21-01/04 Gateway East, Singapore 189721, Singapore

Preface

It was a pleasure for us to organize the 13th Conference on Image and Graphics Technologies and Applications (IGTA 2018). The conference was organized under the auspices of Beijing Society of Image and Graphics, and was held during April 8–10, 2018, at Beihang University in Beijing, China. The conference series is a premier forum for image processing, computer graphics, and related topics, including but not limited to image analysis and understanding, computer vision and pattern recognition, big data mining, virtual reality and augmented reality, and image technology applications. It provides an excellent platform for exchanging new ideas, new approaches, new techniques, new applications, and new evaluations.

The conference program includes keynotes presentations, oral papers, posters, demos, and exhibitions. This year we received a total of 138 submissions for technical presentation. Each of the manuscripts was assessed by at least two reviewers, with some of them being assessed by three reviewers. After careful evaluation, a total of 64 manuscripts were selected for oral and poster presentations.

We are grateful for the efforts of everyone who helped to make this conference a success. We are grateful to the reviewers who completed the reviewing process on time. The host, Beihang University, took care of the local arrangements for the conference, and extended a warm welcome to all the attendees.

The conference continues to provide a leading forum for cutting-edge research and case studies in image and graphics. We hope that you will also find the conference proceedings inspiring and useful.

April 2018   Yongtian Wang

Organization

General Conference Chairs

Yongtian Wang   Beijing Institute of Technology, China
Zhiguo Jiang   Beihang University, China

Executive and Coordination Committee

Guoping Wang   Peking University, China
Chaowu Chen   The First Research Institute of the Ministry of Public
     Security of P.R.C., China
Mingquan Zhou   Beijing Normal University, China
Shengjin Wang   Tsinghua University, China
Chenglin Liu   Institute of Automation, Chinese Academy of Sciences,
     China
Yao Zhao   Beijing Jiaotong University, China
Qingming Huang   University of Chinese Academy of Sciences, China

Program Committee Chairs

Yuxin Peng   Peking University, China
Zhenwei Shi   Beihang University, China
Ran He   Institute of Automation, Chinese Academy of Sciences,
     China

Organizing Chairs

Yue Liu   Beijing Institute of Technology, China
Fengying Xie   Beihang University, China
Xiaoru Yuan   Peking University, China

Research Committee Chairs

Xiaohui Liang   Beihang University, China
Xiangyang Ji   Tsinghua University, China
Jian Yang   Beijing Institute of Technology, China

Publicity and Exhibition Committee Chairs

Lei Yang   Communication University of China
Fengjun Zhang   Software Institute of the Chinese Academy of Sciences,
     China

Program Committee Members

Henry Been-Lirn Duh	La Trobe University, Australia
Takafumi Taketomi	NAIST, Japan
Jeremy M. Wolfe	Harvard Medical School, USA
Yiping Huang	Taiwan University, China
Youngho Lee	Mokpo National University, South Korea
Nobuchika Sakata	Osaka University, Japan
Seokhee Jeon	Kyunghee University, South Korea
Xiaoru Yuan	Peking University, China
Ran He	Institute of Automation, Chinese Academy of Sciences, China
Jian Yang	Beijing Institute of Technology, China
Xiangyang Ji	Tsinghua University, China
Yue Liu	Beijing Institute of Technology, China
Huimin Ma	Tsinghua University, China
Kun Zhou	Zhejiang University, China
Xin Tong	Microsoft Research Asia
Liang Wang	Institute of Automation, Chinese Academy of Sciences, China
Yanning Zhang	Northwestern Polytechnical University, China
Huijie Zhao	Beijing University of Aeronautics and Astronautics, China
Danpei Zhao	Beijing University of Aeronautics and Astronautics, China
Cheng Yang	Communication University of China, China
Jun Yan	Journal of Image and Graphics
Shihong Xia	Institute of Computing Technology, Chinese Academy of Sciences, China
Weiqun Cao	Beijing Forestry University, China
Kaichang Di	Institute of Remote sensing and Digital Earth, Chinese Academy of Sciences, China
Xucheng Yin	University of Science and Technology Beijing, China
Fuping Gan	Ministry of Land and Resources of the People's Republic of China
Xueqiang Lv	Beijing Information Science and Technology University, China
Jianbo Liu	Communication University of China
Hua Lin	Tsinghua University, China
Xiaozhu Lin	Beijing Institute of Petrochemical Technology, China
Hua Li	Institute of Computing Technology, Chinese Academy of Sciences, China
Yan Jiang	Beijing Institute of Fashion Technology, China
Jing Dong	Institute of Automation, Chinese Academy of Sciences, China
Yankui Sun	Tsinghua University, China
Li Zhuo	Beijing University of Technology, China
Qingyuan Li	Chinese Academy of Surveying and Mapping, China

Jiazheng Yuan	Beijing Union University, China
Yiding Wang	North China University of Technology, China
Aiwu Zhang	Capital Normal University, China
Mingzhi Cheng	Beijing Institute of Graphic Communication, China
Yahui Wang	Beijing University of Civil Engineering and Architecture, China
Guoqiang Yao	Beijing Film Academy, China
Siwei Ma	Peking University, China
Liang Liu	Beijing University of Posts and Telecommunications, China
Bin Liao	North China Electric Power University, China

Contents

Visual Simulation of the Interaction Between Spray Droplets
and Plant Canopy 1
  Wei-long Ding, Yan Xu, Zang-xin Wan, Lin-feng Luo, and Jin Meng-jie

An Improved Weighted-Least-Squares-Based Method for Extracting
Structure from Texture. 11
  Qing Zuo and Lin Dai

A Method for Detecting Flower Collision Based on Spherical Projection 22
  Tingrong Cao, Ling Lu, Wenli Wang, Lihua Li, and Lei Wang

The Research on AGV Visual Guided Under Strong Noise 35
  Xiaohong Zhang, Yifan Yang, Wanli Xing, and Hong Zhang

Schatten-p Norm Based Linear Regression Discriminant Analysis
for Face Recognition 45
  Lijiang Chen, Wentao Dou, and Xia Mao

A Framework for Multi-view Feature Selection via Embedding Space 57
  Junhao Zhang, Yuan Wan, and Yuting Pan

Image Mosaic Based on Pixel Subtle Variations 70
  Siqi Deng, Xiaofeng Shi, and Xiaoyan Luo

Object Detection Based on Multiscale Merged Feature Map 80
  Zhaohui Luo, Hong Zhang, Zeyu Zhang, Yifan Yang, and Jin Li

Characterization of Kinoform X-Ray Lens Using Image Stitching Method
Based on Marked Structures. 88
  *Wenqiang Hua, Keliang Liao, Zhongzhu Zhu, Qili He, Weifan Sheng,
  Peiping Zhu, Qingxi Yuan, and Jie Wang*

AMGE: A Tongue Body Segmentation Assessment Method
via Gradient Energy 98
  Jing Qi, Zhenchao Cui, Wenzhu Yang, Gang Xiao, and Naimin Li

A Study of Preschool Instructional Design Based on Augmented
Reality Games 106
  Xiaodong Wei, Dongqiao Guo, and Dongdong Weng

Research on Gas-Liquid Mixing Method Based on SPH 114
  Mingjing Ai, Aiyu Zheng, and Feng Li

Improving Authentic Learning by AR-Based Simulator   124
  Xiaodong Wei, Dongqiao Guo, and Dongdong Weng

Multimodal Visual Analysis of Vector-Borne Infectious Diseases   135
  Xiaohui Qiu, Fengjun Zhang, Hongning Zhou, Longfei Du, Xin Wang,
  and Geng Liang

The Research of Dongba Culture Virtual Museum Based on Human
Factor Engineering   146
  Yuting Yang and Houliang Kang

A Novel Algorithm of Contour Tracking and Partition
for Dongba Hieroglyph   157
  Yuting Yang and Houliang Kang

Real-Time Soft Shadow by A-Buffer.   168
  Dening Luo and Jianwei Zhang

Rock-Ring Accuracy Improvement in Infrared Satellite Image
with Subpixel Edge Detection.   180
  Huan Zhang, Cai Meng, and Zhaoxi Li

A Combined Local-Global Match for Optical Flow   192
  Yueran Zu, Wenzhong Tang, Xiuguo Bao, Ke Gao, and Mingdong Zhang

Progressive Cross-Media Correlation Learning   201
  Xin Huang and Yuxin Peng

Spatio-Temporal Context Tracking Algorithm Based on Master-Slave
Memory Space Model   212
  Xu Li, Yong Song, Yufei Zhao, Yun Li, Shangnan Zhao, Guowei Shi,
  and Xin Yang

Synthesizing Training Images for Semantic Segmentation   220
  Yunhui Zhang, Zizhao Wu, Zhiping Zhou, and Yigang Wang

A Solution to Digital Image Copyright Registration Based
on Consortium Blockchain   228
  Jing Zeng, Chun Zuo, Fengjun Zhang, Chunxiao Li,
  and Longshuai Zheng

Scene Classification of High-Resolution Remote Sensing Image Using
Transfer Learning with Multi-model Feature Extraction Framework.   238
  Guandong Li, Chunju Zhang, Mingkai Wang, Fei Gao,
  and Xueying Zhang

A Novel Image Encryption Scheme Based on Hidden Random Disturbance
and Feistel RPMPFrHT Network. 252
   Guozhen Hu, Xuejing Kang, Zihui Guo, and Xuanshu Luo

Fall Detection System Based on Mobile Robot 263
   Pengfei Sun, Anlong Ming, Chao Yao, and Xuejing Kang

Detecting Infrared Target with Receptive Field and Lateral Inhibition
of HVS 272
   *Yufei Zhao, Yong Song, Shangnan Zhao, Yun Li, Guowei Shi,
   and Zhengkun Guo*

A Novel System for Fingerprint Orientation Estimation 281
   *Zhenshen Qu, Junyu Liu, Yang Liu, Qiuyu Guan, Ruikun Li,
   and Yuxin Zhang*

A Method for Segmentation and Recognition of Mature Citrus
and Branches-Leaves Based on Regional Features. 292
   Sa Liu, Changhui Yang, Youcheng Hu, Lin Huang, and Longye Xiong

Accurate Depth of Field Rendering with Integral Image. 302
   *Yang Yang, Yanhong Peng, Huiwen Bian, Lanling Zeng,
   and Liangjun Wang*

Image Matching for Space Objects Based on Grid-Based Motion Statistics. . . 310
   Shanlan Nie, Zhiguo Jiang, Haopeng Zhang, and Quanmao Wei

CNN Transfer Learning for Automatic Image-Based Classification
of Crop Disease 319
   *Jingxian Wang, Lei Chen, Jian Zhang, Yuan Yuan, Miao Li,
   and WeiHui Zeng*

Learning to Segment Objects of Various Sizes in VHR Aerial Images 330
   *Hao Chen, Tianyang Shi, Zhenghuan Xia, Dunge Liu, Xi Wu,
   and Zhenwei Shi*

Deep Multi-scale Learning on Point Sets for 3D Object Recognition 341
   Yang Xiao, Yanxin Ma, Min Zhou, and Jun Zhang

Maneuver Detection of Uncooperative Space Objects with Space-Based
Optical Surveillance 349
   Shufeng Shi, Peng Shi, and Yushan Zhao

RGB-T Saliency Detection Benchmark: Dataset, Baselines, Analysis
and a Novel Approach. 359
   *Guizhao Wang, Chenglong Li, Yunpeng Ma, Aihua Zheng, Jin Tang,
   and Bin Luo*

Double δ-LBP: A Novel Feature Extraction Method for Facial
Expression Recognition   370
   Fang Shen, Jing Liu, and Peng Wu

Temporal-Spatial Feature Learning of Dynamic Contrast Enhanced-MR
Images via 3D Convolutional Neural Networks.   380
   *Xibin Jia, Yujie Xiao, Dawei Yang, Zhenghan Yang, Xiaopei Wang,
   and Yunfeng Liu*

Long-Term Tracking Algorithm with the Combination of Multi-feature
Fusion and YOLO.   390
   *Sicong Jiang, Jianing Zhang, Yunzhou Zhang, Feng Qiu,
   Dongdong Wang, and Xiaobo Liu*

An Image Retrieval Method Based on Color and Texture Features
for Dermoscopy Images.   403
   Xuedong Song, Fengying Xie, Jie Liu, and Chang Shu

A Discriminative Feature Learning Based on Deep Residual Network
for Face Verification   411
   Tong Zhang, Rong Wang, and Jianwei Ding

Abnormal Event Detection by Learning Spatiotemporal Features in Videos. . . .   421
   Xiaofeng Zhang, Rong Wang, and Jianwei Ding

Template-Guided 3D Fragment Reassembly Using GDS   432
   Congli Yin, Mingquan Zhou, Yachun Fan, and Wuyang Shui

Automatic Mass Detection from Mammograms with Region-Based
Convolutional Neural Network   442
   *Yifan Wu, Weifeng Shi, Lei Cui, Hongyu Wang, Qirong Bu,
   and Jun Feng*

Study on Comfort Prediction of Stereoscopic Images Based
on Improved Saliency Detection   451
   Minghan Du, Guangyu Nie, Yue Liu, and Yongtian Wang

Deep Convolutional Features for Correlation Filter Based Tracking
with Parallel Network   461
   Jinglin Zhou, Rong Wang, and Jianwei Ding

Robust and Real-Time Visual Tracking Based on Single-Layer
Convolutional Features and Accurate Scale Estimation.   471
   Runling Wang, Jiancheng Zou, Manqiang Che, and Changzhen Xiong

A Method of Registering Virtual Objects in Monocular Augmented
Reality System   483
   Zeye Wu, Pengrui Wang, and Wujun Che

A Fusion Approach to Grayscale-Thermal Tracking with Cross-Modal
Sparse Representation   494
    Lin Li, Chenglong Li, ZhengZheng Tu, and Jin Tang

Image Set Representation with Robust Manifold Regularized
Low-Rank Approximation   506
    Bo Jiang, Yuan Zhang, Youxia Cao, and Bin Luo

Adaptively Learning Background-Aware Correlation Filter
for Visual Tracking   517
    Zichun Zhang, Xinyan Liang, and Chenglong Li

Quality Assessment for Pansharpening Based on Component Analysis   527
    Liangyu Zhou, Xiaoyan Luo, and Xiaofeng Shi

Deep Belief Network Based Vertebra Segmentation for CT Images   536
    Syed Furqan Qadri, Mubashir Ahmad, Danni Ai, Jian Yang,
    and Yongtian Wang

Semantic Segmentation of Aerial Image Using Fully
Convolutional Network   546
    Junli Yang, Yiran Jiang, Han Fang, Zhiguo Jiang, Haopeng Zhang,
    and Shuang Hao

Research of Opinion Dynamic Evolution Based on Flocking Theory   556
    Shan Liu and Rui Tang

Research of User-Resource Relationship Based on Intelligent Tags
in Evolution Network   566
    Shan Liu and Kun Huang

A Method of Detecting Human Head by Eliminating Redundancy
in Dataset   578
    Chao Le and Huimin Ma

Application of Ghost Images for Object Detection and Quality Assessment . . .   586
    Nan Hu, Huimin Ma, and Xuehui Shao

An Effective and Efficient Dehazing Method of Single Input Image   596
    Fu-Qiang Han, Zhan-Li Sun, and Ya-Min Wang

Study on User-Generated 3D Gestures for Video Conferencing System
with See-Through Head Mounted Display   605
    Guangchuan Li, Yue Liu, Yongtian Wang, and Rempel David

A Novel Exhibition Case Description Method of Virtual
Computer-Aided Design   616
    Xinyue Wang, Xue Gao, and Yue Liu

An Automatical Camera Calibration Method Based
on Coded Ring Markers.   626
    Yulan Chang and Hongmei Li

A Survey on Dynamic Hand Gesture Recognition Using Kinect Device.   635
    Aamrah Ikram and Yue Liu

Collaborative Simulation Method for Research of Armored Equipment
Battle Damaged   647
    Jun-qing Huang, Wei Zhang, Wei Liu, and Tuan Wang

Author Index   657

Visual Simulation of the Interaction Between Spray Droplets and Plant Canopy

Wei-long Ding[✉], Yan Xu, Zang-xin Wan, Lin-feng Luo,
and Jin Meng-jie

College of Computer Science and Technology,
Zhejiang University of Technology, Hangzhou, China
wlding@zjut.edu.cn

Abstract. Spraying pesticides for crops is a common phenomenon in the management process of crop planting, and a key factor influencing the development of plants and plant ecosystems. An effective method is therefore proposed to visually simulate the interaction between spraying droplets and a plant canopy. In this method, a model to describe spraying droplets was first built and then the spraying scene was simulated by using the technique of Particle Systems. The smoothed particle hydrodynamic (SPH) method was employed to simulate the physical laws of the spraying. The plant model was discretized to a skeleton with control points and the deformation of the plant under the influence of the spraying droplets was simulated. The experimental results showed that the proposed method can simulate this deformation.

Keywords: Spray model · Plant canopy · Scene interaction
Virtual plant model · Visualization

1 Introduction

The interaction between plants and environmental factors is a key direction in the research of virtual plants. At present, many researchers have devoted themselves to the interaction of plants with environmental factors such as light, wind, raindrops, or spraying droplets. Spraying pesticides is common in crop management. By utilizing virtual plant models, the transmission and deposition processes of spray droplets in the plant canopy can be simulated [1]. The behavior of spray droplets interacting with plant leaves can be analyzed through this kind of model [2]. Besides, the use of virtual plant models can help agronomic experts to analyze the diffusion rule of pathogens [3, 4] and the biology of insect pests [5] in a crop community intuitively and effectively, and can also reduce the dosage of pesticides.

In the interactive simulation of plants and spray droplets, related studies have been done. By combining the droplet motion model with the three-dimensional structure of plants, Dorr *et al.* developed a model which can simulate the status of droplets drifting around the different plant structures [6]. However, their plant structure model is simple and assumes that once the droplet is intercepted by blades, it adheres to the leaves without any other actions. In fact, the behavior of a droplet hitting a leaf may include adhesion, splitting, and splashing, so their models have difficulty simulating the physical

© Springer Nature Singapore Pte Ltd. 2018
Y. Wang et al. (Eds.): IGTA 2018, CCIS 875, pp. 1–10, 2018.
https://doi.org/10.1007/978-981-13-1702-6_1

principles involved in this process. In subsequent studies, they used an improved process-based model to predict the interaction between the leaves and the spray droplets, as well as the droplet deposition on plant leaves [7]. Mercer et al. established a physical model to describe the droplet retention on the leaves of different plant species [8]. The model has four aspects: the trajectory description of the droplet, the collision of the droplets with the leaves, the drop of the droplets, and the description of the structure of the canopy. However, the simulation of canopy structure is only in two-dimensional space. Therefore, it is very difficult for their work to simulate the deposition and drift of the droplets in the 3D canopy. Yang et al. presented an approach to animate realistic interactions between tree branches and raindrops, based on physical theory [9], but they did not consider the properties and the actions after collision of raindrops.

A new method to simulate the interaction between spray droplets and a plant canopy is proposed in this paper. It produces better spray visualization effects, maintains the physical law of the spray scene, and reduces the computational cost required for the spray model simulation. The deformation of a rice plant under the influence of spray droplets is done by using GPU, which improves rendering efficiency and realizes real-time rendering.

2   The Construction of the Spray Model

The interaction between the spray droplets and a plant is very complex, because the movements of the droplets may have many possibilities, such as adhesion, rebound or splitting, and the plant may deform and shake under the influence of the droplets. So it is difficult to simulate this common phenomenon realistically. In order to improve the spray visualization effects and retain the physical characteristics of particle motion as much as possible, two types of particles with different properties are used in this article: (1) the physical properties inside the spray scene are simulated by using Smoothed Particle Hydrodynamics (SPH) [10, 11], to calculate the stress deformation of plants from spray impact, and (2) the visualization effect is simulated by using a particle system without the flow dynamics properties.

2.1   Building the Spray Model Based on SPH

SPH is a meshless Lagrangian method to simulate a fluid [10]. Compared with traditional spray simulation methods such as the Euler or Lagrangian methods, SPH is simple and quick. SPH discretizes the fluid into many particles, which particles interact with each other to form a complex fluid motion. The SPH algorithm consists of two parts, particle force movement and physical quantity transfer between particles.

(1) Particle force movement: The force of the particle in the spray scene is computed as shown in Eq. 1:

$$F = F_{ex} + F_p + F_v \tag{1}$$

Where F_{ex} is the external force such as gravity, air resistance, and so on. If we only consider gravity, $F_{ex} = mg$ is given by the Newton's second law of motion, where m represents the mass of the particle and g represents gravity. F_p is the force produced by the pressure difference inside the spray model, and is the negative gradient of the pressure field. So $F_p = -\nabla P$, where ∇P is the gradient of the pressure field of the fluid. F_v is the traction force brought about by the difference between the particles' velocities. Its value is related to the viscosity coefficient of the droplet and the velocity Laplacian, $F_v = \mu \nabla^2 u$, where μ represents the viscosity coefficient inside the spray and u represents the viscosity. Substituting these three equations into Eq. 1, the result is shown in Eq. 2 [12, 13]. After dividing by ρ, the acceleration of the particle in the spray model can be obtained as shown in Eq. 3, and then the speed of the particles can be resolved to update the position of the particles.

$$\rho a = \rho g - \nabla p + \mu \nabla^2 u \tag{2}$$

$$a = g - \frac{\nabla p}{\rho} + \frac{\mu \nabla^2 u}{\rho} \tag{3}$$

(2) Transmission of the physical quantity between particles: In order to solve the problem of interaction between particles, SPH introduced the smoothing kernel. The smoothing kernel means that the scalar and vector physical properties of a particle will gradually spread to the surrounding particles, and the farther the distance from the particles, the smaller impact will be. This function, which gradually decreases as the distance increases, is referred to as the smoothing kernel function, and the maximum radius that a particle can affect is called the smoothing kernel radius. As showed in Fig. 1, for the particle P_0, the radius of the dotted circle is its smoothing kernel radius, so only P_1, P_2, P_3, and P_4 can be affected by P_0. For every point in the spray scene (whether it is a particle or not), any physical quantity can be computed simply by summing the values of that quantity at nearby particles, weighted by the smoothing kernel (see Eq. 4 below).

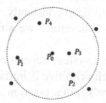

Fig. 1. Schematic diagram of SPH smoothing kernel

As we can get a physical quantity at every point easily, the force of the spray on the plant can be calculated. Moreover, the acceleration of every point of the plant and its position information can be updated.

For any point P_0 in the spraying scene, there are particles P_1, P_2, P_3 ..., P_n in the range of the smoothing kernel radius r, and the physical quantity S is calculated as follows [14]:

$$S(P_0) = \sum_n S_n \frac{m_n}{\rho_n} W(P_0 - P_n, r)$$ (4)

Where m_n and ρ_n are the mass and density of the particle P_n, r is its radius of influence, and $W()$ is the smoothing kernel function, which represents the influence from P_n. It is necessary to calculate the density ρ, the pressure P and the velocity u in order to obtain acceleration information of every point in the spray.

From the Eq. 1 we can see that the force at every point in the spray scene is the sum of the external force F_{ex}, the pressure F_p and the viscous force F_v, so if we compute each of these force, the Eq. 1 can be expanded as follow [12, 13]:

$$a_0 = g + \frac{45mK}{\pi h^6} \sum_n \frac{\rho_0 + \rho_n}{\rho_0 \rho_n} (r - d)^2 + \frac{45m\mu}{\pi r^6} \sum_n \frac{u_0 - u_n}{\rho_0 \rho_n} (r - d_n)$$ (5)

Where g is the direction of gravity, K is the temperature-dependent spray parameter, and μ is the viscosity coefficient of the spray. By using Eq. 5, the movement of every object in the spray can be derived. This equation is derived using one of the smoothing kernel functions [12, 13]:

$$W = \begin{cases} \frac{15}{2\pi r^3} \left(-\frac{d^3}{2r^3} + \frac{r^2}{h^2} + \frac{h}{2r} - 1 \right), & (0 \leq d \leq r) \\ 0, & (d < 0, d > r) \end{cases}$$ (6)

2.2   Spray Visualizations Using Particle System

Particle Systems simulate objects with large deformations, such as smoke, by controlling a large number of primitives. Primitives can be drawn fast and accurately as textured billboards using the parallelism of a GPU. So a particle system is utilized for the visualization of the spray model. Spray scenes are mainly composed of two parts; one is the large droplets, which will drop constantly. The other is small droplets, such as spray near large droplets [15]. Therefore, we simulate the spray by mixing two particle systems.

All the properties of the particle system depend on the time t. At the beginning of the particle system, the state of each primitive is initialized, including position, texture, trajectory, and so on. The primitive's initial position is $P(x, y, z)$. The trajectory of the primitive is based on the Newtonian mechanics formula $P_t = P + u\Delta t$, where P_t is the updated position, P is the current position, u is the velocity of primitive, and Δt is the frame update time. The velocity u of the primitive is calculated by the Newtonian mechanics acceleration formula $u_t = u + F_e\Delta t$. Here F_e is the force on the primitive, which is gravity in this paper, u_t is the updated speed, and u is the current speed. The billboard texture library is generated with unique styles of textures for the particles and textures are matched randomly from the library when initialize the texture of the primitive in order to make the visualization of the spray model more varied. A primitive is considered to be dead and popped from the render queue when its position is lower than the ground, at $y = 0$. For each new time t, first, primitives are initialized and pushed into the render queue, second, dead primitives are removed, and finally, positions of the primitives are updated according to the trajectories.

3 Simulation of the Interaction Between Spray Scene and a Rice Plant

Skeletal animation is already used to simulate human motion [16]. Here it is expanded to plant models. Using a GPU and the technique of skeleton animation to simulate the deformation of rice plants, and adding skeletons and control points according to morphological characteristics of rice models, we can complete the simulation of the deformation effectively.

3.1 Discretization of the Rice Model

In this paper, the skeleton is inserted on the basis of the rice model in [17]. First, the traces of rice leaf and stem are described by baselines. Second, the skeleton is added and control points are added to the skeleton's joints. Then the skeleton is optimized by adding new control points to the rice model for more realism. The specific steps are listed as follows:

Step 1: In order to elaborate the algorithm conveniently, the rice model is simplified as shown in Fig. 2a. Firstly, a curve called the baseline is used to mark the midline of the leaf and stem of rice. Then the baseline is used to mark and number leaves and stems, as showed in Fig. 2b. Where curve s represents the baseline of the main stem of the rice model, s_i is the ith line segment of primary branch bottom up the main stem. If there are branches on the segment s_i, then the baseline of nth branch segment from the growth point of s_i is represented as s_{in}, and so on. l is the baseline of the leaves, numbered starting from the growth point of the stem where the leaves are growing, e.g., l_i is the ith leaf of the stem counting from the growth point, and the leaves on the branch are numbered in the same way. In Fig. 2b, s is the baseline of the main stem of the rice plant, respectively, l_1, l_2, l_3, l_4 and l_5 are the baselines of leaves of the main stem of the rice plant.

Step 2: After obtaining the baselines of rice leaves, we should add control points at the beginning and end of the baselines and connect them as the skeleton. As showed in Fig. 2c, point A, B, ..., F are control points, line segment AC, DE (blue line in the Fig. 2) and so on are skeletons of the rice model. For example, for the baseline l_3, the point D and E are control points, and the line segment DE is l_3's skeleton.

Step 3: Because of some baselines with too large a curvature, the rice model cannot be described exactly by simply adding control points at the endpoints, e.g., baseline l_2 and skeleton AC in Fig. 2c. As the curvature of l_2 is too large, the morphology of this rice leafs can't be described by one skeleton. So, baseline l_2 needs to be described as multiple end-to-end brother skeletons, by adding new control points between A and C. Figure 3 shows two different curvature baselines. The baseline's curvature of Fig. 3a is relatively gentler, but Fig. 3b shows a baseline requiring new control points between control point A and B. The specific method is shown in Fig. 3b: find the point C with the largest distance d to the baseline AB. If d is greater than a certain value ε, we put a control point at point C, and then connect CB and CA. We repeat doing this process until the maximum such distance is less than ε.

Step 4: Add control points and skeleton for all baselines. The results are shown in Fig. 2d. The line segment AH is the plant's root skeleton. The line segment AC, DF, and DE is each other's brother-skeleton, and they are all sub-skeletons of the line segment AM. Control points connect skeletons, and make up the whole skeleton of rice.

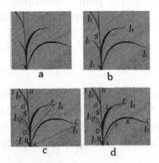

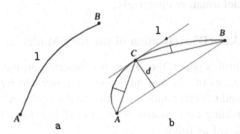

Fig. 2. Rice plant skeleton addition   **Fig. 3.** Add a new control point for baseline

3.2 Deformation of Rice Model

After adding the skeleton for a rice plant model, the force analysis is carried out for each control point. We calculate the force and acceleration in the spray scene in order to calculate the movement of the control point, and complete the deformation of rice model in the spray scene. The specific steps are listed as follows:

Step 1: At the control point A inside the spray scene, as showed in Fig. 4, find the SPH particles in its smoothing kernel radius, which are P_1, P_2, P_3 and P_4 in the figure.

Step 2: Calculate the acceleration of the control point A in the spray scene. Since the rice model the control point is located at is keeping a dynamic equilibrium without spraying, the gravity is compensated by its support. This means the external force F_{ex} is 0, so the external force factor is removed.

Step 3: The displacement amount Δd of the control point A is obtained from the calculated acceleration, so update the position of the control point A to the position A'. The position of the skeleton I is changed into I' (the red line) as given in Fig. 4.

Step 4: For every point m on I', the further distance from its own root node, the greater degree of bending it has. So, for every point m on I', its displacement is calculated as $s = \Delta d * \frac{Bm}{BA'}$, where Bm is the distance from every point m to the control point, BA' is the length of the skeleton the control point is located at. Final position m' of the point m is calculated as shown in Fig. 4, to finally obtain the bending effect as the green line.

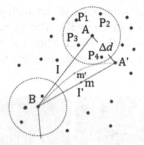

Fig. 4. Movement of the control points in spray scene

4 Simulation Results and Analysis

This article simulates a spray scene based on Unity3D. With C# scripting language, we use SPH to complete the simulation of the physical quantity inside the spray scene, and the visualization effect of the spray scene is completed with the particle system. The computer hardware is Intel(R) Core(TM) i5-3230 M CPU @ 2.60 GHz, 8 GB RAM, NVIDIA GeForce GT 650 M GPU.

Figure 5 indicates the effect of different initialization number n for each frame; they are respectively 10, 25, 50, and 100. As a result of using two different particle systems to respectively simulate the large droplets and small droplets, the spray scene appears hazy and is more realistic. As the primitive is just a two-dimensional texture, this paper uses billboard technology in order to see the whole spray from different viewpoints, which makes the direction of the viewpoint always orthogonal to the primitives so that the number of required primitives is reduced without affecting the rendering effect.

Fig. 5. Variation of the spray effect of different number primitives

Compared with the previous work, our method uses a particle system to simulate the visualization effect of the spray, instead of using SPH to reconstruct a surface when simulating the spray scene, which greatly reduces the amount of calculation. Also, the number of primitives is decreased by the use of billboard technology. The fps during the simulation is maintained at 15 frames or more, which conform to real-time rendering requirements.

This paper is based on skeleton animation and GPU hardware acceleration. The skeleton and control points are attached to the existing rice model, the force analysis and displacement of the control points are carried out to produce the rice model's deformation. Finally, the visual simulation of interaction between the spray and the canopy of the rice is completed in Unity3D. The visual effect of the simulation is shown in Fig. 6, where Fig. 6a is the effect when the rice model is not forced, and Fig. 6b shows the effect that the rice model starting to deform and swing as it is forced.

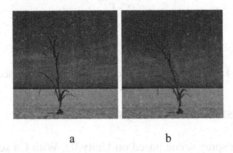

a   b

Fig. 6. The rice model is subjected to force deformation in the spray

It can be seen from Fig. 6b that the rice model is deformed in the spray scene. The main stem has deviated from the original position, which results in a swinging effect. The leaves of rice have bending of different degrees, which correlates with the deformation of a rice plant in real life. Compared with the traditional SPH method, this method achieves higher efficiency of spray scene rendering by separating numerical simulation and scene rendering. Besides, compared with other method based only on particle systems [19], this method can accurately describe the movement of spray droplets in the scene.

5 Discussion and Conclusions

Comparable simulations of plant foliage deformation in a rain or spray scene [9, 18] could not achieve real-time rendering due to the large amount of calculation. This paper reduces the amount of computation for the deformation and improves the efficiency of rendering by introducing a method based on GPU acceleration and skeleton animation.

In the aspect of spray simulation, this paper uses a particle system to simulate the visualization effect of the spray, and the billboard textures for the spray particles reduce the number of graphics primitives and improve the rendering efficiency. But the contact pattern between the spray model and the air cannot be obtained exactly, so that the spray scene cannot be subjected to force deformation analysis, for example, the spray scene should be deformed when affected by wind. In the future, we intend to divide the primitives into surface primitives and internal primitives in order to simulate the wind force on the spray.

When adding control points for the rice model, a new control point is added to the middle of the leaves because of the fact that a single skeleton cannot be used to describe accurately the morphology of the leaves whose curvature is too large, as shown in Fig. 3. The value of ε determines whether the control points are added or not. On the choice of ε, this article simply makes visualization affect a standard to select the value of ε, which is certainly not rigorous enough. Therefore, we intend to determine the value of ε in future work by experimenting with the leaves in the real world and observing the deformation of the blades by applying pressure.

In this paper, a spray simulation algorithm combining particle system with smoothed particle hydrodynamics (SPH) is proposed for the interaction between spray and rice canopy. Based on GPU skeleton animation, the force deformation of rice plants in a spray scene was simulated. First, the skeletons and control points are added to the virtual model of rice. Second, the acceleration of the control point in the spray scene is calculated to obtain the displacement of the control point. Finally, the deformation of the rice model is obtained.

A plant canopy has a complex topology that greatly increases the difficulty of simulating the interaction of spray and rice. The work in this paper is just a beginning; there are still many problems to be studied in the future. Based on the droplet deposition simulation model, we can study the efficiency and cost of a droplet propagation path tracking algorithm in order to track the physical processes in which each droplet particle propagates within the canopy of the plant. Moreover, the visualization algorithm of droplet behavior based on graphics processor will be studied so as to simulate deformation process, splash process, aggregation process, and slip process on the blade.

Acknowledgments. This work was supported by the National Natural Science Foundations of China (31471416, 61571400) and the Natural Science Foundations of Zhejiang Province (LY18C130012). The authors are grateful to the anonymous reviewers whose comments helped improve this paper.

References

1. Dorr, G.J., et al.: Combining spray drift and plant architecture modeling to minimize environmental and public health risk of pesticide application. In: Proceedings of 2005 International Congress on Modeling and Simulation. Melbourne, Australia, pp. 279–285 (2005)
2. Mercer, G., Sweatman, W.L., Elvin, A., et al.: Process driven models for spray retention by plants. In: Proceedings of the 2006 Mathematics in Industry Study Group, pp. 57–85. Mathematics in Industry study group Press, New Zealand (2006)
3. Robert, C., Fournier, C., Andrieu, B., Ney, B.: Coupling a 3D virtual wheat (Triticum aestivum) plant model with a Septoria tritici epidemic model (Septo3D): a new approach to investigate plant–pathogen interactions linked to canopy architecture. Funct. Plant Biol. **35** (1–2), 997–1013 (2008)
4. Li, J., Tang, L., Chen, C.: Visualization of canopy endophytes space distribution based on virtual plant. J. Central South Univ. Forest. Technol. **32**(6), 138–141 (2012)

5. Hanan, J., Prusinkiewicz, P., Zalucki, M., et al.: Simulation of insect movement with respect to plant architecture and morphogenesis. Comput. Electron. Agric. **35**, 255–269 (2002)
6. Dorr, G., Hanan, J., Adkins, S., Hewitt, A., O'Donnell, C., Noller, B.: Spray deposition on plant surfaces: a modeling approach. Funct. Plant Biol. **35**, 988–996 (2008)
7. Dorra, G.J., Kempthorneb, D.M., Mayob, L.C., et al.: Towards a model of spray–canopy interactions: interception, shatter, bounce and retention of droplets on horizontal leaves. Ecol. Model. (2013). https://doi.org/10.1016/j.ecolmodel.2013.11.002
8. Mercer, G., et al.: Process driven models for spray retention by plants. In: Proceedings of the 2006 Mathematics-In-Industry Study Group, New Zealand, Auckland, pp. 57–85 (2006)
9. Meng, Y., En-Hua, W.: Approach for physically-based animation of tree branches impacting by raindrops. J. Softw. **22**(8), 1934–1947 (2011)
10. Stam, J., Fiume, E.: Depicting fire and other gaseous phenomena using diffusion processes. In: Proceedings of SIGGRAPH, Los Angeles, pp. 129–136 (1995)
11. Desbrun, M., Gascuel, M.P.: Smoothed particles: a new paradigm for animating highly deformable bodies. In: Boulic, R., Hégron, G. (eds.) Computer Animation and Simulation 1996. Eurographics, pp. 61–76. Springer, Vienna (1996). https://doi.org/10.1007/978-3-7091-7486-9_5
12. https://thecodeway.com/blog/?p=161
13. https://wenku.baidu.com/view/2c1750b8f121dd36a32d823e.html
14. Monaghan, J.J.: An introduction to SPH. Comput. Phys. Commun. **48**(1), 89–96 (1988)
15. Nielsen, M.B., Sterby, O.: A two-continua approach to Eulerian simulation of water spray. ACM Trans. Graph. **32**(4), 67 (2013)
16. Ji, Z., Zhang, J.: Programmable GPU technology in skeletal animation. Comput. Eng. Appl. **44**(22), 77–80 (2008)
17. Weilong, D., Tao, X., Lifeng, X., et al.: Calculation method of rice canopy leafarea based on virtual model. Trans. CASE **33**(2), 192–198 (2017)
18. Frasson, R.P.M., Krajewski, W.F.: Rainfall interception by maize canopy: development and application of a process-based model. J. Hydrol. **489**, 246–255 (2013)
19. Ding, W., Chen, S., Wu, F.: An simulation algorithm for simulate splashing process of raindrops based on physical laws. J. Zhejiang Univ. Technol. **42**(5), 586–590 (2014)

An Improved Weighted-Least-Squares-Based Method for Extracting Structure from Texture

Qing Zuo$^{(\boxtimes)}$ and Lin Dai

China Digital Video (Beijing) Limited, Beijing, China
{zuo_qing,dai_lin}@cdv.com

Abstract. Extracting meaningful structures from textured images is an import operation for further image processings such as tone mapping, detail enhancement and pattern recognition. Researchers have pay attention to this topic for decades and developed different techniques. However, though some existing methods can generate satisfying results, they are not fast enough for realtimely handling moderate images (with resolution $1920 \times 1080 \times 3$). In this paper, we propose a novel variational model based on weighted least square and a very fast solver which can be highly parallelized on GPUs. Experiments have shown our method is possible to operate images with resolution $1920 \times 1080 \times 3$ realtimely.

Keywords: Texture · Structure · Weighted least squares · GPU

1 Introduction

Many images of natural scene or human-created art contain texture, such as dry river bed and graffiti on wall bricks. Decomposing an image into a structure layer and a texture layer is an important operation for subsequent image processing, such as tone mapping, detail enhancement, image understanding and other tasks. Over the last decades, many researchers have contributed to exploring structure-preserving methods.

We roughly classify these structure-preserving methods into two groups. The first group is local filters which explicitly computes a filtering output as a weighted average of local neighbor pixels. The early work is bilateral filter [1], and later many researchers have improved it by accelerating the computation speed [2–4] or using different computation models [5–7]. This group of methods are typically efficient. When parameters are chosen, the computational complexity is often a linear-time dependent on the number of image pixels only. However, a common limitation of these essentially local filters is that they cannot fully determine whether or not some of the edges should be removed.

The second group of structure-preserving methods are based on global optimization. They build an energy model which usually includes a data term and a smoothness term [8–13]. The data term prevents the result image go far from

© Springer Nature Singapore Pte Ltd. 2018
Y. Wang et al. (Eds.): IGTA 2018, CCIS 875, pp. 11–21, 2018.
https://doi.org/10.1007/978-981-13-1702-6_2

the input, and the smoothness term penalizes the energies of edges. Thanks to seeking the output image in such a global manner, the optimization-based methods often achieve the state-of-the-art results in a large range of image processing tasks. However, the speed of the optimization-based methods are much slower than the local filters.

In this paper, we propose a variational model based on weighted least squares (WLS) for extracting the structure layer of an image with texture. With different weighting schemes, our model can handle different type of image processing tasks. And, as will be elaborated later, Farbman's WLS model [10] and Xu's RTV model [11] can be seen as special cases of our model using certain weighting scheme. Moreover, to obtain comparable computational performance with the local filters, we develop a highly efficient solvers to solve our model which can be parallelized on GPUs.

2 Variational Model

Structure-texture decomposition problems that do not require extensive texture information are often formulated as minimizing an energy function comprising the data term and prior smoothness term. We start with a basic formulation for the structure-preserving image smoothing task which serves as a simple example to provide some intuition.

In image smoothing, given an input image I^* (for simplicity, we only consider single channel images), a desired output I is obtained by minimizing the following weighted least squares (WLS) energy function

$$E(I) = E_{data}(I) + \lambda E_{sm}(I), \tag{1}$$

where λ is a coefficient. And the data term E_{data} and smoothness term E_{sm} are given as

$$E_{data}(I) = \int_\Omega |I(t) - I^*(t)|^2 dt, \tag{2}$$

$$E_{sm}(I) = \int_\Omega \psi(t)|(\partial_x I)(t)|^2 + \phi(t)|(\partial_y I)(t)|^2 dt. \tag{3}$$

Here Ω is the image domain, and ψ, ϕ are weighting fields for $\partial_x I$ and $\partial_y I$ respectively. The data term is to make the extracted structures similar to those in the input image. And by choosing different weighting fields of ψ and ϕ, one can obtain different smoothed results.

Here, we give a general model of ψ, ϕ as

$$\psi = g_1 * \frac{g_2 * |\partial_x I|^r}{|g_3 * (\partial_x I)|^s + \epsilon}, \quad \phi = g_1 * \frac{g_2 * |\partial_y I|^r}{|g_3 * (\partial_y I)|^s + \epsilon}, \tag{4}$$

where g_1*, g_2*, g_3* are Gaussian filtering operations, s and t are two norms, and $\epsilon \geq 0$ is a small value.

By setting the norms of data term and smoothness term to $0 < p \leq 2$ and $0 \leq q \leq 2$ respectively, a more complex energy model can be derived as following.

$$E(I) = \int_{\Omega} |I(t) - I^*(t)|^p dt$$
$$+ \lambda \int_{\Omega} g_1 * \frac{g_2 * |\partial_x I|^r}{|g_3 * (\partial_x I)|^s + \epsilon} |\partial_x I|^q dt + \lambda \int_{\Omega} g_1 * \frac{g_2 * |\partial_y I|^r}{|g_3 * (\partial_y I)|^s + \epsilon} |\partial_y I|^q dt. \quad (5)$$

3 Method

In this section, we first present the approach to solve a simple form of the variational model. Setting ψ and ϕ to some known values α and β respectively, and using quadratic energy for data term and smoothness term, we obtain the following simple formulation

$$E_0(I) = \int_{\Omega} |I(t) - I^*(t)|^2 dt + \lambda \int_{\Omega} \alpha(t)|(\partial_x I)(t)|^2 + \beta(t)|(\partial_y I)(t)|^2 dt. \quad (6)$$

This model is the same as Farbman's WLS model [10] except the latter is in a discrete form.

The Euler-Lagrange equation of Eq. 6 is

$$I - I^* = \lambda \partial_x(\alpha I_x) + \lambda \partial_y(\beta I_y). \quad (7)$$

This is a linear system which can be solved very fast which will be described later.

3.1 Iterative Approach

The complex model described by Eq. 5 is hard to solve. Alternatively, we use an iterative approach to handle the high nonconvexity in ψ and ϕ. In the kth ($k >= 1$) iteration, ψ and ϕ are computed using the result I^{k-1} of the last iteration (let $I^0 = I^*$). Thus ψ and ϕ are known values in the kth iteration. Moreover, when the data term is not quadratic, we change it to the following form

$$E_{data}(I^k) = \int_{\Omega} \frac{1}{|I^{k-1}(t) - I^*(t)|^{2-p} + \epsilon} \cdot |I^k(t) - I^*(t)|^2 dt. \quad (8)$$

Similarly, the smoothness term is changed to

$$E_{sm}(I^k) = \int_{\Omega} \psi(t) \frac{1}{|(\partial_x I^{k-1})(t)|^{2-q} + \epsilon} \cdot |(\partial_x I^k)(t)|^2$$
$$+ \phi(t) \frac{1}{|(\partial_y I^{k-1})(t)|^{2-q} + \epsilon} \cdot |(\partial_y I^k)(t)|^2 dt. \quad (9)$$

Donate

$$\alpha = \psi \frac{1}{|\partial_x I^{k-1}|^{2-q} + \epsilon}, \quad \beta = \phi \frac{1}{|\partial_y I^{k-1}|^{2-q} + \epsilon}, \quad \gamma = \frac{1}{|I^{k-1} - I^*|^{2-p} + \epsilon}.$$

The complex model of Eq. 5 in the kth iteration is simplified to Eq. 10.

$$E(I^k) = \int_\Omega \gamma(t)|I^k(t) - I^*(t)|^2 dt + \lambda \int_\Omega \alpha(t)|(\partial_x I^k)(t)|^2 + \beta(t)|(\partial_y I^k)(t)|^2 dt. \quad (10)$$

The Euler-Lagrange equation of Eq. 10 is

$$\gamma(I^k - I^*) = \lambda \partial_x(\alpha I_x^k) + \lambda \partial_y(\beta I_y^k). \quad (11)$$

It is very similar to Eq. 7.

3.2   Fast Linear Solver

Traditionally, the linear systems are solved by using iterative solvers such as Preconditioned Conjugate Gradient (PCG) [10,11]. This type of solvers needs to explicitly build the matrices and a GPU implementation cannot achieve high speedup.

   To solve the linear system fast, we deploy Successive Over Relaxation (SOR) method which is a fast version of the Gaussian-Seidel iteration method [14]. The term $\partial_x(\alpha I_x)$ is discretized as (with an inner forward derivative and an outer backward derivative)

$$(\partial_x(\alpha I_x))[i,j] = \alpha[i,j]I[i,j+1] - \alpha[i,j]I[i,j] + \alpha[i,j-1]I[i,j-1] - \alpha[i,j-1]I[i,j],$$

where i is the row index and j is the column index. Similarly, $\partial_y(\beta I_y)$ is discretized as

$$(\partial_y(\beta I_y))[i,j] = \beta[i,j]I[i+1,j] - \beta[i,j]I[i,j] + \beta[i-1,j]I[i-1,j] - \beta[i-1,j]I[i,j].$$

Algorithm 1. Red-Black Iteration

Input: Input image I with resolution $W \times H$, weighting fields α, β, γ, parameter
       $\omega \in [1,2)$, num of iteration $nIter$
Output: Output image I
1: **for** $i = 1 : nIter$ **do**
2:     $I = RedBlackKernel(I, W, H, \alpha, \beta, \gamma, \omega, 0)$;
3:     $I = RedBlackKernel(I, W, H, \alpha, \beta, \gamma, \omega, 1)$;
4: **end for**

The SOR iteration method does not need to explicitly build any matrix and thus is fast. To further accelerate it on a graphic card, we modify the SOR iteration to a red-black manner. The pixels are distributed into two groups, red group with $mod(i + j, 2) == 0$ and black group with $mod(i + j, 2) == 1$. In each iteration, all red group pixels are first updated, and then black group. A significant advantage of red-black iteration is when handling a pixel in one group, its neighbor pixels are all in the other group. Thus, it can be highly parallelized on GPUs. See Algorithms 1 and 2 for details.

Algorithm 2. Red-Black Kernel

Input: Input image I with resolution $W \times H$, weighting fields α, β, γ, parameter
$\quad\quad\quad\omega \in [1, 2)$, a flag b (0 for Red group, 1 for Black group)
Output: Output image I
1: **for** parallel $i = 1 : H, j = 1 : W$ **do**
2:$\quad$ **if** $mod(i + j) \neq b$ **then**
3:$\quad\quad$ continue;
4:$\quad$ **end if**
5:$\quad$ $\sum = 0, \sigma = 0$;
6:$\quad$ **if** $j > 1$ **then**
7:$\quad\quad$ $\sum = \sum +\alpha[i, j - 1]$;
8:$\quad\quad$ $\sigma = \sigma + \alpha[i, j - 1] * I[i, j - 1]$;
9:$\quad$ **end if**
10:$\quad$ **if** $j < W$ **then**
11:$\quad\quad$ $\sum = \sum +\alpha[i, j]$;
12:$\quad\quad$ $\sigma = \sigma + \alpha[i, j] * I[i, j + 1]$;
13:$\quad$ **end if**
14:$\quad$ **if** $i > 1$ **then**
15:$\quad\quad$ $\sum = \sum +\beta[i - 1, j]$;
16:$\quad\quad$ $\sigma = \sigma + \beta[i - 1, j] * I[i - 1, j]$;
17:$\quad$ **end if**
18:$\quad$ **if** $i < H$ **then**
19:$\quad\quad$ $\sum = \sum +\beta[i, j]$;
20:$\quad\quad$ $\sigma = \sigma + \beta[i, j] * I[i + 1, j]$;
21:$\quad$ **end if**
22:$\quad$ $I[i, j] = \sigma / \sum *\omega + I[i, j] * (1 - \omega)$;
23: **end for**

---

4   Experiments and Comparison

We have tested our method on different input images. We use the same Gaussian
kernel for the three Gaussian filters (i.e. $g1 = g2 = g3$) in each experiment. The
parameter ϵ is fixed to be $1e^{-3}$ for all experiments. Note that a very small value
of ϵ cannot generate smoothed results which is also found by Xu [11] (also see
Fig. 1). In all presented experiments, we vary λ from 0.01 to 1.00 with a step
0.01 and find that the results of $\lambda \in [0.02, 1.00]$ are very similar, larger λ leads
to some blurring in very weak level.

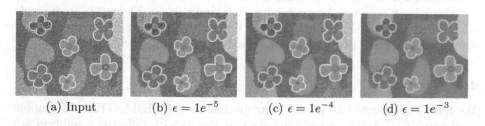

$\quad$(a) Input$\quad\quad\quad$(b) $\epsilon = 1e^{-5}$$\quad\quad\quad$(c) $\epsilon = 1e^{-4}$$\quad\quad\quad$(d) $\epsilon = 1e^{-3}$

Fig. 1. Results with different ϵ.

4.1   Parameters

Iterations. We have tested different parameters of p, q, r, s and found 3–5 iterations of the iterative approach are enough for convergence. The intermediate results are shown in Fig. 2. In the following experiments, we use only 3 iterations if there is no explicit declaration. And the needed iterations for red-black linear solver may depend on the resolution of the input image. However, we found 20 red-black iterations are enough for all images in our experiments.

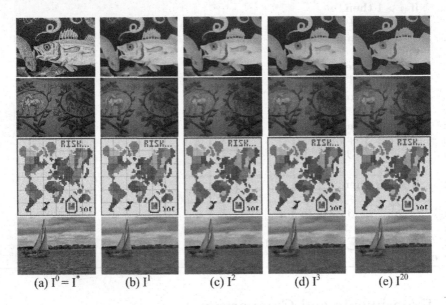

(a) $I^0 = I^*$ (b) I^1 (c) I^2 (d) I^3 (e) I^{20}

Fig. 2. Structure images of different iterations. (Color figure online)

Norms. As Xu's RTV model [11] is one of the best optimization based approaches. We use it (with parameters $p = 2$, $q = 1$, $r = 0$, $s = 1$) as the baseline and adjust the parameters for different results. We fixed $p = 2$, $s = 1$, and only adjust q and r. The result is given in Fig. 3. We can see that when $q + r \leq 1.0$ the output structure images are all satisfying.

Gaussian Filter. When the images have textures in larger scales, we need to use Gaussian filters with larger window and larger sigma. Figure 4 is an example with different Gaussian filters. Gaussian filter with larger window size and larger sigma can eliminate more texture details, but the result is slightly blurred.

4.2   Timing

We have implemented all parts of our method on a NVIDIA GTX1070 graphic card using CUDA [15]. Several images (see Fig. 5) with different resolution are

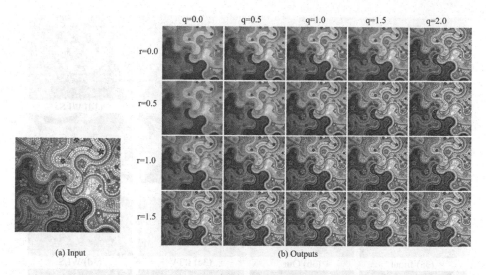

(a) Input   (b) Outputs

Fig. 3. Structure images of different q and r.

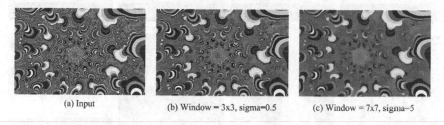

(a) Input   (b) Window = 3x3, sigma=0.5   (c) Window = 7x7, sigma−5

Fig. 4. Structure images of different Gaussian filters.

tested to count the time costs . In Table 1, the first column is the input images, and the second column is the resolution of each image. $nOuterIter$ of the third column means the iterations of the iterative approach, and $nRedBlackIter$ is the iterations of the linear solver. The fourth column is the window size of the Gaussian filter and the last column is the total time of each experiment. From this table, we can see using 3 iterations for the iterative approach, we can obtain 2–5 fps for an image with resolution 1920 × 1080 × 3. We believe that it is possible to achieve realtime performance by using a more powerful graphic card and distributing the iteration more reasonable.

4.3   Comparison

As we have claimed before, Xu's RTV model [11] and Farman's WLS model [10] are two special cases of our model. RTV model is the case with parameter $p = 2$, $q = 1, r = 0, s = 1$ and WLS model is the case with parameter $p = 2, q = 1$, $r = 0, s = 0$. We have found WLS only works well for small textures and RTV

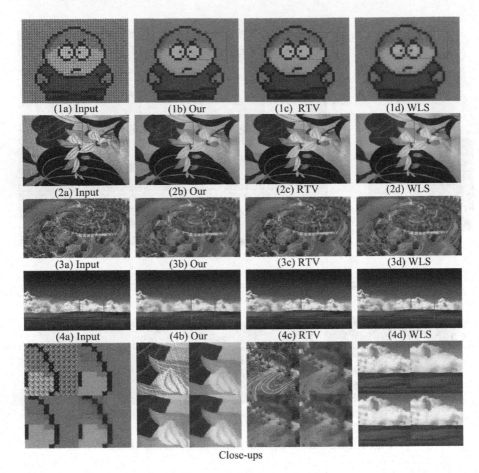

(1a) Input	(1b) Our	(1c) RTV	(1d) WLS
(2a) Input	(2b) Our	(2c) RTV	(2d) WLS
(3a) Input	(3b) Our	(3c) RTV	(3d) WLS
(4a) Input	(4b) Our	(4c) RTV	(4d) WLS

Close-ups

Fig. 5. Images for counting time costs.

works well for more cases than WLS. By tuning parameters, our method work well for most cases. See Figs. 6, 7 and 8 for examples. As Xu et al. have compared the RTV method with the state-of-the-art local methods, we recommend the readers refer to the paper [11].

To handle the same structure images, we can do much faster than existing optimization-base methods, as our linear solver does not build any matrix and can be highly parallelized on GPUs. Min's model [16] is very like ours and also they have developed a faster linear solver than traditional PCG solver. However, we do not see any hope to parallelize their solver on GPU.

Table 1. Timing information.

Image	Resolution	Norms p, q, r, s	nOuterIter, nRedBlackIter	Filter Size	Time
Fig. 5(1b)	$400 \times 324 \times 3$	$1.8, 0.55, 0.45, 1.1$	$3, 20$	3×3	$103\,\text{ms}$
Fig. 5(1c)	$400 \times 324 \times 3$	$2, 1, 0, 1$ (RTV)	$3, 20$	3×3	$160\,\text{ms}$
Fig. 5(1d)	$400 \times 324 \times 3$	$2, 0.5, 0, 0$ (WLS)	$3, 20$	-	$13\,\text{ms}$
Fig. 5(2b)	$720 \times 480 \times 3$	$1.8, 0.55, 0.45, 1.1$	$3, 20$	3×3	$124\,\text{ms}$
Fig. 5(2c)	$720 \times 480 \times 3$	$2, 1, 0, 1$ (RTV)	$3, 20$	3×3	$109\,\text{ms}$
Fig. 5(2d)	$720 \times 480 \times 3$	$2, 0.5, 0, 0$ (WLS)	$3, 20$	-	$34\,\text{ms}$
Fig. 5(3b)	$1280 \times 720 \times 3$	$1.8, 0.55, 0.45, 1.1$	$3, 20$	3×3	$209\,\text{ms}$
Fig. 5(3c)	$1280 \times 720 \times 3$	$2, 1, 0, 1$ (RTV)	$3, 20$	3×3	$193\,\text{ms}$
Fig. 5(3d)	$1280 \times 720 \times 3$	$2, 0.5, 0, 0$ (WLS)	$3, 20$	-	$86\,\text{ms}$
Fig. 5(4b)	$1920 \times 1080 \times 3$	$1.8, 0.55, 0.45, 1.1$	$3, 20$	5×5	$399\,\text{ms}$
Fig. 5(4c)	$1920 \times 1080 \times 3$	$2, 1, 0, 1$ (RTV)	$3, 20$	5×5	$363\,\text{ms}$
Fig. 5(4d)	$1920 \times 1080 \times 3$	$2, 0.5, 0, 0$ (WLS)	$3, 20$	-	$181\,\text{ms}$

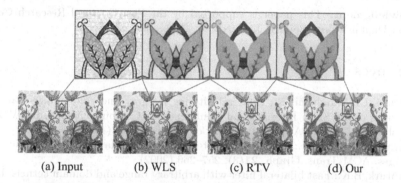

(a) Input   (b) WLS   (c) RTV   (d) Our

Fig. 6. An example where WLS [10], RTV [11] and our method all work well.

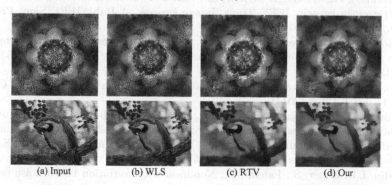

(a) Input   (b) WLS   (c) RTV   (d) Our

Fig. 7. An example where WLS [10] fails while RTV [11] and our method work well.

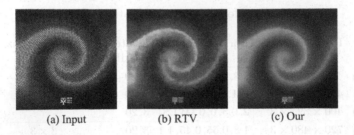

(a) Input   (b) RTV   (c) Our

Fig. 8. An example where RTV [11] does not work well while our method works well.

5   Conclusion

We have proposed an improved method based on weighted least squares to extract structure layers from textured images. Our method can generate results in equal or better quality comparing with state-of-the-art methods, and run much faster than all other existing optimization base approaches.

Acknowledgment. This paper is supported by the Post-Doctoral Research Center of China Digital Video (Beijing) Limited.

References

1. Tomasi, C., Manduchi, R.: Bilateral filtering for gray and color images. In: Proceedings of the Sixth International Conference on Computer Vision, ICCV 1998, Washington, DC, USA, p. 839. IEEE Computer Society (1998)
2. Durand, F., Dorsey, J.: Fast bilateral filtering for the display of high-dynamic-range images. ACM Trans. Graph. **21**(3), 257–266 (2002)
3. Gunturk, B.K.: Fast bilateral filter with arbitrary range and domain kernels. IEEE Trans. Image Process. A Publ. IEEE Sign. Process. Soc. **20**(9), 2690–2696 (2011)
4. Chaudhury, K.N., Sage, D., Unser, M.: Fast $O(1)$ bilateral filtering using trigonometric range kernels. IEEE Trans. Image Process. A Publ. IEEE Sign. Process. Soc. **20**(12), 3376 (2011)
5. Zhuo, S., Luo, X., Deng, Z., Liang, Y., Ji, Z.: Edge-preserving texture suppression filter based on joint filtering schemes. IEEE Trans. Multimed. **15**(3), 535–548 (2013)
6. Cho, H., Lee, H., Kang, H., Lee, S.: Bilateral texture filtering. ACM Trans. Graph. **33**(4), 128:1–128:8 (2014)
7. Zhang, F., Dai, L., Xiang, S., Zhang, X.: Segment graph based image filtering: fast structure-preserving smoothing. In: Proceedings of the 2015 IEEE International Conference on Computer Vision (ICCV), ICCV 2015, Washington, DC, USA, pp. 361–369. IEEE Computer Society (2015)
8. Rudin, L.I., Osher, S., Fatemi, E.: Nonlinear total variation based noise removal algorithms. Phys. D **60**(1–4), 259–268 (1992)
9. Aujol, J.F., Gilboa, G., Chan, T., Osher, S.: Structure-texture image decompositionmodeling, algorithms, and parameter selection. Int. J. Comput. Vis. **67**(1), 111–136 (2006)

10. Farbman, Z., Fattal, R., Lischinski, D., Szeliski, R.: Edge-preserving decompositions for multi-scale tone and detail manipulation. ACM Trans. Graph. **27**(3), 1–10 (2008)
11. Xu, L., Yan, Q., Xia, Y., Jia, J.: Structure extraction from texture via relative total variation. ACM Trans. Graph. **31**(6), 139:1–139:10 (2012)
12. Tan, X., Sun, C., Pham, T.D.: Multipoint filtering with local polynomial approximation and range guidance. In: IEEE Conference on Computer Vision and Pattern Recognition, pp. 2941–2948 (2014)
13. Ham, B., Cho, M., Ponce, J.: Robust image filtering using joint static and dynamic guidance. In: Computer Vision and Pattern Recognition, pp. 4823–4831 (2015)
14. Hadjidimos, A.: Successive overrelaxation (SOR) and related methods. J. Comput. Appl. Math. **123**(1), 177–199 (2000). Numerical Analysis 2000. Vol. III: Linear Algebra
15. Nvidia cuda home page. http://www.nvidia.com/object/cuda_home_new.html
16. Min, D., Choi, S., Jiangbo, L., Ham, B., Sohn, K., Minh, N.D.: Fast global image smoothing based on weighted least squares. IEEE Trans. Image Process. **23**(12), 5638 (2014)

A Method for Detecting Flower Collision Based on Spherical Projection

Tingrong Cao[1], Ling Lu[1,2(✉)], Wenli Wang[1], Lihua Li[2], and Lei Wang[2]

[1] Jiangxi Engineering Laboratory on Radioactive Geoscience and Big Data Technology, East China University of Technology, Nanchang, China
trongcao@yeah.net, luling@ecit.cn,
lovewenlistyle@163.com
[2] Jiangxi Engineering Research Center of Nuclear Geoscience Data Science and System, East China University of Technology, Nanchang, China
lhl@ecit.cn, wlei598@163.com

Abstract. In this paper, a method for detecting and mapping the petals of plant petals is presented. Firstly, the parametric equations are used to represent the initial state of the petals surface. The three - dimensional Cartesian coordinates of each point in the petals are projected onto the spherical coordinates respectively, The discrete values of the projection of the petals are converted to the two-dimensional coordinate plane. Secondly, multiple buffers are used to record the result of each petals projection and the distance of the petals from the origin of the spherical coordinates. According to the value of each buffer, it is determined whether the current petal collides with others, the collides result can be determined the range of collision. Finally, the current petals are deformed or moved to avoid collided with others. Through the collision test between the petals in the process of flower generation, it shows that the detection effect is good.

Keywords: Collision · Projecting · Plant flower · Deforming

1 Introduction

In virtual reality, Collision Detection (CD) is one of the important techniques. Currently. There are four main types of collision detection techniques: collision detection based on space division, collision detection based on bounding volume hierarchy (BVH), collision detection based on distance calculation and collision detection based on image space.

The collision detection based on space partitioning divides the whole space into several small units, and then detect the location relationship of each small unit. In the actual collision detection, if the object has been deformed, but also through this method to achieve the object's own collision detection [1], this collision detection method occupies less computer resources and is more suitable for the scattered distribution of objects in the whole space is more discrete. When a large number of objects are distributed in a small area, the complexity of the detection method may reach $O(n^2)$.

The collision detection based on level bounding box is to put the virtual object into a specific surround box, and by judging the location relation of the surrounding box, it can determine whether the virtual object in the surrounding box collide, the detection accuracy is high [2], At present, there are various kinds of bounding volume, such as oriented bounding box (OBB) [3], discrete oriented polypore (k-DOP) [4], swept sphere volumes [5], bounding sphere [6], dynamic swept sphere volumes [7], axis-aligned bounding box (AABB) [8], this method is more suitable for rigid objects.

The collision detection based on level bounding box is to put the virtual object into a specific surround box, and by judging the location relation of the surrounding box, it can determine whether the virtual object in the surrounding box collide, the detection accuracy is high [2], At present, there are various kinds of bounding volume, such as oriented bounding box(OBB) [3], discrete oriented polypore (k-DOP) [4], swept sphere volumes [5], bounding sphere [6], dynamic swept sphere volumes [7], axis-aligned bounding box (AABB) [8], this method is more suitable for rigid objects.

Collision detection based on distance calculation determines whether objects collide with each other according to the position and distance of the control point of the model. Researchers have studied the distance problems of different surfaces, such as Bezier surface [9], implicit surface [10], ball scan surface [11], NURBS surface [12], pipe surface [13] and so on.

Collision detection based on image space is to project the geometric objects onto the two-dimensional image plane, and then analyze and compare the projection information of the image planes in different phases to determine the possible collisions between the objects. In order reduce the load of CPU, we can use the graphics hardware (graphics acceleration Card) and other technologies. Rossignac et al. [14] make judgment mainly used depth cache and template cache; Myszkowski et al. [15] combine depth cache with template cache; Baciu and et al. [16] combine the collision detection algorithm of bounding box with the collision based on image space Detection algorithm for collision detection; Hoff et al. [17] combine the collision detection techniques based on the graphics space and image space-based collision detection technology.

Collision detection of rigid body is different from collision detection of deformable object, rigid body performs only collision detection, but deformable object performs also need deformation treatment. Some applications of deformable object collision detection such as simulation of cloth [18] and surgical [19] are important. in virtual plants, there are also similar to deformable object collision detection, for example, the collision between petals of a flower during the opening process and the collision between leaves of the plant will deformed the petals or leaves.

In the collision detection of soft body, Tang et al. [20] proposed a bounding box collision detection method based on adaptive ellipsoid, it can quickly handle the fabric with the model of collision simulation results. The surface error of the weighted mean of distance and radial distance of the method is treated with ellipsoid classification. Zhang et al. [21] proposed a collision detection algorithm based on the flow type axial bounding box to the collision of the variable form, which can perform multi-parallel flow calculation on the GPU. Tang et al. [22] proposed a rapid flow algorithm based on GPU for collision detection between the deformation model method. Zhou et al. [23]

proposed a new filter elimination algorithm on the basis of two-stage collision algorithm for the problem of low speed in the detection of large scale complex soft bodies.

This paper is based on the basic graphic deformation method for flower modeling, and proposes a collision detection method which based on spherical coordinate projection for the inter-petal collision, then use of the Gaussian transform to readjust the shape parameters of the petals that collide, so that can prevent the re-styling flower petals from collision again.

2   Collision Characteristics of Petals in Flowers

Flower is a special kind of object, the part of the petals have certain contact between curvature and the petals are very close together, for collision detection between flowers, some of the collision detection methods described above can be used. However, in the process of drawing petals, petals are prone to collision and penetration. Therefore, the previous collision detection algorithm is not suitable for the inter-petal collision detection.

As shown in Fig. 1, in the case of Lily, it has higher petal bending. It is almost ineffective to use the conventional method to divide the whole Lily space, it must be subdivided into each pixel, so the efficiency is very low.

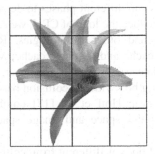

Fig. 1. Split law – lilies.

If we use bounding box technology to achieve collision detection, it is very difficult to build Suitable collision detection bounding box for petal. As shown in Fig. 2a, for a petal, It can quickly build AABB, but when two petals fit very closely, as shown in Fig. 2b, if using AABB. Obviously, the structure of the bounding box is nearly ineffective, and it is effective for petals collision detection to establish a finer bounding box.

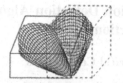

a. one petal bounding box   b. Two petals bounding boxes

Fig. 2. Petal AABB bounding box.

The situation of bounding sphere is similar to that of the AABB, as shown in Fig. 3, it is almost ineffective for detecting collisions between flower petals which closely-fitting curved surfaces.

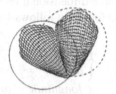

a. one petal surrounded the ball   b. two petal surrounded the ball

Fig. 3. Petals surrounded the ball

The whole petal is a surface, and almost every point's normal vector is different, As shown in Fig. 4, When using the K-DOPS bounding box to establish the plane which bounding box is needed, and almost every point's has to create a directed plane, This leads to the complexity of bounding box building and the large storage space required.

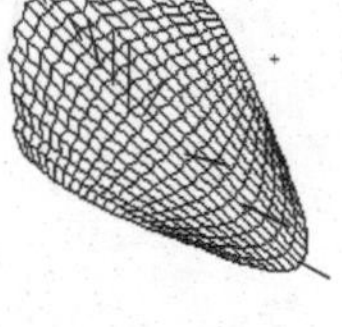

Fig. 4. The normal vector of the surface of the petal

In this dissertation, a collision detection method based on image space is proposed, During the process of modeling petals, the three-dimensional coordinates of each point in the petal surface are respectively projected onto the spherical surface of the geographic coordinate system (Using longitude, latitude and distance from the center of the ball to represent), Multiple buffers were used to record the projection results of each petal and the distance of the petals from the origin of the geographic coordinates. According to the values in each buffer, it is possible to determine whether the current petals collide with other petals.

3 Collision Detection Algorithm Based on Spherical Projection

3.1 Spherical Coordinates

The schematic diagram of the latitude and longitude line adopted in this paper is shown in Fig. 5a. Imitating the geographic coordinate system, the maximum circle in the middle of the sphere is used as the 0 point latitude, and the maximum circle in which the plane is perpendicular to the plane of the circle is taken as the longitude of the 0 point. The latitude above 0 point latitude is from 0 to $\pi/2$ and below is from $\pi/2$ to π. View longitude from above, the anti-clockwise longitude is from 0 to 2π. As shown in Fig. 5b is the case of latitude and longitude within the first quadrant. P is any point on the sphere, then $\angle a$ is latitude, $\angle b$ is longitude.

According to the above method, the formula of the longitude and latitude coordinates of the three-dimensional coordinate point (x, y, z) in the geographic coordinate system can be found as follows Figure.

$$\begin{cases} latitude = \frac{\pi}{2} - arctg\left(\frac{y}{\sqrt{x^2+z^2}}\right) & y > 0 \\ latitude = \frac{\pi}{2} + arctg\left(\frac{|y|}{\sqrt{x^2+z^2}}\right) & y \leq 0 \\ longtitude = arctg\left(\frac{z}{x}\right) & x > 0, z \geq 0 \\ longtitude = \pi - arctg\left(\frac{z}{|x|}\right) & x < 0, z \geq 0 \\ longtitude = \pi + arctg\left(\frac{|z|}{|x|}\right) & x < 0, z \leq 0 \\ longtitude = 2\pi - arctg\left(\frac{|z|}{x}\right) & x > 0, z \leq 0 \end{cases}$$

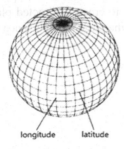

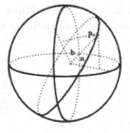

a. Latitude and longitude lines diagram

b. Latitude and longitude co-ordinate system diagram

Fig. 5. Spherical coordinates

3.2 Projection and Collision Detection of Petals

According to the shape feature of a flower, the bounding box of the whole flower can be spherical. This paper uses the method which is shown in Fig. 6 to project the details of petals onto the latitude-longitude coordinate system.

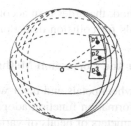

Fig. 6. Composed of petal surface of the small rectangular projection schematic

Each petal plane is projected on the latitude-longitude coordinate system, and the projection of its center point represents the projection of the entire facet. Where p1, p2 and p3 are the center points of three continuous facets, the projection is shown in Fig. 7.

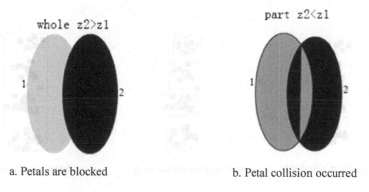

a. Petals are blocked   b. Petal collision occurred

Fig. 7. Petal collision detection diagram

Record the depth, longitude and latitude information of each facet which are composed of the petals, and according to the process of turn from the inside to the outside of the drawing petals, after each petal has been drawn will be recorded in the petals of latitude and longitude depth of maximum value and minimum value of depth. There may be collisions between two petals or they may not collide. As shown in Fig. 8a, it is the case that no collision occurs between two petals. In this case, the depth $z2$ of the second petal must be greater than the depth $z1$ of the first petal at each latitude and longitude. Figure 8b shows the collision of two petals. In this case, the depth $z2$ of the second petal is bound to be less than the depth $z1$ of the first petal at certain longitudes and latitudes.

It can be seen from the above that when drawing the next petal, the current petal's facet projection information can be compared with the original maximum depth value and the minimum depth value. If the depth of the facet projection is between the last petals of maximum depth and minimum depth which has been drawn, then the facet may collide with the original petals.

According to the above method, the order is in accordance with the round from the inside to the outside of the petals for collision detection.

3.3 Collision Detection After the Correction Method

After the collision of the outer wheel petals and inner wheel petals, the external wheel petals are deformed and the deformation function adopts Gaussian function.

Because of the different parameters of petals of various types, the petal parameters u and v that collide after petals projection are also different, as shown in Fig. 8a. The more normal case is the u, v are sometimes continuous, sometimes disconnected points after petals projection. At this moment we have two kinds of schemes to deal with the projection result: The first way is to partition the whole projection according to its continuous condition, obtain the range values of each region respectively, and then perform the Gaussian transformation, as shown in Fig. 8b. The second way is to treat the entire projection as an area, as shown in Fig. 8c.

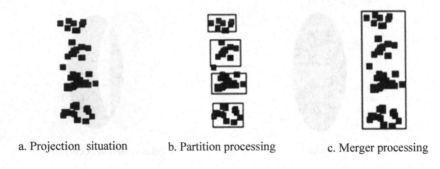

a. Projection situation   b. Partition processing   c. Merger processing

Fig. 8. Collision occurred projection diagram

It is found that the original parameters of petals are transformed by Gauss in the first way, and the results are not satisfactory, so the second method is finally used to deal with the u, v parameters of the projection, The modification of petal parameters is carried out with the following ideas: calculate the *maximum* and *minimum* values of u and v parameters of each petal collision, and the range of parameters u_i and v_i are calculated according to the *maximum* and *minimum* values, Then, according to the intersection of the current petals, the *maximum* cross depth d_i between the petals is obtained, and the parameters u_i, v_i of the center of the whole collision region are obtained, and adjust the parameters of the petal deformation by using Gaussian.

As follows: $u\text{max}_i$ and $u\text{min}_i$ respectively refer to the *maximum* and *minimum* values of the parameter u of the current petal collision, $v\text{max}_i$ and $v\text{min}_i$ respectively refer to the *maximum* and *minimum* values of the parameter v of the current petal collision, $d1_i$ and $d2_i$ respectively refers to the distance between the projection point of the area where the current petal intersects and the center of the circle.

$$\begin{cases} \Delta u_i = u\, \text{max}_i - u\, \text{min}_i \\ \Delta v_i = v\, \text{max}_i - v\, \text{min}_i \\ d_i = \text{max}(d1_i - d2_i) \\ u_i = u\, \text{min}_i + \frac{\Delta u_i}{2} \\ v_i = v\, \text{min}_i + \frac{\Delta v_i}{2} \end{cases}$$

Using two-dimensional Gaussian, according to the parameters obtained earlier, access to the deformation information of petals.

$$g = \sum_i d_i \exp\left(-\frac{(u - u_i)^2}{\Delta u_i^2} - \frac{(v - v_i)^2}{\Delta v_i^2}\right) \tag{1}$$

4 Simulation Experiment Process

The main parameters of the hardware used in the simulation experiments are: CPU1.6 GHz, Memory 2 GB, Video Memory 512 MB, the operating system uses Windows Server 2003, the programming environment is Visual C++ 6.0. The simulation object is peony flower.

As shown in Fig. 9, The initial parameter equation of the initial state of petal surface is as follows [24]:

$$\begin{aligned} x &= au + \Delta x = au + 0.8a(u - 0.5)\sin(\pi v/2 - c) \\ y &= bv + \Delta y = bv + 1.2a(v - 0.5)\sin(\pi u) \\ z &= \Delta z = 5\sin(\pi y/b - 1) + 5\sin(\pi(x - a/2)/a + 0.5) \end{aligned} \tag{2}$$

At the parameter equation: "a" controls the width of the petals, "b" controls the height of the petals, "c" is the phase of deformation, Δx is the deformation function in the x direction, Δy is the deformation function in the y direction, and Δz is the deformation function in the z direction.

The petals are shifted so that the middle part of the petal is located at the origin of

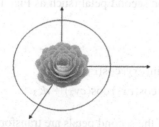

Fig. 9. Cartesian and spherical coordinates

Fig. 10. Initial petals

a. The first petal's location   b. The first petal projection

Fig. 11. The first petal and projection

the coordinates (such as Fig. 10), then rotated around the *x-axis* by an angle cx_1 and translation of an increment dz_1 along the *z-axis*. In order to make it convenient to turn into spherical coordinates, we move the petals downward dy along the *y-axis*, so that the origin of the coordinates approximately in the center of the flower, and the position of the first petal is obtained (such as Fig. 11a, in order to make the three-dimensional effect of flowers obvious, the whole flower was rotated an angle around the *x-axis*). Transformation formula is as follows:

$$
\begin{aligned}
x' &= x \\
y' &= y \cos(cx_1) - z \sin(cx_1) - dy \\
z' &= y \sin(cx_1) + z \cos(cx_1) + dz_1
\end{aligned}
\tag{3}
$$

The center coordinates (x, y) of the first petal facets (the surface consists of multiple facets) are projected onto the spherical coordinates (i, j). And calculates the distance *dis* of the facet from the coordinate origin (which is also the sphere center of the spherical coordinate system). Instead of the value of the current buffer *sphere_z*[i][j], and another *sphere_num*[i][j] is marked. Using the scanning line of computer graphics filling algorithm, the corresponding value of each projection point in the facet is set to the value of its center point. Petals 1 project onto the spherical coordinate surface as shown in Fig. 11b.

According to the second characteristic of petals, change the relevant parameters in parameter Eq. (2), then rotated around the *x-axis* by an angle cx_2, rotated around the *x-axis* by an angle cy_2, move the petals downward dz_2 along the *z-axis*, and move the petals downward dy along the *y-axis*, therefore get the second petal (such as Fig. 12a). Transformation formula is as follows:

$$
\begin{aligned}
x' &= x \cos(cy_2) + z \sin(cy_2) \\
y' &= x \sin(cx_2) \sin(cy_2) + y \cos(cx_2) - z \sin(cx_2) \cos(cy_2) - dy \\
z' &= -x \cos(cx_2) \sin(cy_2) + y \sin(cx_2) + z \cos(cx_2) \cos(cy_2) + dz_2
\end{aligned}
\tag{4}
$$

The coordinates of the center coordinates *(x, y)* of the second petals are transformed to geographic coordinates (i, j). And calculate the distance of the small plane from the origin (which is also the ball center of the spherical coordinate system). If the value of *dis* is greater than that of the current *sphere_z*[i][j], it indicates that the small plane is currently at the outer surface of the sphere, without collision; otherwise it collides with the first petal, Record the distance from the first petal to the radius of the sphere and stored in *sphere_dz*[i][j], then the values of *u* and *v* are stored in *sphere_u*[i][j] and *sphere_v*[i][j]. The corresponding values of each projection point in the small plane are set as the values of their center points. The two petals are projected onto the sphere as shown in Fig. 12b. The red part of the figure shows the extent of the collision. Figure 12a also shows that the second petal crosses the first petal.

The seed filling algorithm is used to calculate the connected area after coalitional

a. The location of two petals   b. Two petal projection

Fig. 12. Two petals and projection

projection and the Δui and Δvi which were *u* and *v* parameters of each area, the maximum cross depth between petals *di*, and the parameters *ui* and *vi* of the center of the area then substitute the Gaussian function of parameter Eq. (1). This is added to the *z* component of the parametric equation for the initial petal.

$$
\begin{aligned}
x &= au + \Delta x \\
y &= bv + \Delta y \\
z &= \Delta z + g
\end{aligned}
\tag{5}
$$

Regenerate the second petal, as shown in Fig. 13a and b.

Similarly, the other petals of the first round of petals are generated. Figure 14a and b show the results of collision detection of the first round of petals and projections, and

a. Corrected position of the two petals.   b. Modified petals and re-projection

Fig. 13. Corrected two petals's positions and re-projected them

Fig. 15 show the results of collision detection with modified petals and re-projection after the first round of petal collision detection, it can be seen from the figure that no collision has occurred.

Figure 16a and b are the results of the modified flower and the re-projected collision detection after the petal collision detection.

a. The first round of petals   b. The projection of the round petals.

Fig. 14. The first round petals and projection

a. Corrected position of the first   b. Modified petals and re-projection
ring of petals

Fig. 15. Modified position of the first ring of petals and re-projected them

Generally, the collision range of inner wheel petals is larger, and the outer wheel petal collision range is small.

a. Corrected complete a flower   b. Modified petals and re-projection
                                                of a flower

Fig. 16. Modified a flower and re-projection it

5 Conclusion

In this paper, we propose a method to detect and plot the petals between the petals of the projection based on the projection. This is a new way to solve the collision problem. In our future research, we will use this to check the collision between flowers, fruit, leaves and branches.

Acknowledgment. This work was funded by two Natural Science Foundation of China (61561003 and 61761003)

References

1. Wu, M., Yu, Y., Zhou, J.: An octree algorithm for collision detection using space partition. Chin. J. Comput. **20**(9), 849–854 (1997)
2. Redon, S., Kim, Y.J., Lin, M.C., et al.: Fast continuous collision detection for articulated models. In: Proceeding Soft the 9th ACM Symposium on Solid Modeling and Applications Airela-Ville Euro graphics Association Press, pp. 145–156 (2004)
3. Gottschalk, S., Lin, M.C., Manocha, D.: OBBTree.: a hierarchical structure for rapid interference detection. In: Computer Graphics Proceedings Annual Conference Series ACM SIGGRAPH, pp. 171–180 (1996)
4. Klosowski, J.T., Held, M., Mitchell, J.S.B., et al.: Efficient collision detection using bounding volume hierarchies of k-DOPS. IEEE Trans. Vis. Comput. Graph. **4**(1), 21–36 (1998)
5. Larse, E., Gottschalk, S., Lin, M.C., et al.: Fast proximity queries with swept sphere volumes. North Carolina University of North Carolina Department of Computer Science (1999)
6. Bradshaw, G., O Sullivan, C.: Sphere-tree construction using dynamic media lax is approximation. In: Proceeding Soft the ACM SIGGRAPH Euro Graphics Symposium on Computer Animation, pp. 33–40 (2002)
7. Corrales, J.A., Candelas, F.A., Torres, F.: Safe human-robot interaction based on dynamic sphere-swept line bounding volumes. Robot. Comput.-Integr. Manuf. **27**(1), 177–185 (2011)
8. Memory-optimized bounding-volume hierarchies. http://www.codecorner.com/Opcod. Accessed 28 Sept 2013
9. Chen, X., Yong, J., Zheng, G., et al.: Computing minimum distance between two Bezier curves/surfaces. Comput. Aided Geom. Des. **25**(3), 677–684 (2006)
10. Chena, X., Yong, J., Zheng, G., et al.: Computing minimum distance between two implicit algebraic surfaces. Comput. Aided Geomet. Des. **38**(4), 1053–1061 (2006)
11. Lee, K., Seong, J.-K., Kim, K.-J., et al.: Minimum distance between two sphere-swept surfaces. Comput. Aided Geomet. Des. **39**(1), 452–459 (2007)
12. Turbull, C., Cameron, S.: Computing distances between NURBS-defined convex objects. In: Proceeding of IEEE International Conference on Robotics and Automation, pp. 236–239 (2008)
13. Ma, Y., Tu, C., Wang, W.: Distance computation for canal surfaces using cone-sphere bounding volumes. Comput. Aided Geomet. Des. **29**(3), 255–264 (2012)
14. Rossignac, J., Megahed, A., Schneider, B.O.: Interactive inspection of solids: cross-section and interferences. In: Computer Graphics Proceedings, Annual Conference Series, ACM SIGGRAPH, pp. 353–360 (1992)

15. Rossignac, J., Megahed, A., Schneider, B.O.: Interactive inspection of solids: cross-section and interferences. Comput. Graph. **10**(4), 181–192 (1999)
16. Baciu, G., Wong, S.K.W., Sun, H.: RECODE.: an image-based collision detection algorithm. J. Vis. Comput. Anim. **10**(4), 181–192 (1999)
17. Hoff III, K.E., Zaferakis, A., Lin, M., Manocha, D.: Fast and simple 2D geometric proximity queries using graphics hardware. In: Proceedings of ACM Symposium on Interactive 3D Graphics, pp. 145–148 (2001)
18. Bridson, R., Fedkiw, R., Anderson, J.: Robust treatment of collisions, contact and friction for cloth animation. ACM Trans. Graph. (TOG) **21**(3), 594–603 (2002)
19. Raghupathi, L., Grisoni, L., Faure, F., et al.: An intestinal surgery simulator: real-time collision processing and visualization. IEEE Trans. Vis. Comput. Graph. **10**(6), 708–718 (2004)
20. Tang, Y., Yang, S., Lu, M., et al.: Adaptive ellipsoidal surround box improvement of fabric collision detection method. Comput. Aided Des. Graph. J. **25**(10), 1589–1596 (2013)
21. Zhang, X.Y., Kim, Y.: Interactive collision detection for deformable models using streaming ABBs. IEEE Trans. Vis. Comput. Graph. **13**(2), 318–329 (2007)
22. Tang, M., Manocha, D., Lin, J., et al.: Collision-streams: fast GPU based collision detection for deformable models. In: Symposium on Interactive 3D Graphics and Games, pp. 63–70. ACM, New York (2011)
23. Zhou, Q., Liu, Y., Cheng, T.: A continuous collision detection algorithm for large soft bodies. J. Chin. Image Graph. **21**(7), 91–912 (2016)
24. Lu, L.: Study of flower color simulation. J. Syst. Simul. **24**(9), 1892–1895 (2012)

The Research on AGV Visual Guided Under Strong Noise

Xiaohong Zhang[1], Yifan Yang[2(✉)], Wanli Xing[2], and Hong Zhang[2]

[1] Luoyang Institute of Electro-Optical Devices, Luoyang 471000, Henan, China
[2] Image Processing Center, Beihang University, Beijing 100000, China
stephenyoung@163.com

Abstract. In this paper, considering the complexity of AGV working environment, the image filtering, segmentation and graph morphology processing are carried out for the high noise of AGV working environment. To solve the problem of uneven light in the process of AGV travel, a dynamic threshold transfer and segmentation method is proposed, which greatly improves the accuracy and efficiency of the segmentation. At the same time, after extracting the morphological gradient of the marking line, the whole inspection method of image acquisition and the label processing of the boundary are established, and a one-sided fast center line searching algorithm is proposed. Compared with the traditional algorithm, the computation cost is reduced by more than 50%.

Keywords: Visual navigation AGV · Strong noise · Fast dynamic threshold Morphological filtering · Center line extraction

1 Introduction

One of the most important parts of vision navigation AGV is the fast and accurate visual navigation algorithm. However, due to the complexity of the AGV working environment, it is easy to appear the strong magnetic field in the working environment, the change of the ambient illumination intensity and the interference of the CCD camera itself. It is inevitable that the guiding line used for a long time will be damaged and tainted, which will have a great impact on the real-time and accuracy of the subsequent AGV visual navigation algorithm. Firstly, we process the image information in order to that path can be partitioned accurately, then we propose a fast path navigation algorithm based on the guarantee of accuracy.

In the past decade, many algorithms for noise removal and segmentation of path images have been proposed, including the use of illumination insensitive HSI color space [1], the improved mean filtering method [2, 3], fuzzy weighting method [4] and

This work was supported by the National Natural Science Foundation of China [Grant No. 61571026] and the National Key Research and Development Program of China [Grant No. 2016YFE0108100].

illumination independent graph denoising method [5]. But these methods failure to meet the requirements of speed, and will severely limit the efficiency of AGV.

In the visual navigation algorithm, we also compare several typical navigation methods [1, 6–8], including sub-region detection, logical direction of the next step [1], using wavelet filter to corrode and extract center line [6], determination of the mean value of the boundary position between the two sides by line scanning method [7] and the center line point determined by scanning the both sides [8]. These methods generally require a large amount of computation, and the accuracy of these methods in sharp turning sections without a boundary information is obviously reduced.

The experimental results show that compared with other image denoising and navigation algorithms, the proposed segmentation and navigation algorithms have obvious advantages in computational complexity and stability. The contributions of this paper can be summarized as follows:

1. A method of dynamic threshold transfer and morphological processing is proposed to judge the variation of light intensity. When there are no light intensity change, it can be directly through the transmission of threshold for fast segmentation, but in the presence of uneven light intensity, the region of light intensity change can be line segmentation. The corresponding relationship between the morphological gradient and the boundary is established by morphological processing.
2. A fast adaptive AGV navigation algorithm with error detection is proposed. By tagging the left and right boundaries, the datum edge is determined by collecting the information quantity of each boundary. Then the change trend of navigation path is determined according to the change trend of reference edge. Experimental results show that this navigation algorithm has obvious advantages over the current visual navigation algorithms in terms of data computation and stability.

The structure of this paper is as follows: In Sect. 2, related work is introduced. In Sect. 3, the image morphology method and threshold transfer segmentation in strong noise path are introduced in detail. In Sect. 4, the algorithm of AGV navigation line is introduced. On the basis of the straight line path, the experiments of left and right turn and sharp turn path are carried out, and the results prove the advantages of the navigation path algorithm proposed in this paper. Finally, with Sect. 5 the conclusion of this paper.

2   Related Work

In the running environment of AGV, it is easy to have uneven illumination. When the global maximum inter-class variance method is used in the case of uneven illumination, the binary image will appear obvious error segmentation after processing. Compared with the global binary method, the local binary method can get better binary images, but there will still be block effect, which leads to the deviation of path segmentation. In order to overcome the phenomenon of uneven illumination, Huang calculates the threshold value of each pixel and reduces the effect of light intensity by using the sum value table and adjusting parameter t [9] and Wellner proposed a method to calculate the threshold value using the weighted mean value of any point around it [10].

The mathematical morphology can make image without noise point and edge smoother [11, 12].

The opened operation is actually to corrode and then expand, the mathematical: expression:

$$dist = open(src, element) = dilate(erode(src, element))$$

The closing operation is actually the expansion and then the corrosion, the mathematical:

$$dist = close(src, element) = erode(dilate(scr, element))$$

The morphological gradient can be said to be the edge information of the path, and the morphological gradient is the difference between the expansion diagram and the corrosion diagram:

$$dist = morph - grad(src, element) = dilate(src, element) - erode(src, element)$$

3 Strong Noise Denoising Filtering

Figure 1 is a strong noise image acquired by a CCD camera, and it includes gradual noises of light intensity [13], the CCD camera noises [14], and the damage to the guide identification line.

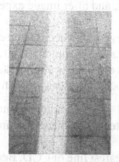   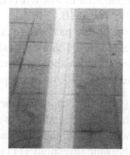

Fig. 1. CCD image acquisition   **Fig. 2.** Image after median filtering

We process the random noise and filter the gray image with median filter, as Fig. 2. Then the optimal global threshold segmentation is carried out [15], as Fig. 3. The random noise has been obviously suppressed, but the noise caused by the gradual change of light intensity has not been handled well. There are still a lot of noise problems in the far side of the AGV.

Fig. 3. Global segmentation image   **Fig. 4.** Dynamically segmented images

The noise problem caused by light intensity gradient, the optimal global threshold to apply only to the image light intensity uniformity [16], so here we use fast segmentation algorithm for a local adaptive dynamic threshold. In order to ensure the processing speed, we propose a fast dynamic threshold calculation method, where the expression of T(i) is:

$$T(i) = \alpha * \sum_{j=0}^{m} A(j)/m + (1 - \alpha) * \sum_{k=0}^{n} B(k)/n \tag{1}$$

Among them, T(i) is the threshold value of the line i. A(j) is the gray value of the line area of the line i. B(k) is the gray value of the background area of the line i. m is the number of pixel points in the line area of the line i. n is the number of pixels points of background area in line i. α is distribution coefficient, and after image experiment, α is generally between 0.45–0.55.

When we get the path image collected by CCD, not every row needs to be calculated and segmented by dynamic threshold transmission because of the continuity of track information. The threshold information in several adjacent lines is similar, so the idea of dynamic threshold transfer is proposed here. The processing steps are as follows:

(1) The global threshold segmentation is performed on the captured images, and whether the segmentation is affected by light is detected. If there is an impact, the following segmentation is carried out.

(2) The dynamic threshold T(1) is obtained from the nearest line of CCD. Because this line is closest to CCD, the information collected is the most accurate, the first line must have a white continuous segment (line area), and then transmit T(1) to T(2).

(3) The second line is divided directly with the transmitted dynamic threshold T(2), and whether there is a continuous white line in a certain length range is detected. If so, the threshold T(2) is passed to the T(3), which is transmitted line by line in turn.

(4) Finally, if the discontinuous white line and too short white line appear after a line is segmented, the fast-dynamic threshold method is used to recalculate the line threshold and segment it. Based on the processing results, the next line is passed or the threshold is recalculated.

This method not only improves the fineness of segmentation, but also propose the thought of transfer threshold, which makes local segmentation speed is greatly accelerated. We process the path information as shown in Fig. 4.

It is clear from the diagram that a large amount of noise caused by the uneven intensity of light has been eliminated, but it can still be seen that there are still noise holes outside the marking line and in the marking line, so we use the open and close operation here. The structural elements should be moderate, because too large structural elements will lead to changes of the target in the image. We adopt a method of calculating the size of the filter structure element [17].

The scale of structure element of open operation is:

$$Ropen = (r-1) * nRrosion + 1 \tag{2}$$

The scale of structure element of closed operation is:

$$Rclose = (r-1) * nDilation + 1 \tag{3}$$

Among them, r is the minimum size of structure element. nRrosion is the times of corrosion and makes the white noise complete removal. nDilation is the times of expansion and makes the black noises complete removal. In Fig. 5, we measured nDilation = 1. In Fig. 6, we measured nRrosion = 1. After calculation of formulas (2) and (3), the opening and closing operation of morphological filtering structure elements are 3 * 3.

Fig. 5. Corrosion   **Fig. 6.** Expansion

It can be seen that without obvious change of target area, the noise and edge noise [18] in the interior of the target are eliminated better, which provides convenience for the extraction of morphological gradient.

Next, we will calculate the morphological gradient of the image. When the structural element is 3 * 3, the edge information of the image can be extracted completely and will not appear condition in which boundary information loses. These images also verifies the correctness of the method for calculating the size of the filter element structure of the binary image.

4   Visual AGV Navigation Algorithm

Our goal is to extract the center line of the mark line by using the boundary information which has been already got above. Here are some common methods.

4.1   Line Scanning

Line scanning method is commonly used, from the first pixel of the first line to the last pixel of the last line. In the same line, finding the path edges coordinates and calculate the mean value of them, then the result is the central point of the line path.

4.2   Median Starting Point Tracing

The idea is similar to that of the first scan method. The difference is that the starting point is the horizontal center point of image [19]. From this point on, it scans both sides simultaneously, and stops at the point where the pixel point at the outermost point of the boundary is 1. Record the boundary coordinate at this time, and take the average of the recorded boundary coordinate to get the position of the middle line.

4.3   Adaptive Fast Center Line Extraction

It can be seen from the first two common methods, each line should be scanned to the two edges, from the first line to the last line, and the boundary is judged by the value of the boundary point is 1. Then the pixel coordinates for 1 are recorded and used to calculate the midpoint, and it does not verify whether the collected image is correct. When there is a problem of image missing information or distortion, it will also process normally, therefore, it will deal with much invalid information.

In view of this situation, we present a fast tracking method with test, including verification part, label processing of left and right boundary, and unilateral scanning part.

4.3.1   Verification Part

In order to make better use of the image boundary information, considering that the driving route of AGV must be driven along the center line of the collected image in the actual operation, we carry on the binary processing to the image collected by the camera. Then scan the pixel points of the nearest five lines of information from AGV, and use the nearest lines of pixels to judge whether the captured image is an effective image. If the five lines of the image detected the midpoint information, the collected AGV path image is valid.

4.3.2   Label Treatment of Left and Right Boundaries

The CCD camera can only capture the information of the side boundary of the marking line. It is impossible to distinguish whether the boundary is left or right simply by using the boundary value of 1. Therefore, we add a label [20] to each of the left and right sides of the boundary, that is, we label the bright spot on the left edge of the mark line at 1 and the bright spot on the right at 2. Because it is the same that binary image is equal to or greater than 1, it will not affect the display of the segmented image. This method can make a very clear sign between the left and right boundary line. When start scanning from the left boundary, the starting point is 1. When from the right boundary, starting point value of 2. This treatment has the corresponding function bwlabel(BW, n) in MATLAB, this function is labeled a category label each connected region BW, n can be set 4 or 8 connectivity.

As shown in Fig. 7, it is a binary local example after the label method, and Fig. 8 is the image matrix information corresponding to the label.

Fig. 7. The image tagging example diagram

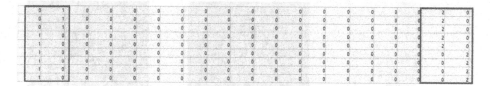

Fig. 8. The image label matrix

4.3.3   Unilateral Scanning Part

In the first five lines, the half value of left boundary to the right boundary is N, where in the N of each picture is changed. In view of the same pictures collected in the AGV path guidance line width is fixed, and the CCD camera to capture a narrow field of vision, so near-large and far-small phenomena can be neglected.

From the line 6, we compare the number of pixels of 1 or 2 in each frame image, and select the edge with more number of pixels to start the scan. Starting from this side (left edge to right, right edge to left), the side coordinate minus N pixels and result is the midpoint position. Figure 9 shows the morphological gradient extracted, and Fig. 10 is the fast center line extraction algorithm for Fig. 9. The method reduces the amount of computation by more than 50% compared with that of the intermediate starting point, which is of great significance for a strong real-time AGV system.

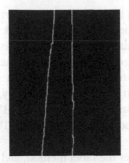

Fig. 9. Mathematical morphology   **Fig. 10.** Center line extraction

4.3.4   Experiment on Navigation Algorithm Under Other Paths

The simulation results of matlab2014a show that the effect of center line extraction from left turn is shown in Fig. 11, and that of center line from right turn is shown in Fig. 12. The extraction effect of the center line of sharp turn is shown in Fig. 13. The three algorithms mentioned in this paper are compared. It is found that the proposed adaptive fast center line extraction algorithm has obvious advantages, and the effect is shown in Fig. 14.

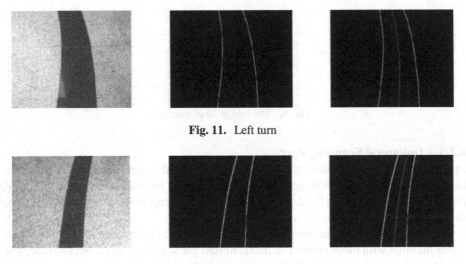

Fig. 11. Left turn

Fig. 12. Right turn

Fig. 13. Sharp turn

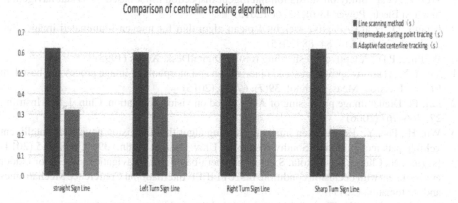

Fig. 14. The times of three algorithms are compared

5 Summary of This Paper

In this paper, a fast center line finding algorithm is proposed after adaptive segmentation in AGV environment. First, median filtering method is used in the noise images obtained by CCD camera to make random noise eliminated. Due to the uneven illumination, we propose a dynamic threshold transfer calculation method and operation steps. Then, morphological processing is carried out to obtain the morphological gradient, and we get the more accurate edge information of the AGV identification line. Then we extract the morphological gradient information to extract the center line and use the nearest five lines of AGV to detect whether the obtained image is an effective image. Finally, the average value of the distance from the boundary to the center point is calculated, and the left and right edges are labeled to find the center point.

References

1. Zhao, K.: Research on visual navigation of intelligent patrol robot in the substation. School of Electrical and Electronic Engineering (2014)
2. Zhu, S., You, C.: A modified average filtering algorithm. Comput. Appl. Softw. **12**, 97–99 (2013)

3. Zhang, X., Chen, S.: A neighborhood mean filter algorithm based on statistical features. SCI/ TECH Inf. Dev. Econ. **15**(2), 146–147 (2005)
4. Zhao, H.: Image denoising based on adaptive fuzzy weighting. Capital Normal University (2008)
5. Shi, H., He, Y.: Navigation algorithm of automated guided forklift based on STM32F103ZET6. Microcontroll. Embed. Syst. **16**, 33–36 (2016)
6. Zhang, L., Duan, Z.: Mobile robot navigation algorithm based on embedded processor. Ind. Control Comput. **23**(6), 65–66 (2010)
7. Zhu, F., Yu, F., Han, Y., Lei, Y., Hu, Y.: Path recognition algorithm for intelligent vehicle based on camera. J. Chin. Agric. Mech. **34**(5), 202–206 (2013)
8. Wei, Z., et al.: Study on substation intelligent inspection robot based on visual navigation. Shaanxi Electr. Power **43**(6), 63–66 (2015)
9. Huang, D., et al.: Adaptive weighted mean algorithm for uneven illuminated image. Sci. Technol. Guide **33**(8), 84–88 (2015)
10. Wellner, P.D.: Adaptive thresholding for the DigitalDesk. Xerox (1993)
11. Chen, X., et al.: Adaptive threshold binarization and morphology image processing based on FPGA. Electron. Meas. Technol. **39**(7), 67–71 (2016)
12. Lei, P.: Digital image processing of AGV based on vision navigation. Chin. J. Sci. Instrum. **27**, 766–767 (2006)
13. Wu, H., Pan, Y.: Research on image processing algorithm for vision navigation intelligent vehicle path recognition. J. Southwest. Norm. Univ. (Nat. Sci. Edn.) **39**(3), 108–115 (2014)
14. Isozaki, N., Chugo, D., Yokota, S., et al.: Camera-based AGV navigation system for indoor environment with occlusion condition. In: 2011 IEEE International Conference Mechatronics and Automation (2011)
15. Nie, R.C., Min, H.E., Zhou, D.M., et al.: Global threshold segmentation algorithm for visual form images. Laser Infrared **47**(02), 234–238 (2017)
16. An, Q., Li, Z., Ji, C., et al.: Agricultural robot vision navigation algorithm based on illumination invariant image. Trans. CSAE **25**(11), 208–212 (2009)
17. Xiao, Q.Z., Xu, K., Guan, Z.Q., et al.: Structuring elements selection in morphology filter. Comput. Eng. Appl. **42**, 49–51 (2007)
18. Xu, S., Yang, X., Jiang, S.: A fast nonlocally centralized sparse representation algorithm for image denoising. Signal Process. **131**, 99–112 (2017)
19. Zhu, Y., Wang, W.C., Wang, M.H.: Research on intelligent vehicle path recognition and tracking algorithm based on Electromagnetism. Sens. World **3**, 008 (2014)
20. Jimenez, A.E., Dabrowski, A., Sonehara, N., Martinez, J.M.M., Echizen, I.: Tag detection for preventing unauthorized face image processing. In: Shi, Y.-Q., Kim, H.J., Pérez-González, F., Yang, C.-N. (eds.) IWDW 2014. LNCS, vol. 9023, pp. 513–524. Springer, Cham (2015). https://doi.org/10.1007/978-3-319-19321-2_39

Schatten-p Norm Based Linear Regression Discriminant Analysis for Face Recognition

Lijiang Chen, Wentao Dou, and Xia Mao[✉]

School of Electronic and Information Engineering, Beihang University,
Beijing 100191, China
moukyou@buaa.edu.cn

Abstract. Locality-regularized linear regression classification (LLRC) shows good performance on face recognition. However, it sorely performs on the original space, which results in degraded classification efficiency. To solve this problem, we propose a dimensionality reduction algorithm named schatten-p norm based linear regression discriminant analysis (SPLRDA) for image feature extraction. First, it defines intra-class and inter-class scatters based on schatten-p norm, which improves the capability to deal with illumination changes. Then the objective function which incorporates discriminant analysis is derived from the minimization of intra-class compactness and the maximization of inter-class separability. Experiments carried on some typical databases validate the effectiveness and robustness of our method.

Keywords: Dimensionality reduction · Schatten-p norm · Linear regression
Feature extraction · Face recognition · Discriminant analysis

1 Introduction

Dimensionality reduction has played a key role in many fields such as machine learning, face recognition and data mining. It devotes to excavate the low dimensional features from high dimensional data while preserving the intrinsic information existed in data.

During the past few decades, a lot of dimensionality reduction algorithms using for feature extraction has been proposed. Principal component analysis (PCA) [1] and linear discriminant analysis (LDA) [2] are two typical methods. As an unsupervised approach, PCA projects high dimensional data onto a variance preserving subspace. In contrast, LDA, as a supervised method, aims to minimize within-class scatter and maximize between-class scatter to extract more discriminative features using labeled class information. However, it often suffers from small sample size (sss) [4] problem resulting from the singularity of within-class scatter. However, the above linear algorithms do not have the capabilities to capture the nonlinear structure embedded in image matrix. A lot of nonlinear feature extraction algorithms have been proposed to excavate the manifold structure of data, such as isometric mapping (ISOMAP) [5], Laplacian eigenmaps (LE) [6] and locally linear embedding (LLE) [7]. ISOMAP extends multidimensional scaling by incorporating the geodesic distances imposed by a weighted graph. LE finds the low-dimensional manifold structure by building a graph,

© Springer Nature Singapore Pte Ltd. 2018
Y. Wang et al. (Eds.): IGTA 2018, CCIS 875, pp. 45–56, 2018.
https://doi.org/10.1007/978-981-13-1702-6_5

whose node and connectivity are data points and proximity of neighboring points. LLE determines the low-dimensional representations of data by focusing on how to pre-serves the locally linear structure and minimizes the linear reconstruction error. However, the so called out-of-sample problem often occurs in those nonlinear algo-rithms. To solve the out-of-sample problem, locality preserving projection (LPP) [8] was proposed. LPP minimizes the local reconstruction error to preserve local structure and obtain the optimal projection matrix.

After feature extraction, data classification is another step for face recognition. Many classification methods have been proposed, such as nearest neighbor classifier (NNC) [9] and linear regression classification (LRC) [10]. More recently, Brown et al. proposed a locality-regularized linear regression classification (LLRC) [11] method using a specific class as the neighbor of a training sample to classify and improve the accuracy of classification.

Although the above feature extraction and classification methods obtain great performances, each of them are designed independently. Therefore, they may be not fit each other perfectly. Using the rule of LRC, Chen et al. proposed reconstructive discriminant analysis (RDA) [12]. In 2018, Locality-regularized linear regression discriminant analysis (LLRDA) [13] deriving from LLRC was proposed to extract features. LLRDA ameliorates the LLRC by performing intra-class and inter-class scatter in the feature subspace, which brings more appropriate features for LLRC. However, in the feature subspace, LLRDA measures the reconstruction error utilizing L2 norm, which causes the strong sensitiveness to illumination changes and outliers. To alleviate the deficiency of L2 norm based methods, many algorithms basing on schatten-p norm have been developed. To improve the robustness to illumination changes and outliers, two-dimensional principal component analysis based on schatten-p norm (2DPCA-SP) [14] was presented using shatten-p norm to measure the recon-struction error. Incorporating the discriminant analysis and schatten-p norm to extract discriminative and robust features, two-dimensional discriminant analysis based on schatten-p norm (2DDA-SP) [15] was proposed. In 2018, Shi et al. proposed robust principal component analysis via optimal mean by joint 2, 1 and schatten p-norms minimization (RPOM) [16] imposing an schatten-p norm based regularized term to suppress the singular values of reconstructed data. Motivated by the above methods, we propose an LLRC based feature extraction method named schatten-p Norm based linear regression discriminant analysis (SPLRDA) utilizing schatten-p norm to improve the robustness to illumination changes. The main advantages of out algorithm are listed below: (1) Features are directly extracted from matrix rather than vectors reshaped from original image; (2) A specific class is assumed to be the neighborhood of a training sample instead of selecting from all samples when calculating the reconstruction vector β; (3) Discriminant analysis is incorporated to obtain discriminative features; (4) In the feature subspace, we measure the similarity distances by schatten-p norm whose parameter p is adjustable, which is more robust to illumination changes and outliers.

The rest parts of this paper are organized as follows. Sect. 2 briefly reviews the background knowledge of LRC and LLRC. The presented SPLRDA method is introduced in Sect. 3. The experimental results and analysis are arranged in Sect. 4. Finally, Sect. 5 concludes this paper.

2 Related Work

Suppose $X = [x_1, x_2, \ldots, x_n]$ be a set of n training images of C classes. Given the number of images in ith class is n_i, therefore, we have $\sum_{i=1}^{C} n_i = n$. x_i denotes the ith reshaped image whose dimension N is the product of the row and column numbers of original ith image. In this section, LRC and LLRC are reviewed briefly.

2.1 LRC

LRC [10] is based on the assumption that a sample can be represented as a linear combination of samples from same class. The task of LRC is finding which class the testing sample y belongs to. Let y be a test sample from the ith class, then it can be reconstructed approximately by:

$$y = X_i \beta_i \tag{1}$$

where $\beta_i \in R^{n_i \times 1}$ is the reconstruction coefficient vector with respect to training image set of class i. β_i is calculated by least square estimation (LSE) method as:

$$\beta_i = \left(X_i^T X_i\right)^{-1} X_i^T y \tag{2}$$

Utilizing the estimated β_i, y can be reconstructed as:

$$\hat{y}_i = X_i \left(X_i^T X_i\right)^{-1} X_i^T y \tag{3}$$

Since $\hat{y}_i$ should approximate to y, the reconstruction error based on Euclidean norm is defined as:

$$l(y) = \min_i \|y - \hat{y}_i\|^2$$
$$= \min_i \left\|y - X_i \left(X_i^T X_i\right)^{-1} X_i^T y\right\|^2 \tag{4}$$

where $l(y)$ represents the class label of y.

2.2 LLRC

Different from LRC, LLRC [11] pays more attention to the local linearity of each sample and considers it to be more important than global linearity. Therefore, images from a specific class instead of all samples are supposed to be the neighborhood of a image sample based on this principle, Brown et al. presented an constraint of locality regularization on LRC by sorely involving k closest images to the query image based on Euclidean distance measure.

The k nearest neighbors set of testing sample y in class i is denoted by $\tilde{X}_i = [x_{i1}, x_{i2}, \ldots, x_{ik}] \in R^{N \times k}$. Similar to the LRC, the label of y is computed by minimizing the reconstruction error as below:

$$l(y) = \min_i \left\| y - \tilde{X}_i (\tilde{X}_i^T \tilde{X}_i)^{-1} \tilde{X}_i^T y \right\|^2 \tag{5}$$

3   Our Method

3.1   Problem Formulation

Suppose $x_i^j \in R^{a \times b}$ be the jth training sample of ith class, then its intra-class and inter-class reconstruction error are defined respectively as:

$$\sum_{i,j} e_i^j = \sum_{i,j} \left\| x_i^j - \tilde{X}_i^j \tilde{\beta}_i^j \right\|_{sp}^p \tag{6}$$

$$\sum_{i,j,m} e_{im}^j = \sum_{i,j,m} \left\| x_i^j - \tilde{X}_{im}^j \tilde{\beta}_{im}^j \right\|_{sp}^p \tag{7}$$

where $\tilde{X}_i^j$ and $\tilde{X}_{im}^j$ denote the k nearest neighbors set of x_i^j in class i and class m respectively. Class m is one of the K nearest heterogeneous subspaces of x_i^j. The intra-class scatter characterizes the compactness of each training samples class, while the inter-class scatter describes the separability between different classes. $\|\bullet\|_{sp}$ denotes the schatten-p norm. Since we know that the singular value decomposition of x is defined as:

$$U \begin{bmatrix} \sigma_1 & 0 & \cdots & 0 \\ 0 & \sigma_2 & \cdots & 0 \\ \cdots & \cdots & \cdots & \cdots \\ 0 & \cdots & \cdots & \sigma_{\min(m,n)} \end{bmatrix} V^T = SVD(x) \tag{8}$$

The schatten-p norm can be represented by [15]:

$$\|x\|_{sp} = \left(\sum_{i=1}^{\min(m,n)} \sigma_i^p \right)^{\frac{1}{p}} = \left[Tr(xx^T)^{\frac{p}{2}} \right]^{\frac{1}{p}} \tag{9}$$

where σ_i is the ith singular value of x. If the parameter p was set to be 1, the schatten-p norm becomes the nuclear norm, which is famous for its capability for solving illumination changes. In the experiments, we can adjust p to the value that attains best performance for face recognition. Suppose the optimal projection matrix be denoted by $A \in R^{b \times s}(s < b)$. In the feature subspace, the corresponding data can be replaced by:

$$y_i^j = x_i^j A \tag{10a}$$

$$Y_i^j = \left[\tilde{X}_i^{j(1)} A, \tilde{X}_i^{j(2)} A, \ldots, \tilde{X}_i^{j(k)} A \right] \tag{10b}$$

$$Y_{im}^j = \left[\tilde{X}_{im}^{j(1)} A, \tilde{X}_{im}^{j(2)} A, \ldots, \tilde{X}_{im}^{j(k)} A \right] \tag{10c}$$

where $y_i^j \in R^{a \times s}$, $Y_i^j \in R^{a \times ks}$ and $Y_{im}^j \in R^{a \times ks}$. Therefore, to find an optimal projection matrix which projects the original data into feature subspace, the function performed in the feature subspace should be maximized:

$$f(A) = \left[\sum_{i,j,m} \left\| y_i^j - Y_{im}^j \tilde{\beta}_{im}^j \right\|_{sp}^p - \sum_{i,j} \left\| y_i^j - Y_i^j \tilde{\beta}_i^j \right\|_{sp}^p \right] \quad \text{s.t. } A^T A = I_s \tag{11}$$

3.2 Problem Solving

As analyzed in the last subsection, the optimization problem can be formulated and simplified as:

$$
\begin{aligned}
\arg\max_{A} f(A) &= \arg\max_{A} \left[\sum_{i,j,m} \left\| y_i^j - Y_{im}^j \tilde{\beta}_{im}^j \right\|_{sp}^p - \sum_{i,j} \left\| y_i^j - Y_i^j \tilde{\beta}_i^j \right\|_{sp}^p \right] \\
&= \arg\max_{A} \left[\sum_{i,j,m} \left\| x_i^j A - \tilde{X}_{im}^j \tilde{\beta}_{im}^j A \right\| - \sum_{i,j} \left\| x_i^j A - \tilde{X}_i^j \tilde{\beta}_i^j A \right\|_{sp}^p \right] \\
&= \arg\max_{A} \left\{ \sum_{i,j,m} Tr \left[B_{ij}^m A A^T \left(B_{ij}^m \right)^T \right]^{\frac{p}{2}} - \sum_{i,j} Tr \left[W_{ij} A A^T \left(W_{ij} \right)^T \right]^{\frac{p}{2}} \right\} \\
&\qquad\qquad\qquad\qquad\qquad\qquad\qquad\qquad\qquad s.t. \, A^T A = I_s
\end{aligned} \tag{12}
$$

where $B_{ij}^m = x_i^j - \tilde{X}_{im}^j \tilde{\beta}_{im}^j$ and $W_{ij} = x_i^j - \tilde{X}_i^j \tilde{\beta}_i^j$. Based on the objective function, the Lagrangian function can be built as:

$$L(A, \Lambda) = \sum_{i,j,m} Tr \left[B_{ij}^m A A^T \left(B_{ij}^m \right)^T \right]^{\frac{p}{2}} - \sum_{i,j} Tr \left[W_{ij} A A^T \left(W_{ij} \right)^T \right]^{\frac{p}{2}} - Tr \left[\Lambda \left(A^T A - I_s \right) \right] \tag{13}$$

Taking the derivative of L with respect to A, we have:

$$\frac{\partial L}{\partial A} = 2 \sum_{i,j,m} \left(B_{ij}^m \right)^T D_{ij}^m B_{ij}^m A - 2 \sum_{i,j} \left(W_{ij} \right)^T H_{ij} W_{ij} A - 2 \Lambda A \tag{14}$$

where $D_{ij}^m = \frac{p}{2}\left[B_{ij}^m AA^T \left(B_{ij}^m\right)^T\right]^{\frac{p-2}{2}}$ and $H_{ij} = \frac{p}{2}\left[W_{ij}AA^T\left(W_{ij}\right)^T\right]^{\frac{p-2}{2}}$. $\Lambda \in R^{s \times s}$ is the symmetric Lagrangian multiplier matrix. To look for the maximum point of objective function, (14) is set to be zero, then the Eq. (14) is changed to:

$$(S_b - S_w)A = A\Lambda \tag{15}$$

where $S_b = \sum_{i,j,m}\left(B_{ij}^m\right)^T D_{ij}^m B_{ij}^m$ and $S_w = \sum_{i,j}\left(W_{ij}\right)^T H_{ij}W_{ij}$. Both S_b and S_w rely on A. If $(S_b - S_w)$ is a known constant matrix and considering the orthogonal constraint $A^T A = I_s$, the optimal projection matrix A can be calculated by solving the eigen value decomposition problem as below:

$$A^T(S_b - S_w)A = \Lambda \tag{16}$$

According to (15), since $(S_b - S_w)$ is symmetric and each element in the diagonal of Λ is an eigen value of $(S_b - S_w)$, A is formed by the s eigen vectors corresponding to s largest eigen values of $(S_b - S_w)$. Since the objective function is bounded by $A^T A = I_s$ and it increases after each iteration, the convergence of this algorithm can be realized. Based on these analyses, we propose an iterative algorithm to obtain the optimal projection matrix. The algorithm is concluded in Algorithm 1.

Algorithm 1. An efficient iterative algorithm for solving the Eq. (12)

Input: N training image matrices $\left\{x_i^j\right\}$, $i = 1,...,C, j = 1,...,l$ (l denotes the number of training samples per individual); Values of k, K, p, ε; Initialize A such that $A^T A = I_s$; Set $t = 0$.

While not converge:

1. Compute B_{ij}^m, W_{ij}, D_{ij}^m, H_{ij}, S_b and S_w;

2. Perform eigen value decomposition of $(S_b - S_w)$, A is formed by the s eigen vectors corresponding to s the largest eigen values of $(S_b - S_w)$;

3. Check the convergence situation $\left\|A^{t+1} - A^t\right\| < \varepsilon$;

4. $t = t + 1$.

End while

Output: the optimal projection matrix $A = A^t$.

---

4 Experiments

In this section, extensive experiments are conducted on ORL [17] and CMU PIE [18] databases to testify the effectiveness of our method in the condition that $p = 1/4$, $1/2$, $3/4$ respectively. Meanwhile, we compare SPLRDA with other state-of-art feature extraction methods such as PCA [1], LDA [2], LPP [8] and RDA [12]. Different classifiers are adopted to measure the performance of each method. All the algorithms have been run for five times independently to obtain average recognition rates. We only exhibit the highest results for comparison and analysis.

4.1 Experiments on ORL Database

The ORL face database includes 400 face images belonging to 40 individuals. Each person has 10 images distinct from view direction, facial expression (mouth opened or closed, laughing or calm), facial details (with or without glasses) and illumination. Each image has been normalized to the size of 112×92 with 256 gray levels.

Ten samples of one individual are displayed in Fig. 1. In our experiments, we cropped each image manually and resized it to 32×32 pixels. l ($l = 4, 5$) images per person are randomly selected for training while the remainders for testing. Note that k ranges from 1 to $l - 1$ and K ranges from 1 to C − 1. To observe the effect of k, K is fixed to $\lfloor C/2 \rfloor + 1$ and k is varied from 1 to $l - 1$.

Fig. 1. Ten samples of one individual in ORL database

Figure 2 shows the recognition rates of SPLRDA plus LLRC with varied k. The results indicate that out method achieves best performances when k = 2 and k = 3 associating with $l = 5$ and $l = 4$, which demonstrates the effectiveness of exploiting neighborhood structure. Therefore, to detect the effect of K, we fixed k to 3 and 2 corresponding to $l = 4$ and $l = 5$ respectively, and varied K from 3 to C − 1 in increments of 4. Figure 3 displays the recognition rates of SPLRDA plus LLRC with varied K. From Fig. 3, it can be seen that parameter K does affect the performance of our method and they all gain best recognition rates when K achieves highest value. Average recognition rates of all methods are displayed in Table 1. In the experiments, we tested these feature extraction methods under three different classifiers. Experimental results verify that classifier matters the performance of face recognition and our method fits LLRC better than other related methods. From Table 1, we can see that when $l = 4$ and $l = 5$, SPLRDA achieves best recognition rates in the condition that $p = 1/4$, which demonstrates the effectiveness of our method.

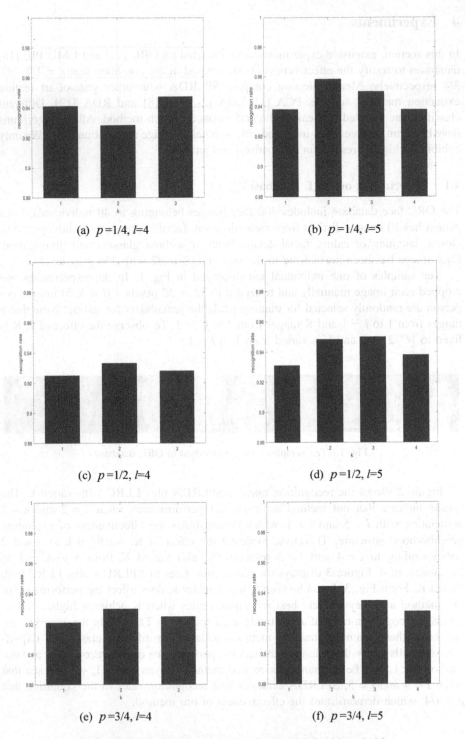

Fig. 2. Recognition rates of SPLRDA plus LLRC with varied k

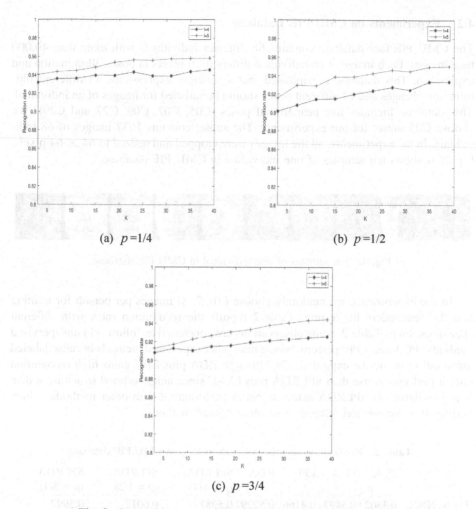

(a) $p=1/4$

(b) $p=1/2$

(c) $p=3/4$

Fig. 3. Recognition rates of SPLRDA plus LLRC with varied K

Table 1. Recognition accuracy of each method in ORL database

		PCA	LDA	LPP	RDA	SPLRDA ($p = 1/4$)	SPLRDA ($p = 1/2$)	SPLRDA ($p = 3/4$)
$l = 4$	NNC	0.8892	0.9125	0.8489	0.9050	0.9050	0.8991	0.8808
	LRC	0.8892	0.9000	0.9000	0.9175	0.9333	0.9300	0.9175
	LLRC	0.8925	0.9083	0.8925	0.9192	**0.9458**	0.9333	0.9300
$l = 5$	NNC	0.9300	0.9250	0.8808	0.9400	0.9350	0.9300	0.9240
	LRC	0.9500	0.9200	0.9200	0.9500	0.9500	0.9400	0.9410
	LLRC	0.9500	0.9333	0.9200	0.9400	**0.9583**	0.9500	0.9440

4.2   Experiments on CMU PIE Database

The CMU PIE face database contains 68 different individuals with more than 40,000 face images. Each image of an individual differs from others in poses, illumination and expression. This database is stipulated that 4 different expressions, 43 different illumination changes and 13 different poses should be satisfied for images of an individual. This database includes five near-frontal poses (C05, C07, C09, C27 and C29). We choose C05 subset for our experiments. The subset contains 1632 images of 68 individuals. In the experiments, all the images were cropped and resized to 64 × 64 pixels. Figure 4 shows ten samples of one individual in CMU PIE database.

Fig. 4. Ten samples of one individual in CMU PIE database

In the experiments, we randomly choose l (6, 7, 8) images per person for training and the remainders for testing. Table 2 reports the recognition rates with different classifiers. From Table 2, some observations are concluded as follow: (1) unsupervised methods (PCA and LPP) perform worse than other supervised methods because labeled information are not be exploited; (2) Although RDA plus LRC gains high recognition rate, it performs worse than SPLRDA plus LLRC since neighborhood structure of data is not utilized; (3) SPLRDA achieves better performance than other methods, which verifies that our method is better than other related methods.

Table 2. Recognition accuracy of each method in CMU PIE database

		PCA	LDA	LPP	RDA	SPLRDA ($p = 1/4$)	SPLRDA ($p = 1/2$)	SPLRDA ($p = 3/4$)
$l = 6$	NNC	0.3302	0.5497	0.4166	0.5229	0.5987	0.6012	0.5997
	LRC	0.5231	0.7116	0.5602	0.7211	0.7271	0.7285	0.7255
	LLRC	0.5044	0.6895	0.5379	0.7071	0.7419	**0.7426**	0.7408
$l = 7$	NNC	0.3837	0.5988	0.4612	0.4533	0.5687	0.5672	0.5683
	LRC	0.6058	0.7532	0.6168	0.8426	0.8345	0.8357	0.8339
	LLRC	0.6113	0.7791	0.6174	0.8391	**0.8627**	0.8581	0.8576
$l = 8$	NNC	0.4912	0.7527	0.5713	0.5947	0.5969	0.5955	0.5937
	LRC	0.7645	0.8504	0.7792	0.9215	0.9224	0.9207	0.9194
	LLRC	0.7539	0.8583	0.7825	0.9203	**0.9298**	0.9226	0.9226

5 Conclusion

In this paper, a novel feature extraction method named schatten-p norm based linear regression discriminant analysis (SPLRDA) has been proposed. It not only incorporates schatten-p norm reducing the interference of illumination changes but also exploits neighborhood structure, which fits LLRC well. Experiments has demonstrated the reliability and effectiveness of our method. It performs better than other related methods.

References

1. Turk, M., Pentland, A.: Eigenfaces for recognition. J. Cogn. Neurosci. **3**(1), 71–86 (1991)
2. Belhumeur, P.N., Hespanha, J.P., Kriegman, D.J.: Eigenfaces vs. fisherfaces: recognition using class specific linear projection. IEEE Trans. Pattern Anal. Mach. Intell. **19**(7), 711–720 (1997)
3. Lee, D.D., Seung, H.S.: Learning the parts of objects by non-negative matrix factorization. Nature **401**, 788 (1999). EP
4. Raudys, S.J., Jain, A.K.: Small sample size effects in statistical pattern recognition: recommendations for practitioners. IEEE Trans. Pattern Anal. Mach. Intell. **13**(3), 252–264 (1991)
5. Tenenbaum, J.B., De Silva, V., Langford, J.C.: A global geometric framework for nonlinear dimensionality reduction. Science **290**(5500), 2319–2323 (2000)
6. Belkin, M., Niyogi, P.: Laplacian eigenmaps for dimensionality reduction and data representation. Neural Comput. **15**(6), 1373–1396 (2003)
7. Roweis, S.T., Saul, L.K.: Nonlinear dimensionality reduction by locally linear embedding. Science **290**(5500), 2323–2326 (2000)
8. He, X., Yan, S., Hu, Y., Niyogi, P., Zhang, H.J.: Face recognition using Laplacianfaces. IEEE Trans. Pattern Anal. Mach. Intell. **27**, 328–340 (2005)
9. Cover, T., Hart, P.: Nearest neighbor pattern classification. IEEE Trans. Inf. Theory **13**(1), 21–27 (1967)
10. Naseem, I., Togneri, R., Bennamoun, M.: Linear regression for face recognition. IEEE Trans. Pattern Anal. Mach. Intell. **32**(11), 2106–2112 (2010)
11. Brown, D., Li, H., Gao, Y.: Locality-regularized linear regression for face recognition. In: Proceedings of the 21st International Conference on Pattern Recognition, ICPR 2012, pp. 1586–1589 (2012)
12. Chen, Y., Jin, Z.: Reconstructive discriminant analysis: a feature extraction method induced from linear regression classification. Neurocomputing **87**, 41–50 (2012)
13. Huang, P., Li, T., Shu, Z., Gao, G., Yang, G., Qian, C.: Locality-regularized linear regression discriminant analysis for feature extraction. Inf. Sci. **429**, 164–176 (2018)
14. Du, H., Hu, Q., Jiang, M., Zhang, F.: Two-dimensional principal component analysis based on Schatten p-norm for image feature extraction. J. Vis. Commun. Image Represent. **32**, 55–62 (2015)
15. Du, H., Zhao, Z., Wang, S., Hu, Q.: Two-dimensional discriminant analysis based on Schatten p-norm for image feature extraction. J. Vis. Commun. Image Represent. **45**, 87–94 (2017)
16. Shi, X., Nie, F., Lai, Z., Guo, Z.: Robust principal component analysis via optimal mean by joint $l_{2,1}$ and Schatten p-norms minimization. Neurocomputing **283**, 205–213 (2018)

17. Samaria, F.S., Harter, A.C.: Parameterisation of a stochastic model for human face identification. In: Proceedings of 1994 IEEE Workshop on Applications of Computer Vision, pp. 138–142 (1994)
18. Sim, T., Baker, S., Bsat, M.: The CMU pose, illumination, and expression (PIE) database. In: Proceedings of Fifth IEEE International Conference on Automatic Face Gesture Recognition, pp. 46–51 (2002)

A Framework for Multi-view Feature Selection via Embedding Space

Junhao Zhang[1], Yuan Wan[1(✉)], and Yuting Pan[2]

[1] Department of Mathematics, Wuhan University of Technology,
Wuhan, Hubei, China
math249810@163.com, wanyuan@whut.edu.cn
[2] School of Law, Guangxi University, Nanning, Guangxi, China
panyvting@sina.cn

Abstract. Multi-view learning has drawn much attention in the past years to reveal the correlated and complemental information between different views. Feature selection for multi-view data is still a challenge in dimension reduction. Most of the multi-view feature selection methods simply concatenate all views together without capturing the information between different views. In this paper, we propose an embedding framework for multi-view feature selection, Embedding Space based Multi-view Feature Selection (ESMFS). ESMFS comes up with a new concept called mapping consensus to embed all views of data to a unified space. By preserving the manifold information, ESMFS captures the fusing views' information. ESMFS is suitable for both supervised and unsupervised feature selection. For practical purpose, we propose two methods ES-LRFS and ES-MAFS to illustrate ESMFS framework. Experiments show that ES-LRFS and ES-MAFS are of inclusiveness and efficiency for multi-view feature selection, thus proving the feasibility of ESMFS.

Keywords: Multi-view · Feature selection · Feature embedding

1 Introduction

With the rapid development of information technology and computer science, getting access to multi-view data has become more and more convenient. Compared to the single view data, multi-view data are described in many different ways, which have totally different intrinsic property from each other. Every *views* can provide compatible and complementary information for data analysis. Thus, one important problem in multi-view data learning is that how to reduce dimension.

Multi-view feature embedding is a technique for feature dimensionality reduction (DR), which can reduce the redundancy among features while preserving the discriminative information. In the past decades, a large family of DR method have been proposed in the attempt to find an appropriate low dimensional subspace of the original high dimensional feature space, such as Locally

© Springer Nature Singapore Pte Ltd. 2018
Y. Wang et al. (Eds.): IGTA 2018, CCIS 875, pp. 57–69, 2018.
https://doi.org/10.1007/978-981-13-1702-6_6

Linear Embedding (LLE [21]), ISOMAP [22], Laplacian Eigenmaps (LE [23]), Hessian eigenmaps (HLLE [24]), and Local Tangent Space Alignment (LTSA [25]). Recently, Researchers have also come up with some methods for multi-view feature embedding, such as Distributed Spectral Embedding (DES [1]), Multi-view Spectral Embedding (MSE [2]), Ensemble Manifold Regularized Sparse Low-rank Approximation (EMR-SLRA [3]), and low-rank discriminant embedding (LRDE [4]), and so on [5]. In this paper, we will show the relationship between multi-view feature embedding and multi-view feature selection.

Multi-view feature selection is another strategy that deals with high-dimensional noisy data and reduces the dimension of data. There are three types: Supervised method [17], Semi-supervised method [18–20] and Unsupervised method. The key challenge of multi-view feature selection is twofold [6]: (1) how to effectively represent the fused information from multiple views; (2) how to choose features that can effectively reveal or maintain the structure of data. There are some of unsupervised multi-view feature selection approaches try to handle these two challenge, such as Adaptive Unsupervised Multi-view Feature Selection (AUMFS [7]), Multi-view Feature Selection (MVFS [8]), Multi-view Feature Unsupervised Feature Selection (MVUFS [9]) and Cross Diffused Matrix Alignment based Feature Selection (CDMA-FS [6]). In this paper, we focus on the first challenge of multi-view feature selection, namely the fusing approach, and propose a framework for multi-view feature selection using multi-view feature embedding method, namely Embedding Space based Multi-view Feature Selection (ESMFS). The main advantages of ESMFS lie in the following:

– ESMFS reveals the relationship between multi-view feature embedding and multi-view feature selection, helping us gain more insight into multi-view feature selection, which provide a new perspective in multi-view feature selection.
– ESMFS deals with the first challenge of fused information, alleviating the conflict between different *views*. Through feature embedding, ESMFS is able to excavate the latent information hiding in multiple *views*.

The remainder of this paper is organized as follows. In Sect. 2, we present the framework of fusing approach of multi-view feature selection, namely Space Embedding Method. In Sect. 3, we perform the feature selection and propose two particular methods namely Embedding Space based Linear Regression Feature Selection Method (ES-LRFS) and Embedding Space based Matrix Alignment Feature Selection Method (ES-MAFS), Experimental results are presented in Sect. 4 and we conclude our work in Sect. 5.

2   Embedding Space Method

To construct a Satisfactory embedding space, it's very crucial to extract information underlying the datum. One prevailing idea is named as Manifold Preserving, which considers inheritance relationship between original space and embedding space. With manifold preserving term, the embedding space can make best use of the structure imformation of original space. Here, we also take use of this method, meanwhile, we proposed a new method called Mapping Consensus, which considers to find high quality mappings between original space and embedding space. In the next subsections, we will show these two methods in detail.

2.1   Manifold Preserving

Different views of features are obtained from different perspectives of the data description, so a good embedding space should have the ability to encode the correlation among those different views. And the correlation between different views can be preserved by the local manifold, which means that datum which are close to each other are also close to each other in the embedding space. Then in the framework of Space Embedding Method, we first consider the factor of local manifold, i.e. Manifold Preserving term.

Just like most of the existing methods [2,3,10], the multi-view manifold preserving term can be formulated as,

$$E_L = \sum_{v=1}^{V}(\lambda^v)^r tr(TL^v T^T), \quad \sum_{v=1}^{V}\lambda^v = 1 \tag{1}$$

where λ^v reflect the importance of view v, L^v is the Laplacian matrix of the vth view, i.e., $L^v = D^v - W^v$ and D^v is a diagonal matrix whose entries are column sums of W^v, W^v is the kernel matrix in vth *view*, and T is the target mapping result of data in the original feature space.

2.2   Mapping Consensus

As we can see, by adopting a mapping from each *view* in the original space to a common latent embedding space, we easily solve the problem of fusing information. However, it obviously leads to a new problem, how to measure the quality of those mappings? Locality preserving term measures the mapping by how well the locality property a mapping can hold.

In this paper, we provide a new perspective, namely mapping consensus, it mainly deals with the problem of multi-mapping disagreements. Since every data point can locate in different *views*, so according to the mapping process, representations of the same data point from every *view* can be mapped into the latent embedding space. In this occasion, mapping conflict may occur, the reason is that the data point is unique, but different mapping in different *views* maybe lead to different mapping results. The aim of mapping consensus is preserving validity of mappings and avoid mapping conflict. An example of canonical mappings with mapping consensus is showed in Fig. 1.

In order to deal with the aforementioned issue, we think reversely, supposing there is a group of perfect maps without mapping conflict. Let X be the datum matrix with each row x_i being the ith data instance. x_i^v represents the vth view of data x_i. Considering of a fixed object x_i represented in different *views* x_i^v ($v = 1, 2, \cdots$), we have $\phi^v : x_i \rightarrow T_i, \phi^v \in V$, where T_i the true representation of this point in latent embedding space and ϕ^v is the latent embedding mapping for vth view, the following expression

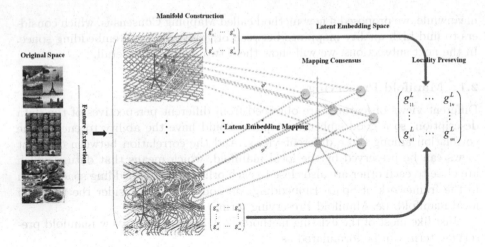

Fig. 1. The diagram of our space embedding method. Through latent embedding mappings, every data in different original feature space is mapped into a common latent embedding space. Mapping consensus ensures the uniqueness of mapping result for each object, while Manifold Preserving ensures the locality geometry structure of datum's manifold in original feature space.

$$E_{C(i)} = \sum_{v=1}^{V} \|\phi^v(x_i^v) - T_i\|^2 \tag{2}$$

should be zero. Now we utilize this character, that is a good set of maps should force this term as small as zero to their utmost. And (2) is called mapping consensus optimizing term.

To prevent the target result from being affected by noisy data, we adopt parameter γ_i^v to achieve this goal, thus we can reformulate mapping consensus term as,

$$
\begin{aligned}
E_{C(i)} &= \sum_{v=1}^{V} \|\phi^v(x_i^v) - T_i\|^2 \gamma_i^v \\
&= tr\left(\begin{pmatrix} \phi^1(x_i^1) - T_i \\ \vdots \\ \phi^V(x_i^V) - T_i \end{pmatrix} (\phi^1(x_i^1) - T_i \cdots \phi^V(x_i^V) - T_i) diag(\gamma_i) \right) \\
&= tr\left(Z_i \begin{pmatrix} -e_{V+1}^T \\ I_{V+1} \end{pmatrix} diag(\gamma_i) \left(-e_{V+1} \ I_{V+1} \right) Z_i^T \right) \\
&= tr(Z_i C_i Z_i^T)
\end{aligned}
\tag{3}
$$

where $Z_i = \left(T_i \ \phi^1(x_i^1) \cdots \phi^V(x_i^V) \right)$, where $\phi = diag(\phi^1 \cdots \phi^V)$. And $C_i = \begin{pmatrix} -e_{V+1}^T \\ I_{V+1} \end{pmatrix} diag(\gamma_i)(-e_{V+1} \ I_{V+1})$. γ_i^v can be as small as 0 when the mapping result of x_i in vth view thought to be outlier, to dismiss the effect of the noisy point.

Thus, considering of whole data set by summing over $E_{C(i)}$, we can formulate the multi-view mapping consensus as,

$$E_C = \sum_{i=1}^{N} E_{C(i)} = \sum_{i=1}^{N} tr(Z_i C_i Z_i^T) \tag{4}$$

Denote $Z = (T \; \phi^1(x_1^1) \; \cdots \; \phi^V(x_1^V) \; \cdots \; \phi^1(x_N^1) \; \cdots \; \phi^V(x_N^V))$, and $Z_i = ZS_i$, S_i is the selection matrix, i.e., $S_i = (e_i^T \; \cdots \; e_{N+(i-1)V+1}^T \; \cdots \; e_{N+iV}^T)$, E_C can be reformulated as,

$$E_C = \sum_{i=1}^{N} tr(ZS_i C_i S_i^T Z) \tag{5}$$
$$= tr(ZCZ^T)$$

where C is defined as $C = \sum_{i=1}^{N} S_i C_i S_i^T$. Through some algebraic manipulation, we have $C = D - \Gamma$, where Γ is a matrix connecting the target mapping points and original data points,

$$\Gamma = \begin{pmatrix} G & \gamma \\ \gamma^T & 0 \end{pmatrix} \tag{6}$$

where

$$\gamma = \begin{pmatrix} \gamma_1^1 \cdots \gamma_1^V & & O \\ & \cdots & \\ O & & \gamma_n^1 \cdots \gamma_n^V \end{pmatrix} \tag{7}$$

and D is a diagonal whose entries are column sums of Γ. We further manipulate E_C as

$$E_C = tr(ZCZ^T)$$
$$= tr\left((T \; \Phi) \begin{pmatrix} C_{11} & C_{12} \\ C_{21} & C_{22} \end{pmatrix} \begin{pmatrix} T^T \\ \phi^T \end{pmatrix} \right) \tag{8}$$
$$= tr(TC_{11}T^T) + tr(\Phi C_{21}T^T) + tr(TC_{12}\Phi^T) + tr(\Phi C_{22}\Phi^T)$$

where $\Phi = (\phi^1(x_1^1) \; \cdots \; \phi^V(x_1^V) \; \cdots \; \phi^1(x_n^1) \; \cdots \; \phi^V(x_n^V))$.

2.3   Optimization Method

Based on the aforementioned optimization term, we conclude the objective function as,

$$\min_{\phi,C,\lambda,T} E = E_C + E_L$$
$$= tr(ZCZ^T) + \alpha C \odot C + \beta \sum_{v \in V} (\lambda^v)^r tr(TL^v T^T) \tag{9}$$
$$= tr(TC_{11}T^T) + tr(\Phi C_{21}T^T) + tr(TC_{12}\Phi^T) + tr(\Phi C_{22}\Phi^T)$$
$$+ \alpha C \odot C + \beta \sum_{v \in V} (\lambda^v)^r tr(TL^v T^T), \quad \sum_{v \in V} (\lambda^v)^r = 1$$

where $\odot$ is the Hadamard product, the term $\alpha C \odot C$ is introduced to help adaptive learning of the structure of C [11].

Now, we give the optimization procedure.

Optimize ϕ, Fixed C, λ, T. Recall the nature of Φ and the aim of our optimization, we can optimize E for fixed C, λ, T through controlling the following term, which will reduce lots of computation expense and be of high efficiency,

$$
\begin{aligned}
\mathcal{L}(\phi) &= \|\Phi - T'\|_F^2 \\
&= \|X\phi' - T'\|_F^2
\end{aligned}
\tag{10}
$$

where $\phi' = diag(\phi, \cdots, \phi)$, $X = (\, x_1^1 \cdots x_1^V \cdots x_N^1 \cdots x_N^V \,)$, $T' = (\, T_1 \cdots T_1 \cdots T_N \cdots T_N \,)$, Setting $\frac{\partial \mathcal{L}}{\partial \phi'} = 0$, we get

$$
\frac{\partial \mathcal{L}}{\partial \phi'} = 2(X\phi' - T')X = 0
\tag{11}
$$

which leads to the updating formula for ϕ'

$$
\phi' = X^{-1}T'
\tag{12}
$$

Optimize C, Fixed ϕ, λ, T. The original expression can be rewritten as,

$$
min\,\mathcal{L}(C) = tr(ZCZ^T) + \alpha C \odot C,
\tag{13}
$$

the optimization of $\mathcal{L}(C)$ can be solved in the same routine mentioned in [11]. For the sake of avoiding overelaborating, readers may find the solution in [11].

Optimize λ, Fixed ϕ, C, T. The original expression can be rewritten as,

$$
\begin{aligned}
min\,\mathcal{L}(\lambda) &= \sum_{v \in V} (\lambda^v)^r tr(YL^vY^T), \\
\sum_{v \in V} (\lambda^v)^r &= 1
\end{aligned}
\tag{14}
$$

Rewrite the constrained optimization problems in the form of Lagrange Multiplier,

$$
min\,\mathcal{L}(\lambda^v, \eta) = \sum_{v \in V} (\lambda^v)^r tr(YL^vY^T) - \eta(\sum_{v \in V} \lambda^v - 1).
\tag{15}
$$

by setting the derivative of $\mathcal{L}(\lambda, \eta)$ with respect to λ and η, we get,

$$
\begin{cases}
\dfrac{\partial \mathcal{L}(\lambda^v, \eta)}{\partial \lambda^v} = r(\lambda^v)^{r-1} tr(YL^vY^T) - \eta = 0 \\[2mm]
\dfrac{\partial \mathcal{L}(\lambda^v, \eta)}{\partial \eta} = \sum_{v=1}^{V} \lambda^v - 1 = 0
\end{cases}
\tag{16}
$$

Therefore, we obtained,

$$
\lambda^v = \frac{(r \cdot tr(YL^vY^T))^{\frac{1}{r-1}}}{\sum_{v \in V}(r \cdot tr(YL^vY^T))^{\frac{1}{r-1}}}
\tag{17}
$$

Optimize T, Fixed ϕ, C, λ. Then the original expression can be rewritten as,

$$
\begin{aligned}
\min \mathcal{L}(T) &= tr(TC_{11}T^T) + tr(\Phi C_{21}T^T) + tr(TC_{12}\Phi^T) \\
&\quad + \beta \sum_{v \in V} (\lambda^v)^r tr(TL^v T^T) \\
&= tr(TC_{11}T^T) + tr(\Phi C_{21}T^T) + tr(\Phi^T C_{12}^T T^T) \\
&\quad + \beta \sum_{v \in V} (\lambda^v)^r tr(TL^v T^T)
\end{aligned}
\tag{18}
$$

setting $\frac{\partial \mathcal{L}(T)}{\partial T^T} = 0$, we get,

$$
2C_{11}T^T + \Phi C_{21} + \Phi^T C_{12}^T + \beta L'T^T = 0
\tag{19}
$$

where $L' = \sum_{v \in V} (\lambda^v)^r L^v$. Therefore, the updating formula for T is

$$
T = \left(-(2C_{11} + \beta L')^{-1} (\Phi C_{21} + \Phi^T C_{12}^T) \right)^T
\tag{20}
$$

The convergence proof of the proposed optimization method is omitted. Similar proof can be found in [2,12].

3 Feature Selection

There are mainly two ways for feature selection whether in multi-view version or in single view version, namely regression method [12,16] and matrix alignment method [6,13]. Embedding Space based Multi-view Feature Selection (ESMFS) combines space embedding and feature selection, where space embedding tries to learn a common latent space over all *view* extracting the fusing information. Adopting the two aforementioned feature selection methods, We propose two specific methods, i.e. ES-LRFS and ES-MAFS, showing the use of linear regression method and matrix alignment method in multi-view feature selection via the framework of Space Embedding method. A illustration of the framework is showed in Fig. 2.

3.1 Regression Method

While assumed that there is a "hard" linear transformation between features and pseudo labels is too strict, because of the existence of nonlinearity, research seek to mitigate this problem, an explicitly "soft" linear constrained transformation [12], which is essentially a regression method.

$$
\min_{W,F} \|X^T W - F\|_F^2 + \beta \|W\|_{2,1},
\tag{21}
$$

where F is the pseudo label and $\| \cdot \|_{2,1}$ is $l_{2,1}$ norm defined as $\|X\|_{2,1} = \sum_{i=1}^{p} \sqrt{\sum_{j=1}^{q} x_{ij}^2}$. And the second term is constraint results in row sparseness property, which is consistent with the ideal feature selection matrix W [7].

3.2   Matrix Alignment

Although regression method considers the nonlinearity of real-world situation as much as possible, it is still a linear method. When encountering a nonlinear distributed datum, the linear way doesn't work well.

[6,13] proposed to use the nonlinearity method called matrix alignment or kernel alignment [26].

$$\min_{s^{(v)}} f = -Tr(HGHK^{(v)})$$

$$s.t. \sum_{p=1}^{D^{(v)}} = d^{(v)} \tag{22}$$

$$s_p^{(v)} \in \{0,1\}, \forall p = 1, \cdots, D^{(v)},$$

where G is the guiding matrix, K is the kernel matrix, H is defined as $H = I - \frac{1}{n}\mathbf{1}\mathbf{1}^T$, $\mathbf{1} = (\,1\,\cdots\,1\,)^T$, $s^{(v)}$ is the feature selection vector, $d^{(v)}$ is the number of selected features in vth view.

4   Experiments

4.1   Data Sets

In experiments, we use two famous real-world data sets.

- NUS-WIDE-OBJECT[1]: It is the object image part from the real-world web image data set from National University of Singapore. Each data sample

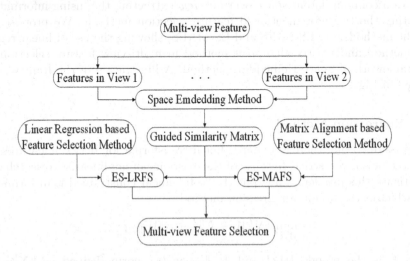

Fig. 2. Flowchart of ESMFS framework based multi-view feature selection

---

[1] http://lms.comp.nus.edu.sg/research/NUS-WIDE.htm.

contains six types of low-level features extracted from these images, including 64-D color histogram, 144-D color correlogram, 73-D edge direction histogram, 128-D wavelet texture, 225-D block-wise color moments and 500-D bag of words based on SIFT descriptions.

- Corel5k[2]: It is collected from real-world by Corel. Corel5k contains 5000 samples, based on 50 different topics, for example, bus, dinosaurs and beaches. In order to keep concordance, we extract the same six types of low-level features.

4.2 Baseline Method

- All Features: It uses all original features without selection for evaluation.
- LS: Laplacian Score [14] selects the features that preserve the local manifold structure.
- MVFS: Multi-view Feature Selection [8] is unsupervised feature selection for multi-view data based on pseudo labels, which are generated as the consensus of spectral clustering on two views.
- CDMA-FS: Cross Diffused Matrix Alignment based Feature Selection [6] selects features for each view by performing alignment on a cross diffused matrix.

4.3 Experimental Settings

We use co-regularized spectral clustering [15] to examine the quality of selected features in unsupervised multi-view feature selection and SVM with RBF kernel for supervised version in multi-view feature selection. In experiment, we repeat co-regularized spectral clustering and SVM for 10 times, number of selected features are in the range between 100 and 600 with step size 50. In convergence test, we show the varying of objective function used in ESMFS, as the iteration times increasing. In sensibility test, because ESMFS focuses on the fusing process for multi-view data, the performance of ESMFS may not be influenced by the category of clustering method and ways of feature selection, we only show the sensibility test in co-regularized spectral clustering using ESLRFS. To better investigate the parameters used in our method, we first test one of the parameter's sensibility while keep the others fixed, then we show the crossing effect of α and β.

In order to evaluating clustering performance, we use normalized mutual information (NMI) as the clustering quality evaluation measure, which gives the mutual information between obtained clustering and the true clustering normalized by the cluster entropies. NMI ranges between 0 and 1 with higher value indicating closer match to the true clustering. Let A be the set of clustering algorithm and B obtained from a clustering algorithm. Their normalized mutual information $MI(A, B)$ can be defined as follows,

$$NMI(A, B) = \frac{1}{max\{H(A), H(B)\}} \sum_{a_i \in A, b_j \in B} p(a_i, b_j) log \frac{p(a_i, b_j)}{p(a_i)p(b_j)}, \quad (23)$$

---

[2] https://github.com/watersink/Corel5K.

where $p(a_i)$ and $p(b_j)$ are the probabilities that a random instance from the data set belongs to a_i and b_j, respectively, and $p(a_i, b_j)$ is the joint probability that the instance belongs to the cluster a_i and b_j at the same time and $H(A)$ and $H(B)$ are the entropy of A and B.

4.4 Experiment Result

The clustering NMI on NUS-WIDE-OBJECT and Corel5k are shown in Fig. 3. The convergence test is shown in Fig. 4. Figures 5 and 6 are the sensitive test for the parameters used in our method.

It can be seen that both ES-MAFS and ES-LRFS are efficient, outperforming other methods on these two data sets, which means that our method are effective in practice. In addition, the convergence of ESMFS is pretty fast and parameters α and β in ESMFS are not very sensitive. The advantages of our method may arise in twofold: (1) ESMFS provide a framework for multi-view selection using feature embedding, allowing further development in multi-view feature selection. (2) ESMFS helps to gain more insight in the feature embedding and feature selection.

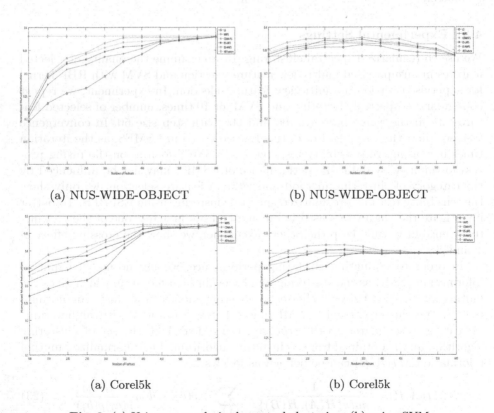

(a) NUS-WIDE-OBJECT   (b) NUS-WIDE-OBJECT

(a) Corel5k   (b) Corel5k

Fig. 3. (a) Using co-regularized spectral clustering, (b) using SVM

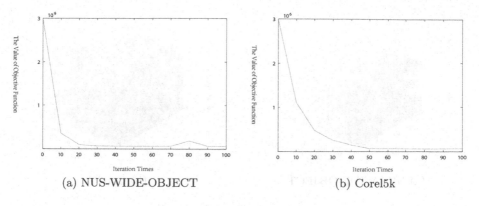

(a) NUS-WIDE-OBJECT   (b) Corel5k

Fig. 4. Convergence test of ESMFS

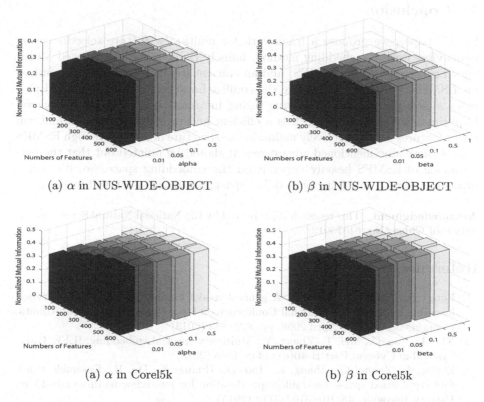

(a) α in NUS-WIDE-OBJECT   (b) β in NUS-WIDE-OBJECT

(a) α in Corel5k   (b) β in Corel5k

Fig. 5. Sensity test for α and β

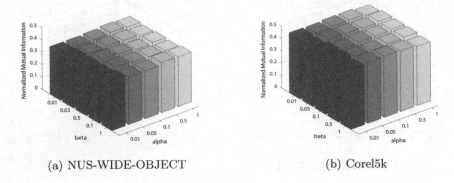

(a) NUS-WIDE-OBJECT   (b) Corel5k

Fig. 6. Sensity test for the crossing effect of α and β

5 Conclusion

In this paper, we propose a framework for multi-view feature selection using multi-view feature embedding method, namely Embedding Space based Multi-view Feature Selection (ESMFS) and an efficient iterative optimization method for ESMFS. ESMFS can alleviate the conflict between different views and provides a new perspective for solving fusing information among multiple views. Experiments show that ESMFS is a efficient and inclusive framework and can select features which effectively maintain the structure of data. Although ESMFS enjoys those aforementioned advantages, it should be pointed out that the performance of ESMFS heavily depends on the embedding space. So, it's still a problem to find a satisfying embedding space, our future work will focus on it.

Acknowledgment. This research is supported by the National Natural Science Foundation of China (No. 61573012).

References

1. Long, B., Yu, P.S., Zhang, Z.: A general model for multiple view unsupervised learning. In: SIAM International Conference on Data Mining, SDM 2008, Atlanta, Georgia, USA, 24–26 April 2008, pp. 822–833 (2013)
2. Xia, T., Tao, D., Mei, T., Zhang, Y.: Multiview spectral embedding. IEEE Trans. Syst. Man Cybern. Part B **40**(6), 1438–1446 (2010)
3. Zhang, L., Zhang, Q., Zhang, L., Tao, D., Huang, X., Du, B.: Ensemble manifold regularized sparse low-rank approximation for multiview feature embedding. Pattern Recognit. **48**(10), 3102–3112 (2015)
4. Li, J., Wu, Y., Zhao, J., Lu, K.: Low-rank discriminant embedding for multiview learning. IEEE Trans. Cybern. **47**(11), 3516 (2017)
5. Wan, Y., Chen, X., Zhang, J.: Global and intrinsic geometric structure embedding for unsupervised feature selection. Expert Syst. Appl. (2017)
6. Wei, X., Cao, B., Yu, P.S.: Multi-view unsupervised feature selection by cross-diffused matrix alignment. In: International Joint Conference on Neural Networks (2017)

7. Feng, Y., Xiao, J., Zhuang, Y., Liu, X.: Adaptive unsupervised multi-view feature selection for visual concept recognition. In: Lee, K.M., Matsushita, Y., Rehg, J.M., Hu, Z. (eds.) ACCV 2012. LNCS, vol. 7724, pp. 343–357. Springer, Heidelberg (2013). https://doi.org/10.1007/978-3-642-37331-2_26

8. Tang, J., Hu, X., Gao, H., Liu, H.: Unsupervised feature selection for multi-view data in social media (2013)

9. Qian, M., Zhai, C.: Unsupervised feature selection for multi-view clustering on text-image web news data. In: ACM International Conference on Conference on Information and Knowledge Management, pp. 1963–1966 (2014)

10. Zhang, T., Tao, D., Li, X., Yang, J.: Patch alignment for dimensionality reduction. IEEE Trans. Knowl. Data Eng. **21**(9), 1299–1313 (2009)

11. Du, L., Shen, Y.D.: Unsupervised feature selection with adaptive structure learning, vol. 37, no. 7, pp. 209–218 (2015)

12. Li, Z., Yang, Y., Liu, J., Zhou, X., Lu, H.: Unsupervised feature selection using nonnegative spectral analysis. In: 模式识别国家重点实验室, vol. 2, pp. 1026–1032 (2012)

13. Wei, X., Cao, B., Yu, P.S.: Nonlinear joint unsupervised feature selection. In: SIAM International Conference on Data Mining, pp. 414–422 (2016)

14. He, X., Cai, D., Niyogi, P.: Laplacian score for feature selection. In: International Conference on Neural Information Processing Systems, pp. 507–514 (2006)

15. Kumar, A., Rai, P.: Co-regularized multi-view spectral clustering. In: International Conference on Neural Information Processing Systems, pp. 1413–1421 (2011)

16. Qian, M., Zhai, C.: Robust unsupervised feature selection. In: International Joint Conference on Artificial Intelligence, pp. 1621–1627 (2013)

17. Chen, X., Zhou, G., Chen, Y., Shao, G., Gu, Y.: Supervised multiview feature selection exploring homogeneity and heterogeneity with $l_{1,2}$-norm and automatic view generation. IEEE Trans. Geosci. Remote Sens. **PP**(99), 1–15 (2017)

18. Chen, X., Liu, W., Su, F., Zhou, G.: Semisupervised multiview feature selection for VHR remote sensing images with label learning and automatic view generation. IEEE J. Sel. Top. Appl. Earth Obs. Remote Sens. **PP**(99), 1–13 (2017)

19. Chen, X., Liu, W., Su, F., Shao, G.: Semi-supervised multiview feature selection with label learning for VHR remote sensing images. In: Geoscience and Remote Sensing Symposium, pp. 2372–2375 (2016)

20. Chen, X., Song, L., Hou, Y., Shao, G.: Efficient semi-supervised feature selection for VHR remote sensing images. In: Geoscience and Remote Sensing Symposium, pp. 1500–1503 (2016)

21. Roweis, S.T., Saul, L.K.: Nonlinear dimensionality reduction by locally linear embedding. Science **290**(5500), 2323 (2000)

22. Tenenbaum, J.B., Silva, V.D., Langford, J.C.: A global geometric framework for nonlinear dimensionality reduction. Science **290**(5500), 2319–2323 (2000)

23. Belkin, M., Niyogi, P.: Laplacian eigenmaps and spectral techniques for embedding and clustering. In: Advances in Neural Information Processing Systems, vol. 14, no. 6 (2001)

24. Donoho, D.L., Grimes, C.: Hessian eigenmaps: locally linear embedding techniques for high-dimensional data. Proc. Natl. Acad. Sci. U.S.A. **100**(10), 5591 (2003)

25. Zhang, Z.Y., Zha, H.Y.: Principal manifolds and nonlinear dimensionality reduction via tangent space alignment. Adv. Manuf. (先进制造进展(英文)) **8**(4), 406–424 (2004)

26. Wang, T., Zhao, D., Tian, S.: An overview of kernel alignment and its applications. Artif. Intell. Rev. **43**(2), 179–192 (2015)

Image Mosaic Based on Pixel Subtle Variations

Siqi Deng[1($\boxtimes$)], Xiaofeng Shi[1($\boxtimes$)], and Xiaoyan Luo[2($\boxtimes$)]

[1] School of Electronic Information Engineering, Beihang University, No. 37 Xueyuan Road,
Haidian District, Beijing, China
{sqdengdeng,shixiaofeng}@buaa.edu.cn
[2] School of Astronautics, Beihang University, No. 37 Xueyuan Road,
Haidian District, Beijing, China
luoxy@buaa.edu.cn

Abstract. Many traditional image mosaic methods focus on image registration, and attempt to provide a discontinuous solution of overlapping images. However, the overlapping areas cannot be captured in some special situation such as airborne line scan camera. For this airborne imaging, we introduce a novel mosaic technique based on pixel subtle variations, which analyses the pixel signal on subtle variations in Taylor series expansion. To construct the correlation between line scan sub-images, the pixels at the same position in each line scan sub-image are viewed as 1D signal, and then the misalignment and displacement among sub-images can be depicted as pixel subtle variations in translational motion. With the reference of previous line scan sub-image, the subtle variations of adjacent sub-images can be evaluated and eliminated. Afterwards, a number of sub-images handled are almost aligned to compose an integral image without seam line. The experimental mosaic results on real sub-images of airborne line scan show the effectiveness of our method in achieving seamless zebra crossing image and the strong robustness to brightness.

Keywords: Image mosaic · Line scan camera · Pixel subtle variations
Taylor series expansion · Signal processing

1 Introduction

The aerial camera is adopted as the main device for aircraft to collect visual data robustly. With flight condition and resolution requirement, the line scan camera is widely used with the advantages of large-width and high-resolution, which is a kind of linear CCD camera with multiple columns but only one row pixels. In order to obtain a complete image, line scan image mosaic becomes an important and challenging issue. If we view each line scan image with only one row pixels as a sub-image, we aim to combine sub-images into a large mosaic image in this paper.

Image mosaic plays a critical role in computer graph and vision. It is the process of combining multiple images to produce a panorama or large image [1, 2]. At present, the commonly used image mosaic is for overlapping images, and the process can be divided into three main parts: feature extraction, image registration and image blending [3, 4]. In [5], Lowe introduces a fully automated panorama image mosaic system. It presents

© Springer Nature Singapore Pte Ltd. 2018
Y. Wang et al. (Eds.): IGTA 2018, CCIS 875, pp. 70–79, 2018.
https://doi.org/10.1007/978-981-13-1702-6_7

a SIFT [6, 7] based alignment technique, with incorporation of RANSAC [8] and probabilistic matching verification to enhance robustness. However, this method requires the multiple handled images are overlapped. In practice, this requirement is not always met. To address this problem, Changying presents a fast mosaic arithmetic method for multi-CCD Image by localizing the calculation to a statistically defined boundary neighbors in [9]. Moreover, as an attempt to exploit remarkable linear features, a feature -based approach [10] is proposed. Nevertheless, the limitation is that the system requires aircraft attitude and geographical coordinates of several feature points to conduct a rough match. Cho et al. [11] explore the problem of reconstructing an image from non-overlapping image patches by jigsaw puzzle problem. Another method for non-overlapping images is proposed by alignment of the extrapolated images in [12]. However, these approaches in [11, 12] are not fit in our case of line scan images with deficiency overlap portion and unknown relative placements.

Therefore, we develop a mosaic method based on pixel subtle variations to create an integral image via assembling a set of line scan sub-images. By analyzing the pixel signal in Taylor series expansion, we construct the correlation among the line scan images to realize sub-images alignment. We formulate the pixels at the same position in each line scan sub-image as 1D signal, so that the misalignment and relative displacement among sub-images can be delineated as pixel subtle variations in translational motion. With the reference of previous line scan sub-image, the subtle variations of adjacent sub-images can be evaluated and then attenuated. Afterwards, a set of sub-images handled are almost aligned to compose a seamless panorama image. This method provides an efficient alignment and mosaic algorithm, which has strong robustness to brightness and outputs reliable results.

The remainder of the paper is structured as follows. Section 2 describes the detail of our pixel-based mosaic method including image alignment and mosaic on the point of subtle variation analysis. Section 3 compares the experimental results on zebra crossing images. In Sect. 4, we discuss the limitations of our processing, and Sect. 5 presents conclusions and ideas for future work.

2   Method

This section describes the automatic line scan image mosaic algorithm for airborne line scan camera. The main process can be divided into three parts: image preprocessing, image alignment based on pixel variation analysis and image stitching, as illustrated in Fig. 1. The image preprocessing is to attenuate the effects of low lighting and enhance the area of interest. To capture the pixel variations at the same location, we consider the corresponding pixels in all sub-images as 1D signal in alignment step, and then the subtle variations of pixel signal is extracted by temporal passband filter before eliminating. Eventually, stitching the aligned line scan sub-images can obtain an integrated image.

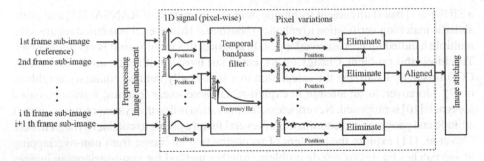

Fig. 1. The mosaic method proposed.

2.1 Image Preprocessing

To decrease the effects of low lighting and enhance the area of interest in the image, our processing includes gray transformation, image binarization and image smoothing.

2.2 Pixel Subtle Variation Analysis

To analyze the pixel subtle variation, we consider the pixels on different time as 1D signal. For a fixed location, the pixel serial signal analysis has been developed in video magnification. For example, Wu et al. [13] exaggerate motion by amplifying the variation of pixel values at fixed positions relying on the first-order Taylor series expansions common in optical flow analyses [14]. Inspired by their work, we aim to find differential approximation between pixels by disposing of pixel variations. Different with traditional image mosaic methods, we only align the sub-images instead of extracting feature points. In order to demonstrate the relationship between sub-image alignment and temporal processing of pixel signal, we briefly introduce translational motion of the 1D signal in first-order Taylor series expansion at first.

2.2.1 Translational Motion of the 1D Signal

Let $I(x, t)$ denote the pixel intensity at position x and time t, so that $I(x, 0) = f(x)$ means the initial intensity. Let $\Delta x(t)$ represent the displacement of the observed intensities, in other words, indicating the variations at position x from time 0 to time t. As a result, we now have a complete description of intensity function:

$$I(x, t) = f(x + \Delta x(t)) \tag{1}$$

The processing aims to acquire the signal:

$$\bar{I}(x, t) = f(x) \tag{2}$$

Assuming that the sub-image can be the first order approximation to Taylor series expansion, we can write the sub-image at time t, $f(x + \Delta x(t))$ in a first-order Taylor expansion about x, as:

$$I(x, t) \approx f(x) + \Delta x(t) f'(x) \tag{3}$$

Where $f'(x)$ is partial derivative for $f(x)$. To find out the displacement variations of pixels, a temporal band-pass filter is applied to $I(x, t)$ at each point x. If the displacement signal $\Delta x(t)$ is almost within the passband of the temporal band-pass filter, the result is shown as follows:

$$B(x, t) \approx \Delta x(t) f'(x) \tag{4}$$

2.2.2　Alignment and Matching

Nevertheless, in more common condition where the displacement signal $\Delta x(t)$ is not entirely within the passband, we eliminate the displacement variations by some displacement factor α. The processed signal is simply.

$$I'(x, t) = I(x, t) - \alpha B(x, t) \tag{5}$$

Where $I'(x, t)$ represents the reconstructed sub-images. Deducing the Eq. (5) by Eqs. (3) and (4), the result is

$$I'(x, t) = f(x) + (1 - \alpha)\Delta x(t) f'(x) \tag{6}$$

Further, using Taylor formula, then we have

$$I'(x, t) = f(x + (1 - \alpha)\Delta x(t)) \tag{7}$$

This process is illustrated for a single signal in Fig. 2.

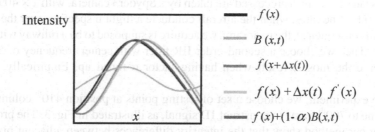

Fig. 2. Temporal processing

Our processing decrease the displacement of the initial $\Delta x(t)$ at time t to $(1 - \alpha)\Delta x(t)$. For completeness, let $\Delta x_i(t)$ denote the different temporal spectral components of $\Delta x(t)$, and σ_i represents the attenuation factor of each $\Delta x_i(t)$ in theory, resulting in a more accurate filtering result $B(x, t)$.

$$B(x, t) \approx \sum_i \sigma_i \Delta x_i(t) f'(x) \tag{8}$$

Combining Eqs. (3), (5), and (8), we have

$$I'(x, t) = f(x + \sum_i (1 - \alpha \sigma_i) \Delta x_i(t) f'(x)) \tag{9}$$

In order to reduce calculation, the displacement factor can be approximately equal to α tuned to process different images.

2.2.3   Temporal Bandpass Filters

We consider the time series corresponding to the value of a pixel in a frequency band and apply a bandpass filter to extract the frequency bands of interest [13]. Second-order IIR filters have passbands with smooth cutoff frequencies, which are efficient to extract the displacement signal by setting center frequency of the IIR filter.

Therefore, broadband temporal bandpass filter, $B(x, t)$, is applied to the original signal $I(x, t)$, resulting in the extracted signal $\Delta x(t) f'(x)$.

2.3   Image Stitching

To mosaic the aligned sub-images in order, we firstly use an empty two-dimensional matrix Das container. Let I_k, indexed by k, represent the k th frame line scan sub-image. When stitching the line scan images, we write the data of each sub-image to the matrix D line by line, resulting in the mosaic result.

$$D = [D; I_1; I_2; I_3 \ldots I_k; I_{k+1}] \tag{10}$$

3   Experimental Results

The line scan sub-images processed are taken by a Spyder3 camera, with 1×4096 resolution, 500 Hz line rates, when the aircraft conducte a flight inspection over the airport runway. In consequence, the panorama we acquire is supposed to be a runway with zebra crossings. Then we choose a second-order IIR filter with center frequency of 500 Hz, and observe the mosaic result when having factor α tuned up. Empirically, we set $\alpha = 0.18$.

In the experiment, we choose a set of testing points at position 410th column from 510th frame to 700th frame to construct 1D signal, as illustrated in Fig. 3. The processed results by our method show that the intensity differences between adjacent pixels are narrowed.

In order to directly compare the basic mosaic method with our algorithm, we used the program of Matlab to reassemble the line scan sub-images, please refer to Figs. 4, 5 and 6 for the mosaic results.

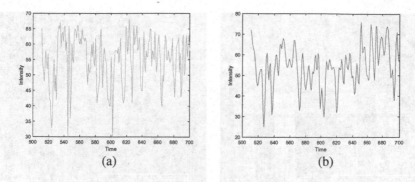

Fig. 3. 1D signal processing. (a) Origin signal. (b) The stitched signal by our method

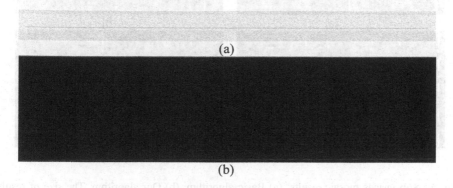

Fig. 4. Stitch the original sub-images with basic algorithm. (a) The original line scan sub-image, and its size is 1×4096 pixel. (b) The result of execution and its size is 1024×4096 pixel.

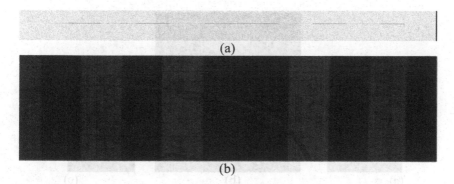

Fig. 5. (a) Result of enhancing the sub-image. (b) Mosaic result of enhanced sub-images.

To verify the excellent performance of the algorithm proposed, we use a set of sub-images to conduct a rough match and compare with other algorithms. Firstly, we carry out the following experiments through feature point extraction and RANSAC algorithm [15]. Start with the general, zoom in to the detail, the seam line shows misalignment by Fig. 7.

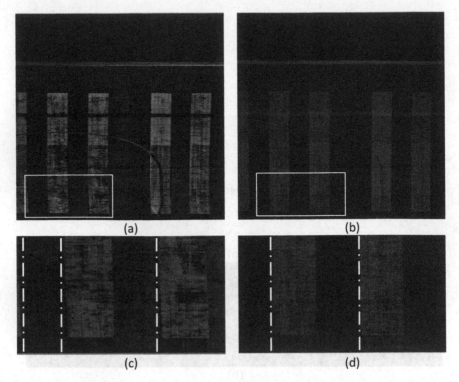

Fig. 6. Sub-images mosaic results. (a) Basic algorithm. (b) Our algorithm. The size of result image is 4096 × 4096 pixel. (c) and (d) are magnified part of the selected portion by white rectangular in (a) and (b).

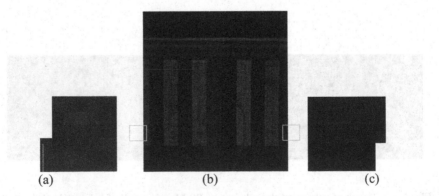

Fig. 7. (a) Misalignment at the left end of seam line. (b) Mosaic result with RANSAC algorithm. (c) Misalignment at the right end of seam line.

Afterwards, we generate a large mosaic image based on SIFT algorithm [16], which is used for automatic image stitching. Through the results of Fig. 8, we can check that this algorithm is not perfect for line scan image mosaic, for the reason that it may lead to image distortion, especially at the edge of the image, and the results are different with different overlapping regions. It can be seen that the Fig. 8(c) reaches a good mosaic effect.

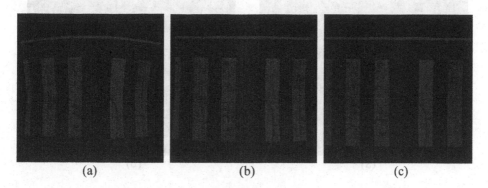

    (a)   (b)   (c)

Fig. 8. Image mosaic results by SIFT algorithm. (a) Overlapping region: 185 lines. (b) Overlapping region: 260 lines. (c) Overlapping region: 340 lines.

Furthermore, we attempt to stitch no-overlapping images using Panorama Maker [17], a commercial image mosaic software, because more overlapping lines means more time and more calculations. However, the results presented in Fig. 9 are not what we expected even if the matching points are adjusted manually.

    (a)   (b)

Fig. 9. Mosaic results by Panorama Maker. (a) Automatic mosaic result. (b) Result of adjusting matching points manually.

Compared with above algorithms, our method has higher stability and suitability for line scan image. The supplemental figures show the mosaic result of other parts of airport runway by our algorithm (Fig. 10).

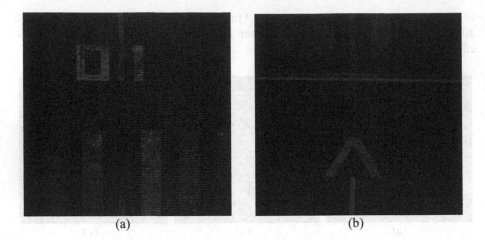

(a)   (b)

Fig. 10. Airport runway images. The size of result is 4096 × 4096 pixel.

Our processing allows line scan sub-images to be aligned smoothly, as well as improves the image alignment stability. Furthermore, intensity transformation can be used to adapt to different lighting conditions. Experimental results demonstrate that the algorithm is efficient and has certain robustness.

4   Discussion and Limitations

This algorithm we mentioned in Sect. 2 is appropriate for low spatial frequencies. For quickly changing image functions, $f(x)$, the first-order Taylor series approximations becomes inaccurate for large values of the perturbation [13]. Hence, if the camera is set to a high frequency, our processing may cause a deviation that we do not anticipate.

Moreover, we need pay more attention and patience to choose an appropriate α when aligning the linear images, because the value of α immediate impacts the alignment effect.

5   Conclusion

Image alignment and mosaic plays a critical role in computer graph and vision. Most studies concentrate on discovering the best feature points matching strategy to align the images. On the contrary, we accomplish the line scan image alignment and mosaic by means of pixel subtle variations in first-order Taylor series expansion.

We formulate the pixels at the same point in each line scan sub-image as 1D signal, extract and attenuate the subtle variations of pixel signal, and then merge the aligned sub-images into a complete image. Our algorithm is simple, intuitive and fast, which can overcome the influence of dynamic environment. Experimental results verify the effectiveness of our algorithm in both accurate alignment and mosaic for line scan images.

References

1. Ma, B., Zimmermann, T., Rohde, M., et al.: Use of Autostitch for automatic mosaicking of microscope images. Micron **38**(5), 492–499 (2007)
2. Pravenaa, S., Menaka, R.: A methodical review on image stitching and video stitching techniques. Int. J. Appl. Eng. Res. **11**(5), 3444–3448 (2016)
3. Xiong, Y.: Eliminating ghosting artifacts for panoramic images. In: IEEE International Symposium on Multimedia. IEEE Computer Society, pp. 432–437 (2009)
4. Taherim, S., Archana, B.: Multiple feature extraction techniques in image stitching. Int. J. Comput. Appl. **123** (2015)
5. Brown, M., Lowe, D.G.: Automatic panoramic image mosaicking using invariant features. Int. J. Comput. Vis. **74**(1), 59–73 (2007)
6. Qu, Z., Lin, S.P., Ju, F.R., et al.: The improved algorithm of fast panorama stitching for image sequence and reducing the distortion errors. Math. Prob. Eng. **2015**, 1–12 (2015)
7. Lowe, D.G.: Distinctive image features from scale-invariant keypoints. Int. J. Comput. Vis. **60**(2), 91–110 (2004)
8. Mach, C.A.C.: Random sample consensus: a paradigm for model fitting with application to image analysis and automated cartography (1981)
9. Wang, C.Y., Zhou, M.Q.: Fast mosaicking arithmetic method for multi-CCD image. Semicond. Optoelectron. **27**(2), 206–209 (2006)
10. Zheng, S.Y., Zhou, Y.: A novel mosaic method for SAR image sequences with deficiency of overlap portion. J. Image Graph. **10**, 023 (2009)
11. Cho, T.S., Avidan, S., Freeman, W.T.: A probabilistic image jigsaw puzzle solver. In: Computer Vision and Pattern Recognition, pp. 183–190. IEEE (2010)
12. Poleg, Y., Peleg, S.: Alignment and mosaicking of non-overlapping images. In: IEEE International Conference on Computational Photography, pp. 1–8. IEEE (2012)
13. Wu, H.Y., Rubinstein, M., Shih, E., et al.: Eulerian video magnification for revealing subtle changes in the world. In: SIGGRAPH (2012)
14. Lucas, B.D., Kaneda, T.: An iterative image registration technique with an application to stereo vision. In: International Joint Conference on Artificial Intelligence, pp. 674–679. Morgan Kaufmann Publishers Inc. (1981)
15. Li, J., Du, J.: Study on panoramic image stitching algorithm. In: Circuits, Communications and System, pp. 417–420. IEEE (2010)
16. Li, Y., Wang, Y., Huang, W., et al.: Automatic image stitching using SIFT. In: 2008 International Conference on Audio, Language and Image Processing, pp. 568–571 (2008)
17. http://www.360doc.com/content/10/1009/09/2001399_59508864.shtml

Object Detection Based on Multiscale Merged Feature Map

Zhaohui Luo, Hong Zhang, Zeyu Zhang, Yifan Yang[✉], and Jin Li

Image Processing Center, Beihang University, Beijing 100191, China
lzhmolly@163.com, Stephenyoung@163.com

Abstract. In object detection, high quality feature map is of great importance for both object location and classification. This paper presents a new network architecture to get higher quality feature map, which combines the feature map from shallow convolution layers with deep convolution layers by up–sampling and concatenating. It adopts a one-stage network, which does not rely on region proposal, to directly predict the location and classification of objects using the high quality feature map. With the input images of size 300 * 300, this network can be trained efficiently to achieve solid results on well-known object detection benchmarks: 77.7% on VOC2007, outperforming a comparable state of the art SSD [1], YOLO [5] and Faster R-CNN [4] model.

Keywords: Object detection · Up-sampling · Concatenating · Feature map

1 Introduction

Convolutional neural networks (CNNs) have made impressive improvements in many computer vision tasks for several years, such as image classification, object detection and semantic segmentation and other tasks. As for object detection, most of current state-of-the-art object detection methods adopt two kind of architecture. One use a Region Proposal Network (RPN) [4] to propose potential bounding boxes that are widely called region proposals, then use a high-quality classification network to detect real objects from those region proposals, as is exemplified in R-CNN [2], Fast R-CNN [3] and Faster R-CNN [4]. The other use a single network that do not rely on region proposal to directly predict the bounding boxes and classification of objects, such as YOLO [5] and SSD [1]. The first kind of method can achieve better results, while it is computationally intensive. The second kind of method is relatively fast and can be applied to real-time applications, but there is still a lot of room for improvement in detection accuracy.

For the second method, it skips the process that generating region proposals to directly detect object from the feature layer. Thereby its performance greatly depend on the quality of feature layer. However there is an imbalance in the depth of feature layer between object location predication and object classification predication. Previous works have shown that feature map from shallow convolution layer capture more fine details of the input objects, which is important for object location predication. However object classification predication usually adopt feature maps from deep convolution layers to have a more accurate judgement in image classification. So the feature map

© Springer Nature Singapore Pte Ltd. 2018
Y. Wang et al. (Eds.): IGTA 2018, CCIS 875, pp. 80–87, 2018.
https://doi.org/10.1007/978-981-13-1702-6_8

from shallow convolution layer lacks for classification information from higher layer, which may yield false positives. This can explain why SSD [1] perform not well in small target detection.

To solve this problem, we present a new network architecture for object detection in this paper, which generate object location predication and classification predication from the new feature maps that combines the feature map from shallow convolution layers with it from deep convolution layers by up–sampling and concatenating. By this way, the new feature map not only preserve fine details of the input objects but also have better object classification information, which is a good solution to the imbalance problem mentioned above.

2 Related Work

2.1 Early Object Detection Networks

With the development of deep convolution neural networks, object detection has made great progress in accuracy. There are two types of object detectors based on deep learning, one way adopt the popular two-stage object detection strategy, which firstly take a region proposal network (RPN [4]) to generate potential bounding box and then use a classification network to recognize the real objects from those region proposal. Another way directly predict object location and classification with a one-stage network that do not relay on region proposals. Methods based on region proposals are firstly used by R-CNN [2], it generates region proposals by a traditional way from Selective Search [6], after that those region proposals are resized into the same size and put into a classical classification network to recognize its categories. With the spatial pyramid pooling layer (SPP net [7]) put forward, Fast R-CNN [3] allow region proposals with different size and scale share the base convolution layer to get features for the later classification process, which largely reduce the convolution computation in feature extraction of region proposals. Afterwards Faster R-CNN [4] no longer uses traditional method Selective Search [6] to extract region proposals, it also use a convolution neural network named RPN [4] to generated region proposals.

In another way, there are also a lot of object detectors that adopt one-stage network and skep the process of extracting region proposals. For example, OverFeat [8] predicts a bounding box directly from each location of the topmost feature map after knowing the confidences of the underlying object categories by a classification network. Lately YOLO [5] begin to predict bounding boxes and the confidence of containing objects at the same time from the topmost feature map, and it share the bounding box for multiple categories. Afterwards SSD [1] do not just take use of the topmost feature map to predict the final result, it begin to adopt multiscale feature maps from different depth convolution layer, which make great improvements to the accuracy of object detectors with one-stage network. Our method try to concatenate those multiscale feature map by up–sampling process to gain higher quality feature map for bounding box prediction and categories prediction.

2.2 Base Network

Almost all image processing and pattern recognition approaches need to extract features from raw image data. In early research, hand-engineered features like Harr [9] features and HOG [10] features are well-designed and widely used. With the development of deep convolution neural networks, object classification network are widely transformed to extract high quality features for different image processing task. Those object classification network are called base network, such as AlexNet [11], VGG [12], and ResNet [13] and GoogLeNet [15–18]. Those base network have different model size and can achieve different precision, we should take the demand of different task into consideration to choose a proper base network to extract features from a large number of raw image data.

2.3 Up-Sampling and Concatenating

Semantic segmentation networks usually combine semantic information with appearance information by the way of up-sampling and concatenating. AS is exemplified in FCN [14], it begins to merge semantic information from a deep, coarse layer with appearance information from a shallow, fine layer to produce accurate and detailed segmentations. It shows that feature map from deeper layer provides classification information while the feature map from shallower layer provides location information. Although object detection task is not as strict as semantic segmentation task to the accurate boundary of objects, it just needs a bounding box to display object location. This architecture can also be applied to object detection to improve the accuracy by merging location information and classification information.

3   Our Approach

3.1 Feature Extraction Network

Figure 1 shows the structure of our detection model, we basically follow the method of SSD 1. Several feature layers are added to the end of the base network VGG16 12, we use the conv4 3, conv7 (fc7), conv8_2, conv9_2, and conv10_2 layer to build the up-sampling and merging architecture. It is processed as follows: the conv10_2 layer is 2x up-sampled and its size changed from 3×3 into 5×5, then concatenated with the conv9_2 layer by a concatenating layer to obtain the new 5×5 feature map with increased channel dimensions. In this illustration the 2x up-sampling layer is initialized by bilinear interpolation. At the same time, the new 5×5 feature map is 2x up-sampled and concatenated with conv8_2 layer to get the new 10×10 feature map. The same up-sampling and merging process is applied to conv7 layer and conv4_3 layer to get the new 19×19 feature map and the new 38×38 feature map. We adopt this up-sampling and merging method to get multiscale high quality feature map, then we predict both location and classifications from those new 5×5, 10×10, 19×19, 38×38 feature map, and the original 1×1, 3×3 feature map. Those new feature maps have fine details of objects appearance and good classification information to accurately detect objects in the image.

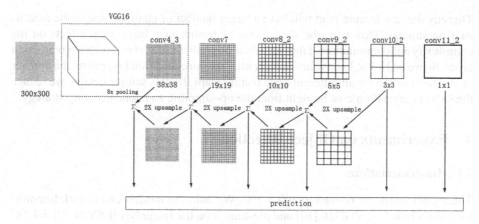

Fig. 1. Key idea of our object detection network.

3.2 Prediction Layer

Since object classification requires larger receptive field, generally it uses the deepest feature map followed by full connection layers to predict object categories. However, when we adopt the method mentioned above that uses different levels of feature maps to predict object classification and object location at the same time, the receptive field of feature map from shallower convolution layer is small, which will lead to a misclassification. To solve this problem, we use deeper convolution network for object classification behind those feature maps to expand its receptive filed. As is shown in Fig. 2, behind that feature map, a deeper convolution network (two 3 × 3 convolution layers) is adopted for object classification, while the location prediction use only one 3 × 3 convolution layer.

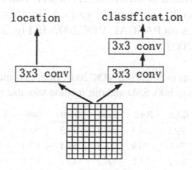

Fig. 2. Key idea of our object detection network.

3.3 Towards a More Efficient Detection Network

In our design, original feature map after the base network is concatenated with the upsampling feature map from deeper convolution layer to generate new feature map.

Thereby the new feature map will have a larger number of channels due to the concatenating strategy. However, the dimensions of feature map have great effects on the complexity and computation of the classification prediction layer and location prediction layer. So we add a 3 × 3 convolution layer after the concatenation layer to fix the number of channels to 256 for all different scale feature maps. By this sample design, we reduce the extra computation cost brought from the up-sampling and concatenating strategy.

4 Experiments on Object Detection

4.1 Implementations

The input images are resized to 300 × 300. We train our models end to end, fine-tune the model based on VGG16 [10] and pre-train it on the ImageNet ILSVRC CLS-LOC 20 dataset. We use SGD with initial learning rate 10 − 3, 0.9 momentum, 0.0005 weight decay, and batch size 24.

4.2 VOC 2007 Detection

On PASCAL VOC 19 dataset, we compare against Fast R-CNN [3] and Faster R-CNN [4], SSD [1] on PASCAL VOC2007 test (4952 images), and trained our model on the union of 2007 trainval and 2012 trainval. Training images are resized into 300 × 300.

Table 1 shows that our method is already more accurate than Faster R-CNN 4 and SSD 1. We can clearly see that our method perform well on majority of categories, especially it improves a lot on the detection of aero plane, bird, person and other categories. However it has much worse performance on the detection of bottle, in large part it is because that bottle usually is not only small but also has a bigger length-width ratio than other categories, while feature map in our design responsible for small objects only has 2 ratio default box so that it is hard to detect objects that has a bigger length-width ratio like bottles. But overall, our method gains a significant improvements on the detection of most categories on PASCAL VOC2007. In Fig. 3 we show some detection results on PASCAL VOC2007.

Table 1. Test detection results in PASCAL VOC2007. Both fast and faster R-CNN resize input images' minimum dimension to 600. SSD and our method take use of 300 × 300 input images.

Method	mAP	Areo	Bike	Bird	Boat	Bottle	Bus	Car	Cat	Chair	Cow
Fast [3]	70.0	77.0	78.1	69.3	59.4	38.3	81.6	78.6	86.7	42.8	78.8
Faster [4]	73.2	76.5	79.0	70.9	65.5	**52.1**	83.1	84.7	86.4	52.0	**81.9**
SSD300[1]	74.1	74.6	80.2	72.2	66.2	47.1	82.9	83.4	86.1	54.4	78.5
Ours	**77.7**	**87.8**	**84.1**	**80.4**	**75.3**	46.0	**89.0**	**88.6**	**87.3**	**55.3**	77.9
Method	mAP	Table	Dog	Horse	Mbike	Person	Plant	Sheep	Sofa	Train	tv
Fast [3]	70.0	68.9	84.7	82.0	76.6	69.0	31.8	70.1	74.8	80.4	70.4
Faster [4]	73.2	65.7	**84.8**	84.6	77.5	76.7	38.8	73.6	73.9	83.0	72.6
SSD300[1]	74.1	73.9	84.4	84.5	82.4	76.1	48.6	74.3	**75.0**	84.3	74.0
Ours	**77.7**	**76.5**	83.7	**87.1**	**87.5**	**79.5**	**55.4**	**76.7**	70.8	**89.1**	76.5

Fig. 3. Samples of detection results on VOC2007. Detections with scores higher than 0.6 are showed and each color corresponds to an object category.

Table 2 shows the speed and accuracy between Faster R-CNN [4], SSD [1] and our method. Our method outperform Faster R-CNN [4] in both speed and accuracy. Although it is slow than SSD300 [1], its accuracy is 3.6% higher than SSD300 [1]. Generally speaking, our object detector can achieve quite high performance, at the same time it runs very fast in the NVIDIA 1080 Ti with 44.8 FPS.

Table 2. The efficiency on VOC2007-test. We test those models on NVIDIA 1080Ti.

Model	mAP	Input size	Times/ms	FPS
Faster [4]	73.2	about 1000 × 600	61.8	16.2
SSD300 [1]	74.1	300 × 300	11.5	87.0
Our method	77.7	300 × 300	22.3	44.8

4.3 Experiments on VOC2007

To get a detection model with high performance and high efficiency, we test our models in different configurations.

Table 3 shows the accuracy of our models in different configurations. If we only adopt up-sampling and concatenating strategy, the model can reach 76.9% mean AP with the VGG16 [12] base network. When different depth of classification and location predication layer is applied, the performance increase by 0.8% mean AP. this strategy use two 3 × 3 convolution layers for object classification, while one 3 × 3 convolution layer for location predication.

Table 3. Effects of various design choices. Up-sampling means model with up-sampling and concatenating feature map. conf&loc means model with different depth of location prediction layer and classification prediction layer.

Model	mAP
Up-sampling	76.9
Up-sampling + conf&loc	77.7

5   Conclusion

We present an object detection network based on multiscale merged feature map. Our system naturally take use of the state-of-the-art image classification models: VGG16 [12] as a base network, it achieves accuracy competitive with the Faster R-CNN [4] and SSD [1]. Our method aims to obtain high quality feature map by up-sampling and concatenating different scale feature map. Moreover high quality feature map is of great importance in other computer vision task, such as object classification and semantic segmentation. We believe that our design principle is not only applicable to object detection but also widely applicable to other computer vision tasks in future work.

References

1. Liu, W., et al.: SSD: single shot multibox detector. In: Leibe, B., Matas, J., Sebe, N., Welling, M. (eds.) ECCV 2016. LNCS, vol. 9905, pp. 21–37. Springer, Cham (2016). https://doi.org/10.1007/978-3-319-46448-0_2
2. Girshick, R., Donahue, J., Darrell, T., et al.: Rich feature hierarchies for accurate object detection and semantic segmentation. In: Proceedings of the IEEE Conference on Computer Vision and Pattern Recognition, pp. 580–587 (2014)
3. Girshick, R.: Fast R-CNN. In: Proceedings of the IEEE International Conference on Computer Vision, pp. 1440–1448 (2015)
4. Ren, S., He, K., Girshick, R., et al.: Faster R-CNN: towards real-time object detection with region proposal networks. In: Advances in Neural Information Processing Systems, pp. 91–99 (2015)
5. Redmon, J., Divvala, S., Girshick, R., et al.: You only look once: unified, real-time object detection. In: Proceedings of the IEEE Conference on Computer Vision and Pattern Recognition, pp. 779–788 (2016)
6. Uijlings, J.R.R., Van De Sande, K.E.A., Gevers, T., et al.: Selective search for object recognition. Int. J. Comput. Vis. **104**(2), 154–171 (2013)
7. He, K., Zhang, X., Ren, S., Sun, J.: Spatial pyramid pooling in deep convolutional networks for visual recognition. In: Fleet, D., Pajdla, T., Schiele, B., Tuytelaars, T. (eds.) ECCV 2014. LNCS, vol. 8691, pp. 346–361. Springer, Cham (2014). https://doi.org/10.1007/978-3-319-10578-9_23
8. Sermanet, P., Eigen, D., Zhang, X., et al.: OverFeat: integrated recognition, localization and detection using convolutional networks. arXiv preprint arXiv:1312.6229 (2013)
9. Ojala, T., Pietikäinen, M., Harwood, D.: A comparative study of texture measures with classification based on featured distributions. Pattern Recogn. **29**(1), 51–59 (1996)
10. Papageorgiou, C.P., Oren, M., Poggio, T.: A general framework for object detection. In: Sixth International Conference on Computer Vision 1998, pp. 555–562. IEEE (1998)

11. Krizhevsky, A., Sutskever, I., Hinton, G.E.: Imagenet classification with deep convolutional neural networks. In: Advances in Neural Information Processing Systems, pp. 1097–1105 (2012)
12. Simonyan, K., Zisserman, A.: Very deep convolutional networks for large-scale image recognition. arXiv preprint arXiv:1409.1556 (2014)
13. He, K., Zhang, X., Ren, S., et al.: Deep residual learning for image recognition. In: Proceedings of the IEEE Conference on Computer Vision and Pattern Recognition, pp. 770–778 (2016)
14. Long, J., Shelhamer, E., Darrell, T.: Fully convolutional networks for semantic segmentation. In: Proceedings of the IEEE Conference on Computer Vision and Pattern Recognition, pp. 3431–3440 (2015)
15. Szegedy, C., Liu, W., Jia, Y., et al.: Going deeper with convolutions. In: Proceedings of the IEEE conference on Computer Vision and Pattern Recognition, pp. 1–9 (2015)
16. Ioffe, S., Szegedy, C.: Batch normalization: accelerating deep network training by reducing internal covariate shift. In: International Conference on Machine Learning, pp. 448–456 (2015)
17. Szegedy, C., Vanhoucke, V., Ioffe, S., et al.: Rethinking the inception architecture for computer vision. In: Proceedings of the IEEE Conference on Computer Vision and Pattern Recognition, pp. 2818–2826 (2016)
18. Szegedy, C., Ioffe, S., Vanhoucke, V., et al.: Inception-v4, inception-ResNet and the impact of residual connections on learning. In: AAAI, pp. 4278–4284 (2017)
19. Everingham, M., Van Gool, L., Williams, C.K., Winn, J., Zisserman, A.: The PASCAL visual object classes (VOC) challenge. IJCV 88, 303–338 (2010)
20. Russakovsky, O., et al.: ImageNet large scale visual recognition challenge. IJCV 115, 211–252 (2015)

Characterization of Kinoform X-Ray Lens Using Image Stitching Method Based on Marked Structures

Wenqiang Hua[1], Keliang Liao[2(✉)], Zhongzhu Zhu[2], Qili He[2], Weifan Sheng[2], Peiping Zhu[2], Qingxi Yuan[2], and Jie Wang[1]

[1] Institute of Shanghai Applied Physics, Chinese Academy of Sciences, Shanghai, China
[2] Institute of High Energy Physics, Chinese Academy of Sciences, Beijing, China
liaokeliang@ihep.ac.cn

Abstract. The unique structure of the kinoform x-ray lens render most image stitching methods difficult to realize the image registration of sub-images acquired by commercial optical microscope with the high power objective, yet it is important to evaluate the fabrication defects using image processing methods in the foundation of the stitched image. In this work we demonstrate the quantitative characterization of the kinoform x-ray lens by using image stitching method based on extracting the geometric features of dedicated marked structures, which could not only avoid the problem of lacking effective features in the lens structure but also provide a reference for the scaling and rotation operations during the image alignment. The proposed stitching method provides us a convenient way to analyze the shape error and various fabrication imperfections for the kinoform x-ray lens.

Keywords: Image stitching · Image process · X-ray optics

1 Introduction

Kinoform lenses (KLs) are promising x-ray nano-focusing optics due to their high efficiency, large aperture and long working distance [1, 2]. The refractive index of materials in the hard x-ray region could be written as $n = 1 - \delta + j\beta$, where δ is the refractive index decrement and β corresponds to the absorption index. As δ and β are on the level of 10^{-5}–10^{-7} and 10^{-7}–10^{-9} respectively, the x-ray refractive lens is inherently with a concave shape of ultra-small radius of curvature. Moreover, in order to minimize the absorption, a KL is formed by removing the excessive materials of an x-ray refractive lens corresponding to an integer multiple of 2π phase shift [3]. Figure 1 shows a typical kinoform x-ray lens.

The difficulty in fabricating high aspect ratio structure is the major obstacle of achieving better spatial resolution for KLs. As a planar micro lens, KL is majorly fabricated using various etching methods, such as LIGA [4, 5] and ion beam etching (IBE) method [6]. During the etching process, defects of the x-ray lens are inevitable. Defect characterization plays a critical role in the optimization of process parameters and evaluating the optical performance of KLs. For a KL with sub-micron spatial resolution, it typically has a feature

© Springer Nature Singapore Pte Ltd. 2018
Y. Wang et al. (Eds.): IGTA 2018, CCIS 875, pp. 88–97, 2018.
https://doi.org/10.1007/978-981-13-1702-6_9

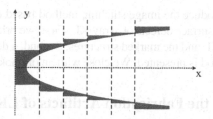

Fig. 1. Schematic of a typical kinoform x-ray lens

size of several microns and a length of several tens of millimeters. The dimension in the longitudinal (x) direction is about two orders larger than that in the transverse (y) direction. Since a commercial microscope only has a field of about several hundreds of microns with a high power objective. Therefore it is straightforward to acquire a series of sub-images along the longitudinal direction and employ image stitching method to get the whole picture of a slender KL. Furthermore, we could apply lots of image process methods to extract the surface shape and evaluate various fabrication imperfections.

Extensive work has been done in the area of image stitching. In fact, image stitching could be treated as a solved problem, which could be summarized as the following steps. (1) After pre-process of the sub-images, different image registration algorithms could be employed to discover the correspondence relationship among the sub-images with varying degrees of overlap. (2) The alignment estimate (or the transform model) among sub-images could be derived based on the above mentioned image registration algorithms. (3) Image blending could be employed to emerge neighboring images and deal with the potential problem of blurring and ghosting related to the varying acquisition conditions for different sub-images. Among the above steps, image registration is the most challenging one and determines the stitching results. A lot of famous registration methods have been proposed, such as the scale invariant feature transform (SIFT) [7] method and Harris corner detection algorithm [8]. In principle, we could apply such registration methods to KLs. However, KL has its own unique structure features, which render the above image registration methods failure to discover the transfer relationship between the neighboring sub-images. First, the KL is composed of many similar sawtooth-like structures [3, 9], which leads to the similarity of the lens structure between neighboring sub-images in both overlapping area and non-overlapping area. Such similarity in the non-overlapping area directly results in the mismatching and renders most image registration algorithms invalid. Second, as illustrated in Fig. 1 the KL structure lacks effective features except for few corners, which means that image registration algorithms based on feature extraction is not appropriate for KLs. Although many commercial optical microscopes are capable of image stitching, they still cannot fulfill the stitching requirements of x-ray KL. In order to characterize the surface defects of kinoform x-ray lens, we adopt the stitching method based on marked structures, in which the geometrical feature of the marked structure was extracted and used for the image alignment. By applying a series of operations, namely pre-process, geometrical feature extraction, rotation, pixel size scaling, cropping, stitching, lens shape extraction, we realize the quantitative characterization of a whole slender x-ray KL.

In this paper, we introduce the image stitching method based on marked structures in order to characterize the surface defects of x-ray KL. First, we briefly introduce the fabrication process of x-ray KL and the marked structures. Second, a detailed discussion about the image stitching method is presented. We close with an outlook of our future work.

2   Characterizing the Fabrication Artifacts of LKLs

2.1   Fabrication Process and Marked Structures

The detailed fabrication process was summarized in our previous work [10]. We herein gave a brief introduction. First, the graph of the KL was transferred to UV photoresist by means of UV lithography technology with a thin gold mask. After development, one then got a UV photoresist structure. Electroplating of gold was performed to get the intermediate mask. Second, an x-ray working mask with a thick layer of gold absorber was formed by means of soft x-ray lithography using the intermediate mask mentioned above. Finally, by applying deep x-ray lithography using the x-ray working mask and a harder x-ray spectrum, the PMMA KL was finally achieved. In fact, in order to increase the numerical aperture of the KLs, compound KLs were fabricated. However, without loss of generality, in this paper we only concentrate on the analysis of a single KL among the fabricated compound KLs.

In order to apply the proposed image stitch method, we added dedicated marked structures in the KL. The dedicated structures were rectangles with edges of 5×10 μm. As shown in Fig. 2, the whole KL structure was divided into 15 sub-images by the rectangle structures. The horizontal and vertical distances of the neighboring rectangle were D_x, D_y respectively. Here, $D_x = 100$ μm, $D_y = 100$ μm.

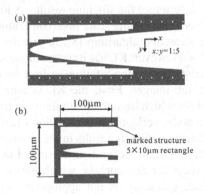

Fig. 2. The schematic of KL and the dedicated marked structures

2.2   Image Stitching Based on Marked Structure

The framework of the image stitching method based on marked structures was illustrated in Fig. 3. As referred to Fig. 2(a), we acquired a series of sub-images in sequence from left to right by using a commercial optical microscope with each sub-image having four rectangular marked structures. The four marked structures were distributed on the four corners. The neighboring two sub-images shared the same two marked structures, which naturally ensured the sufficient overlap region between the two sub-images.

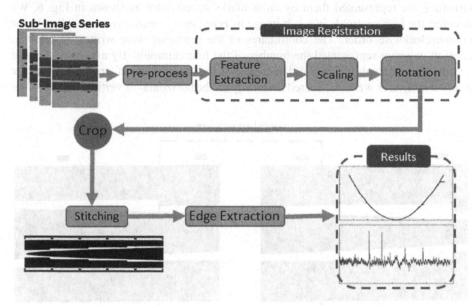

Fig. 3. Framework of the image stitching method based on marked structures.

As shown in Fig. 4(a), there were some obvious scratch on the lens surface, therefore some pre-processing method were employed to diminish them. After a combination of the open and close operation, the phenomenon of surface scratch was effectively improved, as shown in Fig. 4(b). It was followed by grey stretch and image binary, and the corresponding results were shown in Fig. 4(c) and (d) respectively. As depicted in Fig. 4(d), the white part represented the lens material, and the black part corresponded to air. The refractive surface was the curved edge distinguishing the white region from the black region on the KL structure.

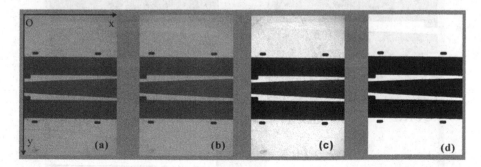

Fig. 4. Pre-process of the KL image series

By clarifying the binary structure, we could select different collected regions and find the four marked structures. As shown in Fig. 5, the neighboring two sub-images shared the same two marked structures. After extracting the centroids of the marked structure, we represented them by cross marks in red color as shown in Fig. 6. We denoted the four centroids in a sub-image as $cent_1$, $cent_2$, $cent_3$, $cent_4$ according to the counterclockwise order. The coordinates of the centroids were written as ($cent_n.x$, $cent_n.y$), where n represented the number of the four centroids. By assuming the four centroids in each sub-image could be treated as the four corners of a rectangle, and the marked structures were distributed uniformly on the horizontal or vertical direction, we

overlap region

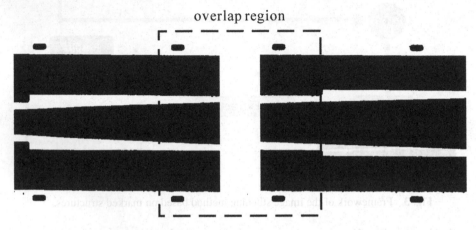

Fig. 5. Two neighboring sub-images with the overlap region marked by the dashed rectangle.

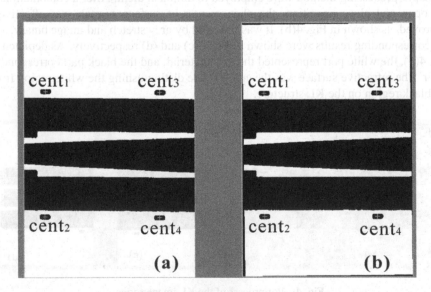

Fig. 6. (a) The centroids of the marked structures were represented by crossed mark in red color; (b) rotation of the sub-image. (Color figure online)

could use them to calibrate the sub-images. We herein majorly applied the rotation and the scaling operation.

If one treated the four centroids as the four corners of a rectangle, one then could get the rotation angle by averaging the tilt angle of the four edges. Therefore the rotation angle could be written as,

$$\tan(\theta) = \frac{1}{4}\left(\frac{cent_4.y - cent_2.y}{cent_4.x - cent_2.x} + \frac{cent_3.y - cent_1.y}{cent_3.x - cent_1.x} + \frac{cent_3.x - cent_4.x}{cent_4.y - cent_3.y} + \frac{cent_1.x - cent_2.x}{cent_2.y - cent_1.y}\right) \tag{1}$$

Moreover, for a sub-image the pixel size was

$$\Delta = \frac{D_x}{cent_3.x + cent_4.x - cent_1.x - cent_2.x} + \frac{D_y}{cent_2.y + cent_4.y - cent_1.y - cent_3.y} \tag{2}$$

By taking the first sub-image as a reference, the scale factor of the nth sub-image could be written as,

$$s_n = \frac{KL_1.\Delta}{KL_n.\Delta} \tag{3}$$

Where $KL_n.\Delta$ represented the pixel size of the n-th sub-image.

After applying the rotation and scaling operations, we then could crop the sub-images to get the effective regions for the following image stitching. As depicted in Fig. 7, the sub-image was cropped with four dashed lines, which were denoted as (up, down, left, right). The corresponding coordinate of the four lines were written as,

$$left = \frac{cent_1.x + cent_2.x}{2} \tag{4}$$

$$right = \frac{cent_3.x + cent_4.x}{2} \tag{5}$$

$$up = \frac{cent_1.y + cent_3.y}{2} - 300 \tag{6}$$

$$down = \frac{cent_2.y + cent_4.y}{2} + 300 \tag{7}$$

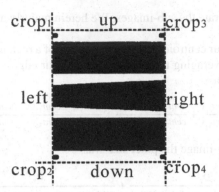

Fig. 7. Crop the sub-images by four dashed lines denoted as (up, down, left, right).

Finally, we obtained the stitched image by matching all the cropped sub-images, which was shown in Fig. 8. With a 5:1 scale ratio in the longitudinal and transverse direction in Fig. 8, we could clearly observe some concave or convex artifacts on the refractive surface. For the convenience of the following analysis, we marked the upper and lower surfaces with dashed arrows in Fig. 8.

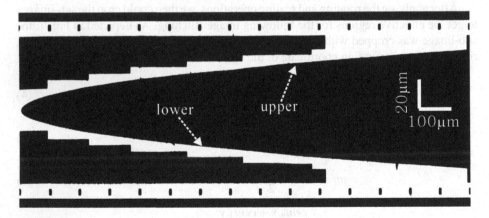

Fig. 8. Stitched KL structure with a 5:1 scale ratio

2.3 Extracting the Lens Shape

Based on the stitched lens structure depicted in Fig. 8, we could employ lots of image processing method to evaluate the fabrication imperfections. As a focusing lens, we herein extracted the refractive surface using edge extraction method. In Fig. 9(a), the extracted curve presented obvious shape error. The most pronounced artifact was shown in Fig. 9(b), which was a concave defect and may be caused by the flaking of lens material during the fabrication process.

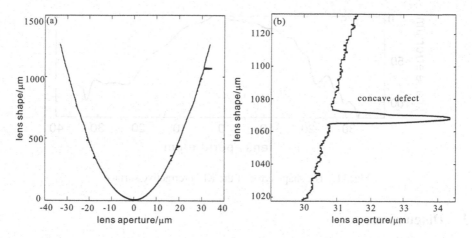

Fig. 9. (a) Concave refractive surface of the KL; (b) The most obvious artifact on the refractive surface.

Furthermore, after subtracting the low frequency component obtained by fitting the curves shown in Fig. 9(a) with 3rd order polynomials, the volatility of the upper and lower refractive surface were shown in Fig. 10(a) and (b) respectively. As depicted in Fig. 10, the root of mean square (RMS) value of the volatility was 80 nm and 240 nm for the upper and lower refractive surfaces.

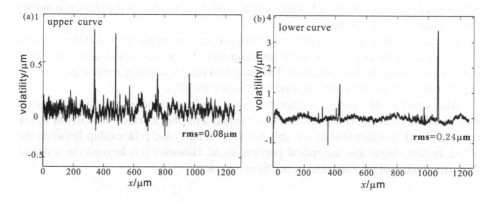

Fig. 10. The volatility of the upper (a) and lower (b) refractive surface

Finally, comparing the fitted refractive curve mentioned above to the ideal lens refractive curve, the lens shape error was shown in Fig. 11, from which shape error larger than 100 μm could be observed.

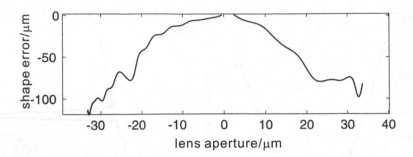

Fig. 11. The shape error of the KL's refractive surface

3   Discussions

Unlike other image registration method based on Harris corner or SIFT, which are on the premise of the similarity only in the overlap region, image stitching method based on dedicated marked structures avoids the problem of similarity in the non-overlap regions. Furthermore, by assuming the four centroids of a sub-image were the corners of a rectangle, we could treat them as accurate references to rotate each sub-image. Moreover, the distance between the neighboring two marked structures provided the same scale for the pixel size scaling among different sub-images. That is to say, the introduction of the four dedicated rectangular structures in each sub-images not only provides effective geometrical features but also could be treated as the reference during the alignment of sub-images.

The calculated shape error of the refractive surface was on the level of 100 μm, which was comparatively large for an x-ray focusing lens. There were also many concave or convex defects on the lens structure. The proposed image stitching method provides us a quantitative characterization method to evaluate the KLs.

Although it is not a general method for image stitching, it indeed provides us a useful way to evaluate the fabrication imperfections and will play a critical role in our future research work. Further studies are still needed to clarify the relationship between the above imperfections and the optical performances. However it is beyond the scope of this paper and will be addressed in our future work.

4   Conclusion and Outlook

In summary, we demonstrated the quantitative characterization of the long kinoform x-ray lens by using image stitching method based on the marked structures. The concave lens shape with ultra-small radius of curvature was extracted. Although this method is based on dedicated marked structures and is comparatively more complicated than other image stitching method, it avoids many difficulties in the case of lacking effective features and similar geometrical shape between non-overlap regions. In our future work, we will feedback the characterization data to the fabrication process and use the useful information to evaluate the focusing or imaging performance of the x-ray lenses.

Acknowledgments. This work is supported by China Postdoctoral Science Foundation (2017M610996), National Key R&D Program of China (2017YFA0403801), National Natural Science Foundation of China (11505278,11675253).

References

1. Alianelli, L., Sawhney, K.J.S., Barrett, R., Pape, I., Malik, A., Wilson, M.C.: High efficiency nano-focusing kinoform optics for synchrotron radiation. Opt. Express **19**(12), 11120–11127 (2011)
2. Evans-Lutterodt, K., et al.: Single-element elliptical hard x-ray micro-optics. Opt. Express **11**(8), 919–926 (2003)
3. Yan, H.: X-ray nanofocusing by kinoform lenses: a comparative study using different modeling approaches. Phys. Rev. B **81**(7), 075402 (2010)
4. Nazmov, V., et al.: LIGA fabrication of x-ray Nickel lenses. Microsyst. Technol. **11**(4–5), 292–297 (2005). https://doi.org/10.1007/s00542-004-0435-y
5. Nazmov, V., et al.: Kinoform x-ray lens creation in polymer materials by deep x-ray lithography. Nucl. Instrum. Methods Phys. Res. Sect. B **217**(3), 409–416 (2004). https://doi.org/10.1016/j.nimb.2003.11.002
6. Nöhammer, B., Hoszowska, J., Freund, A.K., David, C.: Diamond planar refractive lenses for third- and fourth-generation x-ray sources. J. Synchrotron Radiat. **10**(2), 168–171 (2003). https://doi.org/10.1107/S0909049502019532
7. Lindeberg, T.: Scale-space theory: a basic tool for analyzing structures at different scales. J. Appl. Stat. **21**(1–2), 225–270 (1994). https://doi.org/10.1080/757582976
8. Wang, H., Brady, M.: Real-time corner detection algorithm for motion estimation. Image Vis. Comput. **13**(9), 695–703 (1995). https://doi.org/10.1016/0262-8856(95)98864-P
9. Liao, K., Hong, Y., Sheng, W.: Optimized short kinoform lenses for hard x-ray nano-focusing. Opt. Commun. **339**, 53–60 (2015). https://doi.org/10.1016/j.optcom.2014.11.062
10. Liao, K., et al.: Sub-500 nm hard x-ray focusing by compound long kinoform lenses. Appl. Opt. **55**(1), 38–41 (2016)

AMGE: A Tongue Body Segmentation Assessment Method via Gradient Energy

Jing Qi[1], Zhenchao Cui[2(✉)], Wenzhu Yang[2], Gang Xiao[3], and Naimin Li[3]

[1] Beihang University, Beijing, China
qijing@beihang.edu.cn
[2] Hebei University, Baoding, China
cuizhenchao@gmial.com, wenzhuyang@163.com
[3] Harbin Binghua Hospital, Harbin, China

Abstract. Tongue body segmentation is essential for the computerized tongue diagnosis. Several segmentation methods have been developed and some evaluation methods have been used for test the segmentation. However, it is difficult to assess the non-contour parts on the results of segmentation by using the existing assessment methods. To deal with this problem, in this paper, we proposed a novel assessment method for tongue body segmentation based on the characteristics of tongue body contour, called AMGE. In AMGE, There are three steps. Firstly, since of the closed circle structure, the tongue contour is converted into polar coordinate. Secondly, based on the characteristics of tongue body contour, we propose tongue body contour energy which contains radial-based energy function and angle-based energy function. Based on this contour energy function, we can evaluate the tongue body segmentations. Finally, one single threshold is selected to detect the non-contour parts on contour which have high values of energy. Experiments show that the proposed assessment method is superior to the conventional area-based methods and boundary-based methods.

Keywords: Tongue diagnosis · Assessment method · Energy function

1 Introduction

According to the conventional Chinese medicine theory, the changes of tongue present information in one body [1]. Since of the convenient and non-invasive nature, tongue diagnosis is popular diagnosis method [2–4]. However, to achieve correct diagnosis by using tongue diagnosis, Chinese medicine practitioners need years of experience. To deal with this problem, many computerized tongue diagnosis systems have been developed by researchers.

Tongue body segmentation is the first and prerequisite part in computerized tongue diagnosis. Since of the complexity and the similarity between lips and tongue body in texture and color, it is difficult to correctly segment entire tongue bodies from images. Several conventional edge detectors have been adopted for the enhancement of the tongue contours. Considering the shape and grey level characteristics of tongue contour, Zuo et al. [5] proposed a polar edge detector to effectively suppress the adverse

© Springer Nature Singapore Pte Ltd. 2018
Y. Wang et al. (Eds.): IGTA 2018, CCIS 875, pp. 98–105, 2018.
https://doi.org/10.1007/978-981-13-1702-6_10

interference from the lip boundary, tongue fissures, etc. Cui et al. [6] proposed automated tongue body segmentation method to deal with the weak edge on the contour based on 2D Gabor filter and fast marching method. Pang et al. proposed a bi-elliptical deformable template to utilize both the edge enhancement result and the shape of tongue body and active contour model has been used for the tongue contour detection [7]. Wu and Zhang combined region-based and boundary-based methods to segment tongue body [8].

Although several methods have been proposed for edge enhancement and tongue body contour detection, there is no development on assessment method for the results of segmentation. To test the tongue body segmentation methods, several conventional evaluation methods have been used. Boundary-based and area-based [5–7] performance criteria are used for the testing the segmentation results. The similarity between segmentation results and ground-truth can be obtained by using these assessment criteria. However, the results of these criteria cannot assess and locate the non-contour fragments on contours of results.

According to the characteristics of tongue body contour, we propose a tongue body contour assessment method via gradient energy, named AMGE, to deal with the drawbacks of conventional methods. In our method, motivated by the energy function in [9], an energy function is built on each points of the contour, which contains radius-based and angle-based energy, to test the points. The low energy means that the corresponding points of contour is suitable to be parts of tongue body contour, while the high energy presents that the corresponding points of contour is not parts of tongue body contour.

The advantages of AMGE method are represented as follows: (1) non-contour fragments of tongue body can be detected by the method. A single threshold can be used in this assessment method. The points on contour with high energy can easily described as non-contour parts by using a single threshold. (2) The ground-truth is not needed in this evaluation method. For the most exiting methods, testing results can be obtained by using differences between the contour and the ground-truth. For the large image database, it is impossible to obtain the ground-truth. And thus, it is difficult to test segmentation methods by using conventional assessment methods. However, the proposed criterion obtain the rationality of segmentation according to the characteristics of tongue body contour, and it do not need ground-truth of tongue body. Thus the proposed method is suitable to test tongue body segmentation methods.

The remainder of the paper is structured as follows: We describe our tongue body assessment methodology in Sect. 2. Experimental results are provided in Sect. 3. Finally, we conclude in Sect. 4.

2 Tongue Body Assessment Method

Figure 1 shows two typical tongue body contours. One can see that the contours of tongue body have two main characteristics: one is that the contours are smooth curves; the other one is contours of tongues are closed curves. Generally, it is hard to build energy function for closed curves in Cartesian coordinate system. While, polar coordinate system has the natural advantage to represent closed curves. Thus, we build the energy function by using polar coordinate system. Because the tongues are fore-ground in our database as shown in Fig. 1, generally they are required at the center of the images. So we use the center point of image as the origin point of coordinate system to convert the coordinate system into polar coordinate system. Then we can obtain the curve $(\rho(s(n)), \theta(s(n)))$, where s is the parameter of the curve, and $0 \ll s(n) \ll 1, \rho(s(1)) = \rho(0) = \rho(1) = \rho(s(N))$, $\theta(0) = 0$ and $\theta(1) = 2\pi, 1 \leq n \leq N$, N is the number of points on the contour. In polar coordinate system, there are two-dimensional system, thus, we can construct the energy function as follow:

$$En(s) = \alpha f(\rho(s)) + \beta g(\theta(s)) \tag{1}$$

where $f(\rho(s))$ and $g(\theta(s)$ are radius-based energy and angle-based energy respectively. α and β are the parameters for the weights of radius-based energy and angle-based energy respectively.

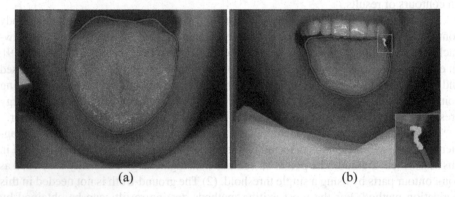

(a)   (b)

Fig. 1. The typical tongue body contour and non-contour fragment

As shown in Fig. 1, the curves of typical tongue body contours are smooth, thus each radius, which is the distance from each point on the contour to the center point of tongue body, is similar with the radius of the neighboring points. In other words, the first-order derivative of radius on s is a small value, but for the non-contour fragments on the contour, the first-order derivatives are different. Thus we define the first-order derivatives of radius as the radius-based energy. In order to enhance the differences of radius, second-order derivative of radius is used in radius-based energy. Finally, the energy function is defined as:

$$f(\rho(s)) = \gamma|\rho_s'|+\delta|\rho_s''| \tag{2}$$

where γ and δ are the parameters of the first-order derivatives of radius on s, ρ_s', and the second-order derivatives of radius on s, ρ_s'' respectively.

2.1 Angle-Based Energy

From $s = 0$ to $s = 1$, the growth of angle for points on contour is monotonically increasing. But for the non-contour fragments, the growth of angle is random. In Fig. 1(b), one can see that the red curve on contour of tongue body is non-contour fragment. One main characteristic id the order of angle growth is not monotonically increasing. Thus, the growth of angle can represent the properties of fragments. By using this characteristic, we define the growth of angle for each point on contour as the angle-based energy, which is presented as: $g(\theta(s)) = |\theta'_s|$. In this paper, we use results of difference instead of the results of first-order derivative. Thus, we can obtain angle-based energy as follow:

$$\overline{g}(\theta(s)) = \theta'_s = \theta_s - \theta_{\overline{s}} \tag{3}$$

where $\overline{s}$ is the next point following s.

The angle-based energy defined by Eq. 3 cannot represent the entire wrong fragment of contour, thus we have to improve the definition. As shown in Fig. 2, we can see that the red fragment on contour is shown in red block in Fig. 2(b). But the energy function cannot present yellow curve, which is also part of wrong fragment of tongue body contour in yellow block as shown in Fig. 2(b). To deal with the detection problem, we propose a novel angle-based energy, which is defined as follow:

$$g(\theta(s)) = |\theta_s - tem| \tag{4}$$

where $tem = \max\{\theta_{(\overline{s}|\overline{s}<s)}$. Since that θ is one monotonic increasing function of s for true tongue body contour, the term *tem* in Eq. 4 is the last point of *s*. In other words, for the right tongue body contour, the point of $\overline{s}$ is close to the point of s. Then Eq. 4 can degenerate into Eq. 3. For the non-contour fragments, the value of *tem* in Eq. 4 do not change, but the value of θ_s increases with the change of s. In this way, the energy $g(\theta(s))$ can indicate the entire non-contour part with a high energy value.

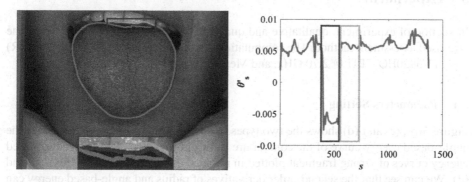

Fig. 2. The typical tongue body contour and the corresponding radius-based energies

2.2 Tongue Body Contour Energy

By using the radius-based energy and angle-based energy, we can obtain the complete assessment energy function for points, $En(s) = \alpha(\gamma|\rho'_s|+\delta|\rho''_s|) + \beta|\theta_s - tem|$. After simplifying the parameters, we can obtain the final energy function:

$$En(s) = \gamma|\rho'_s|+\delta|\rho''_s|+\beta|\theta_s - tem|. \tag{5}$$

The energy for entire contour can be defined as $E = \sum_s En(s)$.
The computation of For.5 is easy, the process is represented in Algorithm 1:

Algorithm 1 AMGE

1: **procedure AMGE** $\theta(s(n)), \rho(s(n)), N, \gamma, \delta, \beta$
2: **while** $n \neq N - 1$ **do**
3:      $E_{\{\rho'\}} \leftarrow \gamma(\rho(s(n + 1)) - \rho(s(n)))$
4:      $E_{\{\rho''\}} \leftarrow \delta(2 \times \{\rho(s(n))\} - \rho(s(n - 1)) - \rho(s(n + 1)))$
5:      **if** $\theta(s(n)) \geq$ tem **then**
6:          tem $\leftarrow \theta(s(n - 1))$
7:          g $\leftarrow$ s(n) - tem
8:      $E(s(n)) \leftarrow E_{\rho'} + E_{\rho''} + \beta\theta(s(n))$
9:          n $\leftarrow$ n + 1
10: **return** $E(s(n))$

From Algorithm 1, one can see all the computational complexities of ρ', ρ'' and $g(\theta)$ are O(N). Thus we can obtain the computational complexity of the final energy is O(N), which means the proposed assessment method has a high computational efficiency.

3   Experiment

In section of experiment, qualitative and quantitative experiments are used to test the proposed assessment method. The computation platform for our experiment is Interl(R) Core i7-6820HQ CPU @ 2.70 GHz, and Memory is 8.00 GB.

3.1   Parameters Setting

Figure 3(b), (c) and (d) shows the two types of energy of the contour of Fig. 3(a). The angle-based energy curve of the contour are shown in Fig. 3(b). And two radius-based energy curves of wrong fragment plotted in red as shown in red block of Fig. 3(c) and (d). We can see that the second-order derivatives of radius and angle-based energy can obviously indicate the wrong fragment, and thus we empirically set the parameter as: $\gamma = 0, \delta = 5, \beta = 20$, and the threshold for detect wrong fragment is 0.55. To obtain the entire fragment on contour of tongue body, we used greedy algrithm to detect the complete wave which contain the results in the curve of energy.

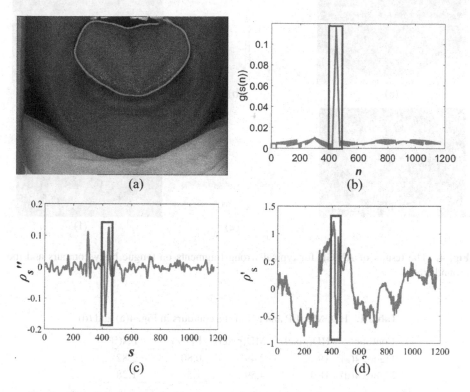

Fig. 3. The typical tongue body contour and the corresponding radius-based energies

3.2 Qualitative Experiment

Figure 4 shows the energy curves of two typical tongue body contour, the curves of these contours, and the ground-truth of the contour. The curves in Fig. 4(b) and (e) is the energy curves of the red fragments in Fig. 4(a) and (d) respectively. The cyan curves in Fig. 4(c) and (f) are the ground-truth of Fig. 4(b) and (e) respectively. Table 1 presents the HD, MD, FP and FN of the Fig. 4(a) and (d). We can see that the values of HD, MD, FP and FN [5] are small, which means the contours in Fig. 4(a) and (d) are close to the ground-truth. Thus the values of HD, MD, FP and FN only state the degree of proximity between the contour and ground-truth. However, the proposed assessment method can detect the wrong fragments on contour, as shown as the red curves in Fig. 4, which means that AMGE is superior to the conventional evaluation criteria, such as HD, MD, FP and FN for tongue body contour detection.

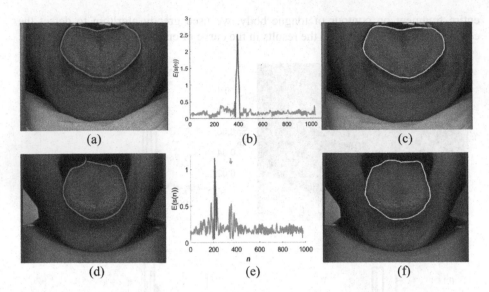

Fig. 4. The results of AMGE for typical wrong fragments on tongue body contours and the ground-truth.

Table 1. HD, MD, FP and FN of the contours in Fig. 4(a) and (d)

Contour	HD(pixel)	MD(pixel)	FP(%)	FN(%)
Figure 4(a)	19.02	2.49	0.80	2.82
Figure 4(d)	18.11	4.59	1.5	1.28

Table 1 shows the means and deviations of CPU time by using existing evaluation methods and proposed method for evaluation of 300 tongue body contours. The low values in Table 1 means that speed of the corresponding method is fast. One can see that the mean of CPU time of HD and MD is 1.57 s. and 1.60 s. respectively, the CPU time of AMGE is 0.87×10^{-2} Sec. Obviously, the speed of proposed evaluation method has a faster speed than HD and MD. And the speed of proposed method is close to the speeds of FP and FN.

4 Conclusion

Considering the characteristics of tongue body contour, we proposed a energy-based evaluation method, AMGE. Two types of energy, radius-based and angle-based energies are used in this method. For the radius-based energy, first-order and second-order derivatives of radius are employed to evaluate the differences of contour on radius. For the angle-based energy, we defined the energy as the difference between the angle of the point and the largest angle in the past points. This function, defined in this way, can expand the difference between non-contour fragments and contour fragments, thus it can make the non-fragments more obviously. The final energy is a weighted sum of angle-based and radius-based energy. The wrong fragments can detect by one certain threshold on the energy. The section of experiment show that our proposed assessment method is superior to the conventional methods, HD, MD, FP and FN, and the speed of proposed is faster than boundary-based methods, HD and MD, and is close to the area-based methods, FP and FN.

Acknowledgment. The work is supported by National Science Foundation of Hebei Province in China under Grant No. F2017201069.

References

1. Wang, K., Li, N., Zhang, D.: Tongue Diagnostics (2011)
2. Wang, X., Zhang, B., Yang, Z., Wang, H., Zhang, D.: Statistical analysis of tongue images for feature extraction and diagnostics. IEEE Trans. Image Process. **22**(12), 5336–5347 (2013)
3. Hu, M.C., et al.: Automated tongue diagnosis on the smartphone and its applications. Comput. Methods Program. Biomed. (2017)
4. Kim, J., et al.: Tongue diagnosis system for quantitative assessment of tongue coating in patients with functional dyspepsia: a clinical trial. J. Ethnopharmacol. **155**(1), 709–713 (2014)
5. Zuo, W., Wang, K., Zhang, D., Zhang, H:. Combination of polar edge detection and active contour model for automated tongue segmentation. In: International Conference on Image and Graphics, pp. 270–273 (2004)
6. Cui, Z., Zhang, H., Zhang, D., Li, N., Zuo, W.: Fast marching over the 2D gabor magnitude domain for tongue body segmentation. EURASIP J. Adv. Signal Process. **2013**(1), 1–13 (2013)
7. Bo Pang, D., Zhang, D., Wang, K.: The bi-elliptical deformable contour and its application to automated tongue segmentation in chinese medicine. IEEE Trans. Med. Imag. **24**(8), 946–956 (2005)
8. Kebin, W., Zhang, D.: Robust tongue segmentation by fusing region-based and edge-based approaches. Expert Syst. Appl. **42**(21), 8027–8038 (2015)
9. Kass, M., Witkin, A., Terzopoulos, D.: Snakes: active contour models. Int. J. Comput. Vis. **1**(4), 321–331 (1988)

A Study of Preschool Instructional Design Based on Augmented Reality Games

Xiaodong Wei[1], Dongqiao Guo[1(✉)], and Dongdong Weng[2]

[1] School of Educational Technology, Northwest Normal University, 967 Anning East Road, Lanzhou 730070, People's Republic of China
1446819657@qq.com
[2] School of Optoelectronics, Beijing Institute of Technology, No. 5, South Zhongguancun Street, Haidian zone, Beijing 100081, People's Republic of China

Abstract. In preschool education, it mostly focused on mobile augmented reality, and there are few games that can be used in kindergarten teaching. In this paper, we were discussed the instructional design on how to use augmented reality game in multimedia teaching environment. Based on the two theories, technicians collaborate with preschool teachers designed an augmented reality game, which can be used in multimedia classroom environment. Preschool teachers wrote the instructional design. The participants were split into two groups. The experimental group worked in an augmented reality environment, while the control group performed the activity in a traditional learning environment. The experimental results show that the experimental group has a better learning effect, and the development of children's multiple intelligences is outstanding. The instructional design, which is discussed in this paper, can have a positive impact on children's learning effects, and can also promote the comprehensive development of children's multiple intelligences.

Keywords: Augmented reality · Preschool education · Instructional design
Multiple intelligence

1 Introduction

Learning content is not easy to forget while students learn in play, so teachers have been looking for new teaching methods to improve students' abilities and trying to use various tools in teaching [1]. Related studies have proved that education and entertainment games also have the characteristics of playing and learning, which help stimulate learners' learning motivation, develop brain thinking and improve their language expression ability.

Augmented Reality (AR) technology has the characteristics of virtual integration, real-time interaction and 3D registration [2], using computer vision technology to overlay the virtual objects on the real scene, so as to construct the fusion reality visual effect. With the operation of real objects, the user can interact with multimedia content, effectively demonstrate concepts of stereo and space-time and bridge real and virtual worlds. Using AR technology in education has provided a new way for teaching. It has been widely used in preschool teaching activities by researchers. In 2007, Dunser and

© Springer Nature Singapore Pte Ltd. 2018
Y. Wang et al. (Eds.): IGTA 2018, CCIS 875, pp. 106–113, 2018.
https://doi.org/10.1007/978-981-13-1702-6_11

Horneker used the fable story as the learning content, and added 3D role, voice and interaction props to observe how children use AR to interact and cooperate learning [3]. In this study, an advantage of this system is that it can be used in modern classroom. However, this study was only designed for storybooks, and didn't involve the instructional design on how to use AR games in the multimedia teaching environment. In China, the field of educational technology generally focuses on the application of AR technology, mostly for macroscopic descriptive introduction, and does not involve research achievements in the field of practice [3].

In view of the above problems, based on the two theories: multiple intelligence and situated learning, preschool teachers wrote the instructional design on how to use the AR game in multimedia teaching environment. In order to validate the education applicability of the instructional design, we also designed and developed an AR game that contains competition elements of game, rich media and good interaction, which can be used in multimedia classroom environment. The pilot experimental results show that the instructional design which is discussed in this paper can have a positive impact on children's learning effects and promote the comprehensive development of children's multiple intelligences.

2   Methodology

2.1   Theoretical Background

Multiple Intelligences (MI). Howard Gardiner, an educational psychologist at the Harvard University, proposed the theory of MI in 1983. MI has only traditionally only emphasized the development of language and logic core intelligence, but that is not intelligence of all human. Gardiner believes that different people have different combinations of intelligences, so he redefined multiple intelligence, pointed out that intelligence is the ability to solve problems in a particular situation and the creativity. And human beings mainly have eight kinds of intelligences: linguistic, logical-mathematical, visual spatial, bodily-kinesthetic, musical, interpersonal, intrapersonal and naturalistic intelligence [4]. The use of multiple intelligence in the AR game activity is shown in Table 1.

Table 1. Application of eight multiple intelligences in AR.

Multiple intelligence	Activities included
Linguistic	The child reads the text on the screen and repeats the learning content
Logical-mathematical	Children should use logic to solve problems
Visual spatial	Children observe and perceive animals from different angles and interact with animals
Bodily-kinesthetic	The teaching content is presented on the card, the child must rotate to locate
Musical	The various sounds appearing in the activity stimulate the children into the situation
Interpersonal	Children's communication and cooperation with teachers and other children
Intrapersonal	The reconstruction of personal knowledge
Naturalistic	Explore the animal and living environment in various ways

Situated Learning. Situated learning is a teaching method that uses specific activity scenarios or provides learning resources, it can create scenarios, arouse students' interest in active learning and improve learning efficiency [5]. In formal learning, the main course why students acquire knowledge or skills are not strong enough is because the experience in formal learning is separated from the situation. AR can provide a vivid and realistic learning situation that enables the students to connect experience and situation together. The pattern of creating situations in the AR game, as shown in Fig. 1.

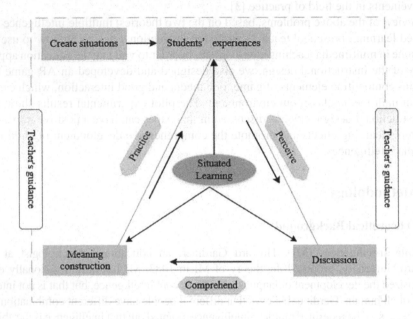

Fig. 1. The pattern of creating situations in the AR game.

2.2 Instructional Design

During kindergarten, knowing about animals is an important part of children's life education, and the amphibian is the content of the middle class syllabus [6]. After investigation, kindergartens have the hardware for AR teaching.

And after we designed the AR game which is used in teaching. To build a happy and efficient classroom for children, the important premise is the teacher's instructional design [7]. First, we analyzed the teaching content, selected four kinds of animals, including frog, toad, newt and caecilian, and designed 3D models, stereo pictures and virtual scenes respectively. Then, teaching activities were designed according to the teaching content. At last we wrote the teaching plan. The instructional design of AR games is shown in Fig. 2. The interaction of teacher and students includes three kinds of games, the first is that children choose animals according to the pictures given by teacher. The second is that children choose animals according to descriptions. And the third is to choose animals based on animal sounds. Finally, under the guidance of teachers, students were introspecting and abstractly generalizing the content of learning, thus promoting the development of their multiple intelligences.

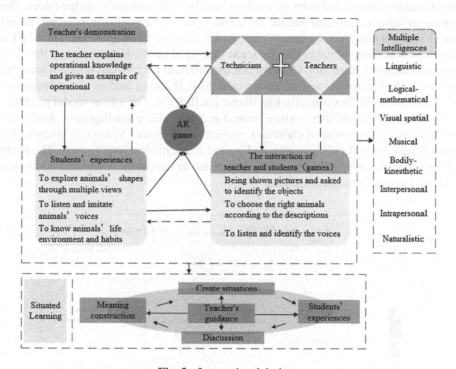

Fig. 2. Instructional design.

In summary, we designed 8 different scenes of AR games. There are 4 amphibious animals and it has two scenes for each animal which are video of 3D animal model and animation scene. We can switch these scenes by recognizing different markers while watching.

2.3 Teaching Aids Design

We prepare the students to use the electronic interactive whiteboard with large screen and marked folders for learning about amphibious animals. According to the guidelines for preschool education, preschool education should fully respect children as the main body of learning experience, respect for their physical and mental development law and their characteristics of study, also should play games as the basic activity, guide them to develop multiple intelligences in an all-around way. Thus, we use marked folders to present 3D animal models and videos in the real world, providing children with immersive experience.

To improve the comprehensive development of children's multiple intelligences, the AR game structure is shown in Fig. 3. A camera is used to capture images, which are then transmitted to the 3D Registration Module and subjected to mark recognition and tracked by the Control Center. The 3D Registration Module is implemented using the Vuforia AR software development kit. The Control Center selectively calls virtual animal models, audios and animation videos based on different marks on the folder. The processed video is converted into the plane and superimposed onto the real scene in real time. Finally, it transmits the virtual scene and the real world image to the Virtual-Real Fusion Module, which makes the AR scene displayed on the large screen of the electronic interactive whiteboard. Children can use different folds to call different teaching contents, which can improve children's positivity. Rotating folders can promote the development of children's bodily-kinesthetic intelligence. The virtual model promotes the development of children's visual spatial and naturalistic intelligences. Audio can improve the development of children's musical intelligence. Video can promote the development of children's linguistic and logical-mathematical intelligences. The game activities organized by AR scenes can promote the development of children's intrapersonal and interpersonal intelligences.

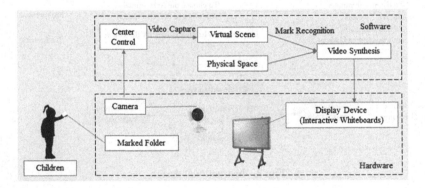

Fig. 3. AR game structure.

2.4 Pilot Study

We designed an AR game that uses a camera to capture image tags, to track virtual objects, and to realize virtual reality fusion. The experiment selected 46 children in middle class, and the average age of the research object is 5 years old. They were randomly divided into two groups. The two groups were taught by the same teacher who has four years' teaching experience and had received AR related content training, which avoided the influence of different teachers' teaching methods on the experimental results. All the students don't have the experience of using AR games for study.

Due to the particularity of children, observation and interview are used to evaluate the students' performance. The purpose of the pre-test is to assess whether the students have the same preparatory knowledge before participating in the experimental activities, and it mainly includes seven questions, with a full score of 100. The post-test aims to assess the degree of knowledge mastery of the students and the changes in all aspects of children after the completion of the experimental teaching. In addition, the staff installed a camera in the classroom to record children's performance in class so that they could be analyzed after the experiment. The teaching activity is shown in Fig. 4.

Fig. 4. The teaching activity.

The interview includes 6 problems of 3 aspects: knowledge feedback, teaching experience and emotional attitude. The questions are as follows. Q1. What amphibious animals do you know today, and what are their sounds like? Q2. What does the newt look like? Q3. Why did the frog in the animated cartoon get angry after being woken up? The last three questions are only suitable for the experimental group A. Q4. Folding pages can make animals, do you think it is fun? Q5. Do you like regular or today's classes? Q6. Why do you like (or dislike) today's class?

3   Results and Discussion

The results of the analysis of Q1–3 are shown in Table 2. The comparison results of Q1 show that using AR (M = 4.65, SD = 0.714) does more than using PPT (M = 4.09, SD = 0.848) in teaching on the integrality of the children's cognitive. Children of the two groups both can guess the animals' category according to their voice and they can also express the animals' sounds, but the AR group guessed faster than the second group, this explains that there is a difference on the music intelligence between two groups. The comparison results of Q2 show that children of AR group can imitate frog vividly and they can organize language more logically. 3D models provide all-round and multi-angle models for children to observe and children can describe things in a visual and stereo way. In conclusion, children of AR group (M = 4.61, SD = 0.583) perform more stable on linguistic, visual-spatial, bodily-kinesthetic and naturalist intelligence than children of PPT group (M = 4.00, SD = 0.853). The comparison results of Q3 show that

Table 2. Variance analysis of children feedback data.

	Groups	N	Mean	Std. deviation	Std. error mean
Q1	Group A	23	4.65	.714	.149
	Group B	23	4.09	.848	.177
Q2	Group A	23	4.61	.583	.122
	Group B	23	4.00	.853	.178
Q3	Group A	23	4.43	.662	.138
	Group B	23	4.22	.795	.166

children of AR group (M = 4.43, SD = 0.662) understand story better than children of PPT group (M = 4.22, SD = 0.759), children of AR group describe the reasons more clearly and perform more stable, which suggests that children of AR group have changes on logic intelligence.

The results of Q4–5 show that the children of AR group can clearly recognize their own learning mood, motivation and changes on the intrapersonal intelligence. Through the observation of the classroom and video, we found that the classroom atmosphere of the experimental group was obviously warmer than the control group, and children generally concentrated on the class, teachers and students also had good interaction with each other.

Therefore, it can be concluded that AR group has better teaching effects and children's multifaceted ability gets better development. AR games have a positive impact on the teaching effect of children.

For Q6, We got different answers, nine children think that "today's lesson is very interesting". Seven children feel "amazing". Five children think that "I made the animals". Two children feel that "small animals are very realistic, but they won't bite". It shows that the AR game stimulates the interests of children and makes them fonder of the classroom.

Therefore, experiential learning stimulates children's learning motivation and enables children to learn knowledge and apply the knowledge into real life in the process of continuous inquiry, which is very important for children's growth.

4   Conclusion

The experimental results show that the AR group has a better learning effect, and the development of children's multiple intelligences is outstanding. It's proved that the instructional design, which is discussed in this paper, can have a positive impact on children's learning effects and meet the needs of teaching.

In addition, there are still many shortcomings during the experiment, such as teachers' more demonstration of AR games and children experience less by themselves. The application of the new technology cannot predict the future stability. Because of the various problems during the teaching experiment of the AR game, the following works are needed in the future research: 1. We will continue to do pilot research to test the stability of AR games. 2. We will develop other types of children's teaching courseware, which would cultivate children's interests and improve the ability of young teachers, thus contributing to the development and popularization of AR technology in preschool teaching.

Acknowledgements. This research was supported by the National Natural Science Foundation of China under Grant No. 11664036.

References

1. Veenema, S., Gardner, H.: Multimedia and multiple intelligences. Am. Prospect 7(29), 69–75 (1996)
2. Azuma, R.T.: A survey of augmented reality. Presence: Teleoper. Virtual Environ. 6(4), 355–385 (1997)
3. Dünser, A., Hornecker, E.: An observational study of children interacting with an augmented story book. In: Hui, K., et al. (eds.) Edutainment 2007. LNCS, vol. 4469, pp. 305–315. Springer, Heidelberg (2007). https://doi.org/10.1007/978-3-540-73011-8_31
4. Zhixian, Z.: Multi intelligence theory and educational technology. E-Educ. Res. **03**, 7–11 (2004)
5. Qiuyi, C.: Literature review of situated learning theory. Basic Educ. Res. **19**, 38–41+63 (2016)
6. Beijing Peihua Talent Training Center: Design of Education Activity in Middle Class Kindergarten (Teacher's Book). China Ocean Press, Beijing (2000)
7. Lilin, L.: Learning science and situated learning for children – the teaching design of happy and efficient classroom. Educ. Res. **34**, 11:81–11:91 (2013)

Research on Gas-Liquid Mixing Method Based on SPH

Mingjing Ai, Aiyu Zheng[✉], and Feng Li

State Key Laboratory of Virtual Reality Technology and Systems,
Beihang University, Beijing 100191, China
zoe_cc@buaa.edu.cn

Abstract. With the continuous development of computer science and technology, the computational ability of computer has been improved a lot. The particle method based on Lagrangian has become a hot spot in water modeling. In this paper, we first implement a standard multiple-fluid mixing framework based on adaptive hierarchical tree-based neighborhood particle search algorithm and simple boundary correction algorithm. On this basis, the gas-liquid mixing mode is expanded, including soluble gas and insoluble gas. We conducted a series of experiments on the computer to verify the effectiveness of the hybrid method.

Keywords: Fluid simulation · Gas-liquid mixing method · SPH

1 Introduction

The authenticity of the water body simulation is mainly reflected in the various details. Water contains a variety of details, such as broken waves, water, foam and so on. Among that, bubbles are an important detail and mainly deal with the interaction of gas and liquid.

At present, the interaction methods of gas and liquid are mainly divided as Eulerian and Lagrangian. Eulerian method treats fluid as a velocity field that varies over time. Given a certain position, a unique velocity vector can be found that characterizes the movement of fluid and bubbles. This velocity field can be obtained by solving the Navier-Stokes equations, which leads to the motion of water and bubbles. There are two main problems of Eulerian. Firstly, bubble's boundary is too thin which may be a few microns or even a few nanometers. The grid-based Eulerian method is difficult to capture such accuracy. Secondly, the calculation of surface tension required to use the explicit method. To achieve numerical stability, it is generally necessary to use a small time step, which leads to a very high computational scale.

Therefore, another kind of method which based on particles has become a hot spot in water modeling recently. The Lagrangian method regards the fluid as a particle system, and the smooth particle dynamics (SPH) makes it possible to discretize fluid. In standard SPH method, however, air does not appear explicitly in the calculation model. The air in the water disappears immediately while the liquid particles take the air out of the way without any obstruction. Thus, in order to model the air surrounded in fluid, we

Y. Wang et al. (Eds.): IGTA 2018, CCIS 875, pp. 114–123, 2018.
https://doi.org/10.1007/978-981-13-1702-6_12

need to add a large number of air particles in the calculation, and there would be a big increase in calculation and complexity.

2 Related Work

As early as 2007, Cleary [1] proposed a gas bubble model generated by dissolved gases and they simulated water and air bubbles independently. At the same time, the interaction between water and gas bubbles was achieved through the pull model, but the effect was rather harsh. Discontinuous density model proposed by Solenthaler [2] is used to simulate the fluid interaction interface with large density changes. In the meantime, Hong [3] and others proposed a hybrid multi-phase flow simulation method to simulate the effect of bubbles. Combined with the new bubble model, SPH was used in combination with the Euler grid to simulate a large number of scenes in which fluid and gas move synchronously. Their new model overcomes the problem of modeling small bubbles. In the multi-phase flow on the grid, they construct the interaction between gas and fluid and the interaction between bubble particles, vividly simulate the scene of a large number of small bubbles in water, but the simulation method is very complex, computational power of the computer made a very high demand.

To solve this problem, Mihalef [4] proposed a mixing model of particles and meshes to simulate bubbles generated by solids. However, the interface between gas and fluid was not satisfactorily handled. Bonnet [5] used the SPH method to simulate the interaction of bubbles and water. They simulate the movement of bubbles in water by establishing a tension model. Shao [6] simulated the details of small–sized water bodies based on the solid-liquid interaction system, implementing a particle-based animation showing the gas flying out of the water. For the first time, this method takes into account the gas concentration and the effect of liquids on the gas.

Since then, people continue to study the impact of water and gas concentration in the interaction process, and work on modeling based on the particle system. Busaryev [7] and Grenier [8] proposed a particle-based algorithm to simulate the formation of bubbles and the interaction between bubbles and liquids. Szewc [9] summarized the issue of sub-kernel spurious interface fragmentation occurring in SPH applied for multiphase flows. Natsui [10] simulated the gas-liquid-liquid flow by using the SPH based multi-phase flow model. The method is obtained by approximating the geometry of the bubble. However, it does not describe soluble gases. Vries [11] shows detailed knowledge about all phenomena involved to predict the behaviour of the bubbles and the implications on the flow.

3 Standard SPH Framework

3.1 Neighborhood Particle Search Algorithm

The SPH method uses the discrete particles around one particle to calculate the relevant physical quantities, and the smooth function specifies the range of the particles affected by other particles. Therefore, an efficient search algorithm is needed to support the particles' huge amount of calculation. At present, there are three kinds of mainstream neighborhood particle search algorithms. That is full search method, space grid search method and adaptive hierarchical tree search method.

The simplest algorithm is the full search method, where all particles are identified by their smooth particle radius. Its complexity reaches $O(n^2)$. Rely on the spatial grid and linked list to search is a more efficient way. Searching the space in advance will greatly reduce the search range, and the algorithm complexity can reach $O(n)$ level under certain conditions. But this method relies on spatial partitioning, the smooth length which controls space partition needs to be a fixed value. Adaptive hierarchical tree search method is currently a more efficient search method. Because of the use of the tree data structure, it has relatively low complexity like $O(n\log n)$ level. The idea of the algorithm is: partition the neighborhood particle problem domain, stop the segmentation if there is only one particle in the divided domain, and repeat the problem domain segmentation if there are multiple particles until there are only unique particle.

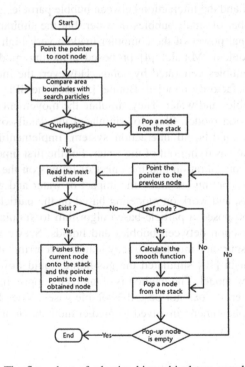

Fig. 1. The flow chart of adaptive hierarchical tree search method

The flow chart of this method is shown in Fig. 1.

After determining the information of the interacting particle pairs, calculating the particle approximation only requires traversing all particle pairs, thus simplifying the calculation.

3.2   Boundary Collision Correction Algorithm

Boundary collision is based on the location and depth of penetration to modify the particle position, then to prevent the purpose of particle penetration. If the particles have penetrated, move the particles through a certain distance in the direction of the normal vector of the contact point. The velocity of the penetrating particle will be reflected by the normal vector of the point, as shown in Fig. 2.

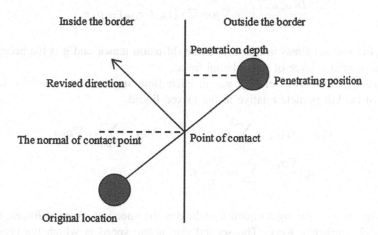

Fig. 2. Collision processing diagram

In order to simulate the kinetic energy lost while water hitting the wall, we use (1) to update the speed.

$$u_i = u_i - (1+c)(u_i \cdot n)n. \tag{1}$$

u_i is the velocity of the particle i. n is the normal vector of the contact point. c is the recovery coefficient from 0 to 1. While c equals to 1, the collision becomes a completely elastic collision without losing kinetic energy.

4   Gas-Liquid Mixing Model

4.1   Liquid Mixing Model

In liquids mixture, we need to calculate the information separately for each type of liquid and then take volume fraction into the standard SPH framework.

The governing equation is shown in Eq. (2).

$$\frac{D\rho_m}{Dt} = \frac{\partial \rho_m}{\partial t} + \nabla \cdot (\rho_m u_m) = 0. \tag{2}$$

ρ_m is the mixing density, u_m is the mixing speed which is described by Eq. (3).

$$u_m = \sum_{k=1}^{n} c_k u_k. \tag{3}$$

k is the current number of particles. c_k is the correlation coefficient, obtained by the ratio of the liquid density to the average density of the k-th particle.

The momentum equation is shown in (4).

$$\frac{D(\rho_m u_m)}{Dt} = -\nabla p + \nabla \cdot (\tau_m + \tau_{Dm}) + \rho_m g. \tag{4}$$

τ_m is the viscous stress tensor. τ_{Dm} is the diffusion tensor and g is the acceleration due to the resultant force of the external force.

Calculate the relative velocity u_{mk} in each time step as shown in (5). It is the velocity of the kth particle relative to the mixed liquid.

$$u_{mk} = v_k(\rho_k - \sum_{k'} c_{k'} \rho_{k'})a - v_k(\nabla p_k - \sum_{k'} c_{k'} \nabla p_{k'})$$
$$- \mu_k(\frac{\nabla \alpha_k}{\alpha_k} - \sum_{k'} c_{k'} \frac{\nabla \alpha_{k'}}{\alpha_{k'}}). \tag{5}$$

The first part of the right equation indicates the speed of external forces, such as gravity and centrifugal force. The second one is the speed at which the pressure is generated, causing the fluid in the high pressure zone to flow to the low pressure zone. The last one expresses the Brownian diffusion, which causes the liquid to flow from the low concentration zone to the high concentration zone. v is the degree of diffusion coefficient. μ is the coefficient of Brownian diffusion. a is calculated by Eq. (6).

$$a = g - (u_m \cdot \nabla)u_m - \frac{\partial u_m}{\partial t}. \tag{6}$$

Diffusion tensor is shown in (7).

$$\tau_{Dm} = -\sum_{k} \alpha_k \rho_k u_{mk} \otimes u_{mk}. \tag{7}$$

$\otimes$ means requesting a tensor product.

The volume fraction is obtained from (8).

$$\frac{D\alpha_k}{Dt} = -\alpha_k \nabla \cdot u_m - \nabla \cdot (\alpha_k u_{mk}). \tag{8}$$

4.2 Gas-Liquid Mixing Model

The gas has a lower density than liquids. Meanwhile, gas is given buoyancy by the surrounding liquids, rapidly changing speed and creating the effect of rising in water.

Gas will also affect the surrounding liquid in the process of rising, resulting in a mixed effect. The computational steps involved in the hybrid model are described below.

4.2.1 Pressure Calculation

The pressure of particles can be expressed in ideal gas as shown in (9).

$$pV = nRT. \tag{9}$$

p is the pressure. V is the reciprocal of the density. n is the molar mass of the gas particles. R is the gas constant and T is the temperature. This article does not consider the impact of temperature. Therefore, the pressure can be simply expressed as shown in (10).

$$p = k\rho. \tag{10}$$

Therefore, the pressure of particles can be expressed by (11).

$$f_i^{pressure} = -\sum_{j \neq i} p_j \frac{m_j}{\rho_j} \nabla W(r_i - r_j, h). \tag{11}$$

However, using (11) to calculate the pressure leads to the problem of unequal pressures between two particles, which violates the basic laws of physics. Therefore, formula (12) is used to ensure that the forces of particles' interaction are equal.

$$f_i^{pressure} = -\rho_i \sum_{j \neq i} (\frac{p_i}{\rho_i^2} + \frac{p_j}{\rho_j^2}) m_j \nabla W(r_i - r_j, h). \tag{12}$$

Because the pressure is calculated by the arithmetic average, the pressure is symmetrical and conforms to Newton's third law.

Because the ideal pressure model is used, resulting in repulsive forces only. In order to achieve the attraction forces between the gas particles, the pressure formula is modified to include a reference value as shown in (13).

$$p = k(\rho - \rho_0). \tag{13}$$

After the reference density is added, the gas particles whose density are smaller than ρ_0 will attract the surrounding particles to increase their density, whereas the gas particles larger than it will repel the surrounding particles. The gas particles whose density are close to it will reduce the attraction and repulsion, so that they can balance the exclusion and attraction between gas particles.

Calculating the pressure by (12), we need to select a suitable smooth function. If we use a smooth kernel $W1$, like (14), the high pressure will causes gas agglomeration. Therefore, we use a more sharp smooth kernel function $W2$, like (15). Because the steep curve can avoid unreasonable particles agglomerate phenomenon, when the particles are too dense.

$$W_1(r, h) = \frac{315}{64\pi h^9} \begin{cases} (h^2 - \|r\|^2)^3 & 0 \leq \|r\| \leq h \\ 0 & \|r\| > h \end{cases} \tag{14}$$

$$W_2(r, h) = \frac{15}{\pi h^6} \begin{cases} (h - \|r\|)^3 & 0 \leq \|r\| \leq h \\ 0 & \|r\| > h \end{cases} \tag{15}$$

4.2.2 Viscosity Calculation

During the process that gas particles move against the shearing force, friction occurs between them. The friction will convert the kinetic energy into thermal energy, thus losing a part of the energy. Viscosity describes the loss of energy due to resistance.

The viscosity between particles is similar to the pressure. The interaction force is asymmetric. The viscosity is related to the velocity between particles. Therefore, we achieve the symmetry of the viscosity between the particles, as shown in (16).

$$f_i^{viscosity} = \mu \sum_{j \neq i} (u_j - u_i) \frac{m_j}{\rho_j} \nabla^2 W(r_i - r_j, h). \tag{16}$$

μ is the coefficient of Brownian diffusion. u_i is the velocity of particle i. m_j is the mass of particle j. ρ_j is the density of particle j. $W(r, h)$ is the smooth kernel function based on particle position r and smooth kernel radius h. Considering that the energy loss due is only related to the velocity between particles, a relatively simplified viscosity calculation is obtained as shown in (15). After the viscosity part is transformed, the SPH method approximation is resumed.

$$f_i^{viscosity} = \frac{\mu}{\rho_j} \sum_j (u_j - u_i) m_j \nabla^2 W(r_i - r_j, h). \tag{17}$$

It should be noted that in the case of constant mass density, (16) can be converted to (17). The density of the gas particle is calculated based on the properties of the adjacent gas particles. Therefore, (16) has higher accuracy, while (17) has a faster calculation speed.

5 Experiments Result

We test our model on Lenovo notebook Y510p, Inter Core i5-4200M. Its memory is 8 GB and the type of video card is NVIDIA GT 755M. Software environment is Windows10. Developed tools is Microsoft Visual Studio 2010, while using the OpenGL library for visualization.

We have achieved the standard water column test, mixed simulation of miscible liquid, mixed simulation of non-miscible liquid, gas-liquid mixture soluble in liquid and non-liquid-soluble gas-liquid mixed simulation. The results verify the efficiency and rationality of the proposed model. Due to the limited space, we only introduced the results of gas-liquid mixing model.

Figure 3 shows the mixture of liquid-soluble gas and liquid.

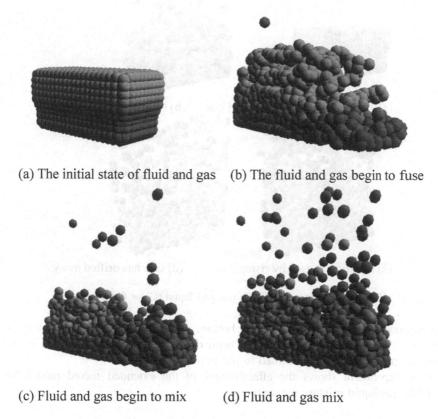

(a) The initial state of fluid and gas   (b) The fluid and gas begin to fuse

(c) Fluid and gas begin to mix   (d) Fluid and gas mix

Fig. 3. Liquid-soluble gas-liquid mixture (Color figure online)

The initial form of water body is rectangle, while the upper part is red fluid and the lower part is blue gas. Then, as the red fluid flows and falls, the blue gas rises and the red liquid at the junction starts to mix resulting in producing purple particles. The liquid then mixed with the newborn liquid to form a large amount of mixture. Some of the blue gas particles floated, but the mixture still appeared purple. Finally, a large amount of blue gas floated, but a large amount of blue gas was still mixed with the red liquid and the mixture appeared purple.

The experiment fully demonstrate the effectiveness and correctness of the hybrid model for simulating the soluble gas-liquid mixture phenomena. The rationality of SPH framework is also verified.

Figure 4 shows a mixture of insoluble gases and liquids.

The initial form of water body is rectangle, while the upper part is red fluid and the lower part is blue gas. As the red fluid flows and falls, the gas rises and the junction encountered a purple-blue gas rose. Then the gas particles rise and affect the liquid particles, resulting in a phenomenon of eruption. We can find that a large number of

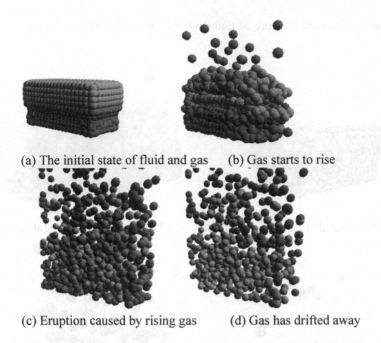

(a) The initial state of fluid and gas   (b) Gas starts to rise

(c) Eruption caused by rising gas   (d) Gas has drifted away

Fig. 4. Mixtures of insoluble gas and liquid (Color figure online)

blue gas particles begin to rise and the bottom of the liquid particles have begun to show red. While the gas particles have been drifting blue, most of the gas particles drifted away and the liquid returned to red finally.

This experiment shows the effectiveness of the extended mixed model for a insoluble gas-liquid mixture scenario.

6   Conclusion

This paper firstly summarizes the real-time gas-liquid mixing simulation methods in recent years. The current mainstream methods are divided into Euler method and Lagrange method. After that, based on the standard SPH framework, we proposes a standard waterbody blending framework based on adaptive stratified tree and boundary correction algorithm, which can significantly improve the efficiency.

Finally, from a physical point of view, we uses the framework to develop a mixing gas-liquid system based on an liquid-liquid mixing model, in which the gas includes both soluble and insoluble gases. This extended hybrid model can intuitively reflect the gas's movement process. At last, we do a series of experiments to verify the effectiveness.

Acknowledgement. This work is supported by the National 863 Program of China under Grant No. 2015AA016403. And the improved shallow water system and all technologies involved are courtesy of the State key Laboratory of Virtual Reality Technology and Systems, Beihang University. We also thank everyone who spent time reading earlier versions of this paper.

References

1. Cleary, P.W., Pyo, S.H., Prakash, M., et al.: Bubbling and frothing liquids. ACM Trans. Graph. **26**(3), 97 (2007)
2. Solenthaler, B., Pajarola, R.: Density contrast SPH interfaces. In: Eurographics/ACM SIGGRAPH Symposium on Computer Animation, SCA 2010, Dublin, Ireland, pp. 211–218 (2008)
3. Hong, J.M., Lee, H.Y., Yoon, J.C., et al.: Bubbles alive. ACM Trans. Graph. **27**(3), 1–4 (2008)
4. Mihalef, V., Metaxas, D., Sussman, M.: Simulation of two-phase flow with sub-scale droplet and bubble effects. Comput. Graph. Forum **28**(2), 229–238 (2009)
5. Bonnet, J.: Animation of air bubbles with SPH. In: GRAPP 2011 - Proceedings of the International Conference on Computer Graphics Theory and Applications, Vilamoura, Algarve, Portugal, March 2016, pp. 225–234 (2016)
6. Shao, X., Zhong, Z., Wei, W.: Particle-based simulation of bubbles in water–solid interaction. Comput. Anim. Virtual Worlds **23**(5), 477–487 (2012)
7. Busaryev, O., Dey, T.K., Wang, H., et al.: Animating bubble interactions in a liquid foam. ACM Trans. Graph. **31**(4), 1–8 (2015)
8. Grenier, N., Touzé, D.L., Colagrossi, A., et al.: Viscous bubbly flows simulation with an interface SPH model. Ocean Eng. **69**, 88–102 (2013)
9. Szewc, K., Pozorski, J., Minier, J.: Spurious interface fragmentation in multiphase SPH. Int. J. Numer. Methods Eng. **103**(9), 625–649 (2015)
10. Natsui, S., Nashimoto, R., Takai, H., et al.: SPH simulations of the behavior of the interface between two immiscible liquid stirred by the movement of a gas bubble. Chem. Eng. Sci. **141**, 342–355 (2016)
11. de Vries, A.W.G.: Path and Wake of a Rising Bubble. University of Twente, Enschede (2017)

Improving Authentic Learning
by AR-Based Simulator

Xiaodong Wei[1(✉)], Dongqiao Guo[1], and Dongdong Weng[2]

[1] School of Educational Technology, Northwest Normal University, 967 Anning East Road, Lanzhou 730070, People's Republic of China
wxd1633@163.com
[2] School of Optoelectronics, Beijing Institute of Technology, No. 5, South Zhongguancun Street, Haidian Zone, Beijing 100081, People's Republic of China

Abstract. In this paper, a simulator based on augmented reality is developed, named ARFLY, for use in China's general high school technology curriculum to improve the authentic learning experience and learning effect. ARFLY replaces a real instrument panel, which is complex and expensive, with a virtual 3D model by means of AR technology. ARFLY includes video see-through head mounted display with a motion tracker to realize 360-degree viewing by relating head tracking information to the display of virtual 3D scenarios. In addition, ARFLY is equipped with an intelligent tutoring system that guides the learning process. A pilot study and questionnaire-based evaluation of ARFLY are conducted. The results of a pilot study show that the proposed simulator can enhance authentic feeling, the immersion sensation, and learning motivation for users when learning control principles.

Keywords: Augmented reality · Learning strategies · Secondary education

1 Introduction

Virtual reality (VR) is a system in which users are immersed in a simulated environment and cannot view the outside world. In contrast, augmented reality (AR), also known as mixed reality (MR), enables users to observe virtual objects that are superimposed on or combined with the real world. That is, AR supplements reality, rather than completely replacing it [1]. AR systems are characterized by the following properties: they combine real and virtual objects in a real environment; they align real and virtual objects with each other; and they operate interactively and in real time [2]. These characteristic benefits enable educators and designers to superimpose virtual graphics over real objects, thereby enabling users to interact with digital content through physical manipulation. This facilitates more effective demonstrations of spatial and temporal concepts and the contextual relationships between real and virtual objects [3].

In view of the above advantages of AR, we direct students to operate a flight simulator with which they can experience the flight process and understand the principles of control. AR can improve authentic learning in high school because: (1) the immersion, interaction, and navigation features of AR improve students' motivation to learn, assist them with knowledge comprehension, and are potentially useful in learning tasks that require experimentation, spatial ability, and collaboration [4–6]; (2) AR can reduce the cognitive workload by integrating multiple sources of information while learning [7]; (3) AR can reduce the cost of experimental courses; in terms of product design, it is becoming a major part of the prototyping process [8] and offers a solution to the expensive problem of building prototypes [9]; and (4) AR can provide more varied interactive modes [10].

Considering the unsatisfactory general technology situation in high schools in China, we applied AR technology to the learning of basic flight control principles in the general technology curriculum. Two constraints currently exist in traditional flight control teaching methods. For one, flight simulators used for actual flight training are relatively expensive. Consequently, owing to the lack of financial support for high school laboratories, students are not afforded the opportunity to use a real flight simulator to study basic flight control principles in authentic learning. Secondly, existing flight simulation games used in authentic learning make it difficult for students to experience a true sensation of flight, such as flying over mountains and operating an aircraft while seated in a real cockpit. The relevant learning effects are too difficult to be achieved because the games are not equipped with an instructional system for learning basic flight control principles.

To address the above problems and improve the authentic learning experience, we developed the ARFLY low-cost flight simulator. Based on AR technology, ARFLY includes an intelligent tutoring system (ITS) that guides the learning process. To evaluate students' authentic feeling, immersion sensation, and learning motivation when using ARFLY, we conducted a pilot study at a high school affiliated with Renmin University, China. We designed and implemented a related questionnaire based on situated learning and flow theory, as well as a questionnaire that evaluated students' comprehension of aircraft component functions and control principles. In Sect. 4, we present the results of our evaluation.

2 Literature Review

2.1 Augmented Reality Flight Simulator

The idea of VR has been the cornerstone of simulation since 1965, when Sutherland conceptualized the visual interface as less of a screen than as a window to a virtual world that looks real, sounds real, and reacts in real time [11]. Flight simulation with VR technology still relies on large, cumbersome, and expensive environments to produce a convincing virtual world: vision is enabled through expensive cameras and almost real-life cockpit avionics; pilot controls are mounted on cockpit-like structures; and the whole structure is moved by heavy, primarily hydraulic-driven motion platforms [12]. Currently, it is still rare for AR to be used to display cockpit avionics. Because AR can naturally superimpose virtual objects on real scenarios, a low-cost aircraft cockpit model can be manufactured that superimposes virtual 'real cockpit avionics'—the most expensive components in the aircraft—on this model with AR technology. Moreover, a virtually real operating scenario can be created through which both the actual manual operation and virtual flying scenes outside can be viewed. Thus, applying AR can reduce the costs of the traditional flight simulator while providing sufficient simulation flight effects. Furthermore, the relevant teaching content can be superimposed on the corresponding positions in the cockpit to achieve a better learning effect.

2.2 Intelligent Tutoring System

An intelligent tutoring system (ITS) is a computer system that provides immediate and customized instruction or feedback to learners typically without intervention from a human teacher [13], thereby fostering learning in meaningful and effective ways. A close relationship exists between intelligent tutoring and cognitive learning theories. There are many examples of ITSs being used in both formal educational and professional settings that have demonstrated their capabilities and limitations.

Schiaffino et al., for example, designed eTeacher, an intelligent agent that supports personalized e-learning assistance. The agent builds student profiles while observing student performances in online courses; the information is then used to suggest personalized strategies to assist student learning processes [14].

Another example of a student-centered ITS is ZOSMAT [15]. It follows the work of students and guides them in different learning stages by recording their progress. It then alters the given program based on the student's performance. ZOSMAT can be used for either individual learning or in a real classroom with the guidance of a human tutor.

3   Method

In this section, we describe the ARFLY system structure and components. We explain the design of its ITS, introduce key aspects of the pilot study, and outline the experiment. We then describe our method for assessing ARFLY's learning effects.

3.1   Flight Simulator for Control Principle Instruction

System Design. ARFLY consists of a full-scale cockpit model, cube green screen, liquid crystal display (LCD) monitor, a video see-through head mounted display (VSTHMD), a Saitek pilot control stick and pedal set (http://www.saitek.com/), and a standard desktop PC. The VSTHMD is comprised of a Sony HMZ-T1 HMD (http://www.sony.com/), Logitech HD Pro C920 webcam (http://www.logitech.com/), and Xsens MTi 10-Series motion trackers (http://www.xsens.com/). The PC runs Windows 7 operating systems and is equipped with Intel Haswell i7 CPUs with relatively high-end graphics cards (NVIDIA GTX770 or better). The HMD motion tracker calculates the angular position of the display and feeds it to the computer; the webcam acquires real images and feeds them to the computer. A virtual instrument panel is superimposed on the instrument panel sticker within a real cockpit, which is used as a tracking marker.

The pilot controls are simple joysticks; the center joystick represents lateral and longitudinal cyclic controls; the side joystick denotes collective control, and its slider controls throttle; and pedals represent the tail rotor control.

The ARFLY system structure is illustrated in Fig. 1. A game engine is the core component. Firstly, the VSTHMD webcam transmits real images of the green screen and cockpit interior to the tracking module, which calculates the position and rotation of the virtual instrument panel in a real scenario according to the captured images. Based on this position and rotation, the game engine superimposes the virtual instrument panel on the real instrument panel sticker within the cockpit. Meanwhile, the tracking module transmits the real-time images to the green screen key module. The module makes the images transparent by deducting the green color data; the processed images are then transmitted to the game engine. From that point, the game engine superimposes the transparent images on all virtual and real scenarios.

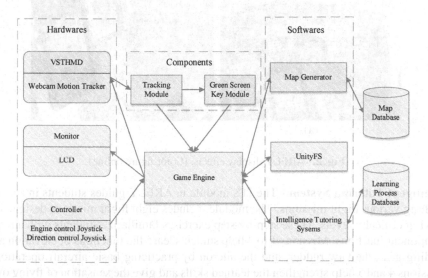

Fig. 1. ARFLY system structure. (Color figure online)

With the above interactive mode, users can view both real cockpit interior scenarios and virtual ones outside the cockpit through the transparent images. Users can simultaneously observe the virtual instrument panel, as shown in Fig. 2(a). In addition, the corresponding dynamic flight scenarios can be rendered through the game engine according to the head motion data recorded by the VSTHMD motion tracker. The ARFLY simulator features a synthetic visual environment as perceived from the pilot's cockpit view. The user has a 360-degree view of the cockpit interior and world surrounding the aircraft through the VSTHMD. This includes pilot controls, cockpit instruments, main rotor rotation, etc. The whole visual environment is integrated through the Unity FS (http://unityfs.chris-cheetham.com/) simulation plug-in. The pilot transmits operation commands through the controller joystick to the game engine. Owing to AR technology, the pilot can observe both his/her manual operations and the virtual instrument panel, as shown in Fig. 2(b). The game engine displays on the LCD monitor the virtual flight scenarios that the pilot perceives in the VSTHMD; therefore, other students can watch. A map generator calculates map data according to the aircraft flight position, calls the given map from a map database, and superimposes it on the flight scenario. When the ARFLY simulator runs, ITS combines multimedia resources stored in the learning process database; rendered by the game engine, these reconstruction resources can guide learning. We developed the flight game, GAMEFLY, to investigate the learning effects of ARFLY. It is similar to flight simulation computer games that do not use a cube green screen, real cockpit, joystick, motion tracker, or HDM. The 3D flight scenarios used in GAMEFLY are the same as those in ARFLY. When playing the game, students view scenarios through the LCD panel but operate the game with a keyboard.

(a)   (b)

Fig. 2.   ARFLY display effects. (Color figure online)

Intelligent Tutoring System. The ITS module in ARFLY guides students in accomplishing various flight missions. The module includes eight flight missions designed in varying difficulty levels. These step-by-step exercises familiarize students with aircraft component functions. Missions 1 to 3 help students learn the functions of elevation and landing gear, the yaw rudder, and the aileron by practicing basic aircraft operations. Missions 4 and 5 help strengthen the learned skills and give the sensation of flying over water and hilly terrain. Missions 6 and 7 guide students in completing more complex flight operations, such as controlling the aircraft during inverted flight. Mission 8 teaches students the importance of the left and right engines and emulates the experience of crashing. A reality explanation video for the latter mission is displayed on the virtual instrument panel with AR technology, as shown in Fig. 2(a), which gives students the feeling of being directed by a real commander. After assessing the completion of a mission, ITS displays a relevant guidance video prepared from the learning resource database, which includes the assigning of new operating missions and a completion notification. The game engine calculates the aircraft altitude, speed, flight time, angle, engine state, and landing gear status to determine the tasks to be achieved; it then notifies ITS to conduct the next task in the schedule. The next operation is initiated only when the former task is complete.

3.2 Participants

We conducted a pilot study to investigate the effect of ARFLY on authentic learning for high school students. From this level, we randomly selected for our study 24 students from 14 classes and placed them in two groups: Group 1 was the control group; Group 2 was the experimental group. Each group was comprised of eight boys and four girls. For Group 1, conventional teaching methods with GAMEFLY were used; as a comparison, Group 2 used only ARFLY.

3.3 Procedure

In this section, we describe our experimental processes. We used general technical teaching procedures as a reference. The proposed ARFLY learning processes were undertaken by Group 2 in three steps. First, the teacher provided a PowerPoint presentation and flight video to respectively explain and illustrate the basic principles of flight control.

The teaching contents include aircraft flight attitude, the composition of the aircraft control system, the working process of the aircraft control system and interference of flight control (http://www.rbloc.cn/). Second, students were then directed to draw a detailed sketch of an aircraft and apply basic flight control principles to analyze how each component works and controls the aircraft. At last, students were directed to operate ARFLY; the study scenario is shown in Fig. 3. The conventional teaching method used by Group 1 was similar to the ARFLY learning method in its first two steps; however, in the last step, Group 1 students played GAMEFLY. At the end of the pilot study, all participants were required to complete two questionnaires that respectively assessed their comprehension and learning experience. Participants were additionally required to complete a comprehension questionnaire before the pilot study to set a baseline.

(a)   (b)

Fig. 3. Learning process using ARFLY: (a) whole learning scene; and (b) local cockpit operating scene.

3.4 Measurements

In an authentic learning environment, student authentic feeling, immersion sensation, and learning motivation play a significant role in teaching effects. We therefore designed the learning experience questionnaire based on situated learning, flow theory, and learning motivation. The questionnaire included 18 questions (Q1–Q18) measuring six dimensions (F1–F6). F1 and F2 related to authentic feeling in and outside of the cockpit. F3 and F4 determined the degree of attention and external influence when operating the simulator or game. F5 related to the sense of time when operating the simulator. F6 assessed learning motivation. A five-point Likert scale was used to score the survey results of each question; a score of 5 denoted "strongly agree" and 1 meant "strongly disagree." The comprehension questionnaire was comprised of ten questions (T1–T10) and was likewise scored based on the five-point Likert scale; a score of 5 denoted "strongly understand" and 1 meant "completely do not understand." T1 through T4 assessed comprehension of basic aircraft component functions; T5 through T10 assessed comprehension of basic control principles. Finally, we calculated the scores of the questionnaires and evaluated the learning effects.

4   Results

4.1   Comprehension Assessment

Each dataset of two groups was collected from different students. Thus, they were uncorrelated and mutually independent; therefore, the independent sample t-test was suitable for analyzing the results obtained from the questionnaires. First, we calculated the mean values of the questionnaire results, as shown in Table 1; a score of 1 denoted "thorough incomprehension" and a 5 meant "thorough comprehension." The pre-test column outlined the baseline comprehension test results; the post-test column outlined comprehension results after completion of the pilot study. The preliminary test results indicated that the mean values in the pre-test column were less than 3.0 and that there was little difference between Groups 1 and 2. That is, students' initial comprehension levels in basic flight control principles were consistent across the two groups; their comprehension was insufficient for both control components and principles. On the other hand, the mean values in the post-test column were all higher than 3.0, indicating that comprehension in control principles had noticeably improved. Meanwhile, the mean values for each question were higher for Group 2 than for Group 1, which suggests that the use of ARFLY was more effective than GAMEFLY in assisting student learning.

We then performed Levene's test on the equality of variances using the data obtained in these two teaching scenarios. If the variance of the two sub-populations was equal, the independent sample t-test employed the pooled variance t-test [16], whereas a separate variance t-test was appropriate if this was not the case.

The test results ($p > 0.05$) from the pre-test indicated that comprehension of control principles did not significantly differ between the two groups. The post-test results of component comprehension, specifically of the aircraft elevator (T1, $t = -2.159$, $p < 0.05$), aileron (T2, $t = -2.378$, $p < 0.05$), and yaw rudder (T3, $t = -2.744$, $p < 0.05$), suggested that Group 2 achieved better comprehension than Group 2. Meanwhile, comprehension of control principles, specifically on transitioning from actual to command indication states (T7, $t = -2.612$, $p < 0.05$), overshooting (T8, $t = -4.330$, $p < 0.01$), reverse overshooting (T9, $t = -3.546$, $p < 0.01$), and operational approaching (T10, $t = -4.022$, $p < 0.01$), was significantly better for Group 2 than for Group 1. On the whole, the comprehension level of Group 2, which used ARFLY, was significantly higher than that of Group 1, which employed conventional learning methods and GAMEFLY.

Table 1. Pre- and post-test results comparison for groups 1 and 2 based on independent-sample t-test for comprehension of basic flight control principles

No.	Group	Pre-test				Post-test			
		Mean	SD	t	Sig. (2-tailed)	Mean	SD	t	Sig. (2-tailed)
T1	1	2.50	0.522	0.394	0.698	4.00	0.426	−2.159	0.042
	2	2.42	0.515			4.42	0.515		
T2	1	2.58	0.515	0.000	1.000	3.92	0.515	−2.378	0.026
	2	2.58	0.515			4.42	0.515		
T3	1	2.58	0.793	0.000	1.000	3.92	0.515	−2.755	0.012
	2	2.58	0.515			4.50	0.522		
T4	1	2.42	0.515	−1.216	0.237	4.25	0.452	−.432	0.670
	2	2.67	0.492			4.33	0.492		
T5	1	2.58	0.515	0.793	0.436	4.17	0.389	−.920	0.368
	2	2.42	0.515			4.33	0.492		
T6	1	2.33	0.492	−1.658	0.111	3.83	0.577	−1.701	0.103
	2	2.67	0.492			4.25	0.622		
T7	1	2.67	0.492	1.216	0.237	3.58	0.515	−2.612	0.016
	2	2.42	0.515			4.17	0.577		
T8	1	2.75	0.452	1.685	0.106	3.50	0.522	−4.330	0.000
	2	2.42	0.515			4.42	0.515		
T9	1	2.67	0.492	1.658	0.111	3.83	0.389	−3.546	0.002
	2	2.33	0.492			4.50	0.522		
T10	1	2.58	0.515	0.793	0.436	3.67	0.492	−4.022	0.001
	2	2.42	0.515			4.50	0.522		

4.2 Learning Experience Assessment

Using the same method described in Sect. 4.1, the mean values for students' learning experience under the two approaches were analyzed; the results are provided in Table 2. The results indicated that the mean values for Group 2 were all greater than 3.5, which were overall greater than the Group 1 values. In particular, the mean values of F1, for authentic feeling in the cockpit, were significantly greater for Group 2 than for Group 1. The mean values of F1 to F5 for Group 2 were additionally greater than those of Group 1. These results suggest that the students in Group 2 had a greater sense of immersion in the learning scenarios.

Table 2. Results comparison for groups 1 and 2 based on independent-sample T-test for learning experience

No.	Group	Mean	SD	t	Sig. (2-tailed)
F1	1	2.83	0.507	−12.800	0.000
	2	4.11	0.319		
F2	1	3.17	0.378	−2.331	0.023
	2	3.44	0.607		
F3	1	2.86	0.683	−9.035	0.000
	2	4.08	0.439		
F4	1	2.81	0.577	−9.567	0.000
	2	4.00	0.478		
F5	1	2.75	0.649	−8.542	0.000
	2	3.94	0.532		
F6	1	3.11	0.622	−2.393	0.019
	2	3.44	0.558		

Independent t-test samples indicated that the Group 2 students more intensely experienced the feeling of sitting in a cockpit (F1, $t = -12.800$, $p < 0.01$), and they experienced the external scenarios as more authentic (F2, $t = -2.331$, $p < 0.05$). Through the use of ARFLY, students demonstrated a higher level of attention (F3, $t = -9.035$, $P < 0.01$), were less influenced by the external environment (F3, $t = -9.035$, $P < 0.01$), experienced time passing more quickly (F5, $t = -8.542$, $p < 0.01$), and showed a greater interest in learning (F6, $t = -2.393$, $p < 0.05$). In summary, the students in Group 2 demonstrated a more authentic and impressive learning experience.

5   Discussion and Conclusions

Because the high school technical course is not included in the college entrance examination, and most teachers implement traditional lecturing as the major teaching strategy, some students are not interested in this course [17]. The unsatisfactory situation of high school general technology in China makes it difficult to gain, sustain, and stimulate students' attention and curiosity to learn [18]. As a result, the learning motivation of this course for students is insufficient. Thus, authentic learning based on new interactive techniques is required to motivate students to participate and learn in the technical course.

The principles of flight control belong to the control theory section of the general technology course (http://www.rbloc.cn/). Most flight simulators are typically more expensive. In addition, no flight simulators exist that are suitable for high school students in a technical course. Hence, most high schools adopt the traditional way of teaching. This disables the course from stimulating students' enthusiasm for the learning of flight control principles; moreover, the students are unable to sufficiently understand the related theory. To overcome this problem and address the related need, the low-cost ARFLY was developed under the guidance of authentic learning theories; its virtual 3D models replace the complex and expensive instrument panels of actual simulators while realizing all operating functions.

Most teaching-aided systems that adopt 2D interfaces rely on the well-established windows, icons, menus, pointers (WIMP) interface metaphor. AR-based user interface techniques and interaction devices are not common in education [19]. In ARFLY, traditional computers and their well-known devices and interfaces disappear from the user's point of view. A new type of AR-based user interface is introduced, enhancing immersion in learning very well. Accordingly, AR can provide a more varied interactive mode, such as with spatial interaction, command-based interaction, virtual control interaction, and physical control interaction [10]. ITS can call and display different flight missions on the virtual instrument panel without influencing the simulation scenarios. In addition, it can estimate the completion of a flight mission and assign a new one, as if directed by a real commander. ITS was independently developed, which reduces external influences and improves students' understanding of the aircraft components and control principles. The ITS in ARFLY uses interactive technology and was specially developed to guide learning. It can reduce the heavy burden on teachers and improve learning effects. During the flight mission, a balance between the challenge and skill is made; the challenge does not exceed the student's current skill level. Therefore, students are not made to feel confused or anxious; conversely, the challenge is not so simple that it engenders boredom and interest loss [20].

Compared to GAMEFLY, ARFLY helps students to form more concrete concepts, develop a greater understanding of aircraft component functions and control principles, and, in particular, more closely grasp the abstract concepts of overshooting, reverse overshooting, and command transacting. A conventional flight simulation game typically displays the flight mission and simulation state simultaneously in menu form. This approach lacks a coherent learning system. When assigning a flight mission, it first blocks or mixes the simulation scenario and then explains the mission through text, audio, images, or video. From that point, the user can finally re-enter the simulation scenario. This easily distracts the user and does not match an actual flight experience, whereas ARFLY displays the information via AR technology. AR gives ITS a natural interactive environment and does not influence flight simulation effects when guiding the learning. Meanwhile, ITS can additionally increase the output of information, such as simultaneously displaying a human-presented explanation video and real-time flight state. With this intelligent-system guided learning, students can obtain task information at any time by watching the instrument panel; the simulation system and ITS can synchronize the work, which entirely fulfills the natural interactive mode. With minimal interference and a strong authentic feeling, students will be prompted to have enhanced attention, greater learning effects, and stronger learning motivations.

Acknowledgements. This research was supported by the National Natural Science Foundation of China under Grant No. 11664036.

References

1. Azuma, R.T.: A survey of augmented reality. Presence Teleoperators Virtual Environ. **6**(4), 355–385 (1997)
2. Azuma, R., Baillot, Y., Behringer, R., Feiner, S., Julier, S., MacIntyre, B.: Recent advances in augmented reality. IEEE Comput. Graph. Appl. **21**(6), 34–47 (2001)
3. Billinghurst, M., Duenser, A.: Augmented reality in the classroom. Computer **45**(7), 56–63 (2012)
4. Dalgarno, B., Lee, M.J.W.: What are the learning affordances of 3-D virtual environments? Br. J. Educ. Technol. **41**(1), 10–32 (2010)
5. Di Serio, A., Ibáñez, M.B., Kloos, C.D.: Impact of an augmented reality system on students' motivation for a visual art course. Comput. Educ. **68**, 586–596 (2013)
6. Dunleavy, M., Dede, C., Mitchell, R.: Affordances and limitations of immersive participatory augmented reality simulations for teaching and learning. J. Sci. Educ. Technol. **18**(1), 7–22 (2009)
7. Neumann, U., Majoros, A.: Cognitive, performance, and systems issues for augmented reality applications in manufacturing and maintenance. In: 1998 IEEE Proceedings Virtual Reality Annual International Symposium, March 1998, pp. 4–11. IEEE (1998)
8. Nee, A.Y.C., Ong, S.K., Chryssolouris, G., Mourtzis, D.: Augmented reality applications in design and manufacturing. CIRP Ann. Manuf. Technol. **61**(2), 657–679 (2012)
9. Carmigniani, J., Furht, B., Anisetti, M., Ceravolo, P., Damiani, E., Ivkovic, M.: Augmented reality technologies, systems and applications. Multimed. Tools Appl. **51**(1), 341–377 (2011)
10. Broll, W., Lindt, I., Ohlenburg, J., Herbst, I., Wittkamper, M., Novotny, T.: An infrastructure for realizing custom-tailored augmented reality user interfaces. IEEE Trans. Vis. Comput. Graph. **11**(6), 722–733 (2005)
11. Sutherland, I.E.: Computer displays. Sci. Am. **222**(6), 57–81 (1970)
12. Yavrucuk, I., Kubali, E., Tarimci, O.: A low cost flight simulator using virtual reality tools. IEEE Aerosp. Electron. Syst. Mag. **26**(4), 10–14 (2011)
13. Psotka, J., Massey, L.D., Mutter, S.A.: Intelligent Tutoring Systems: Lessons Learned. Psychology Press, Hove (1988)
14. Schiaffino, S., Garcia, P., Amandi, A.: eTeacher: providing personalized assistance to e-learning students. Comput. Educ. **51**(4), 1744–1754 (2008)
15. Keleş, A., Ocak, R., Keleş, A., Gülcü, A.: ZOSMAT: web-based intelligent tutoring system for teaching–learning process. Exp. Syst. Appl. **36**(2), 1229–1239 (2009)
16. Carroll, R.J., Schneider, H.: A note on Levene's tests for equality of variances. Stat. Probab. Lett. **3**(4), 191–194 (1985)
17. Davey, G., De Lian, C., Higgins, L.: The university entrance examination system in China. J. Furth. High. Educ. **31**(4), 385–396 (2007)
18. Jiang, S.: Analysis of general technology course teaching and subject construction in senior high schools (article written in Chinese). Educ. Teach. Res. **29**(3), 112–114 (2014)
19. Kaufmann, H., Schmalstieg, D.: Mathematics and geometry education with collaborative augmented reality. Comput. Graph. **27**(3), 339–345 (2003)
20. Chan, T.S., Ahern, T.C.: Targeting motivation: adapting flow theory to instructional design. J. Educ. Comput. Res. **21**(2), 151–163 (1999)

Multimodal Visual Analysis of Vector-Borne Infectious Diseases

Xiaohui Qiu[1,2(✉)], Fengjun Zhang[1], Hongning Zhou[3], Longfei Du[3],
Xin Wang[1], and Geng Liang[1]

[1] Institute of Software Chinese Academy of Sciences, Beijing, China
m15911018925@163.com, {fengjun,wangxin,lianggeng}@iscas.ac.cn
[2] University of Chinese Academy of Sciences, Beijing, China
[3] Yunnan Institute of Parasitic Diseases, Pu'er City, Yunnan, China
zhouhn66@163.com, dulongfei01@163.com

Abstract. In this work, we mainly analyze an infectious disease – dengue, which is transmitted by Aedes aegypti. Here, we propose a visual analysis method based on multiple perspectives. At first, visual analysis is used to calculate the probability of occurrence of new cases of dengue and the relative risk of occurrence of dengue cases influenced by various variables causing dengue. As a result, we find that climatic variables (rainfall, maximum, minimum and average temperature), imported case and density of Aedes aegypti are three major factors affecting outbreak of dengue. Then, prediction model is built based on analysis to realize early warning. At last, various visual methods are used to show prediction results. This whole method is first used in Yunnan province, China. Compared with current methods, our method takes more factors into consideration and bases on machine learning to build prediction model, which can improve the accuracy of prediction.

Keywords: Multi-view visual analysis · Prediction model · Visual display
Dengue

1 Introduction

The global prevalence of dengue has grown dramatically in recent decades. Currently it is estimated that 2.5 billion people – two fifths of world's population – are at risk from dengue (WHO 2010) and up to 500,000 people develop potentially lethal complications called dengue hemorrhagic fever/dengue shock syndrome [1]. The high prevalence, lacking of a registered vaccine or other effective prophylactic measures and an absence of specific treatment make dengue a grave public health threat globally.

Yunnan province is in southern China, located south of the tropic of cancer in the tropical north edge, the tropical monsoon climate, which is warm, sunny, humid and rainy. So it very suitable for Aedes aegypti to survive. At the same time, Yunnan province is adjacent to Myanmar, Laos and Vietnam, which have high prevalence of dengue (we can see from Fig. 1). These countries are in backward economy and poor health care. Therefore, many people in these countries with dengue go to Yunnan province for

© Springer Nature Singapore Pte Ltd. 2018
Y. Wang et al. (Eds.): IGTA 2018, CCIS 875, pp. 135–145, 2018.
https://doi.org/10.1007/978-981-13-1702-6_14

treatment. With "The Belt and Road" promotion in Lancang-Mekong River Sub-region, personnel exchanges and border trade together with tourism are becoming increasingly frequent, which increases the risk of dengue transmission. So how to control dengue is becoming an urgent problem in Yunnan province.

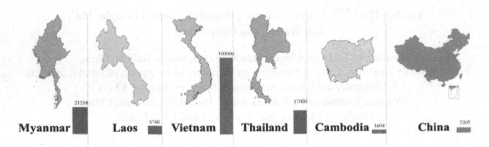

Fig. 1. The distribution of dengue in Yunnan province and its neighboring countries in 2017.

Recently, many studies focus on the impact of climate change on emergence or reemergence of vector-borne infectious diseases such as dengue [2–7]. They mostly utilize statistical analysis to get the influence of different factors on dengue. And few research has been done on dengue in Yunnan province because there is no large sudden outbreak like Guangdong province in 2014, resulting in 45, 224 dengue cases [8] and no rich public data can be got. However, Yunnan province is still facing serious threat of dengue in recent years, which many people die of dengue off and on every year. As we all know, the only way to control dengue is to control vector, so it's important for us to know distribution of vector in advance.

As can be seen from above, it is necessary to take measures to prevent and control dengue. In this paper, we propose a multi-view visual analysis of dengue. We use visual analysis to find major factors leading to dengue, which not only reveals relationship between factors and dengue but also can give people a strong sense of dengue trend to help them take steps. There, we calculate the probability of occurrence of new cases of dengue using many visual methods such as heat map, parallel coordinate plots, scatterplots and color coding to analyze our issue from multiple perspectives (climatic variables, regional distribution and seasonality). Compared with current methods, our prediction model considers more factors and is more reasonable.

2   Related Work

Various studies have shown that there is a strong link between dengue epidemic and climate factors according to the statistical analysis method used in [9, 10]. Climate variables (temperature, rainfall and relative humidity) and global climate indexes are reasonable predictors of pathogens, vectors and dengue cases in previous study [11, 12]. The dengue parasite is transmitted from human to human primarily by bite of Aedes aegypti. Many environmental factors influence sporogonic cycle of Aedes aegypti. For example, temperature affects the rate of pathogen maturation and replication in the mosquitoes, which improves density of vector and increases likelihood of infection. Besides, there are other factors affecting dengue such as seasonality, imported case and dengue Baidu search index [13]. In Singapore, Hales et al. [14] develop a weather-based dengue-forecasting model that allows warning 16 weeks in advance of dengue epidemics. However, dengue epidemics in Yunnan province are generally characterized by low level epidemic caused by imported cases, followed by a sudden and rapid transmission. They have varied greatly in size from year to year, which poses a bigger challenge for prediction than in the stable and endemic regions.

The transmission model of dengue is people-mosquito-human, which has complicated spatiotemporal variability. Due to multi-factors such as multi-scale, randomness and process characteristic refolding, the causal relationship between variables and dengue has strong nonlinear correlation so predicting dengue is difficult. Yang et al. [15] have studied effect of temperature on dengue transmission and calculate density of Aedes aegypti based on meteorological factors. Hales et al. [14] use logistic regression to predict presence or absence of dengue based on meteorological information. Monthly average precipitation, maximum, minimum and average temperature and water vapor pressure are taken as parameters of model. The model can be used to predict outbreak of dengue according to meteorological factors, which provides useful information for predicting and controlling outbreak of dengue in advance. Gharbi et al. [7] propose a seasonal autoregressive model based on time series. These existing studies and classical algorithms mainly base on meteorological factors, lacking of consideration of other factors such as imported cases. Therefore, we analyze this problem from multi-perspectives and take more factors into consideration.

Besides, with development of visualization, this technology has been widely used in many fields such as human mobility [16] and infectious disease [17, 18]. Maciejewski et al. use hotspots to represent spatio-temporal distribution of patients and dynamically display outbreak of the disease in combination with techniques of time-series plots and multivariate interaction [19]. Klemm et al. use 3D regression heat map to fit epidemiological models of multiple traits, which clearly shows the relationship among variables [20]. Most of above analysis methods are passive methods, showing the original characteristics of data without active prediction and analysis. Our method not only visualize relationship among variables but also build prediction model to predict the trend of disease.

3   Method

Compared with current methods, we present a visual analysis method to solve this problem. On the one hand, visualization encodes data as images which can give decision makers intuitive sense. On the other hand, visualization can vividly reveal the relationship between factors and dengue which can make prediction model more accurate. Here, we take four steps to handle this issue. As we mentioned above, there is no public data about dengue in Yunnan province. So first work is to collect data. We cooperate with Yunnan Institute of Parasitic Diseases setting 13 vector (Aedes aegypti) sites and 2 climate sites to get related data of dengue. Then, we take advantage of visual analysis to calculate the probability of all factors that we collect resulting to dengue, which not only helps us get major factors leading to dengue but also assists staff of Yunnan Institute of Parasitic Diseases to take corresponding measures according to the trend of leading factors. After that, we make use of major factors based on our analysis to build prediction model. At last, we dynamically display prediction trend of dengue in Yunnan province day by day.

3.1   Data Collection

Dengue has been a legally notifiable disease in China since 1989 [13]. Daily cases during January 1st, 2012 to December 31st, 2016 in Yunnan province are obtained from Yunnan Institute of Parasitic Diseases. Dengue cases are diagnosed on the basis of China National Diagnostic Criteria for dengue fever [22]. Meanwhile, we gain imported cases by processing raw data according to doctors' remark which indicates patients' infected location.

Meteorological data containing daily minimum temperature, daily maximum temperature, daily average temperature, relative humidity, rainfall, wind speed, air pressure and sunshine time in Yunnan province during January 1st, 2004 to the present are initially collected from the China Meteorological Data Sharing Service System [21]. Because these raw meteorological data are relatively sparse, we can't get meteorological data at some specified places or areas in Yunnan province. We utilize grid interpolating algorithm such as thin plate spline to enrich it. On the other hand, we have deployed meteorological stations in Yunnan province so we can get climate data in real time, which is more accurate and can improve accuracy of calculating relationship between dengue and meteorological factors.

Vector (Aedes aegypti) data during January 1st, 2014 to the present in Yunnan province are got from Yunnan Institute of Parasitic Diseases. The staff in Yunnan Institute of Parasitic Diseases go to various villages making a field survey so that they can obtain raw data such as infected containers and infected houses. Then, we get raw data from them and handle data to compute relative index of vector density.

3.2   Visual Analysis of Various Factors and Dengue

Here, we utilize various visual analysis to project the potential impact of factors on dengue incidence trends. Heat map, parallel coordinate plots, scatterplots and color coding are used in our approach, which can help us get correlation of variables and dengue and make staff in Yunnan Institute of Parasitic Diseases take steps to prevent outbreak of dengue according to variable changing tendency.

Relationship Between Vector Distribution and Dengue. As we all know that a patient is infected with dengue only through bite of Aedes aegypti, which means that controlling the distribution of Aedes aegypti is the most important way to prevent dengue. Therefore, it is necessary to know trend of vector distribution. We simultaneously display vector distribution and dengue distribution in Yunnan province which reveals the relation between them. Here, BI, CI and HI are three vector density indexes.

$$BI = \frac{pos\_con}{sur\_house} * 100 \tag{1}$$

$$CI = \frac{pos\_con}{sum\_con} * 100 \tag{2}$$

$$HI = \frac{pos\_house}{sur\_house} * 100 \tag{3}$$

pos_con indicates the number of infected containers, *sur_house* means the number of inspected houses, *sum_con* is the number of inspected containers and *pos_house* indicates the number of infected houses. BI, CI and HI are three reflex of vector density.

Figure 2 displays distribution of vector and dengue cases at the same time in Yunnan province showing that there is a strong correlation between vector and dengue. The more vectors, the more dengue cases which fits the common sense that dengue is only transmitted by vector. Visual analysis can not only exhibit relationship between vector and dengue, but also reveal changes in vector density and dengue, which excellently helps policy maker make right judgments. Therefore, once we get the distribution of vector, we can predict trend of dengue.

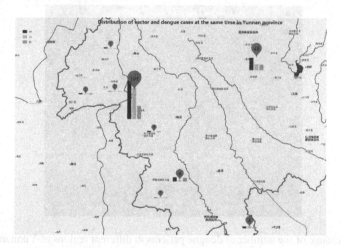

Fig. 2. Distribution of vector and dengue cases at the same time in Yunnan province in August 2016. It shows vector distribution containing three indexes (HI, CI, BI) and dengue cases. Three lines denote vector distribution and the red circle represents dengue cases. (Color figure online)

Relationship Between Meteorological Factors and Dengue. There are many studies showing that meteorological factors like temperature and rainfall are related to dengue, so we take advantage of visual analysis to look into the relationship among them. Here, we mainly show association between temperature and dengue cases, which is the major factor resulting in the change of dengue according to related analysis.

Figure 3 shows that the number of dengue patients has a certain lag relationship to the highest temperature. Therefore, we use some days lag to build dengue prediction model that fits to the actual situation. At the same time, we also analyze other meteorological factors such as rainfall and relative humidity but we don't show here because of limited space. We come to the conclusion that temperature and rainfall are two main factors affecting dengue. Meanwhile, outbreak of dengue has a certain periodicity that the months from September to November show the highest probabilities of the occurrence of new cases throughout the year as Fig. 4.

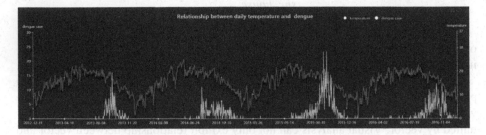

Fig. 3. Relationship between daily temperature and dengue. Red line represents daily temperature and green line indicates daily dengue cases. (Color figure online)

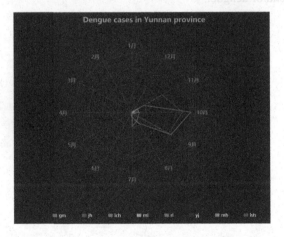

Fig. 4. The change of the number of dengue patients in different regions of Yunnan province in different months. Different color represents different regions. (Color figure online)

Relationship Between Imported Case and Dengue. Yunnan province is located in the southwest frontiers of China and adjacent to Myanmar, Laos and Vietnam which have limited resources to devote to strengthening dengue surveillance systems. The economic conditions prevent these countries building robust formal public health surveillance to control dengue resulting in a sharp rise in these country. Many dengue patients from Myanmar, Laos and Vietnam come to Yunnan province for treatment because of their poor local health care. Therefore, imported case is also a notable factor resulting in the outbreak of dengue in Yunnan province.

Here, we pick two typical cities. One is in interior area of Yunnan province and the other is in border area. As can been seen from Figs. 5 and 6, dengue cases in border area are seriously affected by imported case which is nearly linear. However, there is almost nothing to do with imported case in interior area. Therefore, the weight of imported case in prediction model is large in border area and on the contrary it should be small in inland area. So we need to build different models in border and inland areas of Yunnan province.

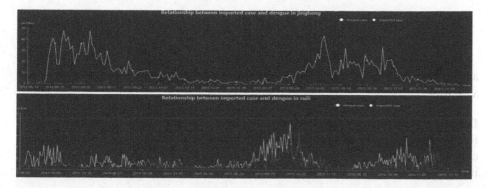

Fig. 5. Relationship between imported case and dengue in two typical regions. The top is in interior area and the bottom is in border area. Red line represents daily imported case and green line indicates daily dengue case. (Color figure online)

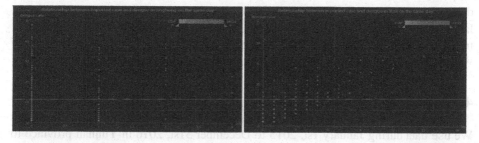

Fig. 6. Relationship between imported case and dengue on the same day. The deeper the color is, the more the dengue case.

3.3 Build Prediction Model

We set up prediction model of vector and dengue separately according to above visual analysis. Vector prediction model can be used to control Aedes aegypti and then prevent dengue. The model of dengue can forecast the situation of dengue in next 14 days.

Vector Prediction Model. For vector prediction model, we take advantage of CUSUM which has been widely used in the field of disease control in past 30 years. The normal distribution or Poisson distribution is the precondition of applying CUSUM. We can get that distribution of vector fits the normal distribution through our statistical analysis so we can use CUSUM here. In the prediction process, sample data is firstly unitarily treated as Eq. (4).

$$Z_t = \frac{y_t - u_t}{\sigma_t} \tag{4}$$

And then we construct S_t meaning accumulative value of deviation.

$$S_t = \max\left(0, S_{t-1} + Z_t - k\right) \tag{5}$$

Here, k is reference value for previous value S_{t-1} that means k is model parameter and is experience value. From Eq. (5), we can easily get S_t is accumulative value and $S_0 = 0$.

Dengue Prediction Model. Dengue prediction model is done through a Poisson Regression Model (PRM) that considers dengue cases as the dependent variable and climatic variables (rainfall, temperature), imported case and history dengue case as independent variables. The model is given by

$$\log(y) = a_1 * temp + a_2 * rainfall + a_3 * temp^2 + a_4 * imported + \log(his\_data) \tag{6}$$

where y is daily dengue situation (divided into 4 grades according to related files [23]), *temp* is the term indicates temperature in last 20 day according to visual analysis that there is delay between temperature and dengue cases, *rainfall* denotes daily rainfall in last 20 days, *imported* denotes daily cumulative imported case in last 7 days, *his_data* means cumulative value of number of dengue cases in last 14 days. a_1, a_2, a_3 and a_4 are weighting factors. As for a_4, the inland area is very different from border area.

4   Result

We use data during January 1st, 2015 to December 31st, 2016 in Yunnan province to train vector prediction model and the other is used to test the model. Figure 7 shows result of vector prediction model, which contains predicting lower and upper bound. BI, CI and HI index are important factors which indicate the living condition of Aedes aegypti. Lower bound and upper bound of the above three indexes can give the staff a much clearer trend of the mosquito vector so the staff can take measures to kill Aedes aegypti based on prediction. Furthermore, the prediction trend of vector can also indicate situation of dengue. So staff can judge whether dengue will erupt according to vector prediction model.

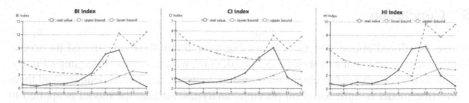

Fig. 7. Result of vector predict model. Red line represents lower bound and upper bound and blue line indicates real value. Here, BI, CI and HI are three indexes of vector density. (Color figure online)

Data during January 1st, 2012 to June 31st, 2015 in Yunnan province is used to train dengue prediction model and the other data is used to test the model. The weights in (6) are set to be $a_1 = 0.0316, a_2 = 0.1563, a_3 = 0.0075$ and $a_4 = 1.06$ in inland area. Table 1 gives the dengue situation of reality and prediction. Daily dengue situation is divided into 4 grades according to related files [23]. From the table, we see that our prediction model mostly can get accurate result. Through our statistics, the accuracy of dengue prediction model is 84%. At last, we apply our model to various regions of Yunnan province to predict dengue situation in each region as Fig. 8.

Table 1. The dengue situation of prediction and reality in October, 2016.

Methods	Time(day)													
	6	7	8	9	10	11	12	13	14	15	16	17	18	19
Real situation	2	3	0	2	2	4	3	2	4	0	3	2	0	0
Predict situation	2	3	0	1	2	4	3	2	2	0	3	1	0	0

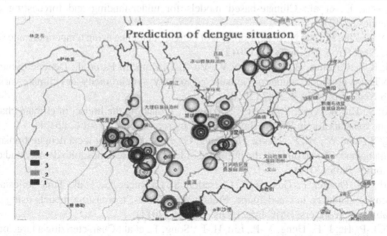

Fig. 8. Prediction of dengue situation. Different color represents different dengue grade.

5 Conclusion

As we mentioned above, dengue is becoming a big threat to people around the world. In this paper, we present a method to analyze dengue, which contains three steps. Firstly, visual analysis is utilized to obtain relationship between factors and dengue. And then, prediction model is built based on previous analytics. At last, the model is applied to actual monitor to assist establishing public health surveillance system. We have used this method in Yunnan province and the result looks good. Compared with current methods, our method can not only give the staff a strong sense on trends of factors that lead to dengue but also predict dengue stages accurately. In the future, we will apply our method in more places to help people in the world and even reduce the threat of dengue.

Acknowledgments. This work was supported by the National Natural Science Foundation of China (No. 61572479), the National Key Research and Development Program of China (No. 2016YFB1001403), the National Natural Science Foundation of China together with the National Research Foundation of Singapore (No. 61661146002), the Science and Technology Program of Guangzhou (Grant No. 201802020015), Key deployment project of the Chinese Academy of Sciences (No. KFZD-SW-316-3), the Strategy Priority Research Program of Chinese Academy of Sciences (No. XDA20080100).

References

1. Kyle, J.L., Harris, E.: Global spread and persistence of dengue. Annu. Rev. Microbiol. **62**, 71–92 (2008)
2. Descloux, E., et al.: Climate-based models for understanding and forecasting dengue epidemics (2012)
3. Hii, Y.L., Zhu, H., Ng, N., et al.: Forecast of dengue incidence using temperature and rainfall. PLoS Negl. Trop. Dis. **6**, e1908 (2012)
4. Thai, K.T., Cazelles, B., Nguyen, N.V., Vo, L.T., Boni, M.F., et al.: Dengue dynamics in Binh Thuan province, southern Vietnam: periodicity, synchronicity and climate variability. PLoS Negl. Trop. Dis. **4**, e747 (2010)
5. Banu, S., Hu, W., Guo, Y., Hurst, C., Tong, S.: Projecting the impact of climate change on dengue transmission in Dhaka, Bangladesh. Environ. Int. **63**, 137–142 (2014)
6. Sang, S., Yin, W., Bi, P., Zhang, H., Wang, C., et al.: Predicting local dengue transmission in Guangzhou, China, through the influence of imported cases, mosquito density and climate variability. PloS (2014)
7. Gharbi, M., Quenel, P., Gustave, J., Cassadou, S., La Ruche, G., et al.: Time series analysis of dengue incidence in Guadeloupe, French West Indies: forecasting models using climate variables as predictors. BMC Infect. Dis. **11**, 166 (2011)
8. Xiao, J.-P., He, J.-F., Deng, A.-P., Lin, H.-L., Song, T., et al.: Characterizing a large outbreak of dengue fever in Guangdong Province, China. Infect. Dis. Poverty **5**, 44 (2016)
9. Mangeas, M., Menkes, C.E., Lengaigne, M., Leroy, A.: Climate-based models for understanding and forecasting dengue epidemics. Plos (2012)
10. Pinto, E., Coelho, M., Oliver, L., Massad, E.: The influence of climate variables on dengue in Singapore. Int. J. Environ. Health Res. **21**, 415–426 (2011)

11. Jansen, C.C., Beebe, N.W.: The dengue vector Aedes aegypti: what comes next. Microbes Infect. **12**, 272–279 (2010)
12. Tabachnick, W.J.: Challenges in predicting climate and environmental effects on vector-borne disease episystems in a changing world. J. Exp. Biol. **213**, 946–954 (2010)
13. Li, Z., Liu, T., Zhu, G., Lin, H., Zhang, Y., He, J., et al.: Dengue Baidu search index data can improve the prediction of local dengue epidemic: a case study in Guangzhou, China. PLoS Negl. Trop. Dis. **11**, e0005354 (2017)
14. Hales, S., de Wet, N., Maindonald, J., Woodward, A.: Potential effect of population and climate changes on global distribution of dengue fever: an empirical model. Lancet **360**, 830–834 (2002)
15. Yang, H.M., Macoris, M.L.G., Galvani, K.C., Andrighetti, M.T.M.: Follow up estimation of Aedes aegypti entomological parameters and mathematical modellings. Biosystems **103**, 360–371 (2011)
16. Wu, W., Xu, J., Zeng, H., Zheng, Y., Qu, H.: TelCoVis: visual exploration of co-occurrence in urban human mobility based on telco data. IEEE Trans. Vis. Comput. Graph. **31**, 935–944 (2016)
17. Quinan, S., Meyer, M.: Visually comparing weather features in forecasts. IEEE Trans. Vis. Comput. Graph. **22**, 389–398 (2016)
18. Liu, S., Maljovec, D., Wang, B., Bremer, P.-T., Pascucci, V.: Visualizing high-dimensional data advances in the past decade. IEEE Trans. Vis. Comput. Graph. **1**, 1249–1268 (2017)
19. Maciejewski, R., et al.: A visual approach to understanding spatiotemporal hotspots. IEEE Trans. Vis. Comput. Graph. **16**, 205–220 (2010)
20. Klemm, P., et al.: 3D Regression heat map analysis of population study data. IEEE Trans. Vis. Comput. Graph. **31**, 81–90 (2016)
21. China Meteorological Data Sharing Service System. http://cdc.nmic.cn/home.do
22. China National Diagnostic Criteria for dengue fever. http://www.nhfpc.gov.cn
23. Technical guidance for dengue epidemic classification prevention and control. Middle disease control transmission and Prevention No. 45 Annex 1 (2015)

The Research of Dongba Culture Virtual Museum Based on Human Factor Engineering

Yuting Yang[1](✉) and Houliang Kang[2]

[1] Culture and Tourism College, Yunnan Open University, Kunming, China
tudou-yeah@163.com
[2] College of Humanities and Art, Yunnan College of Business Management,
Kunming, China

Abstract. The emergence of virtual museum has opened up a new way to protect and inherit the traditional culture. Through extracting a variety of information from artifacts, virtual museum can transform the traditional static artifacts into dynamic digitized information, like sound, images and texts, and visitors can roam or study in the virtual museum breakthrough the limit of time, space and territory. Therefore, we create a Dongba culture virtual museum (DBCVM) based on the real museum in Lijiang. In DBCVM, virtual exhibits combine with physical photos and background knowledge to show the essence of culture in artifacts for visitors. In addition, through combining Human Factor Engineering, the entire system is considered 'user friendly', that is to say the system not only reflects the characteristics of immersion, interaction and imagination of the virtual reality, but also considers the psychological feature, usage habit and learning interest of visitors. DBCVM can fully mobilize visitors' learning initiative by providing them a vivid and visual learning style and promote Dongba Culture breakthrough the limit of time and territory to protect and inherit traditional culture better.

Keywords: Dongba culture · Virtual museum · Human Factor Engineering
Virtual reality

1 Dongba Culture

Dongba culture takes traditional religion Dongba of Naxi nationality as the basic form and the carrier of culture, which is the Naxi traditional culture integrating Naxi Dongba, Dongba hieroglyphic, Dongba scripture, Dongba painting, Dongba crafts, Dongba music, Dongba dance, Dongba divination and sacrifice ceremony into the one [1]. The content of Dongba culture is extensive and profound, involving many aspects, such as geography, history, religion, painting, dance, medicine, literature, etiquette and custom, ethics, ethnic relations and ideas, etc., but also integrating some cultural elements of Bon, Tibetan Buddhism, Taoism and even ancient Persia and ancient India [2], which has high scientific, historical, aesthetic and artistic value, and is known as the "Encyclopedia of ancient society of Naxi nationality". Dongba hieroglyphic is a kind of very primitive picture hieroglyphs, as well as the only surviving hieroglyphs currently in the world, which is known as the "living fossil" of words [3].

© Springer Nature Singapore Pte Ltd. 2018
Y. Wang et al. (Eds.): IGTA 2018, CCIS 875, pp. 146–156, 2018.
https://doi.org/10.1007/978-981-13-1702-6_15

The greatest feature of Dongba culture is that it is closely connect with the production and living style of Naxi nationality. It relies on people and shows itself through scripture, music, dance, painting and other means. Its inheritance approach depends on people carriers by means of oral instruction and rote memory [4]. By using traditional ways, now, Dongba culture is faced with the problems of spreading narrower, protection more difficult, and even appearing the serious hiatus crisis of heritage. Especially, with the accelerated process of urban modernization, the social basis of Dongba culture becomes narrower. The erosion from modern lifestyle, the damage by disaster and constructive both produces varying degrees of harm to Dongba culture, it urgent needs to be protected and inherited [5]. Virtual museum would be a new way to protect and inherit Dongba culture by using a vivid and virtual way to show artifacts and its culture sprite to visitors.

2 Virtual Museum

A virtual museum is a logically related collection of digital objects composed in a variety of media, and because of its capacity to provide connectedness and various points of access, it leads itself to transcending traditional methods of communicating and interacting with the visitor being flexible toward their needs and interests; it has no real place or space, its objects and the related information can be disseminated all over the world [6]. The artifacts can be more dynamic and interactive rather than static [7, 8] in real museum, thus the virtual museum can closer to reality and enhancing the experience for visitors [9].

Currently, the world's developed countries are large-scale convert cultural heritage into digital form in order to preserve permanently and maximize equitable sharing them to the public. UNESCO starts the project – "Memory of the World" in 1992 to promote the digitization of cultural heritage all over the world [10]. It includes the project of "American Memory" in US, the project of Louvre digitization, the project of Michelangelo digitization, the digital project of Grand Theatre in Roam and the digital protection project of lion dance in Japan.

In 1996, the start of the national digital library project in China, begins the digital progress of culture resource. It includes digital protection and restoration of Dunhuang mural [11], 3D display technique of virtual Yin Ruin's museum [12], the research of virtual reality system of ancient architecture [13], reconstruction and exhibition of Chin bell music and choreography for safeguarding of ancient Chu-culture [14], the research of large-scale cultural heritage sites and objects using real geometric data and real texture data [15], the digital civilization heritage reproduction of ZhenGuoQu of Qin dynasty [16] and so on.

Therefore, we create a Dongba culture virtual museum (DBCVM) based on the real museum in Lijiang. In DBCVM, virtual exhibits combine with physical photos and background knowledge to show the essence of culture in artifacts for visitors. In addition, through combining Human Factor Engineering (HF&E), the entire system is considered 'user friendly', that is to say the system not only reflects the characteristics of immersion, interaction and imagination of the virtual reality, but also considers the psychological feature, usage habit and learning interest of visitors. DBCVM can fully mobilize visitors' learning initiative by providing them a vivid and visual learning style and promote Dongba Culture breakthrough the limit of time and territory to protect and inherit traditional culture better.

3   The Design of DBCVM

The virtual museum created is based on Lijiang Dongba Culture Museum. In order to distinguish from other virtual museum and reflect the characteristics of HF&E, this virtual system provides a humanized and easy-to-use environment for visitors and offers a variety of tools to help when entering the system.

The DBCVM consists of two parts: Data and software. The data include the building model, interactive virtual exhibits and virtual avatars. The software is responsible for the interaction between visitors and the virtual system, including data persistence, touring DBCVM, consulting artifacts and handling system logic. Figure 1 illustrates the system framework.

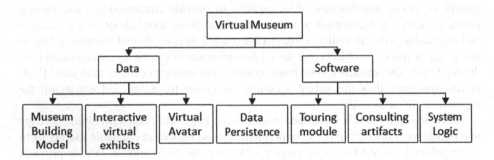

Fig. 1. The system framework

4   Creating Models of DBCVM

4.1   Data Collection

The data include museum building model, interactive virtual exhibits and virtual avatars. The museum building model is based on the real Dongba Culture Museum which has a rich architectural style based on the local Naxi quadrangle dwellings with 'Three Square a Screen Wall'. In Naxi quadrangle, the walls are always white and tiles are gray. Representing Naxi architectural features is very important because it is one of the major characteristics of the museum. In order to build a realistic virtual museum, every kind of texture and material was collected from the real museum and used on the model's surface to make the building look realistic and maintain an authentic style. Figure 2 shows the actual photograph of real museum and Fig. 3 shows the virtual museum.

Dongba culture is the traditional culture of Naxi. Choosing the representative artifacts which can reflect the essence of Dongba culture and the characteristic of Naxi

Fig. 2. The photo of real museum   **Fig. 3.** The screenshot of virtual museum

nationality is very important. In order to ensure the accuracy, availability and objectivity of the artifacts, all the pictures, textures, messages and information we used are from the real museum and the website of Lijiang Dongba Association [17].

4.2 Model Building and Optimizing

The models qualities of virtual exhibits are the key role which decides how much effect the DBCVM could contribute. A model is composed of many polygons. The quantity of polygons is inversely proportional to the operating efficiency of virtual system. That is to say, the more polygons model has, the more real the model rendering, but the more time the virtual system needs to cost [18]. Therefore, two methods are provided to reduce the complexity and scale of the model. One is using texture instead of the original model to reduce the total number of polygons of the model. The other is decreasing the model's detail as much as possible under the premise of good rendering effect. Figure 4 shows the original model and optimized model of net bottle. By

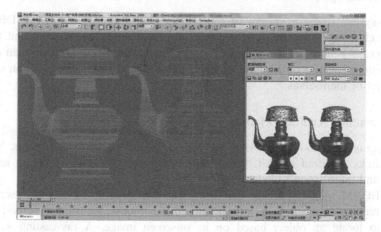

Fig. 4. The original model and optimized model of net bottle

observing the rendering result we found that in the case of significantly reducing the number of polygons did not affect to display model.

5   The Implementation of DBCVM

The software system is considered "user friendly', that is to say, the system pro-vides a convenient, comfortable, practical environment and simple, easy-to-use operational approach for visitors. The software is responsible for the interaction between visitors and the virtual system, including data persistence, touring DBCVM, consulting artifacts and handling system logic. Figure 5 shows the framework of software system.

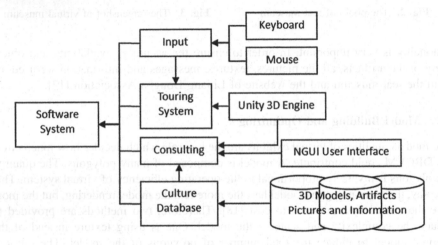

Fig. 5. The framework of software system

5.1   Touring System

Touring system offers a variety of tools to help visitors when entering DBCVM. Through choosing different tools, visitors can obtain different operating and touring experiences. Visitors can travel DBCVM in different perspectives. They can choose first-person perspective or third-person perspective like playing games and can set their own speed by themselves.

5.2   Consulting Artifacts Module

Consulting artifacts module provides pictures and information about artifacts. When a visitor clicks a virtual exhibit, the module will return the corresponding artifact's pictures and information to help visitor to learn it.

In DBCVM, visitor tours the 3D virtual museum through 2D computer screen. In order to realize visitor interacts with 3D museum by mouse, we use the method of ray-casting to locate an object based on its onscreen image. A ray-casting sends an imaginary "laser beam" along the ray from its origin until it hits a collider in the scene. Information is then returned about the object and the point that was hit in a ray-cast hit object [19]. Figure 6 shows the theory of ray-casting.

The core code is as follows:

```
if (Input.GetMouseButtonDown (0))
{    // 1. Create a ray from main camera to mouse
     ray=Camera.main.ScreenPointToRay(Input.mousePosition);
     // 2. Get the Object
     if(Physics.Raycast(ray,out hit))
     {obj=hit.collider.gameObject;
     // 3. Find the father of object
     if(obj.transform.parent!=null)
     {parentObj=obj.transform.parent.gameObject;
     // 4. Convert the variables type from string to enum
     if(parentObj.name.Equals("temp"))
        wenWu=(WenWuFlag)Enum.Parse(typeof(WenWuFlag),obj.name);
     else
        wenWu=(WenWuFlag)Enum.Parse(typeof(WenWuFlag),parentObj.name);
     if(wenWu!=null)
        Application.LoadLevel("introScreen");
..............
```

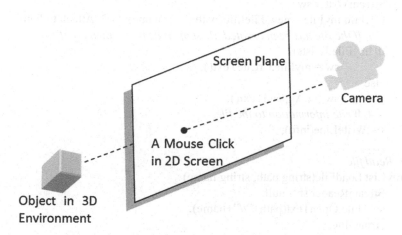

Fig. 6. The theory of ray-casting

In addition, Interactive virtual exhibits are the digitization of artifacts in real museum. The exhibits need to reflect the essence of artifacts and tell visitors the information about the artifacts in a vivid way, so the key features of virtual exhibits are: (a) multiplicity of contexts for the user to connect with the exhibit in a seamless manner; (b) good instructional design; (c) pro-active learning contexts; (d) good balance between learning and leisure; (e) no text-heavy pages to interfere with the learning experience [20]. Therefore, we use NGUI (Next-Generation User Interface kit) to design the consulting interface. NGUI is a powerful UI system and event notification framework for Unity written in C# that closely follows the KISS principle. It features clean code and simple, minimalistic approach to everything. And what you see in the scene view is what you get in the game view [21]. Figure 7 shows the consulting interface of Dongba WuFuGuan.

5.3 Consulting Artifacts Module

Data persistence module is responsible for managing data resources in DBCVM. It includes add, delete update and select data resources by dynamic way. The Module uses unity class – AssetDatabase to handle pictures and uses file stream to handle introduction information and words. The core code is as follows:

```
// Use "AssetDatabase" to load pictures.
UISprite sprite = this.getComponent<UISprite>();
sprite    =    (UISprite)    AssetDatabase.LoadAssetAtPath("Resources/Texture/
WuFuGuan1.jpg", typeof(UISprite));
......
// Use file stream to handle information and words.
// 1. Create file;
void CreateFile(string path, string name, string info)
{       StreamWriter sw;
        FileInfo myFile = new FileInfo(path+"//"+name);  // 2. Attach to Path;
        // 3. If the file has been created, then open it; if not, then create it;
        if(!myFile.Exists)
                sw = myFile.CreateText();
        else
                sw = t.AppendText();
        // 4. Write information to the file.
        sw.WriteLine(info);
        ......
// 5. Read file
ArrayList LoadFile(string path, string name)
{       StreamReader sr = null;
        sr = File.OpenText(path+"//"+name);
        string line;
ArrayList arrlist = new ArrayList();
// Read data line by line.
while((line = sr.ReadLine()) != null)
        arrlist.Add(line);
......
```

东巴"五福冠"

纳西语称"考"。东巴法帽之
一，用布把五片似菱形的纸
牌横向连接而成。用时，使
五片纸牌朝前，以两边的布
条带系在祭司头上。五幅
冠多用于请神攘鬼和开丧超
度仪式中。五片纸牌从左到
右绘的是铎趣构补大神、朗
究大神、东巴什罗大神、答
腊密悲大神、优麻大神。这
五位大神都是东巴教里威力
无比的主要战神。戴上五幅
冠的作用就是借助大神的威

上一幅图 下一幅图 返回

Fig. 7. The consulting interface of Dongba WuFuGuan

6 System Test

The core hardware we used to test DBCVM includes a CPU with Intel Pentium®
3.0 GHz * 2, a graphic card with NVIDIA GeForce GT 610 and a memory with
4 GHz memory size. The core testing software includes unity 3D 4.3.0 and Visual
Studio 2010. DBCVM includes inside scene and outside scene. In order to test and
evaluate the performance of DBCVM, we mainly test it from the following four
aspects:

(1) System start, avatar loaded and initialized. Figure 8 shows the start-up screen of
virtual museum and Fig. 9 shows that visitor enters museum in third- person
perspective.

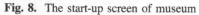

Fig. 8. The start-up screen of museum   **Fig. 9.** Entering in third-person perspective.

(2) Visitor tours DBCVM in different perspective. Figure 10 shows that visitor is touring DBCVM in first-person perspective and Fig. 11 shows in third-person perspective.

Fig. 10. Tour in first-person perspective   **Fig. 11.** Tour in third-person perspective

During the test, the measured maximum was 119 frames per second; the minimum rate was 100 frames per second and with an average of 110.18 frames per second. Figure 12 illustrates the test frame rate of the system.

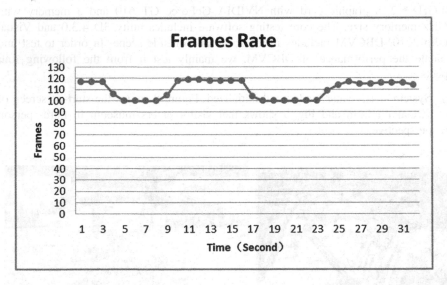

Fig. 12. Frame rate

7 System Test

Virtual museum is a new way to protect and inherit Dongba culture. It breakthrough the limit of time and space, and visitors can tour the whole museum; learn in the museum at any time. DBCVM aims to integrate the actual museum into 3D virtual world and provide visitors with a real experience and comfortable learning environment on virtual museum. Many methods have been used to reduce the scale and complexity of the whole models and to create the virtual museum based on HF&E. DBCVM also considers the psychological feature, usage habit and learning interest of visitors and fully mobilizes visitors' learning initiative by providing them a vivid and visual learning style and promote Dongba Culture in a new method, so that the traditional culture can be protected and inherited better.

Acknowledgments. The authors would like to thank the people who have helped and generously provided materials for this work. The authors also would like to thank the researchers in Lijiang Dongba Museum and Dongba Association.

References

1. He, L.M.: On transition of Dongba culture. Soc. Sci. Yunnan **1**, 83–87 (2004)
2. He, J.G.: The development of Dongba-culture studies of Naxi nationality. J. Yunnan Natl. Univ. **1**, 81–84 (2007)
3. Ge, A.G.: Dongba culture review. Natl. Art Res. **2**, 71–80 (1999)
4. Zhao, H.M.: On the historical opportunity of Dongba culture in Naxi—rethinking about "cultural awareness" under tourist context. Tour. Trib. **7**, 12–18 (2010)
5. Zong, X.L.: New challenges of Dongba culture in the settings of empoldering tourist business. J. Cent. Univ. Natl. (Philos. Soc. Sci. Ed.) **6**, 74–81 (2004)
6. Schweibenz, W.: The virtual museum: new perspectives for museums to present objects and information using the internet as a knowledge base and communication system. In: Zimmermann, H., Schramm, H. (eds.), Proceedings of the 6th ISI Conference, Prague, November 1998, pp. 185–200. UKV, Konstanz (1991)
7. Bergamasco, M., Frisoli, A., Barbagli, F.: Haptics technologies and cultural heritage applications. In: Kawada, S. (ed.), IEEE Proceedings of the CA Conference 2002, Geneva, Switzerland, June 2002, pp. 25–32. IEEE Computer Society Press (2002)
8. Worden, S.: Thinking critically about virtual museums. In: Bearman, D., Trant, J. (eds.), Proceedings of the Conference Museums and the Web, 1997, Pittsburgh, pp. 93–109 (1997)
9. Styliani, S., Fotis, L., Kostas, K., Pertros, P.: Virtual museums, a survey and some issues for consideration. J. Cult. Herit. **10**, 520–528 (2009)
10. Zhang, J., Wang, Y.: The analysis for the related elements of digital cultural heritage protection. J. Lanzhou Jiaotong Univ. **5**, 105–109 (2014)
11. Ke, C.Q., Feng, X.Z., Gu, G.Q.: Three dimensional information restoration of the digital images of the Dunhuang mural paintings. J. Nanjing Univ. (Nat. Sci.) **11**, 628–634 (2006)
12. Duan, X.Y., Liu, X.L., Liu, C.X.: 3D display technique of virtual Yin Ruin's museum. J. Syst. Simul. **9**, 2187–2190 (2005)
13. Zheng, C., Shang, T.: Virtual reality system of ancient architecture based on vega prime. Eng. J. Wuhan Univ. **2**, 83–87 (2006)
14. Yang, C., Sun, S.Q., Su, H.: Reconstruction and exhibition of Chime Bell music and choreography for safeguarding of ancient chu-culture. J. Image Graph. **10**, 1474–1479 (2006)
15. Hu, S.X., Zha, H.B., Zhang, A.W.: Modeling method for large-scale cultural heritage sites and objects using real geometric data and real texture data. J. Syst. Simul. **4**, 951–954, 963 (2006)

16. Yang, A.Q., Yin, Y.W.: The digital civilization heritage reproduction of ZhengGuoQu of Qin dynasty. J. Shaanxi Univ. Sci. Technol. **10**, 112–115 (2004)
17. Lijiang Dongba Association: Dongba Culture, 13 August 2015. http://dongba.lijiang.com/
18. Yang, Y.T., Yang, J.P.: Research of real-time visualization and roaming of virtual campus. Comput. Eng. Sci. **8**, 91–97 (2014)
19. Unity, Rays from the Camera, 27 August 2015. http://docs.unity3d.com/Manual/CameraRays.html
20. Hin, L.T.W., Subramaniam, R., Aggarwal, A.K.: Virtual science centers: a new genre of learning in web-based promotion of science education. In: Proceedings of the 36th Annual HICSS 2003 Conference, pp. 156–165. IEEE Computer Society (2003)
21. NGUI, NGUI: Next-Gen UI Kit, 2 August 2015. http://www.tasharen.com/?page_id=140

A Novel Algorithm of Contour Tracking and Partition for Dongba Hieroglyph

Yuting Yang[1(✉)] and Houliang Kang[2]

[1] Culture and Tourism College, Yunnan Open University, Kunming, China
tudou-yeah@163.com
[2] College of Humanities and Art, Yunnan College of Business Management, Kunming, China

Abstract. Dongba hieroglyph is a kind of very primitive picture hieroglyphs; it has a characteristic of pictograph to express meaning by using pictures, but also has a feature of modern word to express the meaning with simple strokes. In this paper, we analyze the basic structural of the single graphemes in Dongba hieroglyphs. By analyzing the writing methods and habits, a novel algorithm is given based on the chain-connected domain algorithm. It is called connected domain priority marking algorithm, which can be used for both contour tracking and glyphic skeletons partition. Experiments show that the algorithm can extract the correct and ordered contour for the contour-based single graphemes, and solve the problem of sequential extraction of the strokes which are composed of single pixels. For the structure-based single graphemes, the algorithm can achieve the ordered and partitioned skeletons of graphemes by their connected domain, and ensure that the partition results are local consistency for glyphs with the same or similar structure. Therefore, the connected domain priority marking algorithm not only provides a convenient way to analyze the basic structure of Dongba hieroglyphs, but also provides an efficient tool for retrieving isomorphic/variant elements, deformed glyphs, and suffixes of the same basic elements, and lay a foundation for the study of Dongba hieroglyphic structure, glyphs creation, classification detection and reorganization.

Keywords: Connected domain priority marking algorithm
Dongba hieroglyph · Contour tracking · Glyphic partition

1 Dongba Hieroglyph

1.1 Dongba Hieroglyphic Introduction

Dongba hieroglyph is a kind of very primitive hieroglyphs. Naxi call it "Seng Jiu Lu Jiu", which means "imprinting left on the wood and stone" [1], because this hieroglyph is mainly used by the Naxi priests – Dongba to write Dongba scripture which are the national cultural ancient books, therefore, people also call it Dongba hieroglyph [2]. As one of the earliest human text form which transition from hieroglyphic to phonetic transcription, Naxi Dong glyphs not only use pictures to express meaning like pictographs, but also have some features of pictographic, ideographic, self-explanatory

Y. Wang et al. (Eds.): IGTA 2018, CCIS 875, pp. 157–167, 2018.
https://doi.org/10.1007/978-981-13-1702-6_16

and echoism like hieroglyphs. In 2003, Dongba scriptures written by Dongba hiero-glyphics are listed into Memory of the World Heritage List by UNESCO [3, 4].

1.2   The Analysis of Dongba Hieroglyph

Dongba hieroglyphs include 763 single graphemes and 1077 double graphemes. Single graphemes can divided into 442 basic graphemes, 69 deformed graphemes and 252 affixation graphemes. Deformed grapheme refers to transform the basic grapheme to create a new grapheme, and affixation grapheme refers to add somethings like points, lines or blocks to the basic grapheme to compose a new grapheme. Deformed and affixation graphemes are new single graphemes which are created by Naxi ancestors based on the basic graphemes, and they have the related meaning of the original ones. Isomorphic/variant graphemes have many different glyphic forms, but they are not new graphemes. The reason of generating isomorphic/variant graphemes is that the Dongba hieroglyphs have not been developed to a more fixed and unified ideogram [5]. Table 1 shows some examples of isomorphic/variant, deformed and affixation graphemes.

Table 1. Examples of single graphemes and their isomorphic/variant, deformed and affixation graphemes

Basic	Meaning	isomorphic/ variant	Meaning	deformed	Meaning	affixation	Meaning
	people		people, which has the same pronunciation of "rice"		I, which uses finger to self emphasizes "I"		we, which add points to show many people
	bird		bird, which includes the whole body emphasizes flying bird		cuckoo, who is singing means the cultivation of spring has begun.		peck, which add points to show pecking many foods.
	tree		tree, which has the same pronunciation of "singing"		break off, which emphasizes tree breaking off		woods, which add points to show woods have many trees

Therefore, we promote a Chain Code-Based Connected Domain Priority Marking algorithm which can be used to track contour and divide glyphs skeleton into local skeleton curves. The algorithm provides a convenient way to analyze the basic com-position of Dongba single graphemes and provides an efficient preprocessing tool for retrieving basic, isomorphic/variant, deformed and affixation graphemes. And it also lays a solid foundation for the study of Dongba hieroglyphs creation, classification, detection and recognition.

2 Connected Domain Priority Marking Algorithm Based on Chain Code

Based on the glyphic structural [6] of Dongba Hieroglyph, the single graphemes [7, 8] can be subdivided into two types of contour-based single graphemes (CSG) and structure-based single graphemes (SSG). CSG generally express the meaning by drawing the appearance of things or objects, for example: 🌾 (gold), ⚘ (god of mountain), etc. This one has significant features of glyphic outline, so we can handle them from their contour [9]. SSG generally use simple strokes to express the meaning of things or objects [10], for example: 𧘇 (people), 𠂤 (collapse), etc. This one has significant features of character structural, so we can handle them from their topological structure.

Considering the characteristic of different kinds of single graphemes, We combine the processing methods of shapes and handwritten texts to provide a novel algorithm of chain code based connected domain priority marking algorithm which can be used not only to track and sort contour list for CSG, but also used to divide and sort local skeleton curves for SSG.

2.1 Connected Domain Priority Marking Algorithm for Contour Tracking

Chain codes are a form of shape representation that can be used to represent a boundary by means of a connected sequence of straight line segments of specified lengths and directions. This representation is based on the 4-connectivity or 8-connectivity of the segments [11]. The direction of each segment is coded using a numbering scheme, so that we can use a chain code to represent a complete object or curve and computing any shape feature from their chain code [12]. Therefore, the chain code can be used not only to contour tracking, but also to image segmentation, regional filling and other fields [13].

Getting glyphic contour is the basic work of detecting and recognizing single graphemes. In order to get a correct and ordered glyphic contour, we provide a chain code based connected domain priority marking algorithm (CDPM). The algorithm uses 8-connected domain priorities of the specifying point to determine the next neighbor contour point. The algorithm of CDPM must satisfy the following three conditions:

(1) Let horizontal to the right denote the x-axis positive direction, and vertical upward denote the y-axis. And contour tracking is in the counter-clockwise direction.
(2) In contour tracking, the starting point P_1 is the smallest pixels in x-axis. And the next point P_2 is the neighborhood of P_1 traversed in the counter-clockwise direction.
(3) Let $P_i(i \geq 2)$ denote a contour point, the prior neighbor point of P_i is P_{i-1}, and the next is P_{i+1}. So, the vector $\overrightarrow{P_{i-1}P_i}$ is composed of P_{i-1} and P_i, and $\overrightarrow{P_iP_{i+1}}$ is composed of P_i and P_{i+1}.

Analyzing the features of CSG, we find that the contour of glyph always extends in the opposite direction of its center. Thus, P_{i+1} has a higher priority when the direction of $\overrightarrow{P_iP_{i+1}}$ is opposite to the center of the glyph. And when the direction of $\overrightarrow{P_iP_{i+1}}$ is opposite to $\overrightarrow{P_{i-1}P_i}$, P_{i+1} has the lowest priority, because in that case $\overrightarrow{P_{i-1}P_i}$ and $\overrightarrow{P_iP_{i+1}}$ is overlapped, and the direction of $\overrightarrow{P_iP_{i+1}}$ is opposite to the tracking direction.

Table 2 shows the 8-connected priorities of P_i when the direction of $\overrightarrow{P_{i-1}P_i}$ is $v.x > 0$ and $v.y < 0$. We use rectangle to denote the current contour point P_i, and use circle to denote each 8-connected point whose priority is shown in the circle and its coordinate is next to the circle. The larger the value in circle, the higher the priority of 8-connected point is. Therefore, the next potential contour point P_{i+1} should extend as far to the left as possible and then downward, right, and upward, when the direction of $\overrightarrow{P_{i-1}P_i}$ is $v.x > 0$ and $v.y < 0$, and contour tracking is in the direction of counter-clockwise.

So, we can get the following Proposition 1. And Table 2 shows the effects of $\overrightarrow{P_{i-1}P_i}$ on the 8-connected priorities of P_i.

Proposition 1: The 8-connected priorities of P_i are ordered locally in clockwise when the direction of $\overrightarrow{P_{i-1}P_i}$ is $v.x \neq 0$ and $v.y \neq 0$. And the neighbor point P_{i+1} will have the lowest priority when the direction of vector $\overrightarrow{P_iP_{i+1}}$ is opposite to $\overrightarrow{P_{i-1}P_1}$.

There are some glyphs which have the characteristics of both pictorial and structural also, like (ginger), (cuckoo).etc. These CSG have some simple strokes in them which are composed of single pixels. We use the following example to show that our algorithm can also be used to get correctly ordered contour in counter-clockwise for these type and Proposition 1 is satisfied, too.

Table 2. The Effect of different direction of $\overrightarrow{P_{i-1}P_i}$ on the 8-connected priorities of P_i

The direction of $\overrightarrow{P_{i-1}P_i}$	(v.x>0,v.y<0)	(v.x<0,v.y<0)	(v.x>0,v.y>0)	(v.x<0,v.y>0)
The 8-connected priorities of P_i	1 2 3 / 8 Pi 4 / 7 6 5	7 8 1 / 6 Pi 2 / 5 4 3	3 4 5 / 2 Pi 6 / 1 8 7	5 6 7 / 4 Pi 8 / 3 2 1
The direction of $\overrightarrow{P_{i-1}P_i}$	(v.x>0,v.y=0)	(v.x<0,v.y=0)	(v.x=0,v.y>0)	(v.x=0,v.y<0)
The 8-connected priorities of P_i	2 3 4 / 1 Pi 5 / 8 7 6	6 7 8 / 5 Pi 1 / 4 3 2	4 5 6 / 3 Pi 7 / 2 1 8	8 1 2 / 7 Pi 3 / 6 5 4

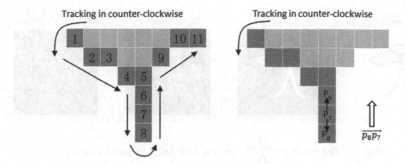

Fig. 1. Mark in single pixel lines

In Fig. 1, we start to calculate the next contour point of $P_i(i = 1)$ based on Proposition 1. The ordered contour list is: $P_1 \rightarrow P_2 \rightarrow P_3 \rightarrow P_4 \rightarrow P_5 \rightarrow P_6 \rightarrow P_7 \rightarrow P_8$. At this moment, P_8 is the end point, and only P_7 is next to it, so P_7 is stored again. We keep going to calculate P_7, now the neighbor points of P_7 are P_8 and P_6. According to the Proposition 1 and the priorities of vector $\overrightarrow{P_8P_7}$ in Table 2, we can calculate that the priority of P_8 and P_6 is 5 and 1, respectively. So, the next contour point is P_6. Figure 2 shows that the final contour list is: $P_1 \rightarrow P_2 \rightarrow P_3 \rightarrow P_4 \rightarrow P_5 \rightarrow P_6 \rightarrow P_7 \rightarrow P_8 \rightarrow P_7 \rightarrow P_6 \rightarrow P_5 \rightarrow P_9 \rightarrow P_{10} \rightarrow P_{11}$. It demonstrates that Proposition 1 can be used when there are some single pixel lines in the glyph. And we can get the following Corollary 1 that is:

Corollary 1: Based on Proposition 1, we can also get the correct and ordered glyphic contour, even if there are some single pixel lines in the glyph.

The CDPM algorithm does not need to add additional access marks to each pixel, and only needs to refer to the direction of vector which is composed of the current point and its previous point to calculate the priorities of all its neighbor points, and the next contour point is the one with the highest priority of them. The CDPM algorithm can be used to track, extract, and sort the outline of CSG, and it has the advantages of calculating faster, implementing simpler and computational complexity lower.

2.2 Connected Domain Priority Marking Algorithm for Skeleton Partition

The characteristic of structure-based single graphemes (SSG) is glyphic structure. It is different from the contour-based single graphemes (CSG), and expressing meaning by using simple strokes. In addition, Table 1 shows that the isomorphic/variant, deformed and affixation graphemes which are derived from the basic SSG have the same structural characteristic, also.

In order to segment skeleton and get ordered local skeleton curves of SSG more easily by using CDPM, we first do some preprocessing for SSG, including glyphic refinement, glyphic skeleton extraction, and additional points remove. Figure 2 shows the result of 🧍 (we) on each stage of preprocessing.

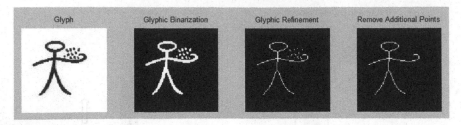

Fig. 2. The result of 🎋 (we) on each stage of preprocessing

The idea of CDPM is that:

(1) Let P_{i-1} and P_i denote the known points, and $\overrightarrow{P_{i-1}P_i}$ is the known vector.
(2) Calculate the 8-connected priorities of P_i based on the Proposition 1.
(3) The next contour or skeleton point is the connected point with the highest priority.
(4) Repeat steps2 and 3 until it meet the end or start point or intersection point.

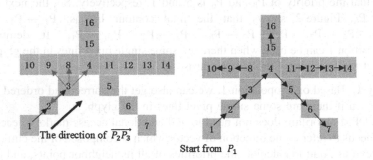

Fig. 3. Glyphic skeleton partition by using connected domain priority marking algorithm

Figure 3 shows the process of dividing the skeleton of a SSG by using CDPM. Among them, P_1 is the start point, and when we track to P_3, the neighbor points of P_3 is P_2, P_9, P_8 and P_4. Combining with the direction of vector $\overrightarrow{P_2P_3}$ and looking up Table 2, we can calculate the priority of each neighbor point, and the values are 1, 3, 4 and 5. So, the next local skeleton point is P_4, while the other three points are stored in the order of priority as candidate starting points for the remaining local skeleton curves in the glyph. Finally, the glyphic skeleton in Fig. 4 is divided into four local skeleton curves; they are Line 1, Line 2, Line 3 and Line 4.

Line 1: $P_1 \rightarrow P_2 \rightarrow P_3 \rightarrow P_4 \rightarrow P_5 \rightarrow P_6 \rightarrow P_7$
Line 2: $P_8 \rightarrow P_9 \rightarrow P_{10}$
Line 3: $P_{11} \rightarrow P_{12} \rightarrow P_{13} \rightarrow P_{14}$
Line 4: $P_{15} \rightarrow P_{16}$

Through analyzing the processing of structure-based single graphemes in Fig. 4, we can find that the 8-connected priorities of point P_i are calculated based on the direction of vector $\overrightarrow{P_{i-1}P_i}$ by using CDPM. So, we can get the following Corollary 2.

Corollary 2: In two Dongba hieroglyphs, if their contour/skeleton points P_i and P_j have the same direction of vectors $\overrightarrow{P_{i-1}P_i}$ and $\overrightarrow{P_{j-1}P_j}$, their 8-connected priorities will be the same. Thus, two different SSG with the same structural features have similar intersect points after division, and their corresponding local skeleton curves also the same.

Corollary 2 illustrates the influence of the direction of vectors on the priorities of connected domain. It is also clear that for the different SSG with the same structural, if the directions of vectors are the same, then the shape of locally segmented skeleton curve should be the same. Taking glyphs of 夭, 夭, 夲, 夭 and 宎 as an example, we divide their skeleton, and find every local skeleton curve from them. Then, we use different colors to mark them. The result is shown in Fig. 4.

Fig. 4. Single glyphs partition by using connected domain priority marking algorithm (Color figure online)

In these glyphs, their head, hand and foot have the same structural. After we divide them by using CDPM, their shapes of corresponding local skeleton curves are the same. The result is consistent with the description in Corollary 2. In addition, these 5 glyphs not only have the same shape of their corresponding local skeleton curves, but the order of the local skeleton curves in each glyph is also the same. So, we can get the following Corollary 3.

Corollary 3: In two different structure-based single graphemes with the same structural, if there are more than one local skeleton curves have the same structural, the order of the local skeleton curves in each glyph should be the same or similar.

2.3   The Analysis of Computational Complexity

CDPM is based on the feature of 8-connected chain code. First of all, we start from the smallest pixels in x-axis named P_1. And the next point P_2 is the neighborhood of P_1 traversed in the counter-clockwise direction. Let P_{i-1} and $P_i(i \geq 2)$ denote two known contour/skeleton points. Then, we calculate their vector $\overrightarrow{P_{i-1}P_i}$ and look up Table 2 to get the 8-connected priorities of P_i. And, we choose the point with the largest priority value as the next new contour/skeleton point. The process is repeated until we meet the end or intersection point in glyph. The pseudo code of the algorithm is as follows:

ConnectedDomainPrioritiesMarking(bwList, type)
1   // bwList denotes a binarization glyphic list
2   // type denotes a glyphic type, 1 denotes structured; 0 denotes contoured;
3   // OrderedList denotes a return values, it is an ordered pixel-points list of glyph
4   if type is 1 // preprocessing the structure-based single grapheme
5   do glyphic preprocess: thin glyph and remove additional points
6   endif
7   P_i=bwlist(1), OrderedList = P_i; // choosing a start point
8   for i = 1to length(bwlist)
9   Find the 8-connected points of P_i, and use neiPoint8 to denote them;
10   if neiPoint8 is empty
11   if type is1
12   sort each local skeleton curve of SSG;
13   else
14   track and sort the contour of CSG;
15   endif
16   elseif the length of neiPoint8 is 1
17   store the neighbor point of P_i in OrderdList;
18   else
19   calculate the direction of $\overrightarrow{P_{i-1}P_i}$;
20   calculate the 8-connected priorities of P_i;
21   choose the point with the largest priority as P_{i+1};
22         $P_i \leftarrow P_{i+1}$;
23   P_i is stored in OrderedList;
24   endif
25   endfor
26   return OrderedList.

Let n denote the total number of contour points. The number of times it uses to calculate the 8-connected priorities of P_i is no more than 8. So, the total computational complexity of the whole algorithm is O(n), and it is linear.

3 Experiment

3.1 Contour Tracking and Sorting for CSG

Dongba Hieroglyphs are different from shapes; it has both the characteristic of pictorial and glyphic strokes. In order to get a correct and ordered contour, the key we need to deal with is that even if there is a single pixel line or contour points which are close to each other in the hieroglyphs, there is no error happened which includes contour point extraction error or points crossing each other, during the process of contour tracking and sorting. We take (gold) as an example to verify the accuracy of CDPM.

Because of the collar button is generally made of metal, so Naxi people use ![glyph] to describe "gold". ![glyph] is a typical CSG, but its four corners contains some single-pixel strokes which are used to depict the decorative pattern. Therefore, it is difficult to track and sort. Figure 5 (left) shows all the pixels (green) that make up the glyph and its contour (read). Figure 5 (right) enlarges the four corners of the glyph. The top left corner is the starting and the ending (right) of the contour. And contour points are sorted counter- clockwise and connected one by one to get the final red contour line. In the four corners, although the outline points are close and the glyphic shape is slender, there is no crossover or extraction error in the contour, which shows that the CDPM algorithm can track, extract and sort the contour correctly.

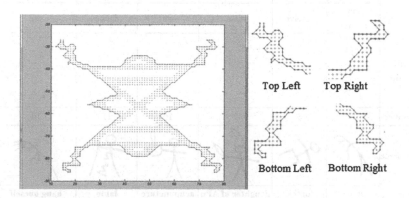

Fig. 5. All Pixels (Green) of ![glyph] and Its contour line (Red) (Color figure online)

3.2 Skeleton Partition and Sorting Locally for SSG

The characteristic of SSG is structure. The structure-based single graphemes with the same or similar structure should have the same results of skeletons partition. We take ![glyph] (people) as the basic grapheme and combine with kinds of its isomorphic/variant, deformed and affixation graphemes to finish the skeletons dividing, and use different colors to mark the different local skeleton curves, as shown in Table 3. According to the result, the partition results for the isomorphic or variant structure-based graphemes evolved from 夫 (people) are better. However, when the glyph changes greatly, such as character rotation (number 6), adding headwear (number 9 and 12), hand holding somethings (number 9 and 10), or local skeleton deforming intensely, the skeleton partition results will be influenced. This is because that the result of CDPM is closely related to the selection of the starting point and the position and number of intersections in the skeleton. When the position or number of intersections in a skeleton changes greatly, the final partition result also changes. However, due to the independence of CDPM, this effect is only reflected in some or some of the local skeleton curve segments and does not affect the other skeleton curve. So, it has little effect on the overall glyphic partition.

Table 3. Deformed glyphs, and suffix glyphs evolved from 夫

number	1	2	3	4	5	6
grapheme						
meaning	people (basic)	receive	raise	we	dance	die
partition result						
number	7	8	9	10	11	12
grapheme						
meaning	stoop	tumble	daughter of APu	acupuncture	lame	hang oneself
partition result						

4 Conclusions

Dongba hieroglyph is a kind of very primitive picture hieroglyph; it has a characteristic of pictograph to express meaning by using pictures, but also has a feature of modern word to express the meaning with simple strokes. In order to deal with these two features at the same time, a connected domain priority making algorithm is presented. Experiments show that for the contour-based graphemes, the algorithm can analyze their features from glyphic pictures and give the correct contour sorted in counter-clockwise direction. At the same time, the algorithm can also start from the structure of structure-based graphemes to carry out the correct skeleton partition and sort each local skeleton curve in counter-clockwise direction. So, our algorithm can be used to analyze and process the Dongba single graphemes with two different types, which lays a solid foundation for the study on the classification, retrieval and recognition of Dongba hieroglyphs.

References

1. He, L.: The research of Dongba culture heritage. Soc. Sci. Yunnan **1**(1), 83–87 (2004)
2. He, J.: The development trend of Dongba culture studies of the Naxi nationality. J. Yunnan Natl. Uni. **24**(1), 81–84 (2007)
3. Ge, A.: Dongba culture review. J. Natl. Artist. Res. **12**(2), 71–80 (1999)
4. He, Z.: Discussing the characteristics of Naxi hieroglyphic—including the different of original pictograph, hieroglyphic and ideograph. Soc. Sci. Yunnan **3**, 71–82 (1982)
5. Zheng, F.: Word research of Naxi Dongba Hieroglyphic, pp. 1–230. Nationalities Publishing House, Beijing (2005)
6. Guo, H., Zhao, J.: Segmentation method for NaXi pictograph character recognition. J. Converg. Inf. Technol. **5**(6), 87–98 (2010)
7. Guo, H., Zhao, J.: Research on feature extraction for character recognition of Naxi pictograph. J. Comput. **6**(5), 947–954 (2011)
8. Guo, H., Yin, J., Zhao, J.: Feature dimension reduction of naxi pictograph recognition based on LDA. Int. J. Comput. Sci. **9**(1), 90–96 (2012)
9. Zhu, Q., Wang, X., Keogh, E., Lee, S.H.: Augmenting the generalized hough transform to enable the mining of petroglyphs. In: Proceeding of ACM SIGKDD International Conference on Knowledge Discovery and Data Mining, pp. 1057–1066 (2009)
10. Zhu, Q., Wang, X., Keogh, E., Lee, S.H.: An efficient and effective similarity measure to enable data mining of petroglyphs. Data Min. Knowl. Discov. **23**(1), 91–127 (2011)
11. Gonzalez, R.C., Woods, R.E.: Digital Image Processing, 2nd edn. Tom Robbins (2001)
12. Onishi, J., Ono, T.: Contour pattern recognition through auditory labels of freeman chain codes for people with visual impairments. In: Proceeding of IEEE International Conference on Systems, vol. 32, no. 14, pp. 1088–1093 (2011)
13. Chunli, D., Yuning, D., Li, W.: Survey of object tracking algorithms based on active contour models. Comput. Eng. Appl. **44**(34), 208–212 (2008)

Real-Time Soft Shadow by A-Buffer

Dening Luo[✉] and Jianwei Zhang

College of Computer Science, Sichuan University, Chengdu 610065, China
loening@stu.scu.edu.cn, zhangjianwei@scu.edu.cn

Abstract. We present a new real-time soft shadow algorithm by A-Buffer in virtual environment. The key idea is to use A-Buffer to store the whole scene information and then to accurately compute soft shadow. In the first pass, the scenes are drawn in the center view of the complex area lights, and the target fragments of per pixel are stored into an A-Buffer. The second is to calculate the occlusion percentage according to the cone which is consisted of the shaded point and area lights from the view of the camera. The occlusion percentage is the ration of blocked area and sampled area within the cone, and it is used to calculate the shadow factor. Our algorithm could produce more realistic shadow effects in real-time and adapt to the complex scenes.

Keywords: Soft shadow · Real-time · A-Buffer · The whole scene information
Area lights

1 Introduction

Shadows rendered correctly and realistically play a very important role in 3D virtual scene, because shadows provide visual clues concerning the spatial relationship of objects and the geometric shapes of the receiver. Meanwhile, they even reveal information hidden from the current point of view. Shadow algorithms mainly base on image-space approach and object-space method or both of them to generate shadows. The shadow volume algorithm [1] is a representative of an object-space approach; shadow mapping [2] is regarded as origination of image-space approach.

As long as shadow algorithms refer to image-space approach, they suffer from some problems which are caused by sampling and resampling issues. This is why shadow mapping leads to self-shadowing artifacts, projection aliasing and perspective aliasing problems. By contrast, object-space solutions avoid aliasing problems of image-based approaches, but it typically comes along with slower speed.

According to this paper's presented algorithm, we improve shadow qualities in image-space and implement real-time soft shadow. At the root of the issue of shadow mapping aliasing is using the finite resolution shadow maps. A-Buffer can store a list fragments per pixel as complete information unit. That is to say, each pixel not only can store the closest layer message, but also can store all fragments' information of the pixel.

National High-tech R&D Program of China (863 Program): Grant No. 2015AA016405.

According to the characteristics of A-Buffer and combining area lights, real-time soft shadow algorithm is presented and the algorithm is irrelevant to the shape and size of the area lights.

2 Related Work

Real-time soft shadow algorithms occupy a half in shadow generation of 3D scenes. Several surveys [3–5] and books or siggraph course [6, 7] on shadow algorithms have carried out a detailed analysis to their advantages and disadvantages. This section mainly overview and summarize algorithms referring to soft shadow by A-Buffer.

Shadow volume and shadow mapping are two most common and also more general techniques for shadow computation. The two techniques have their own advantages and drawbacks. Although the shadow volume was introduced already in 1977, it was not until 1991 [8] that the algorithm was efficiently ported to graphics cards. And shadow mapping has many flaws. First, omnidirectional lights cannot be captured using a single frustum. A second and more severe problem is aliasing artifacts that arise because the sampling of the shadow map and the sampling of the image pixels projected into shadow map usually do not match up. A third problem, incorrect self-shadowing, is caused by under-sampling and imprecisions in the depth information stored in the shadow map for cach texel.

Some algorithms based the standard shadow mapping technique to improve the shadow quality and to reduce errors. Except percentage closer filtering (PCF) [9], percentage-closer soft shadows (PCSS) [10] and other techniques [11, 12] mainly generate perceptually soft shadows, so their effects are little true. Weiskopf et al. [13] take into account these two depths that are closest to the light source and computes an adaptive depth bias to achieve a robust determination of shadowed regions. Wang et al. [14] present an improved depth-map shadow algorithm which does not require a bias for scenes composed of solids and produces accurate shadows with smaller depth maps.

From the above analysis of the algorithm, it can get third layer or second layer of closest to the light source to shadow boundary of shadows or to display shadow detail, and also can utilize multi-layer shadow map to reduce shadow aliasing. Multiple-depth shadow maps [15] use the multi-layer to soften the shadow boundary. Liu et al. [16] encode the depth distribution of the scene into a coarse depth grid in a preliminary pass to record more information and implement a fast soft shadow.

For area light source, linear light source and volume light, some methods turn it into more points light and then sample. However, more and more light sampling cause a waste of time and space. Chen et al. [17] present an algorithm reduced the amount of shadow map by sampling a few key points but using view interpolation in other positions. However, facing complicated area light, its affects is not so well, because this method refers to choice sampling points and to interpolate in others positions.

Soft shadows generation is more complex than hard shadows, because of linear characteristics of light transmission. On the one hand, the accumulation buffer [18] can implement; on the other hand, the percentage of the visual with weights can show how much lights are visible. For a linear light source, Heidrich et al. [19] presents a fast soft method. Its big advantage is using fewer sampling and usually is two vertexes, but this is its big question. If sampling points don't choose fully, it causes error shadow affects. Ying et al. [20] extends this method to apply polygon surface light source.

Except the above sampling algorithms, there are also high efficient to generate fast soft shadow for area light sources. Agrawala et al. [21] presents layered attenuation maps and coherence-based raytracing of depth images to generate high-quality soft shadows from area light sources. Besides Atty et al. [22] and Guennebud et al. [23] present at a time area light soft shadows generation of soft shadow maps. Shadow map is represented a simplified discretization of the scene and each texel stands for underlying occluder of the scene and it is back-project to light source to compute the percentage of the visual.

Basically, an A-Buffer [24] is a simple list of fragments per pixel. Previous methods (depth-peeling, k-buffer, bucket sort depth peeling and so on) to implement it required multiple passes to capture an interesting number of fragments per pixel. For a long time, A-Buffer is not being implemented. But with the development of the hardware level and the graphics technology, a NVIDIA researcher Cyril Crassin [25] implements a fast and accurate single-pass A-Buffer using OpenGL 4.0+ on Icare3D weblog and shows the order independence transparent effects. Similarly, Xu et al. [26] uses a Multi-Layer Occluder buffer to generate accurate soft shadows for complex virtual scenes in real-time.

3 Algorithm Overview

Shadow mapping is more easily comprehended and complemented, and its high efficiency is unable to be replaced by any other algorithms. Even though shadow mapping exist many shortcomings, several methods based on it have been presented and implemented to generate shadows of high-quality and high-efficiency. These methods include using multi-resolution to compute more details in regions with shadow boundaries or computing the shadow map that can effectively store more details in parts of the shadow map that are closer to the eye, and so forth. In order to produce high-quality shadows and reduce aliasing, it is necessary to record even more details of the whole scene.

Figure 1 shows the overlapping pixels of three fragments, so A-Buffer can store them in the rasterization processing stage of the 3D graphics pipeline. Thus A-Buffer records complete information of the whole scene and it is easy to be implemented on the video card supporting the extension "EXT_shader_image_load_store". The extension allows random read or write and atomic operations into global memory and textures to implement an A-Buffer. Each fragment can be written by the fragment shader at its position into a pre-allocated 2D texture array (or a global memory region) with a fixed maximum number of layers. The layer to write the fragment into is given by a counter stored per pixel into another 2D texture and incremented using an atomic increment operation ([image]AtomicIncWrap or [image]AtomicAdd). As a consequence, a pair of 2D texture array and 2D texture can implement a simple A-Buffer.

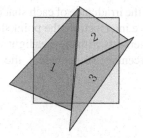

Fig. 1. A-Buffer stores complete information of the whole scene in the rasterizer stage.

In fact, point light sources do not exist in the real world so hard shadows give a rather unrealistic feeling. In contrast, soft shadows are obviously much more realistic than hard shadows. So it's necessary for us to implement a real-time soft shadow algorithm by A-Buffer. Ideally, area lights are regarded as rectangular light sources. In order to determine the shadow factor of a shaded point in the scene, it can be viewed from the point to the light source. So the point and the light source make a cone. Figure 2 shows the basic idea that objects in a cone constituted by any shaded point P in eye and the light source occlude the extent of point P. In other words, only the occluders within cone will block the light ray to reach the point P and impact its shadow factor. In order to count the extent of the occlusion in the cone, it is possible to calculate the occlusion of all the fragments in the cone during fragment shader stage. Assuming the light rays emitted by the rectangular light source converge to the shaded point, since some of the light is obscured by the fragments in the cone, it is possible to calculate how many the light in the cone is blocked and to obtain the occlusion factor according to the Eq. (1).

$$O\_factor = N\_occluder/N\_light \qquad (1)$$

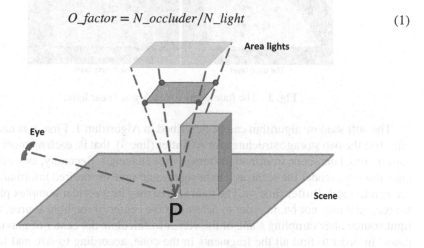

Fig. 2. The basic idea of soft shadow by A-Buffer.

By means of the A-Buffer, we can detect occluded messages of each shaded point. For detecting occluded fragments of a shaded point, sampling its surrounding texel in texture-space and determining which fragments occlude it by the number of layer stored in A-Buffer. Then according to the irradiance of each shaded point along these occluders intersect with area lights, if have intersection, the point should be shadowed or lighted. If the ray directing occluders intersects with the area light sources, the point is shadowed. And finally in terms of the percentage of occluders, the point can be processed a soft shadow.

4   Implementation

From Fig. 3, each layer fragments in A-Buffer are different. Now, A-Buffer stores the normal and depth information from the view of the light and keeps the back-face information. The second layer is the occluder from the ray and we can utilize these layers to implement shadow.

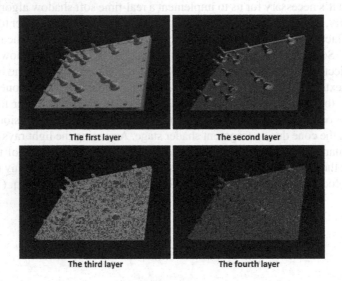

<table>
<tr><td align="center">The first layer</td><td align="center">The second layer</td></tr>
<tr><td align="center">The third layer</td><td align="center">The fourth layer</td></tr>
</table>

Fig. 3. The four layers for each pixel near light.

The soft shadow algorithm can be described in Algorithm 1. First, it is necessary to initialize the two storage structures for A-Buffer (line 3), that is, each memory cell is set zero to avoid the scene information storage miscellaneous. Secondly, as with the SSM algorithm, we render the scene as a light source and save the desired information for the scene into the A-Buffer (line 4). The light source may be a regular complex planar light source, or it may not be, in order to determine the center of the light source, the planar light source after sampling some of the vertex to calculate the center of gravity coordinates. In order to find all the fragments in the cone, according to size and location of light source and cone situation to calculate sampling radius of each shaded point (line 5). Finding all fragments associated with the shaded point in A-Buffer from the sampling area determined in the third step and blocking the effect on the shaded point of the light emitted by the area lights (line 6). This step mainly is to the shaded point in the cone to send light. If the light and area lights intersection that the tablet in the cone, it also shows that it block the light from the light area and ultimately calculate the cone. Finally, we know how many fragments block light rays to the shaded point and obtain the shadow factor for subsequent shading calculation to ultimately draw the scene of the soft shadow effect (line 7).

Algorithm 1 : *Soft shadow by A – Buffer*

1 *void A - BufferSoftShadow*()

2{

3   *initA - Buffer*();

4   *renderSceneFromLightCenter*();

5   det *ectSampleRadius*();

6   *occlusionDetectionInViewFrustum*();

7   *renderSceneFromCamera*();

8 }

4.1   The Whole Scene Information

There are two needed steps which are initializing the A-Buffer and rendering scene from the light source to get A-Buffer data. A-Buffer storage unit can be a memory area, and also is composed of texture units. In order to speed up the access speed, the algorithm chooses the texture unit as the storage structure of A-Buffer. The algorithm generally selects the size of A-Buffer to 16, which is sufficient to store the information of each layer in the scene and it can reduce aliasing and wasted storage. The center of the area lights can be expressed by the Eq. (2). The fragment storage unit of the A-Buffer stores the position information of each fragment in addition to the depth of the light source center in the light source. These data plays an important role in the subsequent shadow factor.

$$\left(\frac{1}{n}\sum_{i=1}^{n}x_i, \ \frac{1}{n}\sum_{i=1}^{n}y_i, \ \frac{1}{n}\sum_{i=1}^{n}z_i\right) \qquad (2)$$

4.2   Sampling Cone

The algorithm starts to render all the scene information in the A-Buffer from the light source center, and only the occluder on the light impact the shaded point. The question of how to accurately find the occluder in the cone is to consider the obstruction in the A-Buffer in terms of the size of the light source. It is a waste of time due to sampling and is not realistic for a large surface light source. Sampling area is a key to the design of the algorithm, sampling adaptive scene. The corresponding A-Buffer sitting in the nearest part of the light source from the location of the world coordinate, the location as the sampling area of the center of the sampling of the cone.

4.3 Sampling Radius

Only to adapt to the scene of the sampling, the appropriate sampling space to find the entire sampling cone, in order to fine simulation of the edge of the soft shadow effect, but also greatly improve the calculation of shadow factor efficiency. The sampling radius of each shaded point has a different size, its radius is not only from the distance between the cover fragments, but also with the light source location, shape and so on. Assume that the planar light source shape is a regular positive quadrilateral with its plane parallel to the receiving surface, as shown in Fig. 4. The plane of the regular quadrilateral light source can be v_1, v_2, v_3, v_4 four vertices. In order to calculate the sampling radius R of the midpoint P of the scene, the light source position information and the point P correspond to the sampling points in the A-Buffer. Sampling radius R is determined by the Eq. (3).

$$R = \frac{\left|\overrightarrow{v_1 v_2}\right| - \dfrac{2d}{\tan \theta}}{2}$$

$$\tan \theta = \sqrt{\frac{1}{\cos^2 \theta} - 1} \tag{3}$$

$$\cos \theta = dot(\frac{\overrightarrow{v_1 P}}{\left|\overrightarrow{v_1 P}\right|}, \frac{\overrightarrow{v_1 v_2}}{\left|\overrightarrow{v_1 v_2}\right|})$$

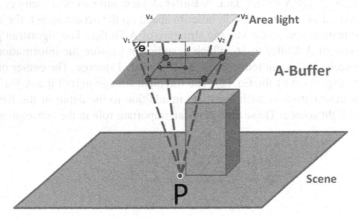

Fig. 4. Sampling radius.

4.4 Search Fragments

Query occluded fragments is the most critical step of this algorithm, which determines the calculation of the shading factor of each shaded point in the scene, and also affects the performance of the whole algorithm. This step is mainly on the scene of the shaded point in the shadow factor calculation, query A-Buffer in those related to the occluded fragment to calculate. For the construction of the color point of the cone query occluded fragments, and according to these occluder elements in the surface under the light source to get the shadow factor.

In intersection stage, the follow formula is to compute whether there are intersections between ray and area lights. We first compute the intersection between the ray $r(t) = 0 + td$ and area light $\pi{:}n_p \bullet x + d_p = 0$, which is easily done by replacing x by the ray. If the denominator, where ε is a very small number, then the ray is considered parallel to the polygon plane and on intersection occurs. Otherwise, the intersection point p of the ray and the polygon plane is compute $d{:}p = o + t \bullet d$, where the t-value is that from the below Equation:

$$n_p \bullet (o + td) + d_p = 0 \Leftrightarrow t = \frac{-d_p - n_p \bullet o}{n_p \bullet d} \tag{4}$$

Thereafter, the problem of deciding whether p is inside the polygon is reduced from three to two dimensions. The pseudocode for an efficient form of the crossings test follows. It was inspired by the work of Joseph Samosky [27] and Mark Haigh Hutchinson. A two-dimensional test point t and polygon P with vertices v_0 through v_{n-1} are compared in algorithm 2. The advantages of the crossings test are that it is relatively fast and robust, and it requires no additional information or preprocessing for the polygon.

Algorithm 2 : *Judge a point whether or not in polygon*

```
1 function bool PointInPolygon(t, P)
2 {
3    bool inside = FALSE;
4    e_0 = v_{n-1};
5    bool y_0 = (e_{0_y} ≥ t_y);
6    for i = 0 to n-1
7       e_1 = v_i;
8       bool y_1 = (e_{1_y} ≥ t_y);
9       if (y_0 ≠ y_1)
10          if(((e_{1_y} - t_y)(e_{0_x} ≥ e_{1_x}) ≥ (e_{1_x} - t_x)(e_{0_y} - e_{1_y})) == y_1)
11             inside = !inside;
12       y_0 = y_1;
13       e_0 = e_1;
14 return inside;
15 }
```

5 Results

The soft shadow algorithm proposed in this paper is implemented on a PC with Intel(R) Core(TM) i3-2100 CPU 950 @ 3.10 GH, NVIDIA GeForce GT 430 with 4096 MB video memory.

The third column of Table 1 shows the performance of soft shadow by A-Buffer on different scene sizes at the same output resolution 800 * 600 and the A-Buffer size 8. The performance of PCF under the same tests is as shown in the fourth column. It can be seen that soft shadow by A-Buffer will have a frame rate of 20%–30% percent decrease with the same conditions compared with PCF algorithms. This is mainly because A-Buffer stores all fragments of the whole scene, but PCF only gets the closest fragments in the light of view. Though A-Buffer's memory occupancy decrease a litter, but no dropped significantly. The memory occupancy of island is greater than chess's, because island loads some textures during rendering scenes.

Table 1. FPS and memory occupancy of A-Buffer and 5 * 5 PCF for different model sizes.

Scene	Faces#	A-Buffer	PCF
Chess	113K	84.2/26.8M	108.3/26.4M
Basketball	324K	45.6/48.4M	67.0/47.8M
Island	81K	92.0/34.0M	116.5/33.1M

The second experiment is employed to compare the performance of soft shadow by A-Buffer and PCF at different output resolutions. The test has 113 K triangles, the FPS at the resolution 800 * 600, 1024 * 1024 and 1280 * 800 are presented in Table 2 respectively. As the resolution increases, A-Buffer doesn't sharp drop in frame rate. A-Buffer's implementation based on the screen-space stored ways.

Table 2. FPS of A-Buffer and 5 * 5 PCF at different resolutions for Chess scene.

Resolution	A-Buffer	PCF
800 * 600	82.2/26.8M	107.4/25.6M
1024 * 1024	43.5/26.9M	95.1/25.6M
1280 * 800	45.5/26.9M	98.0/25.6M

The third experiment is employed to compare the memory occupancy of different scene at different A-Buffer size. The test has Chess, Basketball and Island at the A-Buffer 4, 8 and 12 are presented in Table 3 respectively. From the table, with the crease of the scene complexity, the memory occupancy will gradually increase. But with the A-Buffer size, the indicator does not significant increase. Maybe, with the more complex scenes, the indicator will sharp increase with the A-Buffer size, because of the more layers need to be stored.

Table 3. Memory occupancy of Chess and Basketball at different A-Buffer size for the same resolution.

A-Buffer size	Chess	Basketball	Island
4	26.9M	48.9M	34.2M
8	26.5M	48.9M	34.2M
12	26.9M	48.8M	34.8M

Figure 5 presents comparisons among the shadow mapping (column 1), A-Buffer (column 2), and 5 * 5 FCF (column 3). It can be seen that soft shadow by A-Buffer's effects is better instead of PCF' artifact. But the result has some shortage that light permeability is within the shadows. There are two reasons leading to this result. On the one hand, only as an area of a fixed value to approximate query or inaccurate for occlusion queries is a reason. On the other hand, intersection tests resulted in some blocking the light has not been the easiest way to judge in the course of intersection.

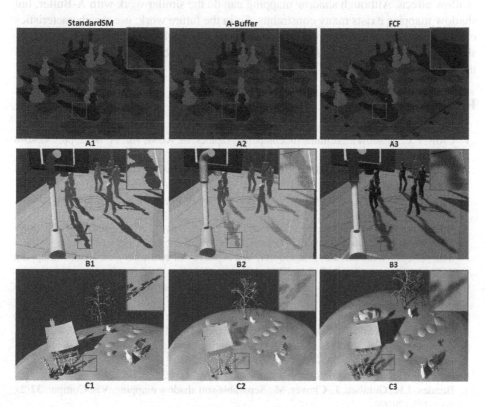

Fig. 5. The results.

6   Conclusions and Future Work

This paper presents the real-time soft shadow algorithm by A-Buffer to generate better soft effects. After that, to use the tool A-Buffer that stores a list of fragments per pixel play a great role in the process of building a better soft shadows. In the shadow of the build process, although we only use the ray that shaded point along the occluders intersection with the area light to simply determine the shadow factor, but it doesn't have to take into account surface properties such as size and shape of the light source, and it can accommodate multiple light sources and dynamic light sources.

However, the soft shadow of A-Buffer also exist some incoming. First we have store the whole information of the scene, but these all information is not used by all, but also leads to the A-Buffer all the features of this tool could not be better use. In the end result, the shadow are light permeability problem needs further improvement.

One interesting future work is to use A-Buffer to generate faster and better soft shadow effects. Although shadow mapping can do the similar work with A-Buffer, but shadow mapping exists many constraints. So in the future work, use the characteristics of A-Buffer presents more algorithms to generate more high-quality and high-efficiency shadow algorithm. And more real-time soft shadow algorithm also will be improved and the effects will be better.

References

1. Crow, F.C.: Shadow algorithms for computer graphics. In: ACM, vol. 11, no. 2, pp. 242–248 (1977)
2. Williams, L.: Casting curved shadows on curved surfaces. ACM, vol. 12, no. 3, pp. 270–274 (1978)
3. Woo, A., Poulin, P., Fournier, A.: A survey of shadow algorithms. IEEE Comput. Graph. Appl. **10**(6), 13–32 (1990)
4. Hasenfratz, J.M., Lapierre, M., Holzschuch, N.: A survey of real-time soft shadows algorithms, vol. 22, no. 4, pp. 753–774. Blackwell Publishing, Hoboken (2003)
5. Scherzer, D., Wimmer, M., Purgathofer, W.: A survey of real-time hard shadow mapping methods. Comput. Graph. Forum **30**(1), 169–186 (2011)
6. Eisemann, E., Schwarz, M., Assarsson, U.: Real-time shadows. CRC Press, Boca Raton (2011)
7. Eisemann, E., Assarsson, U., Schwarz, M.: Efficient real-time shadows. In: ACM, p. 18 (2013)
8. Heidmann, T.: Real shadows, real time. Iris Universe **18**, 28–31 (1991)
9. Reeves, W.T., Salesin, D.H., Cook, R.L.: Rendering antialiased shadows with depth maps. In: ACM, vol. 21 no. 4, pp. 283–291 (1987)
10. Fernando, R.: Percentage-closer soft shadows. In: ACM, p. 35 (2005)
11. Buades, J.M., Gumbau, J., Chover, M.: Separable soft shadow mapping. Vis. Comput. **32**(2), 167–178 (2016)
12. Peters, C., Munstermann, C., Wetzstein, N.: Beyond hard shadows: Moment shadow maps for single scattering, soft shadows and translucent occluders. In: ACM, pp. 159–170 (2016)
13. Weiskopf, D., Ertl, T.: Shadow mapping based on dual depth layers, vol. 3, pp. 53–60 (2003)
14. Wang, Y., Molnar, S.: Second-depth shadow mapping. UNC-CS Technical report TR94-019 (1994)

15. Pagot, C.A., Comba, J.L.D., Oliveira, N.M.M.: Multiple-depth shadow maps. In: 17th Brazilian Symposium on, pp 308–315. IEEE (2004)
16. Liu, X., Hao, X., Huang, M.: Fast soft shadow by depth peeling. In: ACM, p. 126 (2010)
17. Heckbert, P.S., Herf, M.: Simulating soft shadows with graphics hardware. CARNEGIE-MELLON UNIV PITTSBURGH PA DEPT OF COMPUTER SCIENCE (1997)
18. Haeberli, P., Akeley, K.: The accumulation buffer: hardware support for high-quality rendering. ACM SIGGRAPH Comput. Graph. 24(4), 309–318 (1990)
19. Heidrich, W., Brabec, S., Seidel, H.P.: Soft shadow maps for linear lights. In: Péroche, B., Rushmeier, H. (eds.) Rendering Techniques 2000. EUROGRAPH, pp. 269–280. Springer, Vienna (2000). https://doi.org/10.1007/978-3-7091-6303-0_24
20. Ying, Z., Tang, M., Dong, J.: Soft shadow maps for area light by area approximation. In: Pacific Conference on Computer Graphics and Applications, pp. 442–443 (2002)
21. Agrawala, M., Ramamoorthi, R., Heirich, A.: Efficient Image-Based Methods for Rendering Soft Shadows, pp. 375–384. ACM Press/Addison-Wesley Publishing Co. (2000)
22. Atty, L., Holzschuch, N., Lapierre, M.: Soft shadow maps: efficient sampling of light source visibility, vol. 25, no. 4, pp. 725–741 Blackwell Publishing Ltd, Hoboken (2006)
23. Guennebaud, G., Barthe, L., Paulin, M.: Real-time soft shadow mapping by backprojection, pp. 227–234 (2006)
24. Carpenter, L.: The A-buffer, an antialiased hidden surface method. ACM Siggraph Comput. Graph. 18(3), 103–108 (1984)
25. Crassin, C.: Fast and accurate single-pass A-buffer using OpenGL 4.0+ (2010)
26. Xu, Z., Li, B., Cai, X.: Generate accurate soft shadows using complete occluder buffer. In: IEEE, pp. 97–104 (2015)
27. Samosky, J.T.: SectionView–a system for interactively specifying and visualizing sections through three-dimensional medical image data. Massachusetts Institute of Technology, Department of Electrical Engineering and Computer Science (1993)

Rock-Ring Accuracy Improvement in Infrared Satellite Image with Subpixel Edge Detection

Huan Zhang[✉], Cai Meng, and Zhaoxi Li

School of Astronautics, Beihang University, Beijing, China
huanzbuaa@foxmail.com

Abstract. The projection of space circle can be utilized to relative pose measurement of satellite targets. The accuracy of the ellipse parameter is crucial to the pose recovery precision. However, the image quality of space visible image and infrared image are poor. The conventional ellipse detection methods are mainly based on pixel-accuracy-wise edges and the detection accuracy are low which leads to errors in pose recovery. In this paper, a subpixel-accuracy-wise edges based fitting method is proposed to improve the ellipse accuracy. To realize this goal, we design ellipse based subpixel edge detection method. Experimental results show that the ellipse accuracy fitted by subpixel edge coordinate is higher than by pixel edge coordinate, especially when the ellipse is incomplete. Our method is the first one that present and validate that the subpixel edge coordinate is contribute to enhancing ellipse detection accuracy.

Keywords: Ellipse detection accuracy · Subpixel edge detection
Pose recovery

1 Introduction

Pose (position and orientation) estimation, or pose recovery is significant for on-orbit service robot to capture satellite target, or rendezvous and docking. Various methods have been studied to locate satellite pose in rendezvous and docking [1–5].

Among these methods, P1C, which estimates the circle pose by the correspondence of a single circle and its ellipse projection on a calibrated camera [6], attracted most interest, for on satellites the circular part like docking ring can be easily found [7–11]. Luckett studied the differences in pose estimation of non-cooperative satellite with different feature (corners, lines, and ellipses) [9, 14]. He concluded that PnP-based pose estimation was the most accurate but its robustness was the worst. While PnC based pose estimation was the most robust, even under noise situations.

Paper [11] has shown that the accuracy of the ellipse information, (i.e., lengths of major-axis and minor-axis, center position and inclination angle), has a great influence on the precision of pose recovery. However, the quality of the space based image is poor for there is no light diffuse reflection in space, which has great influence on the ellipse detection accuracy. Compared to visual image, the infrared image is less affected by illumination condition. Therefore, IR image is more suitable to be used to locate the satellite. While the resolution of infrared image is lower than visible image, it

© Springer Nature Singapore Pte Ltd. 2018
Y. Wang et al. (Eds.): IGTA 2018, CCIS 875, pp. 180–191, 2018.
https://doi.org/10.1007/978-981-13-1702-6_18

may leads to lower ellipse extraction accuracy. On these basis, this paper devotes to improving the ellipse parameters accuracy on low resolution infrared satellite images.

In the state-of-art ellipse detection methods, most of them are based on the ellipse pixel-wise edge extraction and ellipse fitting. That is, they firstly detect the pixels on the target edge contours, and then fit the ellipse by the coordinate of all these pixels on the edges, where the coordinate is pixel level. There is no concern about the accuracy of ellipse detection. Research [15] shows that the error of fitting ellipse will increase when some of the edge contours are missing, especially when the edges to fit ellipse are in the smooth curvature arcs. By adding condition, the fitted curve can be constrained to be an ellipse, but DLS didn't improve the fitting accuracy [16]. Ellifit studies fitting accuracy while does not utilize the subpixel edges [25].

In this paper, we propose that the ellipse accuracy can be improved by fitting the ellipse with the subpixel-wise edge coordinate. In our method, we first detect the ellipses based on pixel-wise edges. Then for the ellipses with incomplete edge, the subpixel-wise position of the edges are extracted based on the ellipses that previously fitted on pixel-wise edges. Finally these ellipses are refined by fitting them based on the subpixel locations of the edges. The results of the synthetic and real image (visible image and infrared image) experiments showed that the subpixel-wise edge extraction has little influence when the ellipse edge are nearly complete, but have obvious effect when about 50% of the ellipse edge are missing.

2 Ellipse Based Subpixel Edge Detection

Although it is possible to fit an ellipse with a small number of points, there is a prerequisite: the point coordinate must be accurate. The basic premise can't be satisfied in digital images, where the edge point coordinates are discrete rather than actual and precise. This leads to a certain deviation in the solution, especially when the arc segments are very short [17]. If the total points on an ellipse is less than 50% in the image, the error will greatly affect the fitting accuracy of the ellipse. Even more the fitting result is far from the original ellipse. That is why we devote to validate that improving the precision of the edge is helpful for improving the detection accuracy.

Current ellipse detection algorithms could be categorized into three groups: optimization based algorithms [16], Hough transform based algorithms and edge following algorithms [18]. We select the arc-based ellipse detection method [19] as the basic ellipse detection method. The Hough transform based algorithm itself can detect incomplete ellipses, while the high precision coordinate would lead to higher computation cost. And the least square based methods are sensitive to outliners.

We will first introduce our improved arc-based ellipse detection method and then introduce our ellipse-based subpixel edge detection method. As mentioned above, current arc-based ellipse detection and fitting methods are based on the pixel position of the target contours [19, 20], the coordinate is pixel level [21–24]. While we would fit ellipse on the sub-pixel coordinates.

2.1 Ellipse Detection Method

We referred and optimized the edge grouping based ellipse detection algorithm. Original detection algorithm consists of ellipse curve extraction, curve grouping and ellipse fitting.

A. Ellipse Curve Extraction

The ellipse curve extraction include line segmentation and curve segmentation. In line segmentation, canny operator is utilized to extract edge image. In order to reduce the computational complexity, edges are approximated by the DP algorithm. Then edge-contours are divided into curve segments with certain conditions: angle condition, curvature condition and length condition.

B. Curve Grouping and Ellipse Fitting

The grouping approach utilizes the angle and distance relation between the end points of adjacent arc segments to divides arcs from a same ellipse into a group. In real images, one ellipse may be divided into many arcs due to noise or other interference. So they implement global grouping.

2.2 Ellipse Based Subpixel Edge Detection

Our improved subpixel edge detection method would be applied in the ellipse fitting step. The edge pixels on the fitted ellipse are utilized to acquire the subpixel coordinate.

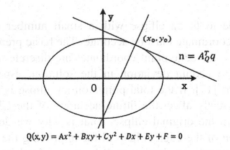

Fig. 1. Sketch map of ellipse based subpixel edge detection method.

As in Fig. 1, elliptic curves can be represented as:

$$Q(x, y) = Ax^2 + Bxy + Cy^2 + Dx + Ey + F = 0 \tag{1}$$

The quadratic equation can also be written as:

$$q^T A_Q q = 0 \tag{2}$$

where q is the homogeneous coordinate vector:

$$q = \begin{bmatrix} x \\ y \\ 1 \end{bmatrix} \quad A_Q = \begin{bmatrix} A & B/2 & D/2 \\ B/2 & C & E/2 \\ D/2 & E/2 & F \end{bmatrix} \tag{3}$$

The normal n of the ellipse is written as:

$$n = A_Q^T q \tag{4}$$

Set the point of tangency on the fitted ellipse as $P(x_0, y_0)$.

If the point P isn't on the edge image, take the closest point on the edge image as P. Then take two points at equal intervals on both sides of the point of tangency respectively, which are defined as P_1, P_2, P_3, P_4. The distance l between P_1 and P_2 is set to 1.4 times of pixel width.

In the image, edges are usually considered as gray scale step. On the edge contour, the place that the gray scale changes most acutely is the precise subpixel location. As in Fig. 3, the coordinate k is corresponding sub-pixel positions of edges. According to the characteristics of grayscale distribution function, the discrete gray values can be fitted into three order polynomial functions:

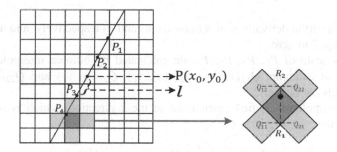

Fig. 2. The adjacent point of tangent point on the normal line.

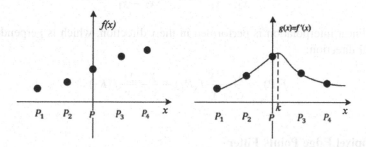

Fig. 3. The characteristics of grayscale distribution.

$$f(x) = a_0x^3 + a_1x^2 + a_2x + a_3 \tag{5}$$

The distance between P and k is:

$$\overline{Pk} = -a_1/3a_0 \tag{6}$$

Set Δx, Δy to be the offset for subpixel location relative to the central pixel:

$$\Delta x = \overline{Pk}\cos\theta \quad \Delta y = \overline{Pk}\sin\theta \quad \theta = \frac{1}{2}\arctan\frac{B}{A-C} \tag{7}$$

The subpixel coordinate can be obtained by:

$$(x + \Delta x, y + \Delta y) \tag{8}$$

Calculating coefficient of three polynomial curve by least square method, and minimize the sum of squared error S.

$$S = \sum_{i=1}^{n}\left(y_i - a_0x^3 - a_1x^2 - a_2x - a_3\right)^2 \tag{9}$$

Calculates partial derivatives of S to a_0, a_1, a_2 and a_3 respectively, and make partial differential equal to zero.

The gray scale of P_1, P_2, P_3, P_4 are calculated by bilinear interpolation. Take point P_4 as an example. $Q_{11}(x_1, y_1)$, $Q_{12}(x_2, y_1)$, $Q_{21}(x_1, y_2)$ and $Q_{22}(x_2, y_2)$ are adjacent pixels, as in Fig. 2.

Linear interpolation is first carried out in the x direction, which is same as the normal direction:

$$f(R_1) \approx \frac{x_2 - x}{x_2 - x_1}f(Q_{11}) + \frac{x - x_1}{x_2 - x_1}f(Q_{21})$$
$$f(R_2) \approx \frac{x_2 - x}{x_2 - x_1}f(Q_{12}) + \frac{x - x_1}{x_2 - x_1}f(Q_{22}) \tag{10}$$

Then linear interpolation is performed in the y direction, which is perpendicular to the normal direction:

$$f(P) \approx \frac{y_2 - y}{y_2 - y_1}f(R_1) + \frac{y - y_1}{y_2 - y_1}f(R_2) \tag{11}$$

2.3   Subpixel Edge Points Filter

Figure 4 left shows some pixel-wise edge positions (red '+' mark) and their subpixel-wise edge positions (blue '*' mark). We sort the elliptic edges pixels according to the deviation difference. The deviation difference is calculated by the city distance between pixel-wise position and its subpixel-wise position:

$$s = |\Delta x| + |\Delta y| \tag{12}$$

Where Δx and Δy are difference of pixel-wise position coordinate and subpixel-wise position coordinate. In our experiment, we choose frontier 80% of the sorted edge pixels. Figure 4 right, shows the subpixel-wise positions of the selected pixels.

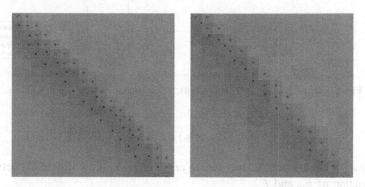

Fig. 4. Pixel coordinate and subpixel coordinate of the subpixel edge detection methods. (Color figure online)

3 Experiment

3.1 Experiment on Synthetic Ellipse Data

In this experiment, we get the edge pixels from a ground-truth ellipse E_g whose center (u_0, v_0) is (30, 30), semi-major axis a and semi-minor axis b length are 25 and 10 respectively, and the inclination angle η is 1.047 rad. The ground truth ellipse is shown as red-lined ellipse Fig. 5.

$$\begin{cases} x = a\cos\theta \\ y = b\sin\theta \end{cases}, \ \theta \in [0, 360°) \tag{13}$$

Then these point coordinates are rounded to its nearest integer to simulate the pixel-wise location of edge points. With these pixel-wise locations, an ellipse is fitted and expressed as E_{pix}. Next these point coordinates are cut to keep only one decimal to simulate the sub-pixel-wise locations. With these subpixel-wise locations, an ellipse is also fitted and expressed as E_{sub}. To compare the fitting accuracy, four criteria are used.

(1) Center distance error Δ_r. 'Center distance error' is the Euclidian distance between the centers of the fitted ellipse E_{fit} and E_g.

$$\Delta_r = \left\| (u_0, v_0)_{E_g} - (u_0, v_0)_{E_{fit}} \right\|_2 \tag{14}$$

(2) Overlap ratio $S_\cap$. Overlap ratio is defined as,

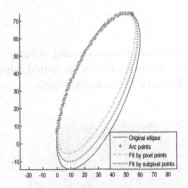 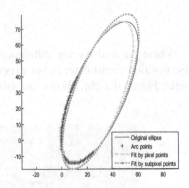

Fig. 5. Fit ellipse on synthetic elliptical arc points. (Color figure online)

$$S_\cap = \left(E_g \cap E_{fit}\right)/\left(E_g \cup E_{fit}\right) \cdot 100\% \tag{15}$$

(3) Inclination angle error Δ_η. Inclination angle error Δ_η is the difference between the inclination of E_{fit} and E_g.

$$\Delta_\eta = \left|\eta_{E_g} - \eta_{E_{fit}}\right| \tag{16}$$

(4) Relative eccentricity. Relative eccentricity error is defined as,

$$\sigma_\varepsilon = \left|\varepsilon_{E_g} - \varepsilon_{E_{fit}}\right|/\varepsilon_{E_g} \cdot 100\% \tag{17}$$

A. Test with Whole Ellipse Edge

In the first comparison test, the whole ellipse edge points are utilized to fit the ellipse. The fitting error of E_{pix} and E_{sub} are shown in Table 1. From this table, it can be drawn that if the edge is complete, the fitting accuracies of pixel-based locations and subpixel-based locations are approximate.

Table 1. Synthetic complete ellipse fitting result.

	Δ_r/pixel	$S_\cap$/%	Δ_η/°	σ_ε/%
E_{pix}	0.094	96.5	0.688	0.47
E_{sub}	0.030	96.5	0.631	0.48

B. Tests with Incomplete Edges

In the following tests, we used different parts of the ground-truth ellipse to fit the ellipse to simulate the incomplete ellipse case. The part of the edge are shown in Fig. 5 with '*'-star mark. The red lined ellipse is E_g, the green shot-line-typed ellipse is E_{pix}, and the blue dot-line-typed ellipse is E_{sub}. From Fig. 5, it is clear that there are notable difference compared to E_g. But E_{sub} is closer to E_g than E_{pix}. The fitting error of E_{pix} and E_{sub} are shown in Table 2. They also indicate that the ellipse fitting accuracy of sub-pixel coordinate is higher than that of pixel coordinate when the ellipse is incomplete.

Table 2. Synthetic elliptical arc points fitting result.

	Δ_r/pixel	$S_\cap$/%	Δ_η/°	σ_ε/%		Δ_r/pixel	$S_\cap$/%	Δ_η/°	σ_ε/%
E_{pix}^1	3.197	79.17	2.159	1.60	E_{pix}^2	3.044	84.59	3.573	1.60
E_{sub}^1	1.412	87.25	0.955	0.75	E_{sub}^2	1.280	91.23	2.312	1.95

3.2 Incomplete Ellipse Detection in Real Images

This experiment aims at detecting ellipse on the incomplete real image. Compare the effect of pixel coordinate and subpixel coordinate on the ellipse detection, which can be seen in Fig. 6 and Table 3. The green ellipses are ground truth. The purple ellipses are detection results by pixel coordinate and the blue ellipses are the results by subpixel coordinate.

3.3 Ellipse Detection in Complex Scene

This experiment is to compare ellipse detection results in real complex scenes. The green ellipses are ground truth. The purple ellipses are detection results by pixel coordinate and the blue ellipses are the results by subpixel coordinate, as seen in Fig. 7.

Table 3. Ellipse detection in satellite models images.

	Δ_r/pixel	$S_\cap$/%	Δ_η/°	σ_ε/%
E_{pix}^1	9.746	94.845	19.84	12.33
E_{sub}^1	**3.037**	94.405	**5.98**	**1.42**
E_{pix}^2	6.240	97.33	14.951	8.07
E_{sub}^2	**2.796**	**97.41**	**1.014**	**3.31**
E_{pix}^3	6.612	96.11	5.233	14.915
E_{sub}^3	**3.200**	**98.01**	**1.473**	**9.845**

The fitting error of E_{pix} and E_{sub} are shown in Table 4. In the complex scenes, there being many interfering, some ellipse cannot be fitted accurately by pixel coordinate. The ellipse detection at subpixel coordinate still outperform that at pixel coordinate.

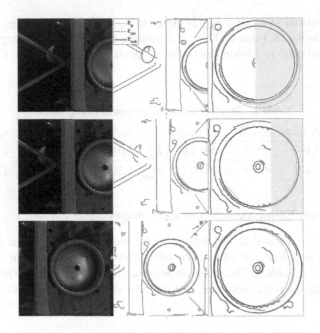

Fig. 6. Ellipse detection in satellite models images. (Color figure online)

Table 4. Ellipse detection in complex satellite images.

	Δ_r/pixel	$S_\cap$/%	Δ_η/°	σ_ε/%		Δ_r/pixel	$S_\cap$/%	Δ_η/°	σ_ε/%
E_{pix}^1	5.506	88.72	4.333	2.63	E_{pix}^2	1.618	97.89	1.097	3.90
E_{sub}^1	**2.306**	86.39	**1.068**	**2.35**	E_{sub}^2	**1.377**	93.78	**1.011**	**1.78**

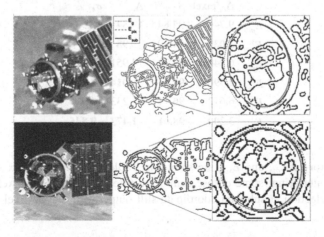

Fig. 7. Ellipse detection in complex satellite images. (Color figure online)

Table 5. Ellipse detection result in infrared images.

	Δ_r/pixel	$S_\cap$/%	Δ_η/°	σ_ε/%		Δ_r/pixel	$S_\cap$/%	Δ_η/°	σ_ε/%
E_{pix}^1	1.985	93.82	38.264	5.91	E_{pix}^4	2.028	95.07	5.027	6.36
E_{sub}^1	**1.799**	**97.11**	42.023	**1.64**	E_{sub}^4	**1.611**	94.42	**2.320**	10.96
E_{pix}^2	2.622	88.89	4.461	36.41	E_{pix}^5	5.258	94.12	6.025	13.09
E_{sub}^2	**1.563**	**99.28**	**0.930**	**3.90**	E_{sub}^5	**2.461**	94.07	6.463	**9.32**
E_{pix}^3	2.404	94.81	11.671	7.32	E_{pix}^6	6.209	96.68	43.845	3.82
E_{sub}^3	**1.550**	**96.27**	**6.981**	**5.50**	E_{sub}^6	**1.599**	95.76	**15.973**	**0.27**

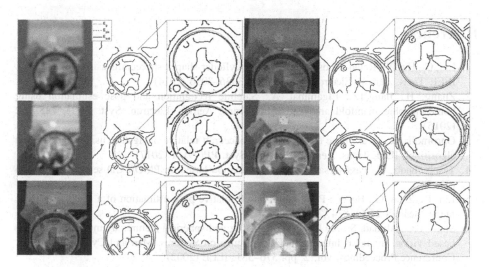

Fig. 8. Ellipse detection in infrared images. Green ellipse are ground truth ellipse. Purple ellipses are fitting by pixel coordinate, and blue ellipse are fitting by subpixel coordinate. (Color figure online)

3.4 Ellipse Detection in Infrared Images

This experiment is to detect ellipse in the infrared images. The image quality of the infrared images is poor, while the ellipse detection at subpixel coordinate method performs better than the detection at pixel coordinate method. Even in the blur image, as in Fig. 8, the ellipse detection at subpixel coordinate still works well. The green ellipses are ground truth. The purple ellipses are detection results by pixel coordinate and the blue ellipses are the results by subpixel coordinate. Quantitative experiment results are present in Table 5.

4   Conclusion

This paper is the first one that validate enhancing ellipse edge precision is helpful to improve the ellipse detection accuracy, especially in incomplete ellipse detection. To validate this hypothesis, we present our subpixel edge detection method. And then we take several experiments on synthetic and real images. Experiments validate that when the edge contours missing lightly, the ellipse fitting accuracy by the pixel coordinate of edge is almost similar to the fitting accuracy by subpixel coordinate of edge. When the edge contours missing largely, the ellipse fitting accuracy by the subpixel coordinate of edge is much higher than the fitting accuracy by pixel coordinate of edge.

References

1. Liu, C., Hu, W.: Relative pose estimation for cylinder-shaped spacecrafts using single image. IEEE Trans. Aerosp. Electron. Syst. **50**(4), 3036–3056 (2014)
2. Zhang, H., Jiang, Z., Elgammal, A.: Satellite recognition and pose estimation using homeomorphic manifold analysis. IEEE Trans. Aerosp. Electron. Syst. **51**(1), 785–792 (2015)
3. Opromolla, R., et al.: Pose estimation for spacecraft relative navigation using model-based algorithms. IEEE Trans. Aerosp. Electron. Syst. **PP**(99), 1 (2017)
4. Tzschichholz, T.: Passive satellite pose estimation based on PMD/CCD sensor data fusion (2015)
5. Liu, L., Zhao, G., Bo, Y.: Point cloud based relative pose estimation of a satellite in close range. Sensors **16**(6), 824 (2016)
6. Shiu, Y.C., Ahmad, S.: 3D location of circular and spherical features by monocular model-based vision. In: IEEE International Conference on Systems, Man and Cybernetics, 1989. Conference Proceedings, vol. 2, pp. 576–581. IEEE (2002)
7. Zheng, Y., Ma, W., Liu, Y.: Another way of looking at monocular circle pose estimation. IEEE In: International Conference on Image Processing, pp. 861–864. IEEE (2008)
8. Wang, G., Wu, J., Ji, Z.: Single view based pose estimation from circle or parallel lines. Pattern Recogn. Lett. **29**(7), 977–985 (2008)
9. Miao, X., Zhu, F.: Monocular vision pose measurement based on docking ring component. Acta Optica Sinica **33**(4), 0412006 (2013)
10. Zhang, L., et al.: Improvement of position and orientation measurement algorithm of monocular vision based on circle features. J. Hefei Univ. Technol. **32**(11), 1669–1673 (2009)
11. Lu, W., Jinhua, Yu., Tan, J.: Direct inverse randomized Hough transform for incomplete ellipse detection in noisy images. J. Pattern Recognit. Res. **1**, 13–24 (2014)
12. Rueda, S., et al.: Evaluation and comparison of current fetal ultrasound image segmentation methods for biometric measurements: a grand challenge. IEEE Trans. Med. Imaging **33**(4), 797–813 (2014)
13. Yao, P., Evans, G., Calway, A.: Using affine correspondence to estimate 3-D facial pose. In: Proceedings of the 2001 International Conference on Image Processing, vol. 3. IEEE (2001)
14. Luckett, J.A.: Comparison of Three Machine Vision Pose Estimation Systems Based on Corner, Line, and Ellipse Extraction for Satellite Grasping. West Virginia University, Morgantown (2012)

15. Matei, B., Meer, P.: Reduction of bias in maximum likelihood ellipse fitting. In: Proceedings of the 15th International Conference on Pattern Recognition, 2000, vol. 3. IEEE (2000)
16. Fitzgibbon, A., Pilu, M., Fisher, R.B.: Direct least square fitting of ellipses. IEEE Trans. Pattern Anal. Mach. Intell. **21**(5), 476–480 (1999)
17. Liu, C., Weiduo, H.: Ellipse fitting for imaged cross sections of a surface of revolution. Pattern Recognit. **48**(4), 1440–1454 (2015)
18. Wong, C.Y., et al.: A survey on ellipse detection methods. In: 2012 IEEE International Symposium on Industrial Electronics (ISIE). IEEE (2012)
19. Nguyen, T.M., Ahuja, S., Wu, Q.M.J.: A real-time ellipse detection based on edge grouping. In: IEEE International Conference on Systems, Man and Cybernetics, 2009, SMC 2009. IEEE (2009)
20. Qiao, Yu., Ong, S.H.: Arc-based evaluation and detection of ellipses. Pattern Recognit. **40** (7), 1990–2003 (2007)
21. Kim, E., Haseyama, M., Kitajima, H.: Fast and robust ellipse extraction from complicated images. In: Proceedings of IEEE Information Technology and Applications (2002)
22. Mai, F., et al.: A hierarchical approach for fast and robust ellipse extraction. Pattern Recognit. **41**(8), 2512–2524 (2008)
23. Chia, A.Y.S., et al.: A split and merge based ellipse detector with self-correcting capability. IEEE Trans. Image Process. **20**(7), 1991–2006 (2011)
24. Cakir, H.I., Benligiray, B. and Topal, C.: Combining feature-based and model-based approaches for robust ellipse detection. In: 2016 24th European Signal Processing Conference (EUSIPCO). IEEE (2016)
25. Prasad, D.K., Leung, M.K.H., Quek, C.: ElliFit: an unconstrained, non-iterative, least squares based geometric ellipse fitting method. Pattern Recognit. **46**(5), 1449–1465 (2013)

A Combined Local-Global Match for Optical Flow

Yueran Zu[1], Wenzhong Tang[1], Xiuguo Bao[2(✉)], Ke Gao[3], and Mingdong Zhang[2]

[1] School of Computer Science and Engineering, Beihang Universtiy, Beijing 100191, China
{yueranzu,tangwenzhong}@buaa.edu.cn
[2] The National Computer Network Emergency Response Technical Team,
Coordination Center of China, Beijing 100029, China
baoxiuguo@139.com, zdm@cncert.org.cn
[3] Institute of Computing Technology Chinese Academy of Sciences, Beijing 100080, China
kegao@ict.ac.cn

Abstract. Optical flow estimation is still an open question in computer vision. Matching is the initialization of the final optical flow results. A good matching is important for the flow. In this paper, a combined local-global matching method is proposed. The local matching method and the global method are integrated together to make a trade-off between the large displacement and local consistency of optical flow. Extensive experiments on state-of-art challenging datasets MPI-Sintel show that the proposed method is efficient and effective.

Keywords: Optical flow · Matching method · Non-local · Global

1 Introduction

The optical flow estimation is a building block of computer vision. The optical flow plays an important role in many video related tasks such as video segmentation [1], video object detection [2], action recognition [3], drive assistance [4, 5], etc. There are abundant literatures of this topic since the pioneering work by Horn and Schunck (HS method) in 1981 [6]. However, it is still an open question, especially in the case of large displacement, motion discontinuities and occlusion, which are often presented in real-world videos.

The optical flow is defined as an energy minimization framework since the HS method proposed. Many effective methods are based on the energy function and different improvements are made to the function. However, these approaches show good performance only in the case of small displacements optical flow and fail in large displacement occasions. The cause of failure is mainly the bad initialization of the energy minimization.

A better initialization for optical flow is very important. Image pyramid scheme is as used in both the traditional minimization function and the modern sparse to dense methods. The traditional coarse-to-fine is proposed in [7]. The modern sparse to dense methods keep leading results in challenging dataset. The sparse step is the matching method and the dense one is the interpolation algorithm. The sparse step can be seen as the initialization of the dense step. As a result, the matching methods play an important

© Springer Nature Singapore Pte Ltd. 2018
Y. Wang et al. (Eds.): IGTA 2018, CCIS 875, pp. 192–200, 2018.
https://doi.org/10.1007/978-981-13-1702-6_19

role in the whole method. Matching techniques have made great advances recently. The two most famous matching methods are the CPM [8] and the DCflow [9]. The CPM is a efficient coarse-to-fine pyramid matching method designed for large displacement optical flow. The DCflow is an accurate matching method by direct cost volume processing which performs well on the MPI-Sintel dataset.

In this paper, a combined local-global matching method is proposed, called LGM, which shows both accuracy and efficiency. The observation of this paper is the CPM performs better than the DCflow in small displacements while the DCflow shows advantage in large displacements than the CPM. As a result, the LGM is proposed to combine the strength of two matching methods in a rather simple way. Extensive experiments show the LGM performs better in the MPI-Sintel dataset. Figure 1 shows the result of the flow.

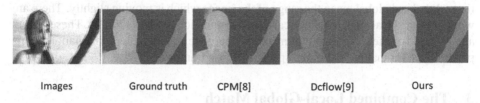

| Images | Ground truth | CPM[8] | Dcflow[9] | Ours |

Fig. 1. Comparison of the state-of-art flow, the proposed flow performs best.

2   Related Work

This paper only discusses the related sparse-to-dense literatures and does not review the whole literatures on optical flow. To see the survey of the entire optical flow publications like [10, 11] are referred. In this section, the related works are reviewed in three parts: matching, interpolation, and the combined local and global methods.

Matching.   The milestone work of Brox and Malik [12] first introduces the descriptor matching term to the traditional minimization function. Since then, several works [13, 14, 15] using matching term are proposed. Xu et al. [13] integrates SIFT descriptor [16] and Patch Match [17] as the initial flow at each coarse-to-fine level. The advantage is preserving the motion detail, however due to the propagation error and sparsity of the matching, they still fail in very large displacements. Weinzaepfel et al. [14] propose dense correspondences matching by means of interleaved convolutions and max-pooling layered operations. The deep matching is limited by its efficiency. The work closely related to this paper is the CPM flow and DCflow. Hu [8] integrates SIFT, Patch Match and image pyramid together to get an efficient coarse-to-fine matching method for optical flow with large displacement. The CPM is global in the coarse layer and local in other layers when searching the correspondence. The DCflow utilizes a semi-global matching method in the feature space, which is more advantage in large displacements. This paper combines the local, global and semi-global together to get a better matching for the optical flow.

Interpolation. In recent works, the interpolation is used widely for optical flow estimation. The most popular one is the Epicflow [18]. It is an edge preserving interpolation method by using the geodesic distance instead of the Euclidean distance after deep matching. To make the interpolation more robust and not vulnerable to input matching noise, the robust interpolation method Ricflow [19] takes superpixel flow as the matching initialization. Moreover, the assumption of the interpolation is each superpixel has the same affine model. Each model is estimated robustly from its support matching neighbors based on a graph constructed. A propagation mechanism is proposed to estimate the models. In this paper, the two interpolation methods are both used as a post processing step.

Combination. The combination of local and global methods for optical flow has last for a long time. As the classical HS method is global and the LK method is local. At first, global and global mean the range of the image which is moving slightly. There are works linking local and global optical flow computation, such as [20, 21]. These papers are all based on the traditional minimization energetic equation, the combination in this paper is just for match used in the sparse to dense framework.

3 The Combined Local-Global Match

In this section, a combined local-global matching method for optical flow is presented. The input of the optical flow is two consecutive images I_1 and I_2. The matches is denoted as $M = \{p_1, p_2\}$, where p1 is the pixel from I_1 and p_2 is the pixel from I_2. The matches are the initial correspondences by the matching method,and the final goal of optical flow is a dense correspondence filed for every pixel of I1, the flow field is F from I_1 to I_2.

In Sect. 3.1, the local matching efficient coarse-to-fine pyramid matching is analyzed. Though the CPM is designed for the large displacement, the experiments show that it takes advantage in small displacement. In Sect. 3.2 the direct column matching is made cleared. A semi-global matching method is used to extend the range of search area, which performs well in large displacement. In Sect. 3.3 the combined local-global match is presented. The proposed LGM method make complementary of local matching and global matching in a simple way.

3.1 The Local Matching

The CPM flow is an efficient coarse-to-fine pyramid matching for large displacement.

It is designed by considering global and local smoothness in different layers. The detailed steps are as follows.

To begin with, the coarse-to-fine pyramid is constructed by downsampling two images I_1 and I_2 with a fixed ratio, like 1/2. About 3 or 5 image layers are constructed. Then, the matching is made from coarse-to-fine layers. In the coarsest layer, the image is very small and the search area of matching method is the maximum image width or height. In the next layers, the search radius is settled to a small value, like 4 pixels. The matching result of each layer is propagated to the next layer as an initialization. The propagation between adjacent layers multiplies the scaling factor of the pyramid and can recover the matching of small structures which is vanished on higher levels. The matching method in each layer is used a patch match like algorithm. The neighborhood propagation and random search are the main processes in a grid structure instead of dense pixels, which make the matching efficient.

Formally, the input two images I_1 and $I_2 \in R^{2}$ and S = $\{s_m\}$ at position $\{p(s_m)\}$ in every d × d non-overlapping block. The matching goal is to find the correspondence position of the seed in I_2. $f(s_m) = M(p(s_m)) - p(s_m)$. $M(p(s_m))$ is the matching result. $f(s_m)$ denotes the flow of the current seed. Flow values are propagated from neighbor seeds n_m to current if they are smaller than the current one. As shown in Eq. (1). The $C(f())$ denotes the match cost of the two patches centered in $p(s_m)$ of I_1 and $p(s_m) + f$ ().of I_2. The cost are computed by SIFT descriptor as SIFT flow [22]. The entire 128 dimensions is used for matching, and the SIFT feature is computed for each pixel on all pyramid layers with a same size patch size 8 × 8.

$$f\left(s_m\right) = \text{argmin} \left(C\left(f\left(s_m\right)\right)\right), s \in \{s_m\} U n_m \tag{1}$$

3.2   The Global Matching

The global matching means the searching area is in wide range. The DCflow is an accurate algorithm by direct cost volume processing. The direct approach benefits the structure of leading stereo matching pipelines. Such approaches have been considered impractical due to the big size of the cost volume. The DCflow make it possible by exploiting the regularity of the volume and adapting semi-global matching.

The procedures of the algorithm is cost volume construction and cost volume processing based on a semi-global matching (SGM). In the cost volume construction step: the four-dimensional cost volume is populated by distances between pairs of feature vectors (f_1, f_2). The feature space embedding F1, F2 $\in R^{MN \times d}$. The feature embedding is computed by a convolutional network [23]. The loss function is as shown in Eq. (2). In the triple loss, the xa is an anchor sampled randomly from the first image, the xp denotes the corresponding positive patch in the second image, and the xn is the negative patch.

$$L(\theta) = 1/|D|^* \text{sum}\{[m+||f(xa_i; \theta)- f(xp_i; \theta)||^2-k||(xa_i; \theta)- f(xn_i;\theta)||^2]\};$$
$$\text{s.t.   } i = 1 \text{ to } |D|. \tag{2}$$

The search space is discrete and rectangular. R = $\{-r_{nax}, r_{max}\}$, and the rmax denotes the maximal displacement. The cost volume of optical flow is $C \in R^{MN \times |R|2}$. The cost can be computed as

$$C(p, v)= 1 - \left(F1_p\right) F2_{p+v.} \tag{3}$$

The SGM is adapted to the optical flow estimation and a discrete energy is defined. For more details, the [8] is referred.

3.3 The Combined Local-Global Matching

Given the local and global match, will the combination of them get a better result? The merit and demerits of each algorithm is analyzed and the combined local-global matching (LGM) is proposed.

The CPM considers local by limited search radius in a small range. The global is considered only in the coarsest layer, and is propagated by the pyramid scheme. Though some large displacements are captured, others with more complex changes or very large ones are lost. And the experiments in Sect. 4 also show that the CPM cannot deal some large displacement.

The DCflow utilize a more large range, and a semi-global matching method. The feature embedding is more robust. However, the small displacements are neglected and easily lost.

As a result, this paper combines the advantages of both matching method. The CPM and the DCflow matching are integrated together by union the matching result together. The proposed LGM makes best use of the complementary advantages of local, semi-global and global. On the feature hand, the CNN feature and the SIFT feature can be made a complementary to each other. As shown in Eq. (4), the match are combined by just union the two matches together. Other methods like the average of them are tried, the union one performs the best.

$$M_{lgm} = M_{cpm} U M_{dc} \tag{4}$$

4 Experiment

The proposed LGM is evaluated on the challenging MPI-Sintel dataset for large displacement optical flow estimation. MPI-Sintel is formed from selected frames with large displacements of an animated movie. There are two versions of datasets, the clean and final version. The final version is more challenging than the clean one which is with motion, deblur and atmospheric effects.

As follows, the analysis of the local and global matching methods is shown in Sect. 4.1, and the results of the MPI-Sintel dataset is shown in Sect. 4.2.

4.1 Analysis of the Matching Method

The matching methods are analyzed by two popular interpolation methods the Epicflow [18] and the Ricflow [19]. The Fig. 2 shows the EPE (end point error) of the four works. The lower of EPE means the better performance. The x axis is the EPE, and the y denotes the group number of the MPI-Sintel training set with 23 groups of images. A statistic is made, the larger EPE means larger displacement optical flow. As presented by Fig. 2(a), the dc match is better than the cpm match in the larger displacements. While as shown in Fig. 2(b), the CPM performs better in small displacements. The two interpolation methods show that the Epicflow performs better than the Ricflow.

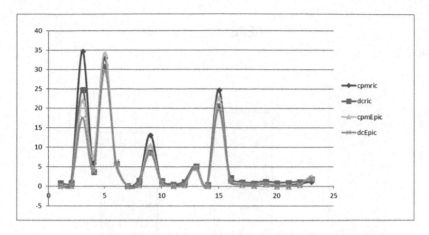

(a)

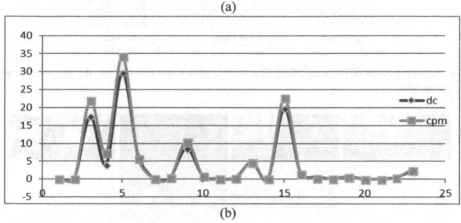

(b)

Fig. 2. Comparisons of four methods, the cpm, dc denotes the two matching algorithm, and the epic and ric denotes two interpolation methods.

4.2 Results on MPI-Sintel

The MPI-Sintel is a challenging dataset for optical flow evaluation. For the interpolation step, the Epic is chosen. The comparison is made on the training set first. As shown in Fig. 3, when using the same interpolation method, the DC performs better than the CPM and the propsed LGM performs the best. It verifies the efficiency of the combined local-global matching, which integrates the merits of CPM and DC into a stronger matching method. Furthermore, Fig. 4 show some quality examples from the training set. It also proves the good performance of the LGM flow.

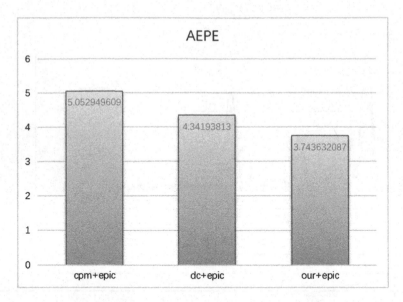

Fig. 3. Comparison of the state-of-art flow on the MPI-sintel training set, the proposed flow performs best.

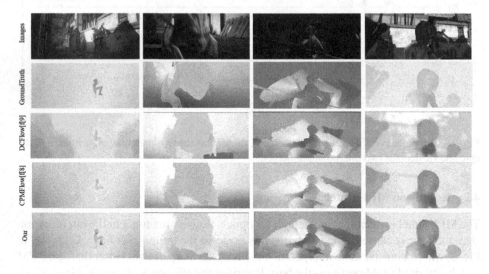

Fig. 4. Quality examples on the MPI-sintel training set. Each column shows from top to bottom: the first image, ground truth, the state-of-art methods and the proposed LGMflow.

Evaluations are made on the test set of MPI-Sintel. The metrics are used as the public assessment website. EPE-all means end point error over the complete frames, EPE matched means endpoint error over regions that remain visible in adjacent frames, EPE unmatched presents endpoint error over regions that are visible only in one of two adjacent frames, d0−10 denotes endpoint error over regions closer than 10 pixels to the nearest occlusion boundary, d10–60 denotes endpoint error over regions between 10 and 60 pixels apart from the nearest occlusion boundary. Table 1 shows the results of 6 state-of-art method on the challenging final version. The proposed LGM flow outperforms all of the method, except 3 metrics from the DCflow. The reason is that, the interpolation we use is not the same with DCflow. The DCflow makes a time consuming post processing step. In this paper, only Epic is used for interpolation.

Table 1. The results on the MPI-sintel test set final pass. EPE-all (end point error over the complete frames), EPE matched (Endpoint error over regions that remain visible in adjacent frames), EPE unmatched (Endpoint error over regions that are visible only in one of two adjacent frames), d0–10 (Endpoint error over regions closer than 10 pixels to the nearest occlusion boundary), d10–60 (Endpoint error over regions between 10 and 60 pixels apart from the nearest occlusion boundary)

Method (final)	EPE all	EPE matched	EPE unmatched	d 0–10	d10–60
DCFlow [9]	5.119	2.283	28.228	4.665	2.108
RicFlow [19]	5.620	2.765	28.907	5.146	2.366
FlowNet2.0 [24]	5.739	2.752	30.108	4.818	2.557
CPM-Flow [8]	5.960	2.990	30.177	5.038	2.419
Epicflow [18]	6.285	3.060	32.564	5.205	2.611
Our	5.195	2.248	29.221	4.556	1.954

5   Conclusion

A local-global matching method for optical flow is proposed in this paper. Two popular matches are analyzed and combined together to get a better match for the optical flow estimation. The local matching and the global matching can be complementary for each other. Experiments on MPI-Sintel dataset show the efficiency of the LGM method than other competing methods. For future search, a better combination between matching and interpolation may improve the optical flow accuracy. Moreover, the traditional algorithms can be integrated with the modern CNN models.

Acknowledgments. This work was supported by National Natural Science Foundation of China(No. 51475025), Beijing Municipal Science and Technology Commission Project Z171100000117010, the National Key Research and Development Plan (Nos. 2016YFB0801203, 2016YFB0801200).

References

1. Ochs, P., Malik, J., et al.: Segmentation of moving objects by long term video analysis. TPAMI **36**(6), 1187–1200 (2014)
2. Xizhou, Z., Wang, Y. et al.: Flow-guided feature aggregation for video object detection. In: ICCV (2017)
3. Simonyan, K., Zisserman, A.: Two-stream convolutional networks for action recognition in videos. In: NIPS, vol. 1, no. 4, pp. 568–576 (2014)

4. Urtasun, R., Lenz, P., Geiger, A.: Are we ready for autonomous driving? The Kitti vision benchmark suite. In: CVPR, pp. 3354–3361 (2012)
5. Menze, M., Geiger, A.: Object scene flow for autonomous vehicles. In: CVPR 2015, pp. 3061–3070 (2015)
6. Horn, B.K.P., Schunck, B.G.: Determining optical flow. Artif. Intell. **17**(1), 185–203 (1981)
7. Lucas, B.D., Kanade, T.: An iterative image registration technique with an application to stereo vision. In: IJCAI, pp. 674–679 (1981)
8. Xu, J., Ranftl, R., et. al.: Accurate optical flow via direct cost volume processing. In: CVPR (2017)
9. Hu, Y., Song, R., et. al.: Efficient coarse-to-fine patch match for large displacement optical flow. In: CVPR, pp. 5704–5712 (2016)
10. Baker, S., Scharstein, D.: Lewis, J.P., et. al.: A database and evaluation methodology for optical flow. Int. J. Comput. Vis. **92**(1), 1–31 (2011)
11. Sun, D., Roth, S., Black, M.J.: A quantitative analysis of current practices in optical flow estimation and the principles behind them. Int. J. Comput. Vis. **106**(2), 115–137 (2014)
12. Brox, T., Malik, J.: Large displacement optical flow: descriptor matching in variational motion estimation. TPAMI. **33**(3), 500–513 (2011)
13. Xu, L., Jia, J., Matsushita, Y.: Motion detail preserving optical flow estimation. In: Computer Vision and Pattern Recognition, pp. 1293–1300 (2010)
14. Weinzaepfel, P., Revaud, J., Harchaoui, Z., Schmid, C.: Deepflow: large displacement optical flow with deep matching. In: ICCV, pp. 1385–1392 (2013)
15. Timofte, R., Gool, L.V.: Sparse flow: sparse matching for small to large displacement optical flow. In: WACV, pp. 1100–1106 (2015)
16. Lowe, D.G.: Distinctive image features from scale-invariant keypoints. Int. J. Comput. Vis. **60**(2), 91–110 (2004)
17. Barnes, C., Shechtman, E., Goldman, D.B., Finkelstein, A.: The generalized patchmatch correspondence algorithm. In: Daniilidis, K., Maragos, P., Paragios, N. (eds.) ECCV 2010. LNCS, vol. 6313, pp. 29–43. Springer, Heidelberg (2010). https://doi.org/10.1007/978-3-642-15558-1_3
18. Revaud. J, Weinzaepfel, P., et al.: Epicflow: edge-preservinginterpolation of correspondences for optical flow. In: CVPR, pp. 1164–1172 (2015)
19. Hu, Y. Li, Y.: Robust interpolation of correspondences for large displacement optical flow. In: CVPR (2017)
20. Niu, Y., Dick, A., Brooks, M.J.: Linking local and global optical flow computation by subspace regularization. Opt. Eng. **52**(3) (2013)
21. Jara-Wilde, J., Cerda, M.: An implementation of combined local-global optical flow. Image Processing On Line. pp. 139–158 (2015)
22. Liu, C., Yuen, J., Torralba, A.: Sift flow: dense correspondence across scenes and its applications. TPAMI **33**(5), 978–994 (2011)
23. Zbontar, J., LeCun, Y.: Stereo matching by training a convolutional neural network to compare image patches. JMLR (2016)
24. Ilg, E., Mayer, N., et al.: Flownet 2.0 evolution of optical flow estimation with deep networks. In: CVPR (2017)

Progressive Cross-Media Correlation Learning

Xin Huang and Yuxin Peng[✉]

Institute of Computer Science and Technology, Peking University,
Beijing 100871, China
pengyuxin@pku.edu.cn

Abstract. Cross-media retrieval aims to retrieve across different media types, such as image and text, whose key problem is to learn cross-media correlation from known training data. Existing methods indiscriminately take all data for model training, ignoring that there exist hard samples which lead to misleading and even noisy information, bringing negative effect especially in the early period of model training. Because cross-media training data is difficult to collect, the common challenge of small-scale training data makes this problem even severer to limit the robustness and accuracy of cross-media retrieval. For addressing the above problem, this paper proposes Progressive Cross-media Correlation Learning (PCCL) approach, which takes a large-scale cross-media dataset with general knowledge (reference data), to guide the correlation learning on another small-scale dataset (target data) via the progressive sample selection mechanism. Specifically, we first pre-train a hierarchical correlation learning network on reference data as reference model, which is used to assign samples in target data with different learning difficulties, via intra-media and inter-media relevance significance metric. Then, training samples in target data are selected with gradually ascending learning difficulties, so that the correlation learning process can progressively reduce the "heterogeneity gap" to enhance the model robustness and improve retrieval accuracy. We take our self-constructed large-scale XMediaNet dataset as the reference data, and the cross-media retrieval experiments on 2 widely-used datasets show PCCL outperforms 9 state-of-the-art methods.

1 Introduction

As the technologies of computer and digital transition have been rapidly developing, data of different media types such as image, text, audio and video is explosively growing and increasingly merging with each other. Human naturally has the ability to receive and integrate information from different sensory channels. For example, visual and auditory information can mutually boost to significantly increase the studying efficiency of human [1]. Therefore, cross-media retrieval has become a key technique of information acquisition, which can retrieve relevant results with different media types by a query of any media type [2]. For instance,

© Springer Nature Singapore Pte Ltd. 2018
Y. Wang et al. (Eds.): IGTA 2018, CCIS 875, pp. 201–211, 2018.
https://doi.org/10.1007/978-981-13-1702-6_20

users can retrieve the relevant images by a query of text. Cross-media retrieval can achieve the collaboration of multimedia information, which is significant for improving the information acquisition for human.

Cross-media retrieval is also a challenging problem, whose main challenge comes from the different representation forms of various media types due to the "heterogeneity gap". For example, we can naturally use visual representations as color and texture for image, which cannot be applied for text. However, although different media types have different representations, they can usually represent the same semantics (e.g., a photo of airplane and its text description). This inspires the mainstream idea of cross-media retrieval: to obtain common representations via correlation learning, so that the cross-media similarity can be directly measured by distance metric.

With this idea, many methods have been proposed, including shallow learning methods [3–5] and depp neural network (DNN) based methods [6–8]. They are all proposed to learn cross-media correlation from known training data, and construct a common space to generate common representations. Existing methods treat all training sample indiscriminately during training process. However, because cross-media correlation is complex and diverse, there often exist hard samples which lead to misleading and even noisy information, bringing negative effect especially in the early period of model training. Because cross-media training data is difficult to collect, the common challenge of small-scale training data makes this problem even severer to limit the robustness and accuracy of cross-media retrieval.

For addressing the above problem, inspired by the idea of curriculum learning (CL) [9], this paper proposes Progressive Cross-media Correlation Learning (PCCL) approach. Given the fact that large-scale data with general knowledge is much more reliable than small-scale data, PCCL takes a large-scale cross-media dataset (reference data) to guide the correlation learning on another small-scale dataset (target data) via the progressive sample selection mechanism. Specifically, we first pre-train a hierarchical correlation learning network on reference data as reference model, which is used to assign samples in target data with different learning difficulties, via intra-media and inter-media relevance significance metric. Then, training samples in target data are selected with gradually ascending learning difficulties, so that the correlation learning process can progressively reduce the "heterogeneity gap"to enhance the model robustness and improve retrieval accuracy. We take our self-constructed large-scale dataset XMediaNet as the reference data, and conduct the cross-media retrieval experiments on 2 widely-used datasets as target data compared with 9 state-of-the-art methods, which shows the effectiveness of PCCL.

2   Related Work

2.1   Cross-Media Retrieval

Cross-media retrieval aims to perform retrieval among different media types, and the mainstream idea is obtaining common representations via correlation learning. Existing methods can be divided into shallow learning methods and DNN-based methods. As for shallowing learning methods, linear projection is regarded as the basic model. Canonical correlation analysis (CCA) [3], as a representative method, aims to learn cross-media correlation via maximizing the pairwise correlation. CCA also has many applications and variants [10,11]. Joint representation learning [4] is proposed to incorporate the graph regularization into correlation learning, and can jointly learn the correlation among up to five media types. Furthermore, Peng et al. [12] propose to analyze the cross-media correlation among patches of media instances, which can effectively capture fine-grained correlations to improve the retrieval accuracy.

As for DNN-based methods, deep neural network serves as the basic model for correlation learning, which have been a research hotspot for cross-media retrieval [6,8,13,14]. An intuitive idea of architecture design is to construct multiple pathways for different media types, which share the same code layer to generate common representations, such as Bimodal deep autoencoder (Bimodal AE) [6]. Deep canonical correlation analysis (DCCA) [15] is proposed as CCA's nonlinear extension, which replaces the linear projection matrices in original CCA with the transformations of DNN. Inspired by transfer learning, cross-media hybrid transfer network (CHTN) [14] is proposed to transfer the knowledge from a large-scale single-media source domain (e.g., ImageNet) to cross-media target domain, which relieves the problem of insufficient cross-media training data and improves retrieval accuracy.

However, existing methods indiscriminately take all data for model training, ignoring that the hard samples can lead to misleading and even noisy information, bringing negative effect especially in the early period of model training. This paper proposes PCCL, which allows the model to first learn from "easy" samples with high intra-media and inter-media relevance significance, and then gradually harder samples. The correlation learning process can progressively reduce the "heterogeneity gap", and address the negative effect brought by hard samples for improving the accuracy of retrieval.

2.2 Curriculum Learning

Curriculum Learning (CL) [9] refers to a kind of training strategy, which has a very intuitive motivation to simulate the progressive learning mechanism of human: to deal with easy samples first, and then learn from gradually harder samples. CL is proposed to avoid the problem that the hard and noisy samples can mislead the model training, especially in the early training period.

Besides determining the order of samples for training [9], CL is also used for determining the order of different tasks to train [16]. A very relevant research topic is Self-paced learning (SPL), which can be seen as CL's implementation [18]. SPL designs a weighted loss term for different samples [17], instead determining the order of training samples in advance. CL has wide applications such as image classification [18] and object tracking [19]. Inspired by CL, this paper assigns different training samples with different learning difficulties for cross-media correlation learning, which are predicted by a reference modal pre-trained on a large-scale cross-media dataset with general knowledge. Such progressive learning strategy aims to learn from samples with gradually ascending learning difficulties, which can enhance the robustness and effectiveness of correlation learning.

3   Progressive Cross-Media Correlation Learning

In this section, we first introduce the hierarchical architecture of correlation learning, and then introduce the strategies of progressive correlation learning. The overview of the proposed PCCL approach is shown as Fig. 1. We denote the reference data as $Ref = \{(i_r^p, t_r^p), y_r^p\}_{p=1}^P$, where (i_r^p, t_r^p) denote the p-th pair of image i_r^p and text t_r^p, and y_r^p denotes the label of the p-th pair. P denotes the pair number in Ref. For target data to perform correlation learning and cross-media retrieval, it includes a training set and a testing set. Similar to the denotation of reference data, the training set is denoted as $T_{tr} = \{(i_t^q, t_t^q), y_t^q\}_{q=1}^Q$, and the testing set is denoted as $T_{te} = \{(i_t^m, t_t^m)\}_{m=1}^M$. The aim is to use Ref to guide the sample selection for T_{tr} to learn cross-media correlation, and generate common representations for T_{te} to perform retrieval.

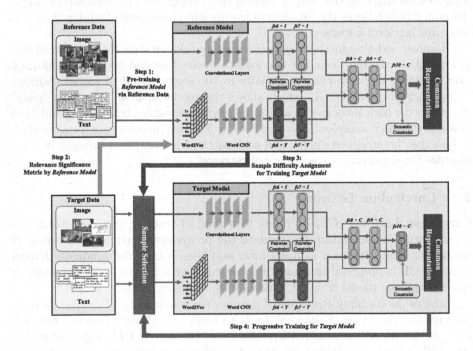

Fig. 1. An overview of our progressive cross-media correlation learning (PCCL).

3.1 Hierarchical Correlation Learning Architecture

As shown in Fig. 1, there is a model for reference data (i.e., reference model) and target data (i.e., target model), respectively. The two networks share the same structure design, so here we take the reference model as an example for description.

The hierarchical architecture includes the separate learning stage for each media type, and the joint learning stage for generating common representations. In separate learning stage, there is one pathway for each media type, respectively. For the pathway of image, we adopt the same structure as the widely-used VGG19 [20] model, except for the last fully-connected layer. Here we denote the two 4,096-d fully-connected layers as $fc6 - I/fc7 - I$. For the pathway of text, we first extract the word embedding of each word via Word2Vec model [21], and then generate representations of 300-d vectors using Word CNN [22]. These 300-d textual vectors will be fed into two additional 4,096-d fully-connected layers, denoted as $fc6 - T/fc7 - T$.

Each image/text pair is used to represent semantics that are closely relevant, so we preserve such coexistence cue via pairwise constraints in separate learning stage. This is achieved by letting the output of corresponding fully-connected layers of image and text be close to each other, and we define the loss term of pairwise constraint as follows:

$$Loss_{(P)} = \sum_{l=l_6}^{l_7} \sum_{p=1}^{P} d^2(i_r^p, t_r^p) \tag{1}$$

where l_6 and l_7 mean the corresponding layers $fc6 - I/fc6 - T$, and $fc7 - I/fc7 - T$. $d^2(i_r^p, t_r^p)$ denotes the Euclidean distance between the corresponding fully-connected layers for pair (i_r^p, t_r^p), which is defined as:

$$d^2(i_r^p, t_r^p) = \|\phi(i_r^p, \theta_I) - \phi(t_r^p, \theta_T)\|^2 \tag{2}$$

where θ_I and θ_T denote the network parameters for image and text pathways, and $\phi(\cdot)$ denotes the output of network layers.

In joint learning stage, we adopt two 4,096-d fully-connected layers ($fc8 - C$ and $fc9 - C$) to learn the semantic consistency of image and text, followed by a classification layer ($fc10 - C$) with the same unit number of semantic categories in Ref. These layers are shared by image and text pathways, so that the common representations (output of $fc10 - C$) can be generated with high cross-media semantic consistency. The semantic constraint loss is defined as:

$$Loss_{(S)} = \frac{1}{p} \sum_{p=1}^{P} f_s(C(i_r^p), y_r^p, \theta_C) + f_s(C(t_r^p), y_r^p, \theta_C) \tag{3}$$

where $f_s(X, Y, \theta)$ is the softmax loss function, $C(i_r^p)$ and $C(t_r^p)$ are the output of $fc10 - C$ for i_r^p and t_r^p, respectively, and θ_C denotes the network parameters.

The target model has the same architecture with the reference model, except that the unit number of $fc10 - C$ is equal to the category number in T_{tr}. Because the architecture of hierarchical correlation learning is end-to-end, the loss terms $Loss_{(P)}$ and $Loss_{(S)}$ can be jointly minimized, which can fully capture both intra-media and inter-media correlation cues.

3.2 Progressive Correlation Learning Strategy

Our aim is to learn correlation on target data T_{tr}, but because cross-media training data for a specific retrieval task is very hard to collect, T_{tr} usually suffers from small scale, and contains hard and even noisy samples which can mislead the correlation learning, especially in the early period of training. Given the fact that large-scale data with general knowledge is much more reliable, we propose to address this problem by sample selection of T_{tr} with the principle of gradually ascending learning difficulties by the guidance of large-scale Ref.

First, we pre-train a hierarchical correlation learning network on all data in Ref to converge as the reference model. This reference model contains general knowledge, which can be used to evaluate the relevance significance of each image/text pair in T_{tr}. The idea is intuitive: if an image/text pair's intra-media and inter-media relevance can be successfully predicted by the reference model, the pair is regarded to be "easy" and the correlation information within it is reliable and "safe". In early period of training, we choose "easy" samples to obtain a robust model, while in late period when the model is already stable, we incorporate "harder" samples to preserve the diversity of correlation learning, which further adapts to target data.

Specifically, we adopt the reference model to generate common representations for T_{tr}. For convenience, we denote the common representations as $C_{tr} = \{(i_c^q, t_c^q), y^q\}_{q=1}^Q$. The intra-media relevance significance for each pair (i_c^q, t_c^q) is obtained by performing single-media retrieval including Image→Image and Text→Text retrieval in T_{tr}. Taking Image→Image as an example, we use cosine distance as the similarity metric between i_c^q and all the other images, and then compute the AP score of the ranking list as:

$$AP(II)^q = \frac{1}{R} \sum_{k=1}^{Q} \frac{R_k}{k} \times rel_k \tag{4}$$

where R is the number of relevant images with i_c^q (with the same label), R_k denotes the relevant image number in top-k results. $rel_k = 1$ if i_c^q and k-th result are relevant, otherwise 0. Similarly we can get $AP(TT)^q$ via Text→Text retrieval, and the intra-media relevance significance is defined as:

$$Sig_{Intra}^q = AP(II)^q + AP(TT)^q \tag{5}$$

As for inter-media relevance significance, because all data in T_{tr} has been converted into common representations with the same dimension, we can easily compute the cosine distance between images and texts, i.e., to perform Image→Text and Text→Image retrieval in T_{tr}. Similar to Eq. (7), we can get $AP(IT)^q$ and $AP(TI)^q$, and the inter-media relevance significance is defined as:

$$Sig_{Inter}^q = AP(IT)^q + AP(TI)^q \tag{6}$$

Therefore, the final relevance significance of (i_c^q, t_c^q) is as follows:

$$Sig^q = Sig_{Intra}^q + Sig_{Inter}^q \tag{7}$$

We re-order all the training data in T_{tr} according to descending order of Sig^q. The training of target model is an iterative process. In $Iter$-th iteration, we select samples with top-$k_{(Iter)}$ largest Sig^q to train the target model for n epoch to obtain $Model_{T(Iter)}$. $k_{(Iter)}$ is computed as follows:

$$k = min(Q, \lfloor \alpha \times (1 + \alpha)^{(Iter-1)} \times Q \rfloor) \tag{8}$$

In the beginning of training, we initialize $Iter = 1$ and obtain $Model_{T(1)}$. Then we set $Iter = 2$, and iteratively update $Model_{T(1)}$ to be $Model_{T(2)}$ by training on the samples with top-$k_{(2)}$ largest Sig^q. It can be seen that as $Iter$ increases, $k_{(Iter)}$ will be larger, and more samples will be selected for training. In this way, the model can gradually learn from the cross-media correlation in T_{tr} with ascending difficulties, which can enhance the model robustness and improve retrieval accuracy.

For network training, PCCL can be trained by stochastic gradient descent (SGD). we set the initial learning rate to be 0.01, and the weight decay 0.0005. As for the parameters of progressive correlation learning, we set α as 0.3 and n as 3, according to the retrieval accuracy of validation data in target data. The maximum value of $Iter$ is set to be 10, and $Model_{T(Iter)}$ with the highest retrieval accuracy on validation data will be recorded to finally perform cross-media retrieval.

4   Experiments

4.1   Dataset Introduction

For reference data, we adopt our self-constructed **XMediaNet** [2] dataset. This is the first large-scale cross-media dataset with more than 100,000 media instances and 5 media types: image, audio, video and 3D model. These instances are manually collected under 200 distinct semantic categories, including 47 animal species like "dog" and 153 artifact species like "airplane" with wordNet hierarchy. In this paper, we choose the training set of image and text data as Ref with 32,000 pairs. Because of the large-scale and general knowledge of XMediaNet dataset, it is proper to serve as the reference data to guide the progressive correlation learning process on target data.

Two widely-used cross-media datasets are respectively adopted as the target data, including **Wikipedia dataset** [10] and **NUS-WIDE-10k dataset** [7]. Wikipedia dataset contains 2,866 image/text pairs with 10 high-level semantic categories, which is randomly split into a training set with 2,173 pairs, a testing set with 462 pairs, and a validation set with 231 pairs following [7]. NUS-WIDE-10k dataset, as a subset of NUS-WIDE dataset [24], contains 10,000 image/text pairs of 10 semantic categories. Similarly, it is also split into a training set with 8,000 pairs, a testing set with 1,000 pairs, and a validation set with 1,000 pairs.

4.2   Compared Methods and Evaluation Metrics

Totally 9 state-of-the-art methods are compared in the experiments, including shallow learning and DNN-based methods: CCA [3], CFA [23], KCCA (with Gaussian kernel) [25], Corr-AE [7], JRL [4], LGCFL [5], DCCA [15], CMDN [8] and Deep-SM [13]. For fair comparison, we use the 4,096-d VGG19 image features (fine-tuned on images in target data) as image input, and use the same 300-d Word CNN text representations (fine-tuned on texts in target data) with our proposed PCCL as text input for all compared methods. There is only one exception that Deep-SM is based on AlexNet and takes pixels as image input, so we replace the AlexNet with VGG19 for Deep-SM to fairly compare with PCCL.

We conduct cross-media retrieval in two directions for evaluation: Image→Text retrieval and Text→Image retrieval. Taking Image→Text as an example, we first generate common representations for images and texts in T_{Te}, and then compute the cosine distance between query images and all texts. After that, we compute the AP scores for all queries according to Eq. (4), and compute the mean average precision (MAP) scores for evaluation. The MAP scores are computed as all queries' mean of average precision (AP), and we compute MAP scores for all results in ranking list.

4.3   Experimental Results

The MAP scores of PCCL and the compared methods are shown in Table 1. We can observe that on both two datasets, PCCL achieves the best MAP scores of 0.494 and 0.535, respectively. Although the training of PCCL takes more time than Deep-SM, it has a significant accuracy advantage. This occurs because PCCL does not take all training samples indiscriminately as the existing methods. Instead, it adaptively selects training samples with gradually ascending learning difficulties for correlation learning, so as to reduce the negative effect brought by hard and noisy samples for improving the accuracy of retrieval.

To further verify the effectiveness of the proposed sample selection strategy, we conduct two baseline experiments: PCCL (All) means that we use all samples in every iteration, and PCCL (Random) means that we assign random Sig^q values to all samples, while the other parts of PCCL keep the same. From Table 2, it can be observed that the accuracies of PCCL (ALL) and PCCL (Random) are close, both of which are clearly lower than complete PCCL. This shows that the proposed sample selection strategy via relevance significance metric by reference model is helpful to distinguish the learning difficulties of samples in target data, and effectively guide the progressive correlation learning process to obtain better retrieval accuracy.

Table 1. MAP scores of our PCCL and compared methods.

Dataset	Method	Task		
		Image→Text	Text→Image	Average
Wikipedia dataset	**Our PCCL**	**0.509**	**0.478**	**0.494**
	Deep-SM	0.478	0.422	0.450
	CMDN	0.487	0.427	0.457
	DCCA	0.445	0.399	0.422
	LGCFL	0.466	0.431	0.449
	JRL	0.479	0.428	0.454
	Corr-AE	0.442	0.429	0.436
	KCCA	0.438	0.389	0.414
	CFA	0.319	0.316	0.318
	CCA	0.298	0.273	0.286
NUS-WIDE -10k dataset	**Our PCCL**	**0.529**	**0.541**	**0.535**
	Deep-SM	0.497	0.478	0.488
	CMDN	0.492	0.542	0.517
	DCCA	0.452	0.465	0.459
	LGCFL	0.453	0.485	0.469
	JRL	0.466	0.499	0.483
	Corr-AE	0.441	0.494	0.468
	KCCA	0.351	0.356	0.354
	CFA	0.406	0.435	0.421
	CCA	0.167	0.181	0.174

Table 2. MAP scores of our PCCL and the baselines.

Dataset	Method	Task		
		Image→Text	Text→Image	Average
Wikipedia dataset	**Our PCCL**	**0.509**	**0.478**	**0.494**
	PCCL (All)	0.485	0.469	0.477
	PCCL (Random)	0.486	0.471	0.479
NUS-WIDE -10k dataset	**Our PCCL**	**0.529**	**0.541**	**0.535**
	PCCL (All)	0.508	0.490	0.499
	PCCL (Random)	0.497	0.511	0.504

5   Conclusion

This paper has proposed Progressive Cross-media Correlation Learning (PCCL) approach. PCCL first pre-trains a hierarchical correlation learning network on reference data (a large-scale cross-media dataset) as reference model, which is used to assign samples in target data (another small-scale dataset) with different learning difficulties, via intra-media and inter-media relevance significance metric. Then, training samples in target data are selected with gradually ascending learning difficulties, so that the correlation learning process can progressively reduce the "heterogeneity gap". The experimental results show that PCCL can effectively enhance the model robustness and improve retrieval accuracy on 2 widely-used cross-media datasets.

As for the future work, we intend to investigate better strategy for sample selection to achieve more effective correlation learning process. We will also explore how to extend PCCL to the unsupervised scenario where the labels of target data is unknown, which brings more scalability for PCCL.

Acknowledgments. This work was supported by National Natural Science Foundation of China under Grants 61771025 and 61532005.

References

1. Gilakjani, A.P.: Visual, auditory, kinaesthetic learning styles and their impacts on english language teaching. J. Stud. Educ. **2**, 104–113 (2012)
2. Peng, Y., Huang, X., Zhao, Y.: An overview of cross-media retrieval: concepts, methodologies, benchmarks and challenges. IEEE Trans. Circ. Syst. Video Technol. (TCSVT) (2017). https://doi.org/10.1109/TCSVT.2017.2705068
3. Hotelling, H.: Relations between two sets of variates. Biometrika **28**(3/4), 321–377 (1936)
4. Zhai, X., Peng, Y., Xiao, J.: Learning cross-media joint representation with sparse and semi-supervised regularization. IEEE Trans. Circ. Syst. Video Technol. (TCSVT) **24**(6), 965–978 (2014)
5. Kang, C., Xiang, S., Liao, S., Xu, C., Pan, C.: Learning consistent feature representation for cross-modal multimedia retrieval. IEEE Trans. Multimedia (TMM) **17**(3), 370–381 (2015)
6. Ngiam, J., Khosla, A., Kim, M., Nam, J., Lee, H., Ng, A.Y.: Multimodal deep learning. In: International Conference Machine Learning (ICML), pp. 689–696 (2011)
7. Feng, F., Wang, X., Li, R.: Cross-modal retrieval with correspondence autoencoder. In: ACM MM, pp. 7–16 (2014)
8. Peng, Y., Huang, X., Qi, J.: Cross-media shared representation by hierarchical learning with multiple deep networks. In: IJCAI, pp. 3846–3853 (2016)
9. Bengio, Y., Louradour, J., Collobert, R., and Weston, J.: Curriculum learning. In: ICML, pp. 41–48 (2009)
10. Rasiwasia, N., et al.: A new approach to cross-modal multimedia retrieval. In: ACM MM, pp. 251–260 (2010)
11. Ranjan, V., Rasiwasia, N., Jawahar, C.V.: Multi-label cross-modal retrieval. In: ICCV, pp. 4094–4102 (2015)
12. Peng, Y., Zhai, X., Zhao, Y., Huang, X.: Semi-supervised cross-media feature learning with unified patch graph regularization. IEEE Trans. Circ. Syst. Video Technol. (TCSVT) **26**(3), 583–596 (2016)
13. Wei, Y., Lu, C., Wei, S., Liu, L., Zhu, Z., Yan, S.: Cross-modal retrieval with CNN visual features: a new baseline. IEEE Trans. Cybern. (TCYB) **47**(2), 449–460 (2017)

14. Huang, X., Peng, Y., Yuan, M.: Cross-modal common representation learning by hybrid transfer network. In: IJCAI, pp. 1893–1900 (2017)
15. Yan, F., Mikolajczyk, K.: Deep correlation for matching images and text. In: CVPR, pp. 3441–3450 (2015)
16. Pentina, A., Sharmanska, V., Lampert, C.H.: Curriculum learning of multiple tasks. In: CVPR, pp. 5492–5500 (2015)
17. Kumar, M.P., Packer, B., Koller, D.: Self-paced learning for latent variable models. In: NIPS, pp. 1189–1197 (2010)
18. Gong, C., Tao, D., Maybank, S.J., Liu, W., Kang, G., Yang, J.: Multi-modal curriculum learning for semi-supervised image classification. IEEE Trans. Image Process. (TIP) 25(7), 3249–3260 (2016)
19. Supancic, J.S., Ramanan, D.: Self-paced learning for long-term tracking. In: CVPR, pp. 2379–2386 (2013)
20. Simonyan, K., Zisserman, A.: Very deep convolutional networks for large-scale image recognition. arXiv preprint arXiv: 1409.1556 (2014)
21. Mikolov, T., Sutskever, I., Chen, K., Corrado, G.S., Dean, J.: Distributed representations of words and phrases and their compositionality. In: NIPS, pp. 3111–3119 (2013)
22. Kim, Y.: Convolutional neural networks for sentence classification. In: EMNLP. 1746–1751 (2014)
23. Li, D., Dimitrova, N., Li, M., Sethi, I.K.: Multimedia content processing through cross-modal association. In: ACM MM, pp. 604–611 (2003)
24. Chua, T.-S., Tang, J., Hong, R., Li, H., Luo, Z., Zheng, Y.: NUS-WIDE: a real-world web image database from National University of Singapore. In: CIVR, No. 48 (2009)
25. Hardoon, D.R., Szedmák, S., Shawe-Taylor, J.: Canonical correlation analysis: an overview with application to learning methods. Neural Comput. 16(12), 2639–2664 (2004)

Spatio-Temporal Context Tracking Algorithm Based on Master-Slave Memory Space Model

Xu Li[1,2], Yong Song[1,2(✉)], Yufei Zhao[1,2], Yun Li[1,2], Shangnan Zhao[1,2], Guowei Shi[3], and Xin Yang[1,2]

[1] School of Optics and Photonics, Beijing Institute of Technology, Beijing 100081, China
yongsong@bit.edu.cn
[2] Beijing Key Laboratory for Precision Optoelectronic Measurement Instrument and Technology, Beijing 100081, China
[3] Institute of Aviation Medicine, AF CPLA, Beijing 100142, China

Abstract. The spatio-temporal context (STC) tracking algorithm has the advantages of high tracking accuracy and speed, but it may update the target template incorrectly under complex background and interference conditions. A spatio-temporal context tracking algorithm based on master-slave memory space model is proposed in this paper. The algorithm introduces the memory mechanism of Human Visual System (HVS) into the template updating process of STC algorithm, and forms a memory-based update strategy by constructing the master and slave memory spaces. Meanwhile, a method for determining the target location from multi peak points of saliency is proposed. Experimental results indicate that the proposed algorithm has comparatively high accuracy and robustness in the case of the target under occlusion, attitude changes, the target missing and appearing, and illumination changes, etc.

Keywords: Memory spaces · Saliency · Spatio-temporal context
Tracking algorithm

1 Introduction

As an important research direction in the field of computer vision, target tracking algorithm has a wide application prospect in video monitoring, human-computer interaction, intelligent transportation and other fields [1].

As a new tracking algorithm based on the correlation of targets and background, the conventional STC algorithm formulates the spatio-temporal relationships between the target and its local context based on a Bayesian framework, according to relationships, the saliency is calculated, and the target location with the maximum likelihood probability is predicted in the saliency. In addition, the Fast Fourier Transform is adopted for fast learning and detection in this algorithm [2].

On the other hand, due to the fact that the conventional STC algorithm uses fixed learning parameters to update the spatio-temporal context template, it may update the target template incorrectly in the case of the target under occlusion, attitude changes,

© Springer Nature Singapore Pte Ltd. 2018
Y. Wang et al. (Eds.): IGTA 2018, CCIS 875, pp. 212–219, 2018.
https://doi.org/10.1007/978-981-13-1702-6_21

the target missing and appearing, illumination changes and so on, which results in low tracking accuracy or even target lost.

Aiming to above problems, some works have been done, but fail to solve the problem completely. For instance, XG Wei combined the STC algorithm with Kalman filter for target tracking. To a certain degree, the target deviation is decreased, but it is hard to avoid wrong updating of the template [3]; XU Jian-Qiang proposed a weighted spatio-temporal context learning algorithm and integrated a weighted map by evaluating the importance of different regions, which improved the robustness, but reduced the processing speed [4].

Memory mechanism of HVS has the characteristics of agility, persistence and standby, which can help to solve above problems in target tracking [5]. In this paper, a spatio-temporal context tracking algorithm based on master-slave memory space model (MSM-STC) is proposed. The algorithm introduces the memory mechanism of HVS into the template updating process of STC algorithm, and forms a memory-based update strategy by constructing the master and slave memory spaces. It solves above problems by remembering the previous scenes. Meanwhile, a method for determining the target location from multi peak points of saliency is proposed. Experimental results indicate that the proposed algorithm has comparatively high accuracy and robustness in the case of the target under occlusion, attitude changes, the target missing and appearing, and illumination changes, etc.

2 MSM-STC Algorithm

2.1 Algorithm Design

The conventional STC algorithm formulates the spatio-temporal context between the target and its surrounding area based on a Bayesian framework, In the proposed algorithm, the memory mechanism of HVS is introduced into the context template updating process of STC algorithm. Figure 1 shows the flow chart of the proposed algorithm.

The proposed algorithm updates in the next frame by following memorizing rules, and combines the spatio-temporal template and the context prior probability to calculate the saliency in the next frame. The new target location with the maximum likelihood probability is predicted in the saliency.

The steps of MSM-STC algorithm are shown as follows:

(1) Learning the spatial context template of the first frame as the spatio-temporal context template of the second frame by initializing the saliency and the context prior probability of the first frame. The saliency can be expressed as:

$$c(x) = h^{sc}(x) \otimes \left(I(x)\omega_\sigma(x - x^*) \right) \tag{1}$$

h^{sc} is the spatial context template, I is image intensity that represents appearance of context and ω_σ is a weighted function. Based on formula (1), The spatial context template of the first frame is presented as (2):

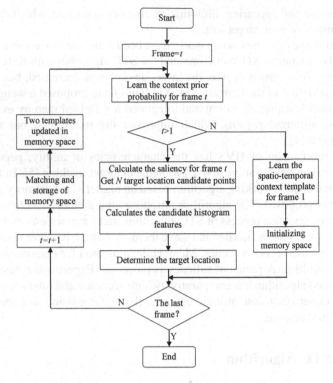

Fig. 1. Flow chart of the proposed algorithm

$$h^{sc}(x) = F^{-1}\left(\frac{F(c(x))}{F(I(x)\omega_\sigma(x-x^*))}\right) \qquad (2)$$

(2) Learning the spatio-temporal context template, matching target location obtained from the frame $t-1$ with the memory space, and updating the spatio-temporal context template of the frame t according to the template updating rule.

(3) Learning the context prior probability of the current frame, and combining the spatio-temporal context template of the frame t to calculate the saliency of the frame t:

$$c_t(x) = F^{-1}\{F(H_t(x)) \odot F(I_t(x)\omega_{\sigma_{t-1}}(x-x_{t-1}^*))\} \qquad (3)$$

H_t is the spatio-temporal context template. Calculating N target location candidate points according to the maximum N peak points of the saliency.

(4) Matching the candidate target area features (color histogram) with the target template, and selecting the target location with the highest similarity of the frame t.

(5) Calculating the color histogram features of the target area determined in the frame t, and matching the template in the master memory space. If the match succeeds,

the spatio-temporal context template in the slave memory space will be updated. Otherwise, it remains the same. Finally, the target location of frame $t + 1$ is determined.

2.2 The Spatio-Temporal Context Template Updating Based on MSM Space Model

As shown in Fig. 2, the model consists of master and slave memory spaces. The master memory space is used to store a color histogram template for determining the matching degree, and the slave space is used to store the spatio-temporal context template. Each memory space constructs three spaces of Ultra-short Time Memory Space (USTMS), Short Time Memory Space (STMS) and Long Time Memory Space (LTMS), in which STMS and LTMS can store R templates respectively.

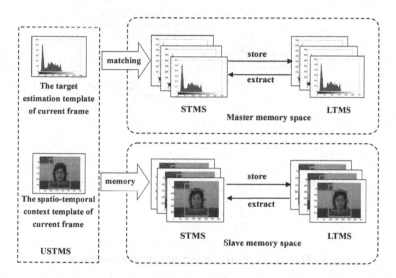

Fig. 2. Master-slave memory space used in the proposed algorithm

The update process of spatio-temporal context template is shown in Fig. 3. If the template in the master memory space matches the target template, the spatio-temporal context template in the slave memory space will be updated. Otherwise it will be not updated. In the master memory space, the estimation template (the target area color histogram feature) obtained from the tracking result of the current frame is stored in USTMS, and sequentially matched with the target template in STMS and LTMS. If the match succeeds, the target template in the master memory space is updated according to update rules, and simultaneously the spatio-temporal context template in the slave memory space is updated. Otherwise, the estimation template in USTMS is memorized in STMS.

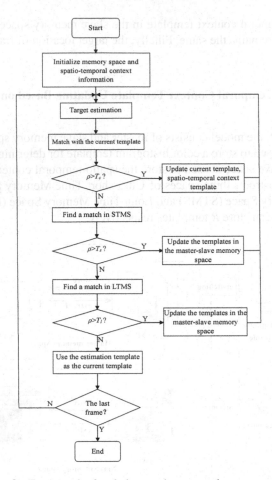

Fig. 3. Framework of updating spatio-temporal context model

2.3 A Method for Determining the Target Location from Multi Peak Points of Saliency

In the conventional STC algorithm, the maximum peak point of the saliency is taken as the target location. Due to the influence of the error in the process of saliency generation, the true target location may be at other peak points, but not at the maximum peak point of the saliency.

In the calculation of the saliency based on STC, the proposed algorithm selects N target location candidate points and chooses the target location with the highest similarity to the target template as the final tracking result. Specifically, calculating the color histogram features of the N target location candidates, marking the i_{th} color histogram as p_i $(i = 1, 2, 3, ..., N)$. The target template stored in memory space is q. Calculating the similarity between p_i and q (p_i and q are L-dimensional vectors). The maximum similarity S is calculated as:

$$S = \max\left(\sum_{j=1}^{L} \sqrt{p_{ij} \times q} \right) \tag{4}$$

Finally, selecting the final target location with the highest similarity.

Using the above method, the influence of saliency error on tracking accuracy is reduced.

3 Experiment and Result Analysis

3.1 Qualitative Analysis

Figure 4 shows the tracking experimental results of four sequences obtained by Partical Filter algorithm (PF), Spatio-temporal context algorithm (STC), compressive tracking algorithm (CT) and the proposed algorithm (MSM-STC).

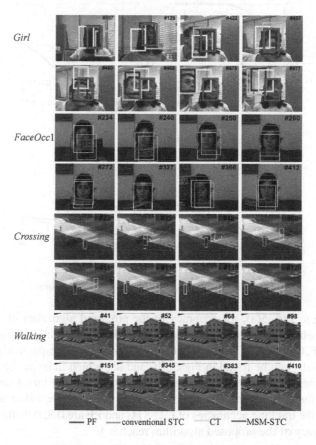

Fig. 4. Tracking results of four sequences

As shown in Fig. 4, the girl of sequence *Girl* is occluded by a man, the PF algorithm, the CT algorithm and the STC algorithm all track the occlusion (male face) while the proposed algorithm tracks the target accurately. In sequence *Walking* and *Crossing*, there are attitude changes and illumination changes, other three algorithms can't track the target (man), they all lose target in the last few frames. However, the proposed algorithm tracks the man robustly.

3.2   Quantitative Analysis

As shown in Fig. 5, the tracking precision plots compares the tracking accuracy of the proposed algorithm with other algorithms. The threshold refers to the distance between the center position of the tracking target and the exact location of the manual calibration, the location error threshold we use is 20 pixels [6]. The precision refers to the percentage of frames that are within the threshold of a given exact value.

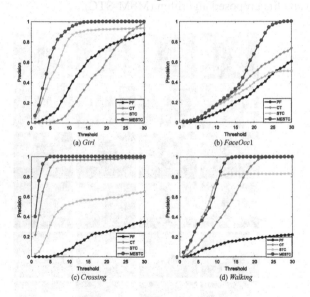

Fig. 5. Tracking precision plots of four algorithms

According to Fig. 5(a), the accuracy of the proposed algorithm of sequence *Girl* reaches 0.99 when the target under occlusion and target attitude changes, while the accuracy of PF, CT and STC algorithm are 0.75, 0.65 and 0.9, respectively. Meanwhile, the similar results can be found in Figs. 5(b) and (c), which indicate that the proposed algorithm has the highest tracking accuracy when the moving target under occlusion repeatedly or the illumination changes. Moreover, the experimental result in Fig. 5(d) indicates that the tracking accuracies of CT, STC and PF are 0.8, 0.9 and 0.2, while the tracking accuracy of the proposed algorithm reaches 1.

4 Conclusion

A spatio-temporal context tracking algorithm based on master-slave memory space model is proposed in this paper. The proposed algorithm uses a spatio-temporal context template updating strategy based on the master-slave memory space models to solve the problem caused by the conventional STC algorithm template update error. Meanwhile, a method for determining the target location from multi peak points of saliency is proposed, thus reducing the influence of saliency error on tracking accuracy. Experimental results indicate that the proposed algorithm has comparatively high accuracy and robustness under complex background and interference conditions, such as target occlusion, attitude changes, the target missing and appearing, and illumination changes, etc.

Acknowledgement. This work is supported by National Nature Science Foundation of China (NSFC) (81671787); Defense Industrial Technology Development Program (JCKY2016208 B001)

References

1. Wu, Y., Lim, J., Yang, M.H.: Online object tracking: a benchmark In: IEEE Conference on Computer Vision and Pattern Recognition, IEEE Computer Society, pp. 2411–2418 (2013)
2. Zhang, K., Zhang, L., Liu, Q., Zhang, D., Yang, M.H.: Fast visual tracking via dense spatio-temporal context learning. In: Fleet, D., Pajdla, T., Schiele, B., Tuytelaars, T. (eds.) ECCV 2014. LNCS, vol. 8693, pp. 127–141. Springer, Cham (2014). https://doi.org/10.1007/978-3-319-10602-1_9
3. Wei, X.G., Zhang, S., Chan, S.C.: A novel visual object tracking algorithm using multiple spatial context models and Bayesian Kalman filter. In: IEEE International Symposium on Circuits and Systems, IEEE, pp. 1034–1037 (2015)
4. Xu, J.Q., Lu, Y.: Robust visual tracking via weighted spatio-temporal context learning. Acta Autom. Sinica **41**(11), 1901–1912 (2015)
5. Kang, H.-B., Cho, S.-H.: Short-term memory-based object tracking. In: Campilho, A., Kamel, M. (eds.) ICIAR 2004. LNCS, vol. 3212, pp. 597–605. Springer, Heidelberg (2004). https://doi.org/10.1007/978-3-540-30126-4_73
6. Babenko, B., Yang, M.H., Belongie, S.: Robust object tracking with online multiple instance learning. IEEE Trans. Pattern Anal. Mach. Intell. **33**(8), 1619–1632 (2011)

Synthesizing Training Images for Semantic Segmentation

Yunhui Zhang[1(✉)], Zizhao Wu[1], Zhiping Zhou[2], and Yigang Wang[1]

[1] Digite Media Interactive Simulation Lab, Hangzhou Dianzi University,
Hangzhou 310018, ZJ, China
zhangyh_data@163.com

[2] School of Computer Science, Hangzhou Dianzi University, Hangzhou 310018, ZJ, China

Abstract. Semantic segmentation is one of the key problems in the computer vision area. Recently, Convolutional Neural Networks (CNNs) have yielded a significant performance for the semantic segmentation task. However, CNNs require a sufficient amount of annotated training images, which is challenging since massive human labour is needed. In this paper, we propose to use 3D models to automatically generate synthetic images with pixel-level annotations. We take advantage of 3D models to generate synthetic images of high diversity in object appearance and background clutterness, by randomly sampling rendering parameters and adding random background patterns. Then, we use the synthetic images to augment training samples for semantic segmentation by combining with publicly available real-world images. Experimental results demonstrate that CNNs trained with our synthetic images improve performance on the semantic segmentation task in the PASCAL VOC 2012 dataset.

Keywords: Semantic segmentation · Synthesizing training images · CNN
Augmentation · Generate synthetic images

1 Introduction

Semantic image segmentation is the problem of labeling each pixel in an image with a semantic class. This is a fundamental problem in computer vision with many applications in scene understanding [4], automatic driving [7], video surveillance [23], etc. Such problem has been addressed in the past using various traditional computer vision techniques [2, 11, 18, 20].

In the recent years, tremendous progress has been made through the use of deep Convolutional Neural Networks (CNNs) due to their rich hierarchical features and an end-to-end trainable framework [1, 5, 26, 27]. For example, the Fully Convolutional Network (FCN) method proposed by Long et al. [13] has been showed that convolutional network architectures that had originally been developed for image classification can be successfully repurposed for dense prediction, which significantly surpasses the prior state of the art by a large margin in terms of accuracy and sometimes even efficiency. However, CNNs require learning many trainable parameters, thus having a sufficient amount of diverse images with class annotations is needed. The training examples should

© Springer Nature Singapore Pte Ltd. 2018
Y. Wang et al. (Eds.): IGTA 2018, CCIS 875, pp. 220–227, 2018.
https://doi.org/10.1007/978-981-13-1702-6_22

cover the huge space of appearance variations, where thousands of images differ greatly in appearance, lighting and occlusion are needed to be properly segmented and labelled at pixel level. This task is considered to be tedious and cumbersome, whereas crowd-sourcing is not a practical option here, because which may cause ambiguous information leading to noisy labels.

Inspired from recent works [3, 17] on synthesizing images for training CNNs, in this work, we use synthetic images to alleviate the bottleneck of training examples facing with CNNs for semantic segmentation. Our synthesizing procedure is mainly based on the render for CNN proposed by Su et al. [21]. We take advantage of a 3D model repository, such as the ShapeNet, to generate synthetic images of high diversity in object appearance and background clutterness, by randomly sampling rendering parameters and adding random background patterns. Then, we use the FCN to perform semantic segmentation, where the training data is composed of the synthetic images and real-world images. Experimental results on the PASCAL VOC 2012 benchmark reveal that models trained with synthetic images and real-world images yield more accurate results than models trained without the synthetic images.

The remainder of this paper is organized as follows. We review the related work in Sect. 2. Section 3 presents the details of the synthesizing procedure and the segmentation technique. The experimental results on benchmark datasets are presented in Sect. 4, followed by conclusions and future work in Sect. 5.

2 Related Work

Semantic Image Segmentation. Semantic segmentation is a key computer vision task and has been studied in a plethora of publications. The early efforts usually adopted Random Forest [2, 18] and Boosting [11, 20] to predict the class probabilities of pixels in a patch, relying on hand engineered features. Recently, the success of CNNs has led researchers to exploit their potential for segmentation tasks. For instance, the FCN [13] has achieved significant improvement over the past methods. This approach transforms the existing and well-known classification models, such as AlexNet [10], VGG [19], GoogLeNet [22], etc., into fully convolutional ones by replacing the fully connected layers with convolutional ones to output spatial maps instead of classification scores. These maps are upsampled using fractionally deconvolutions [26] to produce dense per-pixel labeled outputs. This work is considered a milestone since it demonstrated how CNNs can be trained in an end-to-end manner, and has achieved significant improvements on some popular benchmark datasets.

The performance of FCN has been improve further by integrating context knowledge to make it aware of global information. For example, Zhang et al. [27] introduced the CRF as RNN to refine the segmentation, which reformulates the dense CRF with pairwise potentials as an integral part of the network. Multi-scale deep architectures are also being pursued [5], which allows the models to generalize to different scales.

In addition to the approaches based on supervised learning, several weakly supervised semantic segmentation techniques have been proposed. Hong et al. [9] propose a transfer-learning approach that exploits segmentation annotations of other object classes, and Pinheiro and Collobert [15] perform semantic segmentation based only on image-level annotations in a multiple instance learning framework. Also, Pathak et al. [14] show that even a very little supervision such as one-bit information about object size improves segmentation performance significantly.

Datasets. Generally, CNNs require a large number of annotated images, thus gathering proper and adequate data is critical for any segmentation system based on deep learning techniques. There are some popular large-scale datasets commonly in use for current segmentation techniques. Arguably, the PASCAL Visual Object Classes (VOC) [6] is the most popular dataset for the evaluation of segmentation techniques. Currently, the PASCAL VOC 2012 are categorized in 20 classes with 11,530 images. The dataset is divided into the training set and the validation set. The test set is private for challenge. The Semantic Boundaries Dataset (SBD) [8] is an extended version of the PASCAL VOC, which provides semantic segmentation ground truth for those images that were not labelled in VOC. It contains annotations for 11355 images from PASCAL VOC 2011. The Microsoft Common Objects in Context (COCO) [12] is another image recognition, segmentation, and captioning large-scale dataset. It features various challenges, being the detection one the most relevant for this field since one of its parts is focused on segmentation. The challenge features more than 80 classes, provides more than 82783 images for training.

Despite many open datasets are provided, the images of thest datasets cannot coverage all real-world situations. To alleviate this problem, many researchers resort to generate synthetic images. The SYNTHIA dataset [17] is an example, which provides fine-grained pixel-level annotations of images, rendering from virtual city. GTA [16] is another example, which contains 24966 high quality labeled frames from realistic computer games. Additionally, we note that Chen et al. [3] also present an approach to synthesize training images for boosting 3D pose estimation.

Our work also relates to synthesize training images with CNNs. We differ with them in the task and approach. In our work, we generate synthetic images from 3D models with real-world background rather than from virtual scenes, and towards the semantic segmentation rather than 3D pose estimation.

3   Algorithm

3.1   Training Image Generation

Here we describe how we synthesis a large amount of training images, the synthesizing pipeline is based on the Render For CNN [21]. First, we collect collections of 3D models, such as the ShapeNet repository [24]. Note that the high level features of models in ShapeNet, e.g. the orientation, the symmetry planes, etc., have been extracted and provided, which helps us to generate new models with structure preserving deformation. Then, we render for each model by sampling lighting condition and camera positions to generate rendered images with high diversity. Specifically, for the lighting condition, various lighting models, number and energy of light sources are sampled during the rendering. For the camera setting, the azimuth, elevation and in-plane rotation are sampled and perturbed. The perturbations can be the parameters of azimuth, elevation and in-plane rotation. Gaussian perturbations are also adopted in the sampling process. After that, rendered images of each model can be generated, with high diversity but transparent background. We then resort to the SUN397 dataset [25] as the background dataset, and simply blend a rendered image as foreground and a scene image from SUN397 dataset as background by alpha-composition. As shown in Fig. 1, the synthetic images exhibit a wide variety of appearance. The construction of training data is easily for our synthetic images due to the fact that the foreground and the background have been well assigned in each image.

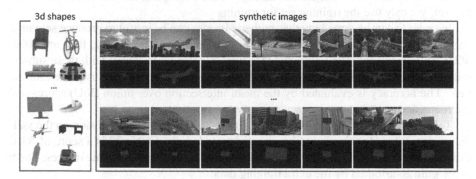

Fig. 1. Our synthetic images. Given a set of 3D shapes, we generate synthetic images with their semantic segmentation results, of high diversity in object appearance and background clutterness. This set is then used to augment the training dataset for semantic segmentation.

We put together the large number of synthetic images, and the real-world images with ground-truth annotations, to form our training set.

3.2   FCN for Semantic Segmentation

Below, we describe the FCN for semantic segmentation based on the training data. In 2014, Long et al. presented the FCN [13], which is a new net architecture for pixel-wise prediction. One advantage of the FCN is the ability to re-interpret existing classification nets as a FCN. Therefore a FCN can benefit from pre-trained CNN models, such as the AlexNet, the VGG, and so on. In order to convert a CNN into a FCN, we replace the fully connected layer by convolutions with a kernel size of 1×1. While the fully connected layer of an image classification net completely discards spatial information and delivers only one feature vector for the image, the fully convolutional layer produces a feature vector for every pixel of the image. Based on the feature map a pixel-wise classification can be performed. This yields a probability map for each class. While pooling improves classification accuracy, it partially neglects spatial information. In general this leads to coarse segmentation maps. Very small objects do not even considered at all. To address this issue, according to [13], we also use the so-called skip net to fuse predictions of different strides to refine the segmentation maps. By combining layers of the feature hierarchy and refining the spatial precision of the output, we achieve the semantic segmentation results.

4   Experimental Results

We employ PASCAL VOC 2012 segmentation dataset for the evaluation. This dataset involves 20 semantic categories of objects. Following previous works, we also use an extra annotation provided by [8]. which contains 10582 images for training, 1449 images for validation and 1456 images for testing. While evaluating the validation set or the test set, we only use the training set for training.

In order to demonstrate how the synthetic images can be useful to produce semantic segmentation results, we fetch out a subset of training data for testing, they are 2000, 4000, and the full set. Then we use 4,000 synthetic images to merge with these subsets individually to make a comparison. The pre-trained VGG-16 network is picked for the task. The accuracy is evaluated by the mean intersection over union (IoU) scores and the mean accuracy scores.

Table 1 compares the results of using different strategies of supervision on the validation set. When 2,000 training images are provided, the FCN yields a score of 53.1, this score is improved to 58.2 when the training set involves our synthetic images. There is 5% gain contributed by the extra training data.

Table 1. Statistical evaluation on the PASCAL VOC 2012 validation. The FCN − 2k denotes the FCN algorithm performing on 2,000 training images, and the FCN − 2k + syn. denotes the FCN algorithm performing on the combination of 2,000 training images and our synthetic images.

Method	FCN − 2k	FCN − 2k + syn.	FCN − 4k	FCN − 4k + syn.	FCN − full	FCN − full + syn.
Mean IoU	53.1	58.2	59.4	61.1	62.1	62.7
Mean acc.	65.0	70.8	72.3	73.9	75.2	76.0

After increasing the real training data, the growth rate of IoU score is degraded. As when 4,000 training images are chosen, we achieve 1% gain contributed by the synthetic images. In this case, we think that training CNN needs a lot of data, as the more input data, the accuracy will be improved, but if the data itself is already a lot, the model prediction ability will gradually reach an upper limit, and the increase of the data will be less. These validate the usefulness of our synthetic images.

Table 2 compares the result of using different light and camera setting. With the different lights and carema setting increased, the mean IoU and mean acc have improved. We also found that as the light source and the amount of position of camera increase, the model gains less. This phenomenon is similar to our previous experiment. This shows that in this task of ours, as the amount of data increases, the predictive power of the model will reach the upper limit, and the benefits of increasing the diversity of data will decrease.

Table 2. Statistical evaluation on the PASCAL VOC 2012 validation. The FCN − 2k only denotes the we only use 2000 training images, and L means lignt, L4 means we use 4 different lights to generate training images, C means Camera, C4 means we use 4 different directions to generate images.

Method	FCN − 2k only	L4 + C4	L4 + C8	L4 + C16	L8 + C16	L16 + C16
Mean IoU	53.1	54.3	55.8	57.1	57.8	58.2
Mean acc.	65.0	66.1	68.2	69.1	69.8	70.8

5   Conclusion

In this paper, we study to use the synthetic images to augment the training images for boosting the performance of semantic segmentation. The results have demonstrated the improvements on the PASCAL VOC 2012 dataset based on our synthetic training images. In the future, we plan to optimize the quality of synthetic images, which is sometimes unreal since we do not perform semantic analysis on the background images, and furthermore, some semantic parts of the background images have been left out when generating the semantic segmentation results of the training data, as is illustrated in Fig. 2.

(a)   (b)   (c)   (d)

Fig. 2. The synthetic images exhibit unrealistic due to lack of semantic analysis on the background images (a) (b) (c), and some semantic parts of the background images have been left out when generating the semantic segmentation results of the training data (d).

Acknowledgments. This work was partially supported by the National Natural Science Foundation of China (No. 61602139) and Zhejiang Province science and technology planning project (2018C01030).

References

1. Badrinarayanan, V., Kendall, A., Cipolla, R.: SegNet: a deep convolutional encoder-decoder architecture for image segmentation. CoRR abs/1511.00561 (2015)
2. Brostow, G.J., Shotton, J., Fauqueur, J., Cipolla, R.: Segmentation and recognition using structure from motion point clouds. In: Forsyth, D., Torr, P., Zisserman, A. (eds.) ECCV 2008. LNCS, vol. 5302, pp. 44–57. Springer, Heidelberg (2008). https://doi.org/10.1007/978-3-540-88682-2_5

3. Chen, W., et al.: Synthesizing training images for boosting human 3D pose estimation. In: Fourth International Conference on 2016 3D Vision 3DV 2016, Stanford, CA, USA, 25–28, October, 2016 pp. 479–488 (2016)

4. Cordts, M., et al.: The cityscapes dataset for semantic urban scene understanding. In: CVPR, pp. 3213–3223 (2016)

5. Eigen, D., Fergus, R.: Predicting depth surface normals and semantic labels with a common multi-scale convolutional architecture. In: ICCV, pp. 2650–2658 (2015)

6. Everingham, M., Gool, L.J.V., Williams, C.K.I., Winn, J.M., Zisserman, A.: The pascal visual object classes (VOC) challenge. Int. J. Comput. Vision **88**(2), 303–338 (2010)

7. Geiger, A., Lenz, P., Urtasun, R.: Are we ready for autonomous driving? The KITTI vision benchmark suite. In: CVPR, pp. 3354–3361 (2012)

8. Hariharan, B., Arbelaez, P., Bourdev, L.D., Maji, S., Malik, J.: Semantic contours from inverse detectors. In: IEEE International Conference on 2011 Computer Vision ICCV , Barcelona, Spain, 6–13, November, 2011 pp. 991–998 (2011)

9. Hong, S., Oh, J., Lee, H., Han, B.: Learning transferrable knowledge for semantic segmentation with deep convolutional neural network. In: CVRP, pp. 3204–3212 (2016)

10. Krizhevsky, A., Sutskever, I., Hinton, G.E.: ImageNet classification with deep convolutional neural networks. In: Advances in Neural Information Processing Systems, pp. 1106–1114 (2012)

11. Ladický, Ľ., Sturgess, P., Alahari, K., Russell, C., Torr, P.H.S.: What, where and how many? combining object detectors and CRFs. In: Daniilidis, K., Maragos, P., Paragios, N. (eds.) ECCV 2010. LNCS, vol. 6314, pp. 424–437. Springer, Heidelberg (2010). https://doi.org/ 10.1007/978-3-642-15561-1_31

12. Lin, T.-Y., Maire, M., Belongie, S., Hays, J., Perona, P., Ramanan, D., Dollár, P., Zitnick, C.L.: Microsoft COCO: common objects in context. In: Fleet, D., Pajdla, T., Schiele, B., Tuytelaars, T. (eds.) ECCV 2014. LNCS, vol. 8693, pp. 740–755. Springer, Cham (2014). https://doi.org/10.1007/978-3-319-10602-1_48

13. Long, J., Shelhamer, E., Darrell, T.: Fully convolutional networks for semantic segmentation. In: IEEE Conference on 2015 Computer Vision and Pattern Recognition CVPR 2015, Boston, MA, USA, 7–12, June, 2015 pp. 3431–3440 (2015)

14. Pathak, D., Krähenbühl, P., Darrell, T.: Constrained convolutional neural networks for weakly supervised segmentation. In: ICCV, pp. 1796–1804 (2015)

15. Pinheiro, P.H.O., Collobert, R.: From image-level to pixel-level labeling with convolutional networks. In: CVPR, pp. 1713–1721 (2015)

16. Richter, S.R., Vineet, V., Roth, S., Koltun, V.: Playing for data: ground truth from computer games. In: Leibe, B., Matas, J., Sebe, N., Welling, M. (eds.) ECCV 2016. LNCS, vol. 9906, pp. 102–118. Springer, Cham (2016). https://doi.org/10.1007/978-3-319-46475-6_7

17. Ros, G., Sellart, L., Materzynska, J., Vázquez, D., Lopez, A.M.: The Synthia dataset: a large collection of synthetic images for semantic segmentation of urban scenes. In: CVPR, pp. 3234–3243 (2016)

18. Shotton, J., Johnson, M., Cipolla, R.: Semantic texton forests for image categorization and segmentation. In: CVPR. IEEE Computer Society (2008)

19. Simonyan, K., Zisserman, A.: Very deep convolutional networks for large-scale image recognition. CoRR abs/1409.1556 (2014)

20. Sturgess, P., Alahari, K., Ladicky, L., Torr, P.H.S.: Combining appearance and structure from motion features for road scene understanding. In: British Machine Vision Conference BMVC, pp. 1–11 (2009)

21. Su, H., Qi, C.R., Li, Y., Guibas, L.J.: Render for CNN: viewpoint estimation in images using cnns trained with rendered 3D model views. In: ICCV, pp. 2686–2694 (2015)

22. Szegedy, C., et al.: Going deeper with convolutions. CoRR abs/1409.4842 (2014)
23. Wang, L., et al.: Temporal segment networks for action recognition in videos. CoRR abs/1705.02953 (2017)
24. Wu, Z., et al.: 3D shapeNets: a deep representation for volumetric shapes. In: CVPR, pp. 1912–1920 (2015)
25. Xiao, J., Hays, J., Ehinger, K.A., Oliva, A., Torralba, A.: SUN database: large-scale scene recognition from abbey to zoo. In: The Twenty-Third IEEE Conference on 2010 Computer Vision and Pattern Recognition CVPR, San Francisco, CA, USA, 13–18 June 2010. pp. 3485–3492 (2010)
26. Zeiler, M.D., Taylor, G.W., Fergus, R.: Adaptive deconvolutional networks for mid and high level feature learning. In: ICCV, pp. 2018–2025 (2011)
27. Zheng, S., et al.: Conditional random fields as recurrent neural networks. In: ICCV, pp. 1529–1537 (2015)

A Solution to Digital Image Copyright Registration Based on Consortium Blockchain

Jing Zeng[1,2]($\boxtimes$), Chun Zuo[1], Fengjun Zhang[1], Chunxiao Li[1],
and Longshuai Zheng[1]

[1] Institute of Software Chinese Academy of Sciences, Beijing 100190, China
zengjing15@otcaix.iscas.ac.cn,
zuochun@sinosoft.com.cn,
{fengjun, chunxiao, longshuai}@iscas.ac.cn
[2] University of Chinese Academy of Sciences, Beijing, China

Abstract. Reliable attribution statement records act as an effective way in which digital image copyright holders provide ownership evidence to defend their rights and interests. The centralized registration from the Copyright Office has shortcomings of high service cost, long processing time and susceptibility to tampering registration records. The decentralized solution based on public blockchain suffers the flaw that registration costs and service availability are susceptible to the prices of the relevant digital currencies as well as the transaction processing costs. In this paper, we propose an applying pattern of consortium blockchain, then put forward a decentralized architecture of digital image copyright registration based upon the applying pattern. Besides, based on the architecture and the registration logic design, a decentralized application prototype, which takes into account stable low service cost, instant registration processing and tamper-proof registration information for digital image copyright, is implemented.

Keywords: Digital image copyright · Blockchain · Consortium blockchain
Decentralized application

1 Introduction

Digital images have become important media for us to record real-world image information and have also been a hot research object in the field of computer science. Internet technologies in the Web 2.0 era, especial the rapid development of the Mobile Internet, makes digital images widely and immediately spread on the internet. About 2.4 billion digital images altogether are uploaded and shared daily only on Facebook, Instagram, Snapchat and WhatsApp [1]. Digital images are information carriers and personal works of creators such as photographers and illustrators, who naturally own the intellectual property of corresponding digital images. Digitalization and Internet make the copying and dissemination of information very convenient and efficient. However, digital images can also be copied and transmitted at very low cost, which makes digital images easily infringed.

Providing evidences of copyright ownership is an inevitable choice for digital image copyright owners to safeguard their own rights and interests. Creditable registration of copyright is an effective way for digital image copyright owners to record their copyright ownership evidence. Copyright registration, that is, information notarized. There are two main types of copyright registration methods currently available, one is the centralized notary method based on the public trusted intermediaries represented by the Copyright Office. The other is based on public blockchain protocols, such as Bitcoin [2] and Ethereum [3], which is a kind of decentralized notarization. The centralized notary registration has the flaws including high price, long processing period and potential risk of being tampered for records. The decentralized method based upon public blockchain, is impacted by the respective cryptocurrency prices and mining costs.

In view of the above facts, this paper proposes a decentralized digital image copyright registration method based on consortium blockchain. Utilizing a notary league corporately constituted by multiple organizations, the method provides consensus maintenance of trusted digital image copyright registration information. The solution takes into account the stable low service cost, instant registration processing and anti-tamper registration information, which provides a new reference solution to the copyright registration protection for digital images. This paper presents an applying pattern of consortium blockchain, then based on this pattern, designs and implements a decentralized digital image copyright registration application prototype.

2 Blockchain

Blockchain is a continuously growing list of records providing a reliable timestamping service based on cryptographic function and distributed consensus that records the history of electronic events occurred in the system. While serving as a kind of distributed ledger technology, it has succeeded in achieving a reliable transaction accounting function under the circumstance of without a centralized trusted authority [4]. The development of blockchain technology is believed to be going through the blockchain 1.0 model represented by cryptocurrency, the blockchain 2.0 model represented by smart contracts, and the more general scenarios beyond cryptocurrency and finance, that is blockchain 3.0 model [5]. Encrypted digital currency system, represented by Bitcoin, realizes the credible verification and record keeping of the ownership of digital currency value information under the circumstance of decentralized transaction institutions. Ethereum utilizes blockchain to reliably maintain the consistent replicated information in a decentralized environment and combines with a Turing-complete contract language to construct a smart contract platform that automates the terms, which enables the blockchain platform to handle computing tasks related to value information in a broader context. Many major research institutes and groups hold a view that blockchain has subversive potential for application in the fields of finance, energy, supply chain, registration confirmation and healthcare [6–11].

According to the different access scope of the network, the blockchain is divided into the public blockchain, the consortium blockchain and the private blockchain [12]. The most valuable types are public blockchain and consortium blockchain. The former has not any identity restriction on the nodes involved in building blockchain networks. It's dependent on the economic incentive mechanism of cryptocurrency and the decentralized consensus mechanism to maintain the consistency and security of network data. It is a completely decentralized pattern represented by Bitcoin and Ethereum. The latter building the network through the alliance of organizations, with the pre-selected maintaining nodes, usually do not need crypto-monetary incentive mechanism. It imposes identity restrictions on the network entities and is presented as a kind of partially decentralized model, which represented by Fabric [13] and Sawtooth [14] in the project Hyperledger under the Linux Foundation.

3 Digital Image Copyright Registration Solution

3.1 Defects in Existing Solutions

The existing registration methods for digital image copyright include the centralized approach and the decentralized one. The former is a mechanism providing copyright registration services for various works at a credible and central institution such as the Copyright Office. The latter currently uses a decentralized public blockchain network protocol to establish a registration service interface at the upper level to write the copyright registration information submitted by the user into the tamper-proof public blockchain data [15].

In the digital image copyright registration scheme based on a central agency, copyright registration services are provided by credible single authority. However, for copyright registration of digital images, even though an online registration interface is provided, this approach also requires a lot of laborious and expensive manual operations at the central office and a long period of registration processing. Due to the need of system maintenance, requests for service are sometimes denied and the centralized copyright registration data also has potential risks of being tampered with. Therefore, the current centralized copyright registration system is not suitable for the digital images whose production and dissemination run very quickly.

Blockchain with the features of decentralization, redundant distribution of evidences and anti-tampering, can be used as a new notarization technology for attribution of rights and interests. Combined with the smart contract, the digital image copyright information can be registered automatically and quickly. Copyright registration scheme based on the public blockchain, such as ascribe [15], writes the copyright statement information into the blockchain transaction data. By using the underlying public blockchain protocol, the transaction data is accepted by the whole network and the corresponding copyright registration information is also recorded into the whole network. The original intention of such proposal was to provide a digital rights registration service that is faster and cheaper than centralized registrations. However, due to the volatile price of cryptocurrencies in the underlying public blockchain and the rising costs of mining, the service fees charged for transactions processing are also not stable [16]. As a result, the cost of copyright registration services has risen and even could affect the registration services availability.

3.2   Architecture Design Based on Consortium Blockchain

Blockchain utilizes tamper resistance and transparent traceability to provide a credible consensus on key electronic data cross multiple institutions and industries. It could be a reference technology for decentralized inter-organization collaboration. To this end, we propose a consortium blockchain applying pattern, which is also an inter-organization collaboration architecture based on the consortium blockchain. Figure 1 shows the structure combining existing systems of organizations with consortium blockchain. In this architecture, the organizations' existing business systems could work normally and need not be completely rebuilt. The consortium blockchain network acts as a "black box" to maintain trusted and tamper-proof data. Existing systems import consensus-maintained data into the blockchain network through the interface layer of the consortium blockchain platform, or obtain trusted data from the blockchain network.

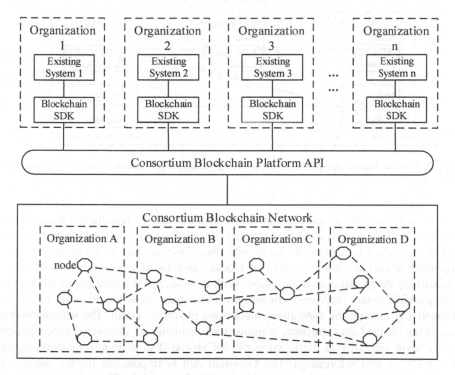

Fig. 1. Consortium blockchain applying pattern

In view of the defects of existing digital image copyright registration schemes and the applying pattern mentioned above, we proposes a digital image copyright registration scheme based on the consortium blockchain. The architecture design of this scheme is shown in Fig. 2. The main components include the digital image copyright registration client, the On-chain API, and the consortium blockchain network which is jointly established and maintained by a plurality of notary organizations.

The digital image copyright registration client provides the users with a digital image copyright registration interface and writes the digital image copyright

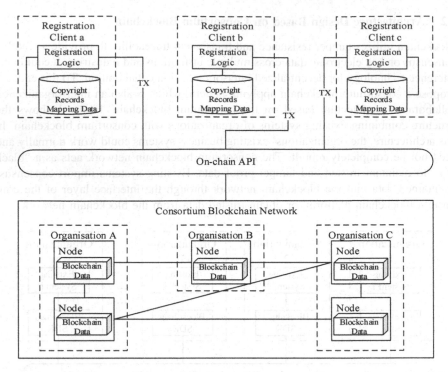

Fig. 2. Digital image copyright registration application framework based on consortium blockchain

information into the blockchain transaction data through its registration logic. Meanwhile, a local database is used as a mapping of the image copyright registration records in the blockchain to provide the users with data corresponding to the tamper-resistant copyright registration information in the blockchain network to support the user queries and display the registration information. With a number of different organizations that can provide notary services, consortium blockchain network is built by nodes respectively running the consortium blockchain platform system. The network makes use of the chained data structure, consensus mechanism and an oversight mechanisms based upon full copy to create tamper-proof shared data to jointly maintain digital image registration information. The On-chain API is responsible for the interaction between the digital image copyright registration client and the consortium blockchain network. It disseminates the blockchain transactions containing digital image copyright registration information to the consortium blockchain network, and returns copyright registration data to the registration client.

Compared with the registration scheme based on a centralized authority, the architecture based upon consortium blockchain changes the structure of the copyright registration notarization from a single center to multi-centers. Each organization that participates in data maintenance in the consortium blockchain can offer registration service, which effectively reduces the risk of denial of service compared to a single-center architecture. At the same time, the anti-tampering feature of the consortium blockchain also eliminates the risk of tampering with the copyright registration information under the single-center structure. Transactions in consortium blockchain can be automatically executed, which make requests for registration of digital rights processed automatically. The registration can be notarized more quickly at less cost to meet copyright registration requirements for digital images.

Compared with the registration scheme based on public blockchain, the framework proposed above takes advantage of consortium blockchain to limit the participation identities for the maintenance of copyright registration data. Consequently, the access permissions need to be granted rather than intrinsically obtained. Without the impacts of digital currency and competitive accounting, the cost and service availability of digital image copyright registration based on consortium blockchain could keep stable.

3.3   Digital Image Copyright Registration Logic

According to the architecture proposed above, we give the logical function design of the digital image copyright registration application system, as shown in Fig. 3.

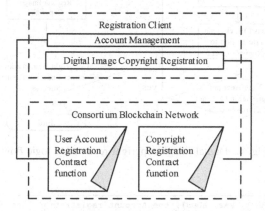

Fig. 3. Digital image copyright registration application logic function design

Registration client mainly provides users with account management as well as digital image copyright registration. Correspondingly, a user account registration contract function and a copyright registration contract function are provided on the consortium blockchain network. The two contract functions both run in all nodes participating in maintaining the consortium blockchain data so that the users could be qualified for registering and the digital image copyright information could be written into the blockchain.

The specific operations of the registration process are shown in Fig. 4. On the client, a user firstly needs to generate an asymmetric key pair and corresponding certificate information to construct blockchain transaction data for registering the corresponding account. Then, the user account registration contract function described as Algorithm 1 in Fig. 5 will be called in the consortium blockchain network. When the account registration is accepted by the blockchain, the user gets the qualification to register digital image copyright. A user selects digital image file and fill the copyright claim information to construct the blockchain transaction data signed by the private key corresponding to his or her account. The copyright registration contract function described as Algorithm 2 in Fig. 6 will be called to put the image copyright information into the consortium blockchain.

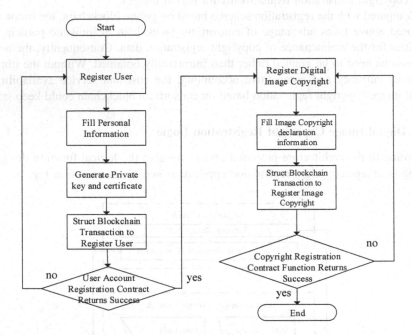

Fig. 4. Digital image copyright registration logic flow

```
Algorithm 1: RA(t, RAs, ADMs), the Account registration function in
Copyright Registration Authority Management Contract

Input:   t, a transaction to register a user account.
         RAs, registered accounts, RAs=[a₁,...,aₙ],a=(a_id, a_cert).
         ADMs, Administrators with authority to register a common account,
         ADMs=[adm₁,...,admₙ],adm=(adm_id,adm_cert).
Output:  r, the identity of the account registered suceessfully or null.
1    adm_cert ← getADMCert(ADMs, t.initiator_id)
2    r ← null
3    if adm_cert and verify(adm_cert.pubkey, t, t.sig)
4        and t.cert complies with X.509 standards
5        and verify(t.cert.pubkey, t.cert, t.cert.sig) then
6            a_id ← hash(t.cert)
7            a ← (a_id, t.cert)
8            if a ∉ RAs then
9                RAs ← {a} ∪ RAs
10               r ← a_id
11           end if
12   end if
13   return r
```

Fig. 5. The user account registration contract function algorithm

```
Algorithm 2: RC(t, CRs, RAs), the Copyright Registration function in
Digital Image Copyright Registration Contract:
─────────────────────────────────────────────────────────────────────
Input:   t, a transaction to register the copyright of a digital image.
         CRs, registered copyright records, CRs=[r₁, ..., rₙ],r=(rid,
         copyright_claim_info).
         RAs, registered accounts, RAs=[a₁, ..., aₙ],a=(a_id, a_cert).
Output:  r, the copyright registration result, true when success or false
         when fail.
1   account_cert ← getAccountCert(RAs, t.initiator_id)
2   r ← false
3   if account_cert and verify(account_cert.pubkey, t, t.sig) then
4       cr ← (t.copyright.digital_image_file_id,
               t.copyright.copyright_claim_info)
5       if cr ∉ CRs then
6           CRs ← {cr} ∪ CRs
7           r ← true
8       end if
9   end if
10  return r
```

Fig. 6. The copyright registration contract function algorithm

Because all nodes engaging in a consortium blockchain should conserve a consistent copy of the blockchain data, the consideration needs to be given to the amount of storage space required for the blockchain data as well as the network bandwidth resources. We should store meta-data on chain to be publicly accessible [17]. Therefore, we calculate the cryptography hash value of digital image file as its identity and write the identity along with the corresponding copyright statement into blockchain. Formula 1 depicts our copyright record model CR, which is represented as a key-value pair. DIF means a digital image file, Hash means a cryptography hash algorithm, and the result of Hash(DIF) acts as the key of the key-value pair. The value CCI, as shown in Formula 2, indicates the hex encoded copyright claim information including the owner account id ownerID, the description of image imgDesc and the description about the above hash algorithm hashAlgDesc.

$$CR = (\text{Hash}(DIF), CCI). \tag{1}$$

$$CCI = \text{hexEncode}(ownerID, imgDesc, hashAlgDesc). \tag{2}$$

The uniqueness of the hash value of the image file and the tamper-proof property of the blockchain can prove the authenticity of the digital image copyright record.

4 Prototype Implementation

According to the scheme designs above, we implement a digital image copyright registration prototype system. We leverage NodeJS to concrete the copyright registration logic and employ MongoDB to store the copyright registration results locally on the registration client. With ReactJS, the client visualizes the copyright registration information to users. The consortium blockchain network is constructed with Repchain [18], a light consortium blockchain platform developed by Institute of Software Chinese Academy of Sciences. We deploy the platform on nodes imitating different organizations to establish consortium blockchain network.

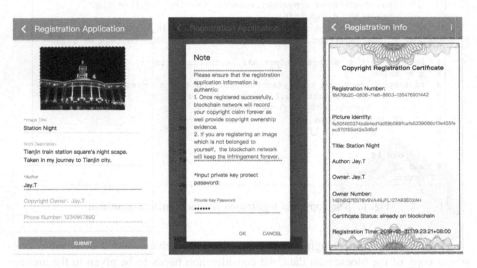

Fig. 7. Digital image copyright registration application visualization interfaces

Figure 7 shows the realization of the digital image copyright registration application visualization interfaces. Within the registration application page, a user could select digital image file and fill his or her copyright statement, then input the corresponding private key protection password to submit the application. In the registration info page, the users could view the respective copyright registration certificate information, such as the registration number, image file identity, author of the image, owner of the copyright and the registration time.

5   Conclusions

In this paper, we propose a solution to digital image copyright registration based upon consortium blockchain. We analysis the existing defects of the centralized scheme based on a single registration authority and the decentralized scheme based on public blockchain, then put forward an improved scheme based on consortium blockchain for digital image copyright registration. We give an applying pattern of consortium blockchain, and design an application architecture based on the pattern for digital image copyright registration. Then, we explain our registration logic, especially the contract functions. Eventually, a prototype system is implemented, which takes into account stable low service cost, instant registration processing and tamper-proof registration information.

The prototype ignores the function of copyright transfer registration,as the future work,we aim to improve the functionality and performance of our smart contracts implementation.

Acknowledgments. This work was supported by the National Natural Science Foundation of China (Grant No. 61572479), the National Key R&D Plan of China (Grant No. 2016YFB1001403), the National Natural Science Foundation of China together with the National Research Foundation of Singapore (Grant No. 61661146002), the Science and Technology Program of Guangzhou (Grant No. 201802020015), Key deployment project of the Chinese Academy of Sciences (Grant No. KFZD-SW-316-3).

References

1. Photo and Imaging Market TREND REPORT. https://www.piv-imaging.com/files/432/Trendreport_2016_EN_Web.pdf
2. Bitcoin: A Peer-to-Peer Electronic Cash System. https://bitcoin.org/bitcoin.pdf
3. Ethereum Whitepaper: A next generation smart contract and decentralized application platform. https://github.com/ethereum/wiki/wiki/White-Paper#ethereum
4. Blockchain. https://en.wikipedia.org/wiki/Blockchain
5. Swan, M.: Blockchain: Blueprint for a New Economy. OReilly Media Inc., Sebastopol (2015)
6. Danezis, G., Meiklejohn, S.: Centrally banked cryptocurrencies. In: 23rd Annual Network and Distributed System Security Symposium, San Diego (2016)
7. Smart Contracts: 12 Use Cases for Business & Beyond. https://digitalchamber.org/wp-content/uploads/2018/02/Smart-Contracts-12-Use-Cases-for-Business-and-Beyond_Chamber-of-Digital-Commerce.pdf
8. Profiles in innovation blockchain putting theory into practice. https://zh.scribd.com/doc/313839001/Profiles-in-Innovation-May-24-2016-1
9. Mills, D., Wang, K., Malone, B., Ravi, A., et al.: Distributed ledger technology in payments, clearing, and settlement. Finance and Economics Discussion Series 2016-095. Board of Governors of the Federal Reserve System, Washington. https://doi.org/10.17016/FEDS.2016.095
10. Scott, B.: How Can Cryptocurrency and Blockchain Technology Play a Role in Building Social and Solidarity Finance? United Nations Research Institute for Social Development (2016)
11. Walport, M.: Distributed Ledger Technology: Beyond Blockchain. UK Government Office for Science (2016)
12. On Public and Private Blockchains. https://blog.ethereum.org/2015/08/07/on-public-and-private-blockchains/
13. Hyperledger Fabric. https://hyperledger-fabric.readthedocs.io/en/latest/
14. Sawtooth. https://sawtooth.hyperledger.org/docs/core/releases/0.8/introduction.html
15. Towards An Ownership Layer for the Internet. https://bravenewcoin.com/assets/Whitepapers/ascribe-whitepaper-20150624.pdf
16. Bitcoin Transaction Fees Are Up More Than 1200% in Past Two Years. https://news.bitcoin.com/bitcoin-transaction-fees-1200-past-two-years/
17. Xiwei, X., Pautasso, C., Liming, Z., et al.: The blockchain as a software connector. In: 13th Working IEEE/IFIP Conference on Software Architecture, pp. 182–191. IEEE Press, New York (2016)
18. Repchain. https://gitee.com/chen4w/repchain

Scene Classification of High-Resolution Remote Sensing Image Using Transfer Learning with Multi-model Feature Extraction Framework

Guandong Li[1], Chunju Zhang[1(✉)], Mingkai Wang[1], Fei Gao[1], and Xueying Zhang[2]

[1] School of Civil Engineering, Hefei University of Technology, Hefei 230009, China
zcjtwz@sina.com
[2] Key Laboratory of Virtual Geographical Environment, Nanjing Normal University, Ministry of Education, Nanjing 210046, China

Abstract. The remote sensing image is full of scene information. Traditional classification methods are based on the artificial extraction feature, can not effectively express the high-level semantic information, and it requires a lot of high-quality training labeled data. However, the labeled data is usually scarce, and difficult to obtain. Transfer learning is a machine learning method that uses existing knowledge to solve those problems different but related. It can effectively solve the learning problem with only a small number of labeled sample data in the target field. ImageNet and remote sensing images have similar characteristics in image texture, lines, color, structure and space. In this paper, we propose a scene classification method of high spatial resolution remote sensing images using transfer learning with multi-model feature extraction network. It designs a combination of multiple pretrained CNN models to extract the features of remote sensing images, and integrates the features into one-dimensional feature vector. This forms a deep feature extraction framework that enriches feature expression and facilitates the capture of remote sensing image features. After feature extraction, a dropout layer and a fully connected layer are used, followed by a classifier. This method achieves a maximum accuracy of 97.38% on the UC Merced dataset and a maximum of 93.97% accuracy on the AID dataset, which is significantly better than the existing method and improves the classification accuracy.

Keywords: Remote sensing image · Convolution neural network
Scene classification · Multi-model integration · Feature extraction and fusion
Transfer learning

This work was supported in part by the National Nature Science Foundation under grant numbers 41401451, 41671456 and 41671393.

1 Introduction

With the advancement of science and technology, the resolution of remote sensing images has been improved. At present, the existing high-resolution satellite (such as IKONOS and QuickBird, etc.) have made the remote sensing image resolution reach the meter level and even the sub-meter level. High resolution remote sensing image not only has a rich spatial and texture features, but also contains a lot of scene semantic information. Due to the enormous increase in the number of remote sensing images and the highly complex geometric structure and spatial pattern, the scene classification of high-resolution images has become a challenging subject, which has attracted wide attention in the field of remote sensing [1]. The solution to the scene classification of high-resolution remote sensing image focus on modeling method based on low-level semantic feature and middle-level semantic feature [2]. These methods include spatial pyramid matching kernel (SPMK) [3], spatial pyramid coexistence kernel (SPCK++) [4], KD-Tree [5], sparse coding [6] and so on. Typically, Based On Visual Words (BOVW), namely through the use of feature descriptors (HOG, SIFT, etc.) to learn the image content of the data characteristics, using clustering method to divide feature words into several categories, each category is equivalent to a visual word and each image is consisted of many visual words, and then, using the statistical word frequency histogram, to get the category of the image. However, the main drawback of these methods is that the general feature descriptor can not extract the effective features fully to describe the complex image structure, and the traditional feature extraction is based on the artificial design of the expert knowledge. Deep learning has proven to have a good effect in the field of image classification [7]. In this case, Convolution Neural Network (CNN) to deal with high-resolution remote sensing images has an outstanding performance. It is progressive extraction of input data from the bottom to the top of the characteristics, and establishing the underlying signal to the high-level semantic mapping, and feature extraction from convolution kernel can be done automatically without manual design. Also, High resolution remote sensing image data grows fast, but the high-quality sample data with labels are often scarce and difficult to obtain. CNN deep learning method can obtain highly accurate classification results based on a larger high-quality sample dataset of remote sensing image. However, when CNN learns limited labeled sample data, it may lead to an over-fitting classification.

In the lack of "expensive" labeled sample data, transfer learning can improve the classification performance with a large number labeled samples with similar distribution. It introduces the information acquired in the original task into the learning of a new task, and allows the computer having ability of cross-domain learning, which makes it possible to effectively reuse information in similar areas. High resolution remote sensing images have similar macroscopic features in image textures, lines, colors, structures, and space with ImageNet. Therefore, this paper proposes a method of scene classification of high-resolution remote sensing image using transfer learning and deep learning.

Based on the principle of transfer learning, the parameters of the CNN model pretrained on the ImageNet dataset are migrated to the high spatial resolution remote sensing image dataset, fully utilizing convolution to understand the image structure.

Based on the similarity degree, So that only a small amount of remote sensing image scene tagged sample data can get a good classification effect. Based on the tests of VGG16, VGG19 [8], Inception-v3 [9], Xception [10], ResNet50 [11], DenseNet [12], it is found that the multiple models are significantly better than single model to extract the feature of remote sensing image. Therefore, this paper proposes a multi-model feature extraction framework that uses multiple combinations of pretrained CNN models to obtain multiple sets of feature vectors, fuses features, and extracts rich feature information for accurate scene classification.

The remaining parts of this paper are organized as follows. In Sect. 2, we present an introduction to pretrained CNN models and transfer learning. Section 3 discusses the process of feature extraction and fusion in our model. Section 4 presents the experimental results, and in Sect. 6, we summarize the paper and discuss future research directions.

2   Principle and Method

2.1   ImageNet Data Set

ImageNet is the world's largest database of image recognition, with 15 million labeled high-definition pictures of the data set, the category is composed by a variety of animals and plants, inanimate objects and so forth, which is more than 22,000 categories. There are many differences among the same category of objects in the shape, perspective, attitude, background, etc. Therefore, the sample with a strong diversity and a wide range of categories covered. The pretrained CNN models used in this paper are trained on this dataset.

2.2   Pretrained CNN Models

CNN is a kind of deep learning method which is specially designed for image classification and recognition based on multi-layer neural network. The structure of CNN is constituted by several sections of the convolution layer, pool layer, activation function layer and the whole connection layer [13]. The model structure tested in this paper includes six kinds of CNN models, such as VGG16, VGG19, Inception-v3, Xception, ResNet50 and DenseNet121, which was pretrained on ImageNet dataset. The VGG-16, VGG-19 is a deep convolution neural network developed by the Computer Vision Group of Oxford University and Google DeepMind. By repeatedly stacking 3×3 small convolution kernels and 2×2 maxpooling layers, VGGNet successfully built a 16–19 layers deep neural network. Continuously using small convolutions to imitate large convolution kernels to locally perceive images, this design can reduce parameters and save computing expenses. VGGNet is highly scalable and the generalization ability to migrate to other data is very good. GooLeNet (Inception-v1) [9] proposed a creative structure of the Inception Architecture, which is a sparse connection structure. This article also uses the Inception-v3 model which is optimized on the basis of Inception-v1. Inception-v3 introduced factorization into small Convolution thought, a larger two-dimensional convolution is disassembled into two smaller one-dimensional convolution, which increases the nonlinear expression ability of the model, and optimizes the structure of Inception Moule. Inception-v3 network structure is complex, but for the image classification has a very good effect. ResNet is proposed by Microsoft, and can be viewed as a combination of parallel and serial multiple models, ResNet has a lot of bypass information that the feeder will enter directly into the back layer, so that the back layer can learn the residuals directly, this structure is called shortcut or skip connections, it looks a bit like RNN, so it can be seen as a better biological neural network model, we use the ResNet50. The Xception model uses the same simple and elegant architecture as ResNet and improves the Inception model. DenseNet directly connects all the layers while ensuring the maximum degree of information transmission between layers in the network. It fully utilizes features, reduces the problem of gradient disappearance, and further suppresses over-fitting. In this paper, six models are tested on the scene classification of remote sensing datasets. Finally, a method of combining multiple models to extract features was proposed.

2.3 Transfer Learning

The goal of knowledge transfer is to extract effective information from the associated tasks to assist in solving new tasks. The fundamental starting point is the sparseness of the data in the target domain, that is, the target training set lacks valid tags or sufficient samples. Knowledge transfer solves the bottleneck problem that the training and test samples of machine learning requirements must follow the same distribution assumption rigorously. Transfer learning allows you to store the knowledge obtained when the source task is resolved in the source domain by applying the label data of some related tasks or domains that already exist and apply it to the target task in the target domain. A domain D consists of a characteristic space X and a marginal probability distribution P(X) on the characteristic space, where X = x1, ..., xn ∈ X. Given a domain D = {X, P(X)}, a task T consists of a label space y and a conditional probability distribution P(Y | X), which is usually obtained from which "feature-label" learns from the training data of (xi ∈ X, yi ∈ Y). Given a source domain Ds, a corresponding source task Ts, a target domain Dt, and a target task Tt, the purpose of the transfer learning is that in the case of Ds $\neq$ Dt, Ts $\neq$ Tt, as well as Ds and Ts information, the conditional probability distribution P(Yt | Xt) in the target domain Dt will be obtained by learning [14]. There are four patterns to achieve transfer learning, including sample transfer, feature transfer, model transfer (also called parameter transfer), and relational transfer [15].

High spatial resolution remote sensing images have similar characteristics in image texture, lines, color, and spatial features with ImageNet to some extent. Therefore, this paper transfers the CNN model's pretrained parameters on the ImageNet dataset to the high spatial resolution remote sensing image dataset. It uses pretrained CNN for feature extraction, and the fully connected neural network for scene classification. Making full use of the understanding of the image structure of convolution, also based on the similarity of ImageNet and remote sensing image data, transfer learning with only a small amount scene labeled data of remote sensing image can get a well classification effect.

3 Multi-model Feature Extraction Framework and Feature Fusion

This paper proposes a multi-model feature extraction framework to extract remote sensing image features. The model generates feature vectors after extracting features, and then merges the generated feature vectors into a set of one-dimensional vectors to achieve the fusion of features. After that, connect a dropout, followed by a 96-D fully connected layer, and finally use the softmax classifier to get the classification results. As shown in Fig. 1.

To explain the effectiveness of this approach, it is basic to answer the following four questions:

1. Are the pretrained models in ImageNet effective on remote sensing datasets?

Based on the principle of transfer learning, pretrained models on ImageNet are used to extract features of remote sensing images. But why would remote sensing image feature extraction benefit from the pretrained model? In [16], The structure of CNN imitates the mammalian visual cortex through a multilayer processing approach. By using this hierarchical structure, pretrained models on ImageNet extended knowledge on low-level spatial descriptors (edge and corner detector) and employ them to describe images in bottom-up manner. This way, pretrained CNNs can trivially "decompose" images into a set of primitive elements and detect similarities on various levels of abstraction among them. These features describe the image in a bottom-up mode, and combine more abstract features in the high-level structure to enable the mapping of feature combinations from low-level to high-level to specific scene labels. This hierarchical image recognition structure ensures the effectiveness of feature extraction for similar sample sources in knowledge transfer. Therefore, the feature extraction process from the low-level to the high-level is also adapted to the feature extraction of remote sensing image data. Only need a small amount of remote sensing image data to train the mapping process, that is, only the classifier needs to be trained. Due to these properties, pretrained models can be easily adapted to new visual tasks.

2. Why do feature extraction at the last level?

In [17], the author used CNN to test the ILSVRC-2012 validation set, and the clustering of the high-level semantic information was very obvious at the last full connection layer. This is compatible with common deep learning knowledge that the first layers learn "low-level" features, whereas the latter layers learn semantic or "high-level" features. The more the features of the back layer are extracted, the higher the accuracy of the model can be improved. Based on this, this paper proposes to save the output of the last layer of the multi-model feature extraction framework as feature vectors and combine the vectors to make full use of the remote sensing data features extracted by the model.

3. Why do we fuse feature vectors into a one-dimensional feature vector?

Since the feature vector of each model in the multi-model is independent, the characteristics of the individual models are not sufficient to describe the classification objects comprehensively. Different feature vectors can provide complementary information to each other. The feature fusion can make the classifier learn more features and improve the accuracy. In our method, the features are combined into a set of one-dimensional vectors.

4. Why add dropout and fully connected layers?

The multi-model feature extraction framework extracts sufficient remote sensing image features, connecting a dropout to prevent over-fitting of the model. Over-fitting can reduce by using "dropout" to prevent complex co-adaptations on the training data. On each presentation of each training case, each hidden unit is randomly omitted from the network with a probability of 0.5, so a hidden unit cannot rely on other hidden units being present [18]. The fully connected layer facilitates the efficient transmission of information associated with classification, and the experimental results demonstrate that the fully connected layer can improve the accuracy of image classification.

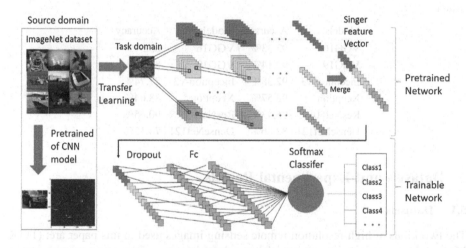

Fig. 1. Multi-model feature extraction framework

4 Model

The multi-model feature extraction network proposed in this paper are tested on UC Merced datasets and AID datasets. The performance of a single model on the dataset is shown in Table 1. Although the six models tested in this paper have obtained good results, we find that the combination of VGG19, Xception, Inception-v3 and ResNet50 models has the best effect on the UC Merced dataset, and the accuracy of the test set is 97.38%. The combination of ResNet50, Inception-v3 and Xception model has the best effect on the AID dataset, and the accuracy rate of the test set reaches 93.97%. This shows that the multi-model feature extraction framework can effectively improve the accuracy of remote sensing image feature extraction. The method can be divided into two parts, the first part is used to extract the feature vector of the joint multiple model, and multiple groups of feature vectors are fused into a set of singer vectors. The second part is that the fused vector is input into the Softmax classifier after dropout and a fully-connected layer to obtain the classification results. As shown in Fig. 1. The first part with the model of pretrained on ImageNet, using pretrained parameters. Before the input of the classifier, use a dropout operation to avoid over-fitting and improve model generalization, and then enters a fully connected layer for information transfer. The final fully connected layers are generally assumed to capture information that is relevant for solving the respective task. The remote sensing image dataset completes the feature extraction in the first stage, and abstracts the original images into more easily classified feature vectors later, and then trains the classifier in the second stage, so that it can achieve good scene classification accuracy with only a few sample data.

Table 1. The performance of a single model on the UC Merced dataset (Left) and AID dataset (Right)

Models	Accuracy	Models	Accuracy
VGG16	93.33%	VGG16	83.37%
VGG19	92.14%	VGG19	81.96%
Inception-v3	92.38%	Inception-v3	87.74%
Xception	93.57%	Xception	88.64%
ResNet50	96.43%	ResNet50	90.65%
DenseNet121	82.86%	DenseNet121	74.12%

5   Datasets and Experimental Results

5.1   Datasets

The two kinds of high-resolution remote sensing images used in this paper are: (1) UC Merced 21 type scene images, which are selected from aerial remote sensing images from different regions of the USGS National City map image, the resolution is about 0.3 m, each class has 100, a total of 2100 pictures, the size is 256×256, the image category has a high degree of repeatability, it has higher intra-class variations and smaller inter-class dissimilarity. The dataset is widely used in aerial image classification tasks, as shown in Fig. 2. (2) AID (Aerial Image DataSet) 30 type scene Image [19], which is produced by Wuhan University, collected from Google Earth. It aims at solving the problem that the algorithm has a saturation in the dataset due to the fact that the UC Merced 21 scenarios have too few images, the resolution is from 0.5–8 m, 220–420 pieces per class, a total of 10000 pictures, the size is 600×600, as shown in Fig. 3.

(a)   (b)   (c)   (d)   (e)

Fig. 2. (a) Airplane (b) building (c) denseresidential (d) Mediumresidentail (e) storagetanks

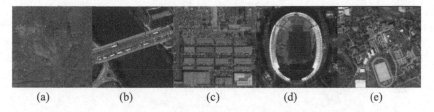

(a)   (b)   (c)   (d)   (e)

Fig. 3. (a) Bareland (b) brige (c) industrial (d) stadium (e) school

5.2   Experimental Results

This paper uses Keras as a deep learning framework. The proportion of training set and test is 8:2. The validation set in training set accounted for 0.2. All the data are trained on a GPU of GTX965.

5.2.1   The Performance of Model Test on UC Merced Dataset

5.2.1.1 Effect of Multi-model Combination

In this paper, we propose pretrained multi-model extraction feature network, the efficiency of feature extraction is further enhanced. The accuracy of single model feature extraction is tested in Table 1. Figure 4 shows the loss value change of six models in the training process, it shows that ResNet50 is the fastest convergent model in six kinds of models. Inception-v3 and Xception models have approximately the same convergence speed. The convergence curves of VGG16 and VGG19 are the slowest and almost the same. It can be seen that the extracted features tend to be consistent, and this also corresponds to a model structure that is close to both of them. This is also demonstrated in the Inception-v3 and Xception two models, both Inception-v3 and Xception contain Inception modules. Figure 5 shows the accuracy changes of the six models during training. The accuracy of the six models is greatly enhanced in the first round of training, while the second round is significantly slowed down, and then the efficiency of feature extraction shows decreasing trend. ResNet50 still achieves good results in remote sensing image feature extraction, while the trend of Inception-v3 and Xception is similar, which is better than the feature extraction efficiency of VGG16 and VGG19. DenseNet121 is the worst. In summary, the proposed multi-model structure can accelerate the feature extraction efficiency in different dimensions, and combine the ResNet50 as the optimal item, Inception-v3 and Xception, VGG16 and VGG19 as two sets of feature extraction models, provide a good guidance for our multi-model feature extraction framework. Table 2 shows the classification accuracy of different combinations on the UC Merced 21 category. The accuracy of the combination of VGG19, Inception-v3, Xception and ResNet is 97.38%, which is significantly better than that of the previous scene classification as shown in Table 3. The multi-model's loss value begins to drop quickly. We trained 100 epoch, and the multi-model achieved the best accuracy at the fastest speed. It saves computing power and improves the efficiency of feature extraction.

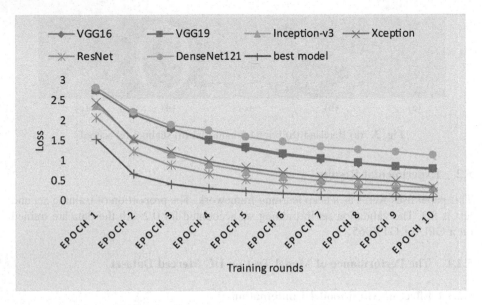

Fig. 4. The loss value variation of the models involved in this paper

5.2.1.2 Effect of Dropout Value

This paper proposes a multi-model to extract features of remote sensing image data, and then fuses the extracted features to form a one-dimensional feature vector. At this point, the multi-model feature extraction framework will extract some repetitive features that may result in over-fitting, so we add the dropout layer. The experiment discussed the influence of different dropout values on the final classification accuracy of the model. As shown in Fig. 6. When the dropout value is set to 0.5, the effect is the best (Using VGG19, Inception-v3, Xception, ResNet combination model).

5.2.1.3 Effect of Fully Connected Layer

The fully connected layer is conducive to the effective transmission of information related to classification. The experiment discusses setting fully connected layers and no fully connected layers, and the final classification accuracy of the model. As shown in Table 4.

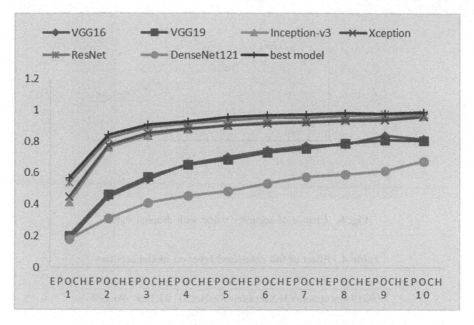

Fig. 5. Acurracy of the models involved in this paper

Table 2. The accuracy of multiple models on the test set

Models	Accuracy
ResNet50+Xception	97.30%
DenseNet121+ResNet50	95.47%
VGG16+Inception-v3+ResNet50	95.71%
VGG16+Xception+ResNet50	96.67%
Inception-v3+Xception+ResNet50	96.90%
VGG16+Inception-v3+Xception+ResNet50	97.14%
VGG19+Inception-v3+Xception+ResNet50	97.38%

Table 3. The accuracy rate of the previous method of UC Merced dataset

Method	Year	Ref	Accuracy (%)
SPMK	2006	[3]	74.0
BOVW	2011	[4]	71.8
SPCK++	2011	[4]	76.0
Sparce Coding	2014	[6]	81.7
Salient Unsupervised Learning	2015	[20]	82.8
Pretrained ConvNet (CaffeNet) with SVM classifier	2015	[21]	93.4
CNN with Overfeat feature	2016	[16]	92.4
Pretrained multi-model extraction feature network (proposed)	2018		97.38

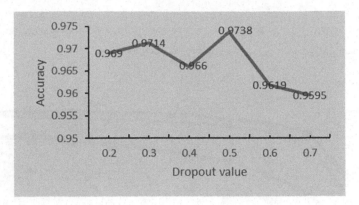

Fig. 6. Change of accuracy value with dropout value

Table 4. Effect of full connected layer on model accuracy

	fc	no fc
VGG19+Inception-v3+Xception+ResNet50	97.38%	96.19%

5.2.1.4 Effect of Activation Function

For deep CNN, a non-linear activation function is connected behind each convolution layer, which is similar to the suppression behavior of real neurons in the human brain to enhance the recognition ability. Commonly used activation functions include sigmoid, Tanh, Relu, etc. In this paper, the sigmoid function is used in the fully connected layer. From the mathematical point of view, the nonlinear sigmoid function has a great effect on the central signal gain, while the signal gain of the two sides is small, it has a good effect on the mapping of the signal's feature space. Nonlinear decision boundary is generated by nonlinear combination of weighted inputs. From the neuroscience point of view, the central region resembles the neuron's excited state, the two sides resemble the neuron's inhibitory state. Therefore, in the process of neural network learning, it is feasible to push the key features to the central area, while the non-key features to the two sides. The experiment tested the Tanh and Relu functions, and the sigmoid function achieved better results, as shown in Table 5.

Table 5. Effects of different activation functions on model accuracy

	Sigmoid	Tanh	Relu
VGG19+Inception-v3+Xception+ResNet50	97.38%	95.48%	93.09%

5.2.1.5 Effect of Feature Vector Extraction

After the multi-model feature extraction process, the high-resolution image forms a 6656-D feature vector, and the dimension totals are shown in Fig. 7. In this paper, we use the t-sne algorithm to reduce the dimension of 6656-D feature vector, as shown in Fig. 8. It can be seen that after the feature extraction, the similar feature of the scene has formed a certain degree of aggregation, and this aggregation provides better guidance for the following training classifier, so that the classifier requires only a few remote sensing image labels to achieve a very high classification accuracy.

Model	VGG16	Inception-v3	Xception	ResNet50	Total
Dimension	512	2048	2048	2048	6656

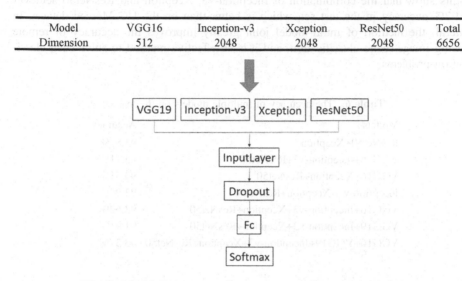

Fig. 7. Model feature extraction process and dimension statistics

Fig. 8. Feature vector reduced dimension image

5.2.2 The Performance of Model Test on the AID Dataset

Based on the effect of multi-model feature extraction framework on the UC Merced dataset, we use the combined model of VGG19, Inception-v3, Xception, ResNet50 to process the AID dataset, set the dropout value to 0.5, add the FC layer, and use the sigmoid activation function, which finally achieve a 91.91% accuracy on the test set. In addition, we also test the multi-model on the AID data set, as shown in Table 6. The results show that the combination of Inception-v3, Xception and ResNet50 achieves 93.97% accuracy in the test set, which is better than on the UC Merced dataset, In general, the method of multi-model joint greatly improves the accuracy of remote sensing image scene classification, and it is an effective method to solve such classification problems.

Table 6. The accuracy of multiple models on the test set

Models	Accuracy
ResNet50+Xception	93.87%
VGG16+Inception-v3+ResNet50	93.11%
VGG16+Xception+ResNet50	93.51%
Inception-v3+Xception+ResNet50	93.97%
VGG16+Inception-v3+Xception+ResNet50	93.62%
VGG19+Inception-v3+Xception+ResNet50	91.91%
VGG16+VGG19+Inception-v3+Xception+ResNet50	93.37%

6 Discussion and Conclusion

This paper proposes a method based on transfer learning and multi-model feature extraction framework for scene classification of high-resolution remote sensing images. The pretrained model on ImageNet is used to extract the feature vectors of remote sensing images. After feature extraction, a dropout layer and a fully connected layer are used, followed by a classifier. This method achieves high accuracy on the test sets of UC Merced and AID datasets, and is not only efficient but also highly migratory.

Future research will further explore the impact of feature extraction structure on high-resolution images based on the multi-model feature extraction framework. And consider using this method on hyperspectral remote sensing images.

References

1. Cheng, G., Han, J., Lu, X.: Remote sensing image scene classification: benchmark and state of the art. Proc. IEEE **105**(10), 1865–1883 (2017)
2. Vailaya, A., Figueiredo, M.A., Jain, A.K., Zhang, H.J.: Image classification for content-based indexing. IEEE Trans. Image Process. **10**(1), 117–130 (2001)
3. Lazebnik, S., Schmid, C., Ponce, J.: Beyond bags of features: spatial pyramid matching for recognizing natural scene categories. In: 2006 IEEE Computer Society Conference on Computer Vision and Pattern Recognition, vol. 2, pp. 2169–2178 (2006)
4. Yang, Y., Newsam, S.: Spatial pyramid co-occurrence for image classification. In: 2011 IEEE International Conference on Computer Vision (ICCV), pp. 1465–1472, November 2011

5. Gueguen, L.: Classifying compound structures in satellite images: a compressed representation for fast queries. IEEE Trans. Geosci. Remote Sens. **53**(4), 1803–1818 (2015)
6. Cheriyadat, A.M.: Unsupervised feature learning for aerial scene classification. IEEE Trans. Geosci. Remote Sens. **52**(1), 439–451 (2014)
7. Krizhevsky, A., Sutskever, I., Hinton, G.E.: Imagenet classification with deep convolutional neural networks. In: Advances in Neural Information Processing Systems, pp. 1097–1105 (2012)
8. Simonyan, K., Zisserman, A.: Very deep convolutional networks for large-scale image recognition. arXiv preprint arXiv:1409.1556 (2014)
9. Szegedy, C., Vanhoucke, V., Ioffe, S., Shlens, J., Wojna, Z.: Rethinking the inception architecture for computer vision. In: Proceedings of the IEEE Conference on Computer Vision and Pattern Recognition, pp. 2818–2826 (2016)
10. Chollet, F. Xception: deep learning with depthwise separable convolutions. arXiv preprint (2016)
11. He, K., Zhang, X., Ren, S., Sun, J.: Deep residual learning for image recognition. In: Proceedings of the IEEE Conference on Computer Vision and Pattern Recognition, pp. 770–778 (2016)
12. Huang, G., Liu, Z., Weinberger, K.Q., van der Maaten, L.: Densely connected convolutional networks. In: Proceedings of the IEEE Conference on Computer Vision and Pattern Recognition, vol. 1, No. 2, p. 3, July 2017
13. Uba, N.K.: Land Use and Land Cover Classification Using Deep Learning Techniques. Arizona State University, Tempe (2016)
14. Pan, S.J., Yang, Q.: A survey on transfer learning. IEEE Trans. Knowl. Data Eng. **22**(10), 1345–1359 (2010)
15. Yosinski, J., Clune, J., Bengio, Y., Lipson, H.: How transferable are features in deep neural networks? In: Advances in Neural Information Processing Systems, pp. 3320–3328 (2014)
16. Marmanis, D., Datcu, M., Esch, T., Stilla, U.: Deep learning earth observation classification using ImageNet pretrained networks. IEEE Geosci. Remote Sens. Lett. **13**(1), 105–109 (2016)
17. Donahue, J., et al.: Decaf: a deep convolutional activation feature for generic visual recognition. In: International Conference on Machine Learning, pp. 647–655, January 2014
18. Hinton, G.E., Srivastava, N., Krizhevsky, A., Sutskever, I., Salakhutdinov, R.R.: Improving neural networks by preventing co-adaptation of feature detectors. arXiv preprint arXiv:1207.0580 (2012)
19. Xia, G.S., et al.: AID: a benchmark data set for performance evaluation of aerial scene classification. IEEE Trans. Geosci. Remote Sens. **55**(7), 3965–3981 (2017)
20. Zhang, F., Du, B., Zhang, L.: Saliency-guided unsupervised feature learning for scene classification. IEEE Trans. Geosci. Remote Sens. **53**(4), 2175–2184 (2015)
21. Hu, F., Xia, G.S., Wang, Z., Huang, X., Zhang, L., Sun, H.: Unsupervised feature learning via spectral clustering of multidimensional patches for remotely sensed scene classification. IEEE J. Sel. Top. Appl. Earth Obser. Remote Sens. **8**(5) (2015)

A Novel Image Encryption Scheme Based on Hidden Random Disturbance and Feistel RPMPFrHT Network

Guozhen Hu[1], Xuejing Kang[2(✉)], Zihui Guo[1,2], and Xuanshu Luo[1,2]

[1] School of Computer Science, Beijing University of Posts and Telecommunications, Beijing 100876, China
claps@claps.com.cn
[2] Institute of Sensing Technology and Business, Beijing University of Posts and Telecommunications, Beijing 100876, China
kangxuejing@bupt.edu.cn

Abstract. In this paper, we propose a novel image encryption scheme based on hidden random disturbance and Feistel RPMPFrHT network, which can improve some common defects of the transform-based methods. At first, we hide some distractive information into the plain image without enlarging the size of the image, which can greatly improve the ability to resist chosen plaintext attack. Then we put the image into Feistel RPMPFrHT network to transform it into two different fractional domain and we will obtain the merits of robustness to noise and data loss. At last we homogenize the numerical distribution and rearrange the pixels by plain-image-dependent chaotic sequences to hide the special statistical characteristics of the image, which can increase the plaintext sensitivity. Simulation results have proved that our proposed encryption scheme shows good performance on most general tests and it makes a great improvement compared with existing image encryption schemes in transform domain.

Keywords: Image encryption · Random disturbance
Feistel network · Fractional Hartley transform

1 Introduction

Image encryption gets growing focus these years because it is a direct and efficient way to meet the security requirements of image information. The study of image encryption schemes based on various transforms, such as fractional Fourier transform (FrFT) [1], Fresnel transform [2], gyrator transform [3] and Mellin transform [4], is a hotspot among researchers because these methods often show the superiority of better performance against noise attack and higher robustness to data loss. However, there are some common defects among these encryption schemes. Firstly, most of them transform the whole original image into another specific domain to process, which results that the cipher image presents some special statistical characteristics corresponding to that domain.

© Springer Nature Singapore Pte Ltd. 2018
Y. Wang et al. (Eds.): IGTA 2018, CCIS 875, pp. 252–262, 2018.
https://doi.org/10.1007/978-981-13-1702-6_25

For example, the histogram of cipher image might show Gaussian distribution [1,4], which may leak some information to attackers. Secondly, many encrypted images in the transform domain are not sensitive enough to plain image, which will cause weaker resistance to chosen plaintext attack. Thirdly, the transform-based encryption schemes are sometimes difficult to implement such as using hardware and embedded system when necessary. Therefore, how to improve the drawbacks of these encryption schemes and simplify the code and circuitry of implementation are worth studying.

In this paper, we proposed a novel image encryption scheme on the basis of reality-preserving multiple-parameter fractional Hartley transform (RPMP-FrHT) aiming to improve the problems above. At first, we proposed the adjoining-pixel encoding and hidden random disturbance scheme to process the plain image. Next we designed the Feistel RPMPFrHT network to transform different blocks of the image into different fractional domains. At last, we proposed the location-dependent unified average gray value (LD_UAGV) to distinguish different plain images and use it to disturb a chaotic system, then homogenize the image by chaotic sequence with bitxor operation. Experiment results have proved the effectiveness of our proposed algorithm in improving the ability to resist chosen plaintext attack and statistical attack.

2   The Proposed Image Encryption Scheme

2.1   The Proposed Hidden Random Disturbance

As we know, a meaningful image has high correlation among adjacent pixels. For four adjoining pixels (2×2 units), it is not rare that some of their gray values are equal. Therefore, we could change the four adjoining pixels into a pattern code and a four-tuple transmission unit, where pattern code encoded all permutations appeared in four adjoining pixels and transmission unit recorded the different gray values.

Suppose the transmission unit is (a, b, c, d), an encoding scheme of pattern code is shown as Fig. 1(a). If we perform adjoining-pixel encoding with this pattern code encoding scheme on image in Fig. 1(b), we will get the result shown as following:

$$C = \begin{pmatrix} 0 & 11 \\ 5 & 1 \end{pmatrix} \ T_a = \begin{pmatrix} 115 & 70 \\ 70 & 71 \end{pmatrix} \ T_b = \begin{pmatrix} 210 & 71 \\ 67 & - \end{pmatrix} \ T_c = \begin{pmatrix} 90 & 210 \\ - & - \end{pmatrix} \ T_d = \begin{pmatrix} 67 & - \\ - & - \end{pmatrix}$$

As we can see, for image G with size $M \times N$, divide G into four-adjoining-pixel units, and then transform each unit into a pattern code and a transmission unit, we will get a pattern code matrix C with size $\frac{M}{2} \times \frac{N}{2}$ and a transmission units matrix T with size $\frac{M}{2} \times \frac{N}{2} \times 4$ (T_a records all values of a, etc.). According to how many different gray values are there in a four-adjoining-pixel unit, some elements in matrix T may have no value (denoted by "-"), which will be filled with random number as random disturbance exactly.

In our encryption algorithm, the pattern code matrix C will serve as a secret key, while the transmission units matrix T will be reshaped to size $M \times N$ as

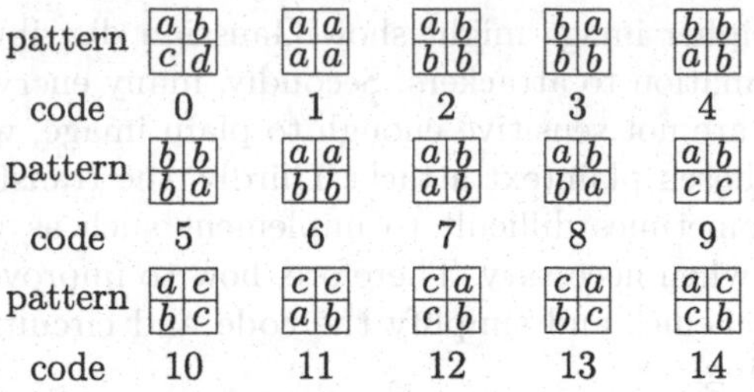

pattern	$\begin{smallmatrix}a&b\\c&d\end{smallmatrix}$	$\begin{smallmatrix}a&a\\a&a\end{smallmatrix}$	$\begin{smallmatrix}a&b\\b&b\end{smallmatrix}$	$\begin{smallmatrix}b&a\\b&b\end{smallmatrix}$	$\begin{smallmatrix}b&b\\a&b\end{smallmatrix}$
code	0	1	2	3	4
pattern	$\begin{smallmatrix}b&b\\b&a\end{smallmatrix}$	$\begin{smallmatrix}a&a\\b&b\end{smallmatrix}$	$\begin{smallmatrix}a&b\\a&b\end{smallmatrix}$	$\begin{smallmatrix}a&b\\b&a\end{smallmatrix}$	$\begin{smallmatrix}a&b\\c&c\end{smallmatrix}$
code	5	6	7	8	9
pattern	$\begin{smallmatrix}a&c\\b&c\end{smallmatrix}$	$\begin{smallmatrix}c&c\\a&b\end{smallmatrix}$	$\begin{smallmatrix}c&a\\c&b\end{smallmatrix}$	$\begin{smallmatrix}c&a\\b&c\end{smallmatrix}$	$\begin{smallmatrix}a&c\\c&b\end{smallmatrix}$
code	10	11	12	13	14

image G with size 4×4:

115	210	210	210
90	67	70	71
67	67	71	71
67	70	71	71

(a) pattern code encoding scheme   (b) image G with size 4×4

Fig. 1. An example of adjoining-pixel encoding

cipher image. In this way, every image will includes some random information when we encrypt it. Thus we will never get the same cipher image even if we encrypt a plain image with the same keys for several times, which causes much difficulties to attackers who use chosen plaintext attack.

2.2 The Proposed Feistel RPMPFrHT Network

The RPMPFrFT has been proved effective to be used in image encryption [1]. Substitute the fractional Fourier transform with fractional Hartley transform (FrHT) [5] and we can get RPMPFrHT. The N-point FrHT kernel $\boldsymbol{H}^a$ is defined as:

$$\boldsymbol{H}^a = \sum_{k=0}^{N-1} e^{-j\pi ak} \boldsymbol{u}_k \boldsymbol{u}_k^T \tag{1}$$

where a is the fractional order, $\boldsymbol{u}_k$ is an eigenvector corresponding to the eigenvalue $e^{-j\pi k}$, and the definition of RPMPFrHT can refer to [1].

The Feistel network [6] is widely used in a large proportion of block ciphers including the Data Encryption Standard (DES). It takes the advantage that encryption and decryption operations are very similar, so that the code or circuitry to implement such a cipher is nearly halved. Split the plaintext into two pieces (L_0, R_0), the construction of a Feistel network in i-th round is defined as:

$$\begin{cases} L_{i+1} = R_i \\ R_{i+1} = L_i \oplus F(R_i, k_i) \end{cases} \tag{2}$$

where F is the round function, k_i are secret keys.

Integrating the Feistel network [6] and the RPMPFrHT [1,5], we design a Feistel RPMPFrHT network shown as Fig. 2. Inherited from the Feistel network, we adopt the block cipher and split the image into two blocks (L_0, R_0). The construction of a Feistel RPMPFrHT network in i-th round is defined as:

$$\begin{cases} L_{i+1} = F_c(\boldsymbol{a}_i, R_i) \\ R_{i+1} = F_r(\boldsymbol{a}_i, L_i) \end{cases} \tag{3}$$

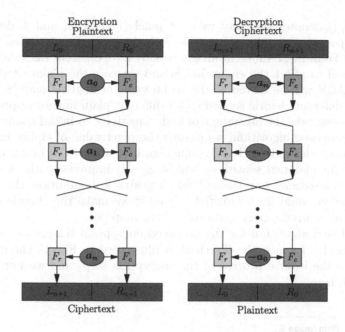

Fig. 2. The proposed Feistel RPMPFrHT network

where a_i is the fractional order of the RPMPFrHT, $F_r(a_i, L_i)$ denotes that perform RPMPFrHT on each row in image matrix L_i with fractional order a_i, while F_c denotes that perform RPMPFrHT on each column. As we can see, an image is transformed into two different fractional domain ultimately, which will confuse attackers.

In our proposed Feistel RPMPFrHT network, we will get the decryption network just by rearranging the fractional oder $(a_0, a_1, \cdots, a_n)$ in reverse order and take the opposite $(-a_n, -a_{n-1}, \cdots, -a_0)$ because of the inverse of RPMPFrHT [1]. This symmetry between encryption and decryption process can be used to simplify the implementation of the system.

2.3 The Proposed LD_UAGV

Many researchers tend to make every pixel influence its subsequent pixels in image encryption to increase the plaintext sensitivity [7]. However, this method is not suitable in transform domain since it will reduce the ability of resistance to noise and data loss attack sharply because of the high coupling among pixels. Our algorithm proposed a better way to satisfy both sides. We define the LD_UAGV of digital image G with size $M \times N$ as:

$$LD\_UAGV(G) = \frac{1}{MN} \sum_{i=1}^{M} \sum_{j=1}^{N} \frac{G(i,j)}{L} \cdot \frac{M \cdot (i-1) + j}{MN} \qquad (4)$$

where $G(i,j)$ denotes the gray value of pixel (i,j) in G, and L denotes the largest supported gray value compatible with the image format, often 255 for 8-bit bitmap. From Eq. 4, different images usually have different LD_UAGV, which could be used to affect the cipher image and increase the plaintext sensitivity. The LD_UAGV will be served as the initial value of Logistic map [8] to generate totally different chaotic sequences for different plain images respectively, as chaotic systems take the advantage of high sensitivity to initial condition.

In our proposed algorithm, we change the pixel value of cipher image with the plain-image-dependent chaotic sequences by conventional bitxor operation. In this way the plaintext sensitivity will be greatly improved without sacrificing the ability of resistance to noise and data loss attack. In addition, the numerical homogenization could be completed as well if we make the chaotic sequences uniformly distributed (apply asymmetric tent map [9]).

The detailed algorithm for the proposed encryption scheme are illustrated as Algorithm 1, of which the flowchart is illustrated in Fig. 3. The decryption algorithm is the inverse process of the encryption steps and we won't go into much detail here.

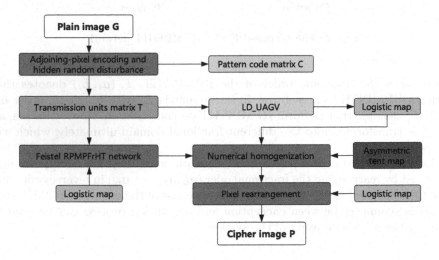

Fig. 3. Flowchart of the proposed encryption scheme

3   Experimental Results and Performance Analysis

To test the performance of our proposed encryption scheme, we implement the encryption-decryption process in MATLAB R2016b, where the hardware parameters of the computer are Intel Core i7-4710MQ CPU and 8 GB RAM. The plain images we use for test are several 8-bit gray images with size 256×256, and the number of rounds n in Feistel RPMPFrHT network is 4. The plain image Lena, encrypted image and decrypted Lena are presented in Fig. 4.

Algorithm 1. The proposed image encryption algorithm

Input: A 8-bit gray image G with size $M \times N$. Number of transform rounds n. Keys:
   $x_{0,i}$, $\mu_{1,i}$ $(i = 1, 2, \cdots, n)$, μ_2, y_0, μ'
Output: Cipher image Q. Plain-image-dependent keys: C, t, R
 1: $[C, T] = HRD(G)$ //$HRD(G)$ denotes hiding random disturbance on G
 2: $t = LD\_UAGV(T)$ //Eq.(4)
 3: $S_0 = T$
 4: **for** $i = 0$ to $n - 1$ **do**
 5:    $a_i = Logistic(x_{0,i}, \mu_{1,i})$ //Logistic map
 6:    $S_{n+1} = Feistel\_RPMPFrHT(S_n, a_i)$ //Eq.(3)
 7: **end for**
 8: $len = M \cdot N$
 9: $\{x'_n\} = Logistic(t, \mu_2)$ with length of len //Logistic map
10: $\{y'_n\} = Tent(y_0, \mu')$ with length of len //Asymmetric tent map
11: $s = \max_{i,j} S_n$
12: $R = \min_r \{r \geqslant s \quad \& \quad r = 2^k, k \in \mathbb{Z}\}$
13: **for** $i = 1$ to len **do**
14:    $x_i = [R \cdot x'_i]$
15:    $y_i = [R \cdot y'_i]$
16:    $j = (i - i \mod M)/M$
17:    $k = i \mod M + 1$
18:    $P(j, k) = \frac{256}{R} \cdot S_n(j, k) \oplus x_i \oplus y_i$ //bitxor on integer part
19: **end for**
20: $\{z_n\} = sort\{x'_n\}$
21: **for** $i = 1$ to len **do**
22:    $m =$ Index of x'_i in $\{z_n\}$
23:    $j = (i - i \mod M)/M$
24:    $k = i \mod M + 1$
25:    $j' = (m - m \mod M)/M$
26:    $k' = m \mod M + 1$
27:    $Q(j, k) = P(j', k')$
28: **end for**

3.1   Key Space

The key space should be large enough to resist the brute-force attack. In our proposed algorithm, the secret keys include $x_{0,i}$, $\mu_{1,i}$ $(i = 1, 2, 3, 4)$, μ_2, y_0, μ', where $x_{0,i}$, y_0, μ' take the range of $(0, 1)$ and $\mu_{1,i}$, μ_2 take the range of $(3.6, 4)$. The sensitivity of each key is higher than 10^{-15}. Thus the key space size of the proposed encryption scheme is more than $10^{15 \times (4+4+3)} = 10^{165}$, which is enough to resist all kinds of brute-force attack.

3.2   Histogram Analysis

Histogram of a digital image shows the distribution of gray value of all pixels. A meaningful image will show obvious characteristic in its histogram. The number of pixels with the same gray value takes a specific percentage. Thus, an ideal

(a) The plain image (b) The encrypted (c) The decrypted
Lena   image   image Lena

Fig. 4. The encryption-decryption result of Lena

cipher image should have an uniform distributed histogram that will never leak any meaningful information to attackers.

However, many image encryption algorithm in transform domain generate a cipher image whose histogram presents normal distribution. This is because the gray value of pixels will change into another domain after transformation and thus show numerical characteristics of the transform domain.

In our proposed algorithm, though we have used RPMPFrHT in our proposed encryption scheme, we do numerical homogenization on image after transformation and get the cipher image with uniformly distributed histogram. We analyzed the histogram of Lena and Baboon as Fig. 5. The results has proved that our approach is effective.

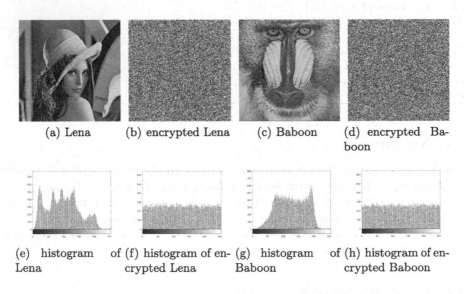

(a) Lena   (b) encrypted Lena   (c) Baboon   (d) encrypted Baboon

(e) histogram of (f) histogram of en- (g) histogram of (h) histogram of en-
Lena   crypted Lena   Baboon   crypted Baboon

Fig. 5. Histogram analysis

3.3   Resistance to Chosen Plaintext Attack

By constructing special plain image to encrypt and find the correspondence among pixels, the chosen plaintext attack is a powerful attack technique. However, most chosen plaintext attack will be useless faced with our proposed encryption algorithm since we hide random disturbance into plain images and will get totally different cipher images even if we encrypt an image with the same keys for several times. When we say "totally different" we tend to use the Number of Pixel Change Rate (NPCR) and the Unified Average Changing Intensity (UACI) to measure the difference between two images. Refer to [10] for formal definition of NPCR and UACI.

For 8-bit gray image, it has been proved that the expect values of NPCR and UACI between two random image (each pixel takes a random number independently) are 99.6094% and 33.4635% [10], respectively.

We encrypted the Lena with the same keys for five times, then tested the NPCR and UACI between each pair of cipher images. The results are listed as Tables 1 and 2.

Table 1. NPCR between each pair of five encrypted Lena

	Cipher 2	Cipher 3	Cipher 4	Cipher 5
Cipher 1	99.60479736%	99.64447021%	99.60021972%	99.62005615%
Cipher 2	-	99.60937500%	99.57122802%	99.59411621%
Cipher 3	-	-	99.64447021%	99.61853027%
Cipher 4	-	-	-	99.64752197%

Table 2. UACI between each pair of five encrypted Lena

	Cipher 2	Cipher 3	Cipher 4	Cipher 5
Cipher 1	33.31254212%	33.65251998%	33.44036514%	33.41965738%
Cipher 2	-	33.48900686%	33.31482157%	33.43866370%
Cipher 3	-	-	33.48728681%	33.66426934%
Cipher 4	-	-	-	33.46462634%

As we can see from the tables above, the NPCR and UACI are close to their expect values, which has proved that we will get a totally different cipher image every time we encrypt an image with the same keys. Thus our proposed algorithm has achieved high resistance to all kinds of chosen plaintext attack.

3.4   Correlation Analysis

A meaningful image has high correlation among adjacent pixels. Thus an important feature for image encryption algorithm is to break this high correlation and make it possible to resist all kinds of statistical attack. To test correlation of image, we randomly select 5000 pairs of adjacent pixels from three different direction (horizontal, vertical and diagonal) in test images, then calculate the correlation coefficient by:

$$CC = \frac{\sum_{i=1}^{N}(x_i - \bar{x})(y_i - \bar{y})}{\sqrt{\left(\sum_{i=1}^{N}(x_i - \bar{x})^2\right)\left(\sum_{i=1}^{N}(y_i - \bar{y})^2\right)}} \tag{5}$$

where $\bar{x} = \frac{1}{N}\sum_{i=1}^{N} x_i$, $\bar{y} = \frac{1}{N}\sum_{i=1}^{N} y_i$. The result is listed in Table 3. As we can see, the plain image Lena and Baboon holds the correlation coefficient close to 1 in all direction, which demonstrates high correlation. After encryption, the correlation coefficient is close to 0. That is, our proposed algorithm has broken the correlation between adjacent pixels.

Table 3. Correlation coefficient

Test image	Horizontal	Vertical	Diagonal
Lena	0.973187	0.960615	0.945709
Encrypted Lena	0.020436	0.044658	0.007289
Baboon	0.807831	0.842404	0.802359
Encrypted Baboon	0.024186	0.007285	0.032444

(a) 25% data loss of encrypted Lena (b) 25% data loss of encrypted Lena (c) 50% data loss of encrypted Lena (d) 50% data loss of encrypted Lena

(e) decrypted Lena from (a) (f) decrypted Lena from (b) (g) decrypted Lena from (c) (h) decrypted Lena from (d)

Fig. 6. Data loss analysis

3.5   Robustness to Data Loss

In actual communication system, some information of the encrypted image may be lost when it is transmitted in channel for all kinds of reasons. Then receivers would like to recover the original image as much as possible from the partial information received in such situation. Thus it is useful if the encryption algorithm shows robustness to data loss, which is exactly a main advantage of image encryption in transform domain.

In our experiment, we let the encrypted Lena lose 25% and 50% information in different pixels, respectively, and then decrypt them with correct keys. The result is shown in Fig. 6. As we can see, the decrypted images have restored most of the original information visually, which has proved the robustness to data loss of our proposed encryption scheme.

4   Conclusion

In this paper, a novel image encryption scheme based on transform domain is proposed aiming to improve the defects in existing algorithms. At first we process the original image by adjoining-pixel encoding and hidden random disturbance with no expanding size of the image. Then we compute the LD_UAGV of the image to generate a plain-image-related chaotic sequence to increase the plaintext sensitivity. Next we put the image into the Feistel RPMPFrHT network to transform it into two fractional domain. The network is symmetrical between encryption and decryption. Finally we homogenize the numerical distribution and rearrange the pixels to get the cipher image. Simulation results proved that our proposed encryption scheme not only reserved the superiority that existing algorithms had such as large key space, robustness to noise and resistance to data loss, but also improved the defects to achieve higher security. By comparison, our algorithm has erased the statistical characteristic corresponding to a specific domain, shown high resistance to chosen plaintext attack and simplified the implementation in some cases.

Acknowledgement. This work was supported in part by National Natural Science Foundation of China (61701036), Fundamental Research Funds for the Central Universities (2017RC52).

References

1. Lang, J.: Image encryption based on the reality-preserving multiple-parameter fractional fourier transform and chaos permutation. Opt. Lasers Eng. **50**(7), 929–937 (2012)
2. Chang, H.T., Hwang, H.E., Lee, C.L., Lee, M.T.: Wavelength multiplexing multiple-image encryption using cascaded phase-only masks in the fresnel transform domain. Opt. Commun. **50**(5), 710 (2011)
3. Singh, N., Sinha, A.: Gyrator transform-based optical image encryption, using chaos. Opt. Lasers Eng. **47**(5), 539–546 (2009)

4. Zhou, N., Wang, Y., Gong, L., Chen, X., Yang, Y.: Novel color image encryption algorithm based on the reality preserving fractional mellin transform. Opt. Laser Technol. **44**(7), 2270–2281 (2012)
5. Jimenez, C., Torres, C., Mattos, L.: Fractional Hartley transform applied to optical image encryption, p. 012041 (2011)
6. Schneier, B., Kelsey, J.: Unbalanced Feistel networks and block cipher design. In: Gollmann, D. (ed.) FSE 1996. LNCS, vol. 1039, pp. 121–144. Springer, Heidelberg (1996). https://doi.org/10.1007/3-540-60865-6_49
7. Wang, X., Liu, L., Zhang, Y.: A novel chaotic block image encryption algorithm based on dynamic random growth technique. Opt. Lasers Eng. **66**(66), 10–18 (2015)
8. Pareek, N.K., Patidar, V., Sud, K.K.: Image encryption using chaotic logistic map. Image Vis. Comput. **24**(9), 926–934 (2006)
9. Abid, S., Hasan, H.: About asymmetric noisy chaotic maps. Int. J. Basic Appl. Sci. **3**(2), 62 (2014)
10. Wu, Y.: NPCR and UACI randomness tests for image encryption. Cyber J.: Multidiscip. J. Sci. Technol. J. Sel. Areas Telecommun. (JSAT) **1**(2), 31–38 (2011)

Fall Detection System Based on Mobile Robot

Pengfei Sun$^{(\boxtimes)}$, Anlong Ming, Chao Yao, and Xuejing Kang

Beijing University of Posts and Telecommunications, Beijing 100876, China
{sunpf,mal}@bupt.edu.cn

Abstract. This paper proposed an accurate fall detection algorithm based on the feature of whole human body. The feature is extracted from convolutional neural network. The implementation of algorithm is integrated into a hardware system based on a visual mobile robot platform. To ensure the robustness and flexibility of algorithm in actual situation, a set of systemic strategies was applied on mobile robot. Finally, sufficient experiments on public dataset were conduct on our algorithm. Moreover, in a real indoor scene, experiment results proved the efficiency and precision of the designed fall detection system.

Keywords: Fall detection · Convolutional neural network
Mobile robot · Deep learning

1 Introduction

For most countries of the world, aging population is becoming a key issue. For example, in the last 20 years, the population over 65 in US has increased by 11%, and it is expected that about 1 in 5 Americans would be elderly by the year 2030 [5]. Relevant statistics [6] show that the fallen event is the main cause of injury to old people. Therefore, for intelligence human-computer interaction, how to implement an effective and accurate fall detection algorithm is particularly important. Recently, many efforts have been made to tackle this problem. General speaking, fall detection methods can be divided into three categories depend on device types: ambient devices [12], wearable devices [2,4] and visual devices [7,8,14]. Specially, RGBD cameras which could provide depth information is commonly used for detection, and enables accuracy rate of recognizing fallen event. Depending on the depth information, the detection system achieves a better understanding on spatial information and human shape, then provides a credible detection result. In [8], the distance between joint points (e.g. head, shoulder center, hip center, ankle right, ankle left) and floor is taken into account for fall detection. Nevertheless, for mobile robot platform, RGBD camera is too

---

X. Kang—This work was supported by National Natural Science Foundation of China under grant of No. 61471343, No. 61701036, Fundamental Research Funds for the Central Universities No. 2017RC52.

© Springer Nature Singapore Pte Ltd. 2018
Y. Wang et al. (Eds.): IGTA 2018, CCIS 875, pp. 263–271, 2018.
https://doi.org/10.1007/978-981-13-1702-6_26

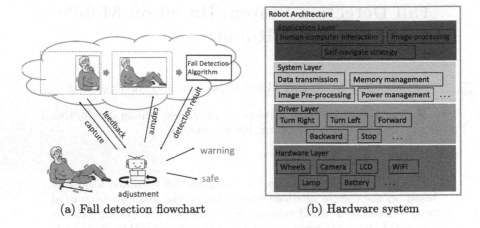

(a) Fall detection flowchart   (b) Hardware system

Fig. 1. Fall detection system framework. (Color figure online)

expensive and has a high requirement for the scene condition, which make it hard to use in practical. Although [11] designed some fall detection methods based on the common RGB image, it still cannot provide an accurate enough detection result in practical applications.

In this paper, to meet the availability requirements of fall detection in practical application, we design a fallen posture recognition algorithm which uses the features of the whole human body. Meanwhile, the proposed fall detection algorithm is integrated into a hardware system based on a visual mobile robot platform, as shown in Fig. 1. To improve the precision of fall detection, several deep learning techniques such as room layout detection and people search, are jointly applied so that some scene information can be used as reference. Otherwise, the navigation function of mobile robot is used to enable that the fallen event is visible in the viewpoint of mobile robot. Finally, the visual mobile robot can auto self-adjust and detect the fallen people in the indoor scene. In the simulation experiments, our proposed system is evaluated in several state-of-the-art public dataset, the subjective and objective results demonstrate the efficiency. Moreover, we also construct a real in-door scene to verify the efficiency of mobile robot platform, the system can provide reliable fall detection results.

2   Fallen People Detection System

2.1   System Architecture

The designed fallen people detection system based on mobile robot is described, as shown in Fig. 1. To support the robot automatically navigate in-door, Fig. 1(b) shows our designed mobile robot platform. Firstly, in the hardware layer, several hardware components are embedded. For example, at least three wheels are used to support robot moving, including forward, backward, turn left and turn right.

Note that, we use an ordinary monocular camera on the head of the robot for image capture. The captured image is with RGB color mode and the resolution is 640 × 480. Secondly, a driver layer is running in the hardware platform, which is developed to drive the embedded hardware components, i.e., to drive the wheels to achieve motion. Then, a system layer is implemented to assign the resource on the hardware platform, such as data transmission, memory management, power management etc. At last, an application layer is implemented to finish the image processing, human-computer interaction control, data transmission and self navigation strategy, etc.

2.2 Fall Detection Algorithm

We formulate the problem of fall detection as posture recognition in still images. But not similar as the state-of-the-art pose estimation approaches which should provide a detailed representation of human bodies, the posture features of the whole body are used to identify the fallen event. In this case, we can make the reasonable assumption that the human body is visible in the robot's field of view. Thus, human detection technique can be applied to obtain the bounding box of person. For the bounding rectangle of a person, significant differences exist between fall and other postures, as shown in Fig. 2. At first, the aspect ratio of bounding rectangle is remarking feature of different posture. For the rectangle, in the ideal situation, the width of rectangle is w, the height is h, then the aspect ratio r can be represented as:

$$r = \frac{w}{h} \tag{1}$$

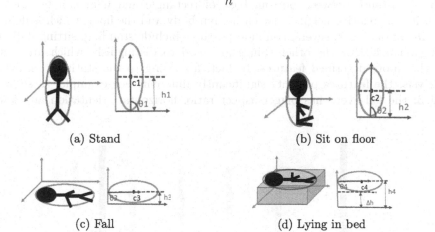

(a) Stand   (b) Sit on floor

(c) Fall   (d) Lying in bed

Fig. 2. Centroid c_i, centroid height h_i, orientation θ_i, and Δh. Grey ellipse is circumscribed ellipse of body. 3D coordinate system is world coordinate system. The 2D coordinate system is the projection of 3D environment and the floor is defined as x-axis.

Secondly, the center of gravity will obviously change while a person is falling. Under fixed frame reference, while a person is walking or standing, the height of a person's centroid is higher than sitting and lying. Generally, a person's body distributes more like an inscribed ellipse than a bounding rectangle. For an image $f(x, y)$, the $p + q$ order moment is given by:

$$m_{pq} = \int_{-\infty}^{+\infty} \int_{-\infty}^{+\infty} x^p y^q f(x, y) dx dy \quad (p, q = 0, 1, 2, ...) \tag{2}$$

For the 1-order and 0-order spatial moments, the center of the ellipse can be figured out by computing the coordinates of centroid $(\overline{x}, \overline{y})$ as follows :

$$\overline{x} = \frac{m_{10}}{m_{00}}, \overline{y} = \frac{m_{01}}{m_{00}} \tag{3}$$

In addition, the inscribed ellipse has directionality which represents the direction of human body. Apparently, the direction of human body is significant different when walking and lying. The orientation θ of human body can be represented by the central moment μ_{pq} as:

$$\mu_{pq} = \int_{-\infty}^{+\infty} \int_{-\infty}^{+\infty} (x - \overline{x})^p (y - \overline{y})^q f(x, y) dx dy \tag{4}$$

$$\theta = \frac{1}{2} \arctan(\frac{2\mu_{11}}{\mu_{20} - \mu_{02}}) \tag{5}$$

For static image, there is not much difference between lying on bed and fall, especially for centroid height, orientation and aspect ratio. As a sequence, the spatial distance between bottom base of rectangle and floor can be used to identify the relative height between human body and the floor, which is defined as Δh. In our work, several common postures include standing, sitting, fall and lying on a bed or the other things are used to distinguish, which are based on the above described features. In fact, according to the statistics and data analysis, the features presents significantly different. For example, as show in Fig. 3, the fall event has bigger aspect ratio, horizontal orientation and lower

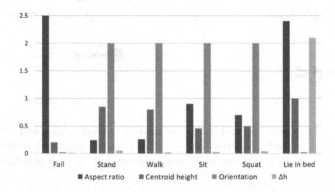

Fig. 3. Statistical results of common postures.

centroid height, compared with the other postures. Therefore, a feature model X based on these features is defined as:

$$X = (r, \bar{x}, \bar{y}, \theta, \Delta h) \tag{6}$$

Here, SVM would be used to implement this 0/1 classification task[1], so that the fall event can be distinguished from the other common postures.

2.3 Implement Details

In this section, some implement details are described. As shown in Fig. 1(a), the mobile robot firstly capture a still image. For a given image, the Room Layout technique [9] and Person Search [13] is applied to calculate features. Note that, to meet the assumption that the whole human body should be visible in the view of mobile robot, a robot control strategy is designed. Figure 4 provides a practical example to adjust the mobile robot, so that the final captured image can be used to detect fallen event.

For posture recognition and camera adjustment strategy, the most import is reference substance. In actual situation, we find that the distribution of floor in image is relatively fixed from robot perspective. And the bounding box of person can be obtained by Person Search. As shown in Fig. 4, the yellow box is the bounding box from Person Search and the area of orange lines is floor. To ensure the completeness of a person's body information, it's necessary to keep a suitable distance and view between robot and person. Here, a 3D cube is defined in the center of projection. As the light blue region shown in Fig. 4. The size of cube is set according to the distribution of floor and experimental data. In an image, the projection of the cube is the light region in Fig. 4. If a person is not in the corresponding region of image, the robot will move according to adjustment strategy until the person locate in the central region. In this way, a precise reference substance and complete information of person body make our detection algorithm more accurate.

3   Experiments and Results

In this section, a complete set of experiments were conducted in a real indoor environment. We validated the effectiveness of algorithm and self-adjustment strategy by testing images of different scenarios, different persons, different poses, different angles of view. To make a comparison, the detection system is evaluated on several public release datasets IASLAB-RGBD Fallen Person Dataset (IASLAB-RGBD) [1] and UR Fall Detection Dataset (URFD) [3]. As the objective evaluation indicators, four common metrics are used: accuracy, precision, recall and $F_{0.5}$ [10].

$$F_{0.5} = \frac{(1 + 0.25) * precision * recall}{0.25 * precision + recall} \tag{7}$$

---

[1] In this work, we justly identify fall or not, the other postures would not be identified.

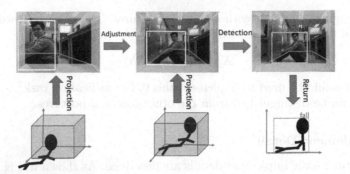

Fig. 4. Process of self-adjustment and detection. Orange is floor outline from Room layout, yellow is bounding box from Person search and red is fallen location. Light region in picture is central region. (Color figure online)

Table 1. Performance comparison on Lab A.

Method	Accuracy	Precision	Recall	$F_{0.5}$
Baseline	0.88	0.65	0.33	0.54
SV	0.90	0.77	**0.78**	0.77
SV+MV	**0.92**	0.87	0.77	0.85
Our method	0.78	**0.96**	0.77	**0.92**

Here, $F_{0.5}$ is an harmonic average of precision and recall promoting a high precision. Finally, a new fall detection was built to further validate the performance of proposed detection algorithm and self-adjustment strategy on complex posture.

3.1 Experiments on Public Dataset

Firstly, lots of experiments were conducted on public dataset IASLAB-RGBD and URFD. IASLAB-RGBD includes both RGB data and depth data, and it sets two different environments: Lab A and Lab B. [1] provides some evaluation results of 3 methods on this dataset, including: Euclidean cluster extraction (baseline), single-view detector (SV) and map verification (MV). As comparison, our algorithm is used to evaluate several objective metrics. Note that our algorithm justly uses the RGB data, not include the depth information. Figure 5 shows the performance of our algorithm, green rectangle is safe and red is fallen. Tables 1 and 2 show the comparison results of different method. The results show that our method has a higher precision but a lower accuracy. It means our method may miss detection in several practical situations. However, our method has highest precision and lowest probability of false detection, which is important to a detection system in practical.

Then we extracted and labeled 1309 images from video sequence frames in URFD. The result is shown in Table 3. Of course, the existing public dataset is

Fig. 5. Performance of our algorithm on IASLAB and URFD. Red rectangle is fallen and green is safe. (Color figure online)

Table 2. Performance comparison on Lab B.

Method	Accuracy	Precision	Recall	$F_{0.5}$
Baseline	0.84	0.64	0.26	0.50
SV	0.89	0.87	0.74	0.84
SV+MV	**0.90**	0.92	0.72	0.87
Our method	0.77	**0.98**	**0.77**	**0.93**

not sufficient enough to support to evaluate the performance of fall detection, which not include enough fall postures or the other similar postures so that we seem to have a very high precision value in measurement.

Table 3. Performance of our algorithm on URFD.

Dataset	Accuracy	Precision	Recall	$F_{0.5}$
URFD	0.89	0.96	0.90	0.95

3.2 Subjective Experiments

As some pictures in Fig. 5 shown, lacking of complete body information often happens during detection. To further validate the effectiveness, accuracy of proposed algorithm and self-adjustment strategy, we build a detection system on mobile robot platform and a new dataset[2] including more complex postures. On

---

[2] We will release a new fallen person dataset in future. It has 2000 pictures containing different scenarios, different persons and different postures.

the robot, an ordinary monocular stationary RGB camera is used to capture visual information. The mobile robot can self-adjust according to the position of person. In addition, we developed a Person Search model for location. In the case of known camera's height, robot's motion parameter and other calibration parameters, the self-adjustment strategy can be implemented precisely.

In common, most of current fall detection algorithm are merely effective when a fallen persons head/shoulder is close to ground. But in the actual situation, a person may pratfall and there is a distance between his head and ground. Besides, many postures may cause some fall detection algorithms false detection, such as cross-legged sitting, squat and lie in bed. Our dataset contains these postures which are not reflected in many datasets and algorithms, but this is a real situation in daily life. The experiment Fig. 6 shows that our algorithm has a great ability to distinguish these complex postures. In addition, further experiments including evolution of self-adjustment strategy were conducted on our own dataset. As shown in Fig. 7, mobile robot will move to an ideal projection point by turning an angle and moving a distance. Then, the final result can be given accurately.

Fig. 6. Kinds of posture like fall and detection results.

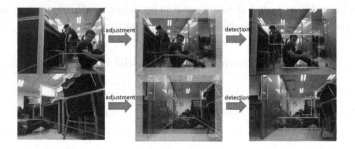

Fig. 7. Experiments on self-adjustment strategy.

4   Conclusion

This paper presented and implemented an accurate and real-time algorithm. The proposed detection algorithm only used ordinary monocular RGB camera.

To evaluate efficiency of the algorithm, a hardware system was built on mobile robot platform. To improve the flexibility of detection system, a set of adjustment strategies for camera was designed. In experimental part, sufficient experiments were conducted to evaluate the effectiveness and precision of the algorithm. And the results showed that our method had lower false detection ratio and a better performance on some complex fall postures.

References

1. Antonello, M., Carraro, M., Pierobon, M., Menegatti, E.: Fast and robust detection of fallen people from a mobile robot. arXiv preprint arXiv:1703.03349 (2017)
2. Hsieh, C.Y., Liu, K.C., Huang, C.N., Chu, W.C., Chan, C.T.: Novel hierarchical fall detection algorithm using a multiphase fall model. Sensors **17**(2), 307 (2017)
3. Kwolek, B., Kepski, M.: Improving fall detection by the use of depth sensor and accelerometer. Neurocomputing **168**, 637–645 (2015)
4. Li, Q., Stankovic, J.A., Hanson, M.A., Barth, A.T., Lach, J., Zhou, G.: Accurate, fast fall detection using gyroscopes and accelerometer-derived posture information. In: 2009 Sixth International Workshop on Wearable and Implantable Body Sensor Networks. BSN 2009, pp. 138–143. IEEE (2009)
5. Liu, C.L., Lee, C.H., Lin, P.M.: A fall detection system using k -nearest neighbor classifier. Expert Syst. Appl. **37**(10), 7174–7181 (2010)
6. Lord, S.R., Sherrington, C., Menz, H.B., Close, J.C.: Falls in Older People: Risk Factors and Strategies for Prevention. Cambridge University Press, Cambridge (2007)
7. Matsuo, K., Aoki, Y.: Depth image enhancement using local tangent plane approximations, pp. 3574–3583, June 2015
8. Mundher, Z.A., Zhong, J.: A real-time fall detection system in elderly care using mobile robot and kinect sensor. Int. J. Mater. Mech. Manuf. **2**(2), 133–138 (2014)
9. Ren, Y., Li, S., Chen, C., Kuo, C.-C.J.: A coarse-to-fine indoor layout estimation (CFILE) method. In: Lai, S.-H., Lepetit, V., Nishino, K., Sato, Y. (eds.) ACCV 2016. LNCS, vol. 10115, pp. 36–51. Springer, Cham (2017). https://doi.org/10.1007/978-3-319-54193-8_3
10. Volkhardt, M., Schneemann, F., Gross, H.M.: Fallen person detection for mobile robots using 3D depth data. In: 2013 IEEE International Conference on Systems, Man, and Cybernetics (SMC), pp. 3573–3578. IEEE (2013)
11. Wang, S., Zabir, S., Leibe, B.: Lying pose recognition for elderly fall detection. Robotics: Science and Systems VII 345 (2012)
12. Williams, A., Ganesan, D., Hanson, A.: Aging in place: fall detection and localization in a distributed smart camera network. In: Proceedings of the 15th ACM international conference on Multimedia, pp. 892–901. ACM (2007)
13. Xiao, J., Xie, Y., Tillo, T., Huang, K., Wei, Y., Feng, J.: IAN: the individual aggregation network for person search (2017)
14. Zerrouki, N., Harrou, F., Houacine, A., Sun, Y.: Fall detection using supervised machine learning algorithms: a comparative study. In: International Conference on Modelling, Identification and Control, pp. 665–670 (2017)

Detecting Infrared Target with Receptive Field and Lateral Inhibition of HVS

Yufei Zhao[1,2], Yong Song[1,2(✉)], Shangnan Zhao[1,2], Yun Li[1,2], Guowei Shi[3], and Zhengkun Guo[1,2]

[1] School of Optics and photonics, Beijing Institute of Technology,
Beijing 100081, China
yongsong@bit.edu.cn
[2] Beijing Key Laboratory for Precision Optoelectronic Measurement Instrument
and Technology, Beijing 100081, China
[3] Institute of Aviation Medicine, AF CPLA, Beijing 100142, China

Abstract. In this paper, we proposed an infrared (IR) target detection method based on the receptive field (RF) and lateral inhibition (LI). In this method, the direction parameters of Gabor filter is adaptively determined according to the gradient direction. And a background prediction method based on LI is used for regulating the gray value in image so as to achieve background suppression and target enhancement. Experimental results indicate that the proposed method can extract both small and area target from complex background, and the target detection ability is satisfactory.

Keywords: Detection · Infrared · Digital image processing
Pattern recognition

1 Introduction

Recently, there are two problems in IR target detection field. One is that the captured infrared target generally has a complex background. Another is that the target detection methods are not suitable for various size. At present, the existing methods generally detect infrared target from perspectives of spatial domain [1], frequency domain [2], mathematical morphology [3] and two-dimensional least-mean-square (TDLMS) [4]. However, these methods have poor detection ability when detecting IR target from complex background. And it is hard to find a detection method which is appropriate for both small and area target in the existing infrared target detection methods.

Utilizing the signal processing mechanisms of Human Visual System (HVS) in IR target detection field is beneficial to improve the anti-interference ability and target detection ability of target detection methods. Utilizing visual attention mechanism can achieve high detection probability, low false alarm probability and robustness in the IR dim and small target detection [5]. Therefore, utilizing the HVS mechanism is considered as a significant way to solve the mentioned

© Springer Nature Singapore Pte Ltd. 2018
Y. Wang et al. (Eds.): IGTA 2018, CCIS 875, pp. 272–280, 2018.
https://doi.org/10.1007/978-981-13-1702-6_27

problems in IR target detection field. On the other hand, RF and LI are significant mechanisms of HVS. The application of RF and LI will do great helpful to detect target of various size in complex background.

In this paper, we proposed an IR target detection method based on the RF and LI of HVS. Firstly, two-dimensional Gabor function is used as the model of RF of simple cells. Then, the gradient direction of each pixel is determined, and the direction parameter of Gabor filter is adaptively determined by the gradient direction of each pixel. Meanwhile, LI is applied to predict the background of IR image, and the gray values of background and target are regulated according to the residual value obtained by background prediction process. Experimental results show that the proposed method can extract both small target and area target in complex background, and it has satisfactory target detection ability.

2 Theory

The two-dimensional Gabor function [6] can be used for describing the model of RF, we take its real component to model the spatial properties of simple RF in the visual cortex, which can be expressed by Eq. 1:

$$\begin{cases} G(x,y) = \exp[-\frac{\mu^2+\lambda\nu^2}{2\sigma^2}]\cos[2\pi f\mu + \varphi] \\ \mu = x\cos\theta + y\sin\theta, \nu = -x\sin\theta + y\cos\theta \end{cases} \tag{1}$$

where σ^2 is the spatial variance, f is the optimal spatial frequency, λ is the spatial aspect ratio. The parameter of $\varphi \in (-\pi, \pi)$ is a phase offset that we set $\varphi = -\pi/2$ in our investigation. And $\theta \in [0, \pi)$ is the direction parameter of Gabor filter.

The response $R(x,y)$ of simple cells to an input image $I(x,y)$ is calculated by convolution filtering, and the frequency and direction characteristics of IR image can be extracted through convoluting with Gabor function. The expression of convolution filtering is shown in Eq. 2:

$$R(x,y) = G(x,y) * I(x,y) = \sum_{x=0}^{M-1}\sum_{y=0}^{N-1} G(x-x_\tau, y-y_\tau) I(x_\tau, y_\tau) \tag{2}$$

where $R(x,y)$ is the output image processed by Gabor function, $G(x,y)$ is the Gabor function, and $I(x,y)$ is the input image of dimension $M \times N$.

LI was first discovered and confirmed by Hartline in 1932 [7]. Dai has proposed a method for simulating the distribution of LI coefficient by exponential function [8], which described the relationship between LI coefficient and the distance between two receptors, and the expression is shown in Eq. 3.

$$\begin{cases} h_{mn}(p,q) = \exp\left(-\frac{d_{ij,pq}}{\rho}\right) \\ \rho = \frac{1}{I(x,y)} \end{cases} \tag{3}$$

where $h_{mn}(p,q)$ is LI coefficient, $I(x,y)$ represents the input image, $d_{ij,pq}$ is the distance between pixel (i,j) and central pixel (p,q) in one inhibition field.

3   Method Design

3.1   Adaptive Gabor Filter

In this part, we proposed an adaptive Gabor filter. First, the gradient direction of each pixel is calculated according to image information. Then, the direction parameter θ is adaptively determined by the calculated gradient directions. Finally, the complete edges corresponding to different directions can be extracted.

Meanwhile, the direction parameter θ is determined by Sobel operator in the proposed adaptive Gabor filter. Specifically, the gray value of each pixel in four neighborhoods are weighted, and then the gradient direction is calculated by the difference computation. The partial derivatives f_x and f_y of Sobel operator can be determined using Eq. 4.

$$f_x\left(x,y\right) = \begin{bmatrix} -1 & 0 & 1 \\ -2 & 0 & 2 \\ -1 & 0 & 1 \end{bmatrix}, f_y\left(x,y\right) = \begin{bmatrix} -1 & -2 & -1 \\ 0 & 0 & 0 \\ 1 & 2 & 1 \end{bmatrix} \tag{4}$$

where $f(x,y)$ is the gray value of pixel (x,y). Then, the gradient direction angle θ of pixel (x,y) can be calculated by Eq. 5.

$$\theta = \arctan\left[\frac{f_y\left(x,y\right)}{f_x\left(x,y\right)}\right] \tag{5}$$

Finally, the Eq. 5 is substituted into Eq. 1, a Gabor filter with adaptive direction parameter is achieved, as shown in Eq. 6:

$$\begin{cases} G(x,y) = \exp\left[-\dfrac{\mu^2 + \lambda\nu^2}{2\sigma^2}\right]\cos[2\pi f\mu + \varphi] \\ \mu = x\cos\theta + y\sin\theta \\ \nu = -x\sin\theta + y\cos\theta \\ \theta = \arctan\left[\dfrac{f_y\left(x,y\right)}{f_x\left(x,y\right)}\right] \end{cases} \tag{6}$$

3.2   Background Prediction Based on LI

In this part, we used LI network to achieve background prediction. The model of background prediction is shown as follows:

$$E\left(x,y\right) = I\left(x,y\right) - \sum_{(p,q)\in S} W\left(p,q\right)I\left(m - p, n - q\right) \tag{7}$$

where $E(x,y)$ is the residual value between input image and predicted image, $I(x,y)$ is input image, S is the filter window, $W(p,q)$ is the weight matrix.

Then, the gray value of each pixel in image is regulated according to the residual value $E(x, y)$ of background prediction, as shown in Eq. 8:

$$f_{\text{out}}(x, y) = (1 + K \cdot E(x, y)) \cdot f_{\text{in}}(x, y) \qquad (8)$$

where $E(x, y)$ is the residual value, $f_{\text{in}}(x, y)$ and $f_{\text{out}}(x, y)$ are the input image and output image. K is the regulatory factor. Finally, Eq. 8 is substituted into the Eq. 2 to obtain the final output results, and the expression is shown as Eq. 9:

$$\begin{aligned} R(x, y) &= (1 + K \cdot E(x, y)) \cdot (G(x \cdot y) * I(x, y)) \\ &= (1 + K \cdot E(x, y)) \cdot \sum_{x=0}^{M-1} \sum_{y=0}^{N-1} G(x - x_\tau, y - y_\tau) I(x_\tau, y_\tau) \end{aligned} \qquad (9)$$

where $R(x, y)$ is the output image, $E(x, y)$ is the residual value of background prediction, $G(x, y)$ is the proposed adaptive Gabor filter, and $I(x, y)$ is the input original image.

3.3 Method Process

Firstly, the gradient direction angle of each pixel is calculated by Sobel operator according to Eq. 5, and the direction parameter θ of Gabor filter is determined according to the calculated gradient direction angle. Secondly, LI coefficient is calculated by LI model according to Eq. 3, and the weight matrix W of background prediction is adaptively determined by the calculated LI coefficient. Then, the predicted image is subtracted from the corresponding input image to obtain the residual value by using Eq. 7. The target or background can be predicted according to the obtained residual value. Finally, the image is processed by adaptive Gabor filter and the residual value of background prediction based on LI simultaneously by using Eq. 9, in which the adaptive Gabor filter is calculated according to Eq. 6.

4   Expriments and Results

In our experiments, if the size of target is less than 81 (9×9) pixels, it is defined as small target [9], otherwise it is defined as area target. Meanwhile, signal to clutter ratio gain (SCRG) and background suppression factor (BSF) are selected as the evaluation parameters. Additionally, the receiver operation characteristic (ROC) curves are drawn for reflecting the varying relationship between the detection probability P_d and the false alarm rate P_f.

We compared the proposed method to top-hat method, max-mean method, max-median method [3], TDLMWS [4] and Shi's method [10]. The parameters in Eq. 1 are set as follows: $\sigma = 1.2$, $f = 0.47$, $\lambda = 0.5$ [11], and the size of Gabor filter template is selected as 5×5. Meanwhile, the regulatory factor K in Eq. 9 is set to 60.

4.1 Small Target Detection

The input experiment images and result images of the different methods are also shown in Fig. 1. Meanwhile, Fig. 2 shows the corresponding results of SCRG and BSF, and Fig. 3 is the corresponding ROC curves.

From Fig. 1, the proposed method has excellent performance on target enhancement and background suppression. According to Column 2, top-hat method works poor in target enhancement when the target is very dim; According to Column 3 and Column 4, the max-mean method and max-median method have poorer abilities on enhancing target and suppressing background compared

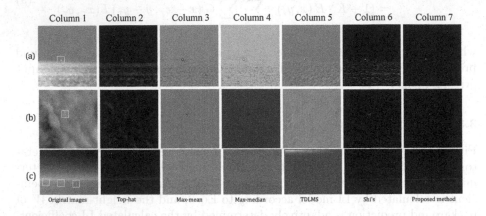

Fig. 1. Original images and detection results processed by the different methods.

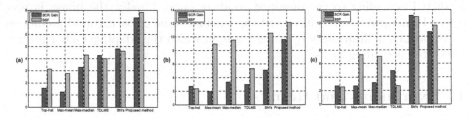

Fig. 2. SCRG and BSF of different methods for each original image in Fig. 1.

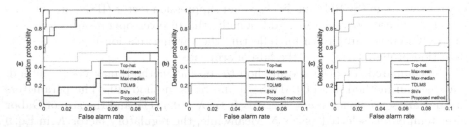

Fig. 3. ROC curves of different methods for each original image in Fig. 3.

to the proposed method; According to Column 5, the result of TDLMS has good background suppression ability. However, there are still many clutter backgrounds remained when the backgrounds are complex; According to Column 6, Shi's method has good performance on extracting small targets from complex background. However, when original image has lots of noises, it still remains a lot of noise. According to Column 7, the dim small targets are extracted accurately from complex background and the result images have less clutters and noises, which indicates that the proposed method has excellent performance on enhancing target and suppressing background. Moreover, from the experimental results in Fig. 2, it can be seen that the proposed method has obtained the better SCRG and the higher BSF than the compared methods for Fig. 2(a).

On the other hand, according to Fig. 3, it can be found that the P_d of the proposed method is higher than the others under the same P_f, which also shows the advancement of the proposed method.

Furthermore, we evaluated the running time of the proposed algorithm and the comparison algorithm, which are shown in Table 1.

Table 1. The running times of the different methods for each original image in Fig. 1.

	Top-hat	Max-mean	Max-median	TDLMS	Shi's	Proposed
Fig. 1(a)	0.2934	0.5932	2.6890	0.1899	0.7956	0.5394
Fig. 1(b)	0.3025	0.9536	3.3857	0.1985	1.1822	0.6815
Fig. 1(c)	0.2869	0.4602	1.8769	0.1541	0.5964	0.3542

4.2 Area Target Detection

Fig. 4 shows the original images with complex clutters and the corresponding result images of our area target detection experiments, in which the original image of Fig. 4(a) contains one area target and two small targets, and Fig. 4(b) and (c) contain one area target.

According to the results of Fig. 4(a), the original image contains an area target and two small targets, top-hat method can extract the targets but remain some background clutters. Max-mean and max-median methods work poor on enhancing the area target region. TDLMS method remains many clutters when the step size of the weight matrix is not appropriate for the original images; Additionally, the results of Shi's method remains a lot of clutters and noises. Compared with the above methods, the proposed method can extract contour of IR targets, while most of the background clutters and noises are suppressed through the adaptive Gabor filter and background prediction process. Similarly, as for the original images of Fig. 4(b) and (c), which contain an area target with different sizes, the corresponding results also indicate that the proposed method has better performance on target enhancement and background suppression than the compared methods.

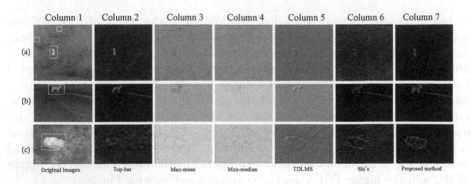

Fig. 4. Original images and detection results processed by the different methods.

Figure 5 shows the corresponding results of SCRG and BSF, which show that the proposed method has obtained better SCRG and higher BSF than the compared methods. Additionally, according to the ROC curves shown in Fig. 6, the P_d of the proposed method is higher than the compared methods under the same P_f, which indicates that the proposed method is robust and effective in the area target detection in complex background.

Similarly, we evaluated the running time of the proposed algorithm and the comparison algorithm, which are shown in Table 2.

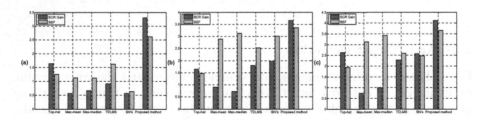

Fig. 5. SCRG and BSF of the different methods for each original image in Fig. 4.

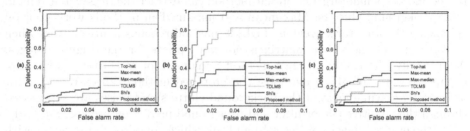

Fig. 6. ROC curves of the different methods for each original image in Fig. 4.

Table 2. The running times of the different methods for each original image in Fig. 4.

	Top-hat	Max-mean	Max-median	TDLMS	Shi's	Proposed
Fig. 4(a)	0.3036	1.4711	4.8534	0.3219	1.8225	1.0213
Fig. 4(b)	0.2325	1.0834	4.3820	0.2205	1.4534	0.8131
Fig. 4(c)	0.2488	0.9334	3.1338	0.2527	1.1205	0.6802

5   Conclusion

Aiming to the problems of target detection in complex background, we proposed an IR target adaptive detection method based on RF and LI of HVS. In the proposed method, an adaptive Gabor filter based on the model of RF of simple cells is used for detecting the edges of different directions in image. The direction parameters of Gabor filter is adaptively determined by the gradient direction of each pixel. Meanwhile, the weight matrix of background prediction is adaptively determined according to LI coefficient. Then, the predicted image is subtracted from the corresponding input image to obtain the residual value so as to predict the target or background. Finally, the gray values of background and target are regulated according to the residual value. Experimental results show that the proposed method can extract both small target and area target in complex background, and it is superior in SCRG, BSF and ROC curve comparing with the compared methods (top-hat, max-mean, max-median, TDLMS and Shi's method), which indicate that the proposed method has potential and beneficial applications in aircraft navigation, vehicle navigation and robot vision, etc.

Acknowledgement. This work is supported by National Natural Science Foundation of China (NSFC) (81671787); Defense Industrial Technology Development Program (JCKY2016208B001).

References

1. Venkateswarlu, R.: Max-mean and max-median filters for detection of small targets. Proc. SPIE - Int. Soc. Opt. Eng. **3809**, 74–83 (1999)
2. Yang, L., Yang, J., Yang, K.: Adaptive detection for infrared small target under sea-sky complex background. Electron. Lett. **40**(17), 1083–1085 (2004)
3. Yang, C., Ma, J., Qi, S., Tian, J., Zheng, S., Tian, X.: Directional support value of gaussian transformation for infrared small target detection. Appl. Opt. **54**(9), 2255–65 (2015)
4. Soni, T., Zeidler, J.R., Ku, W.H.: Performance evaluation of 2-D adaptive prediction filters for detection of small objects in image data. IEEE Trans. Image Process. A Publ. IEEE Sign. Process. Soc. **2**(3), 327 (1993)
5. Wang, X., Lv, G., Xu, L.: Infrared dim target detection based on visual attention. Infrared Phys. Technol. **55**(6), 513–521 (2012)
6. Daugman, J.G.: Uncertainty relation for resolution in space, spatial frequency, and orientation optimized by two-dimensional visual cortical filters. J. Opt. Soc. Am. A Opt. Image Sci. **2**(7), 1160–1169 (1985)

7. Hartline, H.K.: The response of single optic nerve fibers of the vertebrate eye to illumination of the retina. Am. J. Physiol. **121**(2), 400–415 (1938)
8. Dai, S., Liu, Q., Li, P., Liu, J., Xiang, H.: Study on infrared image detail enhancement algorithm based on adaptive lateral inhibition network. Infrared Phys. Technol. **68**, 10–14 (2015)
9. Zhang, W., Cong, M., Wang, L.: Algorithms for optical weak small targets detection and tracking: review. In: International Conference on Neural Networks and Signal Processing, vol. 1, pp. 643–647 (2004)
10. Shi, M., Peng, Z., Zhang, Q., Li, Q., Lin, Z.: Dim infrared target detection based on adaptive lateral inhibition network. High Power Laser Part. Beams **23**(4), 906–910 (2011)
11. Grigorescu, C., Petkov, N., Westenberg, M.A.: Contour detection based on nonclassical receptive field inhibition. IEEE Trans. Image Process. A Public. IEEE Sign. Process. Soc. **12**(7), 729–739 (2003)

A Novel System for Fingerprint Orientation Estimation

Zhenshen Qu[1], Junyu Liu[1], Yang Liu[1($\boxtimes$)], Qiuyu Guan[1], Ruikun Li[1], and Yuxin Zhang[2]

[1] Department of Control Science and Engineering, HIT, Harbin, China
miraland@hit.edu.cn,
{17s004086,17s004024}@stu.hit.edu.cn
[2] Cross-Strait Tsinghua Research Institute, Beijing, China

Abstract. Orientation field extraction is a basic and essential task in an Automated Fingerprint Identification System (AFIS). Previous works failed when dealing with latent images due to the complicate background and strong noise. In this paper, an algorithm system specific for fingerprint orientation extraction is proposed, combining the domain and contexture information. Our system consists of three parts, preprocessing, foreground acquisition and a fully convolutional DNN. Preprocessing decrease the strength of noise in input latent fingerprints, making higher quality inputs for foreground acquisition and DNN. Foreground masks are necessary for eliminating effect of background on orientation extraction. DNN makes use of the foreground information and pre-processed input to produce higher quality outputs. Testing results on our dataset shows that proposed method overperforms state-of-the-art algorithms in accuracy after training with the same image set and weak labels, and groundtruth labels will lead to better results.

Keywords: Orientation field · Fingerprint · Fully convolutional DNN

1 Introduction

Fingerprint is of great importance in personal identity. It has the advantage of high reliability, easy acquisition and convenient operation. Since the 1990s, algorithms of each part of Automated Fingerprint Identification System (AFIS) have been continuously improved [1–3]. Fingerprint analysis mainly includes fields like fingerprint enhancement, feature extraction and fingerprint matching. Among these research fields, orientation field extraction [4–6] is a basic and essential task. Precise orientation field is the guarantee of high quality fingerprint. Current methods can obtain the orientation field of high-quality fingerprint image accurately, but these methods are easily affected by noise and background factors.

Fingerprint orientation field extraction algorithms mainly include: gradient-based methods, model-based methods, filter-based methods, and Convolution Neural Network (CNN)-based ones. In [7], a simple mathematical model is developed which computes fingerprint local ridge orientation from core and delta positions. This model provides an intelligent tool for resolving ambiguities due to the periodic nature of

© Springer Nature Singapore Pte Ltd. 2018
Y. Wang et al. (Eds.): IGTA 2018, CCIS 875, pp. 281–291, 2018.
https://doi.org/10.1007/978-981-13-1702-6_28

orientation, in algorithms for interpreting fingerprint patterns. The orientation field model uses heuristic knowledge to predict the general trend of the global ridge through the location of singularities. Conversely, the predicted ridge does not necessarily represent the true orientation of the ridge, and two fingerprint images with the same singularity may have distinctly different ridge direction fields. It can be seen that the model-based method depends on accurate detection of singularities heavily.

Gradient-based orientation field estimation method was first found in [8]. This method can describe good quality fingerprint orientation accurately, but has the disadvantage of this algorithm is its low tolerance to noise. Many researchers contributed improvements to gradient-based methods. Mei *et al.* [9] proposed a gradient-based method for the computation of fingerprint orientation field. Compared with gradient-based method, the filter-based methods [10–12] shows better noise immunity, but generally only a limited number of filters can be designed, which results in the calculated directional field being inaccurate. When estimating the orientation of the point, the output of each filter needs to be calculated and compared. It is less effective.

Convolutional neural networks are well-known for their ability to extract features from images [13–15]. Some scholars try to apply CNN to feature extraction of fingerprint images. Cao *et al.* [16] proposed a ConvNet-based approach for latent orientation field estimation. 128 representative orientation patterns are learnt from a large number of orientation blocks and the orientation regression problem is converted to a classification task. The disadvantage of this method is that the pattern sets' quality is directly affected by the quality of database. In 2017, a novel network for fingerprints called FingerNet is proposed by Yao *et al.* [17]. FingerNet combine domain knowledge and the representation ability of deep learning, while preserving end-to-end differentiability. In terms of orientation field, a classification network based on DeepLab v2 [18] is adopted. This pipeline achieves better results with expert network-marked labels, but its performance is weakened when trained with low-condition labels.

Inspired by the good characteristic of CNN, We proposes an effective orientation estimation algorithm system for latent fingerprint. The system is divided into three parts to make full use of latent images' domain knowledge and contextual features. The first part is latent fingerprint image preprocessing. TV decomposition, band-pass filter, and log-Gabor as a combination is adopted to preprocess pictures in order. It can also eliminate the influence of errors in weak labels. In the second part, we propose a spatial algorithm to acquire the foreground mask of latent fingerprints. With preprocessed fingerprints and foreground masks as inputs, a Convolutional Neural Network works as the last part of the system, estimating orientation fields more quickly and precisely.

2 Proposed Method

2.1 Methods Overview

In this work, we are aiming to construct a reliable system for fingerprint orientation extraction. Recent years, mainstream of algorithms tends to make use of both domain knowledge of traditional methods and contextual information extracted by DNN structure. Following this trend, our system consists of three parts. Preprocessing decrease the strength of noise in input latent fingerprints, making higher quality inputs for foreground acquisition and DNN. Foreground masks are necessary for eliminating effect of background on orientation extraction. DNN makes use of the foreground information and preprocessed input to produce higher quality outputs. The whole system is shown in Fig. 1.

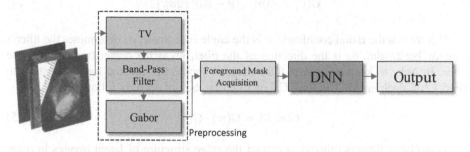

Fig. 1. Flow chart of proposed system.

2.2 Preprocessing

Preprocessing is the first step of our system. De-noising by traditional algorithms, this process enhance the quality of inputs to following steps and decrease the risk for them to be misled by wrong labels. Firstly, total variation (TV) model [19] is utilized to remove the cartoon component (or large scale background noise) while keeping the texture component representing the friction ridge information. Rudin *et al.* proposed this model for image decomposition using the full variation as a regularization term in 1992:

$$min \int |\nabla u| dx + \lambda \int (u - f)^2 dx \qquad (1)$$

Where u and f are output image and input image respectively. The above formula consists of two parts. The first part $TV(u) = \int |\nabla u| dx$ is the total variation of the image, which is the TV energy. It is a regularization term, depending on the magnitude of the image's variation. The second is the fidelity term, which controls the difference between the input image and the output image. λ is a Lagrange multiplier weighting factor, which plays an important balancing role.

Secondly, we use a band-pass filter to perform noise reduction on pictures, and also limit the frequency of fingerprint images to a fixed range. Band-pass filtering of the image can attenuate noise effects while preserving edge profile information. The bandpass filter can be expressed as follows:

$$H(u,v) = \begin{cases} 0 & D(u,v) < D_0 - W/2 \\ 1 & D_0 - W/2 \le D(u,v) \le D_0 + W/2 \\ 0 & D(u,v) > D_0 + W/2 \end{cases} . \qquad (2)$$

Thirdly, a frequency domain Gabor filter called Log-Gabor, is adopted for texture analysis. Its transfer function is defined as two parts:

$$G(w) = exp\left(-[ln(w/w_0)]^2/2[ln(k/w_0)]^2\right). \tag{3}$$

$$G(\theta) = exp\left(-(\theta - \theta_0)^2/2\sigma_\theta^2\right). \tag{4}$$

Where w is the radial coordinate, θ is the angle coordinate, σ_θ determines the filter's angular bandwidth, θ_0 is the direction of the filter, w_0 is the center frequency of the filter. In order to keep a constant filter shape, k should be adjusted for different w_0 to keep k/w_0 unchanged. The final Gabor filter can be obtained as follow:

$$G(w, \theta) = G(w) \cdot G(\theta). \tag{5}$$

Log-Gabor filter is utilized to extract the ridge structure of latent images in overlapping blocks of size 64 × 64 pixels. To avoid edge effect of filters, only 16 × 16 pixels at the center of each block are taken to obtain the whole image.

2.3   Foreground Mask Acquisition

Latent fingerprints' background and noisy regions are in complex patterns. If not separated from original image, it will lead the following steps of the algorithm system to wrong results. For this reason, before orientation prediction, latent images need to be masked to make gray scale of bad areas into zeros. It's easy to get the observation that there's rarely dominant orientation in area of background and noisy regions, except sparse linear background noise (such as arrows, trace of writing, *etc.*) We propose a spatial algorithm for foreground mask acquisition based on this observation. The whole process is displayed by Fig. 2.

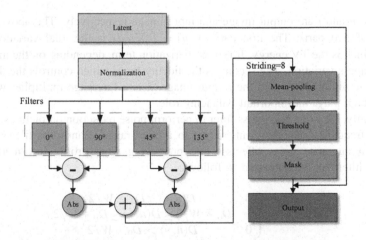

Fig. 2. Flow chart of foreground mask acquisition.

After normalization, input preprocessed image is filtered by 5×5 gradient operators of 0, 45, 90 and 135 degrees. For simplicity, results are named img_{1-4} respectively. These results represents the dominant orientation strength of 5×5 partial areas rather than single pixels, which can eliminate the effect of local sparse linear noise. The next step is displayed by (7):

$$img_k = I * F_k, k = 1, 2, 3, 4. \tag{6}$$

$$r1 = |img_1 - img_3|, r2 = |img_2 - img_4|, r = r1 + r2. \tag{7}$$

In the formulas, * represents convolution operation, $r1$ is the absolute difference of partial area's difference in 0 and 90 degree, and $r2$ is that of 45 and 135 degree. Visual results of $r1$ and $r2$ are shown in Fig. 3(c) and (d). It's clear that amplitude difference of dominant direction area and background is significant. In $r1$, response near vertical or horizontal direction are strengthened and $r2$ enhances patches close to 45° or 135°. To make use of wider area's information and downsample the matrix to fit the orientation field's size, striding 8 mean-pooling [20] is implemented. Then the region mask is threshold and upsampled to the scale of original image. By these steps, minimum units of the mask are 8×8 blocks, which guaranteed each orientation mark in the output orientation fields represents a complete 8×8 block of fingerprint. We use Otsu's

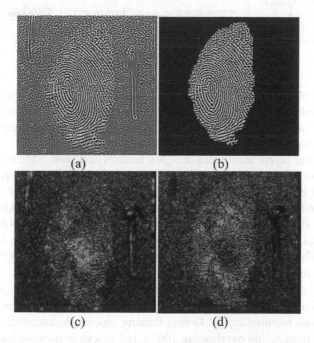

(a)   (b)

(c)   (d)

Fig. 3. (a) original image (b) final output of foreground acquisition (c) (d) Intensity of $r1$ and $r2$. Pixels along vertical and horizontal direction get larger response in $r1$, and pixels with direction near 45° and 135° are brightest in $r2$.

optimal thresholding [21] technique to automatically determine the threshold, then partial noise still remain in the mask is eliminated by region growing. The masked result is as Fig. 3(b) shows.

2.4   CNN Structure

To generate the contextual information of latent images, a fully convolutional neural network is chosen in this work. Usually in a CNN, the last layers are fully connected layers to fetch global features. But in many works, fully connected layers are replaced by convolutional layers. Recent works implements pixel level classification on images, and has been the mainstream in semantic segmentation tasks [18, 22, 23]. Fully convolutional neural network has the advantage of fitting with input fingerprints are of different size and aspect ratio and effectively diminishes parameter number.

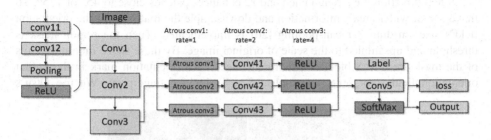

Fig. 4.   Structure of adopted CNN.

The first 3 blocks are of the same Conv-pooling-ReLu structure for local feature learning. According to the results in [24], kernel size of the first part has been adjusted to 7 * 7, 5 * 5 and 3 * 3 respectively to fit the fingerprints' texture frequency. Totally 8-time downsampling is done after these blocks.

The following layers learn more complex features and predict the orientation field. Figure 4 shows the whole structure of the network. As fingerprints have strong semantic inner relationship and orientations change gradually in large scale, we find multi-scale feature will help. ASPP [18] layers are used in 3 scales. Extracted features of three pipes are combined by Conv layer 5 and finally passed to Softmax layer as output. Softmax layer's size is the same with 8-time downsampling input, and has 128channels. The output in the i-th channel ($i = 0, 1 \ldots 127$) represents the probability of angle to be in range from $\left(i \cdot \frac{180}{128}\right)$ to $\left((i+1) \cdot \frac{180}{128}\right)$.

Preprocessed latent fingerprints are used as inputs. Latent fingerprints' Label quality were worse than library fingerprints, but fingerprint patterns and background were similar with required inputs. During training process, as latent sample is limited, we segmented images into overlapping 160×160 blocks to increase sample capacity. Images are disposed with masks obtained in foreground mask acquisition process. Loss function is of cross-entropy type and is the average loss of all pixels. n is the batch size, y is label and a is our network's output.

$$cross\ entropy = -\frac{1}{kMN}\sum\nolimits_{k=1}^{K}[ylna + (1 - y)ln(1 - a)].\tag{8}$$

In testing process, whole latent images are fed into the network directly to control edge effect. Formula of accuracy rate is defined as below. c = −1 means *argmax* is operated on the last channel of *a* or *y*.

$$accuracy = 1 - \frac{1}{kMN}\sqrt{(\mathop{argmax}\limits_{i\in[0,127]}a(i) - \mathop{argmax}\limits_{j\in[0,127]}y(j))^2},\ i,j \in N.\tag{9}$$

3 Experiments

3.1 Database

Our fingerprint database is divided into 2 groups: library fingerprints and latent fingerprints. Every latent image is matched with a library fingerprint, and the total number is 2164 pairs. Each latent fingerprint is 512 × 512 pixels in size and 500 ppi in this paper, and library fingerprints are 640 × 640 pixels and 500 ppi. Among all the images in the database, 500 pairs are made into testing samples and the rest are used for training. Latent images' orientations are to be detected and used to enhance input latent fingerprints. For lack of ground truth orientation information, we produce labels by *Hisign Technology Co., Ltd.*'s SDK program, which won the FVC-Ongoing competition in 2017. In general, library fingerprints' labels are more accurate, while bad quality images' output labels will include more mistakes. Examples of two kinds of images are shown in Table 1.

3.2 Algorithm Performance

Without groundtruth information, the only objective way to confirm performance of fingerprint orientation algorithms is to reinforce latent fingerprints with each methods and test matching rate with library fingerprints. Gabor-based algorithm extracts orientation field on Gabor phase. template-based algorithm extracts orientation fields by first constructing label block templates using clustering Algorithm, and then classifying fingerprint blocks into templates with a learned deep learning network. Following the control variable principle, FingerNet (yellow) is re-trained and tested using the same data set with ours. FingerNet extract orientation fields with a learned fully convolutional network based on DeepLab v2. As the labels for training are all produced by a SDK program, performance of this method is also analyzed. The same reinforcement algorithm is implemented after collecting outputs of all methods mentioned above. Finally SDK is adopted for fingerprint matching process and evaluate performance of each method. Results are shown in Table 2. *Top n* means two fingerprints are matched after *n* attempts.

We finally make the Cumulative Match Characteristic (CMC) curves of all methods above on 500 test samples, as shown in Fig. 5. FingerNet is re-trained and tested all by

Table 1. Examples of database

Library	Latent	Library	Latent

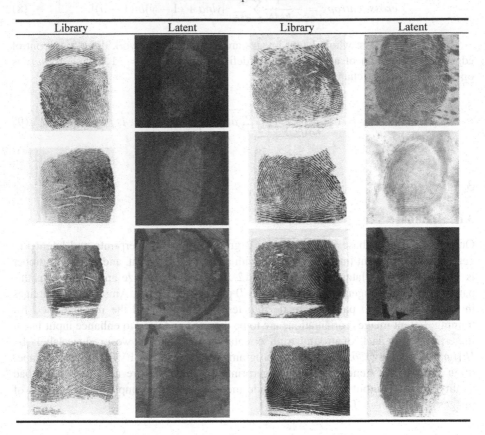

Table 2. Matching performance of each method

Method	Top1	Top5	Top20	Top50
SDK result	430/500	462/500	476/500	483/500
Gabor	406/500	441/500	462/500	471/500
Cao et al.	239/500	275/500	296/500	304/500
FingerNet (retrained)	419/500	449/500	469/500	478/500
FingerNet (Groundtruth)	439/500	468/500	480/500	486/500
Proposed	427/500	459/500	473/500	481/500
Proposed (no preprocess)	421/500	452/500	470/500	478/500

our database as the original model was trained by high level labels and can't provide fair evaluation in this test process. Owing to the clear polarization in CMC curve, the results of high quality methods are placed separately in another graph for a clearer compare.

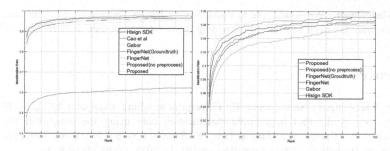

Fig. 5. Performance (CMC curves) of different algorithms on test latents

Proposed method clearly outstrips method in Cao *et al.* or Gabor method. Test result shows our system makes an accuracy of over 85% in top 1 matching test, approximately 1.6 percent higher than the result of FingerNet's outputs. Preprocessing contributes about 0.012% increase in accuracy. Although proposed method's statistic is slightly lower than SDK, considering the performance of FingerNet trained with groundtruth labels, we believe higher quality labels will lead to better results.

Figure 6 exhibits visualized results of proposed method and SDK. Proposed method shows stronger context continuity than SDK. Note that the orientation field belonging to non-ROI region is set to zero and is not displayed.

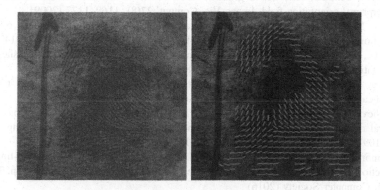

Fig. 6. Result comparison of different methods.

4 Conclusion and Future Work

In this paper, we propose a system for latent fingerprint orientation extraction. The system includes preprocessing, foreground mask acquisition and DNN parts, combining the domain knowledge and contextual features of fingerprints. According to the result in Sect. 3, our method defeats state-of-the-art open source algorithms and performance will improve with higher level labels.

Future work will include (1) integration of the whole system, (2) optimization of the network and preprocess, (3) extending this system to reinforcement and matching.

Acknowledgement. We would like to thank *Beijing Hisign Technology Co., Ltd.* and *Cross-strait Tsinghua Research Institute* for providing the resource and support to us.

References

1. Jain, A.K., Feng, J., Nandakumar, K.: Fingerprint matching. Computer **43**(2), 36–44 (2010)
2. Conti, V., et al.: Fast fingerprints classification only using the directional image. In: Apolloni, B., Howlett, R.J., Jain, L. (eds.) KES 2007. LNCS (LNAI), vol. 4692, pp. 34–41. Springer, Heidelberg (2007). https://doi.org/10.1007/978-3-540-74819-9_5
3. Jiang, X., Liu, M., Kot, A.C.: Fingerprint retrieval for identification. IEEE Trans. Inf. Forensics Secur. **1**(4), 532–542 (2006)
4. Cappelli, R., Lumini, A., Maio, D., et al.: Fingerprint classification by directional image partitioning. IEEE Trans. Pattern Anal. Mach. Intell. **21**(5), 402–421 (1999)
5. Bazen, A.M., Gerez, S.H.: Systematic methods for the computation of the directional fields and singular points of fingerprints. IEEE Trans. Pattern Anal. Mach. Intell. **24**(7), 905–919 (2002)
6. Zhang, L.: Extraction of direction features in fingerprint image. Appl. Mech. Mater. **518**, 316–319 (2014)
7. Sherlock, B.G., Monro, D.M.: A model for interpreting fingerprint topology. Pattern Recogn. **26**(7), 1047–1055 (1993)
8. Kass, M., Witkin, A.: Analyzing oriented patterns. Comput. Vis. Graph. Image Process. **37**(3), 362–385 (1987)
9. Mei, Y., Sun, H., Xia, D.: A gradient-based combined method for the computation of fingerprints' orientation field. Image Vis. Comput. **27**(8), 1169–1177 (2009)
10. Khan, M.A.U., Ullah, K., Khan, A., et al.: Robust multi-scale orientation estimation: directional filter bank based approach. Appl. Math. Comput. **242**, 814–824 (2014)
11. Jin, C., Kim, H.: Pixel-level singular point detection from multi-scale Gaussian filtered orientation field. Pattern Recogn. **43**(11), 3879–3890 (2010)
12. Gupta, P., Gupta, P.: Fingerprint orientation modeling using symmetric filters. In: Applications of Computer Vision, pp. 663–669. IEEE (2015)
13. Krizhevsky, A., Sutskever, I., Hinton, G.E.: ImageNet classification with deep convolutional neural networks. In: International Conference on Neural Information Processing Systems, pp. 1097–1105. Curran Associates Inc. (2012)
14. Redmon, J., Divvala, S., Girshick, R., et al.: You only look once: unified, real-time object detection. In: IEEE Conference on Computer Vision and Pattern Recognition, pp. 779–788. IEEE Computer Society (2016)
15. Liu, W., et al.: SSD: single shot multibox detector. In: Leibe, B., Matas, J., Sebe, N., Welling, M. (eds.) ECCV 2016. LNCS, vol. 9905, pp. 21–37. Springer, Cham (2016). https://doi.org/10.1007/978-3-319-46448-0_2
16. Cao, K., Jain, A.K.: Latent orientation field estimation via convolutional neural network. In: International Conference on Biometrics, pp. 349–356. IEEE (2015)
17. Tang, Y., Gao, F., Feng, J., et al.: FingerNet: an unified deep network for fingerprint minutiae extraction (2017)
18. Chen, L.C., Papandreou, G., Kokkinos, I., et al.: DeepLab: semantic image segmentation with deep convolutional nets, atrous convolution, and fully connected CRFs. IEEE Trans. Pattern Anal. Mach. Intell. **PP**(99), 1 (2017)
19. Chan, T.F., Shen, J.: Mathematical models for local nontexture inpaintings. SIAM J. Appl. Math. **62**(3), 1019–1043 (2001)

20. Simonyan, K., Zisserman, A.: Very deep convolutional networks for large-scale image recognition. Comput. Sci. (2014)
21. Otsu, N.: A threshold selection method from gray-level histogram. IEEE Trans. SMC **9**(1), 62–66 (1979)
22. Badrinarayanan, V., Kendall, A., Cipolla, R.: SegNet: a deep convolutional encoder-decoder architecture for image segmentation. IEEE Trans. Pattern Anal. Mach. Intell. **PP**(99), 1 (2015)
23. Shelhamer, E., Long, J., Darrell, T.: Fully convolutional networks for semantic segmentation. IEEE Trans. Pattern Anal. Mach. Intell. **39**(4), 640 (2014)
24. Schuch, P., Schulz, S.-D., Busch, C.: ConvNet regression for fingerprint orientations. In: Sharma, P., Bianchi, F.M. (eds.) SCIA 2017. LNCS, vol. 10269, pp. 325–336. Springer, Cham (2017). https://doi.org/10.1007/978-3-319-59126-1_27

A Method for Segmentation and Recognition of Mature Citrus and Branches-Leaves Based on Regional Features

Sa Liu[1], Changhui Yang[1,2(✉)], Youcheng Hu[1], Lin Huang[1],
and Longye Xiong[1]

[1] College of Mechanical Engineering, Chongqing University of Technology,
Chongqing 400054, China
yangchanghui@cqut.edu.cn
1225116748@qq.com
[2] College of Mechanical Engineering, Xi'an Jiaotong University,
Xi'an 710049, China

Abstract. A novel method based on the regional feature of mature citrus is proposed for segmentation and recognition in order to achieve the segmentation and identification of mature citrus and branches-leaves in Harvesting robots. Feature mapping table is used to reduce the dimension of the feature vector. The ROI (region of interest) size of the target object is determined by the size of picking up the working space of the manipulator, the binocular camera field and the citrus. According to the scores, the consistency of the primary ROI is sorted to a greater degree, and the ROI with the largest score is chosen as the optimal area. The experimental results show that the accuracy of recognition is 94% and the time required for single image segmentation is 0.24 s. This method is better than many existing methods.

Keywords: Mature citrus · Feature vector · SVM segmentation
Region of interest

1 Introduction

Citrus, as one of the most widely planted fruits in China, is a sort of fruit with a largest trade in the world. As an agricultural product, the trade of citrus is only inferior to that of wheat and corn [1]. Fruit picking in citrus production is a more complex link and accounts for a larger proportion of all production operations. It is precisely because of the complexity of picking operations, resulting in a lower degree of automation, so the citrus picking is often picked by hand, not only labor-intensive, but also have a lot of labor costs [2]. Therefore, using the picking robots instead of artificial picking can not only reduce the labor intensity, save the limited labor resources, but also save the manpower costs and improve the labor productivity.

The working environment of citrus picking robots is the unstructured natural environment,where exist various random factors. At present, there are many researches that can accurately recognize and locate fruits. In the actual picking process, picking robots may collide with obstacles, resulting in serious damage to the robot arm [3].

© Springer Nature Singapore Pte Ltd. 2018
Y. Wang et al. (Eds.): IGTA 2018, CCIS 875, pp. 292–301, 2018.
https://doi.org/10.1007/978-981-13-1702-6_29

Therefore, it is of great significance to study the identification of robot obstacle in picking, there are few researches and the identification is very difficult [4].

At present, there are many researches on fruit target recognition. For example, Xiong et al. [5] deal with the litchi color image under different light conditions. The Litchi color image is preprocessed using Retinex image enhancement and H component rotation in the HSI color space, and then segmented. Peng [6] proposed a novel method to quickly identify the litchi multi-color objects based on the double-order Ostu algorithm. In these studies, the recognition accuracy of the target fruit is relatively high, and has certain anti-light, but did not consider obstacles.

The research on obstacle recognition in front of fruit mainly includes: Okamoto, Stajnko et al. [7, 8] identified the orchard apple by thermodynamic and hyperspectral respectively, and the method has certain light resistance. But the cost is too high to suitable for agricultural picking robots. Amatya [9] adopted the method of decision tree to realize the segmentation of cherry, foliage and background in the nighttime environment. The recognition rate of cherry and foliage by this method was 89.6% and 73.3%, respectively. Bac [10] divided the green peppers, branches, and background in a nighttime environment by using a categorical regression tree approach. The above segmentation methods are all performed in nighttime environmental experiments. Text extraction of hard and soft obstacle segmentation results is not ideal and cannot be used as a reference for avoiding obstacles.

This paper presents a segmentation method based on regional characteristics of mature citrus fruit and branches-leaves segmentation method, which is divided into two parts: offline training and online recognition, as shown in Fig. 1. The off-line training phase mainly analyzes the color information of citrus fruits under different light conditions [11], extracts three color features under RGB channels and marks them manually to obtain the training sample dataset. Through the experimental reference parameters citrus fruit and leaves identification model. Online recognition mainly determines the size of the ROI by the robot picking space size, the binocular camera field size and the citrus fruit size, and uses the ratio of the R channel and the B channel to obtain the ROI local area of the target area so as to reduce the area of the image segmentation, and the feature is dimensionality reduction and segmentation results are applied to identify citrus fruits, branches-leaves and background.

2 Experimental Materials and Methods

2.1 Experimental Materials

The experimental vision system includes BBX213S2C-60 binocular camera, 1394b acquisition card, 1394b cable, workstations and robotic arm. Computer operating system is ubuntu14.04, the image processing software used is opencv2.4.9, the compiler environment is QT5.0.

A citrus picture was collected at the citrus experimental orchard of Chongqing University of Technology. The resolution of the color camera was 1024×768. A total of 130 pictures were collected and divided into two parts, smooth and backlit. The artificial frame was selected for citrus, branches-leaves, background three Sample images.

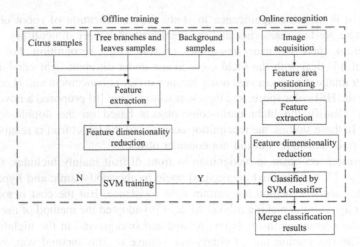

Fig. 1. Identification method flow chart.

The citrus, branches-leaves and background were selected as the training samples under the light and backlight conditions, respectively. As shown in Table 1, the number of pixels between citrus, branches-leaves and background samples was about 1:1:1. In the smooth light, the number of samples under the backlight conditions remained at 1:1. The experimental results show that the training samples selected in this experiment have good balance and diversity.

Table 1. The pixel of three types of sample count tables.

Samples and lighting	Smooth light (pixel)	Backlight (pixel)
Citrus	246232	282323
Branches-leaves	281456	303543
Background	262356	204423

2.2 Citrus Image Feature Extraction

The R, G, B three-channel grayscale information of 100 citrus images were selected respectively for statistics. The R channel grayscale value accounted for 45% between 220–255 and the G channel was more evenly distributed, B channel value of gray value between 20–40, 40–60 accounted for 23.6% and 23.4% respectively. The grayscale values of R, G and B channels of branches-leaves are mainly concentrated in the range of 40–120, and the proportions of grayscale values of R, G and B channels in the range of 40–60, 60–80 and 80–100 Around 13%. The grayscale values of R, G, and B channels in the background are all concentrated in the range of 220–255, accounting for more than 85% of the background.

2.3   The Principle of SVM Algorithm and the Determination of Key Parameters

Support vector machine (SVM) algorithm is a supervised learning algorithm. Support vector machine (SVM) is a classification algorithm, which can improve the generalization ability of learning machine by minimizing the structural risk, minimizing the risk of experience and the scope of confidence. In the case of small sample size, but also to obtain a good statistical rules. In general terms, it is a kind of two-class classification model, its basic model is defined as the largest space in the feature space of the linear classifier, that support vector machine learning strategy is to maximize the interval, and ultimately can be transformed into a convex twice Solving planning problems. SVM algorithm was originally designed for binary classification problem, when dealing with many types of problems, we need to construct a suitable multi-class classifier. At present, there are mainly two kinds of methods to construct the SVM multi-class classifier: one is direct method, which is directly modified on the objective function, and the parameters of multiple classification faces are combined into one optimization problem. The problem "one-off" to achieve multi-category classification by solving this optimization. This method seems to be simple, but its computational complexity is relatively high, more difficult to achieve, only suitable for small problems. The other is indirect method, mainly through the combination of a plurality of two classifiers to achieve multi-classifier construction. The common methods are one to one and one to two. Here uses the one-to-many method (Fig. 2).

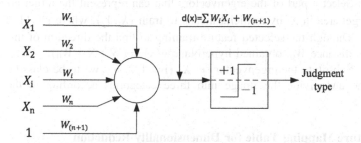

Fig. 2. SVM model.

SVM Hyperplane Model: $g(x) = w^T x + w_0$
The normalization of W and W_0:

$$W^T X + W_0 \geq 1 \quad \forall x \in s_1$$
$$W^T X + W_0 \leq -1 \quad \forall x \in s_1 \tag{1}$$

For each class s_i remember its label t_i, where $t_i = 1, t_i = -1$.
Condition:

$$t_i \cdot \left(W^T x_i + W_0 \right) \geq 1 \quad i = 1, 2, \cdots, N \tag{2}$$

Minimize the solution:

$$c(w) \equiv \frac{1}{2}\|w\|^2 \tag{3}$$

Find the extreme point by Lagrange multiplication:

$$L(w, w_0, \lambda) = \frac{1}{2} w^T w - \sum_{i=1}^{N} \lambda_i \left[t_i \left(w^T x_i + w_0 \right) - 1 \right] \tag{4}$$

Solve the result:

$$w = \sum_{i=1}^{N} \lambda_i t_i x_i \tag{5}$$

$$\sum_{i=1}^{N} \lambda_i t_i = 0 \tag{6}$$

Finally, we can get the optimal parameters of SVM.

Step 1: Draw the image to be segmented and draw the target area by hand, then construct a feature vector X_i through the three channels R, G and B in the area;

Step 2: Select a part of the eigenvectors that can represent the target area and the non-target area in X_i by artificial means to train (X_j, Y_j), where $j \in \{1, 2, \cdots, w\}$;

Step 3: Through the selected feature training to find the direction of the vector W and the distance W_0, obtained hyperplane $g(x) = (W * X + W_0)$;

Step 4: Substitute the eigenvector set X_i; $(i = 1, 2, \cdots, w)$ to be classified into the formula, and divide the image into three categories according to the obtained distance.

2.4   Feature Mapping Table for Dimensionality Reduction

For the processing of color images, generally, the transformation of each pixel in the image may be performed on one pixel or all pixels in a certain neighborhood of a certain pixel at the same time. However, the three color components of a pixel are essentially transformed. Before using the classifier, the mapping table of R, G and B channels should be set up according to the transformation, and the R, G and B channels are indexed during processing, and the corresponding indexes are used directly to classify the data, thus reducing the data dimension and improving the efficiency of image processing. Assuming an array of $W \times H$ pixels for each pixel array to be transformed $P[0 \cdots W - 1, 0 \cdots H - 1]$, pixel $P(i, j)$ after the transformation by f still placed in $P(i, j)$. $P(i, j)$ of the three color components R, G, B recorded as C, then:

$$s = \begin{cases} 255 & f(c) > 255 \\ 0 & f(c) < 0 \\ f(c) & others \end{cases} \tag{7}$$

$$c \in D, f : c \to s \in D, D = \{0, 1, 2, \cdots, 255\}$$

In the transformation f, the color component C is calculated according to the formula f, and then the above rule is modified to obtain the target value S. Only the classification and identification of the target value does not need to identify each pixel for the neighboring pixels. According to the similarity of the S value of the mapping table, the number of identified pixels can be reduced, and the recognition efficiency can be improved. Using the mapping table, the dimension of the eigenvector is reduced. At the same time, the classifier does not need to traverse every point. The method greatly reduces the recognition time but has little effect on the recognition accuracy.

2.5 The Initial Choice of Citrus Regional Characteristics

The number of three-channel image pixels taken by the color camera in this experiment is 786,432, and the number of features is 2,359,296. Using the traditional method of segmentation large amount of computation, will lead to long processing time, it is difficult to achieve real-time. The working space of the robot arm in this paper is a hollow sphere with outer diameter of 780 mm and inner diameter of 245 mm. The orchard spacing of the citrus orchard experimental site is 2800 mm, the distance between the mobile chassis and the trunk is 1400 mm, and the farthest effective distance of the binocular camera is 630 mm.

The farthest citrus is picked, the actual diameters of the three citrus in the picture are 74.22 mm, 75.64 mm and 73.64 mm respectively. The rectangle sizes in the image are respectively 78.7×87.9 pixels and 84.1×98.9 pixels, 76.8×93.36 pixels. Through access to information, citrus actual size range of 55 mm–85 mm [12]. Take the largest citrus 85 mm as the basis for the selection of ROI, robotic picking depth is usually not more than 150 mm. Through calculation, we can draw the conclusion that in the actual picking environment, the maximum size of citrus in the image is 180.375×180.375 pixels. In order to improve its fault tolerance, the area is enlarged by 1.5 times, and the actual ROI size is 270×270 pixels.

Citrus target R channel gray value is mainly concentrated in 220–255, B channel gray value is mainly concentrated in 40–80, with a size of 270×270 pixel ROI traversal image. The R value of R channel is 45% between 220–255 and the B channel is between 40–80 pixels, accounting for 23% of the pixel area, as the initial target ROI. Algorithm calculation process is as follows.

$$P_R = \frac{S_R}{S_{ROI}} \tag{8}$$

$$P_B = \frac{S_B}{S_{ROI}} \tag{9}$$

S_R – The size of the ROI is 270 × 270 pixels, with the number of R channels grayscale values in the range of 220–255 pixels.

S_B – The size of the ROI is 270 × 270 pixels, with the number of B-channel grayscale values in the range of 220–255 pixels.

S_{ROI} – The number of pixels in the ROI of 270 × 270 pixels.

P_R – The proportion of R color features in the ROI.

P_B – The proportion of B color features in the ROI

By judging whether the proportion of R, B color features satisfies the condition (10), it is determined whether it is a valid segmentation region or not.

$$f(P_R, P_B) = \begin{cases} 1 & P_R > 0.45 \; \text{且} \; P_B > 0.23 \\ 0 & others \end{cases} \tag{10}$$

The ROI satisfying the condition (8) has a lot of regions, as shown in Fig. 3. The obtained ROIs are sorted according to the degree of coincidence, and the maximum proportion is obtained as S, as the final segmented ROI, as shown in Fig. 4.

$$S = max\{P_R, P_B\} \tag{11}$$

S in the above equation is the best ROI region.

Fig. 3. Get ROI by color features. (Color figure online)   Fig. 4. Get the highest ROI.

3   Experimental Results and Analysis

3.1   Experimental Results

This article considers the results of the segmentation of the experimenter as accurate. Through the experiment, K-means segmentation algorithm and SVM segmentation algorithm, citrus, branches-leaves and were segmented for thirty images respectively, and the corresponding area was calculated. The experimental results are shown in Table 2, the experimental segmentation results shown in Fig. 5. The experiment uses the following indexes to evaluate the performance of the algorithm, and the definition of recognition accuracy t_P is shown in Eq. (12).

Table 2. Fruit tree target segmentation recognition rate comparison experiment.

Segmentation method and recognition of the target		Citrus	Branches-leaves	Background
Artificial segmentation	Segmentation area (pixels)	3821392	14521668	19994167
K-means segmentation	Segmentation area (pixels)	1843582	6789542	10241678
	Recognition accuracy	48.0%	46.0%	51.0%
SVM segmentation	Segmentation area (pixels)	3770059	14070059	18206866
	Recognition accuracy	98.6%	96.8%	91.0%

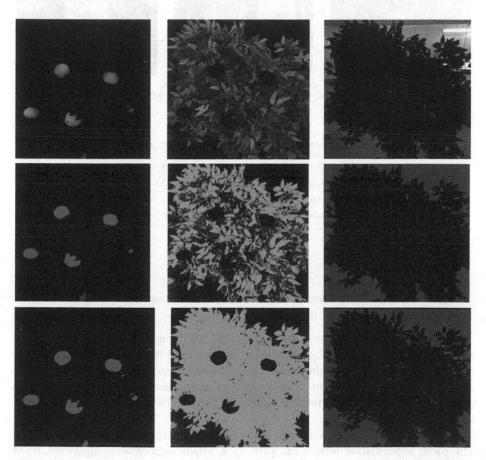

Fig. 5. Comparison of artificial segmentation, K-means segmentation, and SVM Segmentation.

Fig. 6. SVM segmentation based on ROI.

Table 3. Segmentation algorithm to identify the average time.

Segmentation method	Average time (s)
K-means segmentation	0.061853
Whole image SVM segmentation	1779.1
SVM segmentation based on ROI	0.24476

$$t_P = \frac{N_{TP}}{N} \times 100\% \tag{12}$$

N_{TP} – The number of correct identification in the test set.
N – The total number of test samples.

According to analysis the color features and determine the ROI of the target, the segmentation area is reduced, and the color information is reduced by using the feature mapping table to reduce the dimension of the parameters so as to improve the real-time performance of the algorithm. In this paper, changing the light of the segmentation results shown in Fig. 6, the method can be very good segmentation of citrus, branches-leaves and background.

Thirty images were selected and the segmentation experiments were carried out. The mean segmentation time is analyzed by K-means segmentation algorithm, SVM segmentation algorithm and ROI-based SVM feature mapping segmentation method. Table 3 shows the results.

3.2 Experimental Analysis

From the experimental results, we can see that the method proposed in this paper can improve the anti-interference ability under the changing light conditions, the recognition accuracy rate is 94%, the single image segmentation time is about 0.24 s, to meet the real-time and efficient citrus picking.

4 Conclusion

In this paper, a method based on the regional feature of mature citrus is proposed for segmentation and recognition of fruits and leaves. It can solve the problem of identification of mature citrus under the complex environment. Firstly, the mapping relationship of color information is used to reduce the dimension of features and reduce the number of parameters. The best segmentation ROI is obtained to reduce the area of target search and improve the speed of computation, this makes it easy for the picking machine to harvest efficiently.

This method does not distinguish between soft obstacles and hard obstacles (soft obstacles are leaves and hard obstacles are branches). How to make citrus picking robot to avoidance of hardware and software obstacles is the next problem to be solved.

References

1. Yang, S.: China's citrus industry status and development trend. Agric. Eng. Technol. (Agro-Ind.) **04**, 13–17 (2014)
2. Yang, L.: Research on target recognition and positioning technology of citrus picking robot based on binocular vision. Chongqing University of Science and Technology (2017)
3. Xiaojun, Z.: Mathematical picking robot positioning and obstacle detection. Jiangsu University (2009)
4. Jianrong, C., Xiaojun, Z., Feng, W., Qiang, L.: Obstacle identification technology of citrus picking robot. Trans. Agric. Mach. **40**(11), 171–175 (2009)
5. Juntao, X., Xiangjun, Z., Hongjun, W., et al.: Realization of ripe litchi under different light conditions based on Retinex image enhancement. J. Agric. Eng. China **29**(12), 170–178 (2013)
6. Hongxing, P., Xiangjun, Z., Lijuan, C., et al.: Fast identification of field lychee multicolor targets based on double Otsu algorithm. J. Agric. Mechanization **45**(4), 61–68 (2014)
7. Okamoto, H., Lee, W.S.: Green citrus detection using hyperspectral imaging. Comput. Electron. Agric. **66**(2), 201–208 (2009)
8. Stajnko, D., Lakota, M., Hočevar, M.: Estimation of number and diameter of apple fruits in an orchard during the growing season by thermal imaging. Comput. Electron. Agric. **42**(1), 31–42 (2004)
9. Amatya, S., et al.: Detection of cherry tree branches with full foliage in planar architecture for automated sweet-cherry harvesting. Biosyst. Eng. **146**(Suppl. C), 3–15 (2016)
10. Bac, C.W., Hemming, J., van Henten, E.J.: Robust pixel-based classification of obstacles for robotic harvesting of sweet-pepper. Comput. Electron. Agric. **96**, 148–162 (2013)
11. Juntao, X., Xiangjun, Z., Lijuan, C., Aixia, G.: Identification of ripe litchi in natural environment based on machine vision. Acta Autom. Mach. **42**(09), 162–166 (2011)
12. Shun, F.: Design and research of end effector of citrus picking robot. Chongqing University of Science and Technology (2017)

Accurate Depth of Field Rendering
with Integral Image

Yang Yang[✉], Yanhong Peng, Huiwen Bian, Lanling Zeng,
and Liangjun Wang

School of Computer Science and Communication Engineering,
Jiangsu University, Zhenjiang, China
yyoung@ujs.edu.cn

Abstract. Depth of field (DOF) rendering is important in computer graphics, especially in image synthesis and virtual reality applications. Traditionally, a filter with size varying kernels is applied to facilitate DOF rendering, however, the kernel size is approximated by rounding, ignoring the fractional parts, thus causing inconsistencies around the edges. In this paper, we proposed to adapt exact kernel size for depth of field rendering, not only the integral part, but also the fractional part of the kernel size are considered. In addition, we proposed a method to speed up the calculation based on integral images. Experiment results indicate that our proposed method is a practical way for depth of field rendering.

Keywords: Depth of field rendering · Filter · Integral image
Computer graphics

1 Introduction

Depth of field (DOF) rendering refers to the computational methods to sharpen the objects within the focal range while blurring the scenes outside. The DOF effect can guide people's attentions by highlighting the main subjects of the scene. DOF rendering plays an important role in computer graphics, especially in image synthesis and virtual reality applications, for example, it could possibly ease the dizziness caused by views provided by traditional virtual reality applications, as it doesn't force our eyes to focus on every point on the view. Typically, in order to render the DOF effect, the depth information is required, as it provides decision supports for the in-focus areas and out-focus areas. For real world images, the depth information can be obtained by a RGBD camera, or a stereo camera, while for graphics, the depth information is retrieved by 3D modeling.

There are numerous techniques for DOF rendering, among which, a popular method is space varying filtering, i.e., the sizes of the filter kernels change over different positions on the image, if the depth of the points are closer to the front focal plane, they will appear sharp, thus the kernel sizes at the points are smaller, while if the depth of the points are farther to the front focal plane, they will be blurred, thus the kernel sizes at the points are larger. The space varying filtering technique is easy to understand and implement which can produce acceptable DOF effect. In addition, integral image (also known as summed area table) can be explored to improve the

© Springer Nature Singapore Pte Ltd. 2018
Y. Wang et al. (Eds.): IGTA 2018, CCIS 875, pp. 302–309, 2018.
https://doi.org/10.1007/978-981-13-1702-6_30

efficiency, so the space varying filtering is also quite efficient. However, in facilitating DOF rendering, traditional space varying filtering technique approximate the kernel size by rounding, ignoring the fractional part. This results in blur discontinuities, especially inconsistencies around the edges.

To overcome this, in this paper, we proposed a space varying filtering technique for accurate DOF rendering. The proposed method adapts exact kernel size for depth of field rendering, not only the integral part, but also the fractional part of the kernel size is considered. To count in the pixels of fractional parts in the filtering process, additional computation are mandatory, as interpolations are needed to calculate the values of the fractional pixels. Instead of conducting the above time consuming process, an efficient algorithm based on integral images is proposed for the task of accurate DOF rendering. Experiment results indicate that (1) compared with traditional method, our proposed method rendered better DOF effect, as it eliminate the inconsistency around the edges; (2) compared with direct calculation (time + sum), the proposed method based on integral images cost less computational power.

The rest of the paper is organized as follows. In Sect. 2, a literature review about DOF rendering is provided. The details about the proposed method are described in Sect. 3. The experiment results are presented in Sect. 4. Finally, we conclude the paper and present future works in Sect. 5.

2 Related Work

The most direct way to simulate the DOF rendering is to track the light rays through the optical lens. One of the representatives is the work in [1], where they proposed to explore light fields captured by camera arrays for DOF rendering. The method could produce very realistic results, however, the lack of image resolution makes it hard to be widely accepted. [2] proposed an effective ray tracing technique to achieve the bokeh effects produced by parametric aspheric lenses, which simulate mechanical defects in the lens manufacturing process. However, in order to achieve real-time results, some degree of accuracy must be sacrificed, in addition, there are some imperfections in polygon beam tracking and post processing. In the work of [3], the geometric lens model is proposed, which could simulate the DOF rendering with different shapes of the aperture in real time. Lee [4] proposed to synthesize multiple views with a layered image-based scene representation, then accumulate the multi-view to achieve the DOF effect. The method is a good alternative to traditional methods, it can produce high quality DOF blur in reasonable time. [5] introduced an accurate camera lens model and used real lens parameters to simulate the shape and intensity distribution of the DOF effect. This method can be used to analyze and synthesize the DOF effects caused by vignetting.

Many works explore filtering techniques for DOF rendering. [6] developed a novel adaptive filter called adaptive bilateral depth filter to simulate DOF rendering that achieves real-time results with few space requirement, it could further sharpen the boundaries in the focused regions while preserving the blurriness in the out-focus area. However, appropriate parameters must be selected in order to achieve optimistic results. [7] proposed an interactive way to refine the depth map calculated from stereo camera, by filtering the image according to different circles of confusion, the DOF effect is calculated. Nevertheless, users' assistances are needed to refine the depth map. [8] proposed a novel post-processing algorithm that can provide high quality DOF effect in real-time. The filter in this method is controlled by a weighting function defined between two adjacent pixels. However, semi-occlusion areas cannot be robustly processed due to recursive framework and missing scene information. [9] presented a method for DOF rendering based on separable filters, the method could efficiently simulate the DOF effects of polygons such as squares, hexagons and octagons. McGraw [10] proposed low-rank linear filters to render the DOF effect, which reduces the two-dimensional convolution problem to multiple one-dimensional convolutions, thus reducing the computational complexity of the filtering operation.

There are also works beside ray tracing and filtering. [11] proposed a method for depth of field rendering which use nonlinear mipmap interpolation. The method reduces the problem of intensity leakage and blur discontinuity. [12] proposed a new post-processing algorithm that uses the thermal diffusion formula to calculate the exact DOF in real time. The method can be applied for interactive movie preview, but for applications in games, a more advanced GPU may be needed. In the work of [13], eye tracking device is explored to control the depth of the focal plane, it could render the DOF effect based on the gazes. However, in the hardware settings, the accuracy of eye tracker is limited.

3   Proposed Method

In this paper, the DOF effect is achieved by filtering the image with a size-varying all-one matrix, for a specific pixel R_{ij} on the rendered image, it can be calculated with Eq. (1).

$$R_{i,j} = \sum_{m=i-k_{i,j}}^{i+k_{i,j}} \sum_{n=j-k_{i,j}}^{j+k_{i,j}} O_{m,n} \tag{1}$$

Here, $O_{m,n}$ is the pixel on the original image. $k_{i,j}$ is the radius of the kernel at this specific point (i, j) which can be calculated from Eq. (2).

$$k_{i,j} = |A * (disp_{i,j} - disp_f)| \tag{2}$$

A is a coefficient proportional to the size of the aperture. If A is larger, it means that the aperture is relatively large, so that the out-of-focus area is more blurred. On the other hand, if A is smaller, then the out-of-focus region is less blurred. $disp_{i,j}$ is the disparity at point (i, j), $disp_f$ represents the disparity at the focal plane.

Notice that the radius of the kernel $k_{i,j}$ may not be integer, traditional methods typically choose to round it and ignore the fractional part, this certainly will ease the computation, however, it will cause blur discontinuities, especially inconsistency around the edges. Thus in this paper, we will keep the exact value for the radius of the filter kernel $k_{i,j}$, and divide Eq. (1) into two parts, namely the integral part and fractional part, as shown in Eq. (3).

$$R_{i,j} = R_{i,j}^{fint} + R_{i,j}^{frac} \tag{3}$$

This can be clearly shown as the sum of shaded area in Fig. 1. The sum of diamond shaded area is $R_{i,j}^{fint}$, while the sum of the slash and rectangle shaded area is $R_{i,j}^{frac}$.

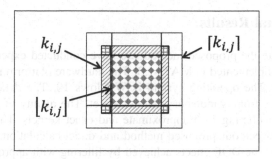

Fig. 1. Filtering with the exact filter kernel (shaded area)

Mathematically, the formula to calculate $R_{i,j}^{fint}$ and $R_{i,j}^{frac}$ are shown in Eqs. (4) and (5) respectively.

$$R_{i,j}^{fint} = \sum_{m=i-\lfloor k_{i,j} \rfloor}^{i+\lfloor k_{i,j} \rfloor} \sum_{n=j-\lfloor k_{i,j} \rfloor}^{j+\lfloor k_{i,j} \rfloor} O_{m,n} \tag{4}$$

$$R_{i,j}^{frac} = f_{i,j}\left(R_{i,j}^{cint} - R_{i,j}^{fint}\right) - f_{i,j}^2 \sum_{m \in \{i-\lceil k_{i,j} \rceil, i+\lceil k_{i,j} \rceil\}} \sum_{n \in \{j-\lceil k_{i,j} \rceil, j+\lceil k_{i,j} \rceil\}} O_{m,n} \tag{5}$$

Here, $R_{i,j}^{cint} = \sum_{m=i-\lceil k_{i,j} \rceil}^{i+\lceil k_{i,j} \rceil} \sum_{n=j-\lceil k_{i,j} \rceil}^{j+\lceil k_{i,j} \rceil} O_{m,n}$, which is the result when the radius of the kernel is $\lceil k_{i,j} \rceil$, $f_{i,j} = k_{i,j} - \lfloor k_{i,j} \rfloor$. Obviously, the direct way to calculate $R_{i,j}$ is very time consuming.

To improve the efficiency, we proposed to adapt integral image. The value for each pixel $I_{i,j}$ in an integral image is the sum of all the top-left values in the original image, as shown in Eq. (6).

$$I_{i,j} = \sum_{m=1}^{i} \sum_{n=1}^{j} O_{m,n} \tag{6}$$

With the integral image, we can calculate $R_{i,j}^{fint}$ and $R_{i,j}^{cint}$ efficiently, as shown in Eqs. (7) and (8).

$$R_{i,j}^{fint} = I_{i+\lfloor k_{ij} \rfloor, j+\lfloor k_{ij} \rfloor} - I_{i+\lfloor k_{ij} \rfloor, j-\lfloor k_{ij} \rfloor} - I_{i-\lfloor k_{ij} \rfloor, j+\lfloor k_{ij} \rfloor} + I_{i-\lfloor k_{ij} \rfloor, j-\lfloor k_{ij} \rfloor} \tag{7}$$

$$R_{i,j}^{cint} = I_{i+\lceil k_{ij} \rceil, j+\lceil k_{ij} \rceil} - I_{i+\lceil k_{ij} \rceil, j-\lceil k_{ij} \rceil} - I_{i-\lceil k_{ij} \rceil, j+\lceil k_{ij} \rceil} + I_{i-\lceil k_{ij} \rceil, j-\lceil k_{ij} \rceil} \tag{8}$$

In this way, for every pixel of the rendered image, we need 13 additions and subtractions, and 3 multiplications, no matter how large is the kernel size. When the size of the kernel is more than 4, our proposed method is deemed to be more efficient in time. Our proposed method requires additional space, since it need to store the integral images, however, the improvement in time complexity is far more significant.

4 Experimental Results

In order to evaluate the proposed method, we have conducted experiments. The proposed method is implemented in MATALB. The hardware platform is an Intel i5 CPU with 8 GB RAM. The operating system is Windows 10. The data involved in this experiment is taken from Middlebury stereo dataset. The quality of the DOF effect is compared between filtering with approximate and exact kernels. The running time is also compared between our proposed method and direct calculation.

Figure 2 shows the DOF effects achieved by filtering with approximate and exact kernels. Both Fig. 2(a) and (b) are DOF effect with $A = 5$, and the focal planes of these two are both set to the depth of the red flower. Figure 2(a) is the result of filtering with approximate kernels. Figure 2(b) is the result of filtering with the exact kernel. It can be observed in Fig. 2(a) that there exists severe artifacts around edges in the image. These artifacts are outlies caused by blur discontinuity and inconsistency. The situation is improved significantly with filtering with exact kernels, as we can see from Fig. 2(b) that most of the artifacts are handled, the edges are smoother.

Fig. 2. The result of the DOF rendering. (a) is the result of filtering with approximated kernel. (b) is the result of filtering with exact kernel.

Figure 3(a) shows the original image. Figure 3(e)–(h), (i)–(l), (m)–(p) illustrate the results of focusing on the red flower, blue flower and orange flower respectively, different aperture sizes are considered in this experiment, i.e., A takes value from the set $\{3, 5, 7, 9\}$. As it can be seen that, the larger the aperture is, the more blurred the out-of-focus area is, the more the main subject of the scene is highlighted. Figure 3(b)–(d) show the running time to focus on the red flower, blue flower and orange flower respectively. As we can see that, compared with direct calculation, the proposed method based on integral image is more efficient, and the gap is getting more obvious as the aperture size increases. In addition, the running time remains constant for our proposed method, while for direct calculation, the running time increases significantly with the aperture size.

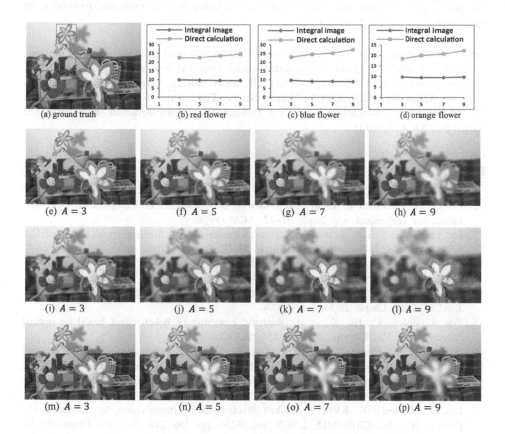

Fig. 3. The comparison of running time between our proposed method and direct calculation and the DOF effect of focusing at different positions. (a) is the original image. (b)–(d) describe the running time of two methods. (e)–(h), (i)–(l), (m)–(p) indicate the results of focusing on the red flower, blue flower and orange flower with different sizes of aperture respectively. (Color figure online)

5 Conclusion and Future Work

In this paper, we proposed a novel method for accurate DOF rendering based on integral image. The DOF effect is achieved by filtering with size varying kernels. Unlike traditional method which only considers the integral part of the kernel size, in this paper, the fractional part of the kernel size is also taking into account. In order to speed up the calculation, integral image is explored. Experiment results indicate that the proposed method could improve the DOF effect significantly, as the artifacts of blur discontinuities and edge inconsistencies produced by traditional method are greatly reduced with our proposed accurate DOF rendering method. In addition, by incorporating integral images, the running time of the proposed accurate DOF rendering method is greatly improved. Thus, it can be concluded that our proposed method is an optimistic way for DOF rendering.

Acknowledgement. This work was supported by National Natural Science Foundation of China (Grant No. 61402205), China Postdoctoral Science Foundation (Grant No. 2015M571688), Jiangsu University (Grant No. 13JDG085), University Science Research Project of Jiangsu Province (Grant No. 16KJB520008), Natural Science Foundation of Jiangsu Province (Grant No. BK20170558), Postgraduate Research & Practice Innovation Program of Jiangsu Province (Grant No. SJCX17_0575).

References

1. Levoy, M., Hanrahan, P.: Light field rendering. In: Conference on Computer Graphics and Interactive Techniques, vol. 2, pp. 31–42. ACM (1996)
2. Joo, H., Kwon, S., Lee, S., et al.: Efficient ray tracing through aspheric lenses and imperfect bokeh synthesis. J. Comput. Graph. Forum **35**(4), 99–105 (2016)
3. Lee, S., Eisemann, E., Seidel, H.P.: Real-time lens blur effects and focus control. In: SIGGRAPH, vol. 29, pp. 1–7. ACM (2010)
4. Lee, S., Eisemann, E., Seidel, H.P.: Depth-of-field rendering with multiview synthesis. J. ACM Trans. Graph. **28**(5), 1–6 (2009)
5. Wu, J., Zheng, C., Hu, X., et al.: Realistic rendering of bokeh effect based on optical aberrations. J. Vis. Comput. **26**(6–8), 555–563 (2010)
6. Wu, S., Yu, K., Sheng, B., Huang, F., Gao, F., Ma, L.: Accurate depth-of-field rendering using adaptive bilateral depth filtering. In: Hu, S.-M., Martin, Ralph R. (eds.) CVM 2012. LNCS, vol. 7633, pp. 258–265. Springer, Heidelberg (2012). https://doi.org/10.1007/978-3-642-34263-9_33
7. Liu, D., Nicolescu, R., Klette, R.: Bokeh effects based on stereo vision. In: Azzopardi, G., Petkov, N. (eds.) CAIP 2015. LNCS, vol. 9256, pp. 198–210. Springer, Cham (2015). https://doi.org/10.1007/978-3-319-23192-1_17
8. Xu, S., Mei, X., Dong, W., et al.: Depth of field rendering via adaptive recursive filtering. In: SIGGRAPH Asia 2014 Technical Briefs, pp. 1–4. ACM (2014)
9. Mcintosh, L., Riecke, B.E., Dipaola, S.: Efficiently simulating the bokeh of polygonal apertures in a post-process depth of field shader. In: Computer Graphics Forum, vol. 31, pp. 1810–1822. Blackwell Publishing Ltd (2012)
10. Mcgraw, T.: Fast Bokeh effects using low-rank linear filters. J. Vis. Comput. **31**(5), 601–611 (2015)

11. Lee, S., Kim, G.J., Choi, S.: Real-time depth-of-field rendering using anisotropically filtered mipmap interpolation. J. IEEE Trans. Vis. Comput. Graph. **15**(3), 453–464 (2009)

12. Kass, M., Lefohn, A., Owens, J.D.: Interactive depth of field using simulated difiusion on a GPU. Pixar Anim. Studios Tech Rep. **2**, 2 (2006)

13. Mantiuk, R., Bazyluk, B., Tomaszewska, A.: Gaze-dependent depth-of-field effect rendering in virtual environments. In: Ma, M., Fradinho Oliveira, M., Madeiras Pereira, J. (eds.) SGDA 2011. LNCS, vol. 6944, pp. 1–12. Springer, Heidelberg (2011). https://doi.org/10.1007/978-3-642-23834-5_1

Image Matching for Space Objects Based on Grid-Based Motion Statistics

Shanlan Nie[1,2], Zhiguo Jiang[1,2], Haopeng Zhang[1,2(✉)], and Quanmao Wei[1,2]

[1] Image Processing Center, School of Astronautics, Beihang University,
Beijing 100191, People's Republic of China
zhanghaopeng@buaa.edu.cn
[2] Beijing Key Laboratory of Digital Media,
Beijing 100191, People's Republic of China

Abstract. Image matching for space objects has attracted wide attention for its importance in applications. Major challenges for this task include the textureless appearance and symmetrical structure of space objects. In this paper, we propose a novel image matching method, aiming to improve the image matching quality for space objects. Our approach consists of three main components, which are grid-based motion statistic (GMS), a contrario-random sample consensus (AC-RANSAC), and constraint of three-view. First of all, GMS is utilized to generate a collection of corresponding points. Subsequently, we adopt AC-RANSAC to eliminate false matches and estimate fundamental matrix. In the end, accurate matches are obtained under the constraint of three-view. Experimental results on simulated images of space objects have quantitatively and qualitatively demonstrated the effectiveness of our approach.

Keywords: Image matching · Space objects
Grid-based motion statistics · AC-RANSAC

1 Introduction

Image matching for space objects plays an important role in many space-related applications, such as pose estimation [1], 3D reconstruction [2], etc. Image matching method is regarded as the first fundamental step in those application researches. By conducting image matching methods, we can estimate the spatial position relationship between images.

Nowadays, a variety of image matching algorithms have been proposed. Most of them consist of two parts, extracting feature points and eliminating false matches. Since the former is the spotlight of researches, we cover a few classic feature points below. One of the most successful feature points is scale-invariant feature transform (SIFT) [3], which is invariant to rotation, scaling, and illumination. SIFT is widely used in image matching methods, due to its high accuracy and strong robustness. Therefore, [2] leveraged SIFT to reconstruct space objects. Subsequently, to increase the efficiency, [4] introduced speeded-up

© Springer Nature Singapore Pte Ltd. 2018
Y. Wang et al. (Eds.): IGTA 2018, CCIS 875, pp. 310–318, 2018.
https://doi.org/10.1007/978-981-13-1702-6_31

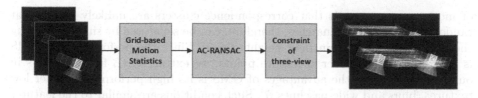

Fig. 1. The pipeline of the proposed approach. Our method consists of three main components, including grid-based motion statistics (GMS), AC-RANSAC, and constraint of three-view.

robust features (SURF). However, the number of SIFT and SURF feature points will decrease dramatically when the baseline of two images of space objects are large. To satisfy the demand of real-time matching, oriented FAST and rotated BRIEF (ORB) [5] was introduced. ORB can generate a large collection of feature points for space objects images, thus making it suitable for image matching for space objects. Researches on feature points extraction are still on-going and a number of deep learning techniques have been adopted; for instance, learned invariant feature transform (LIFT) [6] utilized convolutional neural networks (CNNs) to extract feature points. In the aspect of false matches elimination, most of image matching methods for space objects use RANSAC, which has a problem of setting threshold empirically.

Space objects are man-made structures, which are usually textureless and symmetrical. These two features heavily limit the performance of image matching methods. Lack of textures can deteriorate the feature detectors, thus making the number of feature points decrease largely. Furthermore, symmetrical structures usually cause the feature description of feature points too similar, which induces a bunch of false matches.

In order to improve the image matching for space objects, we propose a new method. We extract ORB feature points and integrate a few constraints into our pipeline to eliminate false matches. As shown in Fig. 1, our approach consists of three main components, namely grid-based motion statistics (GMS) [7], AC-RANSAC [8], and constraint of three-view [9]. We firstly leverage GMS to get a collection of corresponding points. Subsequently, AC-RANSAC is used to eliminate false matches and estimate fundamental matrix. In the end, accurate matches are obtained under the constraint of three-view.

The rest of this paper is organised as follows. In Sect. 2, we describe the process of our method in details. Experimental results on simulated images of space objects are introduced in Sect. 3. The conclusion of this paper is drawn in Sect. 4.

2   Methodology

2.1   Grid-Based Motion Statistics

GMS is a new algorithm of integrating motion smoothness, which is regarded as the statistical likelihood of a certain number of matches in a region. The essence of motion smoothness is that correspondence clusters are unlikely to occur at random. True and false matches, therefore, can be separated by simply counting the number of matches in their neighborhood. Since the performance of GMS is sensible to the number of feature points, we extract ORB feature points in our method. One of the advantages of GMS is its high performance under low textures, blurs and wide-baselines [7]. Such conditions are similar to the features of space objects images, therefore we choose GMS as the first step of our pipeline.

In the first place, one pair of images are set as the input of algorithm. Then the method detects ORB feature points and obtains corresponding points based on their feature descriptors. Subsequently, images are divided by a certain number of grids respectively. When the number of matches between two grids and their neighborhood is larger than the threshold, those matches are considered as true matches. More technical details can be found in [7]. After leveraging GMS, we are able to obtain a large number of matches. Since many false matches exist in the consequence, elimination of false matches is needed afterwards.

2.2 AC-RANSAC

AC-RANSAC, a variant RANSAC algorithms [10], is used to estimate robust model from noisy data that are corrupted by outliers. However, the performance of RANSAC relies heavily on static threshold, which is often set empirically. If the threshold is too small, few points are chosen as inliers. Nevertheless, if the threshold is too large, then outliers will contaminate inliers, which usually induces inaccurate models. Aiming to solve the threshold problem, AC-RANSAC was first introduced in [11]. AC-RANSAC can avoid empirically setting thresholds for inliers/outliers discrimination by introducing number of false alarms (NFA) [12].

$$NFA(M, k) = N_o(n - N_s)\binom{n}{k}\binom{k}{N_s}(e_k^d \alpha_0)^{k-N_s}$$

where n is the total number of input matches. N_s is the number of matches needed to estimate model, which is set as 7 because of the estimation of fundamental matrix. M denotes the model predicted by N_s matches. N_o is the number of models that can be estimated from N_s matches. k denotes the number of hypothesized inlier matches. e_k is the $k - th$ lowest error to the model M among all n matches. d is the dimension of the error, which is set as 1, because we assess point-to-line distance. α_0 is the probability of a random match having error 1 pixel.

Model M is considered as valid if

$$minNFA(M, k) \le \epsilon. \qquad k = N_s + 1...n$$

The target of AC-RANSAC is to find $argmin_M NFA(M)$ among all the models. After finding the final model, we can obtain more precise matches and estimate the fundamental matrix between the pair of images. However, there are still a few false matches. Therefore, our proposed method introduces constraint of three-view to further eliminate the remaining false matches.

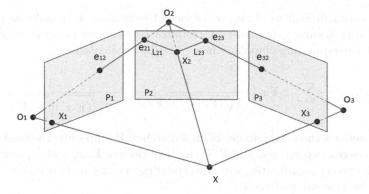

Fig. 2. The constraint of three-view. P_1, P_2, P_3 represent three pictures. O_1, O_2, O_3 denote camera centers of three images respectively. X is a 3D point. And X_1, X_2, X_3 are project points of X in three images. L_{21} and L_{23} are two epipolar lines of X_1 and X_3, whose intersection point is X_2 theoretically.

2.3 Constraint of Three-View

Most of robust model estimations usually adopt the distance between point and epipolar line to discriminate inliers and outliers. However, this epipolar constraint cannot assess the precise position relationship between two corresponding points. Constraint of three-view can be interpreted as the relationship between three points, which is a stronger constraint than the epipolar constraint. The constraint of three-view is exhibited in Fig. 2. In theory, the intersection point of epipolar line L_{21} and L_{23} is X_2 [13]. Therefore, we are capable of obtaining the relationship between three points. With the strong spatial position relationship of three points, more accurate matches can be retained in the end.

After the procedure of AC-RANSAC, we can get a collection of matches and the fundamental matrices. Three images are fed into this component. Assumed that we have three points X_1, X_2, X_3 in three images P_1, P_2, P_3. X_1 and X_2, X_2 and X_3 are corresponding points calculated after AC-RANSAC. By using the fundamental matrix of P_1 and P_2, we can obtain the epipolar line L_{21} of X_1 in P_2. The epipolar line L_{23} can be calculated in the same way. Subsequently, we can get the intersection point of two epipolar lines. In the end, if the distance between intersection point and X_2 is less than the threshold, the matches are regarded as the true matches.

3 Experiments

To demonstrate the effectiveness of our proposed approach, we divide experiments into three parts. First of all, we test the feasibility of our method. Secondly, the robustness to angle interval is evaluated. In the end, we conduct experiments to exhibit applications of the method. It should be mentioned that the images used in our experiments are all from space objects dataset BUAA-SID1.0 [14], since it's quite difficult to obtain real space objects images. In order to measure the matching accuracy, the average distance between all the matching points and their corresponding epipolar Lines (ADPL) is calculated [9].

$$ADPL = \frac{1}{N} \sum_{i=1}^{N} \left| x_i' \mathbf{F} x_i \right| \left(\frac{1}{2\sqrt{(\mathbf{F}x_i)_1^2 + (\mathbf{F}x_i)_2^2}} + \frac{1}{2\sqrt{(\mathbf{F}'x_i')_1^2 + (\mathbf{F}'x_i')_2^2}} \right)$$

where N denotes the total number of final matches. $\mathbf{F}$ represents the fundamental matrix between two images, and $\mathbf{F}'$ is the transpose of $\mathbf{F}$. x_i and x_i', represented by homogeneous coordinates, are corresponding points in two images. $(\mathbf{F}x_i)_1$ denotes the first value of vector.

3.1   Feasibility of Method

In order to assess the feasibility of our approach, two scenes, named Cube and Dsp, are used. Each scene contains 5 images, with a resolution of 1024×1024 pixels, and the angle interval between two adjacent images is $15°$. Figure 3 exhibits some examples of experimental results, and more measurements are shown in Table 1.

The consequence has revealed that our method can obtain a larger collection of matching points than SIFT+AC-RANSAC. Furthermore, SIFT+AC-RANSAC usually leads to false matches under the large angle interval, while ADPL of our method is smaller under such condition. It indicates that our method can get a more accurate result under the large angle interval. Both images and measurements prove that our approach is feasible and has the potential to conduct image matching for space objects, regardless of low textures and wide baseline.

Table 1. Comparison between AC-RANSAC and our method

Satellite	Angle	SIFT+AC-RANSAC		Proposed method	
		Points number	ADPL	Points number	ADPL
Cube	Img1–Img2	30	1.3507	232	**0.8377**
	Img2–Img3	43	**0.5237**	232	0.7750
	Img3–Img4	39	1.1194	432	**0.7129**
	Img4–Img5	29	0.8669	432	**0.7433**
	Average	35	0.9652	332	**0.7672**
Dsp	Img1–Img2	57	1.3949	171	**0.8405**
	Img2–Img3	60	**0.7508**	171	0.9371
	Img3–Img4	61	1.2734	281	**1.0216**
	Img4–Img5	55	1.0785	281	**1.0236**
	Average	59	1.1244	226	**0.9557**

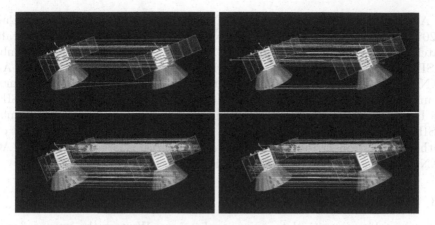

Fig. 3. Some examples of image matching results. Images in the first row are generated by SIFT+AC-RANSAC [8], and images in the second row are the consequences of our approach. The red circles denotes the positions of matching points. And green lines stand for the relationship of matches. Our method can obtain a larger number of matching points and a more accurate result. (Color figure online)

3.2 Robustness to the Angle Interval

In application, because of the relative motion between camera and space objects, two images of space objects usually have certain angle interval, which requires that our algorithm is capable of dealing with certain angle interval. During this part, we evaluate the robustness to angle interval of images. Angle interval in our experiments ranges from 5° to 20° (Cube) or 25° (Dsp), in increments of 5°. In order to make the result more reliable, we choose five images for each angle interval and average the corresponding outcomes as the final result. The average ADPL of five images is measured in Table 2.

Table 2. Performance comparison in different angle intervals.

Satellite	Angle	SIFT+AC-RANSAC		Proposed method	
		Points number	ADPL	Points number	ADPL
Cube	5°	64	**0.3176**	1372	0.7582
	10°	38	**0.5376**	521	0.7055
	15°	35	0.9652	332	**0.7672**
	20°	-	-	272	**0.9733**
Dsp	5°	119	**0.3533**	1418	0.6042
	10°	81	**0.5848**	548	0.8897
	15°	59	1.1244	226	**0.9557**
	20°	38	1.2051	95	**1.0637**
	25°	-	-	74	**1.8507**

As shown in Table 2, SIFT+AC-RANSAC fails when angle interval of Cube is 20° or angle interval of Dsp is 25°. Nevertheless, our method can get stable matching consequences. When the angle interval increases gradually, the number of SIFT feature points becomes less, which leads to the failure of SIFT+AC-RANSAC. It should be mentioned that SIFT+AC-RANSAC can get a more accurate result when the angle interval is small. The main reason is that SIFT can be more robust than ORB under such conditions, even though the number of SIFT is far smaller than that of ORB. Therefore, it can be concluded that our method has a stronger robustness when angle interval is large, while SIFT+AC-RANSAC is more accurate when angle interval is small.

3.3 Application

Image matching is critical to many applications. We test the proposed approach in 3D reconstruction. To evaluate the effect of image matching algorithm,

Table 3. Comparison of the number of dense cloud points

Satellite	SIFT+RANSAC	Proposed method
Cube	11603	**15658**
Dsp	6238	**9851**

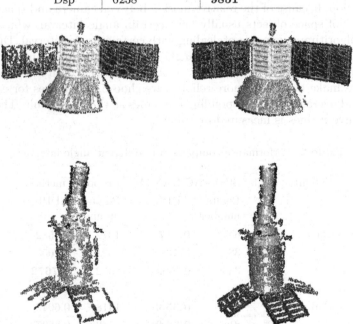

Fig. 4. The comparison of dense 3D reconstruction by using different matching methods. The left ones are generated by SIFT+AC-RANSAC, while the right ones are obtained by our proposed method. Our method can get more dense 3D point clouds and a more complete structure.

we replace the image matching part of 3D reconstruction. 3D reconstruction used in our experiments is sequential structure from motion (SFM) [8], which starts from a minimal reconstruction and incrementally adds new views using pose estimation and 3D point triangulation algorithm. Based on the feature points, SFM can produce sparse 3D point clouds. In order to obtain a dense 3D reconstruction result, the patch-based multi-view stereopsis algorithm (PMVS) [15] is leveraged. The input images are the same images used in the first experiment. Figure 4 displays the result of PMVS and the number of dense point clouds is exhibited in Table 3.

As shown in Fig. 4, one of the solar arrays of Cube is not well-reconstructed by using SIFT+AC-RANSAC, while our method is able to get a more complete structure of Cube. For Dsp, our approach can reconstruct three solar arrays and the structure of solar arrays is more accurate. Moreover, Table 3 indicates that the number of dense point clouds generated by our method is almost 1.5 times larger. The 3D reconstruction consequence can validate the effectiveness of our method.

4   Conclusion

In this paper, a novel image matching of space objects is proposed, aiming to improve the matching quality. Our approach is made up of three components. Firstly, GMS is responsible to extract ORB feature points and obtain a collection of initial matches. Subsequently, we utilize AC-RANSAC to eliminate the remaining false matches and estimate fundamental matrix. To get more accurate matches, constraint of three-view has been integrated into our method in the end. In the experiment, we test the feasibility and robustness of the method and exhibit 3D reconstruction consequences. The experimental results illustrate that our approach is more accurate when the baseline of images is large and can obtain a better 3D reconstruction when it is integrated in 3D reconstruction pipeline.

Acknowledgements. This work was supported in part by the National Natural Science Foundation of China (Grant Nos. 61501009, 61771031 and 61371134), the National Key Research and Development Program of China (2016YFB0501300, 2016YFB0501302) and the Aerospace Science and Technology Innovation Fund of CASC (China Aerospace Science and Technology Corporation).

References

1. Zhang, H., Jiang, Z., Elgammal, A.: Satellite recognition and pose estimation using homeomorphic manifold analysis. IEEE Trans. Aerosp. Electron. Syst. **51**(1), 785–792 (2015)
2. Zhang, H., Wei, Q., Jiang, Z.: 3D reconstruction of space objects from multi-views by a visible sensor. Sensors **17**(7), 1689 (2017)
3. Lowe, D.G.: Distinctive image features from scale-invariant keypoints. Int. J. Comput. Vis. **60**(2), 91–110 (2004)

4. Bay, H., Ess, A., Tuytelaars, T., Van Gool, L.: Speeded-up robust features (SURF). Comput. Vis. Image Underst. **110**(3), 346–359 (2008)
5. Rublee, E., Rabaud, V., Konolige, K., Bradski, G.: ORB: an efficient alternative to sift or surf. In: 2011 International Conference on Computer Vision, pp. 2564–2571, November 2011
6. Yi, K.M., Trulls, E., Lepetit, V., Fua, P.: LIFT: learned invariant feature transform. In: Leibe, B., Matas, J., Sebe, N., Welling, M. (eds.) ECCV 2016. LNCS, vol. 9910, pp. 467–483. Springer, Cham (2016). https://doi.org/10.1007/978-3-319-46466-4_28
7. Bian, J., Lin, W.Y., Matsushita, Y., Yeung, S.K., Nguyen, T.D., Cheng, M.M.: GMS: grid-based motion statistics for fast, ultra-robust feature correspondence. In: 2017 IEEE Conference on Computer Vision and Pattern Recognition (CVPR), pp. 2828–2837, July 2017
8. Moulon, P., Monasse, P., Marlet, R.: Adaptive structure from motion with *a Contrario* model estimation. In: Lee, K.M., Matsushita, Y., Rehg, J.M., Hu, Z. (eds.) ACCV 2012. LNCS, vol. 7727, pp. 257–270. Springer, Heidelberg (2013). https://doi.org/10.1007/978-3-642-37447-0_20
9. Cong Li, Hong Rui Zhao, and Gang Fu. 3-D reconstruction of image sequence based on independent three-view. In: Advanced Materials Research, vol. 989, pp. 3844–3850. Trans Tech Publications (2014)
10. Fischler, M.A., Bolles, R.C.: Random sample consensus: a paradigm for model fitting with applications to image analysis and automated cartography. In: Readings in Computer Vision, pp. 726–740. Elsevier (1987)
11. Moisan, L., Stival, B.: A probabilistic criterion to detect rigid point matches between two images and estimate the fundamental matrix. Int. J. Comput. Vis. **57**(3), 201–218 (2004)
12. Moisan, L., Moulon, P., Monasse, P.: Automatic homographic registration of a pair of images, with a contrario elimination of outliers. Image Process. On Line **2**, 56–73 (2012)
13. Hartley, R., Zisserman, A.: Multiple View Geometry in Computer Vision. Cambridge University Press, Cambridge (2003)
14. Gang, M., Zhiguo, J., Zhengyi, L., Haopeng, Z., Danpei, Z.: Full-viewpoint 3D space object recognition based on kernel locality preserving projections. Chin. J. Aeronaut. **23**(5), 563–572 (2010)
15. Furukawa, Y., Ponce, J.: Accurate, dense, and robust multiview stereopsis. IEEE Trans. Pattern Anal. Mach. Intell. **32**(8), 1362–1376 (2010)

CNN Transfer Learning for Automatic Image-Based Classification of Crop Disease

Jingxian Wang[1,2,3]($\boxtimes$), Lei Chen[1,2,3], Jian Zhang[1,2,3], Yuan Yuan[1,2,3], Miao Li[1,2,3], and WeiHui Zeng[1,2,3]

[1] Institute of Intelligent Machines, Chinese Academy of Sciences, Hefei 230031, China
wjx2016@mail.ustc.edu.cn, {chenlei,jzhang,yuanyuan}@iim.ac.cn
[2] University of Science and Technology of China, Hefei 230026, China
[3] Key Laboratory of Agricultural Internet of Things, Ministry of Agriculture, Beijing, People's Republic of China

Abstract. As the latest breakthrough in the field of computer vision, deep convolutional neural network(CNN) is very promising for the classification of crop diseases. However, the common limitation applying the algorithm is reliance on a large amount of training data. In some cases, obtaining and labeling a large dataset might be difficult. We solve this problem both from the network size and the training mechanism. In this paper, using 2430 images from the natural environment, which contain 2 crop species and 8 diseases, 6 kinds of CNN with different depths are trained to investigate appropriate structure. In order to address the overfitting problem caused by our small-scale dataset, we systemically analyze the performances of training from scratch and using transfer learning. In case of transfer learning, we first train PlantVillage dataset to get a pre-trained model, and then retrain our dataset based on this model to adjust parameters. The CNN with 5 convolutional layers achieves an accuracy of 90.84% by using transfer learning. Experimental results demonstrate that the combination of CNN and transfer learning is effective for crop disease images classification with small-scale dataset.

Keywords: CNN · Transfer learning · Crop disease
Image-based classification · Over-fitting

1 Introduction

Rapid and accurate diagnosis of crop diseases is significant to develop the treatment technique while substantially improving agricultural production and ensuring food safety. Traditionally, the diagnosis of crop diseases is mainly through agricultural experts, which increases labor costs and limited the rapid development of modern agriculture. With the development of computer vision, the performance of intelligent identification research in crop diseases has made great

© Springer Nature Singapore Pte Ltd. 2018
Y. Wang et al. (Eds.): IGTA 2018, CCIS 875, pp. 319–329, 2018.
https://doi.org/10.1007/978-981-13-1702-6_32

achievements. Zhang et al. [1] extracted its color, shape, and texture features after division of disease spot, and then the extracted features are provided for the K-nearest-neighbor classifier to recognize the corn leaf diseases. Rumpf et al. [2] achieved the classication of crop diseases using Support Vector Machine algorithms. The accuracy was between 65% and 90% depending on the type and stage of sugar beet diseases. Also, some diseases classication tasks have been completed based on other hand-engineered features and intelligent algorithms [3, 4].

The traditional machine learning methods mainly use low-level visual features combined with a variety of classification algorithms. Even though these methods have achieved good classification, they suffer from some limitations. Most of them rely on hand-crafted features, which can't solve the problem of semantic gap [5]. Besides, the segmentation work will be difficult when the background of the image is complex or the leaves appear powdery. CNN as a deep learning model can automatically discover increasingly higher level features from data [6] and it have achieved significant success in many diverse domains [7,8]. Recently, there have been some researchers using CNN method for plant disease diagnosis.

Srdjan et al. [9] built a deep CNN to recognize 13 different types of plant diseases, which can also distinguish plant leaves from their surroundings. In the same year, Mohanty et al. [10] trained deep CNN models to classify 14 crop species and 26 diseases by using PlantVillage dataset(www.plantvillage.org) consisting of 54,306 images collected under controlled conditions. Similarly, Amara et al. [11] classified banana leaf diseases using LeNet architecture and demonstrated the effectiveness of the approach. Furthermore, CNN is also used for plant disease severity estimation. Wang et al. [12] evaluated the performances of shallow networks trained from scratch and deep models fine-tuned by transfer learning. The result can get an overall accuracy of 90.4% by using the deep VGG16 model trained with transfer learning.

These methods have achieved good classification effects in plant diseases classification. However, these large-scale deep CNNs will quickly become overfitted to the training data when there are limited amount of crop disease images. In response to this problem, we can construct the networks with less layers and more strategies to reduce the over-fitting phenomenon. Inspired by this, we used CNN of different depths to find out which nets are best suited to classify our crop diseases. Moreover, we can also reduce over-fitting from the perspective of training mechanism. Transfer learning technique that transfer the classification knowledge into the new tasks have been proven helpful [13]. Most of the studies applied transfer learning methods based on models trained on ImageNet [14] dataset. However, there are many differences in content between the ImageNet dataset and crop diseases dataset. Hence, in our work we make full use of the similarities between PlantVillage dataset and our dataset for transfer learning. The capabilities of correctly identify the crop diseases in the natural environment are compared to explore the best network and training mechanism.

2   Proposed Method

2.1   Architecture of Crop Disease Classification Model

The classification model is composed of four parts, which are convolutional layers, relu layers, pooling layers and fully-connected layers. The convolution layer is the core of CNN, which can extract various abstract features automatically from each disease image. CNN adopts the method of local connection and weight sharing to reduce the number of weight parameters. And different convolution kernels can obtain the features under different mapping. The size of the convolution kernel is manually specified, but the parameters in the convolution kernel need to be learned continuously. Following convolution layer are relu layer and pooling layer. Relu layers can do non-linear mapping to the output. The expression of relu activation function is defined as

$$Relu = \begin{cases} x & if \ x > 0 \\ 0 & if \ x \le 0 \end{cases} \tag{1}$$

Pooling Layers are designed to reduce the data dimension, in which the hyperparameters don't need to be learned. This paper uses max-pooling that computes the maximum value overnonoverlapping rectangular regions to integrate features. Figure 1 shows the operation of max pooling. It can be calculated by Eq. (2).

$$y_{0,0} = Max(x_{0,0}, \ x_{0,1}, \ x_{1,0}, \ x_{1,1}) = Max(1, \ 2, \ 6, \ 7) = 7 \tag{2}$$

Fully-connected layer is placed on the last part of the network, and the parameters to be learned are changed from convolution kernel parameters to the weight coefficients in full connection. The last fully-connected layer in this article is responsible for logical inference, which can take advantage of high-level features to classify the disease images into predened classes.

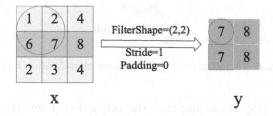

Fig. 1. The operation diagram of max pooling

In addition to the above basic composition, it is necessary to take some measures in the networks to suppress over-fitting because the number of network parameters are still large relative to the size of our dataset. This paper adopts the two strategies of L2 regularization and dropout to reduce over-fitting in the network. L2 regularization is the addition of a regularization term $\frac{1}{2}\lambda w^2$ after

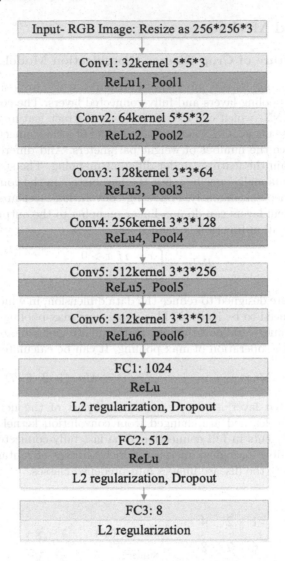

Fig. 2. Visualization of crop disease classification model

the cost function [15]. Assuming that the original cost function is C_0, the cost function and the gradient formula can be respectively expressed as

$$C = C_0 + \frac{1}{2n} \sum_w \lambda w^2 \qquad (3)$$

$$\frac{\partial C}{\partial w} = \frac{\partial C_0}{\partial w} + \frac{\lambda}{n} w \qquad (4)$$

The effect of L2 regularization is to reduce the weights and the feature weight decays a lot when the feature isn't important. This also means that over-fitting can be significantly reduced due to the low complexity of the network. Also in favour of reducing overfitting, dropout was originally proposed by Hinton et al. [16]. The research indicated that the overfitting can be greatly reduced by randomly omitting half of the feature detectors on each training case. Since each neuron has 50% chance of being removed when the network is trained, the appearance of one neuron does not depend on another. Briefly, dropout make a neuron stop working with the probability p. The formulas are as follows:

$$z_i^{(l+1)} = w_i^{(l+1)}(r^{(l)} * y^{(l)}) + b_i^{(l+1)}, \ r_j^{(l)} \sim Bernoulli(p) \tag{5}$$

$$y_i^{(l+1)} = f(z_i^{(l+1)}) \tag{6}$$

According to the above research, we construct six CNNs of different depths and each contains 3–8 convolutional layers. Taking the network with 6 convolutional layers as an example, we present the complete structure and parameter settings in the Fig. 2. In the following sections, we will develop two training mechanisms and conduct experiments based on this network architecture.

2.2   Training Mechanism

In order to overcome the over-fitting problem caused by our small-scale dataset, we compare two training mechanisms based on the above network structure to explore the optimal results. One idea is training from scratch. We put our dataset directly into networks with different depths for training and then evaluate results on the validation set. Another idea is transfer learning. We can make full use of the models trained on the related fields and make some adjustment to reuse in our field. Some researchers have achieved good results by using transfer learning on the trained model of ImageNet [14]. However, compared with ImageNet database, PlantVillage dataset is more similar to our disease dataset. Therefore, this paper takes advantage of the similarity between PlantVillage dataset and our crop diseases dataset to use transfer learning. First, the above network structure is used to train eight plant diseases from PlantVillage dataset to get the pre-trained model. Then the pre-trained model is loaded into the same network to continue training our dataset. The parameters of the network are adapted to our dataset by training and adjusting at this stage. Finally, the experimental results are evaluated on the completed model.

3   Material and Experiment

3.1   Material Preparation

To validate the performance of the proposed approach, we use 8 kinds of diseases from public dataset PlantVillage to obtain pre-trained models. Sample images from PlantVillage dataset are shown in the Fig. 3. Since the plant disease leaves are collected under controlled conditions, the background of these images is relatively simple. There are 10,052 samples in total, and samples of each disease

Fig. 3. Sample images from PlantVillage dataset

Fig. 4. Example each from every crop disease. (1) Cucumber target spot (2) Cucumber powdery mildew (3) Cucumber downy mildew (4) Rice bacterial blight (5) Rice falsesmut (6) Rice blast (7) Rice flax spot (8) Rice sheath blight

are evenly distributed. We will use these images to train a pre-trained model and adjust the parameters based on this model using our dataset.

Our dataset includes 2,430 disease images of cucumber and rice, which have been assigned with 8 classes of labels. Each crop-disease is put in the same folder and it represents a class label. Figure 4 shows some examples from every crop disease in our dataset. These original images are all captured from the natural environment, which have different sizes, shooting angles, poses, backgrounds and illumination. In this work, we resize all the images to 256*256 pixels before they enter the networks. Table 1 lists the number of samples in each crop disease. It can be seen that our dataset is small and the distribution of each disease is uneven. In all the experiments described in the paper, 80% of crop disease images are used for training, and 20% are used for validation. Our task is to classify eight diseases from cucumber and rice without changing the original number of samples.

Table 1. The number of samples in each crop disease

Class	1	2	3	4	5	6	7	8
Number of images	145	201	199	50	47	694	201	893

3.2 Implementation of Experiments

In order to compare the influence of the network depths and training mechanisms, we standardize the hyper-parameters across all the experiments. We use the same hyper-parameters described in Table 2, which are determined by some references and a series of experiments on our dataset. We use Adam optimization algorithm [17] in our model. Adam designed independent adaptive learning rate for different parameters by calculating the first-order moment estimation and second-order moment estimation of the gradient. It can iteratively update the network weights based on training data until optimal results are found to minimize the loss function. The learning rate is set to 0.001, which determines the speed of weight updating. Big learning rate can lead to inaccurate results, and while too small learning rate will require longer training time. Our each experiment runs 20 epochs. All training images have been trained all over the network in one epoch. The optimization algorithm randomly choose a batch of samples in the training set for training. We set the batch size to 64. Dropout has already been mentioned in the above, which is set to 0.5. Tensorflow is adopted to conduct the experiments.

Table 2. The value of hyper-parameters in experiments

Hyper-parameters	Value
Optimization algorithm	Adam
Learning rate	0.001
Epochs	20
Batch size	64
Dropout	0.5

4 Results and Discussion

Figure 5 shows the effect of training mechanisms on classification results under the same CNN. By comparing the green to red lines in the figure, we find the accuracy of training from scratch is higher than using transfer learning when the network depth is shallow. With the increase of network depth, the effect of using transfer learning on our small dataset is better than training from scratch. This is because the network with 3 or 4 convolution layers obtain insufficient features, which can't learn more extensive features from the plantvillage dataset to fit in our dataset. When the network reaches a certain depth, the initial classification accuracy using transfer learning is significantly higher. This shows that deep networks can learn sufficient features, which can be reused in our dataset. Obviously, it is very effective to use transfer learning on networks with convolutional layers of 5–8, and the result is better than training from scratch.

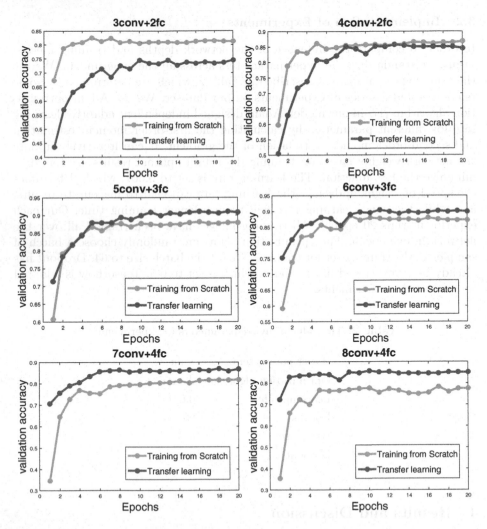

Fig. 5. Validation accuracy using different training mechanisms (3conv + 2fc represents this network contains 3 convolutional layers and 2 fully connected layers, and so on.)

Figure 6 shows the impact of different network depths on classification results under the same training mechanisms. As can be seen from the figure, no matter which training strategy is used, the best results can be obtained on the network with 5 convolution layers. In the case of training starting from scratch, our dataset appears severe over-fitting with the increase of network layers. Generally, fewer network layers can't learn sufficient features, and while more network layers will result in overfitting on the small dataset. This indicates that the depth of network has an important impact on a particular dataset. We should make preliminary judgments about the depth of network based on the scale of our dataset and after that the experimental results are used to verify the suitable network.

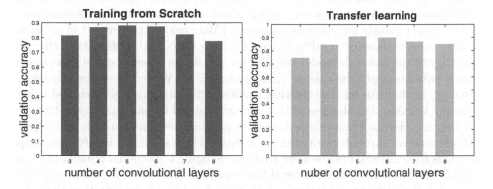

Fig. 6. Validation accuracy using networks of different depths

Table 3 lists the validation accuracy of all experiments. In this paper, we performed 9 experiments for each result. Since the size of the plantvillage dataset is larger than our dataset, the pre-trained models can achieve relatively high accuracy, which shows that the sample size has a great influence on the classification result. For our dataset, it can be seen that using pre-trained model obtained from Plantvillage dataset can achieve higher accuracy than training from scratch when the network reaches a certain depth. Most obviously on the network with 8 convolutional layers, our dataset accuracy can be increased by 7.59% with the help of transfer learning. And on the network with 5 convolutional layers, our dataset can reach the classication accuracy of 90.84% by

Table 3. The validation accuracy of all experiments

	3conv	4conv	5conv	6conv	7conv	8conv
Pre-trained model (%)	0.9490	95.76	98.53	97.93	95.66	94.95
Training from scratch (%)	0.8125	86.83	87.94	87.27	81.91	77.45
Transfer learning (%)	0.7455	84.59	90.84	89.95	86.83	85.04

adjusting parameters on the pre-training model. In fact, our dataset background is more complex than plantvillage dataset. Besides, our data distribution of each disease is't uniform. Better results may be achieved if we reduce the complexity of the background and make the data evenly distributed.

5   Conclusion

The traditional intelligent identification method identifies the disease by manually extracting various features of the leaf spot and selecting specific classification algorithm. This can lead to the semantic gap problem and increase the computational complexity. This paper proposes the method for crop disease images classification by combining CNN and transfer learning, which is applicable not only to leaf diseases, but also to powdery diseases and straw diseases. The contributions of this paper mainly include two aspects: (1) We explored the impact of network depths on classification results. By constructing CNN with different depths, we investigate the network model suitable for our dataset and complete the automatic extraction of crop disease characteristics. (2) We explored the impact of training mechanism on classification results by training from scratch and using transfer learning. For the over-fitting problem caused by our small-scale dataset, we use the relevant Plantvillage dataset to obtain pre-trained models and adjust the parameters through retraining our dataset. Our task is to classify eight crop diseases from natural environment without changing the original number of samples. The CNN with 5 convolutional layers can reach 90.84% classification result by using the training mechanism of transfer learning, demonstrating that the combination of CNN and transfer learning strategy is effective for classification of various crop diseases. In the future, we will collect more crop disease images in natural environment. We hope that we can develop a complete system for crop diseases diagnosis based on this research.

Acknowledgments. The work is partially supported by the National Natural Science Foundation of China (31501223) and Key Laboratory of Agricultural Internet of Things, Ministry of Agriculture, P.R. China.

References

1. Zhang, S.W., Shang, Y.J., Wang, L.: Plant disease recognition based on plant leaf image. J. Anim. Plant Sci. **25**(3), 42–45 (2015)
2. Rumpf, T., Mahlein, A.K., Steiner, U., Oerke, E.C., Dehne, H.W., Plmer, L.: Early detection and classification of plant diseases with support vector machines based on hyperspectral reflectance. Comput. Electron. Agric. **74**(1), 91–99 (2010)
3. Kai, S., Liu, Z., Hang, S., Guo, C.: A research of maize disease image recognition of corn based on BP networks. In: Third International Conference on Measuring Technology and Mechatronics Automation, pp. 246–249 (2011)
4. Sammany, M., Medhat, T.: Dimensionality reduction using rough set approach for two neural networks-based applications. In: International Conference on Rough Sets and Intelligent Systems Paradigms, pp. 639–647 (2007)

5. Wan, J., Wang, D., Hoi, S.C.H., Wu, P., Zhu, J., Zhang, Y., Li, J.: Deep learning for content-based image retrieval:a comprehensive study. In: the ACM International Conference, pp. 157–166 (2014)
6. Lecun, Y., Bengio, Y., Hinton, G.: Deep learning. Nature **521**(7553), 436 (2015)
7. Deng, L., Yu, D.: Deep learning: methods and applications. Found. Trends Sig. Process. **7**(3), 197–387 (2014)
8. Wen, Y., Zhang, K., Li, Z., Qiao, Y.: A discriminative feature learning approach for deep face recognition. In: Leibe, B., Matas, J., Sebe, N., Welling, M. (eds.) ECCV 2016. LNCS, vol. 9911, pp. 499–515. Springer, Cham (2016). https://doi.org/10.1007/978-3-319-46478-7_31
9. Srdjan, S., Marko, A., Andras, A., Dubravko, C., Darko, S.: Deep neural networks based recognition of plant diseases by leaf image classification. Comput. Intell. Neurosci. **2016**(6), 1–11 (2016)
10. Mohanty, S.P., Hughes, D.P., Salath, M.: Using deep learning for image-based plant disease detection. Front. Plant Sci. **7**, 1419 (2016)
11. Amara, J., Bouaziz, B., Algergawy, A.: A deep learning-based approach for banana leaf diseases classification. In: Datenbanksysteme Fr Business, Technologie Und Web, pp. 79–88 (2017)
12. Wang, G., Sun, Y., Wang, J.: Automatic image-based plant disease severity estimation using deep learning. Comput. Intell. Neurosci. **2017**, 2917536 (2017)
13. Pan, S.J., Yang, Q.: A survey on transfer learning. IEEE Trans. Knowl. Data Eng. **22**(10), 1345–1359 (2010)
14. Deng, J., Dong, W., Socher, R., Li, L.J., Li, K., Li, F.F.: ImageNet: a large-scale hierarchical image database. In: IEEE Conference on Computer Vision and Pattern Recognition, CVPR 2009, pp. 248–255 (2009)
15. Massini, M., Fortunato, M., Mancini, S., Tombesi, P.: L2 regularization for learning kernels, vol. 62, no. (4), pp. 109–116 (2012)
16. Hinton, G.E., Srivastava, N., Krizhevsky, A., Sutskever, I., Salakhutdinov, R.R.: Improving neural networks by preventing co-adaptation of feature detectors. Comput. Sci. **3**(4), 212–223 (2012)
17. Kingma, D.P., Ba, J.: Adam: a method for stochastic optimization. Comput. Sci. (2014)

Learning to Segment Objects of Various Sizes in VHR Aerial Images

Hao Chen, Tianyang Shi, Zhenghuan Xia[✉], Dunge Liu, Xi Wu,
and Zhenwei Shi[✉]

Image Processing Center, School of Astronautics, Beihang University,
Beijing, China
{justchenhao, shitianyang, xiwu1000,
shizhenwei}@buaa.edu.cn, maxwell_xia@126.com

Abstract. The goal of semantic segmentation is to assign semantic categories to each pixel in an image. In the context of aerial images, it is very important to yield dense labeling results, which can be applied for land use and land change detection. But small and large objects are difficult to be labeled correctly simultaneously in a single framework. Convolutional neural networks (CNN) can learn rich features and has achieved the state-of-the-art results in image labeling. We construct a novel CNN architecture: Pyramid Atrous Skip Deconvolution Network (PASDNet), which combines features of different levels and scales to learn small and large objects. Secondly, we employ a weighted loss function to overcome class imbalance problem, which improves the overall performance. Our proposed framework outperforms the other state-of-art methods on a public benchmark.

Keywords: Convolutional neural networks (CNNs) · Semantic segmentation
Very high resolution aerial images

1 Introduction

Automated annotation of urban areas in very-high-resolution (VHR) remote sensing imagery contributes to many remote sensing applications, such as land use and land change detection. Semantic segmentation of aerial images is one of the most challenging tasks in remote sensing, which needs to assign every pixel in the image to one specific category. The difficulty is reflected in three ways: (1) Small individual objects lack sufficient pixel description with the corresponding spatial resolution of an aerial image. (2) Objects of the same kind have various scales. (3) Remote sensing images only record the spectrum information on the top side of view of the objects, which limits the possibility of objects to be distinguished.

Deep convolutional neural networks (DCNN) [1] is a popular method for image classification, which extracts features layer by layer to get abstract expressions of the image. DCNN could learn more effective features than hand-crafted ones. Fully convolutional neural networks (FCN) have been used for semantic segmentation of aerial image [2], which replace the original fully connected layers in CNN with convolution layers for pixel-wise classification. FCN inherits the powerful ability of CNN to extract

© Springer Nature Singapore Pte Ltd. 2018
Y. Wang et al. (Eds.): IGTA 2018, CCIS 875, pp. 330–340, 2018.
https://doi.org/10.1007/978-981-13-1702-6_33

the semantic features as well as outputting dense classification results. But the potential of the CNN has not been fully exploited. There are two major shortages of the existing CNN structures (1) Some small objects are not classified correctly due to the lack of spatial information. (2) The center of the large objects failed to be correctly labeled. It is because the size of the receptive field of the network is smaller than that of the object.

Our first attribution is to design a novel semantic segmentation architecture, referred to as PASDNet (Pyramid Atrous Skip Deconvolution Network), which combines features of different resolutions and multiple scales with four strategies. (1) Atrous convolution to enlarge the receptive field. (2) Pyramid sampling to extract multiple scale features (3) Skip connection to fuse the high-level features with the low-level features (4) Deconvolution to produce the classification map of the same size as input.

The second attribution is to employ a weighted loss function which helps to accelerate the training procedure and produce better results compared to the normal one. During training, the minor object has a larger weight to compensate for its substantial quantity.

To validate our idea, we devise another three architectures, (1) ANet, a baseline. (2) PANet to verity features of multiple scales (3) ASDNet to test the features of different levels. We implement all the experiments on Massachusetts [3] dataset and get promising results, demonstrating the competence of the combining of these strategies.

The relation work is given in Sect. 2, and the methodology and design approach are discussed in Sect. 3, including instructions of the four strategies and our proposed architecture. We later preform experimental evaluations in Sect. 4 and draw a conclusion in Sect. 5.

2 Related Work

In this section, we review the applications of CNN both in computer vision and remote sensing.

In computer vision, CNN has been flourishing since 2012 when AlexNet [1] was proposed. Many network structures were designed, e.g. VGG [4], GoogleNet [5], ResNet [6], which have been the foundation of follow-up work. Without fully connected layers, Fully convolution neural networks (FCN) [7] could obtain dense classification maps and has been widely used in semantic segmentation. There are two main derivatives of FCN. (1) Encode-decode method, which encodes the input into low-dimensional features and decodes it to original dimension. One delegate work is SegNet [8]. (2) Encode method which is more efficient without the decode procession and aiming at extracting effective features. Deeplab [9] is one of the most efficacious models.

In remote sensing (RS), mainstream method of VHR image classification before CNN has two stages [10]. (1) Designing the hand-craft features to describe the pattern of objects. (2) Choosing a classifier. Not long ago, CNN was applied in many tasks in RS, such as vehicle detection [11], hyperspectral image classification [12] and land use classification [13–15]. In [13], Penatti uses CNN to extract features and classifies them by SVM. To my best knowledge, Castelluccio [14] is the first to construct an end to end CNN structure for land use classification.

For semantic segmentation of aerial imagery, Mnih [3] proposed a CNN-based classification framework, whose final layer produces an entire dense prediction patch instead of a single prediction. Later on, FCN was used to label RS images in [15, 16]. However, the small objects and detailed edges are labeled poorly due to the lack of spatial information at the end of the network. There is still significant potential in CNN to produce better performance. Therefore, we propose a novel architecture to combine features of different levels and scales to help the network learn better.

3   Method

In this section, we first illustrate the four fundamental strategies, including atrous convolution, skip connection, pyramid sampling and deconvolution. Then, we describe PASDNet in details. In the end, we propose a weighted loss function to address the class imbalance problem.

3.1   Atrous Convolution

In CNN, pooling and striding operation reduce the resolution of the feature map. These down-sampling operations are significant for CNN to identify one object but are the main culprit of losing detailed spatial information. Atrous convolution is one powerful method to balance the tradeoff between category and spatial information. Without down-sampling operation, atrous convolution uses the dilated convolution kernel to obtain a larger receptive field equivalent with that of the same rate of striding and keep more spatial information.

The following formula illustrates the atrous convolution. x is the input feature map, ω is the K × K convolution kernel, y is the output feature map, r is the sample rate. When r = 1, atrous convolution is as same as convolution operation. Figure 1 shows the 1 dimension explanation of atrous convolution.

$$y(i,j) = \sum_{m=-K}^{K} \sum_{n=-K}^{K} x(i+rm, j+rn)\omega(m,n) \tag{1}$$

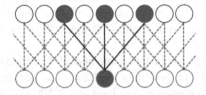

Fig. 1. 1D Atrous convolution with a sample rate r = 2, a kernel size K = 3.

3.2 Skip Connection

Convolutional neural networks have certain translation invariance, which is critical for the precision of classification but a loss of localization information. Skip connection is an intuitive and useful way to address the tradeoff between localization and precision, which extracts features at different levels in a neural network and combines them. There are two ways to merge features. (1) sum, which means to element-wise add features at the corresponding positions to obtain the same dimension feature maps like that of input. (2) concat (short for concatenation), which superimposes multiple input feature maps in the thickness direction. The sum operation adds prior information that the features of all levels are equally important. In fact, the weights of features of different levels can not be the same. With concat, the network retains all the original information and has great potential to explore the magnitudes of different features. Therefore, this paper uses the concat strategy, whose formula is as follows.

$$O = \{v : v \in I_1 \, or \, v \in I_2 \, or \ldots or \, v \in I_n\} \tag{2}$$

$I_1, I_2, \ldots, I_n$ are feature maps to be concatenated, whose element is a feature map. n is the number of groups of feature maps. O is the output feature maps.

3.3 Pyramid Sampling

Considering that objects may have many scales, it is necessary to construct a multi-scale model to describe objects. One way to obtain multi-scale features is to down-sampling the original image in many rates and fuse them at the end, which loses the critical localization information. Atrous convolution with a sampling rate corresponds to a single receptive field. With the combination of several rates, a network can have multiple receptive fields to extract multi-scale features.

Pyramid sampling is a refine method through concatenating feature maps of atrous convolutions at different rates. Figure 2 illustrates pyramid sampling intuitively.

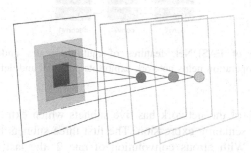

Fig. 2. The blue, light green, yellow circles separately represent neurons with atrous convolution of rate 2, 4, 6. A larger rate denotes a larger size of receptive field. Concatenating the output feature maps to fuse multi-scale features. (Color figure online)

3.4   Deconvolution

There are two kinds of up-sampling methods for increasing the resolution of feature maps. (1) Interpolation. Bilinear interpolation is one popular method which computes each output point according to the values of four nearest points on the input map. (2) Deconvolution, which can be defined as transpose convolution. During backward convolution with stride f, the size of the input gradient map is f times that of the output map. Thus, up-sampling with factor f can be seen as convolution with a fractional stride of 1/f, accomplished by transpose convolution. The advantages of deconvolution include higher efficiency than bilinear interpolation and learnable convolution kernel to achieve high performance.

3.5   PASDNet

Having discussed the four strategies above, we analyze PASDNet in details.

PASDNet is built from VGG-Net and extended by the four strategies. The overall structure is depicted in Fig. 3 and can be split into four parts.

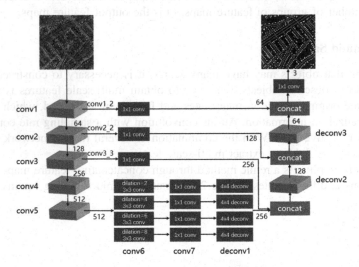

Fig. 3. The structure of PASDNet: features of multiple scales and different levels are concatenated. Concat operation helps network exploit its potential and determine the weights of various features.

(1) The main body of the network has five subnets which extract features layer by layer to obtain semantic expression. The first three subnets have 2 times down-sampling rate. With atrous convolution of rate 2, the last two subsets output features of the same resolution as input. In the end, it outputs features with down-sampling of factor 8 compared to the original input.

(2) AP module. The second part has two subsets. The first subnet is atrous convolutions with four different rates to extract multi-scale features. The second subnet uses 1 × 1 convolution kernel to refine these features.

(3) SD module. The third part has three subnets. Each subset contains factor 2 of up-sampling and concat operation. The first subnet up-samplings the four branches separately, and then concat them with features extracted at the third subnet of the main body. With three times of deconvolution and concat operations, the resolution of feature maps gradually increases to the same size as that of the original input and low-level features make up for the loss of spatial information of high-level features step by step. Concat operation retains the diversity of features and helps network to learn the weight of different features.

(4) Classifier module. Finally, thanks to the high semantic properties of features, we use a 1×1 convolution layer as a linear classifier to predict the final classification maps (the same dimension as the number of categories).

To explore the effectiveness of the four strategies in PASDNet, we design another three networks: ANet, PANet, ASDNet.

ANet is the base-line, which combines the first and the last part of the PASDNet. PANet contains the A, P and classifier module to verify the effect of fusing multi-scale features. Multi-level features are obtained by ASDNet with A, SD and classifier modules.

3.6 Weighted Loss Function

Class imbalance means disproportionate number of class instances and is a common problem in remote sensing, which makes network hard to train, resulting in the poor performance of the minor-class objects. However, we find that the proportions between classes are stable. For example, the road surface is about 9% of the total pixels in urban areas. In a sense, we can construct a category-sensitive loss function to give the minor class a high weight, which is equivalent to increase its quantity.

Considering we have k categories, m samples to be trained together. The weighted loss function is the weighted mean of the cross entropy of the m samples' predicted categories and their real categories and is denoted as follows.

$$J_\omega(\theta) = \frac{-1}{m} \frac{\sum_{l=0}^{k-1} f^{(l)}}{k} \left[\sum_{i=1}^{m} \sum_{j=0}^{k-1} \frac{1}{f^{(j)}} 1\left\{y^{(i)} = j\right\} \log p(y^{(i)} = j | x^{(i)}; \theta) \right] \quad (3)$$

$1\{\cdot\}$ is the indicate function, $p(y^{(i)} = j | x^{(i)}; \theta)$ is the possibility of sample i belongs to category j. θ is the parameter for network to learn. $f^{(j)}$ is the ratio of class j to the total pixels. $\frac{\sum_{l=0}^{k-1} f^{(l)}}{k} \frac{1}{f^{(j)}}$ denotes the weight of the object of category j.

4 Experiments

4.1 Dataset and Evaluation Metrics

We evaluate the aforementioned architectures on the public aerial image labeling dataset: Massachusetts Dataset [3], which was arranged by Dr. V. Mnih and consists of

Massachusetts Roads Dataset and Massachusetts Buildings Dataset. We assembled these two parts of data and generated a dataset containing roads and buildings. Therefore, the types of objects include road, building, and background. The dataset has a total of 151 RGB aerial images of size 1500 × 1500 with 1 m resolution and their corresponding label maps. And there are 141 training samples and 10 test samples.

To evaluate class-specific performance, the paper uses F1 score and overall accuracy as evaluation metrics, which is commonly applied in semantic segmentation tasks in RS. F1 score can be calculated as the harmonic mean between precision and recall. Overall accuracy is the percentage of individuals being corrected classified. To evaluate overall performance, we use mean F1 score of all classes.

4.2   Training Details

Caffe [17] is an important industrial-level deep learning tool that can perform convolutional neural networks well and has been widely used in computer vision. All the experiments in this paper are based on Caffe. Considering the limitations of computer memory, we cut the original aerial samples into a patch size of 500 × 500. At the data layer of the network, we randomly transformed the original image patch with rotation, translation, and Gaussian blur, and then randomly crop a small patch of 321 × 321. These transformations increase the sample diversity and improve the generalization competence of the model.

The networks are trained by stochastic gradient descent with momentum. In each iteration, few patches are fed to the network and losses are backward to update the parameters. Fine-tuning strategy can accelerate the speed of training, so we initialize the network with pre-trained VGG model. In the experiments, we use the poly learning rate policy [9] where learning rate is the product of the base learning rate (Lr) and $\left(1 - \frac{iter}{\max\_iter}\right)^{power}$ (with $Lr = 10^{-4}$, power = 0.9 and max_iter = 10^4). And the momentum term is 0.99, weight decay term is 0.0005, batch size is 5.

4.3   Results and Analysis

In this section, we first present the comparison of PASDNet and its basic architectures: ANet, PANet, ASDNet. And then we compare PASDNet with other methods in works of literature, including Deeplab and SegNet.

(1) Comparison of PASDNet and its original architectures. The numerical results on the validation set is shown on Table 1. Network with a Suffix w means to use the weighted loss function. As we can see, performance with weighted loss strategy is better than that with the normal loss on all metrics. PANet get a higher score of mean F1 than ANet. ASDNet outperforms ANet in all respects, due to the effect of SD module, but is no match for PASDNet. Overall, PASDNet assemblages low-level features, high-level features as well as multiple scale features, and learns the combination of them.

As Fig. 4 shows, the methods without SD module have a poor performance in picture 1 and 2. There exists the adhesion of building results because the pixel size of the distance between small buildings is close to factor 8 of down-sampling rate and the feature maps of low resolution fail to describe small objects. With multi-level features, SD module can handle small objects well. In picture 3, the center pixels of the big house are mislabeled in ANet and ASDNet, due to the insufficient size of the receptive field. With multi-scale features, PAnet and PASDNet perfrom well on the large buildings. As picture 4 shows, there is also adhension of the narrow roads in the results of ANet and PANet. The SD module is the most significant element to label the small objects correctly. We can notice that the annotations of roads with PASDNet are more elegant than that with ASDNet, denoting that AP module is effective in handling multi-scale objects.

(2) Comparison of PASDNet and others methods. As we can see on Table 2, PASDNet is well beyond other means on all metrics, demonstrating the competence of our proposed method.

As is shown in Fig. 5, the results of Deeplab are undesirable with intermittent roads and bonded buildings because of the loss of spatial information with 8 times down-sampling of the network. SegNet does not utilize low-level features to make up for the information loss in high-level features but only uses the pooling index to guide the up-sampling process, which is bound to bring in incorrect instructions. Thus, SegNet outputs wider roads and coarse buildings. Considering features of different scales and levels, PASDNet gets the best results: small buildings, large buildings and narrow roads are labeled well.

Table 1. Numerical results of architectures of PASDNet and its original ones.

	Roads	Buildings	Others	Mean F1	Overall acc.
ANet	52.75	72.44	88.62	71.27	82.86
ANet-w	63.30	76.73	88.59	76.21	83.72
PANet-w	67.12	76.03	87.24	76.80	82.53
ASDNet-w	**73.08**	81.94	91.26	82.09	87.55
PASDNet-w	72.78	**82.71**	**91.48**	**82.33**	**87.76**

Table 2. Numerical results of PASDNet and other methods.

	Roads	Buildings	Others	Mean F1	Overall acc.
Deeplab [9]	60.00	73.50	86.02	73.17	80.37
SegNet [8]	55.67	59.90	81.58	65.71	73.87
PASDNet	**72.78**	**82.71**	**91.48**	**82.33**	**87.76**

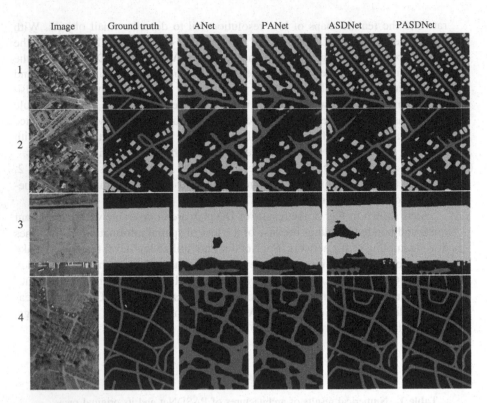

Fig. 4. Comparison of classification results of PASDNet and its basic architectures. Classes: road (red), building (cyan), background (black). (Color figure online)

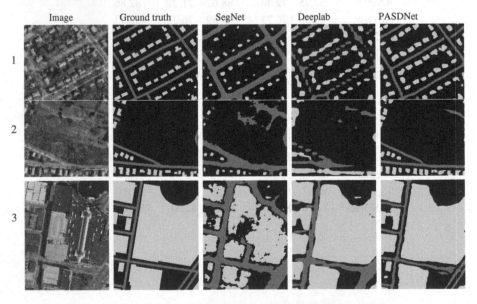

Fig. 5. Comparison of Classification results of different methods.

5 Conclusion

In this paper, we propose a novel architecture for semantic segmentation of VHR aerial images. Our proposed PASDNet combines AP and SD modules. Experiments proves that AP module is helpful for labeling large objects and SD module is significant for classifying small objects. In addition, we deploy a weighted loss function to solve the class imbalance problem. In experiments, PASDNet outperforms others and produces promising outcomes. Nevertheless, the architecture we proposed is more complex than others which calls for a higher amount of calculation. In the future, we hope to utilize the property of objects and construct structure predictions of remote sensing images with lightweight networks.

Acknowledgments. The work was supported by the National Key R&D Program of China under the Grant 2017YFC1405600, the National Natural Science Foundation of China under the Grant 61671037 and the Open Research Fund of State Key Laboratory of Space-Ground Integrated Information Technology under grant NO.2016_SGIIT_KFJJ_YG_03.

References

1. Krizhevsky, A., Sutskever, I., Hinton, G.E.: ImageNet classification with deep convolutional neural networks. Adv. Neural Inf. Process. Syst. **60**(2), 1097–1105 (2012)
2. Volpi, M., Tuia, D.: Dense semantic labeling of subdecimeter resolution images with convolutional neural networks. IEEE Trans. Geosci. Remote Sens. **55**, 881–893 (2016)
3. Mnih, V.: Machine learning for aerial image labeling. Ph.D. thesis, 109 (2013)
4. Simonyan, K., Zisserman, A.: Very deep convolutional networks for large-scale image recognition. In: ICLR, pp. 1–14 (2015)
5. Szegedy, C., et al.: Going deeper with convolutions, pp. 1–12 (2014)
6. Wu, S., Zhong, S., Liu, Y.: Deep residual learning for image steganalysis. Multimed. Tools Appl. **77**, 1–17 (2017)
7. Long, J., Shelhamer, E., Darrell, T.: Fully convolutional networks for semantic segmentation. In: CVPR (2014)
8. Badrinarayanan, V., Kendall, A., Cipolla, R.: SegNet: a deep convolutional encoder-decoder architecture for image segmentation. IEEE Trans. Pattern Anal. Mach. Intell. **39**, 2481–2495 (2017)
9. Chen, L.-C., Papandreou, G., Kokkinos, I., Murphy, K., Yuille, A.L.: DeepLab: semantic image segmentation with deep convolutional nets, atrous convolution, and fully connected CRFs. IEEE Trans. Pattern Anal. Mach. Intell. **40**(4), 834–848 (2018)
10. Yu, H., Yang, W., Xia, G.-S., Liu, G.: A color-texture-structure descriptor for high-resolution satellite image classification. Remote Sens. **8**, 259 (2016)
11. Chen, X.Y., Xiang, S.M., Liu, C.L., Pan, C.H.: Vehicle detection in satellite images by hybrid deep convolutional neural networks. IEEE Geosci. Remote Sens. Lett. **11**, 1797–1801 (2014)
12. Hu, W., Huang, Y., Wei, L., Zhang, F., Li, H.: Deep convolutional neural networks for hyperspectral image classification. J. Sens. **2015**(2), 1–12 (2015)
13. Penatti, A.B., Nogueira, K., Santos, J.A.: Do deep features generalize from everyday objects to remote sensing and aerial scenes domains?, pp. 44–51 (2015)

14. Castelluccio, M., Poggi, G., Sansone, C., Verdoliva, L.: Land use classification in remote sensing images by convolutional neural networks, pp. 1–11 (2015)
15. Marmanis, D., Wegner, J.D., Galliani, S., Schindler, K., Datcu, M., Stilla, U.: Semantic segmentation of aerial images with an ensemble of CNNs. ISPRS Ann. Photogramm. Remote Sens. Spat. Inf. Sci. **III-3**, 473–480 (2016)
16. Maggiori, E., Tarabalka, Y.: Convolutional neural networks for large-scale remote-sensing image classification. IEEE Trans. Geosci. Remote Sens. **55**(2), 645–657 (2017)
17. Jia, Y., et al.: Caffe: convolutional architecture for fast feature embedding (2014)

Deep Multi-scale Learning on Point Sets for 3D Object Recognition

Yang Xiao[1(✉)], Yanxin Ma[1], Min Zhou[2], and Jun Zhang[1]

[1] College of Electronic Science and Engineering,
National University of Defense Technology, Changsha, China
xiaoyang16a@nudt.edu.cn
[2] Branch 72 of No. 32142 Army, Baoding 071000, China

Abstract. In recent years, point cloud data based 3D deep learning has become a popular method for three-dimensional object recognition. In this work, we introduce a multi-scale convolution neural network which takes point cloud as input for 3D object recognition. Our network structure consists of two parts which are the feature extraction structure and the feature processing part. Experiments are conducted on the ModelNet40 dataset with several state-of-the-art methods. The proposed method achieves a higher accuracy on 3D object recognition with 87.1%. Experimental results have demonstrated the superior performance of the proposed multi-scale feature learning network.

Keywords: Point cloud · Multi-scale · Object recognition · Feature learning

1 Introduction

With the development of 3D sensors, such as Microsoft Kinect, Google Tango, etc., 3D data processing has been considered as one of the most important method for interactions between humans and machines. As one of the fundamental task in 3D computer vision, 3D object recognition has achieved a rapid development and been widely used in numerous areas, such as automatic driving, intelligent robots, etc. As deep learning has been widely applied in 2D object recognition, deep learning based 3D object recognition has also achieved much attention.

Before the deep learning was applied to computer vision, it has recently gained meaningfully state-of-the-art performance in tasks involving nature language proposing (NLP), voice recognition and image processing [2]. In recent years, deep learning has also been used for other challenging domains, for example, 3D data processing. Due to the fact that 3D data is not in a regular format, most of researchers prefer to transform 3D data to 2D images, views or regular 3D voxel grids [14].

Deep learning based 3D object recognition methods can be roughly divided into three types of methods, including multi-view based methods [1, 2], volumetric representation based methods [3, 4] and point cloud based methods [6, 16]. The multi-view based methods first project 3D shape to two-dimensional image. Then deep learning is used to extract features from two-dimensional image. These methods can make full use of the superior performance of 2D network architecture, and the existence of massive image data for pre-training. However, the projection loses a part of spatial structure

© Springer Nature Singapore Pte Ltd. 2018
Y. Wang et al. (Eds.): IGTA 2018, CCIS 875, pp. 341–348, 2018.
https://doi.org/10.1007/978-981-13-1702-6_34

information which may bring negative influence for recognition performance. Besides, the multi-view methods only provides a 2D contour representation of the 3D object. And they cannot provide sufficient geometric information of 3D representation because some details of that information are not encoded. 3D volumetric networks give a new direction. Then, voxel convolution neural network, considers 3D shape as the probability distribution in the 2D voxel grid, and thus expresses it as a 2D tensor or 3D tensor. The real breakthrough in this area was made by Wu *et al.* [3] In 2015. The convolution deep belief network was used for 3D object recognition. Besides, Wu *et al.* [3] built a benchmark dataset for 3D object recognition, named ModelNet. Qi *et al.* [4] proposed a volumetric 3D CNN by subvolume supervision to reduce over fitting. Maturana and Scherer [5] designed a convolution neural network for real-time recognition of 3D object by a volumetric convolution neural network named VoxNet. It needs a large amount of calculation, otherwise it will lose more information. For point cloud based methods, Qi *et al.* proposed PointNet [6] to directly process unstructured point cloud data by neural network. And this model can process the depth of point cloud data through learning of network while efficiently completing the 3D point of the transport office identification and segmentation tasks. Although these works have made a great achievement, most of existing deep learning models have high computational cost and complex network architecture. In this paper, we focus on deep learning based multi-scale informative feature extraction from 3D point cloud for 3D object recognition.

PointNet model has successfully achieved an end-to-end model to deal with irregular point clouds and use it as input directly. However, PointNet can only get the local information at one scale for object recognition. With information fusion between multiple scales, a better representation of 3D object can be obtained. Inspired by this simple idea, we propose a multi-scale convolution neural network (MSCNN) for 3D object classification, it utilizes multi-scale information to improve the performance of network.

The main contributions of this work are as follows:

(i)   We propose a 3D CNN, it suits on point set for 3D object recognition. It utilizes multi-scale information to get great improvements as compared to some existing models including Spherical Harmonic descriptor (SPH) [7], 3DshapeNets [3], VoxNet [5], subvolume [4], Light Field descriptor (LFD) [3] and PointNet [6].

(ii) We design two methods to utilize multi-scale information with extracting feature points and enhancing the performance of network.

(iii) Comparative experiments have been conducted on the ModelNet dataset [3]. The experimental results show that proposed model provides a network for 3D object recognition tasks and disorder point clouds processing.

This paper is structured as follows. Section 2 gives a literature review of 3D object recognition methods, especially the CNN based method. Section 3 presents our model and introduces the two methods to utilize multi-scale information and the implementation details. Section 4 the recognition experiments conducted on ModelNet40 dataset. Finally, Sect. 5 concludes this paper.

2   Related Work

The core of 3D object recognition is to extract informative and discriminative features of 3D shape. The classical approach is to design descriptors according to specific tasks and domain knowledge. The main purpose of these methods is to obtain 3D shape features with better discriminating ability, robustness, invariance and computability by extracting the spatial distribution of geometric attributes of 3D object space or using statistical histogram. On the contrary, deep learning automatically learns a common data characteristics from the existing training data, avoiding human intervention.

In recent years, most of methods use hand-crafted [9] 3D shape features to classify. At present, the hand-crafted 3D shape features have been divided into two major categories which are global features and local features. The global feature regards the 3D object as a whole by extracting the entire 3D object global feature information to classify. The advantage of the global feature is that it can make full use of all the information of the object to construct the feature descriptors. In contrast, local feature mainly concerns the local feature information in the neighborhood of the key point. These methods can effectively solve the existence of occlusion and background interference object recognition task. Local feature object recognition can be divided into three categories: point-based methods, histogram-based methods and transform-based methods. The representative algorithms of 3D local shape feature include Snapshot [10], Point Signature [11] and Rotational Projection Statistics (RoPS) [12].

After the number of convolution neural networks have been used to process 2D images and the CNN begin to be applied to 3D object recognition. Shi et al. [12] proposed a convolution neural network (namely, DeepPano) for 3D object recognition, which takes panoramic images of 3D object as input data. Considering that, although neural networks have a certain robustness to translation, the 2D projection will change when the object is rotated, which will have significant influence on CNN based feature extraction. To overcome this negative effect, Shi et al. [12] first projected each 3D object into a panoramic image around the principal axis. The obtained images were fed into a CNN to learn informative feature for object classification. Obviously, DeepPano can preserve the shape information of 3D objects to a certain extent through transformation. However the transformation changes the local and global structures of 3D shapes, resulting in the decrease of feature discrimination. Meanwhile, Su et al. [2] proposed multi-view convolution network structure (MVCNN). Multi-view 2D projections of 3D object was used to extract a concise 3D feature descriptor for the classification and retrieval of 3D shapes. In MVCNN, the projection of 3D shape under twelve different viewpoints was obtained firstly, and then the characteristics of projection images under various viewpoints were studied by using VGG-M convolution neural network. Finally, the multi-view features were pooled and sent to the next CNN network to get the final shape features. The experimental results have shown that multi-view images can get better performance than single-viewpoint images and achieved state-of-the-art performance in 3D object recognition. Johns et al. [17] proposed a convolution neural network using multi-view 2D images without camera trajectory. In this method, the input images were combined in pairs and put into the convolution neural network along with their relative poses. A gray-scale image, a depth image, or both were taken as an input to the proposed network. Specifically, the input image was processed by two convolution neural networks and cascaded together before being input to the fully connected layer. The results on ModelNet40 is better than 3DShapNets [3] and MVCNN [2].

Voxel convolution neural network is another kind of neural network structure which considers 3D shape as a probability distribution in 3D voxel grid and thus represents it as a binary or real-valued 3D tensor. The groundbreaking work in this area was initiated by Wu *et al.* [3] who designed a five-layer Convolution Deep Belief Network (CDBN) named 3DShapeNets. The network took a binary voxelized data as input, where 1 and 0 representing whether the voxel belong to the object or not. Since then, Maturana and Scherer [5] designed a convolution neural network VoxNet for real-time 3D object recognition. Based on this foundation, Sedaghat *et al.* [15] added auxiliary training task of object direction estimation which was transformed into classification problems. As a result, through the training of object classification and directions, the network can make a significant classification from the object direction problems and learn more favorable features for object classification. Qi *et al.* [6] proposed PointNet which solves the problem that deep neural network can not directly process unstructured point cloud data in the past. PointNet can directly deal with point cloud data to efficiently accomplish the classification and segmentation tasks. However, PointNet cannot capture local structure induced by the metric and the network also do not study multi-scale's influence on the results. In our work, we propose our MSCNN to study on multi-scale and we process two methods to compare the results.

3   Model

In this section, our model will be introduced. Our model contains two parts which are the feature extraction structure and the scale changing structure. The former is based on PointNet and utilizes their former half network to input 3D point cloud data. The scale changing structure is realized with two methods including convolution kernel changing and splitting the features. At last, the two parts structure are combined to achieve 3D object recognition.

3.1   Input Data and Feature Extraction

Point cloud is a collection of massive points at the surface of 3D object. It can be used to provide a more complete structural information for 3D object recognition. Specially, 3D point cloud data is expressed in the form of 3D coordinates, which contains spatial information of each point. Due to the existence of massive point cloud data for an object, all cloud point data needs to be prevented from exploding when dealing with point cloud data. Simultaneously, before inputting this data into the network training, the point cloud need to be converted to the regularly input form for most of CNNs.

In our CNN, point cloud is directly input and then put it into a network which named feature extraction network [6], as shown in Fig. 1. The feature extraction network's input is n points, and the input data is $B \times N \times 3$. And then, it needs to apply to input transformation, multilayer perceptron (MLP) and feature transformation. Until we get 1024 dimensional features and now our output data is B × N × 1 × 1024.

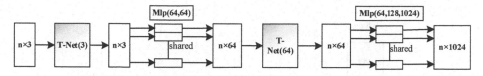

Fig. 1. Feature extraction network

3.2 Multi-filters Based Multi-scale Feature Learning

After getting through the feature extraction, a 1 × 1024 dimensional features is obtained for each point. In next layers, convolution operation is used to transform these features at multiple scales, as shown in Fig. 2.

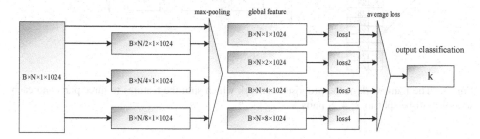

Fig. 2. The framework of the proposed network which changes the convolution kernel size.

In the first layer, we need to do three times convolution operation. From the output size equation, as the Eq. 1 shows. the convolution kernel needs to be set to 2 × 1, 4 × 1, 8 × 1 and the stride needs to be set to 2, 4, 8. So the data outputs are: B × N/2 × 1 × 1024, B × N/4 × 1 × 1024, B × N/8 × 1 × 1024. And at the max pooling layer, different scales of features are sent into the different max pooling layers and each global feature could be got. At last, the fully connected layers to get the loss functions respectively and then fuse them to get the average loss function value and we can classify the object's recognition.

$$outputsize = \frac{n - f + p}{stride}, p = valid \tag{1}$$

3.3 Splitting Based Multi-scale Feature Learning

In this network, as shown in Fig. 3. In the first layer, we use split function cut 1 × 1024 to 2 × 512, 4 × 256, 8 × 128. And the next layer, we need to expand the each features from 512, 256, 128 dimensions to 1024 dimensions. And the next layer, we use concat function to connect these dimensions to $2 \times 1024, 4 \times 1024, 8 \times 1024$. And then send the $1 \times 1024, 2 \times 1024, 4 \times 1024, 8 \times 1024$ dimensional features to max pooling layer and fully connected layer.

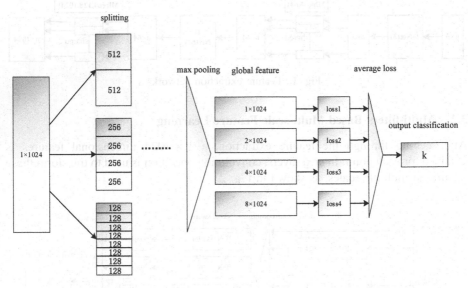

Fig. 3. The framework of the proposed network which split the features to three parts and each section will be split to 2, 4, 8 parts.

Obviously, the 1×1024 dimensional features are cut into $2^M (M = 0, 1, 2, 3)$ equal parts by convolution operation, And then, each part is sent into the different max pooling layers. After that, each feature is expanded to 1024 dimensional features by convolution operation. Next, these features are fused to $1 \times 1024, 2 \times 1024, 4 \times 1024, 8 \times 1024$ dimensional features and generate four loss function values. And finally, average loss function value and the classification result could be got.

4   Experiments and Results

We tested our 3D CNN model on ModelNet40 [3] which is the most of popular 3D object recognition dataset. Princeton ModelNet is a large 3D repository of CAD models (shapes) without noise, and the commonly used datasets are ModelNet10 [3] and ModelNet40. The ModelNet10 dataset contains 4,899 CAD models and the ModelNet40 dataset contains 12,311 CAD models. And the ModelNet40 consists of 9,843 CAD models for training and 2,468 for testing. Meanwhile, the orientation of each object in ModelNet10 has been manually aligned by the authors. So it is a proper benchmark to test these models which apply in orientation estimation and subvolume category prediction tasks so our model was tested in ModelNet40 and our model achieves better performance in spite of the number of various orientations. In this paper, our program uses python programming on the tensorflow platform in Linux environment and the entire program is trained using GPU acceleration.

Our network achieves 3D object recognition through multi-scale feature learning. We evaluate our model on the ModelNet40 shape classification benchmark. Through total correct divide by the total classifications and we can get two indicators: accuracy average class and accuracy overall. The average recognition accuracy achieved by our proposed networks and many other methods on the ModelNet40 dataset are shown in Table 1.

Table 1. Classification results on ModelNet40.

Method	Input	Accuracy average class (%)	Accuracy overall (%)
SPH	Mesh	68.2	-
3DShapeNets	Volume	77.3	84.7
VoxNet	Volume	83.0	85.9
Subvolume	Volume	86.0	89.2
LFD	Image	75.5	-
MVCNN	Image	90.1	-
PointNet	Point	86.2	89.2
PointNet++	Point	-	91.9
Ours (with conv)	Point	87.1	90.4
Ours (with split)	Point	86.8	90.1

It can be observed from Table 1 that the accuracy of our model is better than other existing methods and the two ways obtain a compelling accuracy of 89.9% and 89.4%. This results also shows that our model could achieve 3D object recognition which improves the accuracy compared with that of PointNet. Compared to PointNet++ model (with an accuracy of 91.9%), their model achieves state-of-the-art results. This is because PointNet++ [16] add hierarchical structure and build a hierarchical grouping of points and progressively abstract larger and larger local regions along the hierarchy. Simultaneously, we observed in our experiments that our model has a lower calculation time and the efficiency is acceptable.

5 Conclusion

In this paper, we proposed a multi-scale CNN for 3D object recognition. The proposed networks directly take 3D point cloud as input and learn much more informative feature from 3D data. Our model consists of feature extraction structure and scale changing structure and also our CNN uses two methods to realize the multi-scale processing. Experimental results show that the proposed networks achieve a comparable recognition accuracy with several simple operations.

References

1. Ioannidou, A., Chatzilari, E., Nikolopoulos, S., Kompatsiaris, I.: Deep learning advances in computer vision with 3D data: a survey. ACM Comput. Surv. **50**(2), 20 (2017)
2. Su, H., Maji, S., Kalogerakis, E., Learnedmiller, E.: Multi-view convolutional neural networks for 3D shape recognition, pp. 945–953 (2015)
3. Wu, Z., et al.: 3D ShapeNets: a deep representation for volumetric shapes. In: IEEE Conference on Computer Vision and Pattern Recognition, pp. 1912–1920. IEEE (2014)
4. Qi, C.R., Su, H., Nießner, M., Dai, A., Yan, M., Guibas, L.J.: Volumetric and multi-view CNNs for object classification on 3D data. In: IEEE Conference on Computer Vision and Pattern Recognition, pp. 5648–5656. IEEE Computer Society (2016)
5. Maturana, D., Scherer, S.: VoxNet: a 3D convolutional neural network for real-time object recognition. In: IEEE/RSJ International Conference on Intelligent Robots and Systems, pp. 922–928. IEEE (2015)
6. Qi, C.R., Su, H., Mo, K., Guibas, L.J.: Pointnet: deep learning on point sets for 3D classification and segmentation arXiv preprint arXiv:1612.00593 (2016)
7. Kazhdan, M., Funkhouser, T., Rusinkiewicz, S.: Rotation invariant spherical harmonic representation of 3D shape descriptors. In: Eurographics/ACM SIGGRAPH Symposium on Geometry Processing, pp. 156–164. Eurographics Association (2003)
8. Sun, J., Ovsjanikov, M., Guibas, L.: A concise and provably informative multi-scale signature based on heat diffusion. In: Computer Graphics Forum, vol. 28, pp. 1383–1392 (2009)
9. Guo, Y., Bennamoun, M., Sohel, F., Lu, M., Wan, J.: 3D object recognition in cluttered scenes with local surface features: a survey. IEEE Trans. Pattern Anal. Mach. Intell. **36**(11), 2270–2287 (2014)
10. Malassiotis, S., Strintzis, M.G.: Snapshots: a novel local surface descriptor and matching algorithm for robust 3D surface alignment. IEEE Trans. Pattern Anal. Mach. Intell. **29**(7), 1285 (2007)
11. Chua, C.S., Jarvis, R.: Point signatures: a new representation for 3D object recognition. Int. J. Comput. Vis. **25**(1), 63–85 (1997)
12. Guo, Y., Sohel, F.A., Bennamoun, M., Wan, J., Lu, M.: RoPS: a local feature descriptor for 3D rigid objects based on rotational projection statistics. In: International Conference on Communications, Signal Processing, and Their Applications, pp. 1–6. IEEE (2013)
13. Shi, B., Bai, S., Zhou, Z., Bai, X.: Deeppano: deep panoramic representation for 3-D shape recognition. IEEE Signal Process. Lett. **22**(12), 2339–2343 (2015)
14. Brock, A., Lim, T., Ritchie, J.M., Weston, N.: Generative and discriminative voxel modeling with convolutional neural networks. Comput. Sci. (2016)
15. Sedaghat, N., Zolfaghari, M., Amiri, E., Brox, T.: Orientation-boosted voxel nets for 3D object recognition. arXiv preprint arXiv:1604.03351 (2016)
16. Qi, C.R., Yi, L., Su, H., Guibas, L.J.: Pointnet++: deep hierarchical feature learning on point sets in a metric space. arXiv preprint arXiv:1706.02413 (2017)
17. Johns, E., Leutenegger, S., Davison, A.J.: Pairwise decomposition of image sequences for active multi-view recognition. arXiv preprint arXiv:1605.08359 (2016)

Maneuver Detection of Uncooperative Space Objects with Space-Based Optical Surveillance

Shufeng Shi[✉], Peng Shi[✉], and Yushan Zhao[✉]

School of Astronautics, Beijing University of Aeronautics and Astronautics,
Beijing 100083, China
kkkssf@sa.buaa.edu.cn, {shipeng,yszhao}@buaa.edu.cn

Abstract. This paper explores the maneuver detection method of uncooperative objects with space-based camera. The camera imaging observation model is first described and the observability calculation method is discussed. Then different thrust dynamic models are described in detail and the orbit determination method using space-based observation data is presented. Finally, in order to detect maneuvers of uncooperative objects, the detection algorithms and procedures for different thrust types are presented innovatively. The simulation analyses are made in impulse and continuous thrust conditions, which confirm that the algorithms in this article satisfy task requirements for uncooperative object detection with space-based camera.

Keywords: Space camera · Space-based surveillance · Maneuver detection
Uncooperative objects

1 Introduction

The safe operation of spacecraft always faces serious threat of uncooperative objects like space debris [1]. It is a hard mission to monitor the motion of such space objects, especially when they maneuver due to unpredictable collision or thrust. The basic approaches of space target surveillance include ground-based surveillance and space-based surveillance. The former is the main means of space target detection at present. But ground based surveillance suffers a major disadvantage that the coverage area of ground observation bases is finite, and it is unrealistic to establish enough bases at will. However, space-based optical surveillance is a means of monitoring space objects using cameras on satellite platforms. So the space-based surveillance can observe objects in larger coverage area with the movement of the satellite platform. Moreover, the advantages of optical observation in space orbit are that it increases observation opportunities and observation period, and it improves observation quality without the influence of atmosphere. The Space Based Space Surveillance (SBSS) system has been developed to monitor space targets in the America at present [2]. Related research has been also carried on in other countries.

The mission of space surveillance includes two aspects: orbit determination and maneuver detection. The former has been well studied in a variety of literature. The reduced-dynamic method is widely used in orbit determination and the accuracy has been proved. However the research about maneuver detection is not deep enough.

© Springer Nature Singapore Pte Ltd. 2018
Y. Wang et al. (Eds.): IGTA 2018, CCIS 875, pp. 349–358, 2018.
https://doi.org/10.1007/978-981-13-1702-6_35

Hough [3] studied the maneuver surveillance problem of rockets in the launching section and the reentry section; Aaron [4] analyzed orbit maneuver detection and orbit recovery of ground-based surveillance, which can only be used in the case of large impulse thrust; Hepner [5] presented adaptive filtering algorithm for maneuvering detection, and analyzed the observability of the detection system, but the dynamic model considered was simple; Kelecy [6] studied the orbit determination and maneuver detection under small impulse thrust, and compared the applicability of least square estimation method and Kalman filtering method, but the maneuver detection process was not designed perfectly; Lemmens [7] studied the maneuver detection of low earth orbit using two-line elements, but the work was just a reanalysis of historical data; Johnson [8] also analyzed the problem of orbit recovery under different impulse thrust. Most of these studies just analyzed ground-based circumstances and used simplified simulation model, instead of considering different thrust types and space-based observation.

The main research content of this paper is to solve the problem of maneuver detection using space-based optical surveillance. First, the imaging observation model of the space-based camera is describe and the observability of space-based surveillance is analyzed. Then the orbit determination method using space-based observation data with different thrust dynamic models is presented. Finally, the detection algorithms and procedures for different thrust types are presented and simulations are made to verify the feasibility of the detection algorithms.

2   Observability Analysis of Space-Based Surveillance

An important part of space-based surveillance system includes monitoring platform and monitoring means. The monitoring platform of space-based monitoring system includes satellite and space station. The means of target detection includes optical and radar. Compared with radar, space-based optical detection has many advantages such as short detection wave band, high precision of target extraction, large amount of frame information, and the ability of real-time identification and tracking of multiple targets. In this paper, space-based optical surveillance is used to analyze the maneuver detection problem. The main means of optical surveillance is CCD imaging observation using space cameras [9].

2.1   CCD Imaging Model

The tracking satellite uses CCD cameras to observe space objects. It takes the stars as the background to photograph space objects. The locations of targets in different directions on the negative film are different. As the directions of the stars are known, the coordinate measuring instrument is used to measure the relative positions of space objects and the stars to obtain the directions of the space objects.

The imaging coordinate system is created using the plane of the photographic plate and the main point O after the photographic lens. The projection of the main point O on the plane of the negatives is the bottom point of the imaging D. Based on the original point O, the imaging coordinate system is established, in which the X axis and Y axis are on the plane of the film, and the normal vector is Z axis. The measurement of a star image S in the XY plane is (x_s, y_s), and the measurement of the bottom point D is (x_0, y_0). The relation between the vector of the star image S in the imaging coordinate system and the direction vector in the celestial equatorial coordinate is

$$\lambda A \begin{bmatrix} x - x_0 \\ y - y_0 \\ f \end{bmatrix} = \begin{bmatrix} \cos\alpha\cos\delta \\ \sin\alpha\cos\delta \\ \sin\delta \end{bmatrix}, \tag{1}$$

where $\lambda = [(x - x_0)^2 + (y - y_0)^2 + f^2]^{-1/2}$, A is the rotation matrix of the imaging coordinate to the celestial coordinate system, f is the focal length of the camera lens, (α, δ) is the right ascension and declination of the star which can be get from the star catalog.

There are six parameters to be solved including three coordinate conversion parameters in the rotation matrix A and (x_0, y_0, f). Two independent equations can be get from each calibration star by Eq. (1). So six parameters can be determined using at least three calibration stars. As soon as the parameters are determined, the measurement coordinate of a space object (x_s, y_s) can be converted into the celestial equatorial coordinate (α_d, δ_d).

The tracking of the space objects using space CCD camera is shown in Fig. 1. The target is imaging with the stars at the camera negative at different times. The direction change of the target can be get by real time image negative calculating.

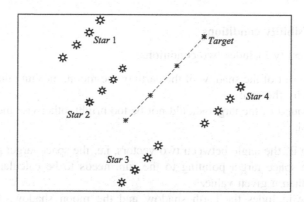

Fig. 1. Direction change of the target and the stars in the camera negative

2.2 Visibility Calculation Method

The visible conditions of space-based cameras for space targets include geometric visibility and optical visibility.

(1) Geometric visibility conditions

Figure 2 shows the schematic diagram of geometric relations between a space object, a tracking satellite and the earth. S represents the tracking satellite with cameras,

D represents the space objects, and the circle with the center point E represents the earth. C is the ground point of the tracking satellite. SA and SB are tangent lines from the satellite to the earth, and α is the half cone angle. The angle between SD and SE is the observation angle β. When $\alpha > \beta$, the object is shielded by the earth, and nothing can be observed in such condition. So the geometric visibility conditions is

$$\alpha < \beta. \tag{2}$$

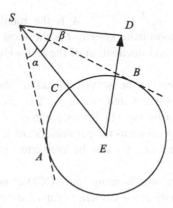

Fig. 2. Geometric relations between a space object, a tracking satellite and the earth

(2) Optical visibility conditions

The optical visibility includes two conditions:

A. The target is out of the shadow of the earth or the moon, meaning the target can be illuminated by the sun;
B. The background of the target should not be too bright, otherwise the target cannot be identified.

In condition B, the angle between two vectors, i.e. the space target pointing to the camera and the space target pointing to the sun, needs to be calculated. The angle should be less than a given value.

The shadow includes the earth shadow and the moon shadow. There are two shadow calculation methods, cylindrical and conical. The conical shadow calculation method is given as follows.

The condition that the target lies in umbra is:

$$\begin{cases} r \cdot \Delta_S > 0 \\ |\alpha_E - \alpha_S| \geq \theta_{ES} \end{cases}. \tag{3}$$

The condition that the target lies in penumbra is:

$$\begin{cases} \boldsymbol{r} \cdot \boldsymbol{\Delta}_S > 0 \\ \alpha_E + \alpha_S > \theta_{ES} > |\alpha_E - \alpha_S| \end{cases}, \tag{4}$$

in which, there are

$$\begin{cases} \alpha_S = \arcsin\left(\dfrac{R_S}{\Delta_S}\right) \\ \alpha_E = \arcsin\left(\dfrac{R_E}{r}\right) \end{cases}, \tag{5}$$

where the radius of the earth is R_E, $\boldsymbol{R}_S$ is the position vector of the sun, $\boldsymbol{r}$ is the position vector of the target, α_S is the angle of the satellite viewing the sun, α_E is the angle of the satellite viewing the earth, $\boldsymbol{\Delta}_S$ is the vector of the target pointing to the sun, θ_{ES} is the angle of earth-target-sun.

3 Orbit Determination Method

3.1 Measurement Model

Tracking data of space-based optical surveillance shows as astronomical angle measurement data including right ascension α and declination δ as described in Sect. 1. It is assumed that the position vectors of the space-based monitor satellite and the space target in the inertial system J2000.0 are respectively $\boldsymbol{R}_s$ and $\boldsymbol{R}_v$, the position component of the space target in the space-based monitor satellite's body coordinate system is (X', Y', Z'), so that

$$\begin{bmatrix} X' \\ Y' \\ Z' \end{bmatrix} = \rho \begin{bmatrix} \cos\alpha\cos\delta \\ \sin\alpha\cos\delta \\ \sin\delta \end{bmatrix}, \tag{6}$$

where ρ is the distance between the space-based satellite and the space target. Let the measurement errors of the right ascension and the declination are respectively ξ_α and ξ_δ. The measurement equation is shown as

$$\begin{cases} \alpha_d = \arctan\left(\dfrac{X'}{Y'}\right) + \xi_\alpha \\ \delta_d = \arcsin\left(\dfrac{Z'}{\sqrt{X'^2 + Y'^2 + Z'^2}}\right) + \xi_\delta \end{cases}, \tag{7}$$

where α_d and δ_d are respectively the right ascension and the declination information obtained from the CCD camera on the space-based satellite.

3.2 Orbit Dynamic Model

The orbit dynamic model under control force is given by

$$\frac{dX}{dt} = \begin{bmatrix} \frac{dr}{dt} \\ \frac{dv}{dt} \end{bmatrix} = \begin{bmatrix} v \\ a_c + a_e + a_s + a_m + a_{srp} + a_{drag} + \ldots + a_{thrust} \end{bmatrix}, \tag{8}$$

where X is the dynamic state variables of the space object including the position vector $r = [r_x, r_y, r_z]^T$ and the velocity vector $v = [v_x, v_y, v_z]^T$ in earth centered inertial (ECI) coordinate system, t is the time, a_c is the central gravitation, a_e is the non-spherical acceleration of the earth, a_s is the gravitational acceleration of the sun, a_m is the gravitational acceleration of the moon, a_{srp} is the solar radiation pressure acceleration, and a_{drag} is the atmospheric drag acceleration. The models of a_{thrust} in different thrust forms are given by

$$a_I = -\frac{\dot{m}}{m_0 - \dot{m}\Delta t} \cdot \frac{1}{\ln\left(1 - \frac{\dot{m}}{m_0}\Delta t\right)} E\Delta v, \tag{9}$$

$$a_F = \frac{I_{sp} g_0 \dot{m}}{m(t)} E\eta = \frac{I_{sp} g_0 \dot{m}}{m(t)} (\eta_R E_x + \eta_I E_y + \eta_C E_z). \tag{10}$$

Table 1. The model and parameter setting of the dynamic model

Items	Models and parameters
Nonspherical gravitation field	EGM96
Third body gravity	Sun and moon (JPL DE405)
Atmospheric resistance	DTM94, resistance coefficient 2.0
Solar radiation pressure	Pressure coefficient 1.2
Tide	Solid tide and sea tide (IERS 2010)
Space-based optical observation error	White noise 10 arcsec

Equation (9) describes the model of maneuvering acceleration under impulse force, and Eq. (10) describes the model of maneuvering acceleration under the action of continuous thrust, where $\Delta v = [v_R, v_I, v_C]^T$ is the increment of velocity pulse in the satellite orbit coordinate system, $\eta = [\eta_R, \eta_I, \eta_C]^T$ is the projection of thrust direction in orbital coordinate system, $E = [E_x, E_y, E_z]^T$ is the attitude conversion matrix of the satellite orbit coordinate system to the ECI coordinate system, $\dot{m}$ is the engine work quality consumption, I_{sp} is the engine specific impulse. The model and parameter setting of the dynamic model is shown in Table 1.

3.3   Orbit Determination Algorithm

Due to shortcomings of batching estimation algorithm in orbit maneuver detection, sequential processing estimation algorithm is used in the orbit determination. Due to the uncertainty of orbit dynamics and observation models during orbit maneuver and the truncation error caused by computer digit restriction during data processing, there are often singular or nearly singular normal equations. Square root information filtering

(SRIF) and square root information smoother (SRIS) use square root matrix to ensure the symmetry and positivity of the covariance matrix, and the numerical range of the variables is shortened. SRIF/SRIS uses Household transform to avoid the inversion of the normal equation and to increase the stability of the numerical solution. It has more stable and higher numerical accuracy than the classical Kalman filtering. SRIF/SRIS has been successfully used in software GIPSY developed by Jet Propulsion Laboratory. Limited to length, detailed theory can be referred to the literature [10].

4   Orbit Maneuver Detection Algorithm and Process

The maneuver detection algorithm should be designed according to the specific thrust type due to the different dynamic models. So two kinds of innovative detection algorithms are proposed corresponding to maneuver in impulse thrust condition and continuous thrust condition separately.

4.1   Maneuver Detection in Impulse Thrust Condition

The satellite position changes continuously in impulse thrust, but the satellite speed jumps at the thrust moment. The intersecting time of orbit position before and after the thrust action can be used as the thrust time, and the corresponding value of the velocity difference of the satellite at this moment is the impulse magnitude. The steps of maneuver detection and analysis of uncooperative objects in unknown pulse thrust are as follows:

(1) The target is normally tracked before the maneuver, and usual orbit determination is carried out;
(2) The velocity of simulation pulse is applied and the observational residuals are increased;
(3) The target is normally tracked and the orbit is re-determined after the orbit maneuver. When the filter reaches the absolute convergence condition, the object orbit is extrapolated backwards to the time before the maneuver;
(4) The forecast orbit before the maneuver and the backward extrapolation orbit after the maneuver are compared to obtain the maneuver moment at the intersection point. The impulse thrust can also be calculated form the velocity difference at the maneuver moment.

4.2   Maneuver Detection in Continuous Thrust Condition

Under the action of continuous large thrust, the thrust acceleration is larger than the orbit perturbation force. The observational residuals will increase significantly when the thrust is applied, based on which the starting time of the thrust can be determined. The steps of maneuver detection and analysis of uncooperative objects in unknown continuous thrust are as follows:

(1) The target is normally tracked before the maneuver, and usual orbit determination is carried out;
(2) The continuous simulation thrust is applied and the observational residuals are increased;
(3) The starting time of the maneuver is determined according to the orbit residual;
(4) The dynamic model of the filter is switched to continuous thrust, and the thrust value is estimated in new model to make sure the observational residuals meet the requirements;
(5) The maneuver period is determined using the estimated thrust.

5   Simulation Examples

The space uncooperative object is set to be in a geosynchronous orbit, and the space-based satellite is set to be in a solar synchronous orbit like SBSS satellites. The orbital elements are shown in Table 2.

Table 2. The initial parameters setting for simulation orbits (1 October 2017 00:00:00.000 (UTC))

Orbit	a/(km)	e	i/(°)	ω/(°)	Ω/(°)	f/(°)
Space base	7178.140	0	98.608	0	120	0
Space object	42170.000	0.0006	1.500	25.000	300.000	250.000

The space object is visible to the space-based camera every day for about 1–2 h. A visible period of 1 h is chosen for the simulation. The simulation period starts at 1 October 2017 06:30:00 (UTC). The maneuver moment is set in the middle of the chosen period.

5.1   Simulation of Impulse Thrust Detection

The impulse thrust is set to be 1 m/s in-track velocity increment at 1 October 2017 07:00:00 (UTC). The maneuver detection process is shown in Fig. 3. The ordinate represents the mutual differences between normal forecast before the impulse maneuver and the backward extrapolation after the impulse. The left figure shows the position difference, in which the position components meet at the impulse maneuver time. In fact, the position difference curve is not strictly intersected at one point, so the time corresponding to the minimum velocity difference is considered to be the maneuver time. And the velocity difference at the maneuver in the right figure is considered to be the velocity increment. The maneuver time calculated by simulation is 1 October 2017 06:30:52 and the impulse thrust is 0.969 m/s. The detection errors in the simulation is acceptable.

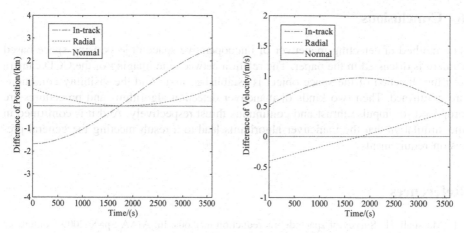

Fig. 3. Mutual differences of orbit prediction in impulse thrust condition

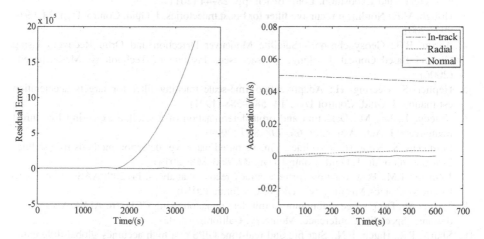

Fig. 4. Detection simulation results in continuous thrust condition

5.2 Simulation of Continuous Thrust Detection

The continuous thrust is set to be 100 N in-track. The thrust starts at 1 October 2017 06:55:00 (UTC) and lasts for 10 min. The maneuver detection process is shown in Fig. 4. The left figure shows the residual error in the tracking progress, in which the residual error grows significantly after the thrust is applied. The moment at which the residual begins to grow at accelerating level is considered to be the starting time of the thrust. The estimated starting time of the thrust in the simulation is 1 October 2017 06:56:20. The right figure shows the curves of acceleration components estimated by the filter with continuous thrust model, and the average acceleration magnitude is 0.048 m/s. The detection errors in the simulation is acceptable.

6 Conclusions

The method of detecting maneuver of uncooperative space objects using space-based camera is discussed in the paper. The relation between the imaging of the CCD camera and the direction of the space object is established first. And the visibility conditions are confirmed. Then two kinds of maneuver detection algorithms and procedures are proposed for impulse thrust and continuous thrust respectively. And it is confirmed in the simulation that the maneuver algorithms lead to a result meeting the general precision requirements.

References

1. Marshall, H.: Survey of space debris reduction methods. In: AIAA Space 2009 Conference and Exposition, pp. 1–11. Pasadena (2009)
2. Rendleman, J.D., Ryals, R.E.: Spacecraft operator duty of care. In: AIAA Space 2011 Conference and Exposition, Long Beach, pp. 28–44 (2011)
3. Hough, M.E.: Nonlinear recursive filter for boost trajectories. J. Guid. Control Dyn. **24**, 991–997 (2001)
4. Aaron, B.S.: Geosynchronous Satellite Maneuver Detection and Orbit Recovery Using Ground Based Optical Tracking. Massachusetts Institute of Technology, Massachusetts (2006)
5. Hepner, S., Geering, H.: Adaptive two-time-scale tracking filter for targets acceleration estimation. J. Guid. Control Dyn. **14**, 581–588 (1991)
6. Kelecy, T., Jah, M.: Detection and orbit determination of a satellite executing low thrust maneuvers. J. Acta Astronaut. **66**, 798–809 (2009)
7. Lemmens, S., Krag, H.: Two line elements based maneuver detection methods for satellites in low earth orbit. J. Guid. Control Dyn. **37**, 860–868 (2014)
8. Johnson, T.M.: Post-maneuver orbit accuracy recovery analysis. In: 20th AAS/AIAA Space Flight Mechanics Meeting, San Diego, California (2010)
9. Vasile, M.: Deep space autonomous orbit determination using CCD. In: AIAA/AAS Astrodynamic Specialist Conference, Monterey, California (2002)
10. Sharp, T.R., Hatch, F.N.: Star fire and real-time GIPSY: a high accuracy global differential GPS system. In: 5th International Symposium on Satellite Navigation Technology and Application, Canberra, Australia (2001)

RGB-T Saliency Detection Benchmark: Dataset, Baselines, Analysis and a Novel Approach

Guizhao Wang, Chenglong Li, Yunpeng Ma, Aihua Zheng, Jin Tang, and Bin Luo[✉]

School of Computer Science and Technology, Anhui University,
No. 111 Jiulong Road, Hefei 230601, China
wgz_ahu@foxmail.com, lcll314@foxmail.com,
670192421@foxmail.com,
{ahzheng214, tj, luobin}@ahu.edu.cn

Abstract. Despite significant progress, image saliency detection still remains a challenging task in complex scenes and environments. Integrating multiple different but complementary cues, like RGB and Thermal (RGB-T), may be an effective way for boosting saliency detection performance. The current research in this direction, however, is limited by the lack of a comprehensive benchmark. This work contributes such a RGB-T image dataset, which includes 821 spatially aligned RGB-T image pairs and their ground truth annotations for saliency detection purpose. With this benchmark, we propose a novel approach, graph-based multi-task manifold ranking algorithm, for RGB-T saliency detection. Extensive experiments against the baseline methods on the benchmark dataset demonstrate the effectiveness of the proposed approach.

Keywords: RGB-T benchmark · Saliency detection
Cross-modality consistency · Graph-based manifold ranking
Multi-task learning

1 Introduction

Image saliency detection is to highlight salient foreground objects automatically from background, and has received increasing attention due to its wide range of applications in computer vision, graphics and artificial intelligence. Despite significant progress, image saliency detection still remains a challenging task in complex scenes and environments (e.g. low lighting conditions and bad weathers). Integrating multiple different but complementary cues, like RGB and Thermal (RGB-T), may be an effective way for boosting saliency detection performance in abovementioned challenges [1, 10]. RGB and thermal information can complement each other and

---

Electronic supplementary material The online version of this chapter (https://doi.org/10.1007/978-981-13-1702-6_36) contains supplementary material, which is available to authorized users.

© Springer Nature Singapore Pte Ltd. 2018
Y. Wang et al. (Eds.): IGTA 2018, CCIS 875, pp. 359–369, 2018.
https://doi.org/10.1007/978-981-13-1702-6_36

contribute to saliency detection in different aspects. On one hand, thermal infrared camera can capture infrared radiation (0.75–13 μm) emitted by subjects with a temperature above absolute zero.

Given the complementary benefits of RGB-T data, however, the research of RGB-T saliency detection is limited by the lack of a comprehensive image benchmark. Therefore, we contribute a comprehensive image benchmark[1] for RGB-T saliency detection in this paper, and take the following two aspects into account: (i) a good dataset should be with reasonable size, high diversity and low bias [17]. Therefore, we establish a RGB-T dataset with multiple attributes of the salient objects in different scenes, environmental conditions for enhancing the diversity and challenge. (ii) RGB-T saliency detection still remains not well investigated. Thus, we implement some baseline methods to provide a comparison platform for RGB-T saliency detection. With the created benchmark, we propose a novel approach, multi-task manifold ranking algorithm, for RGB-T saliency detection. For each modality, we employ the idea of graph-based manifold ranking [22] for the good saliency detection performance in terms of accuracy and speed. Then, we assign each modality with a weight to describe the modal reliability, which is capable of dealing with occasional perturbation or malfunction of individual sources, to achieve adaptive fusion of multiple modalities. To better exploit the relations among modalities, we impose the cross-modality consistent constraints on the ranking functions of different modalities to integrate them collaboratively. Considering the manifold ranking in each modality as an individual task, our method is essentially formulated as a multi-task learning problem.

2 Related Work

To our best, there is no work on studying RGB-T saliency detection, and thus we review some most related works on RGB saliency detection.

Salient object detection has been extensively studied in past decades, and numerous models and algorithms have been proposed based on different mathematical principles or priors [6, 18, 20]. Most of methods measure saliency by exploiting local center-surround contrast and rarity of features over the entire image [6, 7]. In contrast, Gopalakrishnan et al. [5] formulate the object detection problem as a binary segmentation or labelling task on a graph. The most salient seeds and several background seeds are identified by the behavior of random walks on a complete graph and a k-regular graph. Then, a semi-supervised learning technique is used to infer the binary labels of the unlabelled nodes. Different from it, Yang et al. [22] employ manifold ranking technique to salient object detection that requires only seeds from one class, which are initialized with either the boundary priors or foreground cues. Based on the manifold ranking algorithms, Li et al. [9] generate pixel-wise saliency maps via regularized random walks ranking, and Wang et al. [19] propose a new graph model which captures local/global contrast and effectively utilizes the boundary prior.

---

[1] The RGB-T dataset's webpage: https://drive.google.com/file/d/0B4fH4G1f-jjNR3NtQUkwWjF FREk/view.

3 RGB-T Image Saliency Benchmark

In this section, we introduce a newly created RGB-T saliency benchmark, which includes a dataset with statistic analysis, 3 baseline methods with different inputs and 4 evaluation metrics.

3.1 Dataset

Our imaging hardware consists of an online thermal imager (FLIR A310) and a CCD camera (SONY TD-2073). We collect 821 RGB-T image pairs by our recording system. For alignment, we uniformly select a number of point correspondences in each image pairs, and compute the homography matrix by the least-square algorithm. It's worth noting that this registration method can accurately align image pairs due to the following two reasons: (i) we carefully choose the planar and non-planar scenes to make the homography assumption effective. (ii) since two camera views are almost coincident as we made, the transformation between two views is simple. As each image pair is aligned, we annotate the pixel-level ground truth using more reliable modality. The image pairs in our dataset are recorded in approximately 60 scenes with different environmental conditions, and the category, size, number and spatial information of salient objects are also taken into account for enhancing the diversity and challenge, some of which are shown in Fig. 1. Specifically, the following major aspects are considered in creating the RGB-T image dataset:

- *Illumination condition.* The image pairs are captured under different light conditions, such as sunny, snowy, and nighttime. The low illumination and illumination variation caused by different light conditions usually bring big challenges in RGB images.
- *Background factor.* Two background factors are taken into account for our dataset. First, similar background to the salient objects in appearance or temperature will introduce ambiguous information. Second, it is difficult to separate objects accurately from cluttered background.
- *Salient object attribute.* We take different attributes of salient objects, including category (more than 60 categories), size and number, into account in constructing our dataset for high diversity.
- *Object location.* Most of methods employ the spatial information (center and boundaries of an image) of the salient objects as priors, which is verified to be effective. However, some salient objects are not at center or cross image boundaries, and these situations isolate the spatial priors. We incorporate these factors into our dataset construction to bring its challenge.

Considering the above-mentioned factors, we annotate 11 challenges for our dataset to facilitate the challenge-sensitive performance of different algorithms. They are: big salient object (BSO), small salient object (SSO), multiple salient object (MSO), low illumination (LI), bad weather (BW), center bias (CB), cross image boundary (CIB), similar appearance (SA), thermal crossover (TC), image clutter (IC), and out of focus (OF). Due to space limitation, the statistical details and some samples of RGB-T image pairs are presented in **supplementary file**.

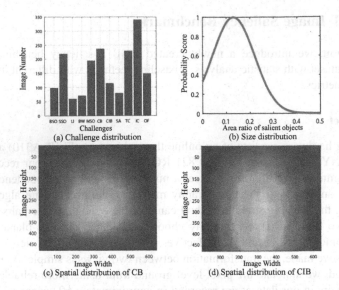

Fig. 1. Dataset statistics.

3.2 Baseline Methods

To provide a comparison platform, we implement 3 kinds of baseline methods with different modality inputs. On one hand, we regard RGB or thermal images as inputs in 12 popular methods to achieve single-modality saliency detection, including MST [18], RRWR [9], CA [12], GMR [22], STM [20], GR [21], NFI [3], MCI [4], SS-KDE [16], BR [14SR [15] and SRM [7]. These baselines can be utilized to identify the importance and complementarity of RGB and thermal information with comparing to RGB-T saliency detection methods. On the other hand, we implement RGB-T baseline methods by fusing the results of some of above-mentioned methods with the equal weights.

3.3 Evaluation Metrics

There exists several metrics to evaluate the agreement between subjective annotations and experimental predictions. In this work, we use (P)recision-(R)ecall curves (PR curves), $F_{0.3}$ metric and Mean Absolute Error (MAE) to evaluate all the algorithms. Given the binarized saliency map via the threshold value within [0, 255], PR curves and $F_{0.3}$ metric are aimed at quantitative comparison, while MAR are better than them for taking visual comparison into consideration to estimate dissimilarity between a saliency map M and the ground truth G, which is defined as $MAE = \frac{1}{t \times h} \sum_{i=1}^{t} \sum_{j=1}^{h} |M(i,j) - G(i,j)|$, where t and h denote the width and height of an image, respectively.

4 Graph-Based Multi-task Manifold Ranking

This section introduces the graph-based multi-task manifold ranking algorithm.

4.1 Graph Construction

Given a pair of RGB-T images, we regard the thermal image as one of image channels, and then generate n non-overlapping superpixels. We take these superpixels as nodes to construct a graph $G = (V, E)$, where V is a node set and E is a set of undirected edges. In this work, any two nodes in V are connected if they follow one of the conditions in [22] for capturing local smoothness cues and reducing the geodesic distance of similar superpixels. It is worth noting that we can explore more cues in RGB and thermal data to construct an adaptive graph that makes best use of intrinsic relationship among superpixels. In detail, if nodes V_i and V_j is connected, we assign it with an edge weight as: $W_{ij}^k = e^{-\gamma^k \|c_i^k - c_j^k\|}$, where c_i^k denotes the mean of the i-th superpixel in the k-th modality, and γ^k is the scaling parameter for k-th modality which controls the edge strength between two superpixel nodes.

4.2 Multi-task Manifold Ranking

We first review the algorithm of graph-based manifold ranking that exploits the intrinsic manifold structure of data for graph labeling [23]. Given a superpixel feature set $X = \{x_1, \ldots, x_n\} \in \mathbb{R}^{d \times n}$, some superpixels are labeled as queries and the rest need to be ranked according to their affinities to the queries. Let $s : X \to \mathbb{R}^n$ denote a ranking function that assigns a ranking value s_i to each superpixel x_i, and can be viewed as a vector $s = [s_1, \ldots, s_n]^T$. In this work, we regard the query labels as initial superpixel weights, and s is thus a superpixel weight vector. Let denote an indication vector, in which if x_i is a query, and otherwise. Given G, the optimal ranking of queries are computed by solving the following problem:

$$\min_s \frac{1}{2} \left(\sum_{i,j=1}^n W_{ij} \left\| \frac{s_i}{\sqrt{D_{ii}}} - \frac{s_j}{\sqrt{D_{jj}}} \right\|^2 + \mu \|s - y\|^2 \right) \tag{1}$$

where $D = diag\{D_{11}, \ldots, D_{nn}\}$ is the degree matrix, and $D_{ii} = \sum_j W_{ij}$. $diag$ indicates the diagonal operation. μ is a parameter to balance the smoothness term and the fitting term. Then, we apply the manifold ranking on multiple modalities, and each modality can be viewed as a individual task, and thus have the following multi-task ranking model:

$$\min_{s^k} \frac{1}{2} \left(\sum_{i,j=1}^n W_{ij}^k \left\| \frac{s_i^k}{\sqrt{D_{ii}^k}} \frac{s_j^k}{\sqrt{D_{jj}^k}} - \right\|^2 + \mu \|s^k - y\|^2 \right) \tag{2}$$

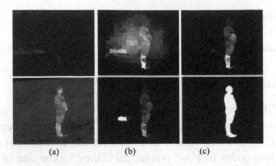

(a)   (b)   (c)

Fig. 2. Illustration of the effectiveness of the introduced modality weights and the cross-modality consistency. (a) Input RGB and thermal images. (b) Results of our method without modality weights and cross-modality consistency are shown in the first and second rows, respectively. (c) Our results and the corresponding ground truth.

inherently indicates that available modalities are independent and contribute equally. This may significantly limit the performance in dealing with occasional perturbation or malfunction of individual sources. Therefore, we propose a novel model for robustly performing salient object detection that (i) adaptively integrates different modalities based on the corresponding modal reliability, (ii) collaboratively computes the ranking functions of multiple modalities by incorporating the cross-modality consistent constraints. The final formulation of the multi-task manifold ranking algorithm is proposed as follows:

$$
\min_{s^k, r^k} \frac{1}{2} \sum_{k=1}^{K} \left((r^k)^2 \sum_{i,j=1}^{n} W_{ij}^k \left\| \frac{s_i^k}{\sqrt{D_{ii}^k}} - \frac{s_j^k}{\sqrt{D_{jj}^k}} \right\|^2 + \mu \sum_{k=1}^{K} \left\| s^k - y \right\|^2 \right.
$$

$$
\left. + \left\| \Gamma \bullet (1-r) \right\|^2 + \lambda \sum_{k=2}^{K-1} \left\| s^k - s^{k-1} \right\|^2 \right) \tag{3}
$$

where $\Gamma = \left[\Gamma^1, \ldots, \Gamma^K \right]^T$ is an adaptive parameter vector, which is initialized after the first iteration, and $r = [r^1, \ldots, r^K]^T$ is the modality weight vector. $\bullet$ denotes the element-wise product, and λ is a balance parameter. The third term is to avoid over-fitting of r, and the last term is the cross-modality consistent constraints. With some simple algebra, Eq. (3) can be rewritten as:

$$
\min_{s^k, r^k} \frac{1}{2} \sum_{k=1}^{K} \left((r^k)^2 \sum_{i,j=1}^{n} W_{ij}^k \left\| \frac{s_i^k}{\sqrt{D_{ii}^k}} - \frac{s_j^k}{\sqrt{D_{jj}^k}} \right\|^2 + \mu \| S - Y \|^2 + \| \Gamma \circ (1-r) \|^2 + \lambda \| CS \|_F^2 \right)
$$

$$
\tag{4}
$$

where $S = [s^1; s^2; \ldots; s^K] \in \mathbb{R}^{nK \times 1}$, $Y = [y^1; y^2; \ldots; y^K] \in \mathbb{R}^{nK \times 1}$, and $C \in \mathbb{R}^{n(K-1) \times nK}$ denotes the cross-modality consistent constraint matrix, which is defined as:

$$
\begin{bmatrix}
I^{2,1} & -I^2 & 0 & \cdots & 0 & 0 \\
0 & I^{3,2} & -I^3 & \cdots & 0 & 0 \\
& \cdots & & & \cdots & \\
0 & 0 & 0 & \cdots & I^{K,K-1} & -I^K
\end{bmatrix}
$$

where I^K and $I^{k,k-1}$ are the identity matrices with the size of $n \times n$. The effectiveness of introducing the modality weights and the cross-modality consistency is demonstrated in Fig. 2. A sub-optimal optimization can be achieved by alternating between the updating of s and r, and we present the detailed optimization algorithm in supplementary file due to space limitation.

5   Two-Stage RGB-T Saliency Detection

In this section, we present the two-stage ranking scheme for unsupervised bottom-up RGB-T saliency detection using the proposed algorithm with boundary priors and foreground queries.

5.1   Saliency Measure

Given an pair of input RGB-T images represented as a graph and some salient query nodes, the saliency of each node is defined as its ranking score computed by (4). In this work, we first employ the widely used boundary prior [22] to highlight the salient superpixels, and select highly confident superpixels as the foreground queries. Then, we perform the proposed algorithm to obtain the final ranking results, and combine them with their modality weights to compute the final saliency map.

5.2   Ranking with Boundary Priors

Based on the attention theories for visual saliency [8], we regard the boundary nodes as background seeds (the labelled data) to rank the relevance of all other superpixel nodes in the first stage. Taking the bottom image boundary as an example, we utilize the nodes on this side as labelled queries, and initialize the indicator y in (3). Given **y**, the ranking values $\{s_b^k\}$ are computed and normalized as $\{\hat{s}_b^k\} \in [0,1]$ by the proposed ranking algorithm. Similarly, given the top, left and right image boundaries, we can obtain the respective ranking values $\{\hat{s}_t^k\}$, $\{\hat{s}_l^k\}$, $\{\hat{s}_r^k\}$. We integrate them to compute the initial saliency map for each modality

$$
s_f^k = (1 - \hat{s}_b^k) \bullet (1 - \hat{s}_t^k) \bullet (1 - \hat{s}_l^k) \bullet (1 - \hat{s}_r^k),
$$
$$
k = 1, 2, \ldots, K
$$

Thus, the final saliency map in the first stage is computed as $\bar{s}_1 = \sum_{k=1}^{K} (r^k s_f^k)$

5.3   Ranking with Foreground Queries

Given s_f^1 for the RGB modality and $\bar{s}_1$, we set an adaptive threshold $T_1 = \max\left(s_f^1\right)$ $-\beta_1$, $T_2 = \max(\bar{s}_1) - \beta_2$ to generate the more robust foreground queries, where $\max(\bullet)$ indicates the maximum operation, and β_k is a constant of the k-th modality. In a specific, we select the i-th superpixel as the foreground query of he k-th modality if $s_{f,i}^k > T_k$. Therefore, we compute the ranking values s_s^k and the modality weights r in the second stage. Finally, the final saliency map $\bar{s}_2$ can be obtained by combining the ranking values with the modality weights $\bar{s}_2 = \sum_{k=1}^{K} \left(r^k s_s^k\right)$.

6   Experiments

In this section, we evaluate the proposed approach on our RGB-T benchmark. The experiments are carried out on a PC with an Intel i7 4.0 GHz CPU and 64 GB RAM.

Table 1. Average precision, recall, and $F0.3$ of our method against different kinds of baseline methods on the newly created dataset. The code type and runtime (second) are also presented. The bold fonts of results indicate the best performance, and "M" is the abbreviation of MATLAB.

Algorithm	RGB			Thermal			RGB-T			Code type	Runtime
	P	R	F	P	R	F	P	R	F		
BR [14]	**0.724**	0.260	0.411	0.648	0.413	0.488	**0.804**	0.366	0.520	M&C++	8.23
SR [15]	0.425	0.523	0.377	0.361	0.587	0.362	0.484	0.584	0.432	M	1.60
SRM [7]	0.411	0.529	0.384	0.392	0.520	0.380	0.428	0.575	0.411	M	0.76
CA [12]	0.592	0.667	0.568	0.623	0.607	0.573	0.648	0.697	0.618	M	1.14
MCI [4]	0.526	0.604	0.485	0.445	0.585	0.435	0.547	0.652	0.515	M&C++	21.89
NFI [3]	0.557	0.639	0.532	0.581	0.599	0.541	0.564	0.665	0.544	M	12.43
SS-KDE [16]	0.581	0.554	0.532	0.510	0.635	0.497	0.528	0.656	0.515	M&C++	0.94
GMR [22]	0.644	0.603	0.587	**0.700**	0.574	**0.603**	0.694	0.624	0.615	M	1.11
GR [21]	0.621	0.582	0.534	0.639	0.544	0.545	0.705	0.593	0.600	M&C++	2.43
STM [20]	0.658	0.569	0.581	0.647	0.603	0.579	-	-	-	C++	1.54
MST [18]	0.627	**0.739**	**0.610**	0.665	**0.655**	0.598	-	-	-	C++	0.53
RRWR [9]	0.642	0.610	0.589	0.689	0.580	0.596	-	-	-	C++	2.99
Ours	-	-	-	-	-	-	0.716	**0.713**	**0.680**	M&C++	1.39

Table 2. Average MAE Score of our method against different kinds of baseline methods on the newly created dataset. The bold fonts of results indicate the best performance.

MAE	CA	NFI	SS-KDE	GMR	GR	BR	SR	SRM	MCI	STM	MST	RRWR	Ours
RGB	0.163	0.126	0.122	0.172	0.197	0.269	0.300	0.199	0.211	0.194	0.127	0.171	**0.109**
T	0.225	**0.124**	0.132	0.232	0.199	0.323	0.218	0.155	0.176	0.208	0.129	0.234	0.141
RGB-T	0.195	0.125	0.127	0.202	0.199	0.297	0.260	0.178	0.195	-	-	-	**0.107**

6.1   Experimental Settings

For fair comparisons, we fix all parameters and other settings of our approach in the experiments, and use the default parameters released in their public codes for other baseline methods. In graph construction, we empirically generate $n = 300$ superpixels and set the affinity parameters $\gamma^1 = 24$ and $\gamma^2 = 12$, which control the edge strength between two superpixel nodes. In addition, we empirically set $\lambda = 0.03$, $\mu 1 = 0.02$ (the first stage) and $\mu 2 = 0.06$ (the second stage).

6.2   Comparison Results

We first report the precision (P), recall (R) and $F_{0.3}$ (F) of our method against other baseline ones on the entire dataset in Table 1. We can observe that the proposed approach substantially outperforms all baseline methods, demonstrating the effectiveness of our approach for adaptively incorporating thermal information. In addition, the thermal data can complement to RGB data by observing the superior performance of RGB-T baselines over single-modal ones. We also report MAE of baseline methods on entire dataset in Table 2. The evaluation results further validate the effectiveness of the proposed approach, the importance of thermal information and the complementary benefits of RGB-T data. The convergence curve and visually comparison results are presented in the **supplementary file**.

6.3   Components Analysis

To justify the significance of the main components of the proposed approach, we implement two special versions for comparative analysis, including: (1) Ours-I, that removes the modality weights in the proposed model and fixes $r^k = \frac{1}{K}$ in (4), and (2) Ours-II, that removes the cross-modality term and sets $\lambda = 0$ in (4). The results are presented in Fig. 3, and we observe and conclude that (1) our method substantially outperforms Ours-I. This demonstrates the significance of the introduced weighted variables to achieve adaptive fusion of different inputs; (2) the complete algorithm achieves superior performance than Ours-II, validating the effectiveness of the cross-modality consistent constraints.

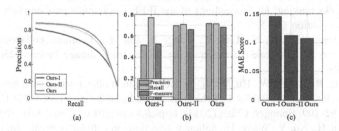

Fig. 3. Evaluation results of the proposed approach with its variants on the entire dataset.

7   Conclusion

In this paper, we create a comprehensive image benchmark for RGB-T saliency detection purpose. With the benchmark, we propose a graph-based multi-task manifold ranking algorithm to achieve adaptive fusion of RGB and thermal data for RGB-T saliency detection. Through analyzing the quantitative and qualitative results, we demonstrate the effectiveness of the proposed approach, and also provided some basic insights and potential research directions.

Acknowledgement. This work was supported in part by the Natural Science Foundation of Anhui Higher Education Institution of China under Grants KJ2017A017, and in part by the National Natural Science Foundation of China under Grants No. 61602006 and No. 61671018, and in part by the Co-Innovation Center for Information Supply & Assurance Technology, Anhui University under Grant Y01002449.

References

1. Conaire, C.O., O'Connor, N., Cooke, E., Smeaton, A.F.: Comparison of fusion methods for thermo-visual surveillance tracking. In: Proceedings of the International Conference on Information Fusion (2006)
2. Desingh, K., Krishna, K.M., Rajan, D., Jawahar, C.: Depth really matters: improving visual salient region detection with depth. In: BMVC (2013)
3. Erdem, E., Erdem, A.: Visual saliency estimation by nonlinearly integrating features using region covariances. J. Vis. **13**(4) (2013)
4. Goferman, S., Zelnik-Manor, L., Tal, A.: Context-aware saliency detection. IEEE Trans. Pattern Anal. Mach. Intell. **34**(10), 1915–1926 (2012)
5. Gopalakrishnan, V., Hu, Y., Rajan, D.: Random walks on graphs for salient object detection in images. IEEE Trans. Image Process. **19**(12), 3232–3242
6. Harel, J., Koch, C., Perona, P.: Graph-based visual saliency. In: Proceedings of the Advances in Neural Information Processing Systems (2006)
7. Hou, X., Zhang, L.: Saliency detection: a spectral residual approach. In: Proceedings of the IEEE Conference on Computer Vision and Pattern Recognition (2007)
8. Itti, L., Koch, C., Niebur, E., et al.: A model of saliency-based visual attention for rapid scene analysis. IEEE Trans. Pattern Anal. Mach. Intell. **20**(11), 1254–1259 (1998)
9. Li, C., Yuan, Y., Cai, W., Xia, Y., Dagan Feng, D.: Robust saliency detection via regularized random walks ranking. In: Proceedings of the IEEE Conference on Computer Vision and Pattern Recognition (2015)
10. Li, C., Cheng, H., Hu, S., Liu, X., Tang, J., Lin, L.: Learning collaborative sparse representation for grayscale-thermal tracking. IEEE Trans. Image Process. **25**(12), 5743–5756 (2016)
11. Peng, H., Li, B., Xiong, W., Hu, W., Ji, R.: RGBD salient object detection: a benchmark and algorithms. In: Fleet, D., Pajdla, T., Schiele, B., Tuytelaars, T. (eds.) ECCV 2014. LNCS, vol. 8691, pp. 92–109. Springer, Cham (2014). https://doi.org/10.1007/978-3-319-10578-9_7
12. Qin, Y., Lu, H., Xu, Y., Wang, H.: Saliency detection via cellular automata. In: Proceedings of the IEEE Conference on Computer Vision and Pattern Recognition (2015)
13. Qu, L., He, S., Zhang, J., Tian, J., Tang, Y., Yang, Q.: RGBD salient object detection via deep fusion. IEEE Trans. Image Process. **26**(5), 2274–2285 (2017)

14. Rahtu, E., Kannala, J., Salo, M., Heikkilä, J.: Segmenting salient objects from images and videos. In: Daniilidis, K., Maragos, P., Paragios, N. (eds.) ECCV 2010. LNCS, vol. 6315, pp. 366–379. Springer, Heidelberg (2010). https://doi.org/10.1007/978-3-642-15555-0_27

15. Seo, H.J., Milanfar, P.: Static and space-time visual saliency detection by self-resemblance. J. Vis. **9**(12), 15 (2009)

16. Tavakoli, H.R., Rahtu, E., Heikkilä, J.: Fast and efficient saliency detection using sparse sampling and kernel density estimation. In: Heyden, A., Kahl, F. (eds.) SCIA 2011. LNCS, vol. 6688, pp. 666–675. Springer, Heidelberg (2011). https://doi.org/10.1007/978-3-642-21227-7_62

17. Torralba, A., Efros, A.: Unbiased look at dataset bias. In: IEEE Conference on Computer Vision and Pattern Recognition (2011)

18. Tu, W.C., He, S., Yang, Q., Chien, S.Y.: Real-time salient object detection with a minimum spanning tree. In: Proceedings of the IEEE Conference on Computer Vision and Pattern Recognition (2016)

19. Wang, Q., Zheng, W., Piramuthu, R.: Grab: visual saliency via novel graph model and background priors. In: Proceedings of the IEEE Conference on Computer Vision and Pattern Recognition, pp. 535–543 (2016)

20. Yan, Q., Xu, L., Shi, J., Jia, J.: Hierarchical saliency detection. In: Proceedings of the IEEE Conference on Computer Vision and Pattern Recognition (2013)

21. Yang, C., Zhang, L., Lu, H.: Graph-regularized saliency detection with convex-hull-based center prior. IEEE Sig. Process. Lett. **20**(7), 637–640 (2013)

22. Yang, C., Zhang, L., Lu, H., Ruan, X., Yang, M.H.: Saliency detection via graph-based manifold ranking. In: Proceedings of the IEEE Conference on Computer Vision and Pattern Recognition (2013)

23. Zhou, D., Weston, J., Gretton, A., Bousquet, O., Scholkopf, B.: Ranking on data manifolds. In: Proceedings of Neural Information Processing Systems (2004)

Double δ-LBP: A Novel Feature Extraction Method for Facial Expression Recognition

Fang Shen$^{(\boxtimes)}$, Jing Liu, and Peng Wu

School of Artificial Intelligence, Xidian University, Xi'an, China
f.shen@qq.com

Abstract. The Local Binary Pattern (LBP) is a widely used descriptor in facial expression recognition due to its efficiency and effectiveness. However, existing facial expression recognition methods based on LBP either ignore different kinds of information, such as details and the contour of faces, or rely on the division of face images, such as dividing the face image into blocks or letting the block centering on landmarks. Considering this problem, to make full use of both detail and contour face information in facial expression recognition, we propose a novel feature extraction method based on double δ-LBP (Dδ-LBP) in this paper. In this method, two δ-LBPs are employed to represent details and the contour of faces separately, which take different kinds of information of facial expression into account. Experiments conducted on both lab-controlled and wild environment databases show that Dδ-LBP outperforms the original LBP method.

Keywords: Facial expression recognition · Local binary patterns
Feature extraction · Principal component analysis · Support vector machine

1 Introduction

The purpose of automatic facial expression recognition is to make the machine recognize different expressions of people, which has been widely used in the area of human-machine interaction. Many algorithms have been proposed for automatic facial expression recognition, in which the most crucial part is feature extraction. Recent successful features in facial expression recognition have been either handcrafted or learned from data. The handcraft feature focuses on constructing informative features manually. A good low-level feature should be both discriminative for inter-expression difference and invariant to intra-expression variations, such as lighting and the same expression of different people.

The Local Binary Pattern (LBP) descriptor has been widely used to both face recognition and facial expression recognition [1]. Existing feature extraction approaches using LBP can be generally grouped into two approaches: dividing face images into regular non-overlapping patches [2–4] and extracting patches centering at key points [5]. The regular non-overlapping dividing method first divides each face image into N overlapping patches with the same size, then applies the LBP to each patch. However, this method may separate the same information into two parts and this is not good for classification. The centering at key points patches method first uses the face alignment method to get landmarks, and then extracts feature centering at the key

© Springer Nature Singapore Pte Ltd. 2018
Y. Wang et al. (Eds.): IGTA 2018, CCIS 875, pp. 370–379, 2018.
https://doi.org/10.1007/978-981-13-1702-6_37

points. It relies largely on the accurate facial landmarks. However, most existing methods of this category present an expression image ignoring different kinds of information like details and the contour, which is crucial for facial expression recognition in reality.

This paper proposes a novel Double δ-LBP (Dδ-LBP) based facial expression recognition approach which applies the key points based method and also takes different kinds of information into consideration. After get the dense landmarks by the face alignment method, we extract patches centering at each landmark, and then apply two δ-LBP to get the detail and contour information respectively.

The performance of Dδ-LBP is validated on four databases: the Extended Cohn-Kanade (CK+) database [6, 7], the Japanese Female Facial Expression (JAFFE) database [8, 9], the MMI database [10] and the Real-world Affective Face Database (RAF-DB) [11]. Experimental results illustrate that Dδ-LBP achieves superior performance in comparison with the single δ-LBP method.

The main contributions of this paper are summarized as follows:

(1) We employ two δ-LBP with two different parameters to obtain two parts of representation for facial expressions, which takes both detail and contour information into consideration and higher accuracies are achieved compared with single δ-LBP methods;
(2) Different feature extraction methods of LBP are compared, which can be taken as a reference in further research;

The organization of the rest of this paper is as follows. Section 2 gives a review on LBP feature extraction methods in facial expression recognition and δ-LBP. Section 3 presents the proposed Double δ-LBP approach. Section 4 shows the experimental results. The conclusion is drawn in Sect. 5.

2 Related Work

In this section, we will first review existing feature extraction methods using LBP. Then, δ-LBP, which is the improved form of LBP is introduced. Also, we explain how we came up with the new feature extraction method Dδ-LBP. The form of LBP and the feature extraction method are two important factors in facial expression recognition using LBP. From the weakness of previous feature extraction methods, combined with advantages of the improved LBP, the Dδ-LBP is proposed.

2.1 Feature Extraction Methods Using LBP

We briefly review feature extraction methods using LBP in facial expression recognition in aforementioned two categories: regular non-overlapping dividing method and centering at key points method.

Considering the problem that an LBP histogram computed over the whole face image encodes only the occurrences of the micro-patterns without any indication about their locations, the regular non-overlapping dividing method equally divides face images into small regions $R_0, R_1, \ldots R_m$ to extract LBP histograms. Shan et al. [2]

divide the 110×150 pixels face images into 18×21 pixels regions. That is, face images are divided into $42(6 \times 7)$ regions and represented by the LBP histograms with the length of 2478, giving a good trade-off between recognition performance and feature vector length. Ahmed et al. [12] partition each image into a number of regions and the proposed CLBP histograms are generated from each of those regions. The histograms of all regions are concatenated to obtain the extended LBP histogram. And the number of regions divided is also estimated in the experiment.

The centering at key points based patches method extracts the feature of facial images centering at landmarks which need to use the face alignment method to get landmarks first. Chen et al. [5] constructed the feature by extracting multi-scale patches centered at dense facial landmarks. After using recent face alignment method, they extract multi-scale image patches centered around each landmark. Each patch is divided into a grid of cells and codes each cell by a certain descriptor. Finally, they concatenate all histograms to form the high-dimensional feature.

2.2 δ-LBP

The original LBP operator was introduced by Ojala et al. [15, 16] and was proved to be a powerful texture description as it can detect even a tiny change of the grayscale value. LBP operator is defined as follows:

$$LBP_{P,R}(x,y) = \sum_{P=0}^{P-1} s(g_P - g_c)2^P, s(x) = \begin{cases} 0, x < 0 \\ 1, x \geq 0 \end{cases} \tag{1}$$

where g_c stands for the grayscale value of the center pixel and g_p $(p = 0, 1, \ldots P - 1)$ represents the neighbor of the center pixel on a circle of radius R, and P denotes the number of the neighbors. In conclusion, the LBP value of a pixel is computed by comparing this pixel with its neighbors.

One fatal weakness of the original LBP operator is that it is sensitive to noise, especially in the near-uniform facial image regions since the thresholds are set exactly to the value of central pixel. To address this problem, Lu et al. [13] proposed the δ-LBP operator. δ-LBP which has 2-valued codes by comparing twice can be considered as the simplified LTP which has 3-valued codes by comparing three times. δ-LBP cut back a formula and in this way, it can greatly reduce the computational burden. δ-LBP is defined as follows:

$$\delta - LBP_{P,R}(x,y) = \sum_{P=0}^{P-1} s(g_P - g_c)2^P$$

$$s(x) = \begin{cases} 0, x \leq \delta th \\ 1, x > \delta th \end{cases}, \delta th \geq 0 \tag{2}$$

Compared with (1), (2) introduces a parameter δ_{th} to describe the difference between the peripheral pixel value and the intermediate pixel value and we can select different values of δ_{th} to achieve different effects. Figure 1 shows the encoding process of δ-LBP. Obviously, when δ_{th} is set to 0, δ-LBP equals to the original LBP.

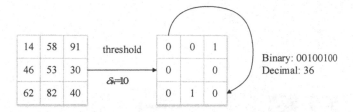

Fig. 1. The encoding process of δ-LBP.

2.3 Motivation of Proposing Dδ-LBP

As mentioned in Sect. 2.1, most existing feature extraction methods using LBP in facial expression recognition did not take different kinds of information like details and the contour into account but relied on selecting patches on face images. In order to more fully extract the information of facial expression, we use two δ-LBP instead of single LBP to represent the features of facial expressions. One is used to extract the features of details, the other to extract the features of contours.

3 Facial Expression Representation Based on Dδ-LBP

The framework of the proposed approach to represent the facial expression based on Dδ-LBP is illustrated in Fig. 2. In this approach, a facial expression image is modeled as a combination of two histograms by applying two δ-LBP with two different δ_{th}. The approach can be described by the following procedure: (1) After pretreatment, e.g. face alignment, patches which have the size of 20×20 are generated centering around the landmarks of an input image. The number of patches equals to the number of landmarks; (2) The first histogram is formed by applying δ-LBP with the smaller parameter δ_{th1} to each patch and concatenate them. This histogram represents the detail information of the facial expression; (3) The second histogram is formed by applying δ-LBP with the larger parameter δ_{th2} to the patches and concatenate them. The second histogram represents the contour information of the facial expression; (4) The first and the second histograms are concatenated to form the final histogram as the representation of the facial expression. The more detailed procedure and the selection of parameters are described below.

3.1 Facial Expression Representation Based on Single δ-LBP

The parameter δ_{th} occupies the most significant position in the δ-LBP. In addition, the choice of δ_{th} affects the representation result. When the value of δ_{th} is small, the texture map obtained by applying δ-LBP operator presents more details of the face. When the value of δ_{th} is large, the texture map shows more contour information for the reason that δ-LBP with larger δ_{th} emphasizes the contrast of the surrounding pixels and the middle pixel value—Only those grayscale value contrasts between the surrounding and the middle pixel are obvious (e.g. edge regions like eyebrows, eyes, and mouth etc.)

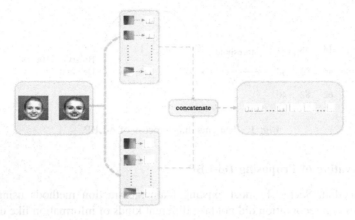

Fig. 2. Representation for the facial expression based on Dδ-LBP.

may be set to 0, while other gentle areas is set to 1. Therefore, the selection of δ_{th} depends on the problem you need to solve. Figure 3 shows the texture map using δ-LBP with different values of δ_{th}.

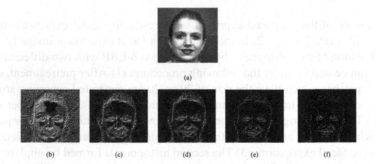

Fig. 3. Examples of texture map using δ-LBP with different δ_{th}. (a) The original face image. (b) The texture map using δ-LBP with $\delta_{th} = 0$. (c) The texture map using δ-LBP with $\delta_{th} = 3$. (d) The texture map using δ-LBP with $\delta_{th} = 5$. (e) The texture map using δ-LBP with $\delta_{th} = 10$. (f) The texture map using δ-LBP with $\delta_{th} = 15$.

3.2   Facial Expression Representation Using Double δ-LBP

The information of facial expression is reflected in two aspects: One is the change of facial features like eyebrows, eyes and mouth, etc., the other is the creation of wrinkles. In this case, we can use a pair of δ-LBP to represent these two different types of information. As illustrated in Fig. 3, δ-LBP with smaller δ_{th} reflects more details of the face, so we can use a δ-LBP with smaller δ_{th} to stand for wrinkles. δ-LBP with larger δ_{th} reflects contours of the face, so a δ-LBP with larger δ_{th} is used to demonstrate facial features. The detailed procedure is described below.

Firstly, we employ the 3000 fps [14] to get 68 landmarks and align faces. Then, the 68 patches which have the size of 20 × 20 are centering on landmarks obtained in the previous step and the boundary points that do not fall in the center of pixels can be estimated by bilinear interpolation. The feature vector of a face image is achieved by concatenate two histograms, each of which has the length of 68 × 59. The first histogram is obtained by δ-LBP with smaller δ_{th} to describe detail information. The secondary histogram is obtained by δ-LBP with the larger δ_{th} to describe contour information.

The most crucial part of the procedure above is the selection of δ_{th1} and δ_{th2}. It derives from the result with the single δ-LBP. The single δ-LBP is similar to the Dδ-LBP and the only different step is that the feature vector is formed with one histogram obtained from δ-LBP with one δ_{th}. We increase the value of δ_{th} from 0 to 40 in the step of 1 to get 41 results of recognition rate using the single δ-LBP method. Then we found that the result has a significant phenomenon: The highest recognition rate is achieved by a smaller δ_{th} and the second highest recognition rate is achieved by a larger δ_{th}. It turns out that smaller δ_{th} preserves more information including details and the contour at the same time. The larger δ_{th} cuts off most noise and can preserve the information of contours of the face, which are the most discriminating features of facial expressions. Chen et al. [5] found that high dimensionality leads to high performance in face recognition because it contains the amount of discriminative information for inter-person difference. To construct informative feature, we form the higher dimensional feature containing both details information with δ_{th1} achieved the best performance using the single δ-LBP and the contour information with δ_{th2} achieved the second-best performance using the single δ-LBP.

3.3 Dimension Reduction and Classification

We construct the high dimensional feature, so before the feature is input to the classifier, the high dimensional feature should be compressed. We use the joint of supervised and unsupervised subspace learning methods, joining Principal Component Analysis (PCA) [17] and Linear Discriminant Analysis (LDA) [18] to compress the high dimensional feature. After the compression, we send the feature into the support vector machine (SVM) [19] to recognize the expression.

4 Experiments

4.1 Database

The Extended Cohn-Kanade (CK+) Database. The database [6, 7] includes 593 sequences from 123 subjects posed or nonposed by 210 people from different area and different genders. The image sequence varies in duration and incorporate the onset to peak formation of the facial expressions.

The Japanese Female Facial Expression (JAFFE) Database. The database [8, 9] contains 213 photos of seven classes of facial expressions (six classes of basic facial expressions + 1 neutral faces) posed by ten Japanese females.

The MMI Database. The MMI database [10] consists of 30 subjects of both sexes (44% female) aged from 19 to 62, including either Asian, European or South American ethnic background and 213 sequences have been labeled with six expressions.

The Real-World Affective Face Database (RAF-DB). The RAF-DB [11] is a large and diverse real-world database that contains 29,672 static face images uploaded by Flickr users worldwide and provides multi-tagged emotional annotations.

4.2   Experiments on Single δ-LBP Method

Before conducting the experiment on Dδ-LBP, we first investigate the single δ-LBP method to determine the two crucial parameters: δ_{th1} and δ_{th2}. In this experiment, we extract image patches centered at 68 landmarks and the patch size is fixed to 20×20. Each patch is further divided into 3×3 cells then each cell is encoded with δ-LBP. 68 histograms calculated from each patch constitute the feature of one image. The dimension of the features is reduced by joint PCA (reserving 90% energy) and LDA. We apply 41 δ_{th} which range from 0 to 40 to evaluate the performance of the single δ-LBP method.

Experiment on CK+ Database. Six basic emotions (remove all "contempt" sequences) and neutral face are used to compare with other methods. For each sequence, the first image (neutral face) and the three peak images are used for prototype facial expression recognition. We construct 10 person-independent subsets by ascending ID order with the step size of 10 based on the subject ID in the dataset. Also, 10-fold cross validation is adopted. The average recognition rate of 7 classes with δ_{th} varying from 0 to 40 is shown in Fig. 4(a). We can find that δ_{th} which performs the best has the value of 2 and δ_{th} which performs the second-best has the value of 11. One has a smaller value and the other one has a larger value.

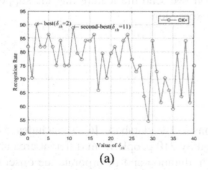 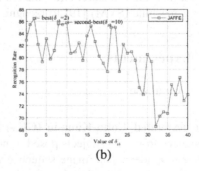

(a)   (b)

Fig. 4. (a) The average recognition rate of 7 classes with δ_{th} varying from 0 to 40 on CK+. (b) The average recognition rate of 7 classes with δ_{th} varying from 0 to 40 on JAFFE.

Experiment on JAFFE Database. All the 213 images are used for 7-class expression recognition. We adopt person-independent facial expression recognition and 10-fold cross-validation. Specifically, we use all images of one person as the validation set and the remaining images as the training set and the experiment is repeated 10 times so that each person is used for testing. The recognition rate with δ_{th} varying from 0 to 40 is shown in Fig. 4(b). We can also easily find that δ_{th} which performs the best has the value of 2 and δ_{th} which performs the second-best has the value of 10. One has a smaller value and the other one has a larger value.

4.3 Experiment on Different Face Region Selection Methods

To decide which face region selection method to use in Dδ-LBP, we test the single δ-LBP in two selection methods: dividing the face into regular non-overlapped patches and patches centering at the key points. In the first method, we divide the face into 6×7 regular patches. In the second method, we use 3000 fps to get the 68 key points. As shown in Table 1, the centering at the key points method performs better than the other method. So we choose centering at the key points method in Dδ-LBP.

Table 1. The comparison between different face region selection methods.

Database	Method	
	Regular patches	Centering at key points
CK+	70.53%	**93.18%**
JAFFE	80.95%	**95.24%**
MMI	52.86%	**56.22%**
RAF-DB	65.79%	**70.83%**

4.4 Experiment on Double δ-LBP Method

We conduct Dδ-LBP experiment on both lab-controlled and wild environment databases. δ_{th1} is set to 2 and δ_{th2} to 11 on four databases.

We also extract the feature centered at each 68 landmarks and each patch is fixed to 20×20. First, we apply δ-LBP with δ_{th1} to all patches and concatenate them together to form the $68 \times 59 = 4012$ dimension feature. Second, we apply δ-LBP with δ_{th2} to all patches and concatenate them together to form the second 4012-dimension feature. Finally, we concatenate the two 4012-dimension features to form the final 8024-dimension feature. This high dimensional feature is reduced by joint PCA (reserving 90% energy) and LDA before it is input to the SVM classifier.

The comparison of recognition rate between single δ-LBP and Dδ-LBP on two databases is reported in Table 2. As shown in Table 2, the improvement of recognition rates due to Dδ-LBP are 2.27%–7.84% on four databases, which shows the effectiveness of the Dδ-LBP method.

Table 2. The comparison between single δ-LBP and Dδ-LBP.

Database	Single δ-LBP	Dδ-LBP
CK+	93.18%	**95.45%**
JAFFE	95.24%	**97.62%**
MMI	70.83%	**78.67%**
RAF-DB	56.22%	**62.84%**

5 Conclusions

A double δ-LBP based facial expression recognition method (Dδ-LBP) is proposed in this paper. Dδ-LBP employs two δ-LBP to represent facial expression with different scales of information into consideration. Considering the most important property of facial expressions, we use two δ_{th} to represent the detail and the contour information separately. Experiments are conducted on four databases to illustrate the effectiveness of the proposed method. Compared with the single δ-LBP method, Dδ-LBP achieves better performance in terms of facial expression recognition accuracy. The key advantages of Dδ-LBP method is that it takes both details and the contour of faces into account, which can fully extract the information of facial expressions. The proposed method can also be applied to other fields, such as face recognition, object detection, and so on.

References

1. Huang, D., Shan, C., Ardabilian, M., Wang, Y., Chen, L.: Local binary patterns and its application to facial image analysis: a survey. IEEE Trans. Syst. Man Cybern. Part C Appl. Rev. **41**(6), 765–781 (2011)
2. Shan, C., Gong, S., Mcowan, P.W.: Facial expression recognition based on local binary patterns: a comprehensive study. Image Vis. Comput. **27**(6), 803–816 (2009)
3. Ahonen, T., Hadid, A., Pietikäinen, M.: Face description with local binary patterns: application to face recognition. IEEE Trans. Pattern Anal. Mach. Intell. **28**(12), 2037–2041 (2006)
4. Kumari, J., Rajesh, R., Pooja, K.: Facial expression recognition: a survey. Int. Symp. Comput. Vis. Internet **58**, 486–491 (2015)
5. Chen, D., Cao, X., Wen, F., Sun, J.: Blessing of dimensionality: high-dimensional feature and its efficient compression for face verification. Comput. Vis. Pattern Recognit. **9**(4), 3025–3032 (2013)
6. Kanade, T., Cohn, J.F., Tian, Y.: Comprehensive database for facial expression analysis. In: 2000 IEEE International Conference on Automatic Face and Gesture Recognition, pp. 484–490 (2000)
7. Lucey, P., Cohn, J.F., Kanade, T., Saragih, J.: The extended Cohn-Kanade dataset (CK+): a complete dataset for action unit and emotion-specified expression. In: 2010 IEEE Computer Society Conference on Computer Vision and Pattern Recognition, vol. 36, no. 1, pp. 94–101 (2010)

8. Lyons, M., Akamatsu, S., Kamachi, M., Gyoba, J.: Coding facial expressions with Gabor wavelets. In: 1998 IEEE International Conference on Automatic Face and Gesture Recognition, pp. 200–205 (1998)

9. Lyons, M.J., Budynek, J., Akamatsu, S.: Automatic classification of single facial images. IEEE Trans. Pattern Anal. Mach. Intell. **21**(12), 1357–1362 (1999)

10. Pantic, M., Valstar, M., Rademaker, R., Maat, L.: Web-based database for facial expression analysis. In: Proceedings of the 2005 IEEE International Conference on Multimedia and Expo, vol. 14 (2005)

11. Deng, W., Hu, J., Zhang, S., Guo, J.: DeepEmo: real-world facial expression analysis via deep learning. In: Visual Communications and Image Processing, pp. 1–4 (2016)

12. Ahmed, F., Hossain, E., Bari, A.S.M.H, Shihavuddin, A.: Compound local binary pattern (CLBP) for robust facial expression recognition. In: IEEE International Symposium on Computational Intelligence and Informatics, pp. 391–395 (2011)

13. Lu, S., Yang, J.H., Zhang, B., Zhang, J.Q.: Infrared target detection based on LBP. J. Changchun Univ. Sci. Technol. **32**(1), 22–24 (2009)

14. Ren, S., Cao, X., Wei, Y., Sun, J.: Face alignment at 3000 fps via regressing local binary features. In: Proceedings of the IEEE Conference on Computer Vision and Pattern Recognition, pp. 1685–1692 (2014)

15. Ojala, T., Pietikäinen, M., Mäenpää, T.: Multiresolution gray scale and rotation invariant texture classification with local binary patterns. IEEE Trans. Pattern Anal. Mach. Intell. **24**(7), 971–987 (2002)

16. Ojala, T., Pietikäinen, M., Mäenpää, T.: A generalized local binary pattern operator for multiresolution gray scale and rotation invariant texture classification. In: Singh, S., Murshed, N., Kropatsch, W. (eds.) ICAPR 2001. LNCS, vol. 2013, pp. 399–408. Springer, Heidelberg (2001). https://doi.org/10.1007/3-540-44732-6_41

17. Jolliffe, I.T.: Principal Component Analysis, vol. 87, pp. 41–64. Springer, Berlin (1986). https://doi.org/10.1007/978-1-4757-1904-8. no. 100

18. Altman, E.I., Marco, G., Varetto, F.: Corporate distress diagnosis: comparisons using linear discriminant analysis and neural networks. J. Bank. Financ. **18**(3), 505–529 (1994)

19. Chang, C.C., Lin, C.J.: LIBSVM: a library for support vector machines. ACM Trans. Intell. Syst. Technol. **2**(3), 27 (2011)

Temporal-Spatial Feature Learning of Dynamic Contrast Enhanced-MR Images via 3D Convolutional Neural Networks

Xibin Jia[1], Yujie Xiao[1], Dawei Yang[2,3(✉)], Zhenghan Yang[2], Xiaopei Wang[2], and Yunfeng Liu[1]

[1] Faculty of Information Technology, Beijing University of Technology, Beijing, China
jiaxibin@bjut.edu.cn,
{xyj,hesoyamlyf}@emails.bjut.edu.cn
[2] Department of Radiology, Beijing Friendship Hospital, Capital Medical University, Beijing, China
Dawei-yang@vip.163.com, yangzhenghan@263.net, wangxiaopei1991@126.com
[3] Beijing Key Laboratory of Translational Medicine on Liver Cirrhosis, Beijing, China

Abstract. Dynamic contrast-enhanced magnetic resonance imaging provide not only the information on the morphological features of the lesions, but also the changes of the lesion's blood perfusion. In this paper, we propose a tensor-based temporal data representation (TTD) model and a multi-channel fusion 3D convolutional neural network (MCF-3D CNN) to extract the temporal and spatial features of dynamic contrast enhanced-MR images (DCE-MR images). To evaluate the performance of the proposed methods, we established a DCE-MR image dataset for non-invasively assessing the differentiation of Hepatocellular carcinoma (HCC). The TTD model achieves the accuracy of 73.96% for non-invasive assessment of HCC differentiation via MCF-3D CNN. Meanwhile, the 3D CNN with TTD achieves accuracy, sensitivity and specificity of 95.17%, 96.33%, and 94.00%, respectively, in discriminating the HCC and cirrhosis. Compared with the normal data representation method, the proposed TTD method is more conducive for 3D CNN to extract temporal-spatial features of DCE-MR images.

Keywords: 3D convolutional neural networks
Tensor-based temporal data representation model
Dynamic contrast enhanced-MR images · Temporal-spatial features
Hepatocellular carcinoma · Non-invasive assessment

1 Introduction

In recent years, 2D Convolutional Neural Networks (CNNs) with powerful feature expression capability have shown their better performance in classification, target detection, and segmentation of natural images than traditional feature extraction

© Springer Nature Singapore Pte Ltd. 2018
Y. Wang et al. (Eds.): IGTA 2018, CCIS 875, pp. 380–389, 2018.
https://doi.org/10.1007/978-981-13-1702-6_38

methods [1–3]. Ji et al. [4] use 3D CNN to extract video spatial characteristics and motion timing characteristics for human action recognition. Meanwhile, the computer aided diagnosis (CAD) technology based on CNN has also been applied to detection, segmentation, and hierarchical diagnosis of brain, retina, breast, lung, and abdominal lesions [5–8].

Hepatocellular cancer (HCC) is an epithelial tumor that originates in the liver. It is the most common primary malignant tumor of the liver and the third most deadly cancer in the world [9, 10]. The World Health Organization (WHO) classifies HCC into three categories, which are well, moderately and poorly based on the heterogeneity of the nucleus and structure of HCC. The differentiation of HCC is one of the most important factors among the multiple factors predicting the recurrence of HCC [11]. Therefore, accurate prediction of HCC differentiation is crucial for selecting treatment plan and prognosis. Liver biopsy is a gold standard for obtaining the differentiation of HCC before surgery, but it cannot be widely used in clinical practice due to its limitations of invasiveness, sampling error and bleeding. Therefore, there is an urgent need for a non-invasive method to accurately assessment the differentiation of HCC. DCE-MRI technology uses high spatial and temporal resolution imaging methods to obtain dynamic continuous images before and after contrast injection, which can simultaneously reflect lesions morphological and perfusion information and provide possibility for the noninvasive assessment of HCC differentiation. Previous study [12] have shown that there is a certain correlation between partial perfusion parameters of DCE-MRI and the differentiation of HCC, but study based on DCE-MRI images to directly predict HCC differentiation have not yet been reported. Therefore, it is necessary to apply CAD technology to achieve non-invasive assessment of HCC differentiation based on DCE-MR images. In the area of CAD based on DCE-MR images, Anna [13] quantified time-intensity curve (TSIC) of DCE-MR images to diagnose prostate cancer and found that TSIC has three major patterns that correspond to the malignant characterization of prostate cancer. Li et al. [14] attempted to describe the dynamic enhancement features of tumor by computing the enhancement rate images, and using 3D CNN to extract the features of the enhancement rate map for distinguishing between malignant and benign breast tumors in DCE-MR images. Zhou et al. [15] proposed that texture features indexed by mean and GLN based on the arterial phase images of DCE-MR images reflect biologic aggressiveness, and may have potential applications in predicting the histological grading of HCC preoperatively. However, there is no relevant work to apply deep learning [16] methods to the assessment of HCC differentiation. Therefore, we use deep learning methods with powerful data representation capability to extract temporal and spatial features of DCE-MR images for the non-invasive assessment of HCC differentiation.

In this study, we proposed a tensor-based temporal data (TTD) representation model and a multi-channel fusion 3D convolutional neural network (MCF-3D CNN) to extract temporal sequence information and spatial texture information of DCE-MR images. Compared with the normal data representation method, the proposed TTD model is more conducive for 3D CNN to extract temporal-spatial features of DCE-MR images. MCF-3D CNN with TTD achieves the accuracy of 73.96% in the non-invasive assessment of HCC differentiation.

2 Methodology

2.1 Tensor-Based Temporal Data Representation

The data used in this paper contains the sequences of DCE-MR images for five periods, each of which has spatial three-dimensional structure, as shown in Fig. 1.

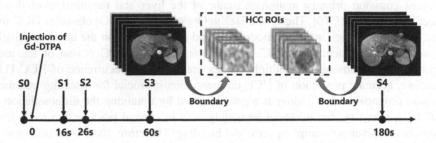

Fig. 1. DCE-MRI images of five phases, including: S0, S1, S2, S3, and S4. S0 represents the MR images acquired before injection of Gd-DTPA contrast agent, and S1, S2, S3, and S4 represent the MR images acquired 16, 26, 60, and 180 s after injection of Gd-DTPA contrast agent, respectively. The collected images are all 3D stereoscopic images.

The three-dimensional spatial boundaries of the cirrhotic area and HCC lesions (ROIs) in DCE-MR images of five periods were labeled by an radiology physician (Dawei Yang) and were examined by a radiology chief physician (Zhenghan Yang). In order to adapt to the neural network, the HCC cross-sectional dimensions size was normalized to size of 32 × 32. On the vertical view, we selected two slices on both sides of the largest region. Therefore, the HCC lesion of each case has five periods, and each period has the size of 32 × 32 × 5. The data for each HCC lesion can be represented using a 4th-order tensor with a size of 32 × 32 × 5 × 5.

When performing convolution operations in 3D CNN, each 3th-order tensor of the input 4th-order tensor are locally multiplied by 3D convolution kernels, and then sum the convolution results. Assuming the input tensor has the shape of I × J × K × C, 3D convolution operation can be expressed as:

$$u_{uv}^{l}(x, y, z) = \sum_{c} \sum_{i,j,k} h_{uc}^{l-1}(x - i, y - j, z - k) W_{uvc}^{l}(i, j, k), \qquad (1)$$

where W_{uvc}^{l} is one of the 3D convolution kernels in the l-th layer which convolves over the 3D feature volume h_{uc}^{l-1}, $W_{uvc}^{l}(i, j, k)$ is the elementwise weight in the 3D convolution kernel. Following (1), a nonlinear activation function is used to generate a feature map of l-th layer:

$$h_{v}^{l} = \sigma \left(\sum_{u} u_{uv}^{l} + b_{v}^{l} \right), \qquad (2)$$

where $\sigma(\cdot)$ is nonlinear activation function, b_{v}^{l} is the bias of the v-th kernel in l-th layer.

Therefore, if the 4th-order tensor was regarded as multi-channel 3D input data of a 3D CNN layer, the 3D convolution kernel can only extract the 3th-order information of the 4th-order tensor at the same time, and make numerical summation at the *4-th* dimension. From the perspective of extracting temporal information and extracting spatial information of the DCE-MR images, we illustrate the following two tensor-based data representation methods, as shown in Fig. 2.

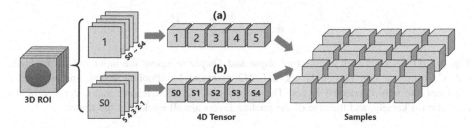

Fig. 2. Tensor-based HCC data representation methods. Solid arrows represent splices N-th-order tensors with the same shape into a (N + 1)-th-order tensor, S0 to S4 are the five phase numbers of DCE-MR images, and 1 to 5 is the cross-sectional slices numbers of each HCC lesion. (a) The proposed TTD model for DCE-MRI, splices each 2D-slice of the five phases of HCC into a 3th-order tensor, and then splices the 3th-order tensors of five slices into a 4th-order tensor. (b) The normal data representation method without structure change, which keeps the 3D structure of the HCC lesion and assembles it into 4th-order tensors according to the time sequence. Finally, the data of all cases were spliced into a 5th-order tensor.

Using the TTD model (Fig. 2(a)) proposed in this paper means that 3D convolution kernels convolve with 5 phase DCE-MR images simultaneously, which is more conducive to the extraction of temporal features in DCE-MR images. When using the traditional data representation method (Fig. 2(b)), the 3D convolution kernel extracts the spatial structure characteristics of each phase of DCE-MR images. Since the samples collected in this paper have a shape of $32 \times 32 \times 5 \times 5$, the shape of the tensor we get by using two data representation method are the same, as well as the numbers of the deep learning model parameters.

2.2 3D Convolutional Neural Networks

In this paper, the 3D CNN is used to extract features of DCE-MR images. A 3D CNN model with input of 4th-order tensor is established with convolutional layer, pooling layer, and fully connected layer. The output layer with softmax classifier will generate the prediction probability of HCC differentiation, as shown in Fig. 3.

It can be seen from Fig. 3 that we use only 6 kernels in the first convolutional layer and 8 kernels in the second convolutional layer, and the number of neurons in the two fully connected layer is 100 and 32, respectively. The purpose of this design is to reduce the number of parameters and avoid overfitting. In the network, a rectified linear unit (ReLU) [17] is used as a nonlinear activation function for the convolutional layer and the fully connected layer. 3D convolution kernels are initialized from the Gaussian

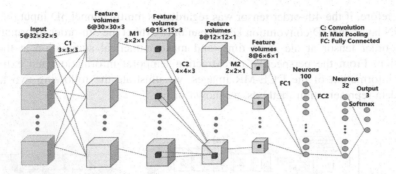

Fig. 3. 3D CNN network architecture. *Input* and *Output* represent the input and output layer, *C1, C2* represent convolution layers, *M1, M2* represent MaxPooling layers, and *FC1, FC2* represent the fully connected layers. The amounts of 3D CNN feature maps, the size of the convolution kernels, and the size of the pooling layers are all marked in the figure.

distribution. Using adaptive moment estimation (Adam) optimization algorithm [18] to adjust the trainable parameters in the network to minimize the cross-entropy loss. Learning rate reduction and dropout method [19] with a ratio of 0.5 are used to prevent overfitting.

2.3   Multi-channel Fusion 3D Convolutional Neural Networks

In order to make full use of the temporal and spatial information of DCE-MR images, we propose a multi-channel fusion 3D convolutional neural network (MCF-3D CNN) to extract the features of the 3th-order tensors using separate convolutional networks with the same structure, and then splice the extracted features, as shown in Fig. 4.

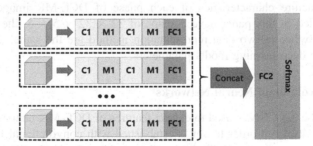

Fig. 4. The architecture of MCF-3D CNN. We split the 4th-order tensor into five 3th-order tensors as the input of five separated 3D CNNs with the same structure. The structure of the C1, M1, C2, M2, and FC1 layers are the same as those in Fig. 3. We splice all the outputs of the FC1 layers as the input of the FC2 layer. Finally, the outputs of the FC2 layer were sent to the softmax classifier to generate probability of each category.

3   Experiments

To evaluate the performance of the proposed method, we established a DCE-MR images dataset for the non-invasively assessing the differentiation of HCC. 51 effective HCC lesions were collected from 48 patients using the GE 3.0T 750 magnetic resonance imaging system in Beijing Friendship Hospital of Capital Medical University. The labels of pathological HCC differentiation were obtained by liver biopsy.

3.1   Data Preprocessing, Augmentation and Sampling

In the preprocessing step, we normalize the volume intensities to the range of [0, 1] using Eq. (3) for the MR images that have higher intensity values than natural images, and there are some sparse noises with high intensity values.

$$I' = (I - I_{min})/(I_{max} - I_{min}),\qquad(3)$$

where I' and I denote the normalized and original intensity values, respectively. I_{min} is the minimum intensity value of the whole volume, and I_{max} is the maximum intensity value after trimming the top 1% gray scale values. This kind of preprocessing has been widely performed in related works [6, 20].

We augmented the data by transposition, rotating and flipping the exacted ROI of the training set and the testing set to prevent over-fitting. The transposition, rotating 90° and flip (horizontal and vertical) can increase the data amount of the original data set by 2, 3 and 2 times, respectively. Therefore, after using the data augmentation methods, the total number of data was 8 times of the original data set.

Due to the limitations of quality, completeness and other factors, a common problem in medical images classify is that some classes have a significantly higher number of examples than other classes. The effect of class imbalance on classification performance of CNN is detrimental [21]. Shen et al. [22] use class-aware sampling in ImageNet2015 competition to reduce the effect of class imbalance. Also in the ImageNet2016 competition, the champion team of the scene classification task uses a label shuffling method to solve the problem of class imbalance. In this study, we uses a compromised label shuffling method to overcome the problem of class imbalance. In detail, we take an appropriate number of samples from each category of samples. This number is between the most and least numbers of all categories.

Specifically, for the task of distinguishing between HCC and liver cirrhosis (Task1), there are 51 samples of HCC and liver cirrhosis. The details of division and augmentation are shown in Table 1. For the task of assessing HCC differentiation (Task2), the number of three categories of HCC samples is imbalance. In addition to data augmentation, we resample the training and testing data by using a compromised label shuffling method. In particular, we randomly sampled (allow repeatedly extract) 128 (64) samples from each category of the augmented training (testing) set. The details of division, augmentation and sampling are shown in Table 2.

Table 1. Details of datasets for discriminating the HCC and cirrhosis

| Datasets | Number of samples \| Augmentation | |
	HCC	Cirrhosis
Training	36 | 288	36 | 288
Testing	15 | 120	15 | 120
Total	51 | 408	51 | 408

Table 2. Details of datasets for non-invasive assessment of HCC differentiation

| Datasets | Number of HCC samples \| Augmentation \| Label Shuffling | | |
	Poorly	Moderately	Well
Training	6 | 48 | **128**	26 | 208 | **128**	4 | 32 | **128**
Testing	3 | 24 | **64**	9 | 72 | **64**	3 | 24 | **64**
Total	9 | 72 | **192**	35 | 280 | **192**	7 | 56 | **192**

3.2 Results

After the data preprocessing, augmentation and sampling, we establish the 3D CNN and MCF-3D CNN models by using Keras and TensorFlow [23], and repeat the experiment ten times independently for Task1 and Task2. In each experiment, we train the 3D CNN and MCF-3D CNN with batch size and epoch of 32 and 1000 on the training set and evaluate the models on the testing set. The inputs of the models have two king of data representation method, TTD (Fig. 2(a)) and Normal (Fig. 2(b)).

Task 1. We evaluate the results of Task1 with the accuracy, the sensitivity, the specificity, and the area under the ROC curve (AUC). The average value and the standard deviation of the 10 test results are shown in Table 3.

Table 3. The results of discriminating the HCC and cirrhosis

Method		Accuracy	Sensitivity	Specificity	AUC
TTD	3DCNN	**0.9517±0.0182**	**0.9633±0.0245**	**0.9400±0.0258**	**0.9992±0.0073**
	MCF-3D	0.9442±0.0117	0.9533±0.0224	0.9350±0.0082	0.9847±0.0090
Normal	3DCNN	0.9417±0.0173	0.9592±0.0234	0.9242±0.0375	0.9919±0.0051
	MCF-3D	0.9358±0.0112	0.9450±0.0205	0.9267±0.0082	0.9567±0.0122

Task 2. We evaluate the results of Task2 with the accuracy, the recall, the precision, and the F1-score on the testing set. The average value and the standard deviation of the 10 test results are shown in Table 4.

Table 4. The results of non-invasive assessment of HCC differentiation

Method		Accuracy	Recall	Precision	F1-score
TTD	3DCNN	0.7188±0.0405	0.7188±0.0405	0.7874±0.0416	0.7014±0.0356
	MCF-3D	**0.7396±0.0104**	**0.7396±0.0104**	**0.8042±0.0198**	**0.7190±0.0098**
Normal	3DCNN	0.6667±0.0195	0.6667±0.0195	0.7463±0.0514	0.6483±0.0092
	MCF-3D	0.5052±0.0210	0.5052±0.0210	0.7332±0.1571	0.4778±0.0405

Feature Maps and Kernels. To provide a comprehensive insight into the learned kernels of 3D conventional layers, all kernels and some samples' feature maps of C1 and C2 convolution layer of 3D CNN are visualized in Figs. 5 and 6.

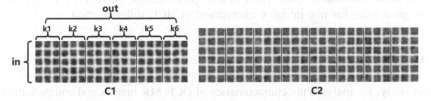

Fig. 5. All the kernels of C1 and C2 convolution layer. For C1 convolution layer, the marker *in* and *out* represent the input and output channels, and *k1, k2, k3, k4, k5,* and *k6* represent the 6 conventional kernels with size of 3 × 3 × 3. The kernels of C2 are arranged in the same way.

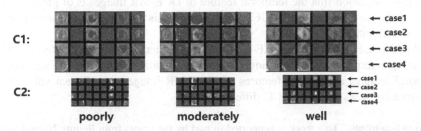

Fig. 6. Feature maps of C1 and C2 convolution layer. For each category of HCC, we use 4 cases to produce the feature maps. For each case, C1 and C2 conventional layer produce feature maps with shape of 30 × 30 × 3 × 6 and 12 × 12 × 1 × 8, respectively. The feature maps of C1 are shown as RGB images and the feature maps of C2 are shown as gray images.

It can be seen from the feature maps in Fig. 6 that the feature maps generated by C1 are similar, while C2 produces discriminative feature maps.

3.3 Analysis

From Tables 3 and 4, the accuracy of the TTD model is higher than the second data representation method in MCF-3D CNN and 3D CNN for the two tasks. Since the TTD-3D model were more conducive for 3D convolution kernels to extract the temporal features of DCE-MR images the second one, which means that the temporal feature is of great value for either distinguishing between HCC and liver cirrhosis or non-invasive assessment of HCC differentiation.

From Table 3, by using the TTD model, 3D CNN achieves the highest accuracy of 95.17% in distinguishing HCC and cirrhosis. Compared to the fusion model (feature level information fusion), 3D CNN, which can be seen as data level information fusion, has fewer parameters (about 1/4 of MCF-3D). A possible explanation is that the differences between HCC and cirrhosis are similar at all the slices of MR images, and it is not necessary for a multiple networks to extract redundant features.

From Table 4, by using the TTD model, MCF-3D obtain the highest accuracy of 73.96% in non-invasive assessment of HCC differentiation, which means that extracting the temporal characteristics of each slice of HCC MR images, and then splicing the features into fused features is more conducive to evaluate the differentiation of HCC. Both the temporal features and spatial features of HCC DCE-MR images are of great value for non-invasive assessment of HCC differentiation.

4   Conclusion

In this study, we analyzes the characteristics of DCE-MR images and compare the two data representation methods. The first tensor-based data representation method (TTD) is convenient for 3D CNNs to extract the temporal features of DCE-MR images, and the other data representation method is more convenient for 3DCNN to extract spatial texture information of DCE-MR images. From the experiment results, We can draw the conclusion that the temporal feature of DCE-MR images is of great value for either distinguishing between HCC and liver cirrhosis or non-invasive assessment of HCC differentiation.

We also use 3DCNN and MCF-3D to extract the temporal-spatial features of DCE-MR images respectively. According to the experimental results, we find that both the temporal features and spatial features of HCC MR images are of great value for the non-invasive assessment of HCC differentiation.

Acknowledgments. This work is supported in part by the grants from Beijing Natural Science Foundation (No.7184199), Capital's Funds for Health Improvement and Research (No. 2018-2-2023), Research Foundation of Beijing Friendship Hospital, Capital Medical University (No. yyqdkt2017-25).

References

1. Krizhevsky, A., Sutskever, I., Hinton, G.E.: ImageNet classification with deep convolutional neural networks. In: International Conference on Neural Information Processing Systems, pp. 1097–1105 (2012)
2. Liu, W., et al.: SSD: single shot MultiBox detector. In: Leibe, B., Matas, J., Sebe, N., Welling, M. (eds.) ECCV 2016. LNCS, vol. 9905, pp. 21–37. Springer, Cham (2016). https://doi.org/10.1007/978-3-319-46448-0_2

3. He, K., Gkioxari, G., Dollár, P., Girshick, R.B.: Mask R-CNN. CoRR, abs/1703.06870 (2017)
4. Ji, S., Xu, W., Yang, M., Yu, K.: 3D convolutional neural networks for human action recognition. IEEE Trans. Pattern Anal. Mach. Intell. **35**, 221–231 (2013)
5. Litjens, G., et al.: A survey on deep learning in medical image analysis. Med. Image Anal. **42**, 60 (2017)
6. Dou, Q., et al.: Automatic detection of cerebral microbleeds from mr images via 3D convolutional neural networks. IEEE Trans. Med. Imaging **35**, 1182–1195 (2016)
7. Lemaître, G., Martí, R., Freixenet, J., Vilanova, J.C., Walker, P.M., Meriaudeau, F.: Computer-aided detection and diagnosis for prostate cancer based on mono and multiparametric MRI: a review. Comput. Biol. Med. **60**, 8 (2015)
8. Kamnitsas, K., et al.: Efficient multi-scale 3D CNN with fully connected CRF for accurate brain lesion segmentation. Med. Image Anal. **36**, 61 (2017)
9. Yang, J.D., Roberts, L.R.: Hepatocellular carcinoma: a global view. Nat. Rev. Gastroenterol. Hepatol. **7**, 448 (2010)
10. Sherman, M.: Hepatocellular carcinoma: screening and staging. Clin. Liver Dis. **15**, 323–334 (2011)
11. Regimbeau, J.M., et al.: Risk factors for early death due to recurrence after liver resection for hepatocellular carcinoma: Results of a multicenter study †. J. Surg. Oncol. **85**, 36–41 (2004)
12. Jiang, T., Zou, Y., Jie-Hua, X.U., Peng, L.R., Shan, H., Radiology, D.O.: Magnetic resonance imaging in predicting histopathological differentiation of hepatocellular carcinoma. J. Sun Yat-Sen Univ. Sci. **37**, 903–911 (2016)
13. Fabijańska, A.: A novel approach for quantification of time-intensity curves in a DCE-MRI image series with an application to prostate cancer. Comput. Biol. Med. **73**, 119–130 (2016)
14. Li, J., Fan, M., Zhang, J., Li, L.: Discriminating between benign and malignant breast tumors using 3D convolutional neural network in dynamic contrast enhanced-MR images. In: SPIE Medical Imaging, p. 1013808 (2017)
15. Zhou, W., et al.: Malignancy characterization of hepatocellular carcinomas based on texture analysis of contrast-enhanced MR images. J. Magn. Reson. Imaging JMRI **45**, 1476–1484 (2017)
16. Lecun, Y., Bengio, Y., Hinton, G.: Deep learning. Nature **521**, 436 (2015)
17. Glorot, X., Bordes, A., Bengio, Y.: Deep sparse rectifier neural networks. In: International Conference on Artificial Intelligence and Statistics, pp. 315–323 (2011)
18. Kingma, D.P., Ba, J.L.: Adam: a method for stochastic optimization. In: International Conference for Learning Representations (2015)
19. Srivastava, N., Hinton, G.E., Krizhevsky, A., Sutskever, I., Salakhutdinov, R.: Dropout: a simple way to prevent neural networks from overfitting. J. Mach. Learn. Res. **15**, 1929–1958 (2014)
20. Chen, H., Yu, L., Dou, Q., Shi, L., Mok, V.C.T., Heng, P.A.: Automatic detection of cerebral microbleeds via deep learning based 3D feature representation. In: IEEE International Symposium on Biomedical Imaging, pp. 764–767 (2015)
21. Buda, M., Maki, A., Mazurowski, M.A.: A systematic study of the class imbalance problem in convolutional neural networks. CoRR, abs/1710.05381 (2017)
22. Shen, L., Lin, Z., Huang, Q.: Relay backpropagation for effective learning of deep convolutional neural networks. In: Leibe, B., Matas, J., Sebe, N., Welling, M. (eds.) ECCV 2016. LNCS, vol. 9911, pp. 467–482. Springer, Cham (2016). https://doi.org/10.1007/978-3-319-46478-7_29
23. Abadi, M., et al.: TensorFlow: large-scale machine learning on heterogeneous distributed systems. arXiv: Distributed, Parallel, and Cluster Computing (2016)

Long-Term Tracking Algorithm
with the Combination of Multi-feature Fusion
and YOLO

Sicong Jiang[1], Jianing Zhang[1], Yunzhou Zhang[1,2(✉)], Feng Qiu[2],
Dongdong Wang[2], and Xiaobo Liu[2]

[1] College of Information Science and Engineering,
Northeastern University, Shenyang 110819, China
jiangsicong1225@gmail.com, zhangjianing313@gmail.com
[2] Faculty of Robot Science and Engineering,
Northeastern University, Shenyang 110819, China
zhangyunzhou@mail.neu.edu.cn,
1264805326@qq.com, 287114064@qq.com, 1807547582@qq.com

Abstract. In recent year correlation filtering based algorithms have achieved significant performance in tracking. In traditional, the previous frame has been trained in order to get the prediction position of the next frame. However, in experiments we find that once the present frame drifts, the latter frame will be affected and accumulate error, which can cause the loss of the target eventually. In that case, the tracker cannot track a target for a long time. To solve these problems and design an efficient long-term tracking algorithm, we propose a long-term tracking algorithm by combining the short-term tracker and the YOLO v2 detector. We use the SURF algorithm to get the similarity of the tracking result and the current contrast template, once the similarity is lower than a threshold, the YOLO v2 will be activated and find the right target through a three-stage cascade selecting mechanism we designed before, then the short-term tracker will be restarted and the contrast template will be updated. In this way, the short-term tracker can be transformed to a long-term tracker which is able to track a target for a long time in complex circumstance. Besides, we also adopt the compound feature to improve our short-term tracker, so our algorithm has better accuracy and robustness. The experimental results demonstrate the proposed approach outperforms state-of-the-art approaches on large-scale benchmark datasets.

Keywords: Computer vision · Long-term tracking · Compound feature
Correlation filters

1 Introduction

Visual tracking, an important problem in computer vision, can be divided into short-term tracking and long-term tracking. In recent years, the short-term tracking field has developed very fast while the long-term tracking hasn't developed so well.

© Springer Nature Singapore Pte Ltd. 2018
Y. Wang et al. (Eds.): IGTA 2018, CCIS 875, pp. 390–402, 2018.
https://doi.org/10.1007/978-981-13-1702-6_39

In the field of short tracking, correlation filtering based methods has been widely used according to their excellent performance. But these methods have a same problem. If drift happens in one frame, the next frame will probably accumulate the error. The drift problem will become more serious from frame to frame. That is why correlation filtering methods are more suitable for short-term tracking rather than long-term tracking.

To solve this problem, we introduce a detector in our tracking algorithm. Among all the detectors, we select YOLO v2 because of its high speed and accuracy. The SURF algorithm is also adopted to determine when to restart the short-term tracker. Besides, we need to update the template which is used to determine the confidence level.

When tracking starts, we first consider the target in the first frame as the template. Then we start the short-term tracker. During the tracking process, we use SURF algorithm to compare the similarity between the present tracking result and the template. We consider the similarity as the confidence of the result, once the confidence is lower than the preset threshold, we will restart the short-term tracker and update the template to record the latest shape of the target. But if the confidence is too low, the tracker may lose the target totally, in that case, we will use YOLO v2 until we find the target again and restart the whole algorithm.

To create a new long-term tracking algorithm, we make the following contributions:

(1) We combine the correlation filter with HOG and CN features, which improve the tracking accuracy.
(2) YOLO v2 is added in tracking system in order to solve drift problem and get better performance.
(3) Using SURF feature points mating algorithm to determine the confidence of the result confidence.
(4) We set up a range of confidence level and train our model to deal with different drift problems according to the range of confidence level.
(5) We formulate a scheme to select the correct target in detection and decide when to update the template.

2 Related Work

Correlation filtering algorithm [1–5] is widely used in tracking area thanks to its ability of fast learning. As a result, KCF [3], DCF [4], CN [5] and other tracking algorithms which are based on correlation filtering are becoming more and more popular. Correlation filtering uses the properties of circulant matrix to solve the ridge regression problem in frequency domain, which greatly speeds up the process. However, these filtering algorithms prefer to adopt artificial feature extraction algorithm, such as HOG [6] features and Gray features.

MOSSE [1] first used Correlation filter as a tool of tracking. It presents a new type of correlation filter, a Minimum Output Sum of Squared Error (MOSSE) filter, which produces stable correlation filters when initialized using a single frame. But the performance of MOSSE is not as good as expected. To get better performance, CSK [2] uses the well-established theory of circulant matrices. It provides a link to Fourier analysis that opens up the possibility of extremely fast learning and detection with the Fast Fourier Transform.

Professor João F. Henriques derived a new Kernelized Correlation Filter (KCF [3]), that greatly improved the speed and accuracy of correlation filter. Building on KCF, they also proposed a fast multichannel extension of linear correlation filters, via a linear kernel, which was called Dual Correlation Filter (DCF [3]).

But in recent years, long-term tracker does not develop as fast as short-term tracker. LCT [7] creatively added a detecting module to the tracker to strengthen the performance of long-term tracking. Also, LCT divided the tracking problem into two parts: the position change and the scale change. However, for some special problems that may occur in the process such as occlusion, LCT did not handle them well. What's more, the detector it combined is not strong enough, making it hard to judge whether the detecting result is reliable.

3 Overview of the Proposed Method

Our tracking task is decomposed into three parts: the correlation filter tracker based on compound feature, the detector of YOLO v2 [8] and the SURF feature points matching part. Using the compound feature, the short-term tracker can perform better. We adopt the SURF feature points matching part to get the similarity of the result and the correct template, if the matching points are not enough, which means that the confidence of the result is to low and we need to enable the detector. With the help of the detection algorithm, the accuracy of the whole tracking algorithm has been greatly improved. The YOLO v2 can select all the targets in the current frame, so we use three-stage cascade selecting mechanism to filter the result and find the most reliable one. If the new target is obtained, we will restart the short-term tracker and update the confidence template to get the latest shape of the target. In general, the whole long-term tracking process is decomposed into multi-step short-term tracking and multiple target re-detecting, which improves the accuracy and robustness of the tracking algorithm.

3.1 Correlation Filter Based on Compound Features

Application of Correlation Filter. The correlation filter target tracking algorithm uses the regularized least squares classifier (RLS classifier) to predict the location of the target.

For all training samples X and expected output Y, the weight W of the classifier is solved by optimizing the target function

$$\min_{w} \sum_{i=1} [f(x_i) - y_i]^2 + \lambda \|\omega\|^2 \tag{1}$$

And the corresponding label data was described by Gaussian function:

$$y(m,n) = e^{\frac{\left(m-\frac{M}{2}\right)^2 + \left(n-\frac{N}{2}\right)^2}{2\sigma^2}} \tag{2}$$

Among them, f is classified function, λ is regularization parameter to prevent overfitting, x_i and y_i denote training samples and expected outputs respectively. In practical applications, mapping the feature space to higher dimensional space can get better classification performance. If the map function is $\varphi(X)$, the weight vector of the classifier will be changed to:

$$W = \sum_I a_i \varphi(x_i) \tag{3}$$

The optimization target is converted to solve:

$$a = \{a_1, a_2, \ldots\}^T \tag{4}$$

Using kernel function can obtain:

$$a = (K + \lambda I)^{-1} Y \tag{5}$$

where I is a unit matrix, and K is a kernel matrix, and the element of the matrix is:

$$K_{ij} = k(x_i, x_j) = <\varphi^T(x_i), \varphi(x_j)> \tag{6}$$

$<,>$ represents the pot product, k is the kernel function. According to the dense sampling algorithm, it can be converted to the Fu Liye frequency domain.

$$\hat{a} = \frac{\hat{y}}{\hat{k}^{xx} + \lambda} \tag{7}$$

F represents Fourier transform. $\kappa(x, x') = \langle \varphi(x), \varphi(x') \rangle$ is the result of the kernel. Y represents the class vector of vector x. We choose the Gauss kernel as the kernel function. The calculation formula is:

$$k^{xx'} = \exp\left\{-\frac{1}{\sigma^2}\left\{\|x^2\| + \|x'\|^2 - 2F^{-1}[F * (x)] \odot F(x')\right\}\right\} \tag{8}$$

To predict the position of the moving target using a pre-trained classifier, we first collect all the positions in the search area as test samples. Then the response outputs of all the test samples are calculated and the new position of the moving target is defined as the position possessing the maximum response output. Specifically, for a given test sample z, the response output $f(z)$ of the classifier can be calculated as

$$f(z) = W^T z = \sum_i^n k(z, x_i) \tag{9}$$

The necessity to compute the response outputs of all the test samples results in a slow computing speed. To tackle this problem, dense sampling algorithm was proposed to perform kernel operations on each test sample in the Fourier Domain and calculate the classifier response output vector of all the test samples as

$$f(Z) = F^{-1}(\hat{K}^{xz} \otimes \hat{a}) \tag{10}$$

Then the location with the maximum response value among all the test samples in response to the vector f(Z) is selected as the next predicted position of the target.

During the object tracking process, the target object can often be affected by the change of the environment. Therefore, the appearance model needs to be updated in time to facilitate the adaptation regarding the change of the target appearance. The parameters updated include both the apparent model parameters for the target (denoted by $\hat{x}$) and the classifier parameters (denoted by $\hat{a}$). The generally adopted linear interpolation method is used to update the parameters, i.e.,

$$\hat{x}^n = (1 - \gamma)\hat{x}^{n-1} + \gamma\hat{x} \tag{11}$$

$$\hat{a}^n = (1 - \gamma)\hat{a}^{n-1} + \gamma\hat{a} \tag{12}$$

where n is the ordinal number of the current frame, γ is the learning rate, $\hat{x}$ represents the apparent model parameters of the predicted position and $\hat{a}$ represents the classifier parameters of the predicted position obtained from the training samples by formula (7).

Compound Features. We combined multiple features in our tracking algorithm to improve the robustness. Considering color information is very significant for visual tracking due to its robustness in illumination, shadows, deformation and so on, we add CN feature to our algorithm. Besides, we also adapt the traditional HOG feature. Because HOG operates on the local grid cell of the image, it can maintain good invariance to the geometric and optical deformation of the image. These two kinds of deformation will only appear in the larger space area.

We proposed a position score function that is a linear combination of color attributes and convolutional features scores:

$$f(\mathbf{x}) = \lambda_{cl}f_{cl}(\mathbf{x}) + \lambda_{hog}f_{hog}(\mathbf{x}) \tag{13}$$

where f_{cl} donates the vote score based on the color attributes and f_{hog} donates the vote score based on convolutional features. λ_{cl} and λ_{hog} are their weighted values, respectively. The two scores are a combinatorial linear function becomes a weighted sum.

Because we use compound features, we can not only extract the shape features of the images, but also extract the color features of the images, which greatly improves the accuracy and robustness of the tracker.

3.2 Selection of Detector

For short-term trackers (such as KCF), the next frame can be easily affected by the previous frame. If the current frame occurs a drift, this problem of drift may be exacerbated in the following frames to affect the performance of a tracking result. In order to alleviate this problem, we add a detection algorithm (Fig. 1).

Fig. 1. The results of YOLO v2

Considering the speed and accuracy of the detection algorithm, we choose a detector called YOLO v2 in our proposed algorithm. Compared with other common detecting algorithms, YOLO v2 performs better, especially on the speed. In the VOC2007 test, the speed of the YOLO v2 algorithm can reach 81FPS with an accurate rate of 73.7%.

3.3   Activation of the Detector According to the Confidence Level

Determination of Confidence. A key problem in our algorithm is when to detect the output target of the tracker. In addition, the detection results are not always correct, and the determination of confidence plays a crucial role in how to select a more reliable result between the result given by detector and another one given by tracker.

We tackle the confidence problem by translating it into the image matching problem in this paper. The higher image matching degree represents higher confidence level. The commonly used image matching algorithms are mainly divided into gray correlation matching and feature based matching. The introduction of SURF [9] feature points matching method can achieve the purpose of image matching.

Similar to Sift [10] feature point matching, SURF also determines the matching degree by calculating the Euclidean distance between two feature points. Shorter Euclidean distance represents higher match degree of two feature points. What differs from Sift feature point matching method is that Surf adds the judgement of the trace of Hessian matrix. If the matrix trace of the two characteristic points is the same, it means that these two features have the same direction contrast change. If the matrix is different, it indicates that the contrast direction of the two feature points is opposite. Through the SURF feature point matching format, we can learn the confidence of the tracking results. More matching points represent higher confidence level.

It is very crucial to select a suitable template to obtain an accurate tracking result. In addition, the determination of the template also directly affects the confidence level. We adopt the method of updating to determine the comparison templates. First, we set the first frame as the current template. Once the detector is activated, the algorithm will compare result given by the detector with another result given by tracker and select the result with higher confidence level to update our template. In this way, the template can be constantly updated to ensure the accuracy of the tracking result.

Threshold Setting. First, we define a range of upper and lower limit of the confidence level according to the performance of the experiments. If the confidence level is above the upper limit, it means that the algorithm is still tracking the correct object and do not need to activate the detector. Otherwise the detector is activated when the confidence level is below the lower limit that the target is lost. However, the confidence level is between the upper and lower limits, there are two possible results:

(1) The target occurs drift, but it's not totally lost.
(2) The tracking target is occluded by some other objects.

For situation 1, we activate the detector to determine the target to track. But as mentioned above, the detector will detect all the objects of the same class in the picture which makes it hard to determine the clear object that we should track. Therefore, we formulate a three-stage cascade selecting mechanism to select the most reliable target.

The multistage selecting mechanism is a central part in our scheme. First, we consider the continuous correlation of object motion, that is, there is no long distance which one object to move from the current frame to the next frame. In that case, we select out the objects that are far away from the tracking target in the current frame. Second, the structural rationality of the object is considered in this paper. The scale changes between two frames should not be very huge. In this way, we also select out

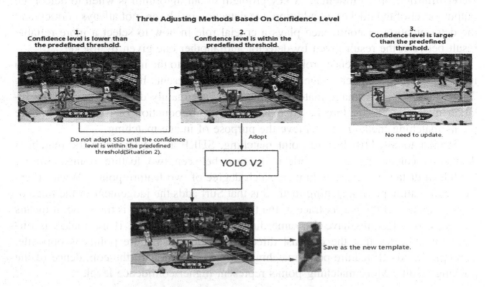

Fig. 2. Three adjusting methods based on confidence level

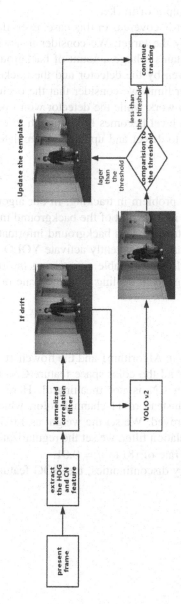

Fig. 3. Flowchart of the long-term tracking algorithm. With the SURF, we can determine the confidence of the result by matching the result with the template. If the confidence is lower than the threshold, we can use the detector to solve the drift problem and if the updated result is reliable, we will update the comparison template, else we will just continue tracking.

some objects whose scale changes too much. Finally, after the above two steps, most of the candidate targets have been selected out and we compare them with the current template using SURF. The target with the highest confidence level will be selected as the output of the detector. The output result is adopted or not depending on the similarity level compared with the output of tracker.

For scenarios 2, the target subject is covered. In this case, even if we activate the detector, it cannot effectively identify the target. We consider that when the target's main body is covered, the target contains a large amount of background information. As a result, the confidence levels given by the detector and the tracker are both very low. If they are both below the upper limit, we consider that the occlusion occurs. In this situation, tracker will continue to work while the detector won't be activated until the occlusion ends. If the confidence level becomes high enough to exceed the upper limit, detector will then be activated to detect and update the templates (Fig. 2).

3.4   The Scale Problem

The scale problem is an unavoidable problem in tracking. In our algorithm, when the target's scale changes, the target will include part of the background information if the tracker don't make appropriate adjustments. This background information will lead to the decrease of the confidence level and consequently activate YOLO V2 to re-detect. And YOLO V2 will change the scale to a suitable size during the detection, which ensures that our algorithm performs good in dealing with the scale problem.

4   Algorithm Process

We show the outline of our algorithm in Algorithm1 and the flowchart in Fig. 3. In this work, the HOG features is 31 bins. And the color space feature(CN) has 11 channels but the color of the 11 channels in CN is not meaningful. Here, we use the 2-dimensional color as representation instead of 11-channel color, which the computational complexity can be greatly improved. We set the weight as 1,0.5 for HOG score map and CN score map. For the correlation filter, we set the regularization parameter of (3) to $\lambda = 10^{-4}$ and set the learning rate of (8) to $\eta = 0.01$.

In addition, to avoid the boundary discontinuities, the HOG features with 31 bins are weighted by a cosine window.

Table 1 Our tracking algorithm.

Inputs: Previous target position P_{i-1} and premade deep
feature template; Position model, and the YOLO v2
detector.

Outputs: target position P_i and current comparison
template; Updated position model.

Repeat

Position estimation

1: Extract HOG features and calculate the response map
    with the correlation filter.

2: Extract CN features and calculate the response map with
    the correlation filter.

3: The final result map is auto weighted stacking.

4: Set T_p to the target position that maximizes y_{posit}

Determinate the confidence of the result

1: Using the SURF to match the current candidate result and
the template.

2: set the good matching point as the confidence value

**Determine whether to enable the detector according to
the confidence**

1: If the confidence of the tracker and the detector is too
low, the target may be lost, then keep detecting until find the
reliable target and restart the algorithm.

2: Else find the most reliable result through three-stage
cascade selecting mechanism and update the template

Until End of video sequence.

---

5 Experimental Results

We implement our tracker in MATLAB R2017a on an Intel Kaby Lake 4 core 2.8 GHz
CPU with 8 GB RAM. We evaluate our method by performing comprehensive
experience in benchmark sequence OTB-13, OTB-15. The trackers are evaluated both
in terms of precision plots and success plots on OPE (one pass evaluation).

5.1 Introduction of the Datasets

In the field of tracking algorithm, more attention is paid to short-term tracking algorithms. Therefore, there is a lack of a sequence of criteria for long-term tracking. The
common sequences of evaluation criteria are OTB [11] and VOT [12]. But the

sequences in VOT is too short to evaluate the long-term tracking algorithm. In comparison, the OTB is more suitable.

5.2   Introduction of Other Contrast Algorithms

At present, the classic tracking algorithms are TLD [13] and LCT. The tracking component of TLD is based on Median-Flow tracker, and the detector of TLD is nearest neighbor classifier. The LCT algorithm upgraded the tracking and detection part. LCT used kernelized correlation filter based on HOG feature as the tracker and used SVM as the detector. Compared with LCT, the TLD doesn't work well. So we did not compare with TLD. Besides, we also compare our algorithm with some short-term tracking algorithms. The contrast algorithms include Staple [14], KCF, Struct [15], VTD [16], VTS [17], CXT [18], LSK [19].

5.3   OTB Results

Figure 4 shows the distance precision rate of one-pass evaluation (OPE) over the videos in the benchmark dataset.

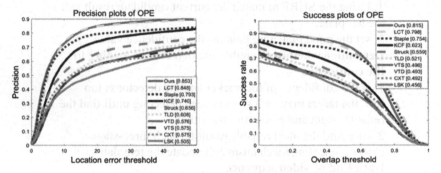

Fig. 4. Distance precision and overlap success plot over benchmark sequences using one-pass evaluation

There are 9 trackers compared with our method. We can see that our algorithm performs well against state-of-the-art trackers. Our method provides a competitive accuracy compared with the other trackers.

Attribute-Base Evaluation. We also evaluate the performance of our method under different video attributes, such as background clutter, occlusion, fast motion and so on. The figure shows the OPE result of our algorithm under these conditions. From the result of we can make some conclusions. First, our method performs very well in the ground clutter while the LCT cannot find the target effectively. LCT both use the correlation filtering algorithm, but we adopt deep features, which can help the tracker distinguish the target from the background better. Besides, our algorithm ranks the first under the occlusion and deformation video attributes because we use YOLO to re-start our trackers, even we lose the target temporarily, we can also find it later. In that case, we can track the target for a long time very well and we can deal with a variety of complex scenes (Fig. 5).

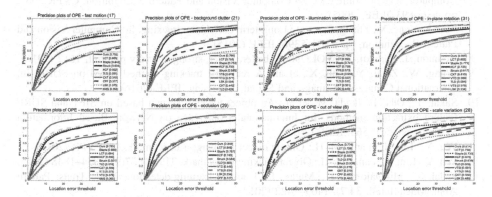

Fig. 5. Distance precision and overlap success plot over benchmark sequences using one-pass evaluation under special conditions

6 Conclusion

In this study, we propose a long-term tracking algorithm, which can track some spatial target, such as a person, for a long time. We combine an object detector and a short-term tracker based on compound feature to track the target and we propose a way to determine the confidence level of the tracking result with the SURF. And the experience shows that our algorithm has high accuracy and strong robustness.

Acknowledgement. Supported by National Natural Science Foundation of China (No. 61471110, 61733003), National Key R&D Program of China (No. 2017YFC0805000/5005), Fundamental Research Funds for the Central Universities (N172608005, N160413002).

References

1. Bolme, D.S., Beveridge, J.R., Draper, B.A., et al.: Visual object tracking using adaptive correlation filters. In: Computer Vision and Pattern Recognition, pp. 2544–2550. IEEE (2010)
2. Henriques, J.F., Caseiro, R., Martins, P., Batista, J.: Exploiting the circulant structure of tracking-by-detection with kernels. In: Fitzgibbon, A., Lazebnik, S., Perona, P., Sato, Y., Schmid, C. (eds.) ECCV 2012. LNCS, vol. 7575, pp. 702–715. Springer, Heidelberg (2012). https://doi.org/10.1007/978-3-642-33765-9_50
3. Henriques, J.F., Caseiro, R., Martins, P., et al.: High-speed tracking with kernelized correlation filters. IEEE Trans. Pattern Anal. Mach. Intell. **37**(3), 583–596 (2015)
4. Song, T.E., Jang, K.H.: Visual tracking using weighted discriminative correlation filter. J. Korea Soc. Comput. Inf. **21**(11), 49–57 (2016)

5. Danelljan, M., Khan, F.S., Felsberg, M., et al.: Adaptive color attributes for real-time visual tracking. In: IEEE Conference on Computer Vision and Pattern Recognition, pp. 1090–1097. IEEE Computer Society (2014)
6. Dalal, N., Triggs, B.: Histograms of oriented gradients for human detection. In: IEEE Computer Society Conference on Computer Vision and Pattern Recognition, CVPR 2005, pp. 886–893. IEEE (2005)
7. Ma, C., Yang, X., Zhang, C., et al.: Long-term correlation tracking. In: Computer Vision and Pattern Recognition, pp. 5388–5396. IEEE (2015)
8. Redmon, J., Farhadi, A.: YOLO9000: better, faster, stronger. arXiv preprint, 1612 (2016)
9. Wang, W., Zhou, Y., Zhu, X., et al.: A real-time tracking method based on SURF. In: International Congress on Image and Signal Processing. IEEE (2016)
10. Sakai, Y., Oda, T., Ikeda, M., et al.: An object tracking system based on SIFT and SURF feature extraction methods. In: International Conference on Network-Based Information Systems, pp. 561–565. IEEE (2015)
11. Wu, Y., Lim, J., Yang, M.-H.: Online object tracking: a benchmark. In: CVPR (2013)
12. Wu, Y., Lim, J., Yang, M.-H.: Object tracking benchmark. TPAMI 37(9), 1834–1848 (2015)
13. Kalal, Z., Mikolajczyk, K., Matas, J.: Tracking-learning-detection. IEEE Trans. Pattern Anal. Mach. Intell. 34(7), 1409–1422 (2012)
14. Bertinetto, L., Valmadre, J., Golodetz, S., et al.: Staple: complementary learners for real-time tracking, 38(2), 1401–1409 (2015)
15. Hare, S., Saffari, A., Torr, P.H.S.: Struck: structured output tracking with kernels. In: International Conference on Computer Vision, pp. 263–270. IEEE Computer Society (2011)
16. Kwon, J., Lee, K.M.: Visual tracking decomposition. In: Computer Vision and Pattern Recognition, pp. 1269–1276. IEEE (2010)
17. Dinh, T.B., Vo, N., Medioni, G.: Context tracker: exploring supporters and distracters in unconstrained environments. In: Computer Vision and Pattern Recognition, pp. 1177–1184. IEEE (2011)
18. Kwon, J., Lee, K.M.: Tracking by sampling trackers. In: IEEE International Conference on Computer Vision, pp. 1195–1202. IEEE (2011)
19. Liu, B., Huang, J., Yang, L., et al.: Robust tracking using local sparse appearance model and K-selection. In: IEEE Conference on Computer Vision and Pattern Recognition, pp. 1313–1320. IEEE Computer Society (2011)

An Image Retrieval Method Based on Color and Texture Features for Dermoscopy Images

Xuedong Song[1], Fengying Xie[1(✉)], Jie Liu[2], and Chang Shu[2]

[1] Beijing Advanced Innovation Center for Biomedical Engineering, Image Processing Center, Beihang University, Beijing 100083, China
{owensong,xfy_73}@buaa.edu.cn

[2] Department of Dermatology, Peking Union Medical College Hospital, Beijing 100730, China

Abstract. Dermoscopy image retrieval can assist dermatologists to make a diagnosis by reference to confirmed cases, which can improve the accuracy of the diagnosis result. This paper proposed a retrieve method based on the combination of color and texture. The proposed method uses the color moments and Gabor wavelet to extract features and implements retrieval function by SKLSH hash code. In the experiments stage, we retrieve dermoscopy images including 4 kinds of skin diseases from the datasets which are pigmented nevus, seborrheic keratosis, psoriasis and eczema. Besides, we compared our methods with other color and texture features, as well as other dermoscopy image retrieval method, and the results show that our method obtains the best retrieval result.

Keywords: Dermoscopy image · Image retrieve · Computer-aided diagnosis
Color feature · Texture feature

1 Introduction

Skin is the largest organ and contacts with the outside world frequently and close. Skin diseases make people uncomfortable and may cause chronic disabilities, even threatening life [1]. Dermoscopy is a non-invasive microscopic image analysis technique which allows doctor observing the subsurface structures [2]. It is an effective auxiliary diagnosis tool for detection of a variety of skin diseases [3]. But it is subjective and easy to cause eye fatigue for observing the skin lesion by naked eye. By contrast, computer aided dermoscopy image analysis system is objective and repeatable, which can assist dermatologists to make a diagnosis [4].

Formerly, researches about dermoscopy image processing technique almost focused on the segmentation and classification of skin lesion. In 2012, Sadri et al., from Isfahan University, used wavelet network to segment the skin lesion in dermoscopy images [5]. In 2017, Yang et al., from Institute of High Performance Computing, Singapore, used a multi-task deep neural network to achieve the lesion segmentation and two independent

This work was supported by the National Natural Science Foundation of China under Grants 61471016.

© Springer Nature Singapore Pte Ltd. 2018
Y. Wang et al. (Eds.): IGTA 2018, CCIS 875, pp. 403–410, 2018.
https://doi.org/10.1007/978-981-13-1702-6_40

binary lesion classifications at the same time [6]. In 2008, Cheng et al. achieved a classification accuracy of 86% for detecting malignant melanoma by using the best features of some relative color features [7]. The above methods are usually processed based on different data sets, and the test images are small sample size. In 2017, Stanford university collected 130000 dermoscopy images and clinical images. The same year [8], Esteva et al., from Stanford University Artificial Intelligence Laboratory, used a deep convolutional neural network (CNN) to achieve a dermatologist-level classification of skin diseases. They validate the algorithm using a three-class disease partition and a nine-class disease partition, achieving 72.1% and 55.4% overall accuracy respectively. This research makes dermoscopy image computer-aided diagnostic technique being extended to multi-classification task. Our group member, Zhou [4], proposed a novel dermoscopy image classification method based on CNN with residual structures, which can classify 6 kinds of lesion skin diseases. Their works allowed the dermoscopy images analysis diagnosis technique to make great progress. But as far as I know, at present there is no computer aided diagnosis system which meets the standard of clinical application.

A reliable dermoscopy image retrieval system can effectively assist dermatologists in diagnosing [9]. With the development of the dermoscopy image processing technique, in recent years, the retrieval system of dermoscopy image began to arouse people's attention. In 2006, Rahman et al. presented a content-based image retrieval system for dermoscopy image as a diagnostic aid to the dermatologists for skin cancer recognition [1]. In 2016, Sun proposed a pigmented skin image retrieval system based on the content, deep convolutional neural network and deep semantic hash [10]. Compared with the classification of dermoscopy image, there are not so much researches about dermoscopy image retrieval research. The Existing retrieval accuracy is not high, which has plenty of room for improvement.

In this paper, a highly robust dermoscopy images retrieval method based on low-level features is proposed. We aimed at these four common skin disease, which are pigmented nevus, seborrheic keratosis, psoriasis and eczema. Based on traditional methods of image feature extraction, we designed an optimal feature combination, which includes features of color and texture. (In addition, we proposed an effective hash code method to achieve the rapid retrieval function). With 0.6180 retrieval accuracy, our method outperforms other traditional low-level features.

The rest of this paper is organized as follows: Sect. 2.1 introduces the methods of extracting features. Section 2.2 introduces the methods of retrieve. Section 3 lists the experiments, results and analysis. Section 4 presents our conclusions.

2   Proposed Method

As the different skin diseases are different in colors and textures, the method we proposed based on extracting the color and texture features through color moments and Gabor filtering, which has a better retrieval performance than other low-level features or their combinations. Color feature is one of the most widely used features in image retrieval and texture feature provides important information of the image [11].

2.1 Feature Extraction

Color Moments [12]. Color moments has no relationship with image's size, orientation and viewing angle, which has high robustness. The first moment, the second central moment and the central third moment can effectively express the image of color distribution. We implement this approach by calculating the first three moments of each color channel of a RGB image. If the value of the i-th color channel at the j-th image pixel is $p_{i,j}$, then the first moment (μ_i), the second central moment (σ_i) and the central third moment (s_i) are defined as:

$$\mu_i = \frac{1}{N} \sum_{j=1}^{N} p_{i,j} \tag{1}$$

$$\sigma_i = \left(\frac{1}{N} \sum_{j=1}^{N} \left(p_{i,j} - \mu_i \right)^2 \right)^{\frac{1}{2}} \tag{2}$$

$$s_i = \left(\frac{1}{N} \sum_{j=1}^{N} \left(p_{i,j} - \mu_i \right)^3 \right)^{\frac{1}{3}} \tag{3}$$

Then we can have 9 floating point numbers as a feature vector.

Gabor Wavelet [13]. Gabor filter which can extract spatial local frequency characteristics is an effective tool to detecting texture. Gabor filter consist of Gaussian kernel function in the two-dimensional spatial domain. Gabor filter is a sinusoidal plane wave that is formulated as follow:

$$G(x, y) = \exp\left(-\frac{x'^2 + \gamma^2 y'^2}{2\sigma^2} \right) \exp\left(i2\pi \frac{x'}{\lambda} + \psi \right) \tag{4}$$

Where:

$$y' = x\cos\theta + y\sin\theta \tag{5}$$

$$x' = -x\sin\theta + y\cos\theta \tag{6}$$

G is Gabor filter kernel at spatial coordinate x, y with a certain dimension, and the other parameters described as:

- σ: standard deviation
- ψ: phase offset
- θ: waves orientation
- γ: aspect ratio
- λ: wavelength of sinusoidal factor
- i: complex number (a + bi)

In this paper, we just compute the imaginary part separately. Afterwards, we compute the convolution of the original images with the imaginary part of Gabor kernel. The imaginary part of Gabor kernel is formulated as follow:

$$G_{imag}(x, y) = \exp\left(-\frac{x'^2 + \gamma^2 y'^2}{2\sigma^2}\right) \cos\left(2\pi\frac{x'}{\lambda} + \psi\right) \tag{7}$$

The Gabor kernel we used uses 5 scales and 6 orientations as follow (Fig. 1):

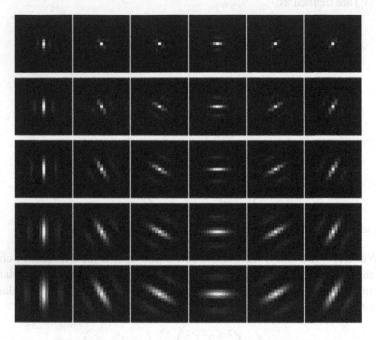

Fig. 1. Gabor Kernel using 5 Scales and 6 orientations

Then we computed the mean and the variance value of these result images of the convolution of the original images with the imaginary part of Gabor kernel. So we have 60-dimensional feature vector. Because of the information redundancy, we reduced dimensions to 6 (99% contribution) dimensions based on Principle Component Analysis (PCA).

Finally, we put the color moments (9-dimensions) and the texture feature (6-dimensions) together, which consist of a 15-dimensions feature vector.

2.2 Retrieve Method Based on Hashing Codes

Because of the large-scale of the retrieval system's database and the large amount of calculation of retrieving images, retrieving image has high real-time requirements. It is essential to retrieve the interested content from huge amounts of data rapidly. Hash code can map high-dimensional features to hamming space, which is convenient to calculate the hamming distance by bitwise operation [14].

We chose the locality-sensitive binary codes from shift-invariant kernels (SKLSH) [15] to map the features to hamming space. This method is based on the random features mapping for approximating shift-invariant kernels. Given a Gaussian kernel

$$K(s) = \exp\left(-\frac{\gamma \|s\|^2}{2}\right) \tag{8}$$

we can get the random map $F_{t,\omega,b} : R^D \rightarrow \{0, 1\}$ through

$$F_{t,\omega,b}(x) \triangleq \frac{1}{2}\left[1 + Q_t(\cos(\omega \cdot x + b))\right] \tag{9}$$

where $t \sim \text{Unif}[-1, 1]$, $\omega \sim P_K$, $b \sim \text{Unif}[0, 2\pi]$ and $Q_t : [-1, 1] \rightarrow \{-1, +1\}$ via $Q_t(u) \triangleq sgn(u + t)$, where we let $sgn(u) = -1$ if $u < 0$ and $sgn(u) = +1$ if $u \geq 0$.

3 Experiments Results and Analysis

A series of experiments are conducted using MATLAB 2014 on Win10 with i7 2.50 GHz quad-core CPU and 8 GB RAM. Our image datasets are selected from the Beijing Union Medical College Hospital's dermoscopy images, which contains pigmented nevus,

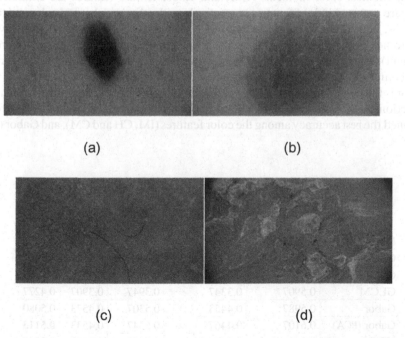

(a)   (b)

(c)   (d)

Fig. 2. Dermoscopy Images with 1872 × 1053 pixels (a) pigmented nevus; (b) seborrheic keratosis; (c) psoriasis; (d) eczema

seborrheic keratosis, psoriasis and eczema, as shown in Fig. 2. There are 700 images of each skin disease and 2800 images totally, which are solution of 1872×1053 pixels. The ground truths (GT) of the images in the datasets are obtained from an experienced dermatologist.

To evaluate the performance of our retrieve method, mean average accuracy of top-k retrieval images is used, which is defined as (Table 1):

$$\text{mean Average Accuracy} = \frac{TP}{TP + FP} = \frac{TP}{k} \tag{10}$$

Table 1. Definitions of True/False Positive/Negative

Ground truth image	Retrieval image	
	True	False
True	True Positive (TP)	False Negative (FN)
False	False Positive (FP)	True Negative (TN)

A satisfactory retrieve method has high values of mean average accuracy of top-k retrieval images.

3.1   Comparison with Other Common Features

In our method, color moments (CM) and Gabor texture features are extracted. We compare our two kinds of features respectively with other widely used color and texture features, which contain color histogram (CH), Invariant Moments (IM), gray level co-occurrence matrix (GLCM). At the same time, the popular HOG (histogram of oriented gradient) feature and SIFT+BOW (scale invariant feature transform, bag of word) are also compared. Table 2 gives the accuracy by different features on the dataset, where Gabor is the 60-dimensional feature vector and Gabor (PCA) is the result of dimensional reduction by PCA, and the latter is used in our method. It can be seen that CM feature obtained the best accuracy among the color features (IM, CH and CM), and Gabor (PCA)

Table 2. The average accuracy of using different single features

	Pigmented Nevus	Seborrheic Keratosis	Psoriasis	Eczema	Average accuracy
IM	0.7533	0.2787	0.4480	0.1013	0.3953
CH	0.6413	0.5680	0.4760	0.4813	0.5417
CM	0.6573	0.5333	0.5920	0.4933	**0.5690**
GLCM	0.5907	0.3347	0.3947	0.3907	0.4277
Gabor	0.5987	0.4453	0.5307	0.4573	0.5080
Gabor (PCA)	0.6107	0.4467	0.5347	0.4533	**0.5113**
HOG	0.2440	0.2640	0.2453	0.2653	0.2547
SIFT (BOW)	0.3480	0.3173	0.4573	0.4747	0.3993

obtained better accuracy than other texture features (GLCM and Gabor without PCA dimensional reduction). And the other two popular features HOG and SIFT+BOW obtained a lower accuracy compared with these color and texture features. In addition, limited by the paper space, we just list the mean average accuracy of top-5 retrieval images.

We combine the CM features with Gabor (PCA) features together, and compare them with other color and texture feature combination. The results are given in Table 3. It can be seen that when combining color feature with texture features, the retrieval performance can be improved. And with 63.37% of accuracy, our combination has the highest retrieval accuracy in these different combination.

Table 3. The average accuracy of our method and other feature's combinations

	Pigmented Nevus	Seborrheic Keratosis	Psoriasis	Eczema	Average accuracy
CM & Gabor	0.6533	0.5827	0.5733	0.4987	0.5770
CM & GLCM	0.7053	0.5213	0.5880	0.5107	0.5813
CH & Gabor	0.6920	0.5560	0.5173	0.4840	0.5623
CH & GLCM	0.6880	0.5653	0.5253	0.4493	0.5570
Ours	0.7667	0.6120	0.6440	0.5120	**0.6337**

3.2 Comparison with Another Method

Compared with the classification of dermoscopy images, the literature about dermoscopy image retrieval is very few. In [10], Sun proposed two dermoscopy image retrieval methods which are based on multi-features combination and deep learning respectively. Since our features are extracted using traditional method, we compared our method with Sun's multi-features combination method, which combines Gabor, local binary patterns (LBP) and edgehistogram (EH) together through weight coefficient, and used Euclidean metric to retrieve the images. The result is shown in Table 4. It can be seen that Sun's method only obtained the accuracy of 48.90%, while our method yielded the accuracy of 63.37%. Therefore, our method greatly outperforms the compared method.

Table 4. The average accuracy of our method and Sun's

	Pigmented Nevus	Seborrheic Keratosis	Psoriasis	Eczema	Average accuracy
Sun's	0.7587	0.4227	0.3933	0.3813	0.4890
Ours	0.7667	0.6120	0.6440	0.5120	**0.6337**

4 Conclusions

A novel retrieve method based on the combination of color and texture is proposed for dermoscopy images in this paper. The proposed method is able to extract high robust features, map the features to a binary code by SKLSH and retrieve similar images in appearance to one that is given as a query. For these four kinds of skin disease including pigmented nevus, seborrheic keratosis, psoriasis and eczema, the proposed method has the better retrieval performance than the compared method. Besides, due to the small datasets, the improvement of retrieval speed by hash code is not obvious. In the future, we will expand the size of datasets to analyze the retrieval performance through different hash code methods.

References

1. Rahman, M.M., Desai, B.C., Bhattacharya, P.: Image retrieval-based decision support system for dermatoscopic images. In: Computer Society, pp. 285–290 (2006)
2. Sabbaghi, S., Aldeen, M., et al.: A deep bag-of-features model for the classification of melanomas in dermoscopy images. Eng. Med. Biol. Soc. 16–20 (2016)
3. Menizies, S., Crotty, K., McCarthy, W., et al.: An Atlas of Surface Micorscopy of Pigmented Skin Lesion: Dermoscopy, 2nd edn. The McGraw-Hill Companies Inc., New York (2003)
4. Zhou, H., Xie, F., Jiang, Z., et al.: Multi-classification of skin diseases for dermoscopy images using deep learning. Imaging Syst. Tech. 1–5 (2017)
5. Sadri, A.R., Zekri, M., et al.: Segmentation of dermoscopy images using wavelet networks. Bio-med. Eng. 60, 1131–1141 (2012)
6. Yang, X., Zen, Z., Yeo, S.Y., et al.: A novel multi-task deep learning model for skin lesion segmentation and classification. In: Computer Vision and Pattern Recognition, pp. 1025–1028 (2017)
7. Cheng, Y.I., Swamisai, R., Umbaugh, S.E., et al.: Skin lesion classification using relative color features. Skin Res. Technol. 14, 53–64 (2008)
8. Esteva, A., Kuprel, B., Novoa, R.A., et al.: Dermatologist-level classification of skin cancer with deep neural networks. Nature 542, 115–118 (2017)
9. Baldi, A., Murace, R., Dragonetti, E., et al.: CBIR system for dermoscopy images. Bio-med. Eng. 8, 8–18 (2009)
10. Sun, Y.: Research of Processing and Content-Retrieval Based on the Images of Pigmented Skin Lesions. University of Electronic Science and Technology of China, Chengdu, Sichuan, China (2016)
11. Liu, Y., Zhang, D., et al.: A survey of content-based image retrieval with high-level semantics. Pattern Recogn. 40, 262–282 (2007)
12. Stricker, M., Orengo, M.: Similarity of color images. In: SPIE Proceedings, pp. 381–392 (1995)
13. Nurhadiyatna, A., Latifah, A.L., et al.: Gabor filtering for feature extraction in real time vehicle classification system. In: International Symposium on Image and Signal Processing and Analysis, pp. 19–24 (2015)
14. Maithiili, K., Elakkiy, P., et al.: Content based image retrieval with hash codes. Int. J. Adv. Res. Comput. Eng. Technol. 4, 1292–1295 (2015)
15. Raginsky, M., Lazebnik, S., et al.: Locality-sensitive binary codes from shift-invariant kernels. In: Neural Information Processing Systems, pp. 1509–1517 (2009)

A Discriminative Feature Learning Based on Deep Residual Network for Face Verification

Tong Zhang, Rong Wang[✉], and Jianwei Ding

People's Public Security University of China, Beijing, China
jwxxzt@gmail.com, dbdxwangrong@163.com

Abstract. The face verification system based on deep convolutional neural networks (DCNNs) has achieved great success. The architecture of existing methods is somehow shallow because of the insufficient convolutional layers. And the softmax loss function does not enlarge inter-class variations and minimize the intra-class variations. In this paper, a residual network was adopted as the core architecture to extract the discriminative features and it was trained with joint supervision of center loss and softmax loss. The public available CASIA-Webface dataset was used as the training data to train our model for face verification, and the model was tested on LFW and CAS-PEAL-R1 datasets. Experimental results show that our method achieves higher accuracy on LFW and has better robustness than the shallow model such as VGG Face.

Keywords: Convolutional neural network · Face verification
Residual network · Center loss

1 Introduction

Convolutional neural network (CNNs) have advanced the computer vision in these decades, achieving state-of-art performance in various tasks, such as image classification [1, 2], object detection [3, 4], object segmentation [5, 6], object tracking [7] and so on. In the filed of face recognition, CNNs have already surpassed human-level performance on several face benchmarks [8, 9].

The general pipeline for face verification application consists of detecting face and facial landmarks, face aligning, extracting and features comparing. It is essential to make the intra-class features closer with each other and inter-class features further apart from each other. To solve this problem, researchers have adopted two strategies.

As for the first approach, different CNNs architectures are used to extract the discriminative features across categories and the polymerized features with only one class. Taigman et al. [9] designed 2 convolutional layers, 1 max-pooling layers, 3 subsequent layers and 2 fully-connected layers to train the DeepFace model. The DeepID series proposed by Sun et al. [11–13] (except DeepID3 [13]) is composed of 4 convolutional layers. Schroff et al. [14] used Zeiler and Fergus [15] style networks and Inception [16] type networks as the core architectures. Parkhi et al. [17] used the VGG

© Springer Nature Singapore Pte Ltd. 2018
Y. Wang et al. (Eds.): IGTA 2018, CCIS 875, pp. 411–420, 2018.
https://doi.org/10.1007/978-981-13-1702-6_41

[18] to accomplish the face verifications. Liu et al. [19] proposed the Sphereface model with the ResNet [2] type network as the basic framework.

In the second approach, different loss functions were proposed to improve the performance of face verification by decreasing the distance of positive pair features and enlarging the distance of negative pair features. Most of the methods [9, 12, 17] train deep convolutional neural network with softmax loss. Sun proposed the contrastive loss [12] to enhance the discrimination power of features. Schroff et al. [14] adopted the triplet loss to separate the positive pair from the negative one by a distance margin and decrease the positive pair's distance. Wen et al. [20] combined the softmax loss with center loss to train the CNNs. The softmax loss enlarges the inter-class variations and the center loss minimizes the intra-class variations.

Deep convolutional neural networks (DCNNs) can make low/middle/high level features more rich and discriminative. A recent research [19] proved that the ResNet style architecture can be easily trained and achieved state-of-art performance in face verification. To explore the performance of deep residual neural networks in face verification tasks, we used the ResNet-64 as the core architecture to extract the facial features and use the loss function which combines the softmax loss with center loss to learn the polymerized features in one class and discriminative features across categories. We test our model on LFW benchmark and it obtains 98.25% accuracy. In order to demonstrate its effectiveness, we evaluated it on different challenging face verification tasks, such as pose-aware face verification on CAS-PEAL-R1 dataset. The result shows that our model achieves higher accuracy than VGG Face and indicates that our model achieves very competitive results.

The subsequent of this paper is organized as follows: We introduce our model in Sect. 2. In Sect. 3, we perform experiment, present results, analysis and compare our method with others. Finally, we draw the conclusions and discuss future research in Sect. 4.

2 Proposed Method

The pipeline for training face verification system using our method is shown in Fig. 1. Before training the network, we use the MTCNN algorithm [21] to process the face images from the CASIA-Web face dataset [22] as the training datasets. Given the processed face images and corresponding labels, the ResNet-64 DCNNs is trained as classification task and the network learns the facial features through a simple face image. And the combination of center loss and softmax loss is used for training the network.

In the testing phase, feature $f(x_p)$ and $f(x_n)$ are extracted by the pair of test face images x_p and x_n which are from LFW face datasets [8] using trained ResNet-64 CNNs and normalized to vectors. Then, the similarity score is computed on the feature vector by cosine distance, as given Eq. 1. If the similarity score is greater than the threshold, the face pairs are the same person:

$$s = \frac{f(x_p)^T f(x_n)}{\left\|f(x_p)\right\|_2 \left\|f(x_n)\right\|_2}. \tag{1}$$

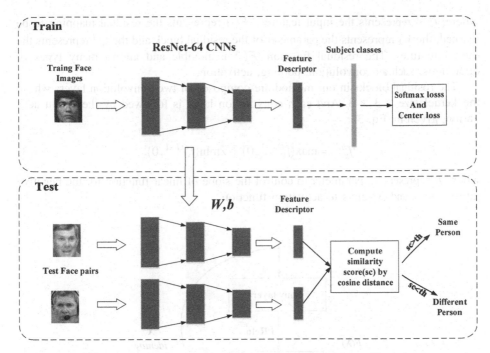

Fig. 1. The pipeline of our methods for training and testing a face verification system, using ResNet-64 CNNs as core architecture and combining center loss with sofmax loss as loss function.

2.1   CNNs Architecture

A recent study [16] shows that the CNNs depth is very important and a deeper CNN could achieve better result on the challenge ImageNet dataset [23]. However, with the network depth increasing, the complexity of the network is also increasing, which makes the network harder to converge and the accuracy gets saturated then degrades rapidly. The residual type network [2] provides a solution to these problems.

Instead of stacking the layers directly, the residual learning framework provides the shortcut connections, as shown in Fig. 2. And the shortcut connections are the type of skipping one or more layers' connections.

The underlying mapping in the common CNNs is $\mathcal{H}(x)$ and the residual learning mapping fits $\mathcal{F}(x) := \mathcal{H}(x) - x$. Therefore, the original mapping is formulated as $\mathcal{F}(x) + x$ which is implemented with identity mapping. Identity shortcut connections don't need extra parameter or computation can be easily trained by SGD backpropagation. In the residual mapping, the input features are added to the outputs of the stacked layers $\mathcal{F}(x)$. Finally, the residual block output can be showed as Eq. 2:

$$f_x^{R,l} = f_x^{l-p} + \mathcal{F}(f_x^{l-p}, \{W_k\}). \tag{2}$$

where, f_x^{l-p} represents the input features, $\mathcal{F}(\cdot)$ represents the residual mapping to be learned, the W_k represents the parameter of the residual block and the $f_x^{R,l}$ represents the output features. The residual function $\mathcal{F}(\cdot)$ is flexible and allows many types of operations, such as convolution, pooling, activation.

The residual blocks in our method are composed of two convolution layers whose the kernel size is 3×3. And each convolution layer is followed by the PRelu activation, given by Eq. 3.

$$f_x^{A,l} = \max(f_x^{O,l-1}, 0) + \lambda \min(f_x^{O,l-1}, 0). \tag{3}$$

where λ represents a parameter to control the slope of linear function for the negative input values and A refers to activation function.

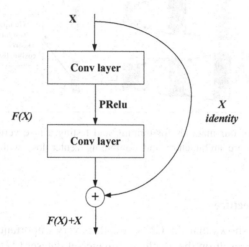

Fig. 2. Residual learning framework: shortcut connections.

2.2 Loss Function

The DCNNs are trained by loss function. The softmax loss is common used as the loss function to train the network and can be easily implemented in deep learning framework such as Caffe [24] and Tensorflow [25]. The extracted features are more separable for face verification without any extra methods and make the network converge quickly. However, it ignores the intra-class similarity and fails to meet the verification need of enlarging the inter-class variations and minimizing the intra-class variations. So many researchers adopted metrics learning on top of features extracted by softmax loss or trained with other types of loss function, such as contrastive loss, triplet loss, center loss and so on. The contrastive loss and triplets can affect the learning of polymerized feature in one class in some extent. However, they are not easily to implemented and have some restrictions on the input images and batch size. They respectively implemented loss for image pairs and triplet which made the results converge slowly and instability. Recent research [20] proposed center loss to learn polymerized features more powerfully. Besides, it can be easily implemented, converges quickly and have stable result. And it achieved better performance in face verification. So in this paper, we combine the center loss with softmax loss to train the model.

The softmax loss encourages the separability of features and is widely used for classification:

$$\mathcal{L}_{softmax} = -\frac{1}{M}\sum_{i=1}^{M} \log \frac{e^{W_{y_i}^T f(x_i) + b_{y_i}}}{\sum_{j=1}^{C} e^{W_j^T f(x_i) + b_j}}. \tag{4}$$

where M is the training batch size, C refers to the number of classes, x_i refers the ith input face image in the batch, $f(x_i)$ refers output of the penultimate layer of the DCNN, y_j is the corresponding the real category label, and W_j, b_j refer to the weights and bias for the last layer of network.

Table 1. Architecture of our model.

Layer name	Our model (Input 3 × 112 × 96)	Output size
conv1	3 × 3, 64 conv, stride 2, pad 1	56 × 48
conv1_x	$\begin{pmatrix} 3 \times 3, 64 \\ 3 \times 3, 64 \end{pmatrix} \times 3$	56 × 48
conv2	3 × 3, 128 conv, stride 2, pad 1	28 × 24
conv2_x	$\begin{pmatrix} 3 \times 3, 128 \\ 3 \times 3, 128 \end{pmatrix} \times 7$	28 × 24
conv3	3 × 3, 256 conv, stride 2, pad 1	14 × 12
conv3_x	$\begin{pmatrix} 3 \times 3, 256 \\ 3 \times 3, 256 \end{pmatrix} \times 16$	14 × 12
conv4	3 × 3, 512 conv, stride 2, pad 1	7 × 6
conv4_x	$\begin{pmatrix} 3 \times 3, 512 \\ 3 \times 3, 512 \end{pmatrix} \times 3$	7 × 6
Classification layer	Fully connected layer, softmax+center loss	1 × 1

The center loss minimizes the intra-class distance while keeping the features of different categories separable. The center is computed by averaging the corresponding category features during each iteration. We set a hyperparameter α to control the learning rate of the center to avoid the influence taken by the mislabeled samples. The center loss is formulated in Eq. 5:

$$\mathcal{L}_{center} = \frac{1}{2}\sum_{i=1}^{M} \left\| x_i - c_{y_i} \right\|_2^2 \tag{5}$$

where c_{y_i} denotes the center of the feature of the y_i class, x_i denotes the feature of the ith class and m denotes the number of mini-batch.

We combine the center loss with softmax loss as supervision signal to train DCNNs and the λ is used to balance two loss functions. The formulation is given in Eq. 6:

$$\mathcal{L} = \mathcal{L}_{softmax} + \mathcal{L}_{center} = -\frac{1}{M}\sum_{i=1}^{M}\log\frac{e^{W_{y_i}^T f(x_i)+b_{y_i}}}{\sum_{j=1}^{C}e^{W_j^T f(x_i)+b_j}} + \frac{1}{2}\sum_{i=1}^{M}\left\|x_i - c_{y_i}\right\|_2^2. \quad (6)$$

Our CNNs model use the residual learning framework as the core architecture and consist of 62 convolution layers and 2 fully connected layers. Each kernel size of convolution layer is 3×3 and each convolution layer is followed by PRelu activation function. We use a 512 neurons fully connected layer after the last convolutional layer. Finally, we adopt the joint softmax loss with center loss as supervision signal to computer and optimize loss. Our model is given fully details in Table 1.

3 Experiments

In this section, we use the MTCNN algorithm to process the images and train our model on CASIA-WebFace dataset. Then, we use the pre-trained model to exact the facial feature and perform face verification. For verifying the effectiveness, the model is tested on several datasets, such as LFW and CAS-PEAL-R1.

3.1 Implementation Details

Processing. Before training, the face images and landmarks are detected by the MTCNN algorithms which is proposed in [21]. We use 5 landmarks (two eyes, two mouth corners and nose) to process the similarity transformation. If the image in the training datasets fails to be detected, it will be removed from the datasets. When the image is in testing datasets, it will be detected by the landmarks which are provided in the datasets. All the face images are cropped to $112 \times 96 \times 3$ RGB images. And each image is normalized by subtracting 127.5 and dividing by 128.

Training. We implement our model on caffe [24] and use the public available web-collected dataset CASIA-WebFace [22] to train our model. CASIA-WebFace dataset contains 494,414 images of 10,572 subjects. The dataset is cleaned using the multi-task cascaded convolutional network (MTCNN) algorithm mentioned in [21]. In the training phase, all face images are horizontally flipped for data augmentation and only use 10,572 individuals because there are three identities appearing in testing dataset. Compared with FaceNet [14] (200M), VGGFace [17] (2M) and DeepFace [9] (4M), the training data(0.49) which we use is a small scale training set. The model is trained with batch size of 64 because of the GPU memory limitations on one Nvidia 1080Ti GPU. We use the SGD to train our model and the momentum is set to 0.9. The learning rate begins with 0.1 and is divided by 10 at the 6k, 30k iterations. And the model is finished at 50k iterations.

3.2   Experiments on LFW

The LFW dataset [8] consists of 13,233 images of 5,759 different identities, with large variations of pose, expression and illuminations. All the images are collected from the Internet. We follow the unrestricted labeled outside data protocols on LFW and test on 6,000 face pairs which are divided into 10 folds and report the accuracy in Table 2.

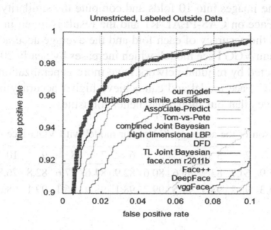

Fig. 3. ROC curve of face verification on LFW.

Table 2. Accuracy on LFW of our method (%)

Fold	1	2	3	4	5	6	7	8	9	10	AVE
ACC	98.33	97.84	97.83	97.67	97.00	98.33	98.50	97.83	99.67	99.50	98.25

Table 3. Verification performance of different methods on LFW

Method	Datasets	Net	Acc %
DeepFace	4M	3	97.35
FaceNet	200M	1	99.65
DeepID2+	300K	1	98.70
VGG Face	2.6M	1	98.00
Softmax loss	WebFace	1	97.88
Our method	**WebFace**	**1**	**98.25**

Table 3 and Fig. 3 provide the results of our method compared with others and our method achieves significant accuracy, despite the fact that Facenet and DeepID2+ used 200M and 300K images to obtain 99.65% and 98.70%, whereas the number of images in our experiment is 0.49M. Our method achieves more than human performance (97.53%) and the results confirm the validity of our model.

3.3   Experiments om CAS-PEAL-R1

The CAS-PEAL-R1 is a large-scale Chinese face dataset which contains 30,863 images of 1040 individuals (595 males and 445 females). All images are controlled by pose, expression, accessory and lighting variations. We use the POSE dataset consists of 21,840 images of 1040 individuals as the test dataset to verify the robustness of our model. For each individual, images across 21 different poses and the images are all gray. We divide the images into 10 folds and compute the similarity. We evaluate our model and VGG Face on CAS-PEAL-R1 and the result is given in Table 4.

Table 4 shows the accuracy of each fold and the average accuracy of our model in dataset is higher than VGG Face model, which increases by nearly 20%. It indicates the face features extracted by residual network have more generalization than the shallow model such as VGG Face model and can achieve higher accuracy in pose-aware face verification. It proves that our model has better robustness.

Table 4. Comparison of the accuracy (%) of our model with VGG face on CAS-PEAL-R1

Fold	1	2	3	4	5	6	7	8	9	10	AVE
VGG	65.9	64.7	83.9	85.6	80.6	82.9	84.6	77.6	82.8	76.8	78.5
Our	96.3	98.2	98.3	99.5	99.2	98.1	98.9	96.1	99.1	98.0	98.2

4   Conclusion

In this paper, we proposed a face verification model which was based on residual network and trained by the joint supervision of center loss and softmax loss. The residual learning framework can learn the rich features and the loss function which combines center loss with softmax loss can learn the discriminative features across categories and polymerized features in one class. We tested our model in LFW and CAS-PEAL-R1 datasets. The experimental results showed that our method has achieved competitive performance and demonstrated the superiority and great potentials. In the future, we will continue to improve the network architecture, using larger face datasets to improve the accuracy and to explore its applicability in different missions.

Acknowledgments. This work is supported by National Key Research and Development Plan under Grant No. 2016YFC0801005 and the National Nature Science Foundation of China (Grant No. 61503388).

References

1. Krizhevsky, A., Sutskever, I., Hinton, G.E.: ImageNet classification with deep convolutional neural networks. In: Advances in Neural Information Processing Systems, pp. 1097–1105 (2012)
2. He, K., Zhang, X., Ren, S., et al.: Deep residual learning for image recognition. In: Proceedings of the IEEE Conference on Computer Vision and Pattern Recognition, pp. 770–778 (2016)

3. Girshick, R., Donahue, J., Darrell, T., et al.: Rich feature hierarchies for accurate object detection and semantic segmentation. In: Proceedings of the IEEE Conference on Computer Vision and Pattern Recognition, pp. 580–587. IEEE Press (2014)
4. Redmon, J., Divvala, S., Girshick, R., et al.: You only look once: unified, real-time object detection. In: Proceedings of the IEEE Conference on Computer Vision and Pattern Recognition, pp. 779–788. IEEE Press (2016)
5. He, K., Gkioxari, G., Dollár, P., et al.: Mask R-CNN. arXiv Preprint arXiv:170306870 (2017)
6. Caelles, S., Maninis, K.K., Pont-Tuset, J., et al.: One-Shot Video Object Segmentation (2016)
7. Henriques, J.F., Caseiro, R., Martins, P., et al.: High-speed tracking with kernelized correlation filters. IEEE Trans. Pattern Anal. Mach. Intell. 37(3), 583–596 (2015)
8. Huang, G.B., Ramesh, M., Berg, T., et al.: Labeled faces in the wild: a database for studying face recognition in unconstrained environments. Technical report 07–49, University of Massachusetts, Amherst (2007)
9. Taigman, Y., Yang, M., Ranzato, M.A., et al.: Deepface: closing the gap to human-level performance in face verification. In: Proceedings of the IEEE Conference on Computer Vision and Pattern Recognition, pp. 1701–1708. IEEE Press (2014)
10. Sun, Y., Wang, X., Tang, X.: Deep learning face representation from predicting 10,000 classes. In: Proceedings of the IEEE Conference on Computer Vision and Pattern Recognition, pp. 1891–1898. IEEE Press (2014)
11. Sun, Y., Chen, Y., Wang, X., et al.: Deep learning face representation by joint identification-verification. In: Advances in Neural Information Processing Systems, pp. 1988–1996 (2014)
12. Sun, Y., Wang, X., Tang, X.: Deeply learned face representations are sparse, selective, and robust. In: Proceedings of the IEEE Conference on Computer Vision and Pattern Recognition, pp. 2892–2900. IEEE Press (2015)
13. Sun, Y., Liang, D., Wang, X., et al.: DeepID3: face recognition with very deep neural networks. arXiv Preprint arXiv:150200873 (2015)
14. Schroff, F., Kalenichenko, D., Philbin, J.: FaceNet: a unified embedding for face recognition and clustering. In: Proceedings of the IEEE Conference on Computer Vision and Pattern Recognition, pp. 815–823. IEEE Press (2015)
15. Zeiler, M.D., Fergus, R.: Visualizing and understanding convolutional networks. arXiv: 13112901 (2013)
16. Szegedy, C., Liu, W., Jia, Y., et al.: Going deeper with convolutions. In: Proceedings of the IEEE Conference on Computer Vision and Pattern Recognition, pp. 1–9. IEEE Press (2015)
17. Parkhi, O.M., Vedaldi, A., Zisserman, A.: Deep face recognition. In: BMVC, vol. 1, p. 6 (2015)
18. Simonyan, K., Zisserman, A.: Very deep convolutional networks for large-scale image recognition. arXiv Preprint arXiv:14091556 (2014)
19. Liu, W., Wen, Y., Yu, Z., et al.: SphereFace: deep hypersphere embedding for face recognition. arXiv Preprint arXiv:170408063 (2017)
20. Wen, Y., Zhang, K., Li, Z., Qiao, Y.: A discriminative feature learning approach for deep face recognition. In: Leibe, B., Matas, J., Sebe, N., Welling, M. (eds.) ECCV 2016. LNCS, vol. 9911, pp. 499–515. Springer, Cham (2016). https://doi.org/10.1007/978-3-319-46478-7_31
21. Zhang, K., Zhang, Z., Li, Z., et al.: Joint face detection and alignment using multitask cascaded convolutional networks. IEEE Sig. Process. Lett. 23(10), 1499–1503 (2016)
22. Yi, D., Lei, Z., Liao, S., Li, S.Z.: Learning face representation from scratch. arXiv Preprint arXiv:14117923 (2014)

23. Deng, J., Dong, W., Socher, R., Fei-Fei, L.: ImageNet: a large-scale hierarchical image database. In: IEEE Conference on Computer Vision and Pattern Recognition, CVPR, pp. 248–255. IEEE Press (2009)
24. Jia, Y., Shelhamer, E., Donahue, J., et al.: Caffe: convolutional architecture for fast feature embedding. In: Proceedings of the 22nd ACM International Conference on Multimedia, pp. 675–678. ACM (2014)
25. Abadi, M., Barham, P., Chen, J., et al.: TensorFlow: large-scale machine learning on heterogeneous distributed systems. arXiv Preprint arXiv:160304467 (2016)

Abnormal Event Detection by Learning Spatiotemporal Features in Videos

Xiaofeng Zhang, Rong Wang[✉], and Jianwei Ding

People's Public Security University of China, Beijing, China
ppsuczhangxfe@163.com, dbdxwangrong@163.com

Abstract. Abnormal event detection from video surveillance is a key issue for social security. At present, the challenge lies in the effective feature extraction of video data. In order to solve the problem, a deep learning method based on convolutional autoencoder was proposed in this paper. Firstly, video data are preprocessed to obtain video volumes for subsequent training. Secondly, the video volumes are put into the convolutional autoencoder to learn the spatiotemporal features. Specifically, the model can capture spatial features by performing convolution and learn temporal features by Long Short-Term Memory (LSTM). Finally, abnormal event detection is carried out according to the normalized reconstruction error, which is adopted as the index of anomaly degree. Experimental results show that the proposed method had higher accuracy and generalization ability on the challenging Avenue and UCSD datasets.

Keywords: Abnormal event detection · Video surveillance
Convolutional autoencoder · Long Short-Term Memory

1 Introduction

The industry of video surveillance has made rapid progress in recent years. Most of the video surveillance systems can record video data very well after events happened. However, they fail to detect abnormal events timely and automatically under unattended circumstances. At the same time, facing the explosion of video data, it is unrealistic to rely on manpower to detect abnormal event. In this case, detecting abnormal events in videos have developed into a novel and vigorous research direction.

Detecting abnormal events in videos is still a very challenging task for the unbounded property of anomaly [1, 2]. The definition of abnormal event would change according to the environment. Therefore, abnormal event detection is generally regarded as a one-class classification problem. The normal class is human-defined, and other classes are all boiled down to the abnormal class. Besides, for video data, dimension is high both in spatial and temporal viewpoints, which makes it difficult for us to extract features and construct model effectively.

The usual method of the abnormal event detection is first learning the normal pattern from training video, and then using it to detect deviations—abnormal event. The method based on sparse coding has been proved to be successful [3, 4]. However, the method needs large amount of computation. In recent years, the method based on deep learning has become a new research direction. Hasan et al. proposed a model

© Springer Nature Singapore Pte Ltd. 2018
Y. Wang et al. (Eds.): IGTA 2018, CCIS 875, pp. 421–431, 2018.
https://doi.org/10.1007/978-981-13-1702-6_42

which can capture the regularities from training videos. A fully convolutional autoencoder was utilized to learn both local features and classifiers [5]. Xu et al. leveraged stacked denoising autoencoders to build Appearance and Motion DeepNet (AMDN), which could learn the motion and appearance representations. Three one-class SVM are separately used and fused together to detect anomaly [6].

In this paper, we propose a deep learning method based on convolutional autoencoder and Long Short-Term Memory (LSTM) to detect abnormal events. In particular, convolutional autoencoder embedding ConvLSTM is adopted to capture the spatiotemporal features in a video sequence. The combination of the two networks form the main model of training and testing. Finally, the normalized reconstruction error of the testing videos is used to detect abnormal events.

The remainder of this paper is organized as follows: the proposed method is discussed in Sect. 2. In Sect. 3, the experimental results are discussed and evaluated. Conclusions are given in Sect. 4.

2 Proposed Methods

As shown in Fig. 1, this work is intended to detect abnormal events from videos based on three main parts, data preprocessing, feature learning, and abnormal event detection. At first, continuous frames are combined into video volumes with a fixed length of time, and simple data preprocessing is carried out. Then, video volumes are put into the model to learn the spatiotemporal features. In model training, the model is optimized by minimizing the reconstruction error of the convolutional autoencoder. Finally, according to the reconstruction error between the input images and reconstructed images, frames with high reconstruction error can be detected as abnormal event.

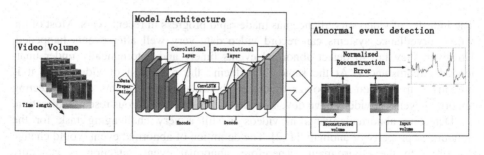

Fig. 1. Overview of the proposed method.

2.1 Data Preprocessing

Considering the experimental efficiency, we just carry out simple data preprocessing. The process can be divided into three parts, resizing images, zero-mean, and generating small video volumes. The process can be seen in Fig. 2.

The specific process is as follows. Firstly, videos from different datasets are all converted to frames and resized to the same size for later training. Secondly, mean frame is calculated among all training frames. After calculating, mean frame is subtracted from the whole training and testing frames. Thirdly, small video volumes are generated. Video volumes contain the continuous images for a fixed time length. As the proposed deep learning model needs a lot of training data, the data are expanded by setting a stride. The stride is used to determine the number of pictures in the intervals. If stride is 2, we select one of every two images in the video volume.

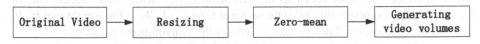

Fig. 2. Flowchart of data preprocessing.

2.2 Convolutional Autoencoder

An autoencoder is a neural network introduced by Rumelhart et al. [7]. The target of autoencoder is to use the output to reconstruct the original input as similar as possible. The optimization goal is to minimize the reconstruction errors. The autoencoder mainly contains two parts, the encoder and decoder part.

Although autoencoder, such as denoising autoencoder (DAE) and sparse autoencoder (SAE) is widely used to detect abnormal events, conventional autoencoder has relatively poor performance in capturing rich image features, especially in crowded scenes. For the case which the proportion of the abnormal event in the entire picture is relatively small, it is difficult to detect anomaly. Inspired by the success of convolutional neural networks, we applied the convolutional autoencoder (CAE) in this work, which was proposed by Masci et al [8]. Convolutional autoencoder adds convolutional operation into the autoencoder. The loss function of the CAE can be written as follows:

$$e(x, y, \mathbf{W}) = 1/2N \sum_{i=1}^{N} \|x_i - y_i\|_2^2 + \lambda \|W\|_2^2. \tag{1}$$

where x_i is input, and y_i is the corresponding reconstruction output. The first term of the function is the Euclidean distance of the reconstruction error. The second term, $\|W\|_2^2$ is the regularization term, and λ is the regularization parameter for $\|W\|_2^2$. The optimization is carried out by minimizing the reconstruction error between input x_i and output y_i. This is a totally unsupervised procedure.

2.3 Convolutional Long Short-Term Memory

Recurrent Neural Network (RNN) is essentially related to a sequence. They are the most natural neural network architecture for such video data. RNN is a network containing loops that allows information to be persisted. However, RNN loses the ability to learn information that is so far away over time. It has limited memory capacity. Besides, error gradients may vanish exponentially fast as the time lag get longer. LSTM solved the problem of long-term dependence and gradients vanish. The LSTM model has achieved some successful applications in many tasks, such as handwriting recognition, sequence generation, machine translation, video analysis and so on. Convolutional LSTM (ConvLSTM) is a variant of LSTM, which was first proposed by Shi et al. in [9]. The specific process can be expressed as follows:

Firstly, the forget gate decides the information to be discarded from cell state:

$$f_t = \sigma\big(W_f * [h_{t-1}, x_t, C_{t-1}] + b_f\big). \tag{2}$$

where x_t means the input vector to the LSTM unit, h_{t-1} denotes the hidden state of $t - 1$, and C_{t-1} expresses the cell state vector at time $t - 1$. W_f is the weight matrix. b_f denotes the bias vector. The operator $*$ denotes the convolution operation.

Secondly, new information was put into cell state:

$$i_t = \sigma(W_i * [h_{t-1}, x_t, C_{t-1}] + b_i) \tag{3}$$

$$\widehat{c_t} = \tanh(W_c * [h_{t-1}, x_t, C_{t-1}] + b_c). \tag{4}$$

In the function, i_t is the new information, and c_t stands for the whole information. Thirdly, cell state is updated:

$$C_t = f_t \otimes C_{t-1} + i_t \otimes \widehat{C_t}. \tag{5}$$

where the operator $\otimes$ expresses the Hadamard product.

Fourthly, output is got according to cell state:

$$o_t = \sigma(W_o[h_{t-1}, x_t, C_{t-1}] + b_o). \tag{6}$$

$$h_t = o_t \otimes \tan(C_t). \tag{7}$$

Through the above process, h_t is final output.

2.4 Model Architecture

The proposed model is a convolutional autoencoder embedding convolutional LSTM layers, which could capture the features both in spatial and temporal dimensions. We construct the model for two reasons. For the first reason, autoencoder has been proved to be successfully applied in abnormal event detection, especially for convolutional autoencoder. By the convolution operation of the kernel, the convolutional layer of the input end can be extracted to the most basic features in the image. It is the best method of spatial feature extraction so far. For the second reason, convolutional architecture cannot mine time association, which restricts its performance in video area. Embedding ConvLSTM layers could make up for the original deficiency, thus enhance the learning ability of the model for video data.

We applied six convolutional and six deconvolutional layers with different filters in autoencoder to capture the spatial features. Three ConvLSTM layers with different filters are embedded into the model to learn temporal correlations. The original input is resized to 224×224. By reconstruction, the output size is 224×224 for each image. T is the time length. See Table 1 for specific parameter settings. For each convolutional and deconvolutional layer, ReLU (rectified linear unit) is adopted as activation function.

2.5 Abnormal Event Detection

We discuss the abnormal event detection by normalized reconstruction error. A detailed description is given of how it leads to the final decision of abnormal events.

Table 1. Architecture of our convolutional autoencoder.

Layer name	Our model (input T × 224 × 224)	Output size
Conv1	3 × 3, 128 filters, stride2, pad 1	T × 128 × 112 × 112
Conv2	3 × 3, 64 filters, stride 2, pad 1	T × 64 × 56 × 56
Conv3	3 × 3, 32 filters, stride 2, pad 1	T × 32 × 28 × 28
Conv4	3 × 3, 16 filters, stride 2, pad 1	T × 16 × 14 × 14
Conv5	3 × 3, 8 filters, stride 2, pad 1	T × 8 × 7 × 7
Conv6	3 × 3, 4 filters, stride 2, pad 1	T × 4 × 4 × 4
ConvLSTM1	3 × 3, 4 filters, stride1, pad 0	T × 4 × 4 × 4
ConvLSTM2	3 × 3, 2 filters, stride 2, pad 1	T × 4 × 4 × 4
ConvLSTM3	3 × 3, 4 filters, stride 1, pad 0	T × 4 × 4 × 4
Deconv1	3 × 3, 4 filters, stride 2, pad 1	T × 4 × 4 × 4
Deconv2	3 × 3, 8 filters, stride 2, pad 1	T × 8 × 7 × 7
Deconv3	3 × 3, 16 filters, stride 2, pad 1	T × 16 × 14 × 14
Deconv4	3 × 3, 32 filters, stride 2, pad 1	T × 32 × 28 × 28
Deconv5	3 × 3, 64 filters, stride 2, pad 1	T × 64 × 56 × 56
Deconv6	3 × 3, 128 filters, stride 2, pad 1	T × 128 × 112 × 112
Output	–	T × 224 × 224

In the testing phase, testing frames are put into the model to reconstruct the original input through the parameters learned during the training process. In this procedure, events that similar to the training videos can be successfully reconstructed with a lower reconstruction error. However, frames that have fairly different patterns with the training videos cannot be well reconstructed. This is the premise of the abnormal event detection

We propose the normalized reconstruction error (NRE) to measure the degree of anomaly. The formula is similar to that proposed by Hasan et al. [5], while he studied regularity. Reconstruction error of the proposed convolutional autoencoder is computed, which can be written as:

$$RE_{pixel}(x, y, t) = \|I(X, t) - f(I(X, t))\|_2. \tag{8}$$

where RE_{pixel} represents the reconstruction error of pixels. I is the gray value of the pixel (x, y). X denotes the input matrix, and t is the frame number in videos.

Then, the reconstruction error of each frame can be obtained by summing the reconstruction error of all the pixel positions in a frame. The formula is as follows:

$$RE_{frame}(t) = \sum\nolimits_{(x,y)} RE_{pixel}(x, y, t). \tag{9}$$

where RE_{frame} stands for the frame level reconstruction error. The results can be smoothed by a moving average filter for later result visualization:

$$SRE_f(t) = 1/N \sum\nolimits_{k=0}^{N-1} RE_{frame}(t+k). \tag{10}$$

In the function, SRE_f means the smooth result of the RE_{frame}, N is the sample numbers of the moving average filter.

Finally, we calculate the normalized reconstruction error of each frame, which is used as an index to measure the degree of anomaly:

$$NRE(t) = \frac{SRE_f(t) - \min(SRE_f)}{\max(SRE_f) - \min(SRE_f)}. \tag{11}$$

By the normalization, the values of all reconstruction error are among 0 to 1.

3   Experiment and Analysis

The training of the model was carried out on the Avenue and UCSD datasets. In the experiment, test data were put into the model to reconstruct the original data. The result curves about normalized reconstruction error are generated, which were used to classify normal and abnormal events. The experimental results are compared with the advanced ones.

3.1   Datasets

Two challenging datasets are considered, which are Avenue and UCSD datasets.

The **Avenue** dataset is proposed by Lu et al. [11]. There are 16 training and 21 testing videos in the dataset. The normal scenes mainly contain pedestrians walking between subway entrance. However, abnormal scenes include people running, throwing, loitering, running or walking in opposite direction and etc. Its challenge lies in the slight camera shake, a few outliers in the training videos. Besides, some normal patterns hardly appear in training videos.

The **UCSD** dataset includes two subsets: ped1 and ped2 [12]. Ped1 includes 34 training and 36 testing video clips with the resolution of 238×158 pixels. Ped2 consists of 16 training and 12 testing video clips with the resolution of 360×240 pixels. For the two subsets, the training videos only contain the pedestrians walking, which is the normal class. The abnormal class includes no pedestrians and anomalous pedestrian motion patterns. Its challenge is the variability of crowd density in the walkways.

3.2   Model Training

The model is trained on a machine equipped with a Nvidia 1080Ti GPU accelerator. Tensorflow is used as the framework of deep learning. The objective function of the training is shown in Eq. (2). The optimization algorithm is random gradient descent. In training, epoch is set to 50. After about 10 epochs, the loss value of the training tends to be stable. The decline in loss value can be seen in Fig. 3. The training loss is lesser than loss on validation set.

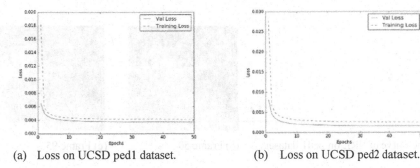

(a)   Loss on UCSD ped1 dataset.   (b)   Loss on UCSD ped2 dataset.

Fig. 3. Training loss on different dataset is given in the above pictures. The solid line, val Loss, represents the loss value on validation set. And the dotted line expresses the training loss.

3.3   Experiment 1: Effect of the Time Length

In order to choose a suitable length of time T, we carry out experiments to analyze the effect of the results. Different time lengths are set in the case of the same conditions. We set the time length to be 5, 10, 15, and 20. It has been found that different time lengths have an impact on the AUC (Area Under the Curve) and EER (Equal Error Rate) of the experiment. Efficiency of training is also considered in this experiment. To better explain the effect of different time lengths, Table 2 is given.

Table 2. Effect of the time length for ped2.

Time length	AUC/EER	Average time of each Epoch(s)
5	87.64%/22.36%	94
10	**89.32%/20.74%**	164
15	88.25%/22.00%	222
20	86.93%/23.01%	260

From the Table 2, as the length of time increases, the average time of each epoch is longer. The corresponding testing time is longer, too. In this sense, the time length should not be very big. As for the performance metrics AUC and EER, we can see that when the time length is 10, the value of AUC is the biggest, at the same time, the value of EER is the smallest. We choose 10 as the time length.

3.4   Experiment 2: Normalized Reconstruction Error for Detecting Anomalies

The normalized reconstruction error is used to determine whether a frame is normal or abnormal. The threshold can be automatically set, and the maximum of performance metric AUC is guaranteed by adjusting the value of the threshold. By normalization, the selection of threshold is relatively simple. To give a clearer description of the experimental results, we selected representative testing videos on each dataset. The resulting curves are displayed, as shown in Figs. 4, 5 and 6.

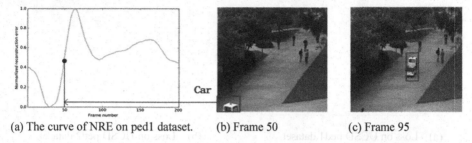

(a) The curve of NRE on ped1 dataset.   (b) Frame 50   (c) Frame 95

Fig. 4. The normalized reconstruction error curve of UCSD ped1 dataset. Two images are given during the abnormal period.

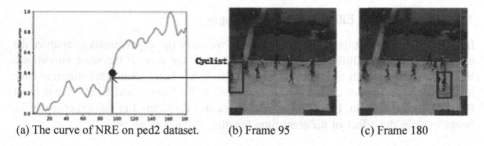

(a) The curve of NRE on ped2 dataset.   (b) Frame 95   (c) Frame 180

Fig. 5. The normalized reconstruction error curve of UCSD ped2 dataset. Two images are given during the abnormal period.

As we talked before, for UCSD dataset, only pedestrians walking on the sidewalk is considered as normal class. In Fig. 4, the car is in the video at around frame 50 to frame 180, which is an abnormal event. In Fig. 5, an abnormal event happened at around frame 95, when a bicycle rider appeared. From the frame 95 to the frame 180, he has been in the video. In Fig. 6, two curves are displayed according to two testing videos. Two videos contain two abnormal events each. For the first video, two running events take place separately at around frame 380 to 428, and frame 649 to 692. For the second video, abnormal events contain a man pushing the cart into the entrance, and a man throwing paper. The abnormal frames are around frame 259 to 286, and 458 to 510 separately.

We can see from the above curves, the frames containing the abnormal events correspond to a larger reconstruction error. To evaluate the performance of our proposed methods, the AUC and EER are compared with the state-of-art methods, which can be seen in Table 3. For ped1, our method is better than which proposed by

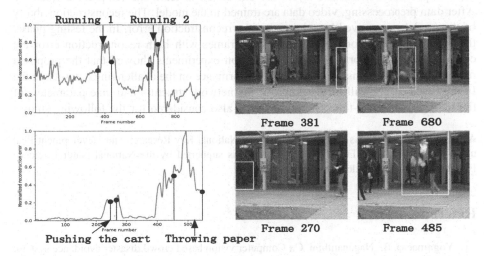

Fig. 6. Two normalized reconstruction error curves of Avenue dataset. On the right of each curve are two corresponding images during the abnormal period.

Table 3. Comparison with other methods

Method	Ped1		Ped2		Avenue	
	EER	AUC	EER	AUC	EER	AUC
MPPCA [13]	40%	59.0%	30%	69.3%	–	–
Social force [14]	31%	76.8%	42%	55.6%	–	–
Detection at 150fps [11]	15%	91.8%	–	–	–	–
Hasan et al. [5]	27.9%	81.0%	21.7%	90.0%	25.1%	70.2%
Proposed	22.8%	84.65%	**20.74%**	89.32%	**22.87%**	**84.20%**

Hasan et al. But our method is worse than the method proposed by Lu et al. [11]. It is possible that the resolution of the images is low, which affects the learning ability. Besides, most videos of the ped1 dataset do not provide groundtruth. For ped2, the EER is smaller than the method proposed by Hasan et al. [5], and the AUC is basically close to Hasan's method. The detection on ped2 has achieved an advanced detection result so far. This might be due to higher resolution for ped2, and all testing videos contains groundtruth. For Avenue dataset, both the AUC and EER are better than Hasan's method. In a comprehensive view, our method can achieve an effective detection on the two challenging datasets.

4 Conclusion

In this paper, we propose a deep learning model for abnormal event detection. By adding convolutional operation in autoencoder, the ability to learn spatial features has been improved. ConvLSTM layers are embedded to learn the temporal correlation. After data preprocessing, video data are trained in the model. The reconstruction ability of the model is improved by minimizing the reconstruction error. In the testing phase, the reconstruction error is calculated. The frames with high reconstruction error are corresponding to abnormal events. Simulation experiments showed that the proposed method is effective considering its good performance on the challenging datasets. In the future research, we will further improve the network structure and tune parameters of the model. Better real-time and reliability is also considered for the following study.

Acknowledgments. This work is supported by National Key Research and Development Plan under Grant No. 2016YFC0801005. This work is supported by the National Natural Science Foundation of China under Grant No. 61503388.

References

1. Yogameena, B., Nagananthini, C.: Computer vision based crowd disaster avoidance system: a survey. Int. J. Disaster Risk Reduct. **22**, 95–129 (2017)
2. Luo, W., Liu, W., Gao, S.: A revisit of sparse coding based anomaly detection in stacked RNN framework. In: IEEE International Conference on Computer Vision (ICCV), pp. 341–349. IEEE Computer Society (2017)
3. Cong, Y., Yuan, J., Liu, J.: Sparse reconstruction cost for abnormal event detection. **32**(14), 3449–3456 (2011)
4. Lu, C., Shi, J., Jia, J.: Abnormal event detection at 150 FPS in MATLAB. In: IEEE International Conference on Computer Vision (ICCV), pp. 2720–2727. IEEE (2013)
5. Hasan, M., Choi, J., Neumann, J., et al.: Learning temporal regularity in video sequences. In: Computer Vision and Pattern Recognition (CVPR), pp. 733–742. IEEE (2016)
6. Xu, D., Yan, Y., Ricci, E., Sebe, N.: Detecting anomalous events in videos by learning deep representations of appearance and motion. Comput. Vis. Image Underst. **156**, 117–127 (2016)
7. Rumelhart, D.E., Hinton, G.E., Williams, R.J.: Learning representations by back–propagating errors. Nature **323**, 533–536 (1986)
8. Masci, J., Meier, U., Cireşan, D., Schmidhuber, J.: Stacked convolutional auto-encoders for hierarchical feature extraction. In: Honkela, T., Duch, W., Girolami, M., Kaski, S. (eds.) ICANN 2011. LNCS, vol. 6791, pp. 52–59. Springer, Heidelberg (2011). https://doi.org/10.1007/978-3-642-21735-7_7
9. Shi, X., Chen, Z., Wang, H., et al.: Convolutional LSTM network. Mach. Learn. Approach Precip. Nowcasting **9199**, 802–810 (2015)
10. Ribeiro, M., Lazzaretti, A.E., Lopes, H.S.: A study of deep convolutional auto-encoders for anomaly detection in videos. Pattern Recogn. Lett. **105**, 13–22 (2017)
11. Lu, C., Shi, J., Jia, J.: Abnormal event detection at 150 FPS in MATLAB. In: Proceedings of the IEEE International Conference on Computer Vision (ICCV), pp. 2720–2727 (2013)
12. Mehran, R., Oyama, A., Shah, M.: Abnormal crowd behavior detection using social force model. In: Computer Vision and Pattern Recognition (CVPR) (2009)

13. Kim, J., Grauman, K.: Observe locally, infer globally: a space-time MRF for detecting abnormal activities with incremental updates. In: Proceedings of the IEEE Conference on Computer Vision and Pattern Recognition (CVPR), pp. 2921–2928 (2009)
14. Mehran, R., Oyama, A., Shah, M.: Abnormal crowd behavior detection using social force model. In: Proceedings of the IEEE Conference on Computer Vision and Pattern Recognition (CVPR), pp. 935–942 (2009)

Template-Guided 3D Fragment Reassembly Using GDS

Congli Yin[1,2], Mingquan Zhou[1,2(✉)], Yachun Fan[1,2], and Wuyang Shui[1,2]

[1] College of Information Science and Technology, Beijing Normal University, Beijing, China
mqzhou@bnu.edu.cn
[2] Key Laboratory of Digital Protection and Virtual Reality for Cultural Heritage, Beijing, China

Abstract. Computer-aided fragment reassembly becomes more and more significant in recent years. The state of the art methods mainly utilize the fracture surface of the fragment. However, some fracture surfaces are often eroded and the features are not discriminative enough for matching. In this paper, we proposed a template-guided 3D fragment reassembly algorithm using Geodesic Disk Spectrum (GDS), which conducts matching between the intact surface of the fragment and the template. A two-step procedure is proposed for the first time with GDS-based matching and ICP-based registration for the reassembly task. The largest enclosed geodesic disk of the fragment is extracted and the matching to the template is found by GDS. In order to reduce the computational complexity, a k-layer Normal Distribution Descriptor (NDD) is also proposed. Transformation of the matched geodesic disks is obtained using the Iterative Closest Points (ICP) algorithm, and the registration between the fragment and the template is achieved. Our algorithm has been tested on various fragments and accurate results are obtained. A higher precision is achieved by comparing with existing algorithms, which proves the efficiency.

Keywords: Fragment reassembly · Template-guided · Geodesic disk spectrum

1 Introduction

With the development of computer-aided model restoration technology, approaches highly assist experts in the fragments reassembly nowadays. Considering the geometric structure of a fragment, the boundary surface can be divided into intact surface and fracture surface. Intact surface is corresponding to the external surface of the original and complete model. Fracture surface refers to those generated due to fracturing. The intact and fracture surface of a fragment are illustrates in Fig. 1. Let T be a template model and F_i be each fragment, we can reassemble fragmented pieces after solving a partial matching problem between F_i and T. 3D fragment reassembly includes fracture surface-based matching and template-guided matching. Fracture surface-based matching methods mainly utilize features of the fracture surface. However, the fracture surface is often eroded which causes difficulties in segmenting and features are not discriminative enough for matching. Therefore, we propose a template-guided 3D fragments reassembly algorithm in this paper, which composes fragmented pieces based on their best match to a complete model using intact surface. The GDS-based matching is

© Springer Nature Singapore Pte Ltd. 2018
Y. Wang et al. (Eds.): IGTA 2018, CCIS 875, pp. 432–441, 2018.
https://doi.org/10.1007/978-981-13-1702-6_43

firstly conducted for the matching. Then we use Iterative Closest Points (ICP) [8] algorithm to find the spatial transformation between matched geodesic disks and obtain the registration result.

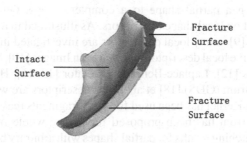

Fig. 1. Intact surface and fracture surface of a fragment.

In summary, the main contributions of this paper are as follows:

(1) A template-guided 3D fragment reassembly algorithm is proposed and accurate reassembly results are achieved.
(2) The geodesic disk spectrum (GDS) is used for matching task for the first time and an optimization strategy is proposed to reduce the computational complexity.

2   Related Work

In this section, the state of the art algorithms for fragment reassembly and 3D shape partial matching are summarized.

2.1   Fragment Reassembly

Fragments reassembly attracts lots of interests in recent years and amounts of algorithms were proposed. The algorithms can be roughly classified into two kinds: fracture surface matching-based methods [1] and template guidance-based methods [2–4]. Fracture surface matching-based approaches exploit similarities in the local fracture geometry of adjacent fragments while template guidance-based approaches compose fragmented pieces based on their best match to a complete model. Each approach has advantages and limitations, and reassembly algorithms in both categories report difficulties in effectively processing small fragmented pieces. Firstly, for small fragments, it is particularly challenging to differentiate and segment intact and fracture surface. Secondly, the number of uncertainly potential matches tends to be large and their effective pruning is difficult [3]. Cooper et al. [5] reassembled 3D pottery fragments by matching the break-curves and shard normal. Willis [6] improved pottery reassembly by applying Bayesian analysis with a semi-automatic matching. Yin et al. [7] used templates to roughly reassemble skull fragments, and performed break-curves analysis to refine the composition. Their method also approximates thin-shell fragments as surface patches, which is not suitable for small fragments [7].

2.2 Partial Matching

Partial matching is commonly conducted using ICP-based [8] methods. However, the methods can only get accurate results if the shapes are similar in size, which are not suitable for matching a partial shape to a complete shape. Other partial matching approaches are based on local shape descriptors. As illustrated in a survey about partial retrieval approaches [9], many local descriptors are investigated in detail. The recently proposed representative local descriptors contain Spin Images [10], Snapshot [11], Local Spherical Harmonics [12], Laplace-Beltrami Operator [13–16], Heat Kernel [17] and Geodesic Disk Spectrum (GDS) [18] et al. These descriptors are widely used in partial matching tasks. Heat Kernel has been used for skull fragments reassembly [19]. In [18], Geodesic Disk Spectrum has been proposed for part-in-whole matching task which achieves accurate matching results for partial shapes with arbitrary boundaries or smooth appearances. GDS describes the region properties and it is more distinctive than other local shape descriptors. In this paper, GDS is used to reassemble the fragments by finding the matching regions between fragments and the template.

3 Geodesic Disk Spectrum (GDS)

In this section, we briefly recap the basic theory and properties of Geodesic Disk Spectrum (GDS) and discuss the suitability for the reassembly task.

3.1 Definition

Shape Index was initially proposed for the graphical visualization of the surface [20]. Dorai et al. [21] employed a modified definition for surface point identifying, which is defined as follows:

$$S_I(p) = \frac{1}{2} - \frac{1}{\pi} \tan^{-1} \left(\frac{\kappa_1(p) + \kappa_2(p)}{\kappa_1(p) - \kappa_2(p)} \right) \tag{1}$$

where $S_I(p)$ ranges during $[0, 1]$, $\kappa_1(p)$ is the maximum normal curvature, $\kappa_2(p)$ is the minimum normal curvature and $\kappa_1(p) > \kappa_2(p)$. Shape Index provides a continuous gradation between salient shapes, such as convex, saddle, concave, and it owns a large vocabulary to describe subtle shape variations. Shape Index is appropriate for the description of the distribution of the disk since the value ranges from $[0, 1]$.

Du et al. [18] proposed Geodesic Disk Spectrum (GDS) for the part-in-whole matching task. Let P be a 3D manifold surface of n vertices, a geodesic disk $GD(p, r)$ with center p and radius r is defined as follows:

$$GD(p, r) = \{v, gd(v, p) \leq r\} \tag{2}$$

where $gd(v, p)$ is the geodesic distance between any point v to the center p. GDS is obtained by counting the distribution of Shape Index for all the points within a geodesic disk. GDS of one geodesic disk is given by:

$$GDS(p, r) = (\frac{n_1}{n}, \frac{n_2}{n}, \dots, \frac{n_N}{n}) \tag{3}$$

where N is the number of bins range in [0, 1] and $n_1, n_2, \dots, n_N$ are the number of points that fall into respective bins.

3.2 Properties of GDS

GDS inherits the excellent characteristics of Shape Index, which is precise and discriminative. Figure 2 shows that the Shape Index distributions of a fragment and the template are almost the same. GDS of two different disks with equal geodesic radius are shown in Fig. 3, which has clearly different distributions.

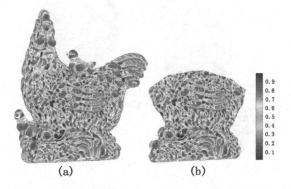

Fig. 2. Distributions of Shape Index of a template (a) and a fragment (b). Colors represent values of Shape Index, which are quite identical. (Color figure online)

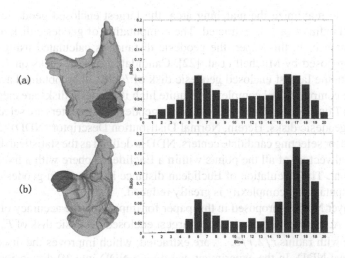

Fig. 3. GDS of two disks (a) and (b) with equal radius are extremely different, the red region are geodesic disks and the histograms represent the distribution of GDS. (Color figure online)

4 Pipeline of the Proposed Algorithm

4.1 GDS-Based Matching

Geodesic Disk Spectrum (GDS) describes the feature of a geodesic disk region, which contains much more information than merely one point. Let T be the template, and F be the intact of T, respectively. Since the fragment is closed, the intact surface needs to be segmented firstly. Herein, we adopt the novel classification method [27] to segment the regions into intact and fracture surfaces based on their statistical properties. The results of segmentation are illustrated in Fig. 4. The intact surface is manually selected for matching.

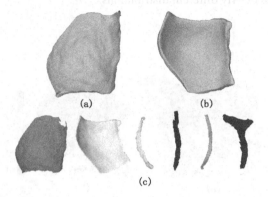

(a)   (b)

(c)

Fig. 4. Segmentation result of a fragment. (a) and (b) The initial fragment. (c) The segmentation result.

In order to maximize the matching area, the largest enclosed geodesic disk with center p and radius r of F is extracted. The computation of geodesic disk depends on geodesic distance. In this paper, the geodesic distance is calculated using the MMP algorithm proposed by Mitchell et al. [22]. Candidate geodesic disks on T which are matched with the largest enclosed geodesic disk of F should be obtained according to p and r. The computational complexity is quite high if geodesic disks are calculated for all points on T one by one. Therefore, candidate geodesic disk centers are selected before computing geodesic disks. Herein, Normal Distribution Descriptor (NDD) [23] is used as a measure for selecting candidate centers. NDD is defined as the statistical distribution of the normal vectors of all the points within a Euclidean sphere with a fixed radius at a certain point. The calculation of Euclidean distance is faster than geodesic distance, and the computational complexity is greatly reduced.

The k-layer NDD is proposed in this paper for improving the accuracy of candidate disk center. According to radius r of the largest enclosed geodesic disk of F, the Euclidean sphere with radius $r/2, r/3, \ldots,$ are extracted, which improves the discrimination of the original NDD. In the experiment, we divide NDD into 10-dimensional vectors with a fixed radius, and a k-layer NDD is obtained as a 10k-dimensional vector. The distance between two vectors is measured using the variance of the difference between each dimension. Generally, we can get more accurate results when $k = 3$.

According to candidate disk centers selected from T, we find the corresponding geodesic disks by the same radius r as that of F. Under the premise of ensuring accuracy, we set $n = 10$ in order to reduce the computational complexity. We use the definitions in Sect. 3.1 to calculate each GDS individually to complete subsequent matching task. For the calculation of GDS, the [0, 1] interval is divided evenly into 20 bins to obtain a 20-dimensional vector. Whether two disks are similar depends on the similarity of the distribution of Shape Index which GDS characterizes. The values of GDS represent the Shape Index distributions. If the difference of each bin is smaller, the two disks are more similar. The differences between the corresponding bins of different disks are evaluated as follows:

$$E_{(GDS_p,GDS_j)}(k) = v_{GDS_p}(k) - v_{GDS_j}(k) \tag{4}$$

where $E_{(GDS_p,GDS_j)}(k)$ is the difference of GDS_p and GDS_j in bin k, $v_{GDS_p}(k)$ indicates the ratio of points in disk GDS_p that fall into bin k, and so is $v_{GDS_j}(k)$. The variance of $E_{(GDS_p,GDS_j)}(k)$ is used to evaluate the differences between two disks to find the most similar geodesic disk on T. By comparing the variance of GDS, the most similar disk is found as shown in Fig. 5.

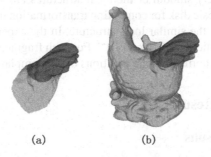

(a)   (b)

Fig. 5. Matching result of the geodesic disk. (a) The fragment. (b) The template. The red region in (a) is the geodesic disk of fragment and that in (b) is the matched geodesic disk with an equal radius. (Color figure online)

4.2 ICP-Based Registration

Iterative Closest Points (ICP) algorithm was proposed by Besl et al. [8]. Let $P = \{p_1, p_2, \cdots, p_i\}$ and $Q = \{q_1, q_2, \cdots, q_j\}$ be the source dataset and the target dataset to be matched in R^3, respectively. The goal of ICP is to find the rotation matrix R and the translation matrix T between the two datasets, which aligns P and Q. The objective function of ICP is given by:

$$f(R, T) = \sum_{i=1}^{n} \left\| q_i - (R * p_i + T) \right\|^2 \tag{5}$$

Given the source dataset, the nearest points on the target dataset are computed iteratively to update the transformation until the average geometric distance is the minimum. In Sect. 4.1, GDS-based matching has obtained two matching geodesic disks, donated as GDS_p and GDS_j. Specific steps of ICP are as follows:

Step 1: Generate the initial correspondences between GDS_p and GDS_j;
Step 2: Calculate the best transformation according to correspondences;
Step 3: Align the two datasets with the best transformation and recalculate corresponddences;
Step 4: Repeat 1–3 until the error of two iterations is less than the given threshold ε.

As we know, the matched geodesic disks GDS_p and GDS_j are almost the same, including the amount of points, the size, and the structure. Therefore, accurate transformation matrix can be obtained through ICP. After that, for the each point $f_i(x_i, y_i, z_i)$ of F, the registration coordinates $f_i'(x_i', y_i', z_i')$ are obtained by the following formula:

$$\begin{pmatrix} x_i' \\ y_i' \\ z_i' \end{pmatrix} = T * \begin{pmatrix} x_i \\ y_i \\ z_i \end{pmatrix} + R \qquad (6)$$

It should be noted that ICP will fall into the local optimum when geodesic disks to be matched are extremely smooth or the local structures are similar. In this case, we propose using $r/2$ geodesic disk for computing transformation matrix, which eliminates the problems caused by the similar local structure. In the experiments, accurate registration results can be achieved when $\varepsilon < 10^{-5}$. For each fragment F_i, the above steps are conducted to obtain the corresponding positions on the template.

5   Experimental Results

5.1   Experimental Results

We test our reassembly algorithm on the dataset provided by [3]. The complete models are scanned firstly as ground truth for result evaluation and then fragments are fractured from complete models. Our algorithm reassembles the digital fragments and we compare our results with the ground truth. Fragments have different tessellations and different positions compared with the complete models (templates). To numerically evaluate reassembly accuracy, the reference error ε_R and the reference error ratio δ_R are defined. Let S, S' be the template model and the reassembled model, respectively. We can measure the reference error ε_R by comparing S and S': compute a displacement field on S to record the distance from each point $x \in S$ to its nearest point on S', then use the average:

$$\varepsilon_R = \sqrt{\sum_{v \in S, v' \in \hat{S}} d^2(v, v')/|S|} \qquad (7)$$

where $|S|$ represents the number of points of S. The reference error ratio δ_R is measured as a percentage of the diagonal length of bounding box.

The proposed algorithm is implemented on a 64-bit PC with an Intel Xeon 2.13 GHz CPU and 6 GB memory. In the GDS-based matching stage, we set $k = 3$ for k-layer NDD and therefore NDD is a 30-dimensional vector. For the number of candidate geodesic disks, we set as $n = 10$ for most cases unless the fragments are extremely small which need to be adjusted according to the specific situation. In the ICP-based registration stage, the iteration error is set as $\varepsilon < 10^{-5}$. Figure 6 shows reassembly of fragmented child model and chicken model. Figure 6(c) is the error distribution of each point. Red represents a large error while blue represents the opposite. We can see that there are some very small pieces and smooth pieces in Fig. 6(a), but our algorithm still get accurate results.

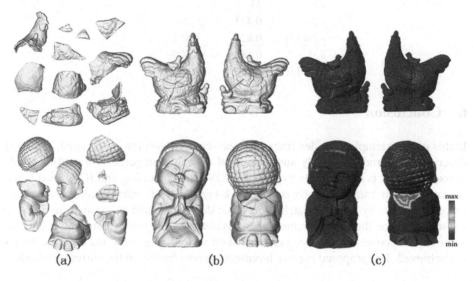

Fig. 6. Reassembly results of fragmented child model and chicken model. (a) The scanned fragments. (b) Reassembly results. (c) The error distribution of each point, red represents a large error while blue represents the opposite. (Color figure online)

5.2 Comparison with Existing Methods

In this section, comparisons with Zhang et al. [3] are conducted. The algorithm proposed in [3] uses Intrinsic Shape Signatures (ISS) [24] and Signatures of Histograms of Orientations (SHOT) [25] for the extracting and matching of feature points, respectively. Amounts of error exist in the initial matching results. They use the RANSAC algorithm [26] for post-processing to remove errors and get a sparse matching result. The accuracy of their algorithm depends on the matching results of the feature points, which leads to failure when the fragment has few features.

Different from the algorithm of Zhang et al. [3], GDS is a descriptor for the fixed region, which is more robust and contains much more information. It can obtain accurate matching results and handle matching problems with smooth appearance or few features. In addition, ICP-based registration finds the transformation matrix using the matched geodesic disk, which also depends on the accurate results of GDS. Quantitative comparisons are shown in Table 1, including reference error ε_R and the reference error ratio δ_R. It can be seen that our algorithm can obtain higher reassembly accuracy than that in [3].

Table 1. Quantitative comparisons. The table shows reference error and reference error ratio of different models. #F is the number of fragments. ε_R and δ_R are reference error and reference error ratio. The reference error ratio is measured as a percentage of the bounding box diagonal length (i.e., reference error/diagonal length $\times$ 100%).

Model	Chicken	Child
#F	11	8
ε_R	0.433	0.518
ε_R of [3]	0.820	0.853
δ_R	0.14%	0.20%
δ_R of [3]	0.27%	0.33%

6 Conclusion

In this paper, a template-guided fragments reassembly algorithm is proposed. The GDS descriptor is introduced firstly and its several desirable properties are analyzed. The reassembly task is divided into two-steps: GDS-based matching and ICP-based registration. In the first stage, we have proposed a k-layer NDD in order to reduce the computational complexity and the matched geodesic disks are found by comparing GDS. In the second stage, the transformation matrix is obtained and thus registration results are achieved. Experiments have been conducted on various fragments and accurate results are achieved. The proposed approach presents improvements to the current methods.

References

1. Huang, Q.-X., Flory, S., Gelfand, N.: Reassembling fractured objects by geometric matching. In: Proceedings of ACM SIGGRAPH 2006 Papers, pp. 569–578. ACM, New York (2006)
2. Zhang, K., Yu, W., Manhein, M.: Reassembling 3D thin shells using integrated template guidance and fracture region matching. In: Proceedings of ACM SIGGRAPH 2015 Posters, pp. 88:1–88:1 (2015)
3. Zhang, K., Yu, W., Manhein, M.: 3D fragment reassembly using integrated template guidance and fracture-region matching. In: IEEE International Conference on Computer Vision, pp. 2138–2146. IEEE Computer Society (2015)
4. Li, X., Yin, Z., Wei, L.: Symmetry and template guided completion of damaged skulls. Comput. Graph. **35**(4), 885–893 (2011)
5. Cooper, D.B., Willis, A., Andrews, S.: Assembling virtual pots from 3D measurements of their fragments. In: Virtual Reality, Archeology, and Cultural Heritage, pp. 241–254 (2001)
6. Willis, A.R., Cooper, D.B.: Bayesian assembly of 3D axially symmetric shapes from fragments. In: CVPR (2004)

7. Yin, Z., Wei, L., Manhein, M., Li, X.: An automatic assembly and completion framework for fragmented skulls. In: International Conference on Computer Vision, pp. 2532–2539 (2011)
8. Besl, P.J., Mckay, N.D.: A method for registration of 3-D shapes. IEEE Trans. Pattern Anal. Mach. Intell. **14**(3), 239–256 (1992)
9. Liu, Z., Shuhui, B., Zhou, K.: A survey on partial retrieval of 3D shapes. J. Comput. Sci. Technol. **28**, 836–851 (2013)
10. Johnson, A.E., Hebert, M.: Using spin images for efficient object recognition in cluttered 3D scenes. IEEE Trans. Pattern Anal. Mach. Intell. **21**(5), 433–449 (2002)
11. Malassiotis, S., Strintzis, M.G.: Snapshots: a novel local surface descriptor and matching algorithm for robust 3D surface alignment. IEEE Trans. Pattern Anal. Mach. Intell. **29**(7), 1285–1290 (2007)
12. Kazhdan, M., Funkhouser, T., Rusinkiewicz, S.: Rotation invariant spherical harmonic representation of 3D shape descriptors. **43**(2), 156–164 (2003)
13. Hu, J., Hua, J.: Salient spectral geometric features for shape matching and retrieval. Vis. Comput. **25**(5–7), 667–675 (2009)
14. Wu, H.Y., Zha, H., Luo, T.: Global and local isometry-invariant descriptor for 3D shape comparison and partial matching. In: Computer Vision and Pattern Recognition, pp. 438–445. IEEE (2010)
15. Dubrovina, A., Kimmel, R.: Matching shapes by eigendecomposition of the Laplace-Beltrami operator. In: Proceedings of the Fifth International Symposium on 3D Data Processing Visualization and Transmission (2010)
16. Lavoue, G.: Bag of words and local spectral descriptor for 3D partial shape retrieval. In: Eurographics Conference on 3D Object Retrieval Eurographics Association, pp. 41–48 (2011)
17. Sun, J., Ovsjanikov, M., Guibas, L.: A concise and provably informative multi scale signature based on heat diffusion. In: Proceedings of Computer Graphics Forum, pp. 1383–1392 (2009)
18. Du, G., Yin, C., Zhou, M.: Part-in-whole matching of rigid 3D shapes using geodesic disk spectrum. Multimedia Tools Appl. **3**, 1–21 (2017)
19. Yu, W., Li, M., Li, X.: Fragmented skull modeling using heat kernels. Graph. Models **74**(4), 140–151 (2012)
20. Koenderink, J.J., Van Doorn, A.J.: Surface shape and curvature scales. Image Vis. Comput. **10**(8), 557–564 (1992)
21. Dorai, C., Jain, A.K.: COSMOS—a representation scheme for 3D free-form objects. IEEE Trans. Pattern Anal. Mach. Intell. **19**(10), 1115–1130 (1997)
22. Mitchell, J.S.B., Mount, D.M., Papadimitriou, C.H.: The discrete geodesic problem. SIAM J. Comput. **16**(4), 647–668 (1987)
23. Martinek, M., Grosso, R., Greiner, G.: Interactive partial 3D shape matching with geometric distance optimization. Vis. Comput. **31**(2), 223–233 (2015)
24. Zhong, Y.: Intrinsic shape signatures: a shape descriptor for 3D object recognition. In: Proceedings of IEEE International Conference on Computer Vision Workshops, pp. 689–696 (2009)
25. Tombari, F., Salti, S., Di Stefano, L.: Unique signatures of histograms for local surface description. In: Daniilidis, K., Maragos, P., Paragios, N. (eds.) ECCV 2010. LNCS, vol. 6313, pp. 356–369. Springer, Heidelberg (2010). https://doi.org/10.1007/978-3-642-15558-1_26
26. Fischler, M.A., Bolles, R.C.: Random sample consensus: a paradigm for model fitting with applications to image analysis and automated cartography. Commun. ACM **24**(6), 381–395 (1981)
27. Andreadis, A., Mavridis, P., Papaioannou, G.: Facet extraction and classification for the reassembly of fractured 3D objects (2014)

Automatic Mass Detection from Mammograms with Region-Based Convolutional Neural Network

Yifan Wu, Weifeng Shi, Lei Cui[✉], Hongyu Wang, Qirong Bu[✉], and Jun Feng

Department of Information Science and Technology, Northwest University, Xi'an 710127, China
chrislei@stumail.nwu.edu.cn, boqirong@nwu.edu.cn

Abstract. Automatic detection of breast mass from mammograms is a challenging task. Recently, Convolution Neural Networks (CNNs) have been proposed to address this task. However, the performance of these CNN-based detection methods is still limited due to high complexity of breast tissue and varying shape of masses. An Automatic Mass Detection framework with Region-based CNN (AMDR-CNN) is presented in this paper, aiming to efficiently exploit informative features from mammograms. Under a hierarchical candidate mass region generation method with a full-size mammogram, the mammogram is greatly simplified and high-quality region proposals are generated. Then, a deeper CNN is introduced, which simultaneously predicts object bounds and scores at each position. In contrast to previous works, the deeper CNN learns the effective features of mass as well as helps produce accurate detection results. The experiments are performed on two public datasets, which achieves a better performance than state-of-the-art algorithms.

Keywords: Mammogram · Mass detection · Region proposal
Convolutional neural network

1 Introduction

Breast cancer is the most common cancer in women and it is the leading cause of deaths from cancer around the world [1]. Screening mammography programs implemented to detect breast cancer at an early stage, which has been shown to increase chances of survival [2, 3]. The mammograms in screening programs has to be inspected for signs of cancer by one or more experienced readers, which is time consuming, costly and most importantly prone to errors, and it has been shown that there is significant amount of variability in radiologists' mammography evaluations [4, 5]. As we all know, mass detection is an important part of screening mammography. In particular, high false positive rates in screening mammography can lead to significant unnecessary cost and patient stress [6, 7]. Therefore, it is necessary and helpful for using computer aided detection (CAD) system to provide reliable advice to doctors as an assistant.

Until recently, the effectiveness of CAD systems still depends on meticulously handcrafted features, and machine learning algorithms for detection on top of these features. However, the disadvantage of pre-defined features is that you need to know which are the most informative features in the detection task. Often the best features are not known,

© Springer Nature Singapore Pte Ltd. 2018
Y. Wang et al. (Eds.): IGTA 2018, CCIS 875, pp. 442–450, 2018.
https://doi.org/10.1007/978-981-13-1702-6_44

and a method of automatic feature discovery could be advantageous. Instead of using pre-defined features, we could learn the most informative image features from the data itself using deep learning techniques. By directly extracting feature information from data, rather than the domain experts, deep learning facilities optimally utilize the increasing amounts of data and reduce human bias. Since 2012, deep convolutional neural networks (CNN) have significantly outperformed the traditional methods in the field of computer vision [8]. Deep CNN have reached or even exceeded human performance in image detection task [9]. Furthermore, CNNs show great potential in medical image analysis. Specifically, several studies have attempted to apply deep learning to analyze mammograms [10–13], but the problem is still far from being solved.

A mammogram is typically in the size of 4000×3000 (height by width) pixels, such as INbreast dataset [14], while the mass lesion or the region of interest (ROI) can be as small as 100×100 pixels. Resizing a large mammogram to a small size to detection, is a common choice of deep learning [15], which makes the ROI too small to be detected. Our research focuses on mass detection from mammograms with full-size images. An Automatic Mass Detection framework with Region-based CNN (AMDR-CNN) is presented in this paper. Our contributions are: (1) To the best of our knowledge, this is the first time that the improved Faster Region-based CNN (Faster R-CNN) is applied to the mass detection from mammograms, which is an end-to-end training network for mass detection. (2) A hierarchical candidate mass region generation method is proposed, which not only reduces the amount of data to be processed, but also improves the accuracy of the mass detection. Moreover, all operations are performed on the original image size without scaling, which solves the shortcoming of image detail loss due to scaling caused by traditional algorithms. (3) According to the characteristic that the size of mammograms is large but mass lesion is very small, we use a deeper CNN (Inception_ResNet_V2) instead of the original basic network VGG-16 of Faster R-CNN to detect the mass regions. (4) The proposed AMDR-CNN framework achieves a good performance on the INbreast [14] and Breast Cancer Digital Repository (BCDR-F03) [16] datasets (INbreast:TP $= 0.88$@FPI $= 0.75$, BCDR-F03:TP $= 0.81$@FPI $= 1.1$).

2   Automatic Mass Detection Framework with Region-Based CNN

In this research, a novel end-to-end framework named AMDR-CNN is proposed, which is divided into two steps. In the first step, we used a hierarchical method coarse-to-fine to produce the candidate mass regions. Inspired by the popular region proposal network (RPN), high-quality region proposals are generated from the simplified mammograms. In the second step, we use a deeper CNN (Inception_ResNet_V2) to predict the boundaries of candidate masses. By sharing convolutional features in the above two steps, AMDR-CNN improves both of region proposal quality and the performance of mass detection. An outline of our framework can be seen in Fig. 1.

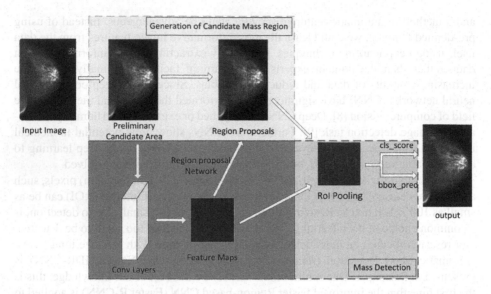

Fig. 1. AMDR-CNN includes two modules, which are generation of candidate mass region (yellow area) and mass detection (blue area). And the green area is the convolutional features shared by the two modules. (Color figure online)

2.1 Hierarchical Candidate Mass Region Generation Method

The mammograms have noise in the background such as tape markings and labels, which can be easily misdetected as masses. In this section, a hierarchical candidate region generation method is proposed to remove the noise and produce high-quality candidate mass regions, which can be divided into two steps. Firstly, we generate a preliminary candidate area that only includes the breast as shown in the Fig. 1. Specifically, a binary image is converted from the mammograms, in which the largest white interconnected area is preserved. Then, the preliminary candidate area is obtained through the position of the preserved interconnected area. Secondly, a RPN is used to provide the accurate candidate lesion regions from the preliminary candidate area, which is generated in the previous step. The RPN is also a fully-convolutional network (FCN). It can be end-to-end trained for the detection task of generating proposal boxes, and can simultaneously predict the boundaries and scores of the object, regardless of the class of the object.

To generate region proposals, we slide a small network over the convolutional feature map output by the last shared convolutional layer. This small network takes as input an n × n spatial window of the input convolutional feature map. Each sliding window is mapped to a lower-dimensional feature. This feature is fed into two sibling fully-connected layer, which are a box-regression layer (reg) and a box-classification layer (cls). It is used to determine whether the proposal is mass or non-mass in this research, and predict the location of the proposal.

At each sliding-window location, we simultaneously predict multiple region proposals, where the number of maximum possible proposals for each location is denoted as k. The k proposals are parameterized relative to k reference boxes, which we called anchors. And the anchor is the center of the sliding window, and is associated with a scale and aspect ratio. By default we use 3 scales and 3 aspect ratios, yielding k = 9 anchors at each sliding position.

2.2 Mass Detection with AMDR-CNN

For classifying and regressing the bounding box of the candidate mass regions, an improved Faster R-CNN named AMDR-CNN is proposed. Faster R-CNN has been successful in detection of natural image, but this is based on the case of large-scale trainable data. The field of medical imaging does not provide large-scale datasets, and the current performance of deep learning methods on different datasets is not stable. And the reason analyzed is that the basic CNN performance of Faster R-CNN is not good enough and it is difficult to learn more robust features for detection. In the past few years, with the emergence and better performance of deeper CNN, such as Residual Network (ResNet) [17]. We propose to use a deeper CNN (Inception_ ResNet_v2) [18] instead of the original VGG16 of Faster R-CNN, which is an improvement over the previous Inception_V3 network. It introduced the idea of ResNet in the original model and added shortcut connections. In this way, the output of each layer is not the mapping of the input in the traditional neural network, but the superposition of mapping and input. In addition, Inception_ResNet_v2 network increases the number of network layers and reduces parallel towers compared to the Inception_v3 network, which has stage 1 with 5 convolution layers and 2 max-pooling layers and an inception module; stage 2 has 5 Inception-Resnet-A modules; stage 3 has a Reduction-A module; stage 4 has 10 Inception-Resnet-B modules; stage 5 has a Reduction-B module; stage 6 has 5 Inception-Resnet-C modules; stage 7 has an average pooling layer, an dropout layer and a softmax layer, the detailed structure of all modules can refer to original [18]. It achieved the best results in the ILSVRC 16-year image classification benchmark.

For training the proposed AMDR-CNN, we assign a binary class label (of being an object or not) to each anchor generated by the hierarchical candidate region generation method. Specific allocation rules can be found in literature [19]. The loss function for an image is defined as:

$$L(\{p_i\}, \{t_i\}) = \frac{1}{N_{cls}} \sum_i L_{cls}(p_i, p_i^*) + \lambda \frac{1}{N_{reg}} \sum_i p_i^* L_{reg}(t_i, t_i^*)$$ (1)

Here, i is the index of an anchor and p_i is the predicted probability of anchor i being an object. The ground-truth label p_i^* is 0 if the anchor is negative, and is 1 if the anchor is positive. t_i is a vector representing the four parameterized coordinates of the predicted bounding box, and t_i^* is that of the ground-truth box associated with a positive anchor. The classification loss L_{cls} is log loss over two classes (object or not object). For the regression loss, we use $L_{reg}(t_i, t_i^*) = R(t_i - t_i^*)$ where R is the robust loss function (smooth L_1) defined in [20]. The term $p_i^* L_{reg}$ means the regression loss is activated only for positive anchors ($p_i^* = 1$) and is forbidden for negative anchors ($p_i^* = 0$). The outputs of the cls and reg layers consist of $\{p_i\}$ and $\{t_i\}$ respectively. The two terms are normalized by N_{cls} and N_{reg} and weighted by a balancing parameter λ. Further details about Faster R-CNN [19] can be found in the original article.

We use the Tensorflow as the backend of our deep learning framework. For end-to-end training the AMDR-CNN, we use backpropagation and stochastic gradient descent with weight decay. The initial model used for training has been pre-trained on the ImageNet dataset. For the two datasets INbreast and BCDR-F03, we trained 40k and 80k steps respectively, because the number of training images in the latter is more than six times of the former. Due to the memory of our GPU, we set the batch_size to 1. The learning_rate is set to 0.0003 in the first 20k steps, between 20k and 30k steps, it is 0.00003 and after 30k steps, it falls to 0.000003. The mass is considered to be detected if the overlap ratio between the bounding box of candidate region and ground truth is 0.2, similar to other works in the field [21–23].

3   Experimental Results

3.1   Datasets Description

The evaluation of our methodology is carried out on two publicly available datasets: INbreast [14] and BCDR-F03 [16]. The INbreast dataset comprises a set of 115 cases containing 410 images, and there are 116 images contain the benign or malignant mass lesions, whereas the rest does not contain any masses. The size of the images are 2560×3328 or 3328×4084 pixels. BCDR-F03 was built as a subset of the BCDR-FM and it is composed of 344 patients with 736 film images containing 426 benign mass lesions and 310 malignant mass lesions, including clinical data and image-based descriptors. The size of the images is 720×1167 pixels. The gray intensity of both datasets is quantized to 8 bits, and each case of these two datasets consist of the two standard views for each breast, Cranio-Caudal (CC) and MedioLateral-Oblique (MLO). We run a five-fold cross validation experiment on INbreast and BCDR-F03 datasets, where we divide the images in terms of the patients in a mutually exclusive manner, with 60% of the cases for training, 20% for validation and 20% for testing.

3.2   Evaluation of the Proposed AMDR-CNN

In order to test the ability to detect and localize masses of AMDR-CNN, we evaluated the performance of predictions on the INbreast and BCDR-F03 datasets using FROC curve. The FROC curve shows the True Positive(TP) as a function of the number of false positive per image(FPI) put on an image Fig. 2. In general on INbreast and BCDR-F03, the true positive performance saturates on the test set at TP of 0.88 at FPI = 0.75 and TP of 0.81 at FPI = 1.1 respectively. The comparison with other methods in Table 1 shows that AMDR-CNN produces the best results in INbreast, and the results of the mass detection on the BCDR-F03 have not been found currently, so we compared the results of other similar datasets for reference.

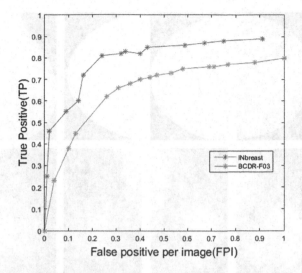

Fig. 2. FROC curve showing the result on various operating point with true positive (TP) against false positive per image (FPI) on INbreast and BCDR-F03.

Table 1. Comparing the performance of AMDR-CNN with state-of-the-art methods

Method	Dataset	Images	Crop	TP@FPI
AMDR-CNN	INbreast	116	Yes	0.88@0.75
Dhungel et al. [24]	INbreast	410	No	0.87@0.8
Kozegar et al. [21]	INbreast	116	No	0.87@3.67
AMDR-CNN	BCDR-F03	736	Yes	0.81@1.1
Dhungel et al. [24]	DDSM-BCRP	158	No	0.70@4
Campanini et al. [25]	DDSM	512	No	0.80@1.1

3.3 Visualization of Mass Detection Results

In our test results, the IOUs of some predictive boxes and ground-truths are less than 0.2 or there are no overlaps. Nevertheless, there is still a possibility that there is a mass in the prediction box. On this point we have received the recognition of professional imaging specialists. The FPI of our detection results is not high when the TP performance saturates on the test set in our result. Therefore, this will not increase too much workload of doctors. Instead, it can provide doctors with good suggestions to minimize the probability of missed masses. In addition, the hierarchical candidate mass region generation method avoids the marks of mammograms being misdetected as masses. We have created a collection of correctly detection, missed lesions and some controversial cases of the INbreast and BCDR-F03 datasets, see in Fig. 3.

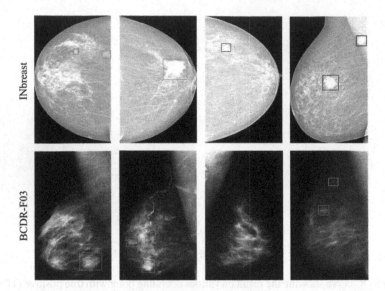

Fig. 3. The first row and the second row are the results of detection on the INbreast and BCDR-F03 datasets respectively. The green boxes represent correctly detection, the red boxes represent missed lesions, and the blue boxes represent false positive but controversial lesion regions. (Color figure online)

4   Conclusion

This research presents an approach to detect masses from mammograms automatically, that are called An Automatic Mass Detection framework with Region-based CNN (AMDR-CNN). We use the AMDR-CNN to perform end-to-end training on mammograms data. The contributions of this research are: (1) An improved Faster R-CNN framework is proposed and applied to the mass detection from mammograms first time. (2) A hierarchical candidate mass region generation method is proposed to produce high-quality proposals. Meanwhile, all operations are performed on the original image size without scaling, which solves the shortcoming of image detail loss due to scaling caused by traditional algorithms. (3) According to the characteristic that the size of mammograms is large but mass lesion is very small, we use a deeper CNN to distill the mass features and further detect masses. (4) The proposed AMDR-CNN framework achieves a good performance on the INbreast and BCDR-F03 datasets. In addition, our method also makes good suggestions for some suspected lesions in the dataset that are not ground-truth, and we have received the recognition of professional imaging specialists. It can be seen from the experimental results that the high TP can be maintained under low FPI, which reflects the effectiveness of our method.

We tried to use a unified method to solve the problem of mass detection and classification, but cannot achieve satisfactory results at the same time. The main work in the future is to combine the mass classification and the diagnosis of breast cancer with the work of this research to complete a system for the mass detection, classification, and diagnosis of breast cancer.

References

1. Ferlay, J., Héry, C., Autier, P., Sankaranarayanan, R.: Global burden of breast cancer. In: Li, C. (ed.) Breast Cancer Epidemiology, pp. 1–19. Springer, New York (2010). https://doi.org/10.1007/978-1-4419-0685-4_1
2. Broeders, M., et al.: The impact of mammography screening on breast cancer mortality in Europe: a review of observational studies. J. Med. Screen. **19**(suppl 1), 14–25 (2012)
3. Tabar, L., et al.: Mammography service screening and mortality in breast cancer patients: 20-year follow-up before and after introduction of screening. Lancet **361**(9367), 1405–1410 (2003)
4. Elmore, J.G., et al.: Variability in interpretive performance at screening mammography and radiologists' characteristics associated with accuracy1. Breast Dis. Year Book Q. **21**(4), 330–332 (2010)
5. Barlow, W.E., et al.: Accuracy of screening mammography interpretation by characteristics of radiologists. J. Natl. Cancer Inst. **97**(12), 1840–1850 (2005)
6. Brewer, N., Salz, T., Lillie, S.E.: Systematic review: the long-term effects of false-positive mammograms. Ann. Intern. Med. **147**(10), 739–740 (2007)
7. Myers, E.R., et al.: Benefits and harms of breast cancer screening: a systematic review. JAMA **314**(15), 1615 (2015)
8. Krizhevsky, A., Sutskever, I., Hinton, G.E.: ImageNet classification with deep convolutional neural networks. In: International Conference on Neural Information Processing Systems (2012)
9. He, K., et al.: Delving deep into rectifiers: surpassing human-level performance on ImageNet classification, pp. 1026–1034 (2015)
10. Kooi, T., et al.: Large scale deep learning for computer aided detection of mammographic lesions. Med. Image Anal. **35**, 303–312 (2017)
11. Becker, A.S., et al.: Deep learning in mammography: diagnostic accuracy of a multipurpose image analysis software in the detection of breast cancer. Investig. Radiol. **52**(7), 434 (2017)
12. Dhungel, N., Carneiro, G., Bradley, A.P.: Fully automated classification of mammograms using deep residual neural networks. In: IEEE International Symposium on Biomedical Imaging (2017)
13. Lotter, W., Sorensen, G., Cox, D.: A multi-scale CNN and curriculum learning strategy for mammogram classification. In: Cardoso, M.J. (ed.) DLMIA/ML-CDS -2017. LNCS, vol. 10553, pp. 169–177. Springer, Cham (2017). https://doi.org/10.1007/978-3-319-67558-9_20
14. Moreira, I.C., et al.: INbreast: toward a full-field digital mammographic database. Acad. Radiol. **19**(2), 236–248 (2012)
15. Ertosun, M.G., Rubin, D.L.: Probabilistic visual search for masses within mammography images using deep learning. In: IEEE International Conference on Bioinformatics and Biomedicine, pp. 1310–1315. IEEE (2015)
16. Arevalo, J., et al.: Representation learning for mammography mass lesion classification with convolutional neural networks. Comput. Methods Programs Biomed. **127**(C), 248–257 (2016)
17. Girshick, R., Donahue, J., Darrell, T., Malik, J.: Rich feature hierarchies for accurate object detection and semantic segmentation. In: IEEE Conference on Computer Vision and Pattern Recognition, CVPR (2014)

18. Szegedy, C., et al.: Inception-v4, Inception-ResNet and the impact of residual connections on learning (2016)
19. Ren, S., et al.: Faster R-CNN: towards real-time object detection with region proposal networks. In: International Conference on Neural Information Processing Systems (2015)
20. Girshick, R.: Fast R-CNN. In: IEEE International Conference on Computer Vision (2015)
21. Kozegar, E., et al.: Assessment of a novel mass detection algorithm in mammograms. J. Cancer Res. Ther. 9(4), 592 (2013)
22. Eltonsy, N.H., Tourassi, G.D., Elmaghraby, A.S.: A concentric morphology model for the detection of masses in mammography. IEEE Trans. Med. Imag. 26(6), 880 (2007)
23. Sampat, M.P., et al.: A model-based framework for the detection of spiculated masses on mammography. Med. Phys. 35(5), 2110–2123 (2008)
24. Dhungel, N., Carneiro, G., Bradley, A.P.: Automated mass detection in mammograms using cascaded deep learning and random forests. In: International Conference on Digital Image Computing: Techniques and Applications (2016)
25. Campanini, R., Dongiovanni, D., Iampieri, E., et al.: A novel featureless approach to mass detection in digital mammograms based on support vector machines. Phys. Med. Biol. 49(6), 961–975 (2004)

Study on Comfort Prediction of Stereoscopic Images Based on Improved Saliency Detection

Minghan Du, Guangyu Nie, Yue Liu$^{(\boxtimes)}$, and Yongtian Wang

Beijing Engineering Research Center of Mixed Reality and
Advanced Display School of Optoelectronics, Beijing Institute of Technology,
Beijing 100081, China
{duminghan, gynie, liuyue, wyt}@bit.edu.cn

Abstract. This paper proposed a saliency-dependent measure to predict visual comfort of stereoscopic. Considering the drawbacks of traditional stereoscopic display visual comfort assessment, a more accurate visual comfort prediction method based on improved stereoscopic saliency detection algorithm was proposed in this paper. The proposed approach includes 3 steps. The first step involves the calculation of region contrast, background prior, surface orientation prior and depth prior which aims to generate a stereoscopic saliency map. The second step is the extraction of visual comfort perception features. Finally, the prediction performance is evaluated by using SVR. The experimental results demonstrate that our method improves the prediction accuracy a lot compared with the related work.

Keywords: Stereoscopic display · Visual comfort · Saliency detection
Assessment system

1 Introduction

Stereoscopic display provides a more immersive and realistic viewing experience by enabling depth perception which has been involved into various areas. However, the visual discomfort of stereoscopic display becomes a growing issue with the wide application of stereoscopic display. Existing researches have shown that binocular parallax is one of the most significant induced factors [1].

As shown in Fig. 1, under the natural environment, the external object image can be mapped in the retina clearly through the convergence and accommodation of human visual system. When parallax occurs, the imbalance of convergence and accommodation will cause visual discomfort [2]. To enlarge the use of stereoscopic display further, it is necessary to research visual discomfort of stereoscopic display.

1.1 Related Work

In the previous studies, the global parallax amplitude and variance of disparity features are the main basis of predicting stereoscopic visual comfort objectively [3].

Lambooij et al. designed an experiment to study that how visual discomfort is built up [4]. Their experiment results showed that the screen disparity influenced visual

© Springer Nature Singapore Pte Ltd. 2018
Y. Wang et al. (Eds.): IGTA 2018, CCIS 875, pp. 451–460, 2018.
https://doi.org/10.1007/978-981-13-1702-6_45

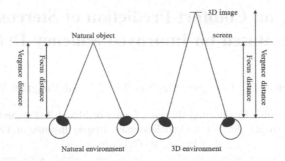

Fig. 1. Binocular parallax theory

comfort a lot in both static and dynamic scenes. Jung et al. proposed a visual comfort objective assessment based on visual importance regions [5]. Perceptually significant disparity features were taken into account to predict the overall degree of visual discomfort after obtaining a saliency-based visual importance map. Their experiment results showed that the method has a higher prediction accuracy. Sohn et al. came up with a visual discomfort prediction method according to object-dependent disparity features [6]. Their experimental results demonstrated that the visual comfort prediction performance was improved by using combined object-dependent disparity features.

It can be seen from the above researches that existing visual comfort prediction methods are mainly based on the visual disparity features. However, these are not enough to describe human stereoscopic visual system. The extracting of visual importance area is one of the significant path to simulate human visual attention mechanism [7]. In this paper, visual salient areas of stereoscopic images will be considered in our model, and more visual comfort perception features will be calculated in the model. The Fig. 2 illustrates the framework of our visual comfort assessment system.

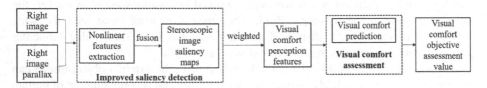

Fig. 2. The flow of our visual comfort assessment system

1.2   Stereoscopic Saliency Detection

Saliency detection has been used in many areas such as object detection, image segmentation and image/video retargeting in recent years. Various saliency detection algorithms based on bottom-up of human visual mechanism were proposed these days [8]. Itti et al. came up with a visual attention system inspired by the neuronal architecture of the early primate visual system [9]. The saliency map was calculated through multiscale image features. Yang et al. proposed a saliency detection model by considering both foreground and background cues instead of foreground only [10]. Li et al. introduced a saliency detection model by considering frequency domain [11]. They proposed a novel bottom-up flow for detecting salient area by using scale-space analysis of amplitude spectrum of images. All the saliency detection methods mentioned above are two-dimension saliency detection algorithms. To predict stereoscopic visual comfort, stereoscopic saliency detection model should be involved in our assessment system.

For stereoscopic image saliency detection, depth features are added into the two-dimension saliency maps usually [12]. Cheng et al. proposed a novel saliency detection method for stereoscopic images which is based on local-global contrast features, followed by surrounded regions and stereo center prior enhancement [13]. Their model achieved a better performance on eye-tracking databases. Tang et al. came up with a structured low-rank matrix recovery model for RGBD salient object detection [14]. The depth information was fused into the RGB result by a Laplacian regularization term. Chen et al. gave a new regional contrast based saliency method which works on depth images based on selective difference [15].

In this paper, an improved stereoscopic saliency detection method was proposed by merging region contrast, background cues, binocular parallax and surface orientation prior features. This improved saliency detection model will be used into the stereoscopic visual comfort prediction system.

2 Improved Saliency Detection Model

Saliency detection, which predicts the area that human will look in an image, has been extensively studied for decades [16]. However, most of the existing methods focused on two-dimension images. To deal with stereoscopic visual comfort problem based on

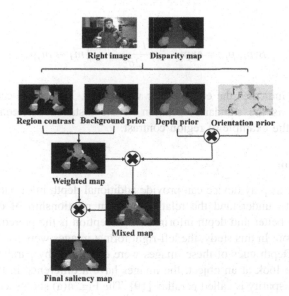

Fig. 3. An overview of the improved saliency model

saliency detection, a stereoscopic saliency detection method is necessary in this study. Ren et al. gave a RGB-D saliency detection model according to global priors in 2015 [17]. Multi-modality imaging data were used in their saliency detection model to improve performance. This paper presents an improved stereoscopic saliency detection model for binocular images instead of RGB-D images inspired by J. Ren's method. The flow of our saliency detection model is shown in Fig. 3.

Three priors, depth, orientation and background prior, were exploited respectively and the region contrast was calculated also. The weighted maps were obtained through region contrast and background prior maps. The mixed maps were calculated by mixing the weighted maps, depth prior maps and orientation prior maps together. Finally, the saliency maps were obtained through the weighted maps and mixed maps.

2.1 Region Contrast

Regional contrast algorithms have been widely used in visual saliency detection area [18]. A region contrast method was used in this model which can simultaneously evaluate global contrast differences and spatial coherence. Depth value was added in the region contrast. We first segmented the image into super-pixel using SLIC when the original image and depth map were calculated by parallax. The contrast of each super-pixel was evaluated to other super-pixels. Here the saliency value was calculated to its color and parallax contrast to all other super-pixel which is shown in formula (1):

$$S_{rc}(p_i) = \sum_{i \neq j} A(p_j) B(p_i, p_j) \tag{1}$$

where i, j are the indexes of region and contained in $\{1, \ldots, n\}$, n is the total region number. $A(p_j)$ is the area of region p_j. The computational formula of $B(p_i, p_j)$ is shown as follows:

$$B(p_i, p_j) = \exp(-\frac{\left\| \vec{c}_i - \vec{c}_j \right\|_2^2}{2\sigma_c^2}) \left\| \vec{m}_i - \vec{m}_j \right\|_2 \tag{2}$$

In which $\vec{m}$ indicates the color vector with depth, $\vec{c}$ denotes each super-pixel's centroid and σ_c is the standard deviation of the distance between two centroids. Figure 7 shows the example of region contrast.

2.2 Depth Prior

The stereoscopic display device can provide additional depth information for the users and help users to understand the relative position relationship of objects in three-dimension space better and depth information perception is the prerequisite for human stereoscopic vision. In this study, the left-right format images were used to calculate the saliency maps. Depth cues of these images were calculated by parallax.

When people look at an object, the images have a difference in the left and right retina, and this disparity is called parallax [19]. The Fig. 4(a) shows a camera model of stereo system. The object O is shoot by two cameras and obtain two images as left and right format images. The baseline distance indicates the parallax.

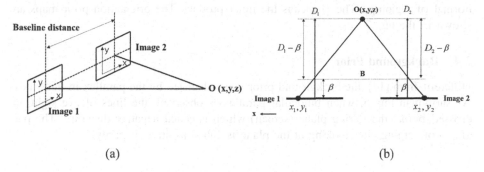

(a)   (b)

Fig. 4. Camera model of a stereo system

The depth is inversely proportional to parallax where x_1 and x_2 are pixel coordinates of the same world point when projected on the stereo image planes. According to the similar triangle, the depth can be calculated by the parallax which is shown in the Fig. 4(b):

Where B is baseline distance and $D - \beta$ is depth. Here we have:

$$X_1 = \frac{x_1}{\beta}(\beta - D_1) \tag{3}$$

$$X_1 + B = \frac{x_2}{\beta}(\beta - D_2) \tag{4}$$

Further deduction can be obtained from the above formulas:

$$D - \beta = depth = \frac{\beta B}{x_1 - x_2} = \frac{\beta B}{parallax} \tag{5}$$

It can be seen from the formula (5) that the depth is proportional to the parallax.

The weighted maps were obtained by adding contrast maps and depth prior maps together which is shown in Fig. 7.

2.3   Surface Orientation Prior

Surface orientation is one of the most important stereoscopic cues in RGB-D methods [17]. Existing measurements used to calculate the relative surface orientation between two super-pixels [20]. In this paper, we conducted surface orientation prior based on the [17] method. The method is based on the direction perpendicular to the principal axis catches the most attention. The orientation prior by:

$$S_{op}(p_i) = \langle \overrightarrow{z}, \overrightarrow{n}(p_i) \rangle \tag{6}$$

Where p_i indicates a region, $\overrightarrow{z}$ is the principal axis and $\overrightarrow{n}(p_i)$ is the unit surface normal of region p_i. The $\langle \rangle$ means the inner product. The orientation prior maps are shown in the Fig. 7.

2.4 Background Prior

Different from [17], the background prior was calculated by the parallax in this study. As shown in Fig. 5, when binocular parallax is observed, the lines of eye sight are crossed before the staring plane (screen) which is called negative disparity. The parallax converging after looking at the plane is called positive disparity.

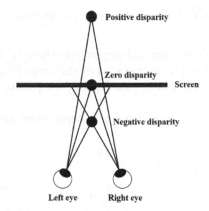

Fig. 5. Three states of binocular parallax

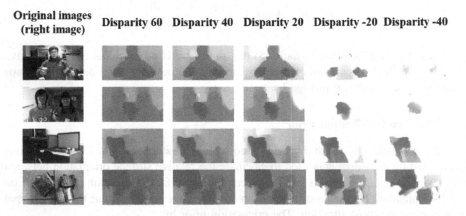

Fig. 6. Foreground extraction by different disparity (Color figure online)

Existing researches show that the foreground objects generally attract more visual attention compared with background objects in a scene [21]. Assuming the salient objects usually closer to the camera than the background when people are taking pictures. According to this point, we used different disparity scale to extract the foreground object and calculate the background prior. The change parameters of disparity and corresponding results are shown in the Fig. 6.

Here we set different zero disparity plane and extracted the foreground objects by translating the plane. As the Fig. 6 shown, the red areas of images are foreground objects in different disparity scale. The deep red illustrates that the area is closer to the camera. The background prior maps were obtained through moving the zero parallax plane.

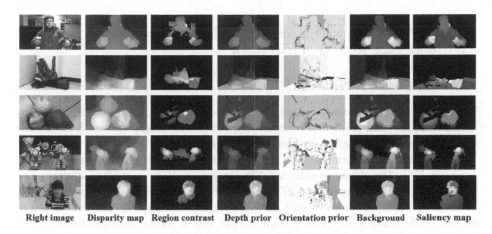

Right image   Disparity map   Region contrast   Depth prior   Orientation prior   Background   Saliency map

Fig. 7. Examples of saliency detection results generated at each step

3   Stereoscopic Images Visual Comfort Assessment

After getting the saliency maps, 4 visual comfort perception features were used and the saliency maps were used as weighted coefficient. Finally, the relationship model between stereoscopic visual comfort and saliency maps was established by SVR.

3.1   Visual Comfort Perception Features

Existing studies show that the parallax features and space frequency can influence visual comfort a lot [22]. Therefore, parallax amplitude eigenvector φ_1, parallax gradient φ_2, disparity standard deviation φ_3 and space frequency φ_4 were used to as visual comfort perception features. The perception features are written as $\xi = [\varphi_1, \varphi_2, \varphi_3, \varphi_4]$ and the features can be calculated as follows:

$$\varphi_1 = \frac{1}{P}\sum_{x=1}^{M}\sum_{y=1}^{N} SM(x, y) \cdot d(x, y) \tag{7}$$

$$\varphi_2 = \frac{1}{P}\sum_{x=1}^{M}\sum_{y=1}^{N} SM(x, y) \cdot |\Delta d(x, y)| \tag{8}$$

$$\varphi_3 = \sqrt{E\left[(D - \mu)^2\right]} \tag{9}$$

$$\varphi_4 = \frac{1}{P}\sum_{x=1}^{M}\sum_{y=1}^{N} SM(x,y) \cdot |c(x, y)| \tag{10}$$

Where P is normalization factor, $\Delta d(x, y)$ is the gradient value of pixel (x, y), $c(x, y)$ is the space frequency of pixel (x, y).

3.2 Visual Comfort Prediction

The visual comfort prediction model was calculated by perception features $\xi = [\varphi_1, \varphi_2, \varphi_3, \varphi_4]$ and prediction function f, where f was trained through SVR. In this study, the radial basis kernel function was used in the SVR.

Our prediction experiment was conducted in the IVY Lab stereoscopic image database [23]. The database includes 120 images in 1920 × 1080 resolution. The images were collected under the ITU-R BT.500 and ITU-R BT.1438 rules and the MOS (mean opinion score) of each image were also involved in this database. The higher MOS means higher visual comfort. The Fig. 8 shows the right image of the database:

Fig. 8. Examples of IVY database

In this study, PLCC (Pearson Linear Correlation Coefficient), SRCC (Spearman Rank-order Correlation Coefficient), KRCC (Kendall Rank-order Correlation Coefficient) and RMSE (Root Mean Squared Error) were used as objective evaluation parameters. The PLCC and RMSE indicate the prediction accuracy of the model and SRCC and KRCC shows the monotonicity. A good prediction model should have high PLCC, SRCC, KRCC and a low RMSE.

The Table 1 shows the contrast results among different models. Except that, different feature groups were also selected to illustrate the influence of different features.

Table 1. The contrast results among different models.

Methods	Evaluation parameters			
	PLCC	SRCC	KRCC	RMSE
Reference [3]	0.6602	0.6750	0.4818	0.6043
Reference [4]	0.7427	0.7689	0.5679	0.5387
Reference [22]	0.7996	0.8192	0.6123	0.4732
$\xi = [\varphi_1, \varphi_2, \varphi_3, \varphi_4]$	0.8681	0.9604	0.8797	0.6117
$\xi = [\varphi_1, \varphi_4]$	0.8720	0.9686	0.8975	0.5995
$\xi = [\varphi_2, \varphi_4]$	0.8666	0.9604	0.8800	0.6178
$\xi = [\varphi_3, \varphi_4]$	0.8649	0.9605	0.8804	0.6240

4   Conclusion

A comfort prediction of stereoscopic images based on improved saliency detection model was proposed in this paper. Three prior calculation and region contrast method were used in the improved saliency model. According to the stereoscopic saliency value, the perception features of stereoscopic visual comfort were obtained. Finally, the SVR was used as regression model. The experiment results show that the model is highly consistent with subjective evaluation results. Our visual comfort assessment model can more accurately reflect the relationship between three-dimension image and visual comfort.

On the basis of this study, the more efficiency saliency detection model and visual comfort perception features will be considered in our future research to enhance the objective classification accuracy of stereoscopic visual comfort.

Acknowledgement. This work has been supported by the National Technology Support Program of China (Grant No. 2015BAK01B05).

References

1. Lambooij, M., Fortuin, M., Heynderickx, I.: Visual discomfort and visual fatigue of stereoscopic displays: a review. J. Imag. Sci. Technol. **53**(3), 30201-1–30201-14(14) (2009)
2. Hoffman, D.M., Girshick, A.R.: Vergence–accommodation conflicts hinder visual performance and cause visual fatigue. J. Vis. **8**(3), 33.1 (2008)

3. Choi, J., Kim, D., Ham, B.: Visual fatigue evaluation and enhancement for 2D-plus-depth video, pp. 2981–2984 (2010)
4. Lambooij, M., Ijsselsteijn, W.A., Heynderickx, I.: Visual discomfort of 3D TV: assessment methods and modeling. Displays **32**(4), 209–218 (2011)
5. Jung, Y.J., Sohn, H., Lee, S.I.: Predicting visual discomfort of stereoscopic images using human attention model. IEEE Trans. Circ. Syst. Video Technol. **23**(12), 2077–2082 (2013)
6. Sohn, H., Jung, Y.J., Lee, S.I.: Predicting visual discomfort using object size and disparity information in stereoscopic Images. Trans. Broadcast. **59**(1), 28–37 (2013)
7. Li, H., Luo, T., Xu, H.: Saliency detection of stereoscopic 3D images with application to visual discomfort prediction. 3D Res. **8**(2), 14 (2017)
8. Fan, X., Liu, Z., Sun, G.: Salient region detection for stereoscopic images. In: International Conference on Digital Signal Processing, pp. 454–458. IEEE (2014)
9. Itti, L., Koch, C., Niebur, E.: A model of saliency-based visual attention for rapid scene analysis. IEEE Trans. Pattern Anal. Mach. Intell. **20**(11), 1254–1259 (1998)
10. Yang, C., Zhang, L., Lu, H.: Saliency detection via graph-based manifold ranking. In: Computer Vision and Pattern Recognition, pp. 3166–3173. IEEE (2013)
11. Li, J., Levine, M.D., An, X.: Visual saliency based on scale-space analysis in the frequency domain. IEEE Trans. Pattern Anal. Mach. Intell. **35**(4), 996–1010 (2016)
12. Peng, H., Li, B., Xiong, W., Hu, W., Ji, R.: RGBD salient object detection: a benchmark and algorithms. In: Fleet, D., Pajdla, T., Schiele, B., Tuytelaars, T. (eds.) ECCV 2014. LNCS, vol. 8691, pp. 92–109. Springer, Cham (2014). https://doi.org/10.1007/978-3-319-10578-9_7
13. Cheng, H., Zhang, J., An, P.: A novel saliency model for stereoscopic images. In: International Conference on Digital Image Computing: Techniques and Applications, pp. 1–7. IEEE (2015)
14. Tang, C., Hou, C.: RGBD salient object detection by structured low-rank matrix recovery and Laplacian constraint. Trans. Tianjin Univ. **23**(2), 176–183 (2017)
15. Chen, Q.X., Fu, L.H., Li, C.C.: A new depth saliency method based on selective difference, vol. 12, p. 03018 (2017)
16. Qu, L., He, S., Zhang, J.: RGBD salient object detection via deep fusion. IEEE Trans. Image Process. **26**(5), 2274–2285 (2016)
17. Ren, J., Gong, X., Yu, L.: Exploiting global priors for RGB-D saliency detection. In: Computer Vision and Pattern Recognition Workshops, pp. 25–32. IEEE (2015)
18. Cheng, M.M., Mitra, N.J., Huang, X.: Salient object detection and segmentation. IEEE Trans. Pattern Anal. Mach. Intell. **37**(3), 1 (2013)
19. Binocular, D.S., Motion, B., Parallax, M.: Perception of three-dimensional space: how do we use information derived from one or both eyes to perceive the spatial layout of our surroundings. In: Perception of the Visual Environment, pp. 257–294. Springer, New York (2002). https://doi.org/10.1007/0-387-21650-2_9
20. Ciptadi, A., Hermans, T., Rehg, J.: An in depth view of saliency. In: British Machine Vision Conference, pp. 112.1–112.11 (2013)
21. Lang, M., Hornung, A., Wang, O.: Nonlinear disparity mapping for stereoscopic 3D. ACM Trans. Graph. **29**(4), 1–10 (2010)
22. Shao, F., Jiang, Q.P., Jiang, G.Y.: Prediction of visual discomfort of stereoscopic images based on saliency analysis. Opt. Precis. Eng. **22**(6), 1631–1638 (2014)
23. IVY Lab stereoscopic image database. http://ivylab.kaist.ac.kr/demo/3DVCA/3DVCA.htm

Deep Convolutional Features for Correlation Filter Based Tracking with Parallel Network

Jinglin Zhou, Rong Wang[✉], and Jianwei Ding

People's Public Security, University of China, Beijing, China
henlouser@163.com, dbdxwangrong@163.com

Abstract. Visual tracking has made great progress in either efficiency or accuracy, but still remain imperfections in accurately tracking on the premise of real time. In this paper, we propose a parallel network to integrate two trackers for real-time and high accuracy tracking. In our tracking framework, both trackers are based on correlation filters running in parallel, with one using hand-crafted features (tracker A) for efficiency and another using deep convolutional features (tracker B) for accuracy. And the tracking results are under supervision by a novel criterion. Furthermore, the sample models trained for correlation filter are optimized by controlling sampling frequency. For evaluation, our tracker is experimented on the datasets OTB2013 and OTB2015, demonstrating a higher accuracy than the state-of-the-art trackers on the premise of real time, especially in the situation of object deformation and occlusion.

Keywords: Tracking · Convolutional feature · Correlation filter
Parallel network

1 Introduction

Object visual tracking is the fundamental work in the field of computer vision. With the broad application prospects in high-level visual tasks, such as automatic driving [1] and scene understanding [2], visual tracking has attracted great attentions from researchers [3, 4]. Whereas, suffering from the interference introduced by environment variation, generic visual tracking is still one of the most challenge research in computer vision. A robust tracking algorithm with high accuracy and efficiency becomes a research hotspot nowadays [5].

Since the deep convolutional neural networks have made a significant breakthrough in the field of object recognition [6], researchers have begun to apply the deep neural network architecture to visual tracking. The convolutional neural network based tracking algorithms have demonstrated great advantages in tracking accuracy [7]. Based on deep convolutional neural networks, trackers are pre-trained by relative sequences for a robust end to end tracker [8]. Another application is exacting deep convolutional features for Siamese network [9], aiming at an online learning tracker. The deep convolutional network has made some progress in accuracy, it performs poorly in terms of computation speed [10].

© Springer Nature Singapore Pte Ltd. 2018
Y. Wang et al. (Eds.): IGTA 2018, CCIS 875, pp. 461–470, 2018.
https://doi.org/10.1007/978-981-13-1702-6_46

The tracking algorithms based on the correlation filter have improve the computing efficiency to a certain extent. The first correlation filter based tracking algorithm MOSSE [11] had caused a sensation for its excitement efficiency. Since then, the KCF [12] tracker applies the kernel function and cyclic matrix to the correlation filter, which is the further improvement of this kind algorithm. In the subsequent SRDCF [13] tracker, the scale adaption is introduced for the problem of object transforming scales continuously. Nevertheless, the correlation filter based trackers have an inherent limitation that they resort to low-level hand-crafted features, are easy to affected by the interference when target is occluded or blurred.

In this paper, deep convolutional neural feathers and online sample model optimization mechanism are introduced for a correlation filter based tracker, aiming at both real-time and high accuracy tracking. Firstly, features are exacted from the first frame and integrated to the sample model for correlation filters. Secondly, based on a parallel implementation architecture, two tracker which based on correlation filter but with different features do tracking alternately and have complementary advantages. The tracker with hand-crafted features executed tracking in most frames under supervise and the other tracker with deep convolutional features would be activated to rectify the tracking results when the results from the former are considered to unreliable. Finally, the tracking results are selected to update the sample model under supervise, for the online training of correlation filters which would be used for the next frame.

The proposed tracker is evaluated on the popular datasets OTB2013 and OTB2015, comparing to 8 state-of-the-art trackers. The experiments show that our tracker have advantages in the situation that the target is blurred and under deformation, and could keep a high accuracy in real-time tracking.

2   Method

2.1   Deep Convolutional Neural Network

Convolutional neural network is a classical architecture of deep learning that inspired from visual mechanism of biology, having a great advantage in exacting robust features which are applicable for object rotation, deformation and so on. Furthermore, without designing, the convolutional neural network could achieve different dimensional features.

According to above, we employ the Very Deep Convolutional Network [14] (which is notated as VGG Net in later parts of this paper) as the convolutional neural network we exacted features from. There are 19 weight layers in the VGG Net we employed, as shown in Fig. 1.

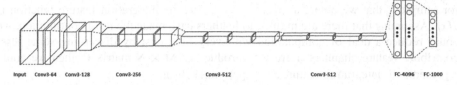

Input   Conv3-64   Conv3-128   Conv3-256   Conv3-512   Conv3-512   FC-4096   FC-1000

Fig. 1. The structure of the VGG Net, including 19 weight layers. There are 16 convolutional layers, 3 fully-connected layers and 5 max-pooling layers.

To exact features, we pre-trained the VGG Net on the ImageNet dataset. Experiments show that the deep layers have achieve richer semantic information and less detail texture, whereas the shallow layers achieved the reverse. The visualization of the features exacted from different layers have been shown in Fig. 2.

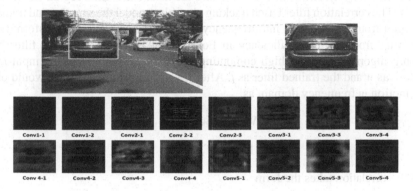

Fig. 2. The visualization of features exacted from every layer in VGG Net. With the deepening of the layer, we could obtain more semantic information and less details. For a complete expression of samples, we employ features from both shallow and deep layers in this paper.

2.2 Multi-features Integration

To make the best of the advantages in diverse features, we select features from multiple layers. According to experiments, we employ the feathers exacted from conv1-1, conv2-2 and conv5-2. And we also employ hand-craft feathers including HOG and color names features to improve the efficiency of the algorithm. The convolutional features and the hand-craft feathers work in a parallel framework, and more detail discussion we would made in Sect. 3.1.

As there are more than one features in each streams, the integration of multiple features should be taken into account. The traditional method is utilizing features by integrating all feature maps, with massive computation.

The other method proposed by [4] performs more efficient. Their method reduce computation by transforming different features into a continuous spatial domain. According to this method, we defines $x_1, x_2, \ldots, x_i$ that represent the training samples for correlation filter from image patches. For each samples, there are n feature channels for sample x_i that we notate as $x_i^1, x_i^2, \ldots, x_i^n$. And the integration feature function is $J\{x\}$. Assuming that there are m (m < n) feathers have made the most contribution, we could reduce a deal of computation with very little cost by discarding some less-contribute feature channels. Here we introduce an M × N matrix P, then we could represents the integration feature $J\{x\}$ approximately as

$$J\{x\} = P^T J_n\{x^n\}. \tag{1}$$

2.3 Correlation Filter

The correlation Filter is usually applied to evaluate the correlation between two signals in communication filed. Extending to visual tracking problem, it is a realistic solution that considering object tracking as searching the most correlation region between two frames. The correlation filter based tracking algorithm model the samples and transform the signal from time domain into frequency domain by Fast Fourier Transform (FFT). Benefiting from the high efficiency in Fourier domain, the correlation filter based tracking algorithm enjoy a high computing speed. Here, we denote the input image window as w and the trained filter as f. After Fourier transformation, we would obtain the function in frequency domain as

$$W = \mathcal{F}(w). \tag{2}$$

$$F = \mathcal{F}(f). \tag{3}$$

The correlation takes the form

$$G = W \odot F^*. \tag{4}$$

Where the $\odot$ indicates element-wise multiplication and the * indicates the complex conjugate. The location corresponding to the maximum value of G represents the new position in the current frame. Base on deduction in Sects. 3.2 and 3.3, there is

$$G = W \odot F^* = f * P^T J_n\{x^n\}. \tag{5}$$

According to above, the tracking task have been transformed to finding the position that the maximum correlation responding to. Furthermore, the filter would update online based on the sample obtained from the new frame.

3 Our Tracking Framework

3.1 Architecture

Our tracking framework consist of two trackers. Both of the trackers are based on the correlation filter, with one of them using deep convolutional features (Tracker A) and the other one using hand-craft features (Tracker B). Tracker B has advantage in computation efficiency, along with Tracker A represents more reliable on tracking accuracy.

Each tracker performs its own functions in parallel, aiming at both high accuracy and real-time tracking. Here we employ the SRDCF [13] tracker as our baseline tracker.

As shown in Fig. 3, tracker A executes tracking task and evaluates whether its result is reliable in every frame. The tracking task would continue if the result was considered to be confidence. Otherwise, a request would be sent to tracker B, asking for a more reliable result from tracker B who is based on deep convolutional feathers. The tracker B would not execute tracking unless received request. At the rest of time, tracker B only updates the sample model based on the tracking results from tracker A.

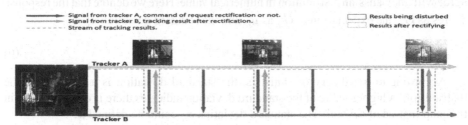

Fig. 3. The pipeline of our tracking framework. The two trackers work in parallel under supervision. The tracker A do tracking in most frames and request of rectifying would be sent to tracker B if the results from tracker A is considered to be unreliable.

3.2 Confidence Embedding

According to the theory of the correlation filter based trackers, the location of maximum correlation responding would be considered to be the position of target. But with the interference such an illumination variation or occlusion, the location of maximum correlation responding might not be the most appropriate position to the target. What is more, there is a serious risk that the tracking results occurred to drift in serval frames letter when the mistaken is accumulated without rectifying promptly, as shown in Fig. 4.

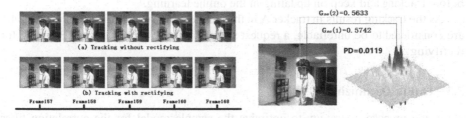

Fig. 4. A comparison of tracking with rectifying and without rectifying. The tracking results is drifting when errors from interference were not rectified promptly. The response map on the right demonstrates the correlation response in frame 157 where errors started accumulate, suffering a low level of PD.

In order to detect the problematic tracking results and rectify it timely, we employ two criteria to judge whether tracking results are reliable or not. One of them is the value of G which has discussed in Sect. 2.3, the other one is a measure we creatively proposed.

By repeating experiment, the problematic tracking results always happened to the situation that there exist several regions similar to the target in appearance nearby. Reflected on the convolutional correlation response maps, there would be several peaks distributing on the map. Nevertheless, under normal conditions there is only one peak on the correlation response map that the value this peak responding to is much higher than the other value is. In view of this, we could evaluate the reliability of the tracking results by analyzing the distribution of the correlation response scores on the map.

In every frame, there are 2809 (53 × 53) response scores being calculated, which agree with the Gaussian distribution in numerical value. Here we denote that the response scores as G_{sc}, the expectation of G_{sc} as μ_{sc} and the standard deviation as σ_{sc}.

$$G_{sc} \sim N\left(\mu_{sc}, \sigma_{sc}^2\right) \tag{6}$$

According to the theory of statistics, the standard deviation is a measure of the distribution. A higher value of the standard deviation indicates there is only one peak in the map instead of several. The standard deviation σ_{sc} could be defined as

$$\sigma_{sc} = \sqrt{\sum \left(G_{sc} - \mu_{sc}\right)^2}. \tag{7}$$

Here we obtain a new measure to evaluate the distribution of the peaks on the map as Peaks Distribution (PD)

$$PD = \sigma_{sc}. \tag{8}$$

On the basis of above, we could consider a high value of PD indicates that the maximum response is significant and the noise is small. In other words, the tracking results are reliable in the situation of the value of PD is high enough.

Here we propose the conditions which must be satisfied in the situation of tracking results considered to be reliable: $G > T_1 \ and \ PD > T_2$. Where T_1 and T_2 is pre-setting before tracking and keep on updating in the online learning.

As the tracking results in tracker A in the architecture we have discussed in Sect. 4.1 are considered to be unreliable, a request signal would be sent to tracker B asking for rectifying.

3.3   Online Optimizing

Here, we propose a strategy to optimize the sample model for the correlation filter training. Most correlation filter based trackers update the sample model in every frame, without considering whether the updates are necessary. Whereas, the unreliable updating would bring about errors and frequent updating would lead to overfitting.

Picking up the appropriate samples for correlation filter training instead of every exacted samples could not only improve the accuracy rate of tracking, but also reduce the computational complexity effectively, especially for the tracker which is based on deep convolutional features.

Our strategy of the sample model optimization is updating model under online learning. For avoiding the overfitting, we distribute the samples in groups. The successive similar samples are divided into one group (as shown in Fig. 5) and the frequent in different group is unequable. Here we introduce a criteria learning rate ζ to indicate the frequency of sampling. The more samples accumulated in one group, the lower the learning rate ζ is in this group. To ensure the reliability of samples, the correlation filter would simply be trained when results are considered to be confidence. Here we employ the measure PD we have discussed in Sect. 3.1.

$$\zeta = \begin{cases} 0 \, (PD < T_3) \\ \dfrac{k}{PD}(k > 0, PD > T_3) \end{cases} \tag{9}$$

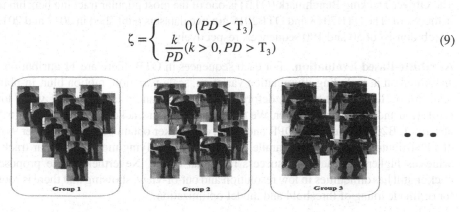

Fig. 5. An example of grouping the samples. The successive similar samples are divided into group, for reducing the computation and avoiding overfitting.

4 Experiments

We extensively evaluate our tracker on the most popular visual tracker benchmark nowadays, the Object Tracking Benchmark (OTB) [16]. The OTB consists of two datasets, OTB2013 and OTB2015, which consist of 50 and 100 sequences respectively. For the purpose of comparison, we employ 8 state-of-the-art trackers, including ECO [15], DeepSRDCF [13], SRDCF [13], Staple [17], LCT [18], DCFNet [8], MEEM [19] and KCF [12], as shown in Fig. 6.

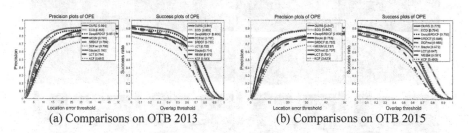

(a) Comparisons on OTB 2013   (b) Comparisons on OTB 2015

Fig. 6. Comparisons with state-of-the-art tracking trackers on OTB2013 and OTB2015 with the DPR and OSR.

4.1 Implementation Details

Our tracker is implemented in a numerical computing environment, Matrix Laboratory (Matlab) in version 2016b. The experiments is validated on a machine equipped with an Intel Core i7 running at 2.50 GHz with 16 GB memory.

4.2 Experiments on OTB2013 and OTB2015

The Object Tracking Benchmark (OTB) is one of the most popular tracking benchmark in the word. The OTB2013 and OTB2015 are two datasets published in 2013 and 2015, which consist of 50 and 100 sequences, respectively.

Attribute-Based Evaluation. For each sequences in OTB, there are 11 attribution is annotated on it, including illumination variation, scale variation, motion blur, in-plane rotation, occlusion, fast motion, deformation, out-of-plane rotation, out of view, low resolution and background clutter. We further analyze our tracker under different attributes in OTB2015. In terms of DPR and OSR, our tracker obtain best results under 9 out of 11 attributes. Owing to the parallel network and rectifying mechanism, our tracker achieves higher accuracy and success rate than others. Nevertheless, the proposed tracker still has difficulties in low resolution and out-of-view, showing that there is room for online learning of threshold and model optimization.

Qualitative Evaluation. Figure 7 demonstrates qualitative comparisons of our tracker with eight state-of-the-art trackers on four sequences selected from OTB2013. Compared with the correlation filter based tracker, our tracker performs more reliable in sequences with deformation and rotation. The deep convolutional feature based trackers could deal with these cases, but failed in sequences with occlusion. Our tracker performs the best in these sequence, benefiting from the parallel architecture.

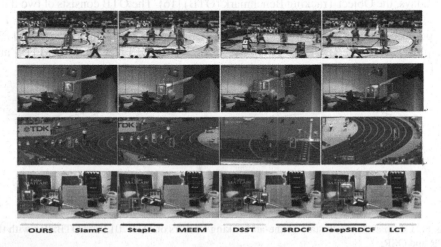

Fig. 7. Qualitative evaluation of the proposed tracker and other eight state-of-the-art trackers on four sequence in OTB2015 (from top to bottom: *Basketball*, *Coke*, *Bolt*, and *Sylvester*).

5   Conclusion

In this paper, we propose a novel real-time object tracking method by integrating deep convolutional features with correlation filter using a parallel network. A strategy is proposed to verify the current tracking results according to convolution response and rectify the results by the deep features based component. Making the best of high efficiency from correlation filter and reliability from deep features. Furthermore, we construct an online sample model optimizing strategy to reduce computation toward more efficiency tracking. The encouraging results are demonstrated in experiments performed on OTB2013 and OTB2015, achieving a state-of-the-art performance both on accuracy and on speed. Further work would involve the improvement of the rectified performance by introducing a more reliable tracker for rectifying.

Acknowledgments. This work is supported by National Key Research and Development Plan under Grant No. 2016YFC0801005. This work is supported by the National Natural Science Foundation of China under Grant No. 61503388.

References

1. Pohlen, T., Hermans, A., Mathias, M., Leibe, B.: Full-resolution residual networks for semantic segmentation in street scenes. In: IEEE Conference on Computer Vision and Pattern Recognition, pp. 3309–3318. IEEE Press, Hawaii (2017)
2. Bagautdinov, T., et al.: Social scene understanding: end-to-end multi-person action localization and collective activity recognition. In: IEEE Conference on Computer Vision and Pattern Recognition, pp. 3425–3434. IEEE Press, Hawaii (2017)
3. Galoogahi, H.K., et al.: Learning background-aware correlation filters for visual tracking. In: IEEE International Conference on Computer Vision, Venice, pp. 1135–1143 (2017)
4. Danelljan, M., Robinson, A., Shahbaz Khan, F., Felsberg, M.: Beyond correlation filters: learning continuous convolution operators for visual tracking. In: Leibe, B., Matas, J., Sebe, N., Welling, M. (eds.) ECCV 2016. LNCS, vol. 9909, pp. 472–488. Springer, Cham (2016). https://doi.org/10.1007/978-3-319-46454-1_29
5. Fan, H., Ling, H.: Parallel tracking and verifying: a framework for real-time and high accuracy visual tracking. In: IEEE International Conference on Computer Vision, Venice, pp. 5486–5494 (2017)
6. Krizhevsky, A., Sutskever, I., Hinton, G.E.: ImageNet classification with deep convolutional neural networks. In: International Conference on Neural Information Processing Systems, pp. 1097–1105 (2012)
7. Nam, H., Han, B.: Learning multi-domain convolutional neural networks for visual tracking. In: IEEE Conference on Computer Vision and Pattern Recognition. IEEE Press, Las Vegas (2016)
8. Valmadre, J., Bertinetto, L., Henriques, J., Vedaldi, A., Torr, P.H.S.: End-to-end representation learning for correlation filter based tracking. In: IEEE International Conference on Computer Vision, Venice, pp. 5000–5008 (2017)
9. Bertinetto, L., Valmadre, J., Henriques, J.F., Vedaldi, A., Torr, P.H.S.: Fully-convolutional siamese networks for object tracking. In: Hua, G., Jégou, H. (eds.) ECCV 2016. LNCS, vol. 9914, pp. 850–865. Springer, Cham (2016). https://doi.org/10.1007/978-3-319-48881-3_56

10. Kang, K., et al.: Object detection from video tubelets with convolutional neural networks. In: IEEE Conference on Computer Vision and Pattern Recognition, pp. 817–825. IEEE Press, Las Vegas (2016)
11. Bolme, D.S., Beveridge, J.R., Draper, B.A., Lui, Y.M.: Visual object tracking using adaptive correlation filters. In: IEEE Conference on Computer Vision and Pattern Recognition, pp. 2544–2550. IEEE Press, San Francisco (2010)
12. Henriques, J.F., et al.: High-speed tracking with kernelized correlation filter. In: IEEE Transactions on Pattern Analysis and Machine Intelligence, vol. 37, pp. 583–596 (2015)
13. Danelljan, M., Hager, G., Khan, F.S., Felsberg, M.: Learning spatially regularized correlation filters for visual tracking. In: IEEE International Conference on Computer Vision, pp. 4310–4318 (2016)
14. Simonyan, K., Zisserman, A.: Very deep convolutional networks for large-scale image recognition. Comput. Sci. (2014)
15. Danelljan, M., et al.: ECO: efficient convolution operators for tracking. In: IEEE Conference on Computer Vision and Pattern Recognition, pp. 6931–6939. IEEE Press, Hawaii (2017)
16. Wu, Y., Lim, J., Yang, M.-H.: Object tracking benchmark. IEEE Trans. Pattern Anal. Mach. Intell. 37(9), 1834–1848 (2015)
17. Bertinetto, L., et al.: Staple: complementary learners for real-time tracking. In: IEEE Conference on Computer Vision and Pattern Recognition, pp. 1401–1409. IEEE Press, Las Vegas (2016)
18. Ma, C., Yang, X., et al.: Long-term correlation tracking. In: IEEE Conference on Computer Vision and Pattern Recognition, pp. 5388–5396. IEEE Press (2016)
19. Zhang, J., Ma, S., Sclaroff, S.: MEEM: robust tracking via multiple experts using entropy minimization. In: Fleet, D., Pajdla, T., Schiele, B., Tuytelaars, T. (eds.) ECCV 2014. LNCS, vol. 8694, pp. 188–203. Springer, Cham (2014). https://doi.org/10.1007/978-3-319-10599-4_13

Robust and Real-Time Visual Tracking Based on Single-Layer Convolutional Features and Accurate Scale Estimation

Runling Wang[1(✉)], Jiancheng Zou[1], Manqiang Che[2], and Changzhen Xiong[2]

[1] School of Sciences, North China University of Technology, Beijing 100144, China
1573112241@qq.com
[2] Beijing Key Laboratory of Urban Intelligent Control Technology, North China University of Technology, Beijing 100144, China
1229462669@qq.com

Abstract. Visual tracking is a fundamental problem in computer vision. Recently, some methods have been developed to utilize features learned from a deep convolutional neural network for visual tracking and achieve record-breaking performances. However, deep trackers suffer from efficiency. In this paper, we propose an object tracking method combining the single-layer convolutional features with correlation filter to locate and speed up. Meanwhile accurate scale prediction and high-confidence model update strategy are adopted to solve the scale variation and similarity interfere problems. Extensive experiments on large scale benchmarks demonstrate the effectiveness of the proposed algorithm against state-of-the-art trackers.

Keywords: Object tracking · Correlation filter · Convolutional features
Scale pyramid · Model update

1 Introduction

Visual tracking addresses the problem of identifying and localizing an unknown target in a video given the target specified by a bounding box in the first frame. It has attracted increasing interest in the past decades due to its importance in numerous applications, such as intelligent video surveillance, vehicle navigation, and human-computer interaction. Despite the significant effort that has been made to develop algorithms [1–4] and benchmark evaluations [5, 6] for visual tracking, it is still a challenging task owing to complicated interfering factors like heavy illumination changes, shape deformation, partial and full occlusion, large scale variations, to name a few.

Owing to the high complexity of deep learning, most deep trackers suffer from low tracking speed, and thus are impractical in many real-world applications. Some new deep trackers with smaller network structure achieve high efficiency while at the cost of significant decrease on precision. In Fig. 1, we display the relationship between tracking speed and accuracy of some deep state-of-the-art trackers [1–4, 7–12]. For better illustration, only those trackers with accuracy higher than 0.82 are reported.

© Springer Nature Singapore Pte Ltd. 2018
Y. Wang et al. (Eds.): IGTA 2018, CCIS 875, pp. 471–482, 2018.
https://doi.org/10.1007/978-981-13-1702-6_47

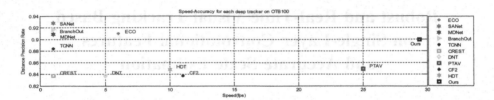

Fig. 1. Speed and accuracy plot of deep state-of-the-art visual tracking on OTB100

Obviously, SANet [2], MDNet [3] and BranchOut [4] utilizing robust deep features for appearance representation obtain highest accuracies than 0.9, but the speeds are around 1 fps; ECO [1] introduces factorized convolution operator to reduce the number of model's parameters but only gets slight increase in speed; CF2 [11] combines the hierarchical features from VGG-19 [13] network with fast shallow tracker based on correlation filters, and achieves high accuracy but 11 fps in speed which is far from practical; PTAV [10] runs in real-time and the performances are barely satisfactory.

Though afore mentioned progresses in either accuracy or speed, real-time and robust trackers remain rare. In this paper, we consider the problems mentioned above and propose an algorithm based on single-layer convolutional features and accurate scale estimation to seek a trade-off between speed and accuracy. The main contributions of our work can be summarized below:

- We decrease the hierarchical layers and adopt a single-layer convolutional features to speed up.
- We change the Gaussian distribution of the samples to match the selected layer by tinkering with the Gaussian bandwidth of label function for training samples.
- We introduce an accurate scale estimation method to predict the scale variation of the object, expecting to further improve the performance.
- We utilize the high-confidence model update strategy, which is beneficial to precision improvement, to prevent our proposed model from drifting due to serious occlusion or interference of similar objects.

The framework of our tracker is shown in Fig. 2, which consists of translation prediction and scale estimation.

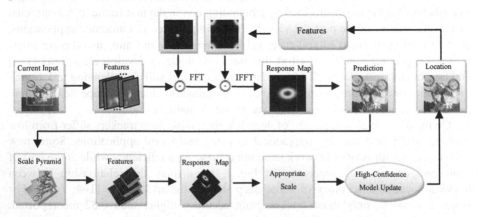

Fig. 2. Framework of proposed algorithm

2 Related Work

CNN Based Trackers. Visual representations play a very important role in object tracking. Numbers of hand-crafted features used to represent the target appearance such as Histogram of Oriented Gradient (HOG) and Color Names (CN) achieve great success. Since 2013, deep-learning methods spur in the field of visual tracking and exceed hand-crafted methods gradually. Wang et al. [14] propose a deep learning tracker (DLT) using a multi-layer auto-encoder network for the first time and solve the problem of insufficient training data through the idea of "offline pre-training and online fine tuning". Hong et al. [15] learn target-specific saliency map using a pre-trained CNN. On the other hand, Wang et al. [16] use feature maps for target tracking from a two-layer neural network, whose earlier and last hierarchical features are complementary in semantic and spatial information. Held et al. [17] make full use of labeled videos and images to train a completely offline universal target tracker and achieve pleasant speed of 100 frames per second, while the precision is notoriously ineffective. Nam et al. [3] design the shallow "shared layers + domain-specific layers" framework for the acquisition of target representation and classification respectively, recommending with the introduction of hard negative mining and bounding box regression approaches. Therefore, they historically obtain the high accuracy, but regretfully only 1 frame per second in speed.

Correlation Filters Based Trackers. Correlation filters for visual tracking have attracted considerable attention due to the high computational efficiency with fast Fourier transforms (FFT). Bolme et al. [18] learn a Minimum Output Sum of Squared Error filter over luminance channel for fast visual tracking. Henriques et al. [19] propose CSK algorithm based on correlation filter by introducing kernel methods and employing ridge regression, but the simplicity of gray features for learning and training makes it lower accuracy. Subsequently they put forward the Kernelized Correlation Filters (KCF) [20], extending the input features from single channel to multiple channels namely HOG, but there is no ideal effect when faced with challenges of multi-scale and fast motion. Xiong et al. [21] propose a kernelized correlation filters tracking based on adaptive feature fusion, which combines global CN features and local HOG features, solving the problem of tracking failure caused by simple feature due to deformation and illumination. Danelljan et al. [22] figure out the fast scale estimation problem by learning separate filters for translation and scale estimation. Ma et al. [11] adaptively learn correlation filters on three convolutional layers to encode the target appearance and hierarchically infer the maximum response of each layer to locate targets. Wang et al. [23] propose to transfer the features of image classification to visual tracking domain via convolutional channel reductions, which significantly increases the tracking speed to real-time performances. Chi et al. [9] integrate the hierarchical feature maps in different layers with an edge detector, and update it with stochastic and periodic methods. Wang et al. [24] make full use of the strong discriminative ability of structured SVM and advantage of correlation filter in speed, combining with multimodal target detection and high-confidence update strategy to improve the speed and accuracy effectively. Danelljan *et al.* [1] introduce a factorized convolution operator to reduce dimensions of features and propose a compact generative model to better the diversity of training samples, which effectively prevents the samples from being contaminated by backgrounds and wrong targets.

3 Correlation Filters

A correlation filter based algorithm learns a discriminative classifier and estimates the translation of the target by searching the maximum value of correlation response map in the search window. Here, we denote x as the feature vector of size $M \times N \times D$, where M, N and D indicate the width, height and the number of channels, respectively. Algorithms based on correlation filters use cyclic offset to generate numbers of training samples $x_{m,n} = \{0, 1, \cdots, M-1\} \times \{0, 1, \cdots, N-1\}$, where m, n indicate shifted position of the samples in the directions of width and height. The core problem of correlation filters is to minimize the square error of the regression function $f(x) = w_t x$, that is to solve the following problem:

$$w^* = \arg\min \sum_{m,n} \left\| w \cdot x_{m,n} - y(m,n) \right\|^2 + \lambda \|w\|_2^2, \tag{1}$$

where w_t is classifier parameter of frame t, w^* is classifier parameter when the error is minimized, w is classifier parameter, $\cdot$ is the inner product which is induced by a linear kernel in the Hilbert space, y is Gaussian labeled function of training samples and λ is a regularization parameter. According to [19], we obtain the closed-loop solution quickly in the Fourier domain by sampling the circulant matrix with shifting so can get the classifier parameters of data's filter on the d-th channel:

$$W^d = \frac{Y \odot \overline{X}_d}{\sum_{d-1}^{D} X_d \odot \overline{X}_d + \lambda}, \tag{2}$$

where Y is the Fourier transformation of the Gaussian labeled function y, the bar indicates complex conjugation and d is the dimension. The operator $\odot$ means Hadamard product.

Given a new image patch, we note z_d as the convolutional feature. Therefore the response for its Fourier transformation Z_d and the classifier parameter W^d can be computed by

$$f = \mathbb{F}^{-1}\left(\sum_{d=1}^{D} W^d \odot \overline{Z}_d\right) \tag{3}$$

The operator $\mathbb{F}^{-1}$ denotes the inverse FFT. And therefore the target location can be estimated by searching for the maximum value of the correlation response map f.

4   Robust and Real-Time Visual Tracking Based on Single-Layer Convolutional Features and Accurate Scale Estimation

4.1   Single-Layer Convolutional Features and Bandwidth Adjustment Strategy

According to [11], the last convolutional layer encode the semantic information and such representations are robust to significant appearance variations; in contrast, earlier layers provide precise localization but are less invariant to appearance changes. So it encodes the object appearance with features extracted from multiple layers (C3-4, C4-4 and C5-4). But redundant features and amounts of computation make the tracking speed rather poor, which is a big trouble for practical application. Therefore, we propose to decrease to a single layer to speed up.

Along with the VGG-19 forward propagation, the semantic discrimination between objects from different categories is strengthened, as well as a gradual reduction of spatial resolution for precise localization. While in visual tracking task, we need features extracted not only possess abundant semantic information to better adapt to appearance variations, but also retain spatial information so as to localize targets. Thus, compared with C3-4 which has better resolution while poor semantic information and C5-4 which is in verse, we take layers before or after C4-4 into account, namely C4-3, C4-4, C5-1, C5-2, C5-3 (more semantic information for appearance variations).

The VGG-19 network is trained by large-scale classification databases. But the difference between classification and tracking lies in the former regarding the similar objects as a category, while the other sorting out representations in all angles and directions of an object from other objects. Therefore, there exist serious interferences from backgrounds when applying the network to tracking. So we take the distribution of training samples into account to increase their diversity to better the discriminative ability for interferences.

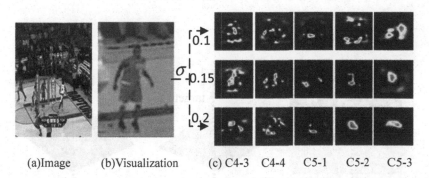

(a)Image   (b)Visualization   (c) C4-3   C4-4   C5-1   C5-2   C5-3

Fig. 3. Visualization of convolutional layers' features with different σ. (a) Image from *Basketball* sequence and ground truth foreground mask. (b) Visualization of the input image patch. (c) Feature map extracted from layers C4-3, C4-4, C5-1, C5-2, C5-3 with different bandwidths of the Gaussian labeled function of training samples.

For each shifted sample, there exists a Gaussian labeled function

$$y(m, n) = \exp(-\frac{(m - M/2)^2 + (n - N/2)^2}{2\sigma^2}),$$

where σ (generally set to 0.1) is the Gaussian kernel bandwidth, determining the pixels' classification. The lager bandwidth is, the more diversely the sample distributes, which makes the classification of pixels more prominent (target or background) and is of benefit to tracker. Figure 3 shows the relationship between the bandwidth σ and the layers in feature extraction of the input image. When increase the bandwidth σ of Gaussian labeled function to change the degree of concentration of the target and backgrounds, the diversity of training samples will be changed and match the required need of different layers. And thus we increase the value of σ with the interval 0.05 and find the layer C5-2 with bandwidth $\sigma = 0.2$ performs excellently. Therefore, we only extract features for tracking task from a single layer.

4.2 High-Confidence Model Update

Most existed trackers update at each frame without considering whether the detection is accurate or not. The ideal response map should have only one sharp peak and be smooth in all other areas when the detected target is extremely matched to the correct target as shown on the right in Fig. 4. However, the unimodal detection will regard the highest peak as the target leading to false detection especially faced with interference of similar object as shown in the middle. To guarantee the robustness, we exploit the high-confidence model update [24] to tackle the challenging problems of occlusion and interference of similar object. We define the average peak-to-correlation energy (APCE) measure, which indicates the fluctuated degree of response maps and the confidence level of the detected target, as

$$APCE = \frac{|f_{\max} - f_{\min}|^2}{mean(\sum_{w,h} (f_{w,h} - f_{\min})^2)}, \tag{4}$$

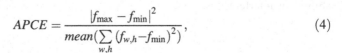

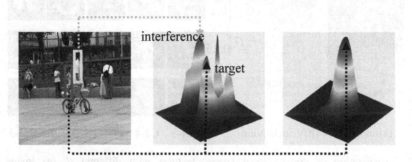

Fig. 4. Illustration for interference of similar object in sequence *Girl2*. The red bounding box indicates the correct location of target while the yellow is interference. Apparently, the response of the target is weaker. (Color figure online)

where f_{max}, f_{min} and $f_{w,h}$ denote the maximum, minimum response score of the response map and the w-th row h-th column elements of f.

When there are occlusion, interference and target missing, APCE will significantly decrease. While when f_{max} and APCE are both greater than their respective historical average values with certain ratios ρ_1, ρ_2, the tracking result in the current frame is considered high confidence and then the proposed tracker will be updated online using a moving average:

$$A_t^d = (1 - \eta)A_{t-1}^d + \eta Y \odot \bar{X}_t^d,$$
$$B_t^d = (1 - \eta)B_{t-1}^d + \eta \sum_{i=1}^{D} X_t \odot \bar{X}_t, \tag{5}$$
$$W_t^d = \frac{A_t^d}{B_t^d + \lambda},$$

where η is the learning rate and W_t^d is the correlation filter of t-th frame and d-th dimension of the features.

4.3 Accurate Scale Prediction

To better accommodate useful features of the target in different scales, the accurate scale estimation on a scale pyramid [22] is adopted. In visual tracking scenarios, the scale difference between two frames is typically smaller compared to the translation filter. Therefore, we first apply the translation filter W^d given a new frame. According to the scale pyramid which is constructed the size of the target at its estimated scale, each image patch is zoomed into the appropriate scale. Let w $\times$ h donate the target size in the current frame and S be the size of the scale filter. For each $i \in \{-\frac{S-1}{2}, \ldots, \frac{S-1}{2}\}$, we exact an image patch J_i of size $s_d w \times s_d h$, where $s_d > 1$ denotes the scale factor between feature layers, centered around the target position predicted by the translation filter. Afterwards, the scale filter W_s is applied at the new target location. An example x computed by extracting features using variable patch size centered around the target is extracted from this location. By maximizing the correlation output (4) between W_s and x, we obtain the scale difference. That is

$$s = \arg\max(\max(f_1), \max(f_2), \cdots, \max(f_i)), \tag{6}$$

where f_i is response map of scale filter. In addition, to obtain a robust approximation, (5) is used to update the scale filter with the new sample x.

5 Experiments

We implement out algorithm in Matlab R2015b underlying Ubuntu 16.04 system, and utilize the MatConvNet toolbox in this work. Our implementation runs at 29.4 frames per second on a computer with an Intel I5-4590K 4.00 GHz CPU, 8 GB RAM, and a GeForce GTX1070 GPU card. All the following experiments are carried out with the fixed parameters: the tradeoff parameter is set to $\lambda = 0.0001$; the learning rate is set to

$\eta = 0.01$; the Gaussian kernel bandwidth for translation filter is 0.2, while $S = 33$ number of scales with a scale factor of $s_d = 1.02$ with kernel bandwidth 0.1. We set value of ρ_1, ρ_2 in high-confidence model update 0.3 and 0.6 respectively.

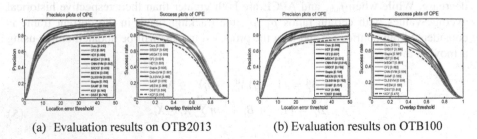

(a) Evaluation results on OTB2013   (b) Evaluation results on OTB100

Fig. 5. Average precision plots and success plots over 50 and the entire 100 benchmark sequences

We compare our algorithm with 11 recent state-of-the-art trackers: MEEM [25], DLSSVM [26], KCF [20], SRDCF [27], SAMF [28], Staple [29], DSST [22], CF2 [11], MSDAT [23], CNN-SVM [15], HDT [12]. Among them, MEEM is developed based regression and multiple tracker, DLSSVM is structured SVM based method, KCF, SRDCF, SAMF, Staple, DSST are CF based methods, these above are designed with conventional hand-crafted features, while CF2, MSDAT, CNN-SVM, HDT are based on CNN features.

Comparison with State-of-the-Art Trackers

To fully assess our method, we use one-pass evaluation (OPE) metric on a large object tracking benchmark dataset OTB100 which contains 100 image sequences. For completeness, we also report the results on the benchmark OTB2013 [5], which is a subset of benchmark OTB100 [6].

To verify the contribution of each component in our algorithm, we implement and evaluate three additional variations of our tracking algorithm on OTB100—Ours with the Gaussian bandwidth $\sigma = 0.1$ ($\sigma = 0.1$); Ours without APCE model update strategy (noapce) and Ours without APCE model update strategy and scale estimation (noapcescale). The performance of all the variations are not as good as our full algorithm (Ours) and each component in our tracking algorithm is helpful to improve performance. The detailed results are illustrated in Fig. 6.

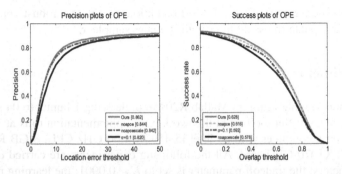

Fig. 6. Precision and success plots on OTB100 for the internal comparisons

Quantitative Evaluation. We evaluate the proposed algorithm with comparisons to 11 state-of-the-art trackers. Figure 5 illustrates the precision plots and success plots under OPE metric. Obviously, the proposed algorithm performs favorably against the state-of-the-art methods. Moreover, we present the quantitative comparisons of average distance precision rate (DPR), average overlap success rate (OSR) and average center location error (CLE) on two benchmarks [3, 4] in Table 1. The first, second and third best values are highlighted in color. Among the trackers, ours achieves the best results and obtains the lower CLE of 21.3 pixels over 100 video sequences compared to the baseline CF2 with 22.8 pixels.

Table 1. Comparisons of average DPR, OSR and CLE with state-of-the-art trackers on OTB2013 and OTB100.

		Proposed	Deep trackers				Correlation-filters based trackers					Others	
		[Ours]	CF2	MSDAT	CNN-SVM	HDT	KCF	SRDCF	SAMF	DSST	Staple	MEEM	DLSSVM
OTB2013	DPR (%)	91.0	89.1	86.3	85.2	88.9	74.0	83.8	78.5	74.0	79.3	83.0	82.9
	OSR (%)	81.9	74.0	74.1	73.4	73.7	62.3	78.1	73.2	67.0	75.4	69.6	72.4
	CLE (pixels)	11.8	15.7	14.6	17.9	15.9	35.5	35.2	30.1	41.2	30.6	20.9	24.1
OTB100	DPR (%)	86.8	83.7	82.1	81.4	84.8	69.6	78.9	75.1	68.0	78.4	78.1	76.2
	OSR (%)	78.1	65.5	65.5	65.1	65.7	55.1	72.8	67.4	60.1	70.9	62.2	62.4
	CLE (pixels)	21.3	22.8	20.5	21.8	20.1	45.0	38.6	36.5	50.4	31.5	27.8	32.9

Attribute-Based Evaluation. To thoroughly evaluate the robustness of the proposed algorithm in various scenes, we summarize the performances based on OTB100 dataset, where all videos are annotated with 11 different attributes, namely: illumination variation (IV), out-of-plane rotation (OPR), scale variation (SV), occlusion (OCC), deformation (DEF), motion blur (MB), fast motion (FM), in-plane rotation (IPR), out-of-view (OV), background cluttered (BC) and low resolution (LR). For clarity, we report the results in Table 2. Our tracking algorithm achieves the best performances under 9 out of 11 attributes in terms of DPR and obtains 10 out of 11 when it comes to OSR but doesn't perform well in handling fast motion and low resolution, which can be explained that features from a single layer can't contain rich spatial details from earlier layers and semantics from last layer simultaneously. Overall, compared with other state-of-the-art tracking algorithms, ours can better locate the target object.

Qualitative Evaluation. We present some tracking results of the top performing tracking methods in Fig. 7: DSST [21], Staple [29], CF2 [11], MSDAT [23], KCF [20] and the proposed algorithm on 12 challenging sequences. KCF learns a kernelized correlation filter over HOG features. It doesn't perform well in deformations (*Couple, Girl2, Skiing, Bolt2*), motion blur and fast motion (*BlurCar2*). DSST performs well in sequences with scale variations (*Shaking, Lemming*), but fails when there are in-plane rotation (*Diving, MotorRolling*) and background clusters (*DragonBaby, Freeman4, Couple* and *Bolt2*) occur. Staple combines a correlation filter (using HOG features) with a global color histogram and thus achieves excellent performance to challenging

Table 2. Average DPR and OSR of our tracker and other top five trackers on different attributes. The first and second highest values are highlighted by bold and underline.

Attributes	DPR (%) on eleven attributes						OSR (%) on eleven attributes					
	Ours	HDT	CF2	MSDAT	CNN-SVM	SRDCF	Ours	HDT	CF2	MSDAT	CNN-SVM	SRDCF
IV	**86.7**	82.0	81.7	82.5	79.5	79.2	**78.2**	60.8	61.6	63.5	61.5	74.7
OPR	**84.7**	80.5	80.7	79.7	79.8	74.2	**74.2**	62.7	62.9	63.6	64.9	66.4
SV	**82.8**	80.8	79.9	77.1	78.7	74.5	**71.1**	51.4	51.9	50.8	52.9	66.7
OCC	**79.4**	77.4	76.7	74.0	73.0	73.5	**70.2**	61.1	60.6	59.7	60.6	68.4
DEF	**83.1**	82.1	79.1	79.2	79.3	73.4	**71.7**	61.8	60.3	60.4	63.4	66.7
MB	**81.5**	78.9	80.4	76.1	75.1	76.7	**77.7**	68.9	69.8	65.9	71.5	72.9
FM	79.9	**81.7**	81.5	74.4	74.7	76.9	**73.9**	66.4	66.8	63.4	64.9	71.7
IPR	**87.8**	84.4	85.4	85.4	81.3	74.5	**76.0**	65.7	66.2	67.6	65.7	66.2
OV	**71.5**	66.3	67.7	62.7	65.0	59.7	**61.6**	54.7	54.0	56.0	59.1	55.8
BC	**86.6**	84.4	84.3	83.3	77.6	77.5	**77.8**	71.3	72.1	72.5	68.1	70.1
LR	83.3	88.7	84.7	85.0	**92.5**	76.5	52.9	35.4	32.7	35.9	29.3	**66.8**
Overall	**86.8**	84.8	83.7	82.1	81.4	78.9	**77.6**	65.7	65.5	65.5	65.1	72.8

Proposed ——— DSST ——— Staple ——— CF2 ——— MSDAT ——— KCF ———

Fig. 7. Qualitative evaluation of the proposed algorithm and other five state-of-the-art trackers on twelve challenging sequences (from left to right and top to bottom are *Sylvester, DragonBaby, BlurCar2, MotorRolliing, Bolt2, Shaking, Couple, Diving, Skiing, Freeman4, Girl2, Lemming*)

situations exhibiting motion blur (*BlurCar2*, *DragonBaby*) but notoriously sensitive to deformation (*Diving*, *Girl2*, *MotorRolling*, *Skiing*) as hand-crafted features are not effective in accounting for large appearance changes. CF2 is the baseline of MSDAT and Ours. Both of the two use deep features to represent object appearance so that they could fully exploit the semantic and fine-gained information as we do and can deal with these cases to some degree. Nevertheless, they still fail when heavy occlusion happens with other situations such as deformation and fast motion (*BlurCar2*, *Girl2*). Compared with these trackers, our approach accurately estimates the target scale and translation despite the mentioned factors.

6 Conclusions

In this paper, we propose an object tracking method combining the CNNs features with correlation filter. Hence the proposed algorithm absorbs the powerful representation ability from convolutional features and speeds up by correlation filter algorithm significantly. The accurate scale prediction and high-confidence model update strategy are adopted to improve the precision. It is worth to emphasize that our proposed algorithm not only performs superiorly, but also runs at a speed of 29.4 which is sufficient for real-time applications.

Acknowledgments. This work is supported in part by National Key R&D Program of China, 2017YFC0821102, in part by North China University of Technology Students' Technological Activity.

References

1. Danelljan, M., Bhat, G., Khan, F.S., Felsberg, M.: ECO: efficient convolution operators for tracking. In: Computer Vision and Pattern Recognition, pp. 6931–6939 (2017)
2. Fan, H., Ling, H.: SANet: structure-aware network for visual tracking. In: CVPR Deep Vision Workshop, pp. 2217–2224 (2016)
3. Nam, H., Han, B.: Learning multi-domain convolutional neural networks for visual tracking. In: Computer Vision and Pattern Recognition, Las Vegas, pp. 4293–4302 (2016)
4. Han, B., Sim, J., Adam, H.: BranchOut: regularization for online ensemble tracking with convolutional neural networks. In: IEEE Conference on Computer Vision and Pattern Recognition, Las Vegas, pp. 521–530 (2017)
5. Wu, Y., Lim J, Yang M.: Online object tracking: a benchmark. In: Computer Vision and Pattern Recognition, Portland, pp. 2411–2418 (2013)
6. Wu, Y., Lim J, Yang M.: Object tracking benchmark. In: Computer Vision and Pattern Recognition, pp. 1834–1848 (2015)
7. Nam, H., Baek, M., Han, B.: Modeling and propagating CNNs in a tree structure for visual tracking. http://arxiv.org/abs/1608.07242
8. Song, Y., Ma, C., Gong, L., Zhang, J., Lau, R.W., Yang, M.: CREST: convolutional residual learning for visual tracking. In: IEEE International Conference on Computer Vision, pp. 2574–2583 (2017)
9. Chi, Z., Li, H., Lu, H.: Dual deep network for visual tracking. IEEE Trans. Image Process. **26**, 2005–2015 (2017)

10. Fan, H., Ling, H.: Parallel tracking and verifying: a framework for real-time and high accuracy visual tracking. http://arxiv.org/abs/1708.00153v1

11. Ma, C., Huang, J., Yang, X.: Hierarchical convolutional features for visual tracking. In: Computer Vision and Pattern Recognition, Boston, pp. 3074–3082 (2015)

12. Qi, Y., Zhang, S., Qin, L., Yao, H., Huang, Q., Lim, J.: Hedged deep tracking. In: Computer Vision and Pattern Recognition, pp. 4303–4311 (2016)

13. Simonyan, K., Zisserman, A.: Very deep convolutional net works for large-scale image recognition. In: International Conference on Learning Representations, San Diego (2015)

14. Wang, N., Yeung, D. Y.: Learning a deep compact image representation for visual tracking. In: International Conference on Neural Information Processing Systems, pp. 809–817. Curran Associates Inc. (2013)

15. Hong, S., You, T., Kwak, S.: Online tracking by learning discriminative saliency map with convolutional neural network. In: Computer Science, pp. 597–606 (2015)

16. Wang, L., Ouyang, W., Wang, X.: Visual tracking with fully convolutional networks. In: IEEE International Conference on Computer Vision, Santiago, pp. 3119–3127 (2015)

17. Held, D., Thrun, S., Savarese, S.: Learning to track at 100 FPS with deep regression networks. In: Leibe, B., Matas, J., Sebe, N., Welling, M. (eds.) ECCV 2016. LNCS, vol. 9905, pp. 749–765. Springer, Cham (2016). https://doi.org/10.1007/978-3-319-46448-0_45

18. Bolme, D., Beveridge, J., Draper, B.: Visual object tracking using adaptive correlation filters. In: Computer Vision and Pattern Recognition, California, pp. 2544–2550 (2010)

19. Henriques, J.F., Caseiro, R., Martins, P., Batista, J.: Exploiting the circulant structure of tracking-by-detection with kernels. In: Fitzgibbon, A., Lazebnik, S., Perona, P., Sato, Y., Schmid, C. (eds.) ECCV 2012. LNCS, vol. 7575, pp. 702–715. Springer, Heidelberg (2012). https://doi.org/10.1007/978-3-642-33765-9_50

20. Henriques, J.F., Rui, C., Martins, P.: High-speed tracking with kernelized correlation filters. IEEE Trans. Pattern Anal. Mach. Intell. 37, 583–596 (2015)

21. Xiong, C., Zhao, L., Guo F.: Kernelized correlation filters tracking based on adaptive feature fusion. J. Comput.-Aided Des. Comput. Graph. 1068–1074 (2017). (in Chinese)

22. Danelljan, M., Häger, G., Khan, F.: Accurate scale estimation for robust visual tracking. In: Proceedings of British Machine Vision Conference, Nottingham, pp. 65.1–65.11 (2014)

23. Wang, X., Li, H., Li, Y.: Robust and real-time deep tracking via multi-scale domain adaptation. In: IEEE International Conference on Multimedia and Expo, Hong Kong, pp. 1338–1343 (2017)

24. Wang, M., Liu, Y., Huang, Z.: Large margin object tracking with circulant feature maps. In: Proceedings of IEEE International Conference on Computer Vision and Pattern Recognition, Hawaii, pp. 4800–4808 (2017)

25. Zhang, J., Ma, S., Sclaroff, S.: MEEM: robust tracking via multiple experts using entropy minimization. In: Fleet, D., Pajdla, T., Schiele, B., Tuytelaars, T. (eds.) ECCV 2014. LNCS, vol. 8694, pp. 188–203. Springer, Cham (2014). https://doi.org/10.1007/978-3-319-10599-4_13

26. Ning, J., Yang, J., Jiang, S.: Object tracking via dual linear structured SVM and explicit feature map. In: Computer Vision and Pattern Recognition, Las Vegas, pp. 4266–4274 (2016)

27. Danelljan, M., Gustav, H., Fahad, S.: Learning spatially regularized correlation filters for visual tracking. In: IEEE International Conference on Computer Vision, Santiago, pp. 4310–4318 (2015)

28. Li, Y., Zhu, J.: A scale adaptive kernel correlation filter tracker with feature integration. In: Agapito, L., Bronstein, M.M., Rother, C. (eds.) ECCV 2014. LNCS, vol. 8926, pp. 254–265. Springer, Cham (2015). https://doi.org/10.1007/978-3-319-16181-5_18

29. Bertinetto, L., Valmadre, J., Golodetz, S.: Staple: complementary learners for real-time tracking. In: Computer Vision and Pattern Recognition, Las Vegas, pp. 1401–1409 (2016)

A Method of Registering Virtual Objects in Monocular Augmented Reality System

Zeye Wu[1,2], Pengrui Wang[1], and Wujun Che[1,3(✉)]

[1] Institute of Automation, Chinese Academy of Sciences, Beijing 100190, China
{wuzeye2016,wujun.che}@ia.ac.cn
[2] School of Computer and Control Engineering, University of Chinese Academy of Sciences, Beijing 100049, China
[3] AICFVE of Beijing Film Academy, Beijing 100088, China

Abstract. A flexible novel method of registering virtual objects in monocular AR system is presented in this paper. Monocular AR systems use SLAM-related techniques to obtain the camera pose, of which the translation component is on a random scale. We add a scale calibration process to acquire the scale factor from the SLAM map to the real world and provide a closed-form solution of the transformation between two coordinate systems with different scales. We also describe the framework of an AR system based on our method with implementation. The proposed system can easily initialize virtual objects' position, orientation and size by using a known reference in the real scene and the reference is no longer needed in the later process. Our method is flexible, simple to set up and easy to control. The results show the proposed method can apply to real-time interactive AR applications.

Keywords: Augmented reality · Monocular SLAM · Virtual objects registration
Scale calibration

1 Introduction

Augmented Reality (AR) is a technology of overlaying virtual objects on real scenes which can interactive with the environment in real-time. It has huge application potential in the fields of medicine, military, education and entertainment [1–5]. AR registration consists of two aspects: tracking the observer's pose relative to the environment and correctly locating the virtual objects on the real scene.

Tracking is an essential process of AR and has been the most popular research topic of AR in recent years [6]. SLAM (Simultaneous Localization and Mapping) is an attractive option of tracking since it can provide accurate pose estimation in an unknown environment without any marker. Commercial AR solutions including Magic Leap [7] and ArKit [8] have applied SLAM-related techniques in their devices. One of the most convenient sensors for SLAM is a single camera due to its low cost, minimal size and wide deployment in personal terminals. Therefore, researchers have also been interested

© Springer Nature Singapore Pte Ltd. 2018
Y. Wang et al. (Eds.): IGTA 2018, CCIS 875, pp. 483–493, 2018.
https://doi.org/10.1007/978-981-13-1702-6_48

in monocular visual SLAM-based AR [9–12]. Several monocular visual SLAM solutions have been suggested to use in AR including MonoSLAM [13], PTAM [10], ORB-SLAM [14], RKSLAM [11].

In marker-less monocular SLAM-based AR, a common way to locate virtual objects in the environment is to detect planar surfaces from point clouds recovered by SLAM and register virtual objects to random or manually-selected positions on these surfaces [12, 15, 16]. It makes it inconvenient to register virtual objects accurately.

Besides, such methods have to face the scale ambiguity problem which is inherent for monocular visual SLAM. Since the estimated map by monocular SLAM usually has an unknown scale, it cannot provide sufficient information for registration. For example, when supposed to place an avatar of actual human size, the monocular AR system may display a mini-size avatar. In that case, manual fine-tuning is needed to obtain the exact desired result. To solve the ambiguity, it has been popular to fuse visual camera with extra sensors including IMU or depth sensors [17–20], but these solutions undermine the largest advantages of monocular configuration in equipment size and power cost. As for vision-only solutions, additional prerequisites were introduced to calibrate the scale, including non-holonomic constraints [21], a planar road assumption for indoor or on-road scenes [22, 23]. A closed-form solution using a 2D-3D correspondence was given in [24]. [25] proposed a metric monocular SLAM by initializing the system's scale with a known chessboard pattern.

The main contributions of our work are summarized as follows. First, we propose a registration method with a scale calibration process for monocular AR by combining SLAM-based tracking with marker-based object localization. The scale calibration consists of a theoretical solution and a random sample optimization. Second, we present a monocular AR system based on the proposed registration method. It can flexibly overlay a virtual object in real scenes with easy control of its actual position, orientation and size. Our method is also applied to an interactive AR application to demonstrate its validness and effectiveness.

The paper is organized as follows. Section 2 describes the registration method. Section 3 describes a monocular AR system with the proposed registration process embedded in it. Section 4 provides the experimental results and the conclusion is given in Sect. 5.

2   Method of Scale Calibration and Registration

Visual monocular SLAM has two basic process: tracking and mapping. The tracking process computes the trajectory of the camera through unipolar geometry model, however, losing the depth information of the image points [26]. For example, if scaling up the scene and the motion of the camera at the same time, the observation of the camera will not change. Therefore, the depth of real-scene points is estimated up to a scale factor in mapping process.

We compute camera pose again by solving a PnP problem based on Iterative algorithm [27]. The 3D coordinates of four coplanar points in the real scene are needed so that we can obtain a camera translation with the same scale as the scale of the real world.

The translation information is used to calibrate the scale factor of SLAM coordinate system.

2.1 Relationship Between Coordinate Systems with Different Scales

The coordinate system built by SLAM is denoted by C_s. The coordinate system of the coplanar points is denoted by C_p. Suppose that the camera moves from position 1 to position 2. Figure 1 illustrates the relationship between the coordinate systems mentioned above. By Iterative algorithm, we can solve the two camera poses relative to C_p and the camera coordinate systems in position 1 and position 2 are denoted by C_1 and C_2 respectively. An arbitrary 3D point in coordinate system C_p is denoted by $X_p = (x_p, y_p, z_p)$, and in coordinate system C_1 it is denoted as $X_1 = (x_1, y_1, z_1)$, in coordinate system C_2 it is denoted as $X_2 = (x_2, y_2, z_2)$. The projective coordinates of X_p is denoted by $\overline{X}_p = (x_p, y_p, z_p, 1)$ and similarly, the projective coordinates of X_1 by $\overline{X}_1 = (x_1, y_1, z_1, 1)$, the projective coordinates of X_2 by $\overline{X}_2 = (x_2, y_2, z_2, 1)$. The relationship between $\overline{X}_p$ and $\overline{X}_1$ is expressed as

$$[R_1 | T_1]\overline{X}_p = \overline{X}_1. \tag{1}$$

where $[R_1 | T_1]$ is the rotation and translation from C_p to C_1.

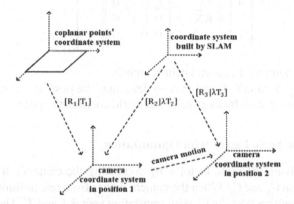

Fig. 1. An explanation of the relationships between the coordinate systems.

The inverse matrix of the camera poses computed by the SLAM system in position 1 and 2 are denoted by $[R_2 | T_2]$ and $[R_3 | T_3]$ respectively. Let λ denote the scale factor between C_s and the real world coordinate system C_p. The 'real' translation from C_s to C_1 and C_2 are λT_2 and λT_3 respectively. So we have

$$[R_2 | \lambda T_2]\overline{X}_s = \overline{X}_1 \tag{2}$$

$$[R_3 | \lambda T_3]\overline{X}_s = \overline{X}_2 \tag{3}$$

where $\overline{X}_2$ is the projective coordinates of the 3D point in C_2.

From (1) and (2), we have

$$\overline{X}_s = [R_2|\lambda T_2]^{-1} [R_1|T_1]\overline{X}_p = [R_2^{-1}| - \lambda T_2][R_1|T_1]\overline{X}_p$$
$$= [R_2^{-1}R_1| - \lambda T_2 + T_1]\overline{X}_p.$$

Combining with (3), we have

$$\overline{X}_2 = [R_3|\lambda T_3][R_2^{-1}R_1| - \lambda T_2 + T_1]\overline{X}_p$$
$$= [R_3 R_2^{-1}R_1|\lambda T_3 - \lambda T_2 + T_1]\overline{X}_p. \tag{4}$$

2.2   Registering a Virtual Point in an Augmented Image

In formula (4), the scale factor λ is the only unknown parameter. Supposing we have measured the value of λ by some means, $\overline{X}_2$ can be computed using formula (4). Knowing $\overline{X}_2$, the pixel coordinates (u, v) of point X_p are obtained by applying the camera pinhole model:

$$z_2\begin{bmatrix} u \\ v \\ 1 \end{bmatrix} = K\overline{X}_2 = \begin{bmatrix} f_x & 0 & c_x & 0 \\ 0 & f_y & c_y & 0 \\ 0 & 0 & 1 & 0 \end{bmatrix}\begin{bmatrix} x_2 \\ y_2 \\ z_2 \\ 1 \end{bmatrix}, \tag{5}$$

where K is the augmented camera intrinsic matrix.

Consequently, formula (4) and (5) can determine the pose of a virtual object in the SLAM coordinate system by its pose in the world coordinate system.

2.3   Solving the Scale Factor with Optimization

We are now solving the scale factor λ by computing the camera's translation in the coordinate system C_p and C_s. When the camera moves from one position to another, we can obtain two camera poses in C_p with translation vector T and T'. The corresponding poses in C_s have translation vector t and t', respectively. The scale factor λ makes the following formula true:

$$T - T' = \lambda(t - t'). \tag{6}$$

The above formulas provide a theoretical method to register a virtual object in the image by assigning a real position for it. However, physical instruments and SLAM system always have errors and deviations. We can refine the result by statistical means. First, to reduce errors caused by small distance, we sample the captured images according the camera translation from last sampled image. Specifically, we ensure that the real distance between two adjacent samples is on a certain range of (0.05 m, 0.2 m) so that we obtain a sequence of translations in C_p, denoted by $\{T_n\}$, and a sequence of translations in C_s, denoted by $\{T'_n\}$. We compute other two sequences $\{S_n : S_n = T_{n+1} - T_n\}$ and $\{S'_n : S'_n = T'_{n+1} - T'_n\}$. The scale factor's sequence is expressed as $\left\{\lambda_n = \dfrac{S_n}{S'_n}\right\}$.

Supposing $\{\lambda_n\}$ has errors following a normal distribution, then $\{\lambda_n\}$ also follows a distribution denoted as $N(\mu, \sigma^2)$, where λ is an unknown constant. Take the average value μ_n of $(\lambda_i)_{i=1}^n$ as the nth estimator of μ and the standard deviation σ_n of $(\lambda_i)_{i=1}^n$ as the nth estimator of σ. $\lambda_i (i \in N, i \leq n)$ is seen as an outlier when it is out of the range of $(\mu_n - \sigma_n, \mu_n + \sigma_n)$. We seek to find a normal distribution so that it is a stable distribution with small deviation and also its confidence interval contains most of the sequence data. Therefore, a sampling algorithm inspired by RANSAC [28] is performed as illustrated in Algorithm 1. When the existing data cannot provide a satisfying result, take more samples as input to approximate the accurate result.

Algorithm 1: Random Sample Estimator

Input: Sequence $S = \{\lambda_i : i = 1, \dots, n\}$
Loop:
    Compute the average value μ, the standard deviation σ of S;
    Update Sequence S by Sampling $S = \{\lambda_i : \lambda_i \in (\mu - \sigma, \mu + \sigma)\}$;
End Loop While ($\sigma <$ threshold or #S < 3)
If ($\sigma <$ threshold & #S > 2n/3):
    Output μ;
Else:
    Add 10 inputs s.t. $S = \{\lambda_i : i = 1, \dots, n + 10\}$;
    Back to Loop;
End If

---

3   AR System Based on the Proposed Method

In this section, we describe a monocular AR system with the proposed registration process. As shown in Fig. 2, it consists of four processes: monocular SLAM tracking, scale calibration, virtual object registration and rendering. We use the proposed method in the section above for scale calibration process and registration process.

SLAM Tracking. As mentioned in Sect. 2, monocular visual SLAM computes camera pose in a different scale from the scale of real world. In the AR system, we use ORB-SLAM system, which defines its 'unit length' by the distance between the first two keyframes [14]. We solve the problem by adding a scale calibration process.

Scale Calibration. In scale calibration, the system detects an ArUco marker in the real scene and extracts its four corner points as the four coplanar points [29]. The world coordinate system is defined as shown in Fig. 2c: the red, green and blue axes are the x axis, y axis, and z axis respectively; the origin is the left-top corner point of the marker; the coordinates of other 3 corner points is determined by its real distance relative to the

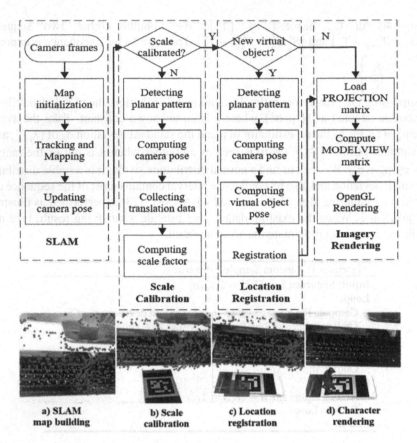

Fig. 2. The overview of our AR system with an image illustration for each process. The points in the image are map points. (Color figure online)

origin. With the four 2D-3D point correspondences, we use Iterative algorithm in [27] to compute an optimal camera pose relative to the marker.

At the same time, the system records the camera translation computed by SLAM module. The local average scale factor is computed based on formula (6) and the post process described in Sect. 2.2. If SLAM module has built the scene map with a closed loop optimization, i.e. has optimized the scale-drift problem, the scale calibration process only need to be carried out once. Otherwise, everytime a new virtual object is added to the scene, the scale calibration process should be performed. That is because the SLAM module has local optimization which makes the scale in a local map be consistent.

Virtual Object Registration. After the scale factor is determined, the ArUco marker is used to assign a real-scene position and orientation as where the virtual object should be. The concrete steps are the following:

(a) place the marker to the desired position,
(b) extracts its four corner points from the captured frame,

(c) solve the marker pose relative to the camera,
(d) compute the marker pose in SLAM coordinate system using formula (4).

This process ensures any virtual object has the same size in the rendering scene as it is in the marker's coordinate system, which means we can easily control the size of it. Once the marker pose is saved, the marker can move out of position. We can register one or more virtual objects by moving one marker to those appointed positions. Moreover, it is feasible to register the location of a moving marker in real-time.

Rendering. We use OpenGL to render virtual imagery over the real-scene image. The MODELVIEW matrix, which describes the relationship between the virtual object to be rendered and the camera, is the projective matrix of the marker pose saved in the registration process. The PROJECTION matrix is computed using the intrinsic parameters of the camera.

4   Experiments

First, we verify the validity of the proposed method by comparing the rendering results of the proposed AR system with and without scale calibration process. Then, we evaluate the registration accuracy of the proposed method by the reprojection errors. Finally, we apply the system to an AR application which can have real-time interaction with the real world. Experiments are run in an Intel i5-347, 3.2 GHz quad-core desktop with 24 GB of RAM and graphics card of NVIDIA GeForce GTX 670, under Windows 10 operating system. The camera frame input is at 30 Hz with resolution of 640 * 480 pixels. The SLAM module in the proposed system is implemented based on the open source code of ORB-SLAM.

4.1   Performance Analysis

Marker-based AR registration method is used as a baseline in our experiments. Marker-based AR usually detects a marker first, then computes the camera pose relative to the marker and finally renders a virtual object over the marker for every frame. We use both methods to render a surrounding rectangle of the marker in the augmented scene as shown in Fig. 3. The ground truth data, i.e. coordinates of the four corner points, are produced by directly detecting the four corner points with manual fine-tuning.

The registration error of one point is defined as the normalized distance between the real point's pixel-coordinates and the computed pixel-coordinates of the registered point. Suppose the pixel coordinate of one of the detected marker's corner is denoted by $P = (u_{pi}, v_{pi})$, $i = 1, 2, 3, 4$ and the pixel coordinate of the origin computed by our system is denoted by $Q = (u_{qi}, v_{qi})$, $i = 1, 2, 3, 4$. The registration error for one frame is defined as

$$error = \sum_{i=1}^{4} sqrt\left(\left(\frac{u_{pi} - u_{qi}}{w}\right)^2 + \left(\frac{v_{pi} - v_{qi}}{h}\right)^2\right)/4,$$

where w, h are the pixel width and height of the input image.

Fig. 3. Sample pictures of registering a surrounding rectangle of the marker in the augmented scene. The pink filled rectangle is registered using our method. The green rectangle is registered by marker-based method. (Color figure online)

Figure 4 shows a comparison of the registration errors of both methods when the marker can be observed. Our method performs better when the camera is moving away from the marker and rotating. In addition, our method still works when the marker disappears or is under occlusion. Figure 5 illustrates this effectiveness by registering a surrounding rectangle of the partly occluded marker, in which the keyboard is taken as the background texture for SLAM mapping. The marker is used to suggest the correct position. Under this condition, the marker-based method cannot detect the marker for registration process. Consequently, we make it more flexible to register a virtual moving character, i.e. once registered, even if the camera cannot observe the marker, the character can have a correct relationship with the environment when moving. See Sect. 4.2 for details.

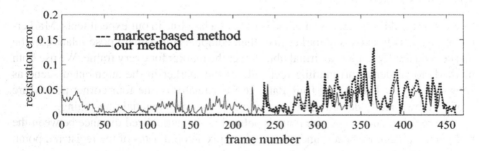

Fig. 4. The relative registration errors of 461 frames in the test. When taking the first 237 frames, the camera is close to its initial position and the marker-based method has a better accuracy. When the camera is moving away from the marker and rotating after 237th frame, our method does better in registration accuracy.

Fig. 5. The left-top image shows the initial position of the marker. The others show registering a surrounding rectangle of a partly occluded marker by our method, in which the marker-based method fails.

The runtime performance has also been tested. The average runtime of scale calibration is 1032.9 ms. Since the scale calibration process is performed only once, its runtime has little negative effect on the real-time rendering of virtual objects. It costs 21.22 ms to compute one virtual object's pose in average for current frame and the maximum computing time is 32 ms, which can satisfy the requirements of real-time (30 fps) applications.

4.2 Interactive Application

Figure 6 shows a simple AR application based on our system. The application can place a virtual character on a selected position in the real scene and control the character's walking directions in real-time using a marker. The character's motion control is based on the PFNN framework by [30]. When the application is running, it will load or build the scene map first. When camera is moving, the application seeks the marker in the

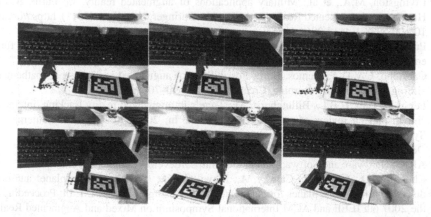

Fig. 6. Real-time interactive AR application using our registration method. The character walks towards the left-top corner point of the marker.

scene and automatically calibrate the scale factor. After that, stop the camera's moving for 2 s and the virtual character appears over the marker. Then the character starts to chase after the marker if user move the marker to another position.

5   Conclusion and Future Work

This paper has proposed a registration method for monocular SLAM-based AR system, which can conveniently register virtual objects in the augmented scene. We use a planar marker to calibrate the scale of the SLAM map and to control the position, orientation and size of the registered object. Different from marker-based AR which needs to capture markers for every frame, the proposed system only uses a marker for calibration and initial localization and no marker is needed for later location process. Therefore, it is more adaptive to dynamic augmented scenes. The proposed method is flexible, simple to set up and easy to control. Experimental results demonstrate that the proposed method provides real-time accurate registration results and can apply to interactive AR applications. Future work will consider using fingers or gestures to register and control virtual objects as a more convenient way of interaction based on the pipeline of the proposed method.

Acknowledgements. This work is supported by National Natural Science Foundation of China (No. 61471359) and National Key R&D Plan of China (No. 2016YFB1001404).

References

1. Kaufmann, H.: Construct3D: an augmented reality application for mathematics and geometry education. In: ACM Multimedia, pp. 656–657. (2002)
2. Bichlmeier, C., Sielhorst, T., Heining, S.M., Navab, N.: Improving depth perception in medical AR. In: Horsch, A., Deserno, T.M., Handels, H., Meinzer, H.P., Tolxdorff, T. (eds.) Bildverarbeitung für die Medizin 2007. Informatik aktuell, pp. 217–221. Springer, Heidelberg (2007). https://doi.org/10.1007/978-3-540-71091-2_44
3. Livingston, M.A., et al.: Military applications of augmented reality. In: Furht, B. (ed.) Handbook of Augmented Reality, pp. 671–706. Springer, New York (2011). https://doi.org/10.1007/978-1-4614-0064-6_31
4. Pucihar, K.C., Coulton, P.: Exploring the evolution of mobile augmented reality for future entertainment systems. Conf. Comput. Eur. **11**, 1–16 (2013)
5. Carvalho, C.V.D.A., Lemos, B.M.: Possibilities of augmented reality use in mathematics aiming at a meaningful learning. Creat. Educ. **05**, 690–700 (2014)
6. Feng, Z., Duh, H.B.L., Billinghurst, M.: Trends in augmented reality tracking, interaction and display: a review of ten years of ISMAR. In: 2008 7th IEEE/ACM International Symposium on Mixed and Augmented Reality, pp. 193–202 (2008)
7. Detone, D., Malisiewicz, T., Rabinovich, A.: Toward geometric deep SLAM (2017)
8. ARKit Hardware and Software Integration. https://developer.apple.com/arkit/
9. Chekhlov, D., Gee, A.P., Calway, A., Mayol-Cuevas, W.: Ninja on a plane: automatic discovery of physical planes for augmented reality using visual SLAM. In: Proceedings of the 2007 6th IEEE and ACM International Symposium on Mixed and Augmented Reality, pp. 1–4. IEEE Computer Society (2007)

10. Klein, G., Murray, D.W.: Parallel tracking and mapping for small AR workspaces. In: international symposium on mixed and augmented reality, pp. 225–234 (2007)
11. Liu, H., Zhang, G., Bao, H.: Robust keyframe-based monocular SLAM for augmented reality. In: 2016 IEEE International Symposium on Mixed and Augmented Reality (ISMAR), pp. 1–10 (2016)
12. Xue, T., Luo, H., Cheng, D., Yuan, Z., Yang, X.: Real-time monocular dense mapping for augmented reality. In: Proceedings of the 2017 ACM on Multimedia Conference, pp. 510–518. ACM, Mountain View (2017)
13. Davison, A.J., Reid, I.D., Molton, N., Stasse, O.: MonoSLAM: real-time single camera SLAM. IEEE Trans. Pattern Anal. Mach. Intell. 29, 1052–1067 (2007)
14. Murartal, R., Montiel, J.M.M., Tardos, J.D.: ORB-SLAM: a versatile and accurate monocular SLAM system. IEEE Trans. Rob. 31, 1147–1163 (2015)
15. Concha, A., Civera, J.: DPPTAM: dense piecewise planar tracking and mapping from a monocular sequence. In: Intelligent Robots and Systems, pp. 5686–5693 (2015)
16. Gao, Q.H., Wan, T.R., Tang, W., Chen, L., Zhang, K.B.: An improved augmented reality registration method based on visual SLAM. In: Tian, F., Gatzidis, C., El Rhalibi, A., Tang, W., Charles, F. (eds.) Edutainment 2017. LNCS, vol. 10345, pp. 11–19. Springer, Cham (2017). https://doi.org/10.1007/978-3-319-65849-0_2
17. Lupton, T., Sukkarieh, S.: Removing scale biases and ambiguity from 6DoF monocular SLAM using inertial. In: International Conference on Robotics and Automation, pp. 3698–3703 (2008)
18. Kim, O., Kang, D.: A sensor fusion method to solve the scale ambiguity of single image by combining IMU. In: International Conference on Control and Automation, pp. 923–925 (2015)
19. Nutzi, G., Weiss, S., Scaramuzza, D., Siegwart, R.Y.: Fusion of IMU and vision for absolute scale estimation in monocular SLAM. J. Intell. Rob. Syst. 61, 287–299 (2011)
20. Fujimoto, S., Hu, Z., Chapuis, R., Aufrere, R.: ORB-SLAM map initialization improvement using depth. In: International Conference on Image Processing, pp. 261–265 (2016)
21. Scaramuzza, D.: 1-point-RANSAC structure from motion for vehicle-mounted cameras by exploiting non-holonomic constraints. Int. J. Comput. Vis. 95, 74–85 (2011)
22. Kitt, B., Rehder, J., Chambers, A., Schönbein, M., Lategahn, H., Singh, S.: Monocular visual odometry using a planar road model to solve scale ambiguity, pp. 43–48 (2011)
23. Song, S., Chandraker, M.: Robust scale estimation in real-time monocular SFM for autonomous driving. In: Computer Vision and Pattern Recognition, pp. 1566–1573 (2014)
24. Esteban, I., Dorst, L., Dijk, J.: Closed form solution for the scale ambiguity problem in monocular visual odometry. In: Liu, H., Ding, H., Xiong, Z., Zhu, X. (eds.) ICIRA 2010. LNCS (LNAI), vol. 6424, pp. 665–679. Springer, Heidelberg (2010). https://doi.org/10.1007/978-3-642-16584-9_64
25. Li, Y., Wang, S., Yang, D., Sun, D.: Metric online monocular SLAM by using a known reference. In: World Congress on Intelligent Control and Automation, pp. 3002–3006 (2016)
26. Hartley, R.I., Zisserman, A.: Multiple view geometry in computer vision. Kybernetes 30, 1333–1341 (2000)
27. Oberkampf, D., Dementhon, D., Davis, L.S.: Iterative pose estimation using coplanar feature points. Comput. Vis. Image Underst. 63, 495–511 (1996)
28. Matas, J., Chum, O.: Randomized RANSAC with Td, d test. Image Vis. Comput. 22, 837–842 (2004)
29. Garrido-Jurado, S., Muñoz-Salinas, R., Madrid-Cuevas, F.J., Marín-Jiménez, M.J.: Automatic generation and detection of highly reliable fiducial markers under occlusion. Pattern Recogn. 47, 2280–2292 (2014)
30. Holden, D., Komura, T., Saito, J.: Phase-functioned neural networks for character control. ACM Trans. Graph. 36, 1–13 (2017)

A Fusion Approach to Grayscale-Thermal Tracking with Cross-Modal Sparse Representation

Lin Li, Chenglong Li, ZhengZheng Tu, and Jin Tang[✉]

School of Computer Science and Technology,
Anhui University, No. 111 Jiulong Road, Hefei 230601, China
lilin00727@163.com, lcll314@foxmail.com,
jtang99029@foxmail.com

Abstract. Grayscale-thermal tracking receives much attention recently due to the complementary benefits of the visible and thermal infrared modalities in over- coming the imaging limitations of individual source. This paper investigates how to perform effective fusion of the grayscale and thermal information for robust object tracking. We propose a novel fusion approach based on the cross-modal sparse representation in the Bayesian filtering framework. First, to exploit the interdependence of different modalities, we take both the intra- and inter-modality constraints into account in the sparse representation, i.e., cross-modal sparse rep- resentation. Moreover, we introduce the modality weights in our model to achieve adaptive fusion. Second, unlike conventional methods, we employ the reconstruction residues and coefficients together to define the likelihood probability for each candidate sample generated by the motion model. Finally, the object is located by finding the candidate sample with the maximum likelihood probability. Experimental results on the public benchmark dataset suggest that the proposed approach performs favourably against the state-of-the-art grayscale-thermal trackers.

Keywords: Multi-modal · Fusion · Laplacian matrix · Sparse representation
Bayesian filtering

1 Introduction

Visual tracking has been one of the popular research topics in computer vision. Many tracking algorithms have been proposed to address the various of difficulties like background clutter, object changes and low illumination, some of which are produced by the imaging limitations of visible spectrum, and could be addressed by fusing other complementary information. Recently, the fusion of visible and thermal modalities receives increasing attention in computer vision community as the thermal sensors are

---

Electronic supplementary material The online version of this chapter (https://doi.org/10.1007/978-981-13-1702-6_49) contains supplementary material, which is available to authorized users.

Y. Wang et al. (Eds.): IGTA 2018, CCIS 875, pp. 494–505, 2018.
https://doi.org/10.1007/978-981-13-1702-6_49

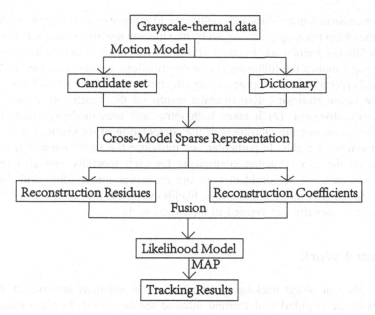

Fig. 1. Flowchart of the proposed tracker.

insensitive to lighting conditions [5, 10], especially for visual tracking (sometimes called grayscale-thermal tracking) [9, 11].

Most of existing grayscale-thermal trackers follows the Bayesian filtering framework [9, 11, 13]. These approaches base on the sparse representation due to its robustness to noises. Wu et al. [13] concatenate multiple modal features, and then employs conventional sparse representation to compute the reconstruction residues for tracking. Liu and Sun [11] perform joint sparse representation on multiple modal inputs, and use the reconstruction coefficients to define the likelihood scores. The two trackers, however, treat each modality equally, and thus may significantly limit the tracking performance on dealing with occasional perturbation or malfunction of individual sources. Li et al. [9] propose a collaborative sparse representation to optimize the modality weights online with the sparse reconstruction coefficients. But this tracker may ignore the importance of both intra- and inter-modality consistency.

In this paper, we propose a two-phase fusion approach based on the cross-modal sparse representation for grayscale-thermal object tracking. In model fusion phase, we propose the cross-modal sparse representation to adaptively make full use of the modal information. In particular, we introduce intra- and inter-modality constraints to compute the modality weights and reconstruction coefficients robustly. For intra-modality constraint, we apply Laplacian and sparse constraints to regularize the reconstruction coefficients and also refine the modality weights. For inter-modality constraint, we pursue the cross-modal consistency by introducing the $l_{2,1}$ norm on the joint sparse coefficient matrix. In likelihood fusion phase, we integrate the reconstruction residues and the reconstruction coefficients to define the likelihood probability for each candidate. With this strategy, our approach is able to utilize the complementary information from the reconstruction residues and coefficients to achieve more robust tracking results. Finally, the object tracking is carried out by maximizing the likelihood probability in the Bayesian filtering framework. Figure 1 shows the flowchart of our tracking approach.

This paper makes the following major contributions to grayscale-thermal tracking and related applications. (1) It proposes an effective approach for RGB-T tracking by a two-phase fusion strategies. Experimental results on the benchmark dataset demonstrate the effectiveness. (2) It takes both intra- and inter-modality constraints into account for improving the robustness of the computation of reconstruction coefficients and the modality weights. In particular, we introduce the Laplacian and sparse regularization on the reconstruction coefficients for each modality and also refine the modality weights. (3) It considers both the reconstruction residues and the reconstruction coefficients in the definition of likelihood probability for each candidate. Its complementary benefits are verified in the experiments.

2 Related Work

Grayscale-thermal object tracking has received more and more attention in the community with the popularity of thermal infrared sensors [1–3]. In [2], Conaire et al. utilize different fusion schemes on manually annotated multi-modal surveillance videos to evaluate tracking performance of appearance model. Algorithms in 2007, including Cvejic et al. [4], investigate the impact of pixel-level fusion of videos from grayscale-thermal surveillance cameras to compare with other trackers in single modality videos; Bunyak et al. [1], which presents a moving object detection and tracking system that fuses grayscale and thermal videos within a level set framework; Conaire et al. [3], not only propose a framework that can efficiently combine features for robust tracking but also instantiate the fusion of thermal infrared and visible spectrum features. In later years, Leykin et al. [8] propose a pedestrian tracker designed as a particle filter based on the proposed background model, in which each pixel is represented as a multi-modal distribution with the changing number of modalities for both grayscale and thermal input. In Wu et al. [13], the image patches from grayscale and thermal sources are concatenated into a one-dimensional vector which is then sparsely represented in the target template space. Liu et al. [11] perform joint sparse representation calculation on both grayscale and thermal modalities and utilize min operation on the sparse representation coefficients to fuse the resultant tracking results. Recently, Li et al. [9] propose a collaborative sparse representation for grayscale-thermal tracking method, which provides a reliable weight for each modality. Compared with the above works, we introduce the intra- and inter-modality constraints for reconstruction coefficients and modality weights to further improve the tracking performance.

3 Cross-Modal Sparse Representation

In this section, we will introduce the model fusion phase. For one grayscale-thermal data, we first construct dictionary with two template bases for each modality, from both the foreground regions and the surrounding background regions. Next we extract candidate set of each modality. The dictionary and the candidate set are served as the input data of the proposed cross-modal sparse representation. Through the proposed algorithm, we obtain sparse coefficients, which are used to calculate the reconstruction residues as well as the reconstruction coefficients in the likelihood fusion phase.

First, we propose a joint sparse representation using multi-modal data. Candidate set is denoted by $\mathbf{X}^m = [\mathbf{x}_1^m, \mathbf{x}_2^m, \ldots, \mathbf{x}_K^m] \in R^{d \times K}$, where $m = 1, \ldots, M$. The operator $[M]$ indicates the set of integers between 1 and $M : [M] = \{1, 2, \ldots, M\}$, e.g., $\mathbf{X}^{[M]} = \{\mathbf{X}^1, \mathbf{X}^2, \ldots, \mathbf{X}^M\}$. Grayscale-thermal data used in this paper is the special case with $M = 2$. d and K denote the feature dimension and the number of candidates, respectively. The positive and negative template bases are denoted by $\mathbf{T}_{pos}^{[M]} = [\mathbf{t}_1^{[M]}, \mathbf{t}_2^{[M]}, \ldots, \mathbf{t}_p^{[M]}]$ and $\mathbf{T}_{neg}^{[M]} = [\mathbf{t}_{p+1}^{[M]}, \mathbf{t}_{p+2}^{[M]}, \ldots, \mathbf{t}_{p+q}^{[M]}]$, where p and q indicate the number of positive and negative templates. Thus, we construct M dictionaries as $\mathbf{T}_{[M]} = [\mathbf{T}_{pos}^{[M]}, \mathbf{T}_{neg}^{[M]}]$ and reconstruct the candidate samples as follows:

$$\min_{\mathbf{C}} \sum_{m=1}^{M} \frac{1}{2} \|\mathbf{X}^m - \mathbf{T}^m \mathbf{C}^m\|_F^2, \tag{1}$$

where $\mathbf{C} = [\mathbf{C}^1; \mathbf{C}^2; \ldots; \mathbf{C}^M]$ serves as the sparse coefficients, $\mathbf{T}^m$ is the dictionary of the m-th modality which consists of both positive and negative basis templates of the m-th modality.

Usually, the reconstruction errors (1) can measure the imaging qualities of different modalities. The smaller the reconstruction error is, the better the modal quality [9]. However, unlike algorithms in [11, 13] which assume that available modalities contribute equally, we introduce the weight variables to represent modal reliabilities [9], improving the ability of dealing with occasional perturbation or malfunction of individual sources. Therefore, we apply the modality weights into (1) to achieve adaptive fusion of different source data:

$$\min_{\mathbf{C}, \alpha^{[M]}} \sum_{m=1}^{M} \frac{(\alpha^m)^2}{2} \|\mathbf{x}^m - \mathbf{T}^m \mathbf{C}^m\|_F^2 + \sum_{m=1}^{M} (1 - \alpha^m)^2, \tag{2}$$

where α^m is the reliable weight for the m-th modality.

In (2), there are still some limitations: (1) The above assumption may go wrong, i.e., smaller reconstruction errors can not insure better modal qualities always [9]. (2) The sparsity of each modality isn't taken into consideration. (3) If candidates share high similarity, their sparse coefficients should be highly consistent. But it usually does not hold due to the effects of noises. To handle above problems while avoiding the influences of previous tracking results [9], we propose the weighted Laplacian sparse representation as follows:

$$\min_{\mathbf{C},\alpha^{[M]}} \sum_{m=1}^{M} (\alpha^m)^2 (\frac{1}{2}\|\mathbf{X}^m - \mathbf{T}^m\mathbf{C}^m\|_F^2 + \Gamma\|\mathbf{C}^m\|_1 +$$

$$\beta\, tr(\mathbf{C}^m\mathbf{L}^m\mathbf{C}^{m,T})) + \sum_{m=1}^{M} (1 - \alpha^m)^2, \qquad (3)$$

where $\mathbf{L}^m = \mathbf{B}^m - \mathbf{D}^m$ is the Laplacian matrix, $\mathbf{B}^m$ is a $k \times k$ diagonal matrix denoted as $\mathbf{B}^m = diag(b_{11}^m, b_{22}^m, \ldots, b_{kk}^m)$ and its i-th diagonal element is $\sum_{j=1}^{k} \mathbf{D}_{ij}^m \cdot \mathbf{C}^{m,T}$ is the transposition of $\mathbf{C}^m$.

The introduced Laplacian constraints and coefficients constraint $\|\mathbf{C}^m\|_1$ can not only be utilized to regularize the sparse coefficients but also refine the modality weights for different modalities.

Through the work above, we have introduced intra-modality constraints only. However, with only intra-modality cooperation, the cross-modal tracker may easily be affected by one modality information. Therefore, to further improve the robustness of our tracker, we introduce inter-modality constraint, which will help further improve the consistency of different modalities.

$$\min_{\mathbf{C},\alpha^{[M]}} \sum_{m=1}^{M} (\alpha^m)^2 (\frac{1}{2}\|\mathbf{X}^m - \mathbf{T}^m\mathbf{C}^m\|_F^2 + \Gamma\|\mathbf{C}^m\|_1 +$$

$$\beta\, tr(\mathbf{C}^m\mathbf{L}^m\mathbf{C}^{m,T})) + \sum_{m=1}^{M} (1 - \alpha^m)^2 + \lambda\|\mathbf{C}\|_{2,1}, \qquad (4)$$

where λ is a balance parameter and $\|\mathbf{C}\|_{2,1}$ encourages that one candidate shares the same pattern across different modalities. The optimization algorithm to (4) are presented in the **supplementary file** due to space limitation.

4   Tracking via Bayesian Filtering

In this section, we will introduce the proposed likelihood fusion phase in Bayesian filtering framework.

4.1   Bayesian Filtering Framework

Let $\mathbf{Z}_t^{[M]} = [\mathbf{z}_1^{[M]}, \mathbf{z}_2^{[M]}, \ldots \mathbf{z}_t^{[M]}]$ denote the observation set generated from M different modalities at time t. Given $\mathbf{Z}_t^{[M]}$ and the state variable $\mathbf{x}_t$, we can compute the optimal state $\hat{\mathbf{x}}_t$ by Maximum A Posterior (MAP) estimation,

$$\hat{\mathbf{x}}_t = \arg\max_{\mathbf{x}_{t,i}} P(\mathbf{x}_{t,i}|\mathbf{Z}_t^{[M]}), \qquad (5)$$

where $\mathbf{x}_{t,i}$ indicates the state of the i-th sample at time t. We factorize (5) by Bayesian rules as follows,

$$P(\mathbf{x}_t|\mathbf{Z}_t^{[M]}) \propto P(\mathbf{z}_t^{[M]}|\mathbf{x}_t)$$
$$\int P(\mathbf{x}_t|\mathbf{x}_{t-1})P(\mathbf{x}_{t-1}|\mathbf{Z}_{t-1}^{[M]})d\mathbf{x}_{t-1}, \tag{6}$$

where $P(\mathbf{x}_t|\mathbf{x}_{t-1})$ and $P(\mathbf{z}_t^{[M]}|\mathbf{x}_t)$ are the motion model and the likelihood model, respectively. Here, six independent affine parameters are utilized, including deformable and translated information, to represent the variation of motion, and model the dynamic process by the Gaussian distribution,

$$P(\mathbf{x}_t|\mathbf{x}_t - 1) = N(\mathbf{x}_t; \mathbf{x}_t - 1, \sigma_p), \tag{7}$$

where σ_p denotes a diagonal covariance matrix whose elements are the variations of the affine parameters, and its setting depends on motion variations of the target object.

According to the motion model, we can predict a set of candidate regions in the next frame base on the current tracking results. The likelihood term $P(\mathbf{z}_t^{[M]}|\mathbf{x}_t)$ will be defined base on the proposed cross-modal sparse representation to measure the confidence of each candidate object region.

4.2   Discriminative Likelihood

In some Bayesian filtering based trackers, the likelihood term $P(\mathbf{z}_t^{[M]}|\mathbf{x}_t)$ is calculated only by reconstruction residues [9] or reconstruction coefficients [18] obtained from the main tracking algorithm. Differently, we introduce a fusion modal for obtaining likelihood score, which integrates both reconstruction residues and reconstruction coefficients. We define our fusion likelihood model as follows,

$$P(\mathbf{z}_t^{[M]}|\mathbf{x}_t) \propto \exp(-S_i), \tag{8}$$

where S_i is the fusion likelihood score, $S_i = \theta_1 S_{e,i} + \theta_2 S_{c,i}$. θ_1 and θ_2 are the fusion parameters. $S_{e,i}$ denotes the i-th candidate score obtained by reconstruction residues and $S_{c,i}$ denotes the i-th candidate score obtained by reconstruction coefficients.

The fusion modal (8) cooperates both reconstruction coefficients and reconstruction residues, which can provide more complete information of one candidate, thus further improve the robustness of our tracker.

To obtain the reconstruction coefficients score, the sparse coefficients $\mathbf{C}$ from the proposed cross-modal sparse representation will be used. However, simply introducing $\mathbf{C}$ may suffer from potential instability. Thus, we refine the sparse coefficients with adaptive weights W_{ij}^m.

$$W_{ij}^m = exp(-\left\|\mathbf{T}_i^m - \mathbf{X}_j^m\right\|) \tag{9}$$

Therefore, for i-th candidate, the reconstruction coefficients scores are defined as

$$s^m_{c,i-pos} = \sum_{k=1}^{l} Max(c^{T,m}_{i-pos} \odot w^m_{i-pos}, k)$$

$$s^m_{c,i-neg} = \sum_{k=1}^{l} Max(c^{T,m}_{i-neg} \odot w^m_{i-neg}, k) \tag{10}$$

where $\mathbf{C}^m = [\mathbf{c}^m_1, \mathbf{c}^m_2, \ldots, \mathbf{c}^m_k] \in R^{k \times k}$, k denotes the number of candidates. $Max(c, p)$ denotes the p-th largest element in c and we set l to be half of the positive templates, which discards some small values that may carry bad influence.

Obtaining scores for both positive and negative candidates, the discriminated score for reconstruction coefficients of i-th candidate is defined as

$$s^m_{c,i} = s^m_{i-neg} - s^m_{i-pos} \tag{11}$$

From (11) we can see that, candidate that shares strong similarity with background will obtain larger discriminated score and vice versa, which is able to differ the target and the background. Then we define the discriminative score for reconstruction coefficients of i-th candidate as $S_{c,i}$,

$$S_{c,i} = \sum_{m=1}^{M} s^m_{c,i} \tag{12}$$

Then, for each candidate region, we utilize the reconstruction residues from both positive basis and negative basis to define reconstruction residues score $S_{e,i}$, In contrast, the past sparse representation based tracking algorithms usually employ positive template only [12, 16]. In particular, their methods are likely to drift when target appearance is similar to the background [17].

For i-th candidate, we obtain the reconstruct errors on the positive and negative templates of m-th modal as..

$$e^m_{i-pos} = \left\| \mathbf{X}^m_i - \mathbf{T}^m_{pos} \mathbf{C}^m_{i-pos} \right\|^2_F$$

$$e^m_{i-neg} = \left\| \mathbf{X}^m_i - \mathbf{T}^m_{neg} \mathbf{C}^m_{i-neg} \right\|^2_F \tag{13}$$

For effective fusion of different modalities, we normalize the reconstructed errors of each modality into $[0, 1]$:

$$\hat{\mathbf{e}}^m = \frac{\mathbf{e}^m - \min(\mathbf{e}^m)}{\max(\mathbf{e}^m) - \min(\mathbf{e}^m)}, \tag{14}$$

where $\min(\mathbf{e}^m)$ and $\max(\mathbf{e}^m)$ denote the minimum and maximum elements of $\mathbf{e}^m$, respectively. Note that this normalization method usually obtain good performance even though different error vectors have different normalization rules. The discriminative score for reconstruction residues of i-th candidate can be defined as follows,

Table 1. Success Score (SS, %) of success plots and corresponding rankings (in parenthesis) with different attributes. Herein, baseline trackers are with grayscale-thermal input. The bold fonts of results indicate the best performance.

	Ours	CSR	SCM	STRUCK	MEEM	CT	L1-PF	TLD
All	**66(1)**	62(2)	56(3)	53(4)	52(5)	48(6)	43(7)	41(8)
LI	**68(1)**	61(2)	56(3)	55(4)	52(5)	49(6)	40(7)	40(7)
TC	**67(1)**	64(2)	56(3)	51(5)	55(4)	43(7)	44(6)	40(8)
Code type	MATLAB	MIX	MIX	C++	MIX	MATLAB	MIX	MIX
FPS	1.5	1.6	0.3	10.8	4.9	31.8	5.1	2.7

$$S_{e,i} = \sum_{m=1}^{M} e_{i-pos}^{m} - e_{i-neg}^{m} \tag{15}$$

Base on the fusion likelihood with reconstruction coefficients and reconstruction residues, the score of one candidate is actually being evaluated twice. Thus, only candidate with both better reconstruction coefficients and reconstruction residues can be chosen to be the target. Such fusion work can enable tracker to alleviate the influence caused by bad reconstruction residues and improve the tracking results.

5 Experiments

The experiments are run on a PC with an Intel i7 4.2 GHz CPU and 32 GB RAM, and implemented on the platform of MATLAB.

5.1 Evaluation Settings

Parameters. For fair comparisons, we fix all parameters and other settings in our experiments. In Bayesian filtering, the number of candidates is generally determined by the trade-off between the computational cost and the variance of the resulting estimates. Here we fix it to be 200 on entire dataset for more fair comparison. Besides, the positive and negative samples are set to be 10 and 190, respectively. Table 2 shows the influence of different β, λ, Γ, θ_1 and θ_2, and thus we set them to be 0.8, 0.0001, 0.0001, 0.6 and 0.4 respectively. Mooveover, we also present the result with different fusion parameters in Table 3.

Datasets. GTOT [9] is a recently proposed standard benchmark dataset for evaluating RGB-T trackers, which includes 50 RGB-T video clips with ground truth object locations under different scenarios and conditions. The dataset is annotated with 7 attributes, including occlusion (OCC), large scale variation (LSV), fast motion(FM), low illumination (LI), thermal crossover (TC), small object (SO), deformation (DEF) [9].

Table 2. Success Score (SS) of the proposed method with different parameters.

Param	Setting	SS	Setting	SS	Setting	SS
β	1.0	62	**0.8**	**66**	0.6	65
λ	0.01	59	0.001	62	**0.0001**	**66**
Γ	0.01	64	0.001	65	**0.0001**	**66**
θ_1	0.7	64	**0.6**	**66**	0.5	62
$\theta2$	0.5	61	**0.4**	**66**	0.3	65

Table 3. Average success scores (SS) of the proposed tracking method against its different fusion parameters.

θ_1	0.0	0.3	0.4	0.5	**0.6**	0.7	1.0
θ_2	1.0	0.7	0.6	0.5	**0.4**	0.3	0.0
SS	63	63	61	58	**66**	61	59

Compared Methods. With the same initialization, we compare our proposed method against the 7 state-of-the-art trackers on GTOT dataset, including CSR [9], Struck [6], SCM [17], MEEM [14], L1-PF [13], TLD [7], CT [15]. Herein, CSR and L1-PF are grayscale-thermal methods, others are only grayscale methods.

5.2 Comparison Results

We first report the Success Score (SS) of grayscale-thermal trackers on entire dataset in Fig. 2 and in attributes LI, TC in Table 1. Note that both LI subsets and TC subsets have quite strong dependence on reliable weights of each modality. LI subset means there is low illumination around the target region, which can bring more challenges in grayscale videos. While in TC subset, the target will have similar temperature with other objects or background, which may lead to ambiguous thermal information in tracking objects. Both these two subsets will have imperfect data in one of the two modalities, which indicates the importance of reliable weights for them. The proposed fusion work for cross-modal sparse representation tracking method is devoted to generate better reliable weights with different modality information. From the evaluation results in Table 1, we can observe that the proposed approach significantly outperforms the baseline trackers.

5.3 Component Analysis

To justify the contributions of the main components of the proposed method, we implement four special versions for experimental analysis: (1) **Ours-I**, which sets the $\beta = 0$ to remove the Laplacian constraints on the weighted sparse representation in (4). (2) **Ours-II**, which sets $\Gamma = 0$ to remove l_1 constraint to sparse coefficients. (3) **Ours-III**, which sets $\lambda = 0$ to remove inter-modality constraint. (4) **Ours-IV**, which sets $\alpha^m = 1(m = 1, 2, \ldots, M)$ to remove the reliable weights for different modality in (4). (5) **Ours-V**, which sets $\theta_1 = 0$, only uses reconstruction residues to obtain likelihood

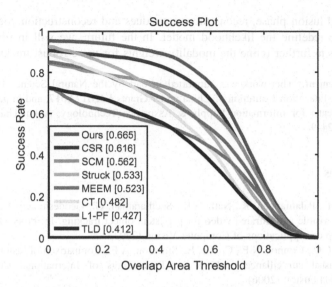

Fig. 2. Presentation of the Success Score (SS) of the proposed cross-modal sparse representation tracker compared with other state-of-the-art grayscale-thermal trackers.

Table 4. Average success scores (SS) of the proposed tracking method against its four different versions. The bold font indicates the best performance.

	Ours	Ours-I	Ours-II	Ours-III	Ours-IV	Ours-V	Ours-VI
SS	**66**	59	64	62	61	63	59

model. (6) **Ours-VI**, which sets $\theta_2 = 0$, only uses reconstruction coefficients to obtain likelihood model.

From the experimental results reported in Table 4, we can draw the conclusions as follows: (1) Comparing Ours and Ours-I, the Laplacian constraints are helpful to reconstruct the sparse coefficients correctly as well as refining the reliable weights. (2) The reliable weights are capable of better integrating information from different modality and can make our method more robust by observing Ours and Ours-IV. (3) The results of Ours, Ours-V and Ours-VI show the effectiveness of our fusion work for reconstruction residues and reconstruction coefficients.

6   Conclusion

In this paper, we propose a two-phase fusion approach base on the cross-modal sparse representation. In model fusion phase, intra- and inter-modality constraints are introduced to refine the sparse representation model. The Laplacian constraints are incorporated to refine both coefficients and weights for intra-modality constraint. For inter-modality constraint, we introduce $l_{2,1}$ norm to the joint sparse coefficients matrix.

In likelihood fusion phase, reconstruction residues and reconstruction coefficients are integrated to redefine the likelihood model. In the future, we will incorporate other prior models to further refine the modality weights for more robust tracking.

Acknowledgement. This work was supported in part by the Natural Science Foundation of Anhui Higher Education Institution of China under Grants KJ2017A017, and in part by the Co-Innovation Center for Information Supply & Assurance Technology, Anhui University under Grant Y01002449.

References

1. Bunyak, F., Palaniappan, K., Nath, S.K., Seetharaman, G.: Geodesic active contour based fusion of visible and infrared video for persistent object tracking. In: Proceedings of IEEE Workshop on Applications of Computer Vision (2007)
2. Conaire, C.O., Connor, N.E., Cooke, E., Smeaton, A.F.: Comparison of fusion methods for thermo-visual surveillance tracking. In: Proceedings of International Conference on Information Fusion (2006)
3. Conaire, C.O., Connor, N.E., Smeaton, A.: Thermo-visual feature fusion for object tracking using multiple spatiogram trackers. Mach. Vis. Appl. **7**, 1–12 (2007)
4. Cvejic, N., et al.: The effect of pixel-level fusion on object tracking in multi-sensor surveillance video. In: Proceedings of IEEE Conference on Computer Vision and Pattern Recognition (2007)
5. Gade, R., Moeslund, T.B.: Thermal cameras and applications: a survey. Mach. Vis. Appl. **25**, 245–262 (2014)
6. Hare, S., Saffari, A., Torr, P.H.S.: Struck: structured output tracking with kernels. In: Proceedings of IEEE International Conference on Computer Vision (2011)
7. Kalal, Z., Mikolajczyk, K., Matas, J.: Tracking-learning-detection. IEEE Trans. Pattern Anal. Mach. Intell. **34**(7), 1409–1422 (2011)
8. Leykin, A., Hammoud, R.: Pedestrian tracking by fusion of thermal-visible surveillance videos. Mach. Vis. Appl. **21**(4), 587–595 (2010)
9. Li, C., Cheng, H., Hu, S., Liu, X., Tang, J., Lin, L.: Learning collaborative sparse representation for grayscale-thermal tracking. IEEE Trans. Image Process. **25**(12), 5743–5756 (2016)
10. Li, C., Wang, X., Zhang, L., Tang, J., Wu, H., Lin, L.: WELD: weighted low-rank decomposition for robust grayscale-thermal foreground detection. IEEE Trans. Circ. Syst. Video Technol. **27**, 725–738 (2016). https://doi.org/10.1109/TCSVT20162556586
11. Liu, H., Sun, F.: Fusion tracking in color and infrared images using joint sparse representation. Inf. Sci. **55**(3), 590–599 (2012)
12. Mei, X., Ling, H.: Robust visual tracking using l_1 minimization. In: Proceedings of IEEE International Conference on Computer Vision (2009)
13. Wu, Y., Blasch, E., Chen, G., Bai, L., Ling, H.: Multiple source data fusion via sparse representation for robust visual tracking. In: Proceedings of International Conference on Information Fusion (2011)
14. Zhang, J., Ma, S., Sclaroff, S.: MEEM: robust tracking via multiple experts using entropy minimization. In: Fleet, D., Pajdla, T., Schiele, B., Tuytelaars, T. (eds.) ECCV 2014. LNCS, vol. 8694, pp. 188–203. Springer, Cham (2014). https://doi.org/10.1007/978-3-319-10599-4_13

15. Zhang, K., Zhang, L., Yang, M.-H.: Real-time compressive tracking. In: Fitzgibbon, A., Lazebnik, S., Perona, P., Sato, Y., Schmid, C. (eds.) ECCV 2012. LNCS, vol. 7574, pp. 864–877. Springer, Heidelberg (2012). https://doi.org/10.1007/978-3-642-33712-3_62

16. Zhang, T., Ghanem, B., Liu, S., Ahuja, N.: Robust visual tracking via multi-task sparse learning. In: Proceedings of IEEE Conference on Computer Vision and Pattern Recognition (2012)

17. Zhong, W., Lu, H., Yang, M.H.: Robust object tracking via sparsity-based collaborative model. In: Proceedings of IEEE Conference on Computer Vision and Pattern Recognition (2012)

18. Zhuang, B., Lu, H., Xiao, Z., Wang, D.: Visual tracking via discriminative sparse similarity map. IEEE Trans. Image Process. 23(4), 1872–1881 (2014)

Image Set Representation with Robust Manifold Regularized Low-Rank Approximation

Bo Jiang, Yuan Zhang, Youxia Cao, and Bin Luo[✉]

Department of Computer Science and Technology, Anhui University,
Jiulong Road. No. 111, Hefei 230601, China
{jiangbo,luobin}@ahu.edu.cn

Abstract. Many problems in computer vision and machine learning area can be formulated as image set representation and learning. In real application, image set data often contains various kinds of noises or missing value corruptions, and are also usually sampled from nonlinear manifolds. These make the representation and learning process of image set data more challengeable. This paper proposes a robust manifold regularized low-rank approximation (MLRA) method for image set recovery and representation. MLRA provides an effective low-rank representation for image set whose elements are sampled from nonlinear manifolds. Comparing with original observed image set, MLRA of image set is generally noiseless and more regular, which can obviously encourage the robust learning and recognition process. We evaluate our method on several datasets to demonstrate the benefits of the method.

Keywords: Manifold learning · Image set · Representation
Low-rank approximation

1 Introduction

Many problems in computer vision and multimedia area can be formulated as object recognition/learning based on visual content information. Recently, image set based object recognition has been widely studied [8,15,24,25]. In real application, image sets of objects are commonly available and can be easily collected by video surveillance, multi-view cameras, photo albums or long term observations. Comparing with single image, image set usually contains more variations of the object appearance and has been demonstrated more effectively and robustly in real applications, such as face recognition, gesture recognition and so on [4,19,20,27,29,34].

In recent years, many methods have been developed for image set representation and learning task [6,11,14,32,36]. Generally, these works can be roughly categorized into three categories: statistical models [1,23,28,32,34], linear (affine) subspace methods [11,13,19,35] and nonlinear manifold based methods [4,5,9,14,31,33,36]. In statistical methods, image sets are usually represented by some statistical distributions, such as Gaussian, GMM and so on.

© Springer Nature Singapore Pte Ltd. 2018
Y. Wang et al. (Eds.): IGTA 2018, CCIS 875, pp. 506–516, 2018.
https://doi.org/10.1007/978-981-13-1702-6_50

Then, the similarity between two image sets can be conducted via metric measurement between two distributions [1,12,23,28,30,32]. For linear (affine) subspace based methods, they generally make the assumption that each image set spans a linear or affine subspace. Then, distance between two image sets can be measured via computing the distance between two subspaces [4,11,13,19,35]. Additionally, recent works also demonstrate that the image samples in an image set are usually lying on a nonlinear manifold and aim to use the metric measurement of manifolds to achieve image set learning tasks [4,5,9,13,14,31,33,36].

In this paper, we propose a new method for image set representation and classification problem. Our method is developed based on the following two observations:

- In real applications, image set data often contains various kinds of noises or corruptions, which makes the representation and recognition process of image set data more challengeable. Therefore, it is desirable to develop a robust representation for image set data which are robust to the noises and corruptions. This inspires us to develop a robust low-rank approximation/reconstruction method to recover clear image set data from original observed noise data.
- Recent studies have demonstrated that the observed image samples in an image set are usually sampled from a nonlinear manifold or several submanifolds [31,33]. Thus traditional linear based representation methods generally fail to deal with them effectively. This further inspires us to exploit a manifold learning method for image set representation.

Based on these two observations, we propose a new manifold regularized low-rank approximation (MLRA) method for image set recovery and representation. One main advantage of MLRA is that it provides an effective low-rank representation for image set data whose elements are sampled from nonlinear manifolds. Thus, comparing with original observed image sets, MLRA of image sets are generally noiseless and more regular, which can significantly encourage the robust learning and recognition process. MLRA aims to use the general manifold learning model for image set data representation. This is also different from many previous works [31,33] who aim to represent image set data using some manifold representations.

It is known that manifold regularized representation and learning methods have been widely used in many traditional single image data based learning tasks in recent years [3,16,18,37,38]. However, to the best of our knowledge, this technique has been not or less studied for image set learning problem. Furthermore, MLRA uses ℓ_1-norm reconstruction function [41] which performs more robustly to the sparse noises and corruptions than ℓ_2-norm function used in previous works [3,16,37,38]. Based on MLRA, we then propose to use covariate-relation graph [7] and Kernel Linear Discriminant Analysis (KLDA) [2] method for image set classification. Experimental results on five datasets demonstrate that the proposed approach yields significantly better performance than the state-of-art methods.

2   Proposed Approach

2.1   Low-Rank Approximation of Image Set

Let $\mathbf{X} = (\mathbf{x}_1, \mathbf{x}_2, ..., \mathbf{x}_n) \in \mathbb{R}^{p \times n}$ be an image set (or video) containing n images. In many applications, the image set data $\mathbf{X}$ usually contains noise, i.e., $\mathbf{X} = \mathbf{Z} + \mathbf{E}$, where $\mathbf{Z}$ is the true signal data and $\mathbf{E}$ is the corruption noise. The aim of low-rank recovery is to find the optimal recovery $\mathbf{Z}$ by minimizing,

$$\min_{\mathbf{Z}} \sum_{i=1}^{n} \|\mathbf{x}_i - \mathbf{z}_i\|_1 = \|\mathbf{X} - \mathbf{Z}\|_1 \quad s.t. \ \ \mathrm{rank}(\mathbf{Z}) \leq k \tag{1}$$

where $\|\mathbf{E}\|_1 = \sum_i \sum_j |\mathbf{E}_{ij}|$ denotes ℓ_1-norm of matrix. Here, we use ℓ_1-norm cost function which is robust to corruption/grossly noises. Since the rank constraint $\mathrm{rank}(\mathbf{Z})$ is difficult to impose in optimization process, many works use a replacement constraint to inexplicitly impose this constraint. One classic way is to use the following matrix factorization [40], i.e.,

$$\min_{\mathbf{Z}, \mathbf{U}, \mathbf{V}} \|\mathbf{X} - \mathbf{Z}\|_1 \quad s.t. \ \ \mathbf{Z} = \mathbf{UV}, \tag{2}$$

where $\mathbf{U} \in \mathbb{R}^{p \times k}$ and $\mathbf{V} \in \mathbb{R}^{k \times n}$. Since $\mathrm{rank}(\mathbf{U}) \leq k$ and $\mathrm{rank}(\mathbf{V}) \leq k$, thus we have $\mathrm{rank}(\mathbf{Z}) = \mathrm{rank}(\mathbf{UV}) \leq k$. This problem is equivalent to the following,

$$\min_{\mathbf{U}, \mathbf{V}} \|\mathbf{X} - \mathbf{UV}\|_1 = \sum_{i=1}^{n} \|\mathbf{x}_i - \mathbf{Uv}_i\|_1 \tag{3}$$

The optimal $\mathbf{Z} = \{\mathbf{Uv}_1, \mathbf{Uv}_2, ..., \mathbf{Uv}_n\}$ provides a low-rank approximation/recovery for image $\mathbf{X} = \{\mathbf{x}_1, \mathbf{x}_2, ..., \mathbf{x}_n\}$. Comparing with original image data $\mathbf{x}_i$, the grossly noise can be suppressed/removed in its low-rank approximation $\mathbf{z}_i$.

2.2   Manifold Regularized Low-Rank Approximation

Motivation and Formulation. The above low-rank method Eq. (3) provides an approximation for image set $\mathbf{X}$ whose images lie on a linear manifold. However, recent studies [31,33] reveal that the images in an image set (or video) are usually sampled from a nonlinear manifold $\mathcal{M}$, i.e., they are generally distributed on a nonlinear manifold $\mathcal{M}$. This motivates us to propose to incorporate manifold structure into the above low-rank approximation process.

One popular way to characterize this manifold structure is to use a neighbor graph which is based on an assumption that the local neighborhood relationship between images on manifold $\mathcal{M}$ can be seen as linear form. Formally, given image set $\mathbf{X} \in \mathbb{R}^{p \times n}$ which are distributed on manifold $\mathcal{M}$, we construct a k nearest neighbor graph $G_{\mathcal{M}}(V, E)$ to encode the nonlinear manifold structure $\mathcal{M}$ of images in $\mathbf{X}$. Each node $v_i \in V$ corresponds to an image $\mathbf{x}_i \in \mathbf{X}$ and an edge $\mathbf{e}_{ij} \in E$ exists between node v_i and v_j if $\mathbf{x}_j$ belongs to the k nearest neighbors of $\mathbf{x}_i$. For each edge $\mathbf{e}_{ij}$, there is a weight $\mathbf{w}_{ij}$ which is used to measure the closeness of two image nodes v_i and v_j, and can be defined by several ways such as binary weight, Heat kernel and dot-product function. After the construction of graph $G_{\mathcal{M}}(V, E)$, many methods can be used to obtain the optimal manifold representation. In this paper, we use graph Laplacian based manifold embedding method which preserves the local geometrical neighborhood relationships in new space and minimizes the smoothness with respect to the intrinsic manifold of the image set $\mathbf{X}$ by minimizing

$$\min_{\mathbf{Y}} J_{\mathcal{M}} = \sum_{i=1}^{n} \sum_{j=1}^{n} \|\mathbf{y}_i - \mathbf{y}_j\|_F^2 \mathbf{W}_{ij} \tag{4}$$

where $\mathbf{Y} = \{\mathbf{y}_1, \mathbf{y}_2, ..., \mathbf{y}_n\}$ is the low-dimensional manifold representation of image $\mathbf{X}$.

By incorporating $J_{\mathcal{M}}$ into Eq. (3), our Manifold regularized Low-Rank Approximation (MLRA) is formulated as,

$$\min_{\mathbf{U}, \mathbf{Y}} J = \sum_{i=1}^{n} \|\mathbf{x} - \mathbf{U}\mathbf{y}_i\|_1 + \alpha \sum_{i=1}^{n} \sum_{j=1}^{n} \mathbf{w}_{ij} \|\mathbf{y}_i - \mathbf{y}_j\|_F^2 \tag{5}$$

where $\mathbf{Y} = (\mathbf{y}_1, \mathbf{y}_2, ..., \mathbf{y}_n)$, and $\alpha \geq 0$ is a parameter balance the contributions of two parts. Using matrix representation, the above model can be reformulated as,

$$\min_{\mathbf{U}, \mathbf{Y}} J = \|\mathbf{X} - \mathbf{U}\mathbf{Y}\|_1 + \alpha \mathrm{Tr} \ \mathbf{Y}(\mathbf{D} - \mathbf{W})\mathbf{Y}^T$$
$$s.t. \ \mathbf{Y}\mathbf{Y}^T = \mathbf{I} \tag{6}$$

The orthogonal $\mathbf{Y}\mathbf{Y}^T = \mathbf{I}$ is used to avoid trivial solution. Comparing the aforementioned low-rank model Eq. (3), the optimal $\mathbf{Z} = \mathbf{U}\mathbf{Y} = \{\mathbf{U}\mathbf{y}_1, \mathbf{U}\mathbf{y}_2, ..., \mathbf{U}\mathbf{y}_n\}$ provides a more effective low-rank approximation for image $\mathbf{X} = \{\mathbf{x}_1, \mathbf{x}_2, ..., \mathbf{x}_n\}$ by further incorporating the geometric manifold structure encoded in graph $G_{\mathcal{M}}(\mathbf{V}, \mathbf{E})$.

Optimization. We present an effective updating algorithm to solve MLRA model. Firstly, Eq. (7) can be rewritten equivalently as

$$\min_{\mathbf{U}, \mathbf{Y}, \mathbf{E}} \ \|\mathbf{E}\|_1 + \alpha \mathrm{Tr}\mathbf{Y}(\mathbf{D} - \mathbf{W})\mathbf{Y}^T$$
$$s.t. \ \mathbf{E} = \mathbf{X} - \mathbf{U}\mathbf{Y}, \mathbf{Y}\mathbf{Y}^T = \mathbf{I} \tag{7}$$

We use the Augmented Lagrange Multiplier (ALM) method to solve this problem. ALM solves a sequences of subproblems

$$\min_{\mathbf{U}, \mathbf{Y}, \mathbf{E}} \|\mathbf{E}\|_1 + \mathrm{Tr}\Omega^T(\mathbf{E} - \mathbf{X} + \mathbf{U}\mathbf{Y}) + \frac{2}{\mu}\|\mathbf{E} - \mathbf{X} + \mathbf{U}\mathbf{Y}\|_2^2 + \alpha Tr\mathbf{Y}(\mathbf{D} - \mathbf{W})\mathbf{Y}^T$$
$$s.t. \ \mathbf{Y}\mathbf{Y}^T = \mathbf{I} \tag{8}$$

where Ω is Lagrange multipliers and μ is the penalty parameter. There are two major parts of this algorithm, i.e., solving the sub-problem and updating parameters (Ω, μ).

First, we rewrite the objective function of Eq. (9) as

$$\min_{\mathbf{U}, \mathbf{Y}, \mathbf{E}} \ \|\mathbf{E}\|_1 + \frac{2}{\mu}\|\mathbf{E} - \mathbf{X} + \mathbf{U}\mathbf{Y} + \frac{\Omega}{\mu}\|_F^2 + \alpha \mathrm{Tr}\mathbf{Y}\mathbf{L}\mathbf{Y}^T \tag{9}$$

where $\mathbf{L} = \mathbf{D} - \mathbf{W}$ is the Laplacian matrix.

Then, we iteratively solve the following sub-problems until convergence.

(1) Solve $\mathbf{U}$ while fixing $\mathbf{Y}, \mathbf{E}$. The problem becomes

$$\min_{\mathbf{U}} J_{\mathbf{U}} = \frac{2}{\mu}\|\mathbf{E} - \mathbf{X} + \mathbf{U}\mathbf{Y} + \frac{\Omega}{\mu}\|_F \tag{10}$$

The optimal solution can be obtained by setting the first deviation to zero, i.e.,

$$\frac{\partial J_{\mathbf{U}}}{\partial \mathbf{U}} = -2(\mathbf{X} - \mathbf{E} - \frac{\Omega}{\mu})\mathbf{Y} + 2\mathbf{U} = 0 \tag{11}$$

Thus, the optimal $\mathbf{U}^*$ is computed as,

$$\mathbf{U}^* = (\mathbf{X} - \mathbf{E} - \frac{\Omega}{\mu})\mathbf{Y}^T$$

Note that, by setting $\mathbf{U} = (\mathbf{X} - \mathbf{E} - \frac{\Omega}{\mu})\mathbf{Y}^T$, the original problem is equivalent to the following,

$$\min_{\mathbf{Y}, \mathbf{E}} \frac{2}{\mu}\|\mathbf{E} - \mathbf{X} + \frac{\Omega}{\mu} + (\mathbf{X} - \mathbf{E} - \frac{\Omega}{\mu})\mathbf{Y}^T\mathbf{Y}\|_F^2 + \mathrm{Tr}\mathbf{Y}\mathbf{L}\mathbf{Y}^T$$
$$s.t. \ \mathbf{Y}\mathbf{Y}^T = \mathbf{I} \tag{12}$$

(2) Solve $\mathbf{Y}$ while fixing $\mathbf{E}$. By some algebra, the above problem is equivalent to

$$\min_{\mathbf{Y}\mathbf{Y}^T = \mathbf{I}} \mathrm{Tr}\mathbf{Y}\left[(\mathbf{X} - \mathbf{E} - \frac{\Omega}{\mu})^T(\mathbf{X} - \mathbf{E} - \frac{\Omega}{\mu}) + \alpha\mathbf{L}\right]\mathbf{Y}^T \tag{13}$$

Thus, the optimal $\mathbf{Y}^*$ can be obtained by computing the eigenvectors corresponding to the first k smallest eigenvalues of the matrix the following $\mathbf{M}$,

$$\mathbf{M} = (\mathbf{X} - \mathbf{E} - \frac{\Omega}{\mu})^T(\mathbf{X} - \mathbf{E} - \frac{\Omega}{\mu}) + \alpha\mathbf{L}$$

(3) Solve $\mathbf{E}$ while fixing $\mathbf{Y}$. This is

$$\min_{\mathbf{E}} \ \|\mathbf{E}\|_1 + \frac{2}{\mu}\|\mathbf{E} - \mathbf{X} - \mathbf{U}\mathbf{Y} - \frac{\Omega}{\mu}\|_F^2 \tag{14}$$

Let $\mathbf{e}_i, \mathbf{a}_i$ be the i-th column of matrix $\mathbf{E}$ and $\mathbf{E} - \mathbf{X} - \mathbf{U}\mathbf{Y} - \frac{\Omega}{\mu}$, respectively. The problem can be decomposed into n independent problems

$$\min_{\mathbf{e}_i} \|\mathbf{e}_i\| + \frac{2}{\mu}\|\mathbf{e}_i - \mathbf{a}_i\|^2 \tag{15}$$

The solution of this proximal operator is known [26] to be

$$\mathbf{e}_i = \max\{1 - \frac{1}{\mu}\|\mathbf{a}_i\|, 0\}\mathbf{a}_i \tag{16}$$

(4) At the end of each ALM iteration, Ω, μ are updated as

$$\mathbf{C} = \mathbf{C} + \mu(\mathbf{E} - \mathbf{X} + \mathbf{UY})$$
$$\mu = \rho\mu \tag{17}$$

where $\rho > 1$. In practice, $\rho = 1.1 - 1.5$ are good choices.

2.3 Image Set Classification

Based on MRLA representation, we then use some traditional set feature extraction methods, such as CDL [32], CRG [7], to achieve image set recognition task. In this paper, we use covariate-relation graph (CRG) based feature extraction method because of its simplicity and effectiveness [7].

Given an image set $\mathbf{X} = \{\mathbf{x}_1, \mathbf{x}_2, ..., \mathbf{x}_n\}$, we first obtain its MRLA $\mathbf{Z} = \{\mathbf{z}_1, \mathbf{z}_2, ..., \mathbf{z}_n\}$ where $\mathbf{z}_i = \mathbf{Uy}_i$. Then, we use CRG to represent $\mathbf{Z}$. Let $\mathbf{u}_i, i = 1, ..., p$ be the i-th covariate denoting the i-th dimension feature throughout the n images of $\mathbf{Z}$, i.e., the i-th row of low-rank representation matrix $\mathbf{Z}$. The aim of CRG is to construct a graph $\mathbf{G} = (\mathbf{V}, \mathbf{E})$, where each node $\mathbf{v}_i, \mathbf{v}_i \in \mathbf{V}$ in $\mathbf{G}$ represents a covariate/feature $\mathbf{u}_i$, and the edge $\mathbf{e}_{ij}$ between node $\mathbf{v}_i$ and $\mathbf{v}_j$ denotes some relationship $\mathbf{r}_{ij}$ between covariate $\mathbf{u}_i$ and $\mathbf{u}_j$. Based on CRG representation, we can define a kind of kernel/similarity between two CRG graphs and thus image sets [7]. At last, we conduct image set classification by using Kernel variant of Linear Discriminant Analysis (KLDA) [2,32] method and nearest neighbor classification method [32].

3   Experiments

3.1   Datasets and Settings

Our method has been compared with some other methods including Discriminant-analysis of Canonical Correlations (DCC) [19], Manifold-Manifold Distance (MMD) [33], Manifold Discriminant Analysis (MDA) [31], Covariate-relation graph (CRG) [7], Covariance Discriminative Learning (CDL) [32], Set to Set Distance Metric Learning (SSDML) [39] and DARG [34]. We test our MRLA method on dataset of YouTube Celebrities (YTC) [17], ETH-80 [22], Honda/UCSD [21] and CMU MoBo [10].

We do the experiments by randomly selecting 70% samples for gallery data and the rest for probe data. We run experiments 20 times for different random selections and compute the average performance. In all experiments, we set the parameter $\alpha = 0.4$.

Table 1. Classification results of different methods on five datasets.

Methods	DCC [19]	MMD [33]	MDA [31]	SSDML [39]	CDL [32]	CRG [7]	DARG [34]	MLRA
YTC	0.6434	0.7751	0.6667	0.7907	0.6589	0.8139	0.7984	**0.8217**
ETH80	0.8750	0.8000	0.8750	0.8333	0.9375	0.9167	0.9500	**0.9583**
Honda	0.9271	0.8974	0.9411	0.7435	0.9487	0.8717	0.9487	**0.9744**
CMU	0.8887	0.7273	0.7651	0.6363	0.8939	0.8788	0.8641	**0.9091**

3.2 Results Analysis

We test different methods on both image set classification and identification tasks. For classification task, we use the Nearest Neighborhood classification method and obtain the average classification accuracies for different methods. For identification task, for each image set in probe data, we first obtain the ranking of all the gallery image sets using the proposed representation and similarity measurement, and then report the Cumulative Match Characteristics (CMC) curve. On CMC curve, the rate at rank n shows the percentage of correct matchings in top n candidates. Table 1 summarizes the average classification results. Figure 1 shows the CMC curves of different methods.

Here, we can note that (1) Comparing with CRG [7], the proposed MRLA image set representation can significantly improve the classification result, which clearly demonstrates the desired benefit and effectiveness of the proposed MLRA method on conducting image set representation problem and thus leads to better classification result. (2) Comparing with some other approaches, the proposed approach obtains the highest classification rate. (3) From Fig. 1, we can note that the proposed approach achieves highest identification rates for all ranks on five datasets, which shows the effectiveness of the proposed image set approach.

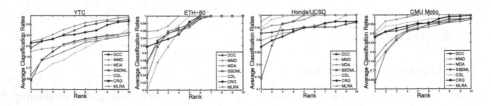

Fig. 1. CMC performance curves for different methods on all datasets.

3.3 Robust to Noise

To evaluate the robustness of MRLA method to the noise possibly appearing in the testing image set data, we randomly add some noise to the image set datasets. We add two kinds of noises including corruption noise and missing value noises. The corruption noise is added as follows. For each image in an image set, we randomly choose some pixels to corrupt and replace these pixels

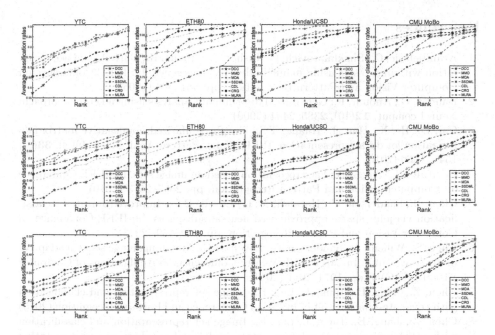

Fig. 2. CMC performance curves for different methods on the corruption datasets. From top row to the bottom row, the corruption percentages are set from 10%, 30% and 50%, respectively.

by using some random values that uniformly range from 0 to 1 (note that the pixel values have been normalized to [0,1]). Figure 2 shows the comparison results across different noise levels on five datasets. Here, we can note that, as the noise level increases, the proposed approach can maintain better results than other comparing methods, which indicates the robustness of the proposed approach.

4   Conclusion

This paper presents a new robust manifold regularized low-rank approximation (MLRA) method for image set representation and recognition problem. MLRA provides an effective low-rank representation for image set by further exploring the manifold structure of image set and thus leads to robust image set learning and recognition result. We test MLRA on five datasets and experimental performance demonstrate the robustness and effectiveness of the method.

Acknowledgement. This work is supported by National Natural Science Foundation of China (61602001, 61472002); Natural Science Foundation of Anhui Province (1708085QF139); Natural Science Foundation of Anhui Higher Education Institutions of China (KJ2016A020).

References

1. Arandjelovic, O., Shakhnarovich, G., Fisher, J., Cipolla, R., Darrell, T.: Face recognition with image sets using manifold density divergence. In: IEEE Conference on Computer Vision and Pattern Recognition, pp. 581–588 (2005)
2. Baudat, G., Anouar, F.: Generalized discriminant analysis using a kernel approach. Neural comput. **12**(10), 2385–2404 (2000)
3. Cai, D., He, X., Han, J., Huang, T.S.: Graph regularized nonnegative matrix factorization for data representation. IEEE Trans. Pattern Anal. Mach. Intell. **33**(8), 1548–1560 (2010)
4. Cevikalp, H., Triggs, B.: Face recognition based on image sets. In: IEEE Conference on Computer Vision and Pattern Recognition, pp. 2567–2573 (2010)
5. Chen, S., Sanderson, C., Harandi, M.T., Lovell, B.C.: Improved image set classification via joint sparse approximated nearest subspaces. In: IEEE Conference on Computer Vision and Pattern Recognition, pp. 452–459 (2013)
6. Chen, S., Wiliem, A., Sanderson, C., Lovell, B.C.: Matching image sets via adaptive multi convex hull. In: 2014 IEEE Winter Conference on Applications of Computer Vision (WACV), pp. 1074–1081 (2014)
7. Chen, Z., Jiang, B., Tang, J., Luo, B.: Image set representation and classification with covariate-relation graph. In: Asian Conference and Pattern Recognition (2015)
8. Chen, Z., Jiang, B., Tang, J., Luo, B.: Image set representation and classification with attributed covariate-relation graph model and graph sparse representation classification. Neurocomputing **226**(C), 262–268 (2017)
9. Cui, Z., Shan, S., Zhang, H., Lao, S., Chen, X.: Image sets alignment for video-based face recognition. In: IEEE Conference on Computer Vision and Pattern Recognition, pp. 2626–2633 (2012)
10. Gross, R., Shi, J.: The CMU motion of body (MoBo) database. Technical report CMU-RI-TR-01-18, Robotics Institute, Carnegie Mellon University (2001)
11. Hamm, J., Lee, D.D.: Grassmann discriminant analysis: a unifying view on subspace-based learning. In: International Conference on Machine Learning, pp. 376–383 (2008)
12. Harandi, M., Salzmann, M., Baktashmotlagh, M.: Beyond gauss: image-set matching on the Riemannian manifold of PDFs. In: IEEE International Conference on Computer Vision (2015)
13. Harandi, M.T., Sanderson, C., Shirazi, S., Lovell, B.C.: Graph embedding discriminant analysis on Grassmannian manifolds for improved image set matching. In: IEEE Conference on Computer Vision and Pattern Recognition, pp. 2705–2712 (2011)
14. Hu, Y., Mian, A.S., Owens, R.: Sparse approximated nearest points for image set classification. In: IEEE Conference on Computer Vision and Pattern Recognition, pp. 121–128 (2011)
15. Ji, Z., Huang, Y., Sun, Q., Cao, G.: A spatially constrained generative asymmetric Gaussian mixture model for image segmentation. J. Vis. Commun. Image Represent. **40**, 611–626 (2016)
16. Jiang, B., Ding, C., Luo, B., Tang, J.: Graph-laplacian PCA: closed-form solution and robustness. In: IEEE Conference on Computer Vision and Pattern Recognition, pp. 3492–3498 (2013)
17. Kim, M., Kumar, S., Pavlovic, V., Rowley, H.: Face tracking and recognition with visual constraints in real-world videos. In: IEEE Conference on Computer Vision and Pattern Recognition, pp. 1–8 (2008)

18. Shahid, N., Kalofolias, V., Bresson, X., Bronstein, M., Vandergheynst, P.: Robust principal component analysis on graphs. In: IEEE International Conference on Computer Vision, pp. 2812–2820 (2015)
19. Kim, T.-K., Kittler, J., Cipolla, R.: Discriminative learning and recognition of image set classes using canonical correlations. IEEE Trans. Pattern Anal. Mach. Intell. 29(6), 1005–1018 (2007)
20. Kim, T.-K., Wong, K.-Y.K., Cipolla, R.: Tensor canonical correlation analysis for action classification. In: IEEE Conference on Computer Vision and Pattern Recognition, pp. 1–8 (2007)
21. Lee, K.-C., Ho, J., Yang, M.-H., Kriegman, D.: Video-based face recognition using probabilistic appearance manifolds. In: Computer Vision and Pattern Recognition (2003)
22. Leibe, B., Schiele, B.: Analyzing appearance and contour based methods for object categorization. In: Computer Vision and Pattern Recognition, pp. 409–415 (2003)
23. Lu, J., Wang, G., Moulin, P.: Image set classification using holistic multiple order statistics features and localized multi-kernel metric learning. In: IEEE International Conference on Computer Vision, pp. 329–336 (2013)
24. Ma, R., Hu, F., Hao, Q.: Active compressive sensing via pyroelectric infrared sensor for human situation recognition. IEEE Trans. Syst. Man Cybern. Syst. 47, 1–11 (2016)
25. Min, R., Kose, N., Dugelay, J.L.: KinectFaceDB: a kinect database for face recognition. IEEE Trans. Syst. Man Cybern. Syst. 44(11), 1534–1548 (2014)
26. Nie, F., Huang, H., Cai, X., Ding, C.H.: Efficient and robust feature selection via joint l2, 1-norms minimization. In: Advances in Neural Information Processing Systems, pp. 1813–1821 (2010)
27. Nishiyama, M., Yamaguchi, O., Fukui, K.: Face recognition with the multiple constrained mutual subspace method. In: Kanade, T., Jain, A., Ratha, N.K. (eds.) AVBPA 2005. LNCS, vol. 3546, pp. 71–80. Springer, Heidelberg (2005). https://doi.org/10.1007/11527923_8
28. Shakhnarovich, G., Fisher, J.W., Darrell, T.: Face recognition from long-term observations. In: Heyden, A., Sparr, G., Nielsen, M., Johansen, P. (eds.) ECCV 2002. LNCS, vol. 2352, pp. 851–865. Springer, Heidelberg (2002). https://doi.org/10.1007/3-540-47977-5_56
29. Song, S., Gong, Y., Zhang, Y., Huang, G., Huang, G.-B.: Dimension reduction by minimum error minimax probability machine. IEEE Trans. Syst. Man Cybern. Syst. 47, 58–69 (2017)
30. Wang, L., Zhong, Y., Yin, Y.: Nearest neighbour cuckoo search algorithm with probabilistic mutation. Appl. Soft Comput. 49, 498–509 (2016)
31. Wang, R., Chen, X.: Manifold discriminant analysis. In: Computer Vision and Pattern Recognition, pp. 429–436 (2009)
32. Wang, R., Guo, H., Davis, L.S., Dai, Q.: Covariance discriminative learning: a natural and efficient approach to image set classification. In: Computer Vision and Pattern Recognition, pp. 2496–2503 (2012)
33. Wang, R., Shan, S., Chen, X., Gao, W.: Manifold-manifold distance with application to face recognition based on image set. In: Computer Vision and Pattern Recognition, pp. 1–8 (2008)
34. Wang, W., Wang, R., Huang, Z., Shan, S., Chen, X.: Discriminant analysis on Riemannian manifold of Gaussian distributions for face recognition with image sets. In: IEEE Conference on Computer Vision and Pattern Recognition, pap. 2048–2057 (2015)

35. Yamaguchi, O., Fukui, K., Maeda, K.-I.: Face recognition using temporal image sequence. In: Proceedings of the Third IEEE International Conference on Automatic Face and Gesture Recognition 1998, pp. 318–323 (1998)
36. Yang, M., Zhu, P., Van Gool, L., Zhang, L.: Face recognition based on regularized nearest points between image sets. In: 2013 10th IEEE International Conference and Workshops on Automatic Face and Gesture Recognition (FG), pp. 1–7 (2013)
37. Zhang, Z., Zhao, K.: Low-rank matrix approximation with manifold regularization. IEEE Trans. PAMI **35**(7), 1717–1729 (2013)
38. Zheng, M., et al.: Graph regularized sparse coding for image representation. IEEE Trans. Image Process. **20**(5), 1327–1336 (2011)
39. Zhu, P., Zhang, L., Zuo, W., Zhang, D.: From point to set: extend the learning of distance metrics. In: International Conference Computer Vision, pp. 2664–2671 (2013)
40. Ke, Q., Kanade, T.: Robust L1 norm factorization in the presence of outliers and missing data by alternative convex programming. In: Computer Vision and Pattern Recognition, pp. 739–746 (2005)
41. Shahid, N., Kalofolias, V., Bresson, X., Bronstein, M., Vandergheynst, P.: Robust principal component analysis on graphs In: IEEE International Conference on Computer Vision, pp. 2812–2820 (2015)

Adaptively Learning Background-Aware Correlation Filter for Visual Tracking

Zichun Zhang, Xinyan Liang, and Chenglong Li[✉]

School of Computer Science and Technology, Anhui University, No. 111 Jiulong Road
Hefei 230601, Anhui, China
188484592@qq.com, lcll314@foxmail.com

Abstract. Correlation filter (CF) trackers have received more and more attention due to their excellent performance while maintaining high frame rates. However, the limited context information might limit the performance of CF trackers as the presence of background effects in or around target bounding box will corrupt CF learning. In this paper, toward improving background-aware CF trackers, we propose a general algorithm that adaptively incorporates background contexts in CF learning to suppress the distractors effectively. Comparing with existing background-aware CF trackers, our approach can adaptively explore background distractors by employing their correlations to the target object which makes our tracker more effective and efficient. Experimental results on large-scale benchmark dataset demonstrate the effectiveness and efficiency of the proposed approach against recent CF trackers.

1 Introduction

Visual tracking is one of the fundamental research problems in computer vision and has been hot and active due to its wide range of practical applications, such as video surveillance, robotics, and human computer interaction. Despite many recent breakthroughs in visual tracking, it is still a challenging problem partly due to background clutter which produces many distractors in or around target bounding box.

To handle background distractors, the context-aware correlation filter tracker (CA) [17] is proposed to allow the explicit incorporation of background context within CF trackers. In particular, CA uniformly samples 4 fixed context patches around the object of interest to be better aware of the surroundings, as shown in Fig. 1(c). These context patches can be viewed as hard negative samples and suppressed in the CF training stage, in which the CF model makes the negative samples regress to zero while the target sample regresses to a regression target and hence suppress the distractors. In real-world scenarios, however, the number and locations of the background distrators usually vary over time, as shown in Fig. 1(a) and (b). Therefore, the context patches with fixed number and locations do not convey real background distractors which might limit the tracking performance when some distractors are not suppressed.

© Springer Nature Singapore Pte Ltd. 2018
Y. Wang et al. (Eds.): IGTA 2018, CCIS 875, pp. 517–526, 2018.
https://doi.org/10.1007/978-981-13-1702-6_51

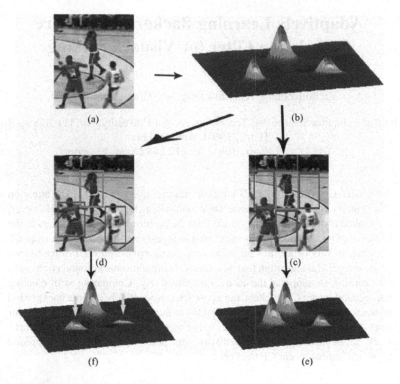

Fig. 1. Illustration of adavantages of our approach over CA [17]. (a) Input frame. (b) Response map generated by CF. (c) Context patches (denoted by the red bounding box) used in CA. (d) Detected context patches in our approach. (e) Response map of CA. (f) Response map of our approach. The results show that our approach can detect reasonable background distractors and our approach thus suppress the background effects more effectively than CA. (Color figure online)

In this paper, we propose an adaptive approach to detect the background distractors for visual tracking. We first generate the response map at the current frame using previous correlation filter. Then, we determine number and locations of background distractors based on the observation that the distractors have a similar appearance to the target object and hence will produce peaks in the response map, as shown in Fig. 1(b). Although the response peaks reflect background disturbance to the target object, it is unreasonable to use all of them to suppress background effects for visual tracking due to the following reasons: (1) Some of them are near close from each other, and thus the corresponding background context patches have large overlap, which brings big information redundancy in CF learning. (2) They are sometimes dense due to background clutter, and integrating all of them into CF learning will result in low tracking speed.

To this end, we propose a simple yet effective strategy to handle these problems. First, we extract all local maxima in the response map, in which the non-maxima suppression is adopted for the robustness. These maxima are treated as the candidate set of background distractors. In many scenarios, the size of the candidate set is large due to the background clutter which brings big information redundancy and also increase computational complexity. Therefore, we select representative distractors from the candidate set as follows: Given the candidate set, we first select the distractor with highest response, and then remove those distractors whose overlap with the selected one are larger than a predefined threshold. The remaining distrators are formed a new candidate set, and we repeat above process until the size of the candidate set reduce to zero. The selected distractors could cover most challenging background contexts and also have a minimum overlaps which make the learned filter more discriminative and efficient. We integrate these distractors into the background-aware CF, and achieve a real-time and effective object tracking. Extensive experiments on large dataset show the effectiveness of our method.

2 Related Work

Correlation filters (CFs) is a most potential research direction in visual tracking due to the excellent performance and high tracking speed. The seminar work, i.e., MOSSE [3], only employs the brightness of images as input features, and might be weak in complicated situations. Major extensions based on MOSSE are about different aspects, such as more powerful features [8, 13, 16], kernel trick [12, 13], scale handling [2, 5, 14], mitigation of boundary effects [6, 11], and integration of context information [10, 17]. In particular, the use of context information for tracking has been proof to be effective way for boosting tracking performance. For example, Xiao et al. [19] utilize multilevel clustering to exploit contextual information of a scene to detect similar objects and other potential distractors. Mueller et al. [17] propose to take global context into account and incorporates it directly into the learned filter. The filter has a closed-form solution, and thus makes the tracker more effective and efficient. However, this method fixes the number and locations of context patches, and thus might not convey the real background distractors.

3 Proposed Tracker

3.1 Review: Context-Aware Correlation Filter Tracker

Since our improvements are based on the work of Context-Aware (CA) method [17], we would like to make a review of the framework first. First of all, the background information of the object has a big impact on tracking performance. Situations like background clutter have shown that the background distraction could easily affect the process of discriminative learning, since the contextual distractors usually possess a high response in response map. To better reduce distractive effect, the contextual information is incorporated into the learned filter. Hence, Mueller et al. [17] propose a framework that adds contextual information to the filter during the learning stage. It suggests to sample context patches uniformly around the target as x_i. The circulant matrices $\mathbf{X_i}$ and $\mathbf{X_0}$ represent the context patches and the target, respectively. These context patches can be treated as hard negative samples. The context patches are incorporated into the standard formulation as a regulaizer. It encourages the learned filter w that has a high response for the target patch and close to zero response for context patches. As a result, the target patch is regressed to **y**, while the parameter λ_2 controls the context patches regressed to zeros. This idea can be formalized as:

$$\min_{w} \left\| \mathbf{X}_0 w - \mathbf{y} \right\|_2^2 + \lambda_1 \left\| w \right\|_2^2 + \lambda_2 \sum_{i=1}^{k} \left\| \mathbf{X}_i w \right\|_2^2 \tag{1}$$

The primal objective function (1) can obtain the following closed-form solution in Fourier domain using the diagonal identity of circulant matrix:

$$\hat{w} = \frac{\hat{x}_0^* \odot \hat{y}}{\hat{x}_0^* \odot \hat{x}_0 + \lambda_1 + \lambda_2 \sum_{i=1}^{k} \hat{x}_i^* \odot \hat{x}_i} \tag{2}$$

Where the matrix inversion can be settled efficiently by element-wise calculation. Although the CA method improve this task to some extent, there are deficiencies in this method that make the proposed trackers unfit those distractors beyond fixed settings. The number and location of the background patches in this method are fixed, respectively set to the up, down, left and right directions as seen in Fig. 1. Thus those potential distractors from other directions are dismissed, causing the tracking process attacked. Even if some moving distractors are incorporated in current frame, the fixed background patches are not able to follow them in the next few frames or just obtain partial information.

3.2 Overview of Our Approach

Unlike the fixed settings of CA work, we learn the number and location of distractors using an adaptive detection, which enable filter to better learn about the global context. We then train the filter with the sampled information using the closed-form solution in CA method [17]. The distractors are suppressed due to the regression to zero in the solution and hence affect the following tracking process in a limited level.

3.3 Distractor Detection

We do detection on the response map $r_p(w, z)$ of current map, which is generated by the search window z and previous correlation filter w. Since the distractors have the similar appearance as target and produce peaks on the response map, our key idea is to we extract all local maxima in the response map whose response score exceed a judging threshold defined by $\tau * \delta$. Here, τ indicates the target response score and δ is a judging parameter.

We involve these maxima into candidate set $M = \{ m_1, m_2, \dots, m_n \}$ during each detection. This process can be formalized as:

$$m_i = S_\delta \left(\tau, r_p(w, z) \right), i = 1, 2, \dots, n \tag{3}$$

Where the m_i refers to the corresponding detected maxima. Function S indicates the detection process. We then select the maxima with highest response as the corresponding distractor X_i. And the remaining maxima are formed the new candidate set $M = \{m_1, m_2, \ldots m_{i-1}, m_{i+1}, \ldots, m_n\}$, and we repeat above process until the size of the candidate set reduce to zero. Noticed that distractors may overlap at the same region. Hence multiple maxima are generated in the same area as seen in Fig. 2. In that occasion, the assigned patches may overlap and cause oversampling and over suppressing. To solve this, we advance our method as: After selecting a maxima, we remove other maxima that are in the same area thus ensure these maxima would not be selected again.

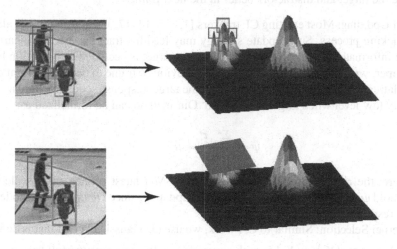

Fig. 2. There are fluctuations around the peak. By simply searching the maximum points, several patches would overlap in the same distractor and cause excess suppressing. Our baffle method remove the patch information once the the maximum point is searched. The distractor thus would only be counted once.

Here, since the distractors can be dense sometimes, we set a range for the patch number as $[n, m]$. The key purpose to do this is that we remain the filter to be discriminative even the background clutter is not significant. The bottom limit n indicates the filter to sample enough background patches around the target. On the other hand, we set the upper limit m in order to maintain the robustness of the framework, since a large variation of patch number i unfit the fixed λ_2 in the Eq. (1). Extensive experiments show that increase the limit m are helpless to performance, since the tracker already samples considerable information of background.

3.4 Tracking

Besides the key method as mentioned, we also add other modules into our method, including target state estimation, model updating, kernel selection and feature representation.

Target State Estimation: Generally, the target hold the maximum score in the generated response map. Through this, we firstly detect the position of maximum point in the map. Then, by estimating the excursion between this position and position of maximum point in the last frame, we could obtain the current position of target. On the other hand, after sampling ample information of distractors, our goal is to train a filter that can suppress the distractors and generate low response score with those distractors in the following tracking. Here, we use the closed-form solution as shown in Eq. (1) to train our filter. The sampled information of detected distractors X_i are regressed to zero in the solution while the target is regressed to a regression target y. Therefore, the trained filter differentiate the target and distractors better in the next frame.

Model Updating: Most existing CF trackers [1, 3, 5, 14, 17, 19] update models all along the tracking process. Such update strategy may lead the tracking model to learn inaccurate information especially when the tracked target is occluded or in motion blur. In this paper, we utilize the feedback from the previous κ frame to decide the right chance of updating. Our key purpose relies on that the target response score drop into a comparatively low level when target is occluded. Our method can be formalized as:

$$\psi = \frac{\Sigma_{i=1}^{\kappa} \tau^i}{\kappa} * \mu \tag{4}$$

Here, the τ^i refers to the target response in $No.i$ latest frame. μ is a scale factor. Threshold ψ determines the right chances of updating, since we update the model if the target response score is above ψ.

Kernel Selection: Similar to CA work, we use the Gaussian kernel that is defined as $\kappa(X_1, X_2) =< \varphi(X_1), \varphi(X_2) >$ with a mapping φ. We compute the full kernel correlation efficiently in the Fourier domain.

Feature Representation: We integrate our method to different kinds of trackers including those who use HOG features, CN features, Grayscale pixel intensity and color histogram. Moreover, extensive experiments have shown that by using more sophisticated features, trackers integrated with our method show higher performance.

4   Experiment

To validate the effectiveness of our methods, we integrate it with four popular and diverse CF trackers. We then benchmark them against their baseline versions. We select the popular object tracking benchmark OTB-100 [18] to evaluate these trackers.

4.1   Baseline Trackers

To demonstrate the effectiveness of our method, we apply our method to these selected CF trackers named MOSSE, DCF, SAMF, STAPLE. The selected trackers follow the standard CF formulation and are different from other selected baselines in terms of features and/or implementation. To depict the improvement of our method, we benchmark the integrated trackers against the baseline versions and the integrated CA method versions. For convenience, we call the trackers integrated our method $MOSSE_{AL}$, DCF_{AL}, $SAMF_{AL}$ and $STAPLE_{AL}$. Similarly, the trackers integrated with the CA method are called $MOSSE_{CA}$, DCF_{CA}, $SAMF_{CA}$ and $STAPLE_{CA}$.

4.2 Experiment Setup

Metrics: In this paper, the precision rate (PR) and success rate (SR) are used to evaluate the performance of trackers. PR is the percentage of frames whose the center error between tracker bounding box and ground truth bounding box is within the given threshold distance. By varying the maximum allowed center error in pixel distance along the x-axis, the percentage of correctly predicted bounding boxes per threshold is plotted on the y-axis. The common pixel distance is set to 20 pixels for ranking trackers. SR is the ratio of the number of successful frames whose the intersection over union (IoU) of tracker bounding box and ground truth bounding box is larger than a threshold. By varying the threshold, the SR plot can be obtained and we employ the area under curve of SR plot to define the representative SR. All trackers are run on the same workstation (Intel CPU I5-5200 2.2 GHZ, 8 GB RAM) using MATLAB. Notice that our workstation may be different from that of previous work (Intel Xeon CPU E5-2697 2.6 GHz, 256 GB RAM), which may cause some slight difference between the general performance of previous work.

Parameter Settings: For fair comparison, all trackers based CA method are run with the standard parameters provided by the authors. We generally set the regularization factor λ_1 to $1e^{-4}$, the discrimination factor δ to 0.4 and regularization factor λ_2 to {5,0.5,2.5,0.5} for $MOSSE_{AL}$, DCF_{AL}, $SAMF_{AL}$ and $STAPLE_{AL}$ trackers, respectively. We empirically set the κ to 200 and μ to 0.6. Combining these two factor with an appropriate learning rate factor σ is essential to global performance. So we set the σ to {0.2,0.01,0.01,0.02} for $MOSSE_{AL}$, DCF_{AL}, $SAMF_{AL}$ and $STAPLE_{AL}$ trackers, respectively. In addition, we also define the up and bottom limit $[n,m]$ of gained distractors and then set them to be [4, 5].

4.3 Comparison Result

Overall Performance: Figure 3 show the results of all CA method trackers and our AL method trackers on the OTB-100. It can be deduced that all AL trackers improve the corresponding CA trackers in PR and SR. We have to mention that since the CA counterpart has already improved for a large amount compared with the baseline version, we focus mainly on the advancement between AL trackers and CA trackers. The absolute improvement ranges from 2.0%/1.5% to 4.4%/3.6% for the most sophisticated CF tracker (STAPLE) and the most basic CF tracker (MOSSE) respectively. For the basic CF tracker (DCF), DCF_{AL} outperforms DCF_{AL} by 5.4%/3.5% in PR/SR. The improvement turns out to be significant with trackers using ordinary features such as the MOSSE or DCF. To visualize the impact our method has on tracking performance, we show examples of each baseline method compared to our AL counterpart on sample videos from

OTB-100 in Fig. 4. Noted that although we finish a detection for distractor in every frame, trackers based on our method still run at the similar speed as CA counterpart.

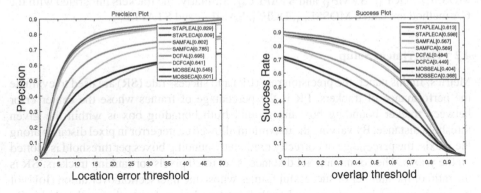

Fig. 3. Average overall performance on OTB-100

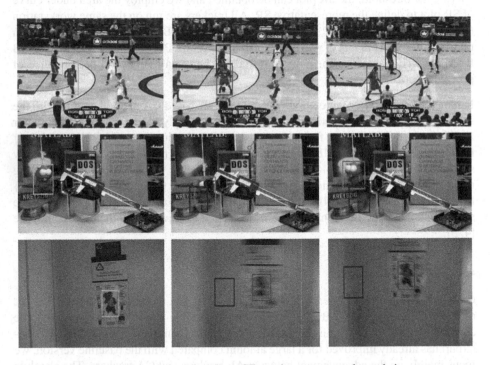

Fig. 4. Tracking results of four baseline CF trackers compared to their context-aware counterparts. To best present our general performance, we select results respectively from background clutter (Basketbal), occlusion (Lemming) and motion blur (BlurOwl) of OTB-100. We use, red and Green, Red to respectively indicate the groundtruth, our results and baseline results (Color figure online)

Attribute-Based Evaluation: Our method improves tracking performance in most scenarios there are certain categories that benefit more than others. In this paper, we mainly select four specific scenarios to illustrate the effectiveness of our methods: background clutter, fast motion, occlusion and motion blur. For convenience, we abbreviate the four scenarios as BC, FM, OC and MB, respectively. The average performance of precision rate is presented in Table 1. From the Table 1, we have the following major observations and conclusions. All trackers based on AL outperform the corresponding CA trackers. It can be illustrated that AL methods can learn well the background distractors compared to CA methods. In particular, trackers integrated AL methods are beneficial against the distractors in BC. Moreover, our performance in drastically object appearance changes (e.g. motion blur, occlusion) is rather significant due to the adaptive template updating method. For most cases, our method outperforms the CA trackers and improve the baseline performance further. There are several more categories including aspect ratio change, deformation, illumination variation, in/out-of-plane rotation, etc. (not listed in table). In these scenarios, our method possess a similar value as the corresponding CA trackers.

Table 1. The average performance of precision rate (PR%) on OTB-100 for 4 typical attributes. The Blue annotation is our method.

Tracker	MOSSE	MOSSE*CA*	MOSSE*AL*	DCF	DCF*CA*	DCF*AL*	SAMF	SAMF*CA*	SAMF*AL*	STAPLE	STAPLE*CA*	STAPLE*AL*
BC	37.0	46.1	53.4	63.6	63.7	68.3	67.4	78.1	78.7	74.9	78.9	80.2
FM	25.7	44.1	48.2	58.3	62.9	63.6	68.4	73.5	74.2	70.6	75.7	76.2
OC	32.0	45.5	50.1	55.3	62.4	67.2	70.4	75.0	77.3	72.2	73.9	74.2
MB	29.3	46.7	49.8	53.5	63.5	68.1	64.2	73.7	76.5	69.9	74.9	75.6

5   Conclusion

In this paper, we mainly propose an adaptive learning approach that can adaptively learn the context patches to integrate into CF tracking framework. In addition, we set a threshold to determine whether the tracking model to update or not. The learned background distractors are incorporated into the filter to suppress distracting effects while discriminatively updating our template. Extensive experiments demonstrated the effectiveness of the proposed approach. Our future work will concentrate on developing a more powerful learning framework, e.g., integrating the current work with deep learning framework such as CNN (convolutional neural network) and expanding our evaluation platform with more challenging video sequences and baseline approaches for facilitating the related research on CF tracking.

References

1. Bertinetto, L., Valmadre, J., Golodetz, S., Miksik, O., Torr, P.H.: Staple: complementary learners for real-time tracking. In: Proceedings of the IEEE Conference on Computer Vision and Pattern Recognition (2016)
2. Bibi, A., Ghanem, B.: Multi-template scale-adaptive kernelized correlation filters. In: Proceedings of the IEEE International Conference on Computer Vision Workshops (2015)

3. Bolme, D.S., Beveridge, J.R., Draper, B.A., Lui, Y.M.: Visual object tracking using adaptive correlation filters. In: 2010 IEEE Conference on Computer Vision and Pattern Recognition (CVPR) (2010)
4. Danelljan, M., Bhat, G., Khan, F.S., Felsberg, M.: ECO: efficient convolution operators for tracking. In: Proceedings of IEEE Conference on Computer Vision and Pattern Recognition (2017)
5. Danelljan, M., Häger, G., Khan, F., Felsberg, M.: Accurate scale estimation for robust visual tracking. In: British Machine Vision Conference, Nottingham, 1–5 Sept 2014
6. Danelljan, M., Hager, G., Shahbaz Khan, F., Felsberg, M.: Learning spatially regularized correlation filters for visual tracking. In: Proceedings of the IEEE International Conference on Computer Vision (2015)
7. Danelljan, M., Robinson, A., Shahbaz Khan, F., Felsberg, M.: Beyond correlation filters: learning continuous convolution operators for visual tracking. In: Leibe, B., Matas, J., Sebe, N., Welling, M. (eds.) ECCV 2016. LNCS, vol. 9909, pp. 472–488. Springer, Cham (2016). https://doi.org/10.1007/978-3-319-46454-1_29
8. Danelljan, M., Shahbaz Khan, F., Felsberg, M., Van de Weijer, J.: Adaptive color attributes for real-time visual tracking. In: IEEE Conference on Computer Vision and Pattern Recognition (CVPR), Columbus, Ohio, USA, 24–27 June 2014
9. Dinh, T.B., Vo, N., Medioni, G.: Context tracker: exploring supporters and distracters in unconstrained environments. In: 2011 IEEE Conference on Computer Vision and Pattern Recognition (CVPR) (2011)
10. Galoogahi, H.K., Fagg, A., Lucey, S.: Learning background-aware correlation filters for visual tracking. In: Proceedings of IEEE Conference on Computer Vision and Pattern Recognition (2017)
11. Galoogahi, H.K., Sim, T., Lucey, S.: Correlation filters with limited boundaries. In: 2015 IEEE Conference on Computer Vision and Pattern Recognition (CVPR) (2015)
12. Henriques, J.F., Caseiro, R., Martins, P., Batista, J.: Exploiting the circulant structure of tracking-by-detection with kernels. In: European conference on computer vision (2012)
13. Henriques, J.F., Caseiro, R., Martins, P., Batista, J.: High-speed tracking with kernelized correlation filters. IEEE Trans. Pattern Anal. Mach. Intell. 37(3), 583–596 (2015)
14. Li, Y., Zhu, J.: A scale adaptive kernel correlation filter tracker with feature integration. In: Agapito, L., Bronstein, M.M., Rother, C. (eds.) ECCV 2014. LNCS, vol. 8926, pp. 254–265. Springer, Cham (2015). https://doi.org/10.1007/978-3-319-16181-5_18
15. Lukezic, A., Vojir, T., Cehovin, L., Matas, J., Kristan, M.: Discriminative correlation filter with channel and spatial reliability. In: Proceedings of IEEE Conference on Computer Vision and Pattern Recognition (2017)
16. Ma, C., Huang, J.B., Yang, X., Yang, M.H.: Hierarchical convolutional features for visual tracking. In: Proceedings of the IEEE International Conference on Computer Vision (2015)
17. Mueller, M., Smith, N., Ghanem, B.: Context-aware correlation filter tracking. In: Proceedings of the IEEE Conference Computer Vision and Pattern Recognition (CVPR) (2017)
18. Wu, Y., Lim, J., Yang, M.H.: Object tracking benchmark. IEEE Trans. Pattern Anal. Mach. Intell. 37(9), 1834–1848 (2015)
19. Xiao, J., Qiao, L., Stolkin, R., Leonardis, A.: Distractor-supported single target tracking in extremely cluttered scenes. In: Leibe, B., Matas, J., Sebe, N., Welling, M. (eds.) ECCV 2016. LNCS, vol. 9908, pp. 121–136. Springer, Cham (2016). https://doi.org/10.1007/978-3-319-46493-0_8

Quality Assessment for Pansharpening Based on Component Analysis

Liangyu Zhou[1], Xiaoyan Luo[1(✉)], and Xiaofeng Shi[2]

[1] Image Processing Center, School of Astronautics, Beihang University,
Beijing, China
luoxy@buaa.edu.cn
[2] School of Electronic and Information Engineering, Beihang University,
Beijing, China

Abstract. The quality assessment for pansharpening is important. Since most existing indexes evaluate the performance of entire fused image either from the spatial aspect or the spectral aspect individually, we introduce an pansharpening metric which separate the fused image into two components to evaluate spectral and spatial quality simultaneously. This can be achieved by pure pixels containing one material and mixed pixels with more than one materials in the multispectral (MS) image. The MS pure pixels can be utilized to evaluate the spectral quality, which are projected to the low-frequency regions in the panchromatic (PAN) image. In contrast, the MS mixed pixels corresponding to the PAN high-frequency regions can be utilized to evaluate the spatial quality. Finally, the pansharpening quality assessment is made by a weighted sum of common existing criteria on pure and mixed components, which generates a pure and mixed index (PM index). Experimental results, carried out on high-resolution GeoEye-1 and WV-2 datasets, demonstrate that the proposed quality assessment is made on fused images in a more comprehensive and objective manner.

Keywords: Pansharpening · Remote sensing · Quality assessment Superpixels

1 Introduction

Satellites such as SPOT and QuickBird usually provide two types of data: panchromatic (PAN) and multispectral (MS) images which are simultaneously captured on the same optical platform [1]. Because of technical limiting, the PAN and MS images are characterized by their high spatial resolution and high spectral resolution respectively. In this context, fusion techniques called pansharpening is to obtain a integrated image which preserves the spectral fidelity of the MS image and contains the high frequency information of the PAN image.

Many remote sensing applications require to combine PAN and MS images at their preliminary step, such as change detection [2] and crop type differentiation [3], so that many pansharpening algorithms have been proposed over the last two decades [4–6]. Generally, they can be divided into two categories: component substitution (CS) and multiresolution analysis (MRA). To convert the upsampled MS image into spatial and

© Springer Nature Singapore Pte Ltd. 2018
Y. Wang et al. (Eds.): IGTA 2018, CCIS 875, pp. 527–535, 2018.
https://doi.org/10.1007/978-981-13-1702-6_52

spectral details, the CS-based methods are based on a decorrelation transform, while the MRA-based approaches draw support from a multiresolution decomposition.

The accurate quality assessment criteria are required to compare different pan-sharpening algorithms. At present, quality indexes have been defined in order to measure the similarity between two images, either scalar or vector [7]. As an example, a Minkowski distance in the order of 2 is used to calculate the median square error (MSE) or the ERGAS indexes [8], the dot product used by the Single Angle Mapper index (SAM) [9] or the cross correlation (CC) [10] on the computation of the Zhou's protocol. Some researchers calculate image statistics to establish a quality assessment as the Q, Q4 or SSIM indexes referring to source images [11], and others implement the Quality with No Reference (QNR) index [12]. However, a quantitative quality assessment constitutes a complex and challenging issue due to the variety of different application requirements and the lack of a clearly defined ground-truth. Hence, it is still an open question to evaluate the pansharpening methods.

Considering the knowledge of information content, the low-frequency and high-frequency regions of the pansharpening result can be viewed as pure and mixed components, which can be utilized to evaluate the spectral and spatial quality respectively. In this paper, we propose a pure and mixed index (PM Index) to assess the performance of different pansharpening methods.

The rest is organized as follows. In Sect. 2, we present the details of our proposed PM index. The experimental analysis of the proposed technique is reported in Sect. 3. Finally, we draw conclusions in Sect. 4.

2 The Proposed PM Index

The goal of pansharpening is to fuse the spatial properties of PAN image with spectral properties of MS image. This concept simply lead us to propose a more accurate pansharpening quality index. Due to the corresponding relationship between MS pixels and PAN blocks, the MS pixels can be categorized into pure pixels containing one material and mixed pixels with more than one materials image based on the structure analysis of the PAN image. Using pure and mixed components in the fused image to represent low-frequency and high-frequency regions respectively, the proposed PM quality assessment is captured in pure and mixed components, as shown in Fig. 1.

2.1 Creation of the Superpixel Map

As is known, superpixels can adhere to image boundaries which correspond to high-frequency information. Hence, the entropy rate superpixel (ERS) method [13] is uti-lized to extract spatial structure information from the PAN image in terms of nonoverlapping superpixels. These superpixels are labeled with superpixel indexes $s = 1, 2, \ldots, L$, where L denotes the number of superpixels.

Generally, the ratio of the pixel sizes of the MS and PAN images is equal to 4. So there exists a corresponding relationship between the MS pixels and the PAN image blocks. Hence, the superpixel indexes $\mathbf{SI} = \{s_1, s_2, \ldots, s_k\}$ of every MS pixel can be obtained from the corresponding block in the superpixel map. As for the m MS pixels

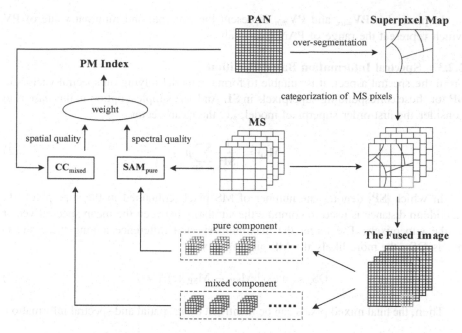

Fig. 1. Flowchart of quality assessment in pure and mixed components

are included in the i th superpixel, they are denoted as $\mathbf{SP}_i = \{\boldsymbol{p}_1, \boldsymbol{p}_2, \ldots, \boldsymbol{p}_m\}$. Finally, the pure and mixed pixels can be distinguished by spectral information in the MS image and spatial information in the PAN image.

2.2 Categorization of MS Pixels

2.2.1 Initial Partition

Considering that superpixels can adhere to image boundaries and maintain homogeneity, the k values of MS mixed pixels in **SI** should be greater than 1. Otherwise, they can be considered as MS pure pixels. However, the k values of some MS pure pixels are also greater than 1 when these superpixels indexes in **SI** represent the same material. Then it is necessary to screen out the truly MS mixed pixels further.

2.2.2 Spatial Information Based Partition

As every MS mixed pixel contain more than one materials, the pixels in corresponding PAN block should have large intensity difference for different materials. Assuming every superpixel can represent a material, the PAN mean values for every superpixel index in the corresponding PAN image block are $\mathbf{PV} = \{pv_1, pv_2, \ldots, pv_k\}$. The larger the maximum difference among these pv values DS_1, the more likely they are mixed pixels which contain more than one materials.

$$DS_1 = \mathbf{PV}_{max} - \mathbf{PV}_{min} \tag{1}$$

In particular, PV_{max} and PV_{min} represent the maximal and minimal value of PV which represent the range of PAN mean values.

2.2.3 Spectral Information Based Partition

From the spectral aspect, it is suitable to format a model relying on spectral vectors in **SP** for these corresponding superpixels in **SI**. And The simplest option in this case is to consider the first-order superpixel model, i.e. the mean vector.

$$\mathbf{M_{SP}} = \frac{1}{|\mathbf{SP}|}\sum_{p \in \mathbf{SP}} p \tag{2}$$

In which $|\mathbf{SP}|$ denotes the number of MS pixels contained in the superpixel **SP**. Euclidean distance is used to compute the similarity between the mean spectral vector of the superpixels. The larger the maximum spectral difference among these super-pixels DS_2, the more likely the MS pixel is mixed.

$$DS_2 = \max(\|\mathbf{M_{SP_i}} - \mathbf{M_{SP_j}}\|_2), i \neq j \tag{3}$$

Then, the final mixed pixels can be identified using spatial and spectral information:

$$T = DS_1 + \beta * DS_2 \tag{4}$$

where $\beta \geq 0$ is the weight to control the contribution of the spatial information term and spectral information term. If T is beyond a threshold τ, the pixel can be regarded as a mixed pixel. The results of categorization of MS pixels are shown in Fig. 2.

2.3 PM Index

Computation of the PM index is performed in two parts of pure component and mixed component. By analyzing the attributes of existing quality indexes and the pure and mixed components, SAM and CC are applied to separate computations of pure component for spectral fidelity and mixed component for spatial fidelity.

$$SAM_{pure} = normalized(\cos^{-1}(\frac{<I_p \cdot MS>}{\|I_p\| \cdot \|MS\|})) \tag{5}$$

$$CC_{mixed} = \frac{\sum_{ij}(I_m - \overline{I_m})(PAN - \overline{PAN})}{\sqrt{\sum_{ij}(I_m - \overline{I_m})\sum_{ij}(PAN - \overline{PAN})^2}} \tag{6}$$

where I_p and I_m are pure and mixed components of the fused image respectively. In this manner, pure component (I_p) compares with MS image and mixed component (I_m) compares with PAN image. Furthermore, considering SAM is usually expressed in degrees (angle between two vectors, 0° for high compatibility and 90° for opposite direction), it is normalized from zero to one and the ideal value is one.

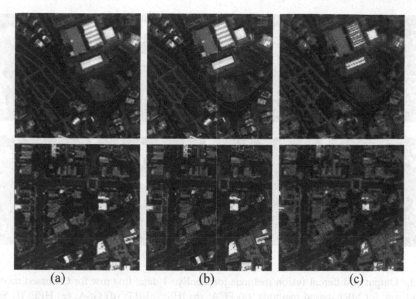

(a)   (b)   (c)

Fig. 2. First row for GeoEye-1 dataset; second row for WorldView-2 dataset. (a) MS image; (b) PAN image; (c) two components: red rectangles represent mixed pixels and others are pure pixels (Color figure online)

In order to evaluate the quality of the fused image, it is necessary to have the PM index in the form of a unique value. The PM index should include both estimated pure and mixed components which requires a weighting procedure to be applied:

$$\mathbf{PM} = \mathbf{W_P} \cdot \mathbf{SAM}_{pure} + \mathbf{W_M} \cdot \mathbf{CC}_{mixed} \tag{7}$$

Where

$$\mathbf{W_P} = \frac{Number\ of\ pure\ pixels\ in\ MS\ images}{Total\ pixels\ in\ MS\ images}$$

$$\mathbf{W_M} = \frac{Number\ of\ mixed\ pixels\ in\ MS\ images}{Total\ pixels\ in\ MS\ images}$$

Obviously, since the sum of the both weights is equal to one, then the PM index carries a normalization characteristic with itself. And the higher quality of PM index tends to one. In this manner, we can estimate and compute performance of each fusion technique in two different aspects. For investigating spatial properties of output result, mixed component of PM index is used. Also, for investigating spectral properties of output result, pure component of PM index is used. In this regard, our method can provide these three values (pure component, mixed component and PM Index). If the goal of application is map updating, the quality assessment of mixed component is more important than pure component.

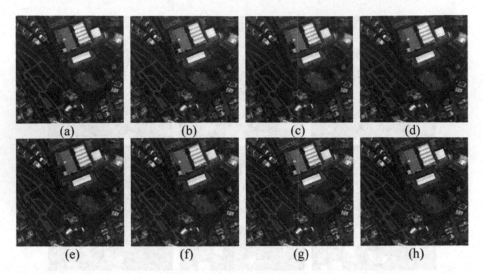

Fig. 3. Output of different fusion methods for GeoEye-1 data: first row for CS-based methods; second row for MRA-based methods. (a) PCA; (b) IHS; (c) BT; (d) GSA; (e) HPF; (f) SFIM; (g) ATWT; (h) AWLP

Table 1. Performance of different fusion methods in GeoEye-1 data.

		PCA	IHS	BT	GSA	HPF	SFIM	ATWT	AWLP
SAM_{pure}	Value	0.9490	0.9505	0.9570	0.9445	**0.9640**	0.9636	0.9564	0.9621
	Rank	7	6	4	8	1	2	5	3
SAM_{ori}	Value	0.9342	0.9374	0.9450	0.9281	**0.9512**	0.9507	0.9417	0.9488
	Rank	7	6	4	8	1	2	5	3
CC_{mixed}	Value	0.9914	0.9840	0.9834	**0.9922**	0.9702	0.9707	0.9727	0.9716
	Rank	2	3	4	1	8	7	5	6
CC_{ori}	Value	0.9867	0.9759	0.9767	**0.9884**	0.9743	0.9745	0.9756	0.9752
	Rank	2	4	3	1	8	7	5	6
PM	Value	0.9604	0.9595	0.9640	0.9573	**0.9657**	0.9655	0.9608	0.9646
	Rank	6	7	4	8	1	2	5	3

3   Experiments and Results

The proposed quality index is evaluated by using very high resolution satellites GeoEye-1 and WorldView-2 which are acquired on Turkey and Washington D.C. respectively. For the parameters in our approach, we empirically set $L = 700$, $\beta = 0.3$, $\tau = 220$. Note that, these parameters mainly affect the balance between pure and mixed components. Furthermore, classical quality parameters are also computed and visual comparisons reported, to assess the reliability and the completeness of the proposed method.

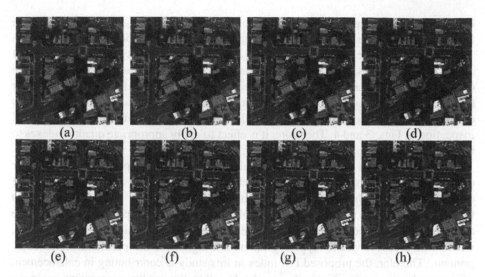

Fig. 4. Output of different fusion methods for WorldView-2 data: first row for CS-based methods; second row for MRA-based methods. (a) PCA; (b) IHS; (c) BT; (d) GSA; (e) HPF; (f) SFIM; (g) ATWT; (h) AWLP

Table 2. Performance of different fusion methods in WorldView-2 data.

		PCA	IHS	BT	GSA	HPF	SFIM	ATWT	AWLP
SAM_{pure}	Value	0.8940	0.8947	0.9027	0.8866	**0.9290**	0.9261	0.9209	0.9236
	Rank	7	6	5	8	1	2	4	3
SAM_{ori}	Value	0.8800	0.8816	0.8887	0.8659	**0.9095**	0.9061	0.8996	0.9020
	Rank	7	6	5	8	1	2	4	3
CC_{mixed}	Value	0.9644	0.9634	0.9670	**0.9928**	0.9642	0.9646	0.9676	0.9663
	Rank	6	8	3	1	7	5	2	4
CC_{ori}	Value	0.9530	0.9509	0.9578	**0.9900**	0.9653	0.9656	0.9680	0.9670
	Rank	7	8	6	1	5	4	2	3
PM	Value	0.9162	0.9163	0.9230	0.9200	**0.9401**	0.9382	0.9356	0.9371
	Rank	8	7	5	6	1	2	4	3

For the purpose of quality assessment in this study, eight well-known pansharpening methods are tested for comparisons, including Principal Component Analysis (PCA) [14], Intensity-Hue-Saturation (IHS) [15], Brovey Transform (BT) [16], Gram Schmidt Adaptive (GSA) [17], High-Pass Filtering (HPF) [14], Smoothing Filter-based Intensity Modulation (SFIM) [18], Additive A Trous Wavelet Transform with unitary injection model (ATWT) [19] and Additive Wavelet Luminance Proportional (AWLP) [20]. The PCA, IHS, BT and GSA belong to the family of CS approach. The HPF, SFIM, ATWT, AWLP are in the family of MRA approach. Vivone et al. [5] give a critical comparison among the existing popular pansharpening methods and develop a benchmark software package. The codes of these pansharpening methods are chosen from this software package, and the settings are chosen as the default.

By comparing the SAM_{pure} and CC_{mixed} with original quality indexes in Tables 1 and 2, they have the same trend of computation to evaluate and assess the performance of the existing pansharpening methods. Specifically, the CS-based methods have higher spectral distortion and lower spatial distortion than MRA-based methods. And it is consistent with previous studies [5]. Besides, it also can be induced from the visual inspection in Figs. 3 and 4. Therefore, it is effect to apply appropriate quality indexes to the pure and mixed components.

To sum up from the experiment results, the proposed approach is feasible for quality assessment of pansharpening methods. According to adopting appropriate quality indexes for the pure and mixed components, the fused images are evaluated from the spatial and spectral aspects simultaneously. More importantly, most of the quality assessment indexes cannot evaluate the fused image in a comprehensive way, which PM index solved by applying different weights for the pure and mixed components. Therefor, the proposed PM index in this study is contributing in enhancement of comprehensiveness. This is due to the fact that the quality assessment has been separated into two pure and mixed components to make it rather objective.

4   Conclusions

In this paper, a new objective index for the quality assessment of Pansharpened datasets has been proposed. More precisely, the proposed PM index has been designed under the assumption of the separate and direct impact of pure and mixed components on the quality of fused image. Hence, the PM index can lead to more comprehensive pansharpening image assessment that evaluate the fused image from spectral and spatial aspects simultaneously.

The assessment results of eight pansharpening methods have been implemented in this study. Results show that the proposed index exhibits a comprehensive capability by taking the spectral and spatial components separately into account as opposed to the previous approaches which took the whole image into analyses.

References

1. Thomas, C., Ranchin, T., Wald, L., Chanussot, J.: Synthesis of multispectral images to high spatial resolution: a critical review of fusion methods based on remote sensing physics. IEEE Trans. Geosci. Remote Sens. **46**(5), 1301–1312 (2008)
2. Bovolo, F., Bruzzone, L., Capobianco, L., Garzelli, A., Marchesi, S., Nencini, F.: Analysis of the effects of pansharpening in change detection on VHR images. IEEE Geosci. Remote Sens. Lett. **7**(1), 53–57 (2010)
3. Gilbertson, J.K., Kemp, J., Van Niekerk, A.: Effect of PAN-sharpening multi-temporal Landsat 8 imagery for crop type differentiation using different classification techniques. Comput. Electron. Agric. **134**, 151–159 (2017)

4. Duran, J., Buades, A., Coll, B., Sbert, C., Blanchet, G.: A survey of pansharpening methods with a new band-decoupled variational model. ISPRS J. Photogram. Remote Sens. **125**, 78–105 (2017)
5. Vivone, G., et al.: A critical comparison among pansharpening algorithms. IEEE Trans. Geosci. Remote Sens. **53**(5), 2565–2586 (2015)
6. Aiazzi, B., Alparone, L., Baronti, S., Garzelli, A., Selva, M.: Twenty-five years of pansharpening: a critical review and new developments. In: Chen, C.-H. (ed.) Signal and Image Processing for Remote Sensing, 2nd edn., pp. 533–548. CRC Press, Boca Raton, FL, USA (2012)
7. Li, S., Li, Z., Gong, J.: Multivariate statistical analysis of measures for assessing the quality of image fusion. Int. J. Image Data Fus. **1**(1), 47–66 (2010)
8. Wald, L.: Data Fusion. Definitions and Architectures-Fusion of Images of Different Spatial Resolutions. Presses des MINES, Paris (2002)
9. Kruse, F.A., et al.: The spectral image processing system (SIPS)-interactive visualization and analysis of imaging spectrometer data. Remote Sens. Environ. **44**(2), 145–163 (1993)
10. Vijayaraj, V., O'Hara, C.G., Younan, N.H.: Quantitative analysis of PANsharpened images. Opt. Eng. **45**(4), 046202 (2006)
11. Wang, Z., Bovik, A.C., Sheikh, H.R., Simoncelli, E.P.: Image quality assessment: from error visibility to structural similarity. IEEE Trans. Image Process. **13**(4), 600–612 (2004)
12. Alparone, L., Aiazzi, B., Baronti, S., Garzelli, A., Nencini, F., Selva, M.: Multispectral and PANchromatic data fusion assessment without reference. Photogram. Eng. Remote Sens. **74**(2), 193–200 (2008)
13. Liu, M.-Y., Tuzel, O., Ramalingam, S., Chellappa, R.: Entropy rate superpixel segmentation. In: Proceedings IEEE Conference Vision and Pattern Recognition, pp. 2097–2104 (2011)
14. Chavez Jr., P.S., Sides, S.C., Anderson, J.A.: Comparison of three different methods to merge multiresolution and multispectral data: landsat TM and SPOT PANchromatic. Photogramm. Eng. Remote Sens. **57**(3), 295–303 (1991)
15. Tu, T.-M., Su, S.-C., Shyu, H.-C., Huang, P.S.: A new look at IHS-like image fusion methods. Inf. Fus. **2**(3), 177–186 (2001)
16. Gillespie, A.R., Kahle, A.B., Walker, R.E.: Color enhancement of highly correlated images —II. Channel ratio and "chromaticity" transform techniques. Remote Sens. Environ. **22**(3), 343–365 (1987)
17. Aiazzi, B., Baronti, S., Selva, M.: Improving component substitution pansharpening through multivariate regression of MS+PAN data. IEEE Trans. Geosci. Remote Sens. **45**(10), 3230–3239 (2007)
18. Wald, L., Ranchin, T.: Comment: Liu 'Smoothing filter-based intensity modulation: a spectral preserve image fusion technique for improving spatial details'. Int. J. Remote Sens. **23**(3), 593–597 (2002)
19. Vivone, G., Restaino, R., Mura, M.D., Licciardi, G., Chanussot, J.: Contrast and error-based fusion schemes for multispectral image pansharpening. IEEE Geosci. Remote Sens. Lett. **11**(5), 930–934 (2014)
20. Otazu, X., González-Audícana, M., Fors, O., Núñez, J.: Introduction of sensor spectral response into image fusion methods. Application to wavelet-based methods. IEEE Trans. Geosci. Remote Sens. **43**(10), 2376–2385 (2005)

Deep Belief Network Based Vertebra Segmentation for CT Images

Syed Furqan Qadri[1], Mubashir Ahmad[2], Danni Ai[2], Jian Yang[2(✉)], and Yongtian Wang[1,2]

[1] School of Computer Science and Technology, Beijing Institute of Technology, Beijing 100081, China
[2] Beijing Engineering Research Center of Mixed Reality and Advanced Display, School of Optics and Electronics, Beijing Institute of Technology, Beijing 100081, China
jyang@bit.edu.cn

Abstract. Automatic vertebra segmentation is a challenging task from CT images due to anatomically complexity, shape variation and vertebrae articulation with each other. Deep Learning is a machine learning paradigm that focuses on deep hierarchical learning modeling of input data. In this paper, we propose a novel approach of automatic vertebrae segmentation from computed tomography (CT) images by using deep belief networks (BDNs) modeling. Using the DBN model, the contexture features of vertebra from CT images are extracted automatically by an unsupervised pattern called pre-training and followed by supervised training called back-propagation algorithm; then segmentation the vertebra from other abdominal structure. To evaluate the performance, we computed the overall accuracy (94.2%), sensitivity (83.2%), specificity (94.8%) and mean Dice coefficients (0.85 ± 0.03) for segmentation evaluation. Experimental results show that our proposed model provides a more accuracy in vertebra segmentation compared to the previous state of art methods.

Keywords: Segmentation · Deep belief network (BDN) · Pre-training Back-propagation algorithm

1 Introduction

Image segmentation is a computer vision branch; its main purpose is to make meaningful regions of an image. To raise diagnoses quality, localize organs and pathology; segmentation has a great clinical appreciation in image analysis. Various medical applications such as surgery, medical image assessment, statistical shape model, pose and biomechanical modeling all are elaborated with segmentation as a vital prerequisite. For achieving the optimum placement of bone transplantation between the transverse processes, a precise and accurate segmentation process is demanded the medical image-guided interventions. In recent years, several automated and semi-automated methods focusing on vertebra segmentation have been developed for CT images. Kadoury et al. [1] proposed a combined methodology of local statistical shape models and global shape appearance for each vertebra. In conversely, Rasoulian et al. [2] developed a method of

© Springer Nature Singapore Pte Ltd. 2018
Y. Wang et al. (Eds.): IGTA 2018, CCIS 875, pp. 536–545, 2018.
https://doi.org/10.1007/978-981-13-1702-6_53

combining all vertebrae together with a statistical pose model into a single shape model. In these cases, both approaches are thought that whole spine acted as a basic unit for statistical shape model construction. Aslan et al. [3] used the level set algorithm for vertebral column segmentation. These all approaches [3–5] did not utilize the shape prior information. Thus these are compromising to leakage then the results of segmentation are less accurate. On the other class of segmentation, there are many vertebral segmentation methodologies that possess the shape prior information. Aslan et al. [6] used the graph cut based framework with the shape prior information. A template base on segmentation approached in proposed by the Suzani et al. [7]. These methods could not gain from the principal modes of variation and only depend on the mean shape information. By using the simple threshold a coarse segmentation is reported by the Herring et al. [8] and then did registration for recomputed spine shape model. A model-based segmentation approach is presented by Klinder et al. [9] with utilizing the appearance model on region-based that have invariance information. Lim et al. [10] introduced a new approach for accurate vertebral segmentation called edge mounted Willmore flow that deals with missing information of noisy images and also an estimator of shale kernel density to the level set segmentation framework. Naegel [11] segmented the vertebra by combining the watershed and morphological approach. Ghebreab and Smeulders [12] built deformed integral spine model for vertebral segmentation. This method showed the vertebral boundaries appearances from training image sets. An automatic vertebra segmentation and spine registration method of 3D ultrasound images are proposed by Hacihaliloglu et al. [13].

Deep learning is a subfield of machine learning and its techniques produce multilevel models of input data with different hierarchical representations. Recently, deep learning paradigms introduced to medical images in multiple applications, including segmentation, tumor classification, histopathological diagnosis etc. The deep belief networks (DBNs) [14] is a deep learning paradigm for an efficient learning technique by stacking the restricted Boltzmann machines (RBMs). DBNs having a number of RBMs layers which are trained by the greedy layer-wise approach. An RBM has unsupervised learning algorithm with a generative undirected graphical model. There are already many methodologies for automatic features extraction using DBNs proposed. For example, the work in [15] presented the medical images analysis by DBNs which have many fruitful applications such as diseases diagnosis correlated to breast, lung, pediatric or musculoskeletal studies etc. In [16] proposed an approach to breast cancer classification with an accuracy of 99.68% by DBNs. Sun et al. [17] did a study for robust lung cancer diagnosis using deep learning algorithms but found the results from DBN was slightly higher than other deep learning methods. The proposed work in [18] identifies the cell segmentation using learning algorithms (i.e., deep belief networks, convolutional neural networks and stacked autoencoders) with histopathological images. It is investigated in [19] to characterize differences in brain morphometric data in schizophrenia by using deep belief network (DBN) modeling that has more accurate as a classifier with accuracy 73.6% than other. A deep learning approach based on deep stack autoencoder for liver segmentation from 2D CT images is presented in [23]. There is developed a deep learning framework by DBNs for RNA binding proteins preferences by incorporating the primary sequences, secondary and tertiary structural kind of profiles in [20]. DBNs has shown permissible results identification of bone disease progression predicting and informative risk factors in [21].

In this paper, it is proposed a novel approach for vertebra segmentation based on DBN model from CT images that can generate more accuracy and efficiency than state of art methods. Feature learning, classification and vertebra segmentation is done by using DBNs. In machine learning, representation of input data is very important so much of work is done on data preprocessing, feature learning and features extraction. In this method, unlabeled data is given for pre-training to extract high-level features and then provided the labeled data for fine-tuning. In the end, post-processing to get the vertebra segmentation results, the details are given in below portion of the paper. Our proposed DBN segmentation methodology can be applied to many fields of medical image analysis.

2   Background Work

2.1   Deep Belief Networks (DBNs)

Deep belief networks (DBNs) is a probabilistic multilayer neural network composed of stacking restricted Boltzmann machine for learning complex data patterns. DBN can be divided into two stages of the learning process. First one is unsupervised learning that is employed by CD algorithm called pre-training to obtain the initial weights from stacked RBMs. The second one is supervised learning implemented by error back-propagation (BP) algorithm called fine-tuning that tunes the initial weights to get the final weights.

In Joint distribution between visible layer x and hidden layer h gained by the energy-based probabilistic model as follows:

$$p(x, h^1, \ldots, h^n) = \left(\prod_{i=1}^{n-2} p(h^i | h^{i+1}) \right) . p(h^{n-1} | h^n) \qquad (1)$$

In the above equation $1 = h^0, p(h^i | h^{i+1})$ is a conditional distribution in RBM for hidden-hidden units corresponding to the kth level of DBNs, and hidden joint distribution in top-level RBM is $p(h^{n-1} | h^n)$ wherein each layer, the calculated output of RBM is used as a next layer input.

2.2   Restricted Boltzmann Machines

Restricted Boltzmann Machines (RBMs) is the basic unit of a DBNs that is treated as generative stochastic graphical and an unsupervised energy-based generative model. RBM is a layer of visible units x and a layer of hidden units h, undirected and connected by symmetrically weighted connections. Each hidden unit of RBM has the capability to encode at least one higher order interaction among inputs.

To represent the problem complexity, RBM requires less hidden units when a specific number of latent reasons given in the input and this scenario can be analyzed by RBM model with contrastive divergence (CD) unsupervised learning algorithms. The model defines the energy function as follow:

$$E(x, h;\theta) = -\sum_{i=1}^{l}\sum_{j=1}^{m} x_i W_{ij} h_j - \sum_{i=1}^{l} b_i x_i - \sum_{j=1}^{m} a_j h_j \tag{2}$$

Where l and m are the number of visible and hidden units and $\theta = \{w\ a\ b\}$ are the model parameters. Specifically, the joint distribution of visible (x) and hidden (h) units are shown as follow:

$$P(x, h;\theta) = \frac{1}{Z(\theta)} exp(-E(x, h;\theta)) \tag{3}$$

In above equation, $Z(\theta)$ is called partition function that is used for normalizing constant for energy function. And analytically computation of conditional probabilities are as follow:

$$p(h_j = 1/x) = \sigma\left(b_j + \sum_{i=1}^{l} x_i w_{ji}\right) \tag{4}$$

$$p(x_i 1/h) = \sigma\left(a_i + \sum_{j=1}^{m} h_j w_{ji}\right) \tag{5}$$

Where σ is a sigmoid function

3   Materials and Methods

It is a challenging task of automatic and robust vertebra segmentation from CT images due to high contrast, varied shape and anatomical complex structure of the vertebra. However, manually segmentation of vertebra is a difficult and time-consuming process. Therefore automatic and robust vertebral segmentation is desired to get accurate and reliable vertebra segmentation on large scale. In this paper, we propose an automated and robust vertebra segmentation methodology from transverse (axial) view. We did our experimental evaluation on thoracic and lumbar vertebrae CT datasets of ten young adults; 16–35 years old age group and 2D slice images thickness are 1 mm and the resolution is between 0.31 and 0.45 mm [22]. We show that consistently accurate vertebra segmentations can be achieved for each of the different thoracic and lumbar vertebrae. An overview of our proposed method is shown in Fig. 1 and details are given in below section.

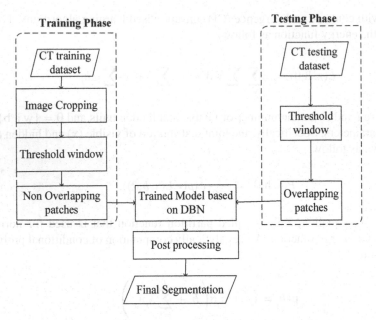

Fig. 1. Proposed vertebra segmentation framework

3.1 Preprocessing

An experimentation process of DBNs is implemented on MATLAB 2017a; Dell personal computer (PC) with Intel Core(TM) i7 4790 processor, 3.60 GHz, 16 GB RAM and windows 7 ultimate operating system. It is used ten CT datasets for experimentation. The DBN was trained using seven datasets contains 3,923 CT slices and three datasets contain 1,642 CT slices for testing. The original 512 × 512 CT images were cropped to 480 × 480 pixels. By doing this, the input size and number of DBN parameters were greatly reduced, which can reduce the risk of over-fitting and potentially improve the training efficiency. Then the cropped image slices are divided into the 32 × 32 non-overlapping patches which were scaled into a one-dimensional vector (1024 neurons) are given as an input into the DBNs model. To discriminate vertebrae from other bone structures and soft tissues, we applied a threshold of 990 to the CT images because the vertebra intensities are higher than other abdominal tissue in CT images which is shown in Fig. 2. We divided the whole dataset into two classes which are foreground and background where foreground belongs to a vertebra and the remaining part is background as shown in Fig. 3.

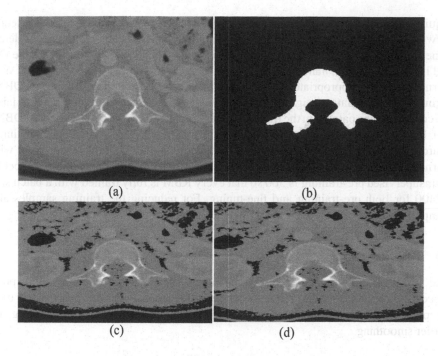

Fig. 2. One example of CT dataset (a) original CT slice image 512 × 512 (b) ground truth slice image (c) applying threshold HU window (d) Resize slice image 480 × 480

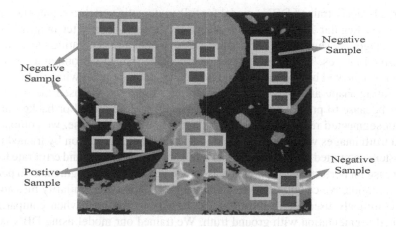

Fig. 3. Training samples as positive (green) and negative (red) extracted from a CT slices (Color figure online)

3.2 Training DBN

In the training process, the input neurons are loaded into DBN followed by the greedy layer-wise unsupervised procedure. Then, with two (vertebra and background) of our required output size, the DBN is unfolded to the neural network and finally, the neural network is trained by backpropagation algorithm through the numbers of epochs determined. The parameters of training and setting up DBNs are the number of visible (X) and hidden (H) layers, number of neurons in each layer, number of epochs, batch size, learning rate and appropriate momentum coefficients. For optimal training of DBNs required the systematic design of the experiment. We selected the center pixel to label the corresponding patches in the training set. The architecture size of our proposed DBNs is a 1024-100-50-20-2, where the dimension of the input data is 1024 called as input neurons and three hidden layers having 100 and 50 and 20 neurons respectively with learning rate 0.0001 and momentum coefficient was set to 0.5. The number of epochs in unsupervised pre-training is 500 so that every RBM is fully trained with a batch size of 400 for both pre-training and fine-tuning. For reducing the training samples and complexity, we used non-overlapping patches.

3.3 Post Processing

Due to misclassification, there are some pixels appeared in the background, post-processing method is used to refine the shape of the vertebra. For this purpose, we used morphological operations [23] to remove the misclassified regions for holes filling and border smoothing.

4 Segmentation and Results

We directly apply trained DBNs model for fully automatic vertebra segmentation from CT images. Regular 32×32 pixel patches (1024 pixels map) after preprocessing of testing images are sent as input to trained DBNs model and generating the articulating transformed images. The location that constructs the trained net output as segmented vertebra is achieved by overlapping of test patches pixel by pixel with stride 1 that can be get fining shape after post-processing. In the testing set, we used the overlapping patches because to predict each pixel of the image as foreground or background. 2D vertebra segmented results are shown in Fig. 4. In the testing case, we compared the ground truth images with the segmented images as result generation by trained model. Our system computed the overall accuracy, sensitivity, specificity and error rate for each testing case for performance evaluation as shown in Table 1. For segmentation performance evaluation, we calculated Dice coefficients (DC) that are similarity measurement index commonly used and a mean 0.85 ± 0.03 were obtained when comparing the computed segmentation with ground truth. We trained our model using DBN because of its unsupervised features learning in pre-training that makes it prominent from other methods. This method is not more time consuming but gives high accuracy.

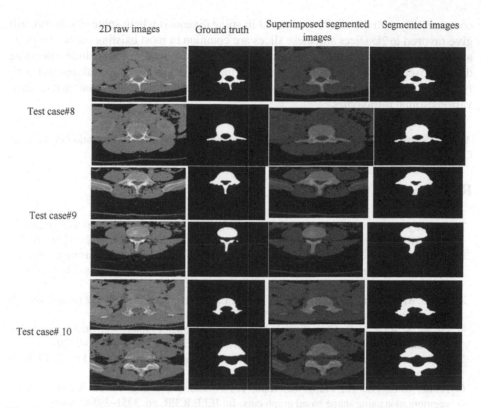

Fig. 4. Segmentation results for specific vertebra in test cases#8, 9, 10 show visual comparison of mid-axial slices.

Table 1. Summarization of performance evaluation parameters of DBN

	Accuracy	Sensitivity	Specificity	Error rate
Deep belief network	94.2%	83.2%	94.8%	5.8%

5   Discussion and Conclusion

In this paper, a methodology for thoracic and the lumbar vertebrae segmentation from CT images has been proposed which is based on deep learning model called DBNs. The proposed method emphasis on 2D vertebra recognition and provides a stable, fast and highly accurate solution for vertebra segmentation. The evaluation performance is done on ten datasets with overall classification accuracy (94.2%), sensitivity (83.2%), specificity (94.8%), error rate (5.8%) and mean Dice coefficients (0.85 ± 0.03) for segmentation evaluation. It is noted that both results of classification and segmentation could be more improved if the model did not fail in few T1 vertebrae that is the same structure of cervical vertebra C7 and in some cases of L5 as similarities to the sacrum. The practical importance of vertebra segmentation is that it is robust and automatic full compatibility with the clinical judgment in spine diagnosis where spine physicians still give favored to 2D slices and these slices are common in most existing medical reports and diagnostics document. Future directions of our research would include extending the proposed method to different spine structures, different image modalities and verifying the proposed frame on large-scale medical Image databases that would have various spinal pathologies.

Acknowledgments. This work was supported by the National Science Foundation Program of China (61527827).

References

1. Kadoury, S., Labelle, H., Paragios, N.: Spine segmentation in medical images using manifold embeddings and higher-order MRFs. Med. Imaging IEEE Trans. **32**(7), 1227–1238 (2013)
2. Rasoulian, A., Rohling, R., Abolmaesumi, P.: Lumbar spine segmentation using a statistical multi-vertebrae anatomical shape+pose model. Med. Imaging IEEE Trans. **32**(10), 1890–1900 (2013)
3. Aslan, M.S., Farag, A.A., Arnold, B., Xiang, P.: Segmentation of vertebrae using level sets with expectation maximization algorithm. IEEE 2010–2013 (2011)
4. Ghosh, S., Alomari, R., Chaudhary, V., Dhillon G.: Automatic lumbar vertebrae segmentation from clinical CT for wedge compression fracture diagnosis. In: SPIE, pp. 1–9 (2011)
5. Narkhede, H.P.: Review of image segmentation techniques. Int. J. Sci. Mod. Eng. 2319–6386 (2013)
6. Aslan, M.S., Ali, A., Farag, A., Rara, A., Arnold, B., Xiang, P.: 3D vertebrae body segmentation using shape based graph cuts. In: IEEE ICPR, pp. 3951–3954 (2010)
7. Suzani, A., Rasoulian, A., Seitel, A., Fels, S., Rohling, R.N.: Deep learning for automatic localization, identification, and segmentation of vertebral bodies in volumetric MR images, vol. 9415, pp. 1–7 (2015)
8. Herring, J., Dawant, B.: Automatic lumbar vertebral identification using surface-based registration. Comput. Biomed. Res. **34**(2), 74–84 (2001)
9. Klinder, T., Wolz, R., Lorenz, C., Franz, A., Ostermann, J.: Spine segmentation using articulated shape models. In: Metaxas, D., Axel, L., Fichtinger, G., Székely, G. (eds.) MICCAI 2008. LNCS, vol. 5241, pp. 227–234. Springer, Heidelberg (2008). https://doi.org/10.1007/978-3-540-85988-8_28
10. Lim, P.H., Bagci, U., Bai, L.: Introducing willmore flow into level set segmentation of spinal vertebrae. IEEE Trans. Biomed. Eng. **60**, 115–122 (2013)
11. Naegel, B.: Using mathematical morphology for the anatomical labeling of vertebrae from 3D CT-scan images. Comput. Med. Imaging Graph. **31**(3), 141–156 (2007)
12. Ghebreab, S., Smeulders, A.: Combining strings and neck- laces for interactive three-dimensional segmentation of spinal images using an integral deformable spine model. IEEE Trans. Biomed. Eng. **51**(10), 1821–1829 (2004)
13. Hacihaliloglu, I., Rasoulian, A., Rohling, R.N., Abolmaesumi, P.: Local phase tensor features for 3-D ultrasound to statistical shape+pose spine model registration. IEEE Trans. Med. Imaging **33**, 2167–2179 (2014)
14. Hinton, G., Salakhutdinov, R.: Reducing the dimensionality of data with neural networks. Science **313**, 504–507 (2006)

15. Khatami, A., Khosravi, A., Nguyen, T., Lim, C.P., Nahavandi, S.: Medical image analysis using wavelet transform and deep belief networks. Expert Syst. Appl. **86**, 190–198 (2017)

16. Abdel-Zaher, A.M., Eldeib, A.M.: Breast cancer classification using deep belief networks. Expert Syst. Appl. **46**, 139–144 (2016)

17. Sun, W., Zheng, B., Qian, W.: Automatic feature learning using multichannel ROI based on deep structured algorithms for computerized lung cancer diagnosis. Comput. Biol. Med. **89**, 530–539 (2017)

18. Hatipoglu, N., Bilgin, G.: Cell segmentation in histopathological images with deep learning algorithms by utilizing spatial relationships. Med. Biol. Eng. Comput. **55**, 1829–1848 (2017)

19. Pinaya, W.H.L., et al.: Using deep belief network modelling to characterize differences in brain morphometry in schizophrenia. Sci. Rep. **6**, 38897 (2016)

20. Zhang, S., et al.: A deep learning framework for modeling structural features of RNA-binding protein targets. Nucleic Acids Res. **44**, e32 (2015)

21. Li, H., Li, X., Ramanathan, M., Zhang, A.: Identifying informative risk factors and predicting bone disease progression via deep belief networks. Methods **69**, 257–265 (2014)

22. Yao, J., Burns, J.E., Munoz, H., Summers, R.M.: Detection of vertebral body fractures based on cortical shell unwrapping. In: Ayache, N., Delingette, H., Golland, P., Mori, K. (eds.) MICCAI 2012. LNCS, vol. 7512, pp. 509–516. Springer, Heidelberg (2012). https://doi.org/10.1007/978-3-642-33454-2_63

23. Ahmad, M., Yang, J., Ai, D., Qadri, S.F., Wang, Y.: Deep-stacked auto encoder for liver segmentation. In: Wang, Y., et al. (eds.) IGTA 2017. CCIS, vol. 757, pp. 243–251. Springer, Singapore (2018). https://doi.org/10.1007/978-981-10-7389-2_24

Semantic Segmentation of Aerial Image Using Fully Convolutional Network

Junli Yang[1(✉)], Yiran Jiang[1], Han Fang[1], Zhiguo Jiang[2],
Haopeng Zhang[2], and Shuang Hao[3]

[1] International School, Beijing University of Posts and Telecommunications,
Beijing 100876, China
{yangjunli,2015212885,fanghan}@bupt.edu.cn
[2] Image Processing Center, School of Astronautics, Beihang University, Beijing 100191, China
{jiangzg,zhanghaopeng}@buaa.edu.cn
[3] Beijing Control and Electronic Technology Institute, Beijing 100038, China
5094478382@163.com

Abstract. Dense semantic segmentation is an important task for remote sensing image analyzing and understanding. Recently deep learning has been applied to pixel-level labeling tasks in computer vision and produces state-of-the-art results. In this work, a fully convolutional network (FCN), which is a variant of convolutional neural network (CNN), is employed to address the semantic segmentation of high resolution aerial images. We design a skip-layer architecture that combines different layers of features in aerial images. This structure integrates the semantic information from deep layer and appearance information from shallow layer to make better use of the aerial image features. Moreover, the FCN can be trained end-to-end and produce segmentation output correspondingly-sized as the input image. Our model is trained on the extended GE-4 aerial image dataset to adapt FCN to the aerial image segmentation task. A full-resolution semantic segmentation is produced for each testing aerial image. Experiments show that our method obtains improvement in accuracy compared with several other methods.

Keywords: Semantic segmentation · Aerial images · Deep learning
Convolutional neural network · Fully convolutional network

1 Introduction

Semantic segmentation for aerial images has been an important and challenging task for remote sensing application. Different from the image categorization which assigns one class label to a whole image, semantic segmentation is a low level computer vision task that involves assigning a class label to each pixel in image. Semantic segmentation produces more expressive representation for remote sensing images, which makes the image easier to be analyzed in tasks like image retrieval or object recognition. But this dense pixel-wise labeling task is much more difficult. There are two challenges in obtaining accurate and detailed semantic segmentation of aerial images: (1) The perspective of aerial images is from top-side-view, which is totally different from the perspective

© Springer Nature Singapore Pte Ltd. 2018
Y. Wang et al. (Eds.): IGTA 2018, CCIS 875, pp. 546–555, 2018.
https://doi.org/10.1007/978-981-13-1702-6_54

in other computer vision tasks. Thus the contextual information contained in aerial images is different from that in general images, which makes objects or landcover classes more difficult to be distinguished. (2) Remote sensing images usually cover large land scale and contain large amount of heterogeneous data. This also improves the difficulty of accurate semantic segmentation. Because of these two reasons, spectral information alone becomes insufficient to discriminate different classes. Moreover, we are addressing aerial images that do not have high spectral resolution in this work, which means the spectrum features of different classes are less distinguishable compared to that of remote sensing images with higher spectral resolution (e.g., hyperspectral images). Therefore, more discriminative appearance features like spatial context or texture features are needed.

In previous literatures, the features are usually manually designed by experts in image processing field, such as SIFT [1] or HAAR [2]. However, the design of a good set of features needs high expertise, and a specific set of features cannot have satisfying performance on classification of various ground objects. Thus the selection of representative features once becomes the bottleneck to improve classification accuracy. Recently with the emergence of deep learning, convolutional neural network (CNN) [3] has achieved state-of-the-art results on a number of computer vision tasks including semantic segmentation [4]. CNN can automatically extract discriminative contextual features at different scales by the organization of multi-layer neurons, which are more effective than hand-crafted features. CNN has been proved effective for remote sensing data [5, 6], but is used for scene categorization or semantic segmentation on a patch level. In the task of semantic segmentation, the down-sampling operation following convolutional layers in CNN usually leads to an output with a lower resolution than the input image.

In this work, we apply the fully convolutional network (FCN) [7], which is a variant of CNN, to address the semantic segmentation of aerial images. By replacing fully connected layers of CNN with convolutional layers, the FCN can maintain the 2-D structure of aerial images and produces dense pixel-to-pixel semantic segmentation, thus can overcome the down-sampling effect of CNN. Moreover, we use the skip structure of FCN-8s [7] to combine multi-scale features in aerial images to fully exploit the contextual and texture information, this strategy further refines the spatial resolution of the output. We fine-tuned the parameters of the ImageNet-pretrained VGG-16 [8] network by back-propagation using triple-waveband high spatial resolution dataset GE-4 [9], to adapt the FCN to our aerial image semantic segmentation task. We perform the FCN semantic segmentation on the testing set from GE-4. Experimental results show that the FCN based method achieves higher accuracy compared to some traditional and state-of-the-art methods.

2 Our Method

In our work, the FCN-8s based on VGG-16 net are applied to address the remote sensing image semantic segmentation task, since the VGG-Net did remarkably well in ILSVRC14. The final classifier layer is discarded, and the fully connected layers are converted to convolution layers, which are followed by the deconvolution layers to up-sample the coarse outputs to pixel-dense output. This strategy transforms the VGG-Net into fully convolutional network that can take input of any size and output correspond-ingly-sized output semantic segmentation maps. We introduce the VGG-Net and the corresponding FCN in detail in the following subsections.

2.1 Advantages of VGG-Net

VGG-16 contains thirteen convolution layers and three fully connected layers, five pooling layers, and other basic components like activation and drop layers. In VGG-Net, the convolution part can be considered as five sections with more than one convo-lution layers per section, but all convolution layers use filters with the same size of 3×3, the convolution stride is 1 and padding is 1. The excellent job of VGG-Net in ILSVRC14 proved that the use of small convolution (like 3×3) and high depth of network can effectively improve the model's performance. Compared to AlexNet in which each section contains only one Convolution layer and the filter is of size 7×7, VGG-Net can achieve the comparable accuracy by reducing the filter size to 3×3 and increasing the number of layers. 3×3 is the smallest convolutional kernel size that captures the left, right, top, bottom, and center concepts and this kind of convolution kernel needs less parameters. And multiple convolution layers with 3×3 kernel have more nonlinearities than one convolution layer with a large size kernel. More ReLU layers can be added after the convolution layers to make the decision function more deterministic.

As the networks go deeper, some problems inevitably occur, such as over-fitting or gradients vanishing problems. Rectified Linear Units (ReLU) function is chosen as a non-linear activation function in VGG-Net to avoid the problem of gradients vanishing. The ReLU function has characteristics of unilateral suppression, a relatively wide excitement boundary, sparse activation and other features, which are better in line with the characteristics of neuroscience and can reduce the training burden of deep learning network.

In addition, VGG-Net uses the maximum pooling layer. And the soft-max function, which is the extension of logistic regression from two-class classifier to multi-class classifier, is employed in the fully connected layer to construct the loss function of supervised training in VGG-Net.

2.2 Network Structure of FCN

In order to implement the fully convolutional network, VGG-Net's three fully connected layers need to be converted into convolutional layers. The convolutional layer, pooling layer and activation function layer map the original data to hidden layer feature space, then the fully connected layer serves to map the learned distributed feature representation to the sample markup space. All learning features are superimposed, and a feature vector is output as the final representation. The traditional VGG-Net's fully connected layers have a fixed number of nodes and discard the original image spatial coordinates. The output is the image classification, i.e. assigning one label to each image, rather than pixel-level classification. However, these fully connected layers can also be taken as convolutions with kernels covering the whole input fields. This converts the VGG-Net into a fully convolutional network. The FCN denotes the three converted layers as convolutional layers, and the sizes of the convolution kernel (the number of channels, width and height) are (4096, 1, 1), (4096, 1, 1), (1000, 1, 1) correspondingly.

After transforming the fully connected layer to convolutional layer, the resulting feature maps need to be up-sampled to obtain the output image with the same size as the input image. After the input image is passed and calculated through the convolution layers and the pooling layers of VGG-Net, the resolution of the image can be reduced by 2, 4, 8, 16 and 32 times correspondingly in order. So for the output image, the FCN-32s [7] add the prediction layer and the deconvolution layer with 32 pixels' stride to up-sample the coarse feature maps to get the pixel-wise prediction correspondingly sized as the input image.

The up-sampling method used by FCN is deconvolution, which reverses the forward and backward processes of convolution. This operation is performed by backpropagation from pixel-level losses for end-to-end learning. The parameters of this kind of deconvolution layer have not to be set fixed and can also be learned to achieve better effects. However, for training and inference in CNN, it is often necessary to fix the size of the input image, whereas the FCN can accept input image of any size and output the correspondingly-sized semantic segmentation result as the input image. Moreover, in optimization, FCN is more efficient than CNN because it can avoid the problem of duplicated storage and convolutional computation caused by the use of patch-wise training. This is very useful for remote sensing images with large amount of information, so FCN is a very suitable model for the dense semantic segmentation of aerial images.

In order to take full advantages of the information contained in aerial images, we use the FCN-8s with skipping structure design. Figure 1 demonstrates the skipping structure of FCN-8s. As mentioned earlier, FCN requires 32 times up sampling in the deconvolution layer to get the same-sized output as the original input image, but this only uses the last convolutional layer's output. FCN creatively combines results from different layers, and the combination of these shallow layers and deep layers make better use of both local and global information, thus can achieve even better semantic segmentation results.

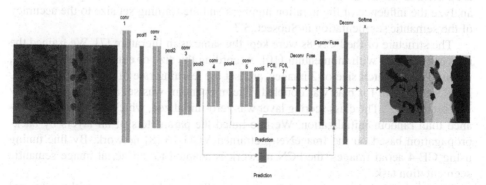

Fig. 1. The skipping structure of FCN-8s

FCN-8s first adds a prediction layer after pool4, pool3, and fc7 and then adds a deconvolution layer with stride of 2 after the fc7 prediction layer. After the fusion of the pool4 prediction and fc7 prediction, the result should be added with the prediction layer. Then the deconvolution layer with 2-pixel stride should be added. After the above results combined with prediction layer behind pool3, one prediction layer should be added, then a deconvolution layer with stride of 8-pixels is added to produce the finally pixel wise segmentation, which is called FCN-8s. Once augmented with skips, the network combines features from coarse layers with those from fine layers to produce each type of probabilistic prediction. Several predictions can be fused that the network are learned jointly and end-to-end.

The final output of FCN is a matrix of size h * w * d, where h is the height of the input image, w is the width of the input image. And d is the number of classes in the output segmentation map, each dimension of which is the probability of current pixel belonging to each class. By choosing the label with the highest probability as the final class of each pixel, we can get the output of FCN and save the semantic segmentation map.

3   Experimental Results

3.1   Experimental Setting

We evaluated the performance of our method on the extended GE-4 dataset [9], which was collected from Google Earth. The GE-4 dataset originally contains 67 triple-waveband high resolution remote sensing images, each of size 500 * 300 pixels. The 67 images were manually labeled with five classes: trees, grass, building, road, and background, and the labeled image are called ground truth. We supplemented 33 images and the corresponding ground truth images to the previous GE-4 dataset, and the extended GE-4 dataset contains 100 images now.

We tuned the iteration numbers of the FCN by line search, and set the iteration numbers as 2500. We randomly chose 90 images from the extended GE-4 dataset and used them as the training set, and the rest 10 images were used as testing set. We will analyze the influence of the iteration numbers and the training set size to the accuracy of the semantic segmentation in Subsect. 3.3.

The structure of the FCN-8s were kept the same as in literature [7]. We trained the network by SGD with momentum [10]. According the size of extended GE-4 dataset, we used a minibatch size of 2 images, and set the learning rate of 10^{-4} by line search. The learning rate for bias was doubled. The momentum was set as 0.9, weight decay was set to be 5^{-4}. The class scoring layer was zero-initialized, which has better performance than random initialization. We fine-tuned the parameters of all layers by backpropagation based on the ImageNet-pretrained VGG-16 [8] network. By fine tuning using GE-4 aerial images, the FCN network is adapted to our aerial image semantic segmentation task.

We give the classification results of our method, and compare it with traditional methods support vector machine (SVM) [11] and conditional random fields (CRF) [12], and also state-of-the-art deep learning method CNN [13] in the following subsections.

3.2 Semantic Segmentation Performance

Figure 2 shows the experimental results of our method on the GE-4 dataset. Here we report the best results achieved. We give the results of all the 10 tested images in two groups, and each group presents 5 images. The first row are the original images, the second row are the manually labeled ground truth images, and the third row are the semantic segmentation results of our FCN based method. We can see that the semantic segmentation results are already very close to the ground truth images, except for some minor errors in small regions. We have to point out that the background class (labeled with black) was not considered here because it actually includes more than one classes, and training with this background class is not going to yield an accurate classifier for it. Therefore we only considered the other four classes. The black regions in the segmentation results were just copied from the corresponding ground truth images.

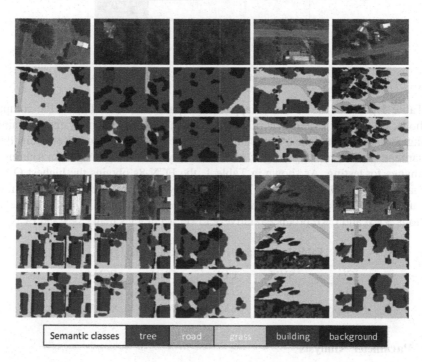

Fig. 2. FCN semantic segmentation result on extended GE-4 dataset.

The OA (overall accuracy, percentage of pixels correctly classified) of this experiment is 92.31% and the Kappa coefficient [14] is 88.21%. The training time is about 16.5 min, and testing time is 1.1 s for 10 testing images. The experiments were conducted in Ubuntu 16.04, on a PC with 12 cores of 2.40 GHz Intel Xeon(R) E5-2620 and a GPU of GeForce GTX1080.

To give the quantitative evaluation, Fig. 3 presents the confusion matrix of the four considered classes: tree, road, grass, building. The numbers on the diagonal are the class-specific accuracies (percentage of pixels correctly classified for each class). We can see the FCN achieves higher accuracies on tree and grass, which are 92% and 94% respectively, and relatively lower accuracies on road and building, which are 87% and 89% respectively. This is because road and building are sometimes similar in texture and color, which makes them difficult to be distinguished.

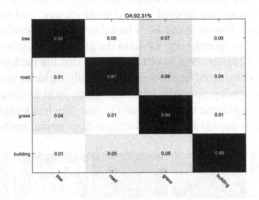

Fig. 3. Confusion matrix on accuracy of the four classes.

Table 1 presents the OA and Kappa of compared methods. For all the compared methods, we ran each experiment fifteen times with different randomly chosen training-testing sets and reported the mean accuracies. The compared methods were trained with the same number of training images, which is to say 90 training images for training and 10 images for testing. As shown in Table 1, the FCN-8s obtains the highest OA and Kappa, which are 89.45% and 82.97% respectively. The CNN gets the second highest OA and Kappa, which are 4.42% and 6.12% lower than that of FCN-8s. The classic methods SVM and CRF produce relatively lower accuracies than CNN and FCN-8s.

Table 1. Comparison of different methods (%)

Classes	SVM	CRF	CNN	FCN-8s
OA	80.62	74.55	85.03	89.45
Kappa	71.94	63.16	76.85	82.97

3.3   Parameter Analysis

Figure 4 shows the influence of iteration numbers to the semantic segmentation accuracies. Here we randomly chose a training set size to be 60, and the rest 40 images were used as testing set. Figure 4(a) and (b) give the OA and Kappa curves of the FCN in relation to different iteration numbers, respectively. Each OA or kappa score reported in the curves is the average value of fifteen runs of experiments, with different randomly chosen 60 images as the training set. The other parameters were kept the same as mentioned in Subsect. 3.1. We can see from the two curves that the accuracies improve dramatically as the iteration number increases at the beginning. But after the iteration number arrives at around 2000, the increments become much slower and the curves even decrease at some point due to overfitting. From the two curves, we can see the highest accuracies appear when the iteration number is 2500, which is set as the final iteration number of the FCN model.

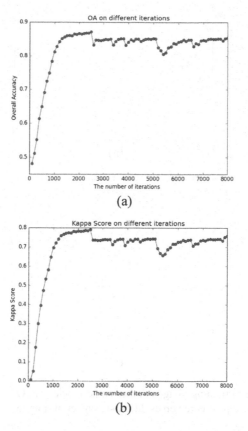

(a)

(b)

Fig. 4. The influence of iteration numbers on accuracies. (a) OA versus different number of iterations, (b) kappa score versus different number of iterations.

Figure 5 demonstrates the influence of training set size to the semantic segmentation accuracies. Figure 5(a) and (b) show the OA and Kappa curves of the FCN in relation to different number of training images, respectively. Here the iteration number was kept as 2500, which was chosen by line search as explained in the last paragraph. Each OA or kappa score reported is also the average value of fifteen runs of random experiments. The other parameters were also set the same as mentioned in Subsect. 3.1. We can see that the curves climb quickly as the number of training images increases at the beginning. But the increments gradually become slower as the number of training images keep increasing. The curves arrive at the highest accuracies when the number of training images is 90, which is the biggest training set size in the curve. The OA is 89.45% and the Kappa is 82.97% at this point.

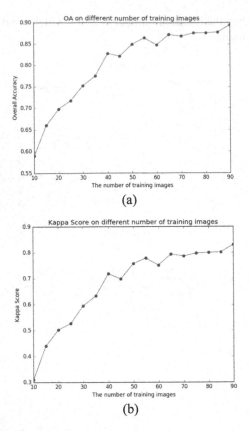

Fig. 5. The influence of training image number on accuracies. (a) OA versus different number of training images, (b) kappa score versus different number of training images.

It is noticeable that the trends of the curves are always going up as the training image keep increasing, which means the FCN can probably achieve even higher accuracies when we can have more training data.

4   Conclusions

In this study, we take advantages of fully convolutional network for dense semantic segmentation, and extend this method for aerial image semantic segmentation. We applied the skip architecture of FCN-8s to combine high-level semantic features from coarse layer and low-level appearance features from fine layer, which fully exploits the local and global information contained in aerial images. We trained the FCN-8s end-to-end on the extended GE-4 aerial image dataset by SGD with momentum. And to adapt the FCN to our aerial image semantic segmentation task, we fine-tuned the parameters of the ImageNet-pretrained VGG-16 net by back-propagation on the extended GE-4 dataset. A semantic segmentation correspondingly-sized as the input aerial image is produced for each testing image. Experiments show that our method has better perform-ance than several other traditional and state-of-the-art methods.

Acknowledgments. This work was supported in part by the National Natural Science Foundation of China (Grant Nos. 61501009, 61771031 and 61371134), the National Key Research and Development Program of China (2016YFB0501300, 2016YFB0501302) and the Aerospace Science and Technology Innovation Fund of CASC (China Aerospace Science and Technology Corporation).

References

1. Zhou, H., Yua, Y., Shi, C.: Object tracking using SIFT features and mean shift. Comput. Vis. Image Underst. **113**(3), 345–352 (2009)
2. Viola, P.: Robust real time object detection. In: International Workshop on Statistical and Computational Theories of Vision – Modeling, Learning, Computing, and Sampling 87 (2001)
3. Krizhevsky, A., Sutskever, I., Hinton, G.E.: ImageNet classification with deep convolutional neural networks. In: International Conference on Neural Information Processing Systems, pp. 1097–1105. Curran Associates Inc. (2012)
4. Lin, G., Shen, C., Reid, I., et al.: Efficient piecewise training of deep structured models for semantic segmentation. In: IEEE Conference on Computer Vision and Pattern Recognition (2016)
5. Penatti, O.A.B., Nogueira, K., dos Santos, J.A.: Do deep features generalize from everyday objects to remote sensing and aerial scenes domains? In: IEEE CVPR Workshops, pp. 44–55 (2015)
6. Maggiori, E., Tarabalka, Y., Charpiat, G., et al.: Convolutional neural networks for large-scale remote-sensing image classification. IEEE Trans. Geosc. Remote Sens. **55**(2), 645–657 (2016)
7. Long, J., Shelhamer, E., Darrell, T.: Fully convolutional networks for semantic segmentation. IEEE Trans. Pattern Anal. Mach. Intell. **39**(4), 640–651 (2017)
8. Simonyan, K., Zisserman, A.: Very deep convolutional networks for large-scale image recognition. CoRR, abs/1409.1556 (2014)
9. Yang, J., Jiang, Z., Quan, Z., et al.: Remote sensing image semantic labeling based on conditional random field. Acta Aeronaut. Et Astronaut. Sin. (2015)
10. Bengio, Y.: Practical recommendations for gradient-based training of deep architectures. In: Montavon, G., Orr, G.B., Müller, K.-R. (eds.) Neural Networks: Tricks of the Trade. LNCS, vol. 7700, pp. 437–478. Springer, Heidelberg (2012). https://doi.org/10.1007/978-3-642-35289-8_26
11. Platt, J.C.: Probabilistic outputs for support vector machines and comparisons to regularized likelihood 405 methods. Adv. Larg. Margin Classif. **10**, 61–74 (1999)
12. Zhong, P., Wang, R.: Jointly learning the hybrid CRF and MLR model for simultaneous denoising and 384 classification of hyperspectral imagery. IEEE Trans. Neural Netw. Learn. Syst. **25**(7), 385, 1319–1334 (2014)
13. Chen, L.-C., Papandreou, G., Kokkinos, I., Murphy, K., Yuille, A.L.: Semantic image segmentation with deep convolutional nets and fully connected CRFs. In: International Conference on Learning Representations (ICLR 2015) (2015)
14. Arora, H., Loeff, N., Forsyth, D., Ahuja, N., et al.: Unsupervised segmentation of objects using efficient 434 learning. In: IEEE Conference on Computer Vision and Pattern Recognition, 2007. CVPR 2007, pp. 1–7, 435. IEEE (2007)

Research of Opinion Dynamic Evolution Based on Flocking Theory

Shan Liu[✉] and Rui Tang

Information Engineering School, Communication University of China, Beijing 100024, China
liushan@cuc.edu.cn

Abstract. Using natural science research methods to study the behavior and phenomenon in complex social groups has attracted great concern in recent years. The opinion refers to the views, choices, or preferences that individual have in one thing. The main study of opinion dynamics is the evolution process of individual views from disorder to order in social groups. Under the background of flocking theory, we proposed an individual opinion impact model based on Agent. We also analyzed the evolution of ideas and emergence of cluster. The effectiveness of proposed model is validated with simulation on the impacts of the opinion's formation and evolution. The simulation results illustrate an effective interpretation of some phenomena in reality.

Keywords: Flocking theory · Opinion dynamics · Continuous opinion
Opinion evolution

1 Introduction

Opinion dynamics, also known as the dynamics of public opinion, is a subject to study the convergence of group opinions or the evolution process and rule of clustering separation phenomena using mathematics, physics and computer, especially Agent based modeling and simulation methods [1]. The opinion refers to the views, choices, or preferences that individual have in one thing. A large number of individual opinions form public opinion. Social groups make their opinions shared and spread in the population through various forms of information capture and interaction. Thus they can affect the opinions of others. The individual opinions evolve, concentrate and ultimately form a series of point cluster. The opinion dynamics considers the formation and evolution of individual opinions, which is influenced by the opinions of other individuals. It tries to establish an opinion evolution model in complex social phenomena in order to analyze and explain all kinds of complicated social phenomena. Opinion dynamics are widely applied in a variety of complex social phenomena, including fashion and trends, the existence and diffusion of minority opinions, the consistency of group decision reached, political elections and political parties, rumors spread, extremism spread and fanatical worship spread [2].

The dynamics of opinions are only a preliminary attempt by the scholars, and so far there is no unified theoretical framework. The first kinetic model proposed by the physicist is Weidlich [3], based on the social dynamics of probability theory. In 1982, the

© Springer Nature Singapore Pte Ltd. 2018
Y. Wang et al. (Eds.): IGTA 2018, CCIS 875, pp. 556–565, 2018.
https://doi.org/10.1007/978-981-13-1702-6_55

most fundamental and widely used Ising model [4] in opinion dynamics is proposed. The model which is inspired from the physics concept put forward the ideal that the change of individual opinion is affected by the surrounding field and there are two groups in the final evolution direction. One is reaching an agreement between two opinion values. The other is two opinions may co-exist within the group. The proposed Ising model makes the model first appear in the opinion dynamics. The original Ising model is used to study the structure of materials, but at the end of twentieth Century, scientists began to apply the model to the economic, biological and social [5–8]. Although the structure of this model is relatively simple, scientists have found many generalized properties with it, or proved some power-law distribution [9–11]. In the last century, physicists are active in the opinion dynamics and put forward many models, such as MR model, Voter model and bounded confidence models. These models also gave a good explanation of some social phenomena, such as the Poland election [12], the politics of Brazil and the economy stock price.

Since the evolution rules of social opinions are very similar to the flocking evolution theory [13], we applied the biological model of flocking to the study of opinion dynamics and established the individual opinion impact model based on Agent. We also analyzed the evolution of ideas and emergence of cluster. The effectiveness of proposed model is validated with simulation on the impacts of the opinion's formation and evolution through MATLAB. The simulation results give an effective interpretation of some phenomena in reality. The author believes that innovation is reflected in the following aspects: 1. combining the biological model with the communication effectively which has never been done before. 2. providing multiple angles to seek the affecting factors of information communication. 3. visual simulation has made the process of opinion evolution more clear and understandable.

2   The Biological Model of Flocking

The Agent based individual opinion impact model derives directly from the group behavior of birds in nature. Group behavior is a common phenomenon in nature, for instance, formations of migrating birds, parade fish with warm cold, collaborative working ant colony and so on. In these cases, all these cooperation will eventually enable all individuals to perform certain complex and functional activities, but each individual cannot do it alone. These phenomena have a common feature. A certain coordinated movement and behavior will emerge through a large number of independent individuals' simple actions or cooperation.

In computer science, the imitation of the birds is mainly based on the group's Flocking model which was proposed by Reynolds in 1987 [13]. In this model, all the agents follow three rules:

a. Separation: Steering away from the other birds to avoid collision.
b. Clustering: Attempting to stay close to the neighbors.
c. Velocity Matching: Aiming to match the speed to the neighbors.

Under these rules, all he individuals in the agents group will have the same moving direction while avoiding collisions and keeping the aggregation. At present, the research of computer simulation has proved that for the flocking behavior, collective leadership, level control, global information and so on is not necessary. The individuals only need to know the local information instead of knowing the global information of the whole group through local perception. Therefore, an important feature of flocking is the coordinated global behavior emerged from simple local rules.

The individual opinion impact model proposed in this paper uses the same simple rules as the flocking theory: agents with similar opinions attract each other, while dissimilar agents repel each other. Finally there will form a series of clusters of opinions and even reach an agreement.

3   Building an Individual Opinion Impact Model

3.1   Main Algorithm

In the individual opinion impact model proposed in this article, each agent represents the opinion value of the individual. Supposing the number of individuals in the set of groups is n. Considering that the group view in the model is formed by a series of repetitive processes over time, we assume that the value of time is a series of discrete points, $T = \{0, 1, 2 \ldots\}$. In order to simplify the process, we assume that the individual opinions can be mapped to any real number within an interval. Let $x_i(t)$ be the opinion for individual i at time t where $1 \leq i \leq n$. At time t, vector $x(t) = \big(x_1(t), x_2(t), \ldots, x_n(t)\big)$ is made up of individual values, which we call the opinion profile at the time t (Table 1).

Table 1. The main algorithm for opinion dynamic system

(1)	Read the n data $x_1(t), x_2(t), \ldots, x_n(t)$
(2)	**While** t in T **do**
(3)	Compute a new position for each of the n agents according to the same local rule
(4)	Move all agents
(5)	**endWhile**
(6)	Output the flock of agents

For an individual i, we suppose that its opinion is average weighted by other individuals within a group. Supposing that the weight coefficient is $a_{ij}, a_{ij} \geq 0$. It represents the impact of j's opinion have on i's opinion. In order to simplify the calculation, we assume that $a_{i1} + a_{i2} + \cdots + a_{in} = 1$ (Table 2). The individual opinions forming formula is as follows:

$$x_i(t + 1) = a_{i1}x_1(t) + a_{i2}x_2(t) + \cdots + a_{in}x_n(t) \tag{1}$$

Table 2. Computing the move of agent i

(1)	Compute i's neighborhood:
(2)	$V(i,x) = \{i \leq j \leq n \mid |x_i - x_j| \leq \varepsilon_i\}$
(3)	**if** V(i)= Ø **then**
(4)	$x_i(t + 1) = x_i(t)$
(5)	**else**
(6)	**for** each agent j∈V(i) **do**
(7)	$x_i(t + 1) = |V(i, x(t))|^{-1} \sum\limits_{j \in I(i, x(t))} x_j(t), t \in T$
(8)	**endfor**
(9)	**endif**

The weight a_{ij} can be 0. For example, if all the individual opinions in the group cannot influence i, then $a_{ij} = 1$ and $a_{ik} = 0(k \neq j)$. If only j's opinion can impact I, then $a_{ij} = 1$ and $a_{ik} = 0(k \neq j)$. It is noteworthy that a_{ij} is not necessarily a real number, and it may be a function that changes with time t or opinion profile x(t). We write a more general form of formula:

$$x(t + 1) = A(t, x(t))x(t), t \in T \tag{2}$$

A(t, x(t)) is a n×n matrix, as is shown below:

$$A(t, x(t)) = \begin{pmatrix} a_{11}(t, x(t)) & \cdots & a_{1n}(t, x(t)) \\ \vdots & \ddots & \vdots \\ a_{n1}(t, x(t)) & \cdots & a_{nn}(t, x(t)) \end{pmatrix} \tag{3}$$

3.2 Local Behavior Rule

So how to ensure that j's opinion can affect i's opinion? In the model we assume that only when two opinions' difference is within a certain range $\left(0 \leq \varepsilon_i \leq 1\right)$, their views can affect each other. We call it the accepted range, which is a collection of opinions for i:

$$V(i, x) = \{i \leq j \leq n \mid \left|x_i - x_j\right| \leq \varepsilon_i\} \tag{4}$$

In the formula above, |·| refers to taking absolute value. In order to simplify the calculation, we assume that the weight coefficient a_{ij} of opinions that have infect on i's opinion is the same. That is $a_{ij} = |V(i, x)|^{-1}, j \in V(i, x)$ where |·| represents the number of elements in set V(i, x). Therefore, the evolution formula of the opinions in the model is shown as follows:

$$x_i(t + 1) = |V(i, x(t))|^{-1} \sum\nolimits_{j \in I(i, x(t))} x_j(t), t \in T \tag{5}$$

4   Simulation

According to the theory of social influence [14], the three main factors, namely the influence of other opinions, their initial opinions, and the external factors from the government policies and mass media, will influence the formation of ideas. Then we will make a MATLAB simulation analysis on how these three factors affect the formation of opinions.

4.1   The Influence of the Acceptable Interval on the Formation of Opinions

In this part, we will present a continuous, one-dimensional, normalized opinion x evolution over time T, $x \in [0, 1]$. In order to show the effects of accepted interval on the formation of group opinion intuitively, we choose 200 opinions between [0, 1] as the initial opinion profile when $t = 0$. Then we discuss the effects of accepted interval $\varepsilon_i \in [0, 1]$ on the formation of group opinion. The longitudinal axis represents the viewpoint value of the group. Considering the need of visualization and subsequent analysis, we use continuous chromatography that range from red (x = 0) to purple (x = 1). The horizontal axis represents time, and only 10 time intervals are shown in the figure below (Figs. 1 and 2).

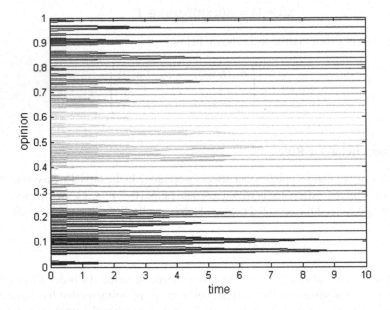

Fig. 1. The changing curves of opinions over time when $\varepsilon_i = 0.01$ (Color figure online)

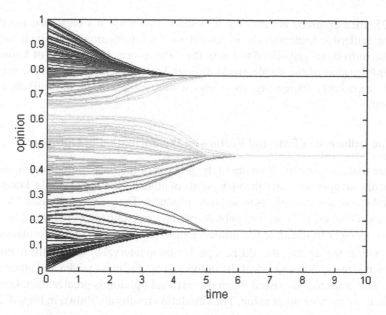

Fig. 2. The changing curves of opinions over time when $\varepsilon_i = 0.15$ (Color figure online)

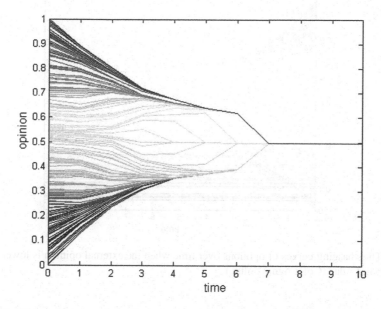

Fig. 3. The changing curves of opinions over time when $\varepsilon_i = 0.25$ (Color figure online)

Obviously, the time of the opinions reaching transient state is less than 10 time intervals. When the acceptable interval of opinion is small ($\varepsilon_i = 0.01$), there are 36 opinions when the system reaches steady state. If we enlarge the acceptable interval ($\varepsilon_i = 0.15$), there are 3 opinions when the system reaches steady state. When

$\varepsilon_i = 0.25$, their opinions are moving forward in harmony. It's clear that the flocking behavior, collective leadership, level control, global information and so on is not necessary. The individuals only need to know the local information instead of knowing the global information of the whole group through local perception. When the acceptable interval is gradually increasing, the views within the group are more likely to reach agreement.

4.2   The Influence of External Factors on the Formation of Opinions

There are usually some mass media in the process of the formation of opinions. These mass media strongly influence the viewpoints of other nodes. For example, businessmen make full use of advertisements to sell their products. The government uses TV or radio to propagate their ideas. Scientists publish articles on certain topics to influence people's opinions. In order to illustrate the influence of external factors on the formation of the group opinion, we suppose that the accepted opinion interval $\varepsilon_i = 0.25$, the hypothetical population size n = 200 and 1/5 of the individual are the mass media and other external factors. The cases are discussed when the external opinion is greater than, equal to or lower than the average point value. The simulation results are shown in Figs. 4, 5 and 6.

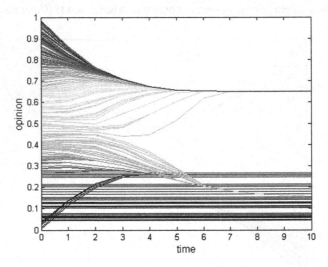

Fig. 4. The changing curves of opinions over time when the external opinion is lower than the average point value (Color figure online)

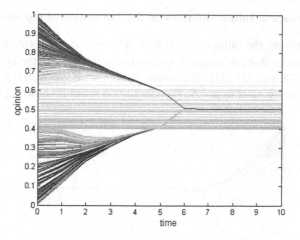

Fig. 5. The changing curves of opinions over time when the external opinion is greater than the average point value (Color figure online)

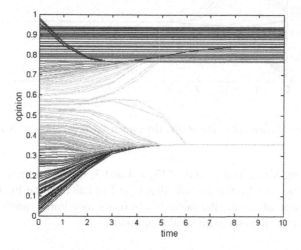

Fig. 6. The changing curves of opinions over time when the external opinion is equal to the average point value (Color figure online)

As you can see from Figs. 4, 5 and 6, when the external views have obvious and firm tendencies, they have a strong influence on the formation of views within the group. When the external opinion deviates from the average value of group viewpoint, a part of those who are similar to external viewpoints accept the view of government policy or mass media, while others do not agree with them. Only when the average value of the external views is the same as the average value of the group opinions, the group opinions can gradually be consistent.

4.3   The Influence of Initial Opinions on the Formation of Opinions

In order to illustrate the influence of initial opinions on the formation of the group opinion, we suppose that the accepted opinion interval $\varepsilon_i = 0.25$, the hypothetical population size n = 200 and 1/5 of the individual opinions are less than 0.5, 4/5 of the individual opinions are greater than 0.5. The simulation result is shown in Fig. 7.

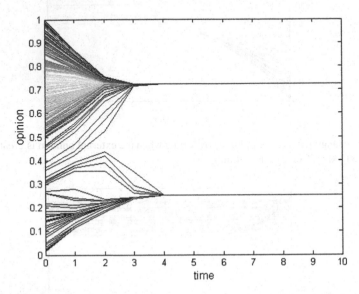

Fig. 7. The changing curves of opinions over time when the initial opinions is not random (Color figure online)

Comparing the simulation results of Figs. 3 and 7, it is not difficult to find that the distribution of the initial opinions will affect the formation of the final group opinion when the other conditions are the same. When one's own initial opinions have a clear tendency, it is easier to agree with similar opinions.

5   Conclusions

In this paper, we research on how other opinions, our initial opinions, and the external factors from the government policies and mass media influence the formation of ideas through building an individual opinion impact model. After analysis, we have got the following conclusions: First, when the acceptable interval is gradually increasing, the views within the group are more likely to reach agreement. Second, when the external views have obvious and firm tendencies, they have a strong influence on the formation of views within the group. Third, when one's own initial opinions have a clear tendency, it is easier to agree with similar opinions.

References

1. Xia, H., Wang, H., Xuan, Z.: Opinion dynamics: a multidisciplinary review and perspective on future research. IGI Global (2011)
2. Jiongming, S.: Continous opinion dynamics evolution on social networks and its application in online prediction. National University of Defense Technology (2014)
3. Weidlich, W.: The statistical description of polarization phenomena in society †. Br. J. Math. Stat. Psychol. **24**(2), 251–266 (1971)
4. Galam, S., Gefen, Y., Shapir, Y.: Sociophysics: a new approach of sociological collective behaviour: I. Mean-behaviour description of a strike. J. Math. Sociol. **9**(1), 1–13 (1982)
5. Stauffer, D., Penna, T.J.P.: Cross over in the Cont-Bounchaud percolation model for mark fluctuations. Phys. A **256**, 284–290 (1998)
6. Schweitzer, F., Hołyst, J.A.: Modelling collective opinion formation by means of active Brownian particles. Eur. Phys. J. B – Condens. Matter and Complex Syst. **15**(4), 723–732 (2000)
7. Higgs, P.G., Derrida, B.: Stochastic models for species formation in evolving populations. J. Phys. A Gen. Phys. **24**(17), L985 (1991)
8. Florian, R., Galam, S.: Optimizing conflicts in the formation of strategic alliances. Eur. Phys. J. B – Condens. Matter Complex Syst. **16**(1), 189–194 (2000)
9. Bak, P., Tang, C., Wiesenfeld, K.: Self-organized criticality: An explanation of the $1/f$ noise. Phys. Rev. Lett. **59**(4), 381–384 (1987)
10. Bak, P., Sneppen, K.: Punctuated equilibrium and criticality in a simple model of evolution. Phys. Rev. Lett. **71**(24), 4083–4086 (1993)
11. Pekalski, A.E., Sznajdweron, K.E.: Exotic statistical physics: proceedings of the 36th Karpacz winter school in theoretical physics held in Ladek Zdrój, Poland 11–19 February 2000
12. Bernardes, A.T., Costa, U.M.S., Araujo, A.D., Stauffer, D.: Damage spreading, coarsening dynamics and distribution of political votes in Sznajd model on square lattice. Int. J. Mod. Phys. C **12**(02), 159–167 (2001)
13. Reynolds, C.W.: Flocks, herds and schools: a distributed behavioral model. In: Conference on Computer Graphics and Interactive Techniques, vol. 21, pp. 25–34. ACM (1987)
14. Lewenstein, M., Nowak, A., Latané, B.: Statistical mechanics of social impact. Phys. Rev. A At., Mol., Opt. Phys. **45**(2), 763 (1992)

Research of User-Resource Relationship Based on Intelligent Tags in Evolution Network

Shan Liu[✉] and Kun Huang

Information Engineering School, Communication University of China,
Beijing 100024, China
liushan@cuc.edu.cn

Abstract. In view of the digitization and networking of the current media resources and users, the relationship between users and media resources is studied to realize the maximum effective utilization of media resources and the accurate recommendation of users as well as the more reasonable classification of users and media resources. Based on the attribute tags of users and media resource, we design an evolutionary model that reflects the inner relationship between users and media resource, and study the relevant indicators in the network. This paper mainly uses the modeling and analysis methods of complex networks to design the evolution mechanism and the main structure of the evolution network of user-resource relations. On this basis, we study the inner relationship between the structure and function of the network and provide the foundation for the research and design of various dynamic behaviors and processes in the network. Lay the foundation for the intelligent tag.

Keywords: Media resources · Intelligent tags · Complex networks

1 Introduction

With the development of Internet technology and the popularization of intelligent devices, the number of media content resources and network users are constantly increasing. People face a mass of media content resources on the Internet, and their daily online behavior generates a lot of information, and establishes their own user relationship network through social networking. At the same time, through the integration and management of media content resources, countless resource management libraries have also been set up to form a media content resource network.

A cluster of users and resources together creates a miniature network in which connections between users and resources reinforce the network's sophistication. The common features or content attributes of the users and resources may be defined as individual tags, thereby implementing the management of the micro-network through the tags. After long-term evolution of the micro-network, the microscopic changes of the related attributes of the users or resources and the change of the intrinsic objects in the whole network will show certain macro characteristics. We use complex networks and other related technologies to study the relevance of users and media content resources, and to achieve accurate recommendations on the user's media content and resources and user management.

© Springer Nature Singapore Pte Ltd. 2018
Y. Wang et al. (Eds.): IGTA 2018, CCIS 875, pp. 566–577, 2018.
https://doi.org/10.1007/978-981-13-1702-6_56

The basis of the label's intelligence lies in the design of the network structure and evolution mechanism. The core of the Tag-based User-Resource Relations Evolution Network is the relationship between users and users, media resource and media resource, users and media resource, and internal dynamics. The designed networks mainly include the actors of the network (nodes), the actors of the network (connections between nodes) and the motivation of the main body of the network (node control mechanism).

2   Contribution

The main contribution of this paper is as follows.

(1) Using the modeling theory of complex networks, and using the Jaccard distance, combining the attributes of users and resources, cleverly analyzing the relationship between the two, and establishing a tag-based user-resource relationship evolution network model of users and media assets based on tags.
(2) The definition of distance is innovatively given to the distance between the user and the media in the network to express the relationship between the objects.
(3) The initial evolution mechanism of the network is designed, including the joining of objects, the analysis of the attributes of objects, and the convergence of objects.

This article lays the foundation for the design and use of intelligent tags, and the intelligentization of intelligent tags.

3   Relevant Theory

3.1   Tab Overview

Tag is a flexible and effective way to classify, and users can make one or more tags for various resources, such as pictures, web pages and so on. Tags and keywords are similar, a description of the resource information. However, there are differences between tags and keywords. The keyword added can only be the creator or publisher of resources. Tags can be added by any interested user, and no longer restricted.

Content-based methods are the basic method of tagging, and other methods are often used in conjunction with content-based methods of recommendation. Content-based recommendation is based on the document content as the basis for the recommendation of the tag. In general, text content is used, which generally includes the following three basic steps: 1. Feature modeling. By extracting content features from the tagged resources, a model describing the resources is created. 2. Similarity comparison. Calculate the similarity between the content features of the resources that have been tagged and get an ordered tag recommendation candidate set. 3. Tag recommendation. According to the tag sorting of the second step, select the top n tags with the highest similarity from the candidate set and recommend them to the user. The types of resources tagged by the social tagging system are various, including webpages, documents, videos, audios and photos. Depending on the type of resource, existing resources can be divided into two broad categories: text/webpage and non-text [1].

In the correlation study, some resource tags are based on the specific content of the media resources on the one hand, and on the other hand, based on a series of attributes that the resource has been browsing through the network for a period of time, including the number of times viewed, the time of establishment, and many more. User tags come from a user's series of attributes, such as gender, region, resource attributes viewed, points of interest, and so on.

3.2 The Basic Concept of Complex Networks, Network Representation

A complex network, that presents a high degree of complexity, consists of a collection of elements (nodes) and a collection of elements (nodes). The elements that make up a complex network are often very simple. However, the interaction mechanism between elements often shows extremely high complexity, including the complexity of network structures, the complexity of network evolution mechanisms, the complexity of connections, the dynamics of dynamics, the complexity of nodes, and the convergence of these complexities [2].

Complex networks have been widely used in various fields such as transportation networks, power networks, the Internet, neural networks, communication networks, social networks, and so on [3]. In recent years, some scholars have proposed a network model and application that combines the idea of community structure for the community structure attributes in the network [4–6]. Clauset et al. apply a network model of machine learning theory, propose a general technique for inferring hierarchical structures from network data, and prove that the existence of hierarchical structures can simultaneously explain and quantitatively reproduce the common topologies of many networks nature [7]. Gupta et al. proposed a framework to explore the periodical patterns of the two aspects of whether the network is weighted and directed and proposed to study the interaction behavior at the micro level in the network [8]. Zhang et al. introduced two methods (link prediction and likelihood analysis) to measure the multiple evolutionary mechanisms of complex networks and applied them from different real world networks to observe how the popularity and the clusters co-evolved [9].

3.3 Jaccard Distance

Intelligent tags are formed by a series of specific text vocabularies or content. In the tag-based user-resource relations evolution network. The object is embodied in the tag. Its attributes are a series of specific tag collections. The measure of the relative distance of objects afterwards depends on the comparison of collections. In view of the diversity of the set, the Jaccard distance is a suitable measure and calculation method.

Jaccard Distance is an indicator used to measure the difference between two sets. It is a complement of Jaccard's similarity coefficient, defined as 1 minus the Jaccard's similarity coefficient. The Jaccard similarity coefficient, also known as the Jaccard Index, is an index used to measure the similarity between two sets [10].

The Jaccard similarity coefficient is defined as the number of elements in the intersection of two sets divided by the number of elements in the union.

$$J(A, B) = \frac{|A \cap B|}{|A \cup B|}$$

Jaccard similarity distance is the complement of Jaccard coefficient, defined as 1 minus the Jaccard similarity coefficient.

$$d_J(A, B) = 1 - J(A, B) = \frac{|A \cup B| - |A \cap B|}{|A \cup B|}$$

The Jaccard distance has two properties: (1) If A and B are empty, then $J(A, B) = 1$; (2) $0 < J(A, B) < 1$. Therefore, the greater the Jaccard coefficient, the more similar the two sets are. It can be deduced that $0 < d_J(A, B) < 1$, and the larger the $d_J(A, B)$, the greater the difference between the two sets.

4 User-Resource Relations Evolution Network Design

4.1 Distance Definition

4.1.1 Distance Definition of the Same Type of Object

Regarding the setting of attribute weights, the current attribute weights are as follows:

(1) User attribute weight setting: except id, name, sex = 0.1, usergroup_age = 0.2, usergroup_career = 0.2, city_work = 0.1, city_born = 0.1, liveness = 0.05, forcus = 0.25;
(2) Resource attribute weight settings: id, name except, type = 0.05, tag = 0.3, brower = 0.05, topic = 0.1, createdtime = 0.05, usergroup_age = 0.15, usergroup_sex = 0.15, usergroup_career = 0.15.

Combined with the concept of the Jaccard distance, the previous definition of the object distance was adjusted and corrected to increase its rationality. The distance for similar objects is designed as follows:

(1) The basic distance of the same type of object is denoted as D_0. Each object has n attributes. One attribute represents the id of the user object or resource object, and one attribute represents the user name or resource name. The distance between the objects is determined by the remaining n−2 attributes.
(2) For two user objects or two resource objects X_n and X_m, the attributes of the objects are compared, and a matrix M_{nm} with n−2 numbers can be obtained, which is defined as an attribute comparison matrix: for only one tag or one numerical value The attribute, if the attributes of the two objects are equal, the corresponding position value is 0; if not, the corresponding position value is 1. For an attribute with multiple tags, that is, the attribute has a tag set. The tag set of the attributes of the two objects uses the concept of the Jaccard distance to obtain the value of the

corresponding position in the attribute comparison matrix. The method is as follows:

(1) The tag set of this property of the two objects is taken as the intersection and a collection of a tag elements is obtained; the collection of tags of the properties of the two objects is taken as a union to obtain a set of a_0 tag elements;

(2) It can be known from the definition of the Jaccard distance that the Jacad distance of these two sets is $1 - \frac{a}{a_0}$, and the corresponding position value is $1 - \frac{a}{a_0}$.

(3) After all the attribute correspondences are compared, it is determined that an attribute comparison matrix M_{nm} is obtained. For different attributes, different weights are set on the influence degree of the distance between two objects. The value of each position in M_{nm} is multiplied by the corresponding weight to obtain a new matrix M'_{nm}, which is defined as the object distance matrix.

(4) To find the modulo D_{nm} for the obtained matrix M'_{nm}, the distance between the objects X_n and X_m is $d_{nm} = D_{nm} * D_0$.

4.1.2 Distance Definition of the Different Type of Object

The distance between the resource and the user is mainly based on the tag of the resource and the relationship between the user's group and the attribute of the user. The reason is that when making a recommendation, the user mainly pays attention to the content of the resource, and the reason why the resource is selected often lies in the user. Its own attributes affect its content. Therefore, the method of measuring the distance between users and resources is tentatively designed as follows.

Current user object attributes include: id, name, sex, usergroup_age, usergroup_-career, city_work, city_born, liveness, focus; resource object attributes include: id, name, type, tag, browser, topic, createdtime, usergroup_age, usergroup_sex, usergroup_career.

For user objects, the attributes sex, usergroup_age, usergroup_career, city_work, city_born are all single-tag words, and focus is a set of tags. For resource objects, tag, topic, usergroup_age, usergroup_sex, and usergroup_career are tag sets.

Calculating the distance method: For the user object A and the resource object B, the property comparison matrix M_{AB} (the matrix is a 1 * 4 matrix) that can calculate the distance is obtained by comparing several attribute contents. The method of determining the value of the matrix corresponding bit is as follows:

(1) User A's sex, usergroup_age, and usergroup_career attributes correspond to resource group usergroup_sex, usergroup_age, and usergroup_career, respectively, if the former three attributes (single tag elements) are contained in the latter three attributes (tag sets), respectively. Then the corresponding bit of M_{AB} is 0; otherwise it is 1;

(2) The city_work, city_born, and focus attributes of the user object A are combined to form a new set user_tag, and the tag and topic attributes of the resource object B are combined to form a new set source_tag, and the two sets are judged using the Jakard distance.

(3) After the attribute correspondence comparison is completed, the attribute comparison matrix M_{AB} is determined. Different weights are set for the influence degree of each attribute on the distance between two objects (the weight of the corresponding bit of the attribute comparison matrix M_{AB} is tentatively set as: 0.2, 0.2, 0.2, 0.4), and the values in each position in M_{AB} are multiplied by the corresponding weights. After a new matrix M'_{AB}, defined as the object distance matrix;

(4) For the obtained matrix M'_{AB} find its modulus D_{AB}, then the distance between the user object A and the resource object B is $d_{AB} = \mu * D_{AB} * D_0$, μ is to eliminate the object overlap due to the fact that the weight is a decimal due to simulation. The distance is not obvious.

4.2 Relationship Evolution Network Structure Design

4.2.1 Model Evolution Process Design

There are two kinds of objects in the network - users and resources, users or resources have their own attributes. The properties of objects are the key to building relationships between users and users, resources and resources, users, and resources, and attributes are essentially tags for users or resources. The life cycle of users and resources for the time being set as eternal.

The nodes in the network are users or resources, and the two are distinguished in the simulation.

The method for the object entering the network is conceived as two kinds: 1. Although in the definition, user objects or resource objects are all in increasing order of sequence numbers. However, when entering the network, the user or resource randomly enters, keeping the sequence number unchanged until all objects enter the network. 2. The order of entering the network is in the order of the initial defined sequence number.

The attributes of the user object include: id, name, sex, usergroup_age, usergroup_career, city_work, city_born, liveness, focus. The attributes of the resource object include: id, name, type, tag, browser, topic, createdtime, usergroup_age, usergroup_sex, usergroup_career. In addition, each object has a variable that is related to the simulation process: degree (k). The program has simulation time steps (t = 0, 1, 2, ..., T).

(1) Initial network (t = 0): several user objects and resource objects (the number will be determined by simulation).

(2) At each time step t, the following events occur: (The segments between objects based on distance are called edges).

① The length of the edge between objects represents the distance between two objects. If there is an edge between the two, the length of the side is the relative distance between the two in the network calculated according to the method defined in this article. In the simulation, if the object properties are not changed, the connection between objects will not change. If the attributes change dynamically, the connection between objects will change.

② Add edges. According to the object distance calculation method defined in this article, there will be a distance value between each object and other objects. At each time step t, each object completes a connection with both objects. The connection is based on the minimum value of the calculated distance and connects the two.

③ Eliminate edges. When the simulation reaches a certain size, part of the edges between objects will be eliminated. The basis is that each object has a certain number (M_0) of connected objects. When the upper bound of the connected object is reached, the distance between all connected objects is compared, the object with the largest distance is removed, and the objects with the relatively shorter distance complete the connection.

④ Reconnect: If some attributes of a user object or a resource object change during the simulation evolution, the calculation value of the distance between objects will be changed. Therefore, the connection of edges between objects also changes.

(3) Perform the above step T times to obtain a tag-based user-media relationship evolution network.

4.2.2   Object Aggregation Design

In an object cluster, there is a node as a leader, and other related nodes randomly exist in an adjacent area and establish a connection with it. The leader node needs to meet certain conditions, that is, several nodes with the highest degree as the core. Other nodes determine which object cluster they belong to based on the distance weight (the smaller the distance weight is, the closer they are).

Specific steps:

(1) Based on the calculated distance matrix and adjacency matrix of the object, statistics the degree distribution of the node.

(2) According to the degree distribution, certain cores are determined. At present, the number of cores is the number of nodes corresponding to the highest and second highest degrees.

(3) After determining the core points, identify other related peers within a circle centered on the core points. When a node is classified into a core area, the distance weight between the node and each core node is compared (the distance weight is determined based on the properties of the same type of object), and the core area with the core point with the smallest distance weight is taken as the area. (The final result is that some resources or users are the core, other resource objects are aggregated with some core resources, and other user objects are converged with some core users.)

Compared with the previous collection of similar objects based on the property distance, this simulation is aimed at the convergence of different types of objects.

Specific steps are as follows:

(1) Calculate the degree distribution of nodes for the calculated distance matrix between objects and the established adjacency matrix;

(2) Targeted distribution, to determine a number of core. At present, the number of cores is the number of nodes on the highest value and the next highest value;

(3) After determining the core point, identify other related heterogeneous nodes in a circle centered on the core point. When a node is classified into a core area, the distance weight between the node and each core node is compared (the distance weight is determined based on the heterogeneous object attribute), and the core area with the core weight with the smallest distance weight is taken as the area. (The final result is that some resources or users are the core, other user objects are aggregated with some core resources, and other resource objects are converged with some core users.)

Focus on the user object, the highest percentage of the proportion of resources, the highest proportion of tag attributes. In the early stages of simulation, the tag attributes of all the resources were collected into a tag library, and the focus attributes of all the users were converged into a focus library.

For all the objects, set the number of simulation steps, each time the focus object of each user object from the focus library to add a tag, each resource tag attribute tag library from a tag. Such a result is equivalent to the inherent properties of the object is constantly changing, the relative distance between each object obtained at each moment will change, the object convergence results will be different from time to time, observe the results of the convergence of objects in each time step.

5 User-Media Asset Relationship Evolution Network Characteristics Analysis

5.1 Network Evolves with Time Step (T)

Based on the design of the network evolution process and the definition of the distance between objects in the previous chapter, several objects are simulated. These object data are set based on the universal attribute values of users and media in the existing network.

In the network model, the actual evolution is simulated and reflected by adjusting the number of simulation time steps. With the growth of time, the number of resources and users, the change of corresponding attribute tags will bring about the change of object relevance and network size, and then analyze the macroscopic characteristics of the network and the changes of local resources and users.

Let T = 6, the simulation results are shown as follows, in which the red dot on behalf of the user object, the blue dot represents the blue object, the object number is also marked next to the point. The red link represents the connection between users, the blue link represents the connection between the media, the green link represents the connection between the user and the media, the connection has no direction, and the online numerical representation represents the calculation based on the object distance the value obtained (Figs. 1 and 2).

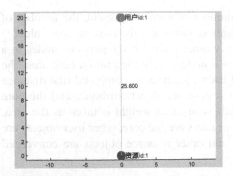

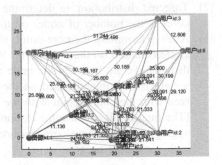

Fig. 1. User/resource object distribution based on attribute distance (T = 1) (Color figure online)

Fig. 2. User/resource object distribution based on attribute distance (T = 6) (Color figure online)

5.2 Introduced Parameter u to Control the Scale of the Network

In reality, there is a limit to the amount of resources a user can focus on, and the number of users recommended for a resource is not unlimited either. In order to simulate this one characteristic, will control the number of nodes in the network to control the scale, but also to adapt to the purpose of user cluster and resource clustering.

In the actual operation of simulation, when the distance between some nodes reaches a certain extent, the necessity of connection and the effectiveness of aggregation will be reduced. Therefore, this time for the inter-node connection conditions added a parameter u, to obtain a distance threshold. When the distance between two nodes is less than or equal to this threshold, the connection is established (Figs. 3 and 4).

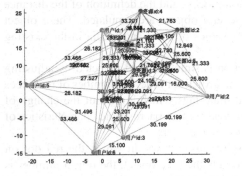

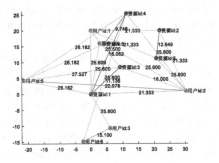

Fig. 3. User/resource object distribution based on attribute distance (u = 1)

Fig. 4. User/resource object distribution based on attribute distance (u = 0.75)

According to the simulation results, it can be concluded that the value of different u will cause the change of the connection number of each node, that is, the change of degree.

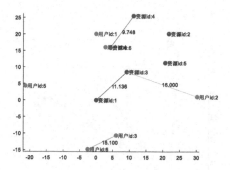
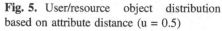

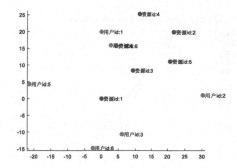

Fig. 5. User/resource object distribution based on attribute distance (u = 0.5)

Fig. 6. User/resource object distribution based on attribute distance (u = 0.25)

Due to the size of the data and the specific value of the object, when u is 0.25, the degree of each node in the network becomes zero. Theoretically, when u = 1, each node in the network is fully connected; when u = 0, each node in the network is completely disconnected from each other.

For the current simulation, in order for the nodes in the network to have a little connection, the value of u = generally needs to be greater than 0.5, and the current value of u is suitably 0.75 (Figs. 5 and 6).

5.3 Object Aggregation Analysis

According to the design of the previous object convergence, the number of simulation steps is set to 6, and the simulation results are as follows (Figs. 7 and 8).

(1) Convergence of similar objects

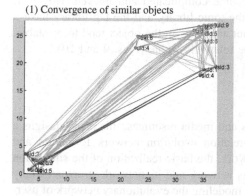
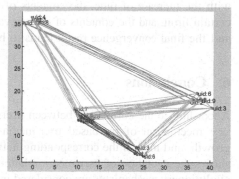

Fig. 7. User/resource object distribution based on attribute distance (T = 1)

Fig. 8. User/resource object distribution based on attribute distance (T = 6)

(2) Convergence of different objects

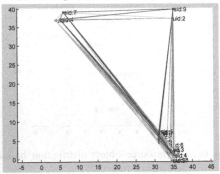
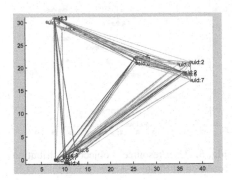

Fig. 9. User/resource object distribution based on attribute distance (T = 1)

Fig. 10. User/resource object distribution based on attribute distance (T = 6)

According to the above two kinds of distribution can be initially inferred the following conclusions:

In some attributes and object data originally set, based on the initial conditions, the convergence distribution will be relatively concentrated in several object clusters. However, with the increasing of time, the object attributes change. Due to the randomness of the set changes, the object clusters in the whole network gradually become more complex and the confusion increases. After the time step continues to increase, the degree of chaos in the entire network begins to decline again and again as the initial state (but the object composition of the object cluster has changed, that is, the new stable convergence result).

According to the simulation results and data reasoning, the reason is that the change of the tag content in the object attribute is indefinite within a certain time step, and the calculated relative distance values also become complicated and uneven. However, with the increase of time, the contents of the topic library and the tag library have a certain limit, and the contents of the relevant attributes in the object tend to be stable, and the final convergence result tends to be relatively stable (Figs. 9 and 10).

6 Conclusions

According to the correlation between users and media resources, this paper designs a key mechanism of tag-based user-media-relation evolution network formation and growth, and models the corresponding network, the basic realization of the simulation shows the evolution of user-media relations network and its network structure. Many evolutionary mechanisms are considered in modeling the evolutionary network of user-media relations, and the parameters set in the model are so large that any changes in the parameters of the simulation will lead to differences in the evolutionary network structure. Therefore, the above simulation result is only the unbalanced state or transient state of the evolution of the network model, which lays the foundation for further investigation of various dynamic behaviors occurring in the evolution network of user-media relations.

References

1. Liu, Z.: Content-based social tag recommendation technology research. Harbin Engineering University (2012)
2. Wang, N.: Research on complex networks in evolution of virtual industrial clusters. Beijing University of Posts and Telecommunications (2010)
3. Wang, X., Li, X., Chen, G.: Complex network theory and its application. Tsinghua University Press, Beijing (2006)
4. Yin, L., Cheng, F., Ren, Y., et al.: Microblogging topics detection based on complex network overlapping community discovery. J. Sichuan Univ. (Nat. Sci. Ed.), **53**(6) (2016)
5. Xian, Z., Tinglei, H., Yi, L.: Network clustering algorithm based on community classification. Comput. Modern. **12**, 1–5 (2017)
6. Guo, Y.: Research on complex network community structure detection algorithm. Jilin University (2017)
7. Clauset, A., Moore, C., Newman, M.E.: Hierarchical structure and the prediction of missing links in networks. Nature **453**(7191), 98 (2008)
8. Gupta, A., Thakur, H.K., Garg, A., et al.: Mining and analysis of periodic patterns in weighted directed dynamic network. Int. J. Serv. Sci. Manage. Eng. Technol. **7**(1), 1–26 (2016)
9. Zhang, Q.M., Xu, X.K., Zhu, Y.X., et al.: Measuring multiple evolution mechanisms of complex networks. Sci. Rep. **5**, 10350 (2015)

A Method of Detecting Human Head by Eliminating Redundancy in Dataset

Chao Le and Huimin Ma[✉]

Department of Electronic Engineering, Tsinghua University, Beijing 100084, China
lec15@mails.tsinghua.edu.cn, mhmpub@mail.tsinghua.edu.cn

Abstract. The method of constructing an image dataset by sampling images from videos with a short interval keeps the information in the video but also brings redundancy and increases the training costs significantly. In this paper, we propose a method to detect human heads with less training cost and higher performance, including: (1) A filtering standard to screen out the useless image in video-based image dataset with almost the same average precision. (2) An effective head detection model with the fusion of shoulder context. We evaluate our method on a human head dataset – HollywoodHeads and achieve reasonably good performance. This result shows that our method is very useful in human head detection task.

Keywords: Convolutional neural network · Dataset filtering
Head detection

1 Introduction

As an important branch of object detection, head detection has been used in many visual tasks, including person identification, action recognition, and crowd counting. On the other hand, current human head detection datasets are usually taken from daily life or movie scenes. Extracting valuable information in the dataset and adopting the algorithm specifically for human head detection can reduce training cost and improve overall performance.

Constructing an image dataset from video data is a common method. For example, the autonomous driving dataset KITTI [3] takes two high-resolution color and grayscale video cameras for image data recording. Head detection datasets usually capture images from specific scenes or categories. Hollywood-Heads [13] and TVHI [8] extract video frames from classic movies clips. Brainwash [12] gets images from a camera on the ceiling of a cafe. In order to avoid the similarity between images, a long interval is taken to sample the video when we have a large amount of data. Brainwash [12] (91146 head annotations/11917 images) dataset extract images from video footage at a fixed interval of 100 s to ensure a considerable variation in images. Relatively, another efficient way is pre-cutting the video into several important fragments and sampling with a short interval in a dataset. A short sampling interval preserves more valid data in the video, but it also results in many duplicates or similar images in some scene without drastic change. The sample interval in HollywoodHeads [13] (369846 head annotations/227740 images) is too short in some simple clips, which results in many similar images in the dataset. Meanwhile, the images and annotations are not enough in complex scenes. In this case, a standard is needed to filter out useless images.

In recent years, head detection algorithms have also undergone the process of development from handcraft feature to convolutional neural network, just like those in object detection. Schmid et al. [10] adopt the upper body region DPM [2] template to get the upper body proposal and then refine them to the head location. Marin et al. [7] utilize 4 different views of head template to make head detection. Vu et al. [13] use R-CNN [4] combined with head and context information, and introduce the positional relation semantics in the video. Stewart et al. [12] treat heads as a sequence, and use LSTM to regress the head location one by one. Other methods introduce additional information and annotations to detect. Aziz et al. [1] use the difference of video to obtain the body area and generate human skeleton map, then regress the location of head with this information. Jafari et al. [5] collect point cloud data from 3D camera and use RGB-D data to detect human head. Recently, Lin et al. [6] propose FPN, a top-down architecture with lateral connections and achieve significant performance in object detection at different scales.

As is shown in Fig. 1, our method first filters out useless images in a dataset by using the box annotations, then uses a convolution neural network based on the context of head and shoulder to detect human head. As a consequence, we evaluate our method on human head detection datasets–HollywoodHeads [13] and achieve an obvious improvement compared with our baseline. These results show that the method to make image filtering on dataset screen out redundant images in dataset efficiently. The approach maintains training accuracy and decreases training time dramatically. The experiment result shows that our method is effective on human detection tasks.

2 The Proposed Method

Our method first filters the dataset by excluding the redundant images from the training set. Then we train a convolutional neural network with shoulder information by using the remaining images, and merge the detection output by the non-maximum suppression method based on bounding box voting to obtain the final detection result.

2.1 Materials

HollywoodHeads is a dataset extracted from video frames about classical movies. This dataset contains 227740 images with 369846 labeled heads. This dataset is composed of movies clips in 15 movies. The author gives three training set with different sizes, each containing 4, 8, 15 movies respectively. We use the training sets including 4 and 15 movies to evaluate our method.

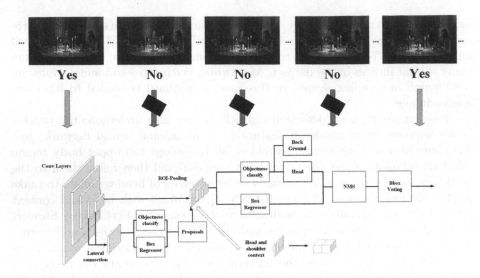

Fig. 1. Overall architecture. Our method first filters the image dataset to construct a new training set by removing redundant images. The new training set is used to train a CNN with shoulder context information. The output boxes are finally merged by NMS based on bbox-voting to obtain the final detection result.

Fig. 2. Here is an example of the duplicate images in HollywoodHeads dataset. Images from mov001007585 to mov001007590 is almost the same because the person is sitting up and speaking without drastic exercises.

2.2   Filter of Dataset

An efficient way to construct an image dataset is to annotate the object in the video, then sample at a regular interval. This method produces duplicate or similar images when the object in the video is stationary. On the other hand, HollywoodHeads is a dataset based on classic movies. The more characters there are in the image, the greater the interactions between characters generate. Figure 2 shows the duplicate Images from mov001007585 to mov001007590 in dataset. Therefore, we formulate the following standard in Algorithm 1 to determine the similarity of the two images by comparing the overlap of head annotation and calculating the maximum number of people.

Algorithm 1. Dataset filtering.

Ensure:

    whether an image should be preserved of removed.

1: Conserve all images have more than 3 objects.
2: **For** each image which has less than or equal to 3 objects:
3:     **if** the current image is the same size and
        same object numbers as the previous one:
4:       Calculate the IOU of two images
        by overlapping head annotation
5:       **if** IOU $\geq$ threshold:
6:         Remove this image
7:       **else:**
8:         Conserve this image
9:     **else:**
10:     Preserve the current image.

Table 1 shows the change of the number of images and head annotations in 4 movies training set and 15 movies training set. The number of images in the dataset is very huge and there is a lot number of redundant images before filtering. After filtering, The remaining images and head annotations are less than 1/3. A large number of unnecessary images and head annotations are removed.

Table 1. The changes in the 4/15 movies training set of HollywoodHeads dataset by our screen method.

Set	Before		After	
	Images	Heads	Images	Heads
4 movies	66155	105080	19627	31895
15 movies	227740	354229	70636	124563

2.3 Implement Details

This part mainly describes the network details of our network. We use resnet-50 as the backbone. The proposal feature map is generated on block 4 by using the lateral connection in the block 4 and 5. Origin block 5 after ROI-Pooling layer is substituted by 2 fully connect layer. By using approximate joint training respectively. We use five scales of anchors corresponding to dataset distributions (64, 96, 144, 256, 512 pixels) by and 5 aspect ratios (1:2, 3:4, 1:1, 4:3, 2:1). The loss function can be written as:

$$Loss = \sum_i p_i^* L_{reg}(t_i, t_{fi}^*) + \sum_i L_{cls}(p_i, p_i^*) \tag{1}$$

In the ROI pooling layer, we use a context-embedding based on the head and shoulder structure to extract the feature map corresponding to the proposal. By extending 25% to the left and right sides, 50% to the down side of the head candidates, we form a corresponding head-and-shoulder context. Then we concatenate this context feature with the head feature. A bounding box voting is used to further improve the positioning accuracy after NMS. In order to further extract difficult samples in the dataset for training, we also use the OHEM [11] method to perform gradient back-transition on objects with the larger loss in each batch. Other parameters are the same as those used in Faster R-CNN.

3 Experiments

3.1 Baseline Methods and Metric

We compare our approach with the method in [4,9,13]. Resnet-50 is taken for backbone network in our and Ren [9]'s method. We conduct an evaluation using the standard protocol based on IOU. A box is considered correct if its IOU with a ground-truth bounding box is larger than 0.5. We also set IOU as 0.7 for experiments to further illustrate the improvement of our approach. We plot recall-precision curves and summarize results in each experiment with average precision (AP).

3.2 Results

There are two aspects of the comparison of our approach.

We first compare the performance of the filtering method by using the Faster R-CNN to train the dataset before and after screening. Table 2 shows the comparison of origin dataset and the dataset after filtering in average precision with 0.5 and 0.7 IOU. From the results, we can see that the performance in test set and validation set do not decline after screening.

Table 3 shows the final results for HollywoodHeads by our fiter method and detection network. Our final method only uses the images after filtered in 4/15 movies for training. Since this is not a human head detection dataset with specific scene, we use origin NMS and bbox voting to fusion output. Compared with Vu'method, our architecture achieves a 17.8% increasement in 4 movies test set, and 13.3/15.3% increasement in the 15 movies test/validation set. Compared with Faster R-CNN, our method archieves a 4.6/5.7% increasement in 4 movies test set with the IOU of 0.5/0.7 and a 3.9/9.9% increasement in 4 movies validation set.

The comparison of PR curves in 15 movies set is shown in Fig. 3. In order to compare these curves clearly, we mark 1-precision as the x-axis and recall as the y-axis. Some detection results of our method are visualized in Fig. 4.

Table 2. Performance (% AP) before and after filter in the 4 movies test/validation sets of HollywoodHeads dataset.

Method	Test		Val	
	IOU 0.5	IOU 0.7	IOU 0.5	IOU 0.7
Origin	76.5	54.1	86.7	59.2
Filtered	76.1	53.5	87.4	60.5

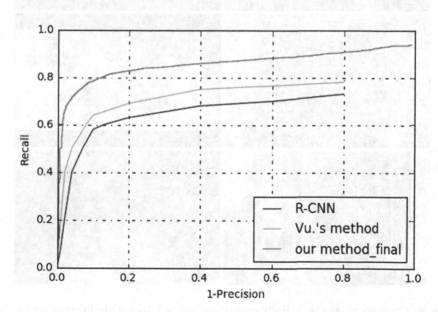

Fig. 3. PR curves in HollywoodHeads dataset. In order to compare these curves clearly, we mark 1-precision as the x-axis and recall as the y-axis.

Table 3. Performance (% AP) in the 4 movies test/validation sets of HollywoodHeads dataset. Our method only uses the images preserved after filter for training.

	IOU 0.5		IOU 0.7	
	Test		Val	
4 movies				
Vu's method [13]	63.3	-	-	-
Our method	81.1	59.8	90.6	69.1
15 movies				
Vu's method [13]	72.7	-	78.5	-
Our method	86.0	63.0	93.8	72.0

Fig. 4. Qualitative results in HollywoodHeads dataset Including different scenes and scales.

4   Conclusion

By reducing the redundancy training images, our method not only maintains a similar average precision, but also reduces the training time significantly. Through the improvement of the network structure, our detection architecture is superior to Faster R-CNN in human head detection task. These results show that our method is very effective on human head detection task.

References

1. Aziz, K.: Head detection based on skeleton graph method for counting people in crowded environments. J. Electron. Imaging **25**(1), 013012 (2016)
2. Felzenszwalb, P., Mcallester, D., Ramanan, D.: A discriminatively trained, multiscale, deformable part model. In: IEEE Conference on Computer Vision and Pattern Recognition, 2008. CVPR 2008, pp. 1–8 (2008)
3. Geiger, A.: Are we ready for autonomous driving? the kitti vision benchmark suite. In: IEEE Conference on Computer Vision and Pattern Recognition, pp. 3354–3361 (2012)
4. Girshick, R., Donahue, J., Darrell, T., Malik, J.: Region-based convolutional networks for accurate object detection and segmentation. IEEE Trans. Pattern Anal. Mach. Intell. **38**(1), 142–158 (2015)
5. Jafari, O.H., Mitzel, D., Leibe, B.: Real-time RGB-D based people detection and tracking for mobile robots and head-worn cameras. In: IEEE International Conference on Robotics and Automation, pp. 5636–5643 (2014)
6. Lin, T.Y., Dollr, P., Girshick, R., He, K., Hariharan, B., Belongie, S.: Feature pyramid networks for object detection (2017)
7. Marin-Jimenez, M.J., Zisserman, A., Eichner, M., Ferrari, V.: Detecting people looking at each other in videos. Int. J. Comput. Vision **106**(3), 282–296 (2014)
8. Patronperez, A., Marszalek, M., Reid, I., Zisserman, A.: Structured learning of human interactions in tv shows. IEEE Trans. Pattern Anal. Mach. Intell. **34**(12), 2441–2453 (2012)
9. Ren, S., He, K., Girshick, R., Sun, J.: Faster R-CNN: towards real-time object detection with region proposal networks. IEEE Trans. Pattern Anal. Mach. Intell. **39**(6), 1137–1149 (2017)
10. Schmid, C., Zisserman, A.: Human focused action localization in video. In: European Conference on Computer Vision, pp. 219–233 (2010)
11. Shrivastava, A., Gupta, A., Girshick, R.: Training region-based object detectors with online hard example mining. In: Computer Vision and Pattern Recognition, pp. 761–769 (2016)
12. Stewart, R., Andriluka, M., Ng, A.Y.: End-to-end people detection in crowded scenes. In: Computer Vision and Pattern Recognition, pp. 2325–2333 (2016)
13. Vu, T.H., Osokin, A., Laptev, I.: Context-aware CNNs for person head detection. In: IEEE International Conference on Computer Vision, pp. 2893–2901 (2015)

Application of Ghost Images for Object Detection and Quality Assessment

Nan Hu[1], Huimin Ma[1(✉)], and Xuehui Shao[2]

[1] Department of Electronic Engineering, Tsinghua University,
Beijing 100084, China
hu-n16@mails.tsinghua.edu.cn, mhmpub@mail.tsinghua.edu.cn,
mhmpub@tsinghua.edu.cn
[2] National Key Laboratory of Science and Technology on Aerospace Intelligent
Control, Beijing 100854, China
zhengli_1217@163.com

Abstract. Ghost imaging uses the high-order correlation of the light field and has the physical properties of entanglement, coherence, and non-locality. With high performance of anti-interference and stability, ghost imaging has important value in theoretical research and practical application. This paper presents the application of ghost data for object detection and quality assessment. Due to the complexity of the real imaging environment, we generated a large number of synthetic images as original materials through a ghost imaging simulation systems. And then we proposed a detection network for ghost data based on convolutional neural network with several fusion strategies. At the same time, a novel non-reference image quality assessment criteria based on detection performance is designed. Experiments on ghost dataset demonstrated that the early fusion network performed better, and the quality evaluation criteria based on this network is simple, reliable, and has usability.

Keywords: Ghost imaging · Object detection · Quality assessment

1 Introduction

Ghost images are obtained by correlating the output of two light paths [1,18]. The first is a single-pixel photodetector with no spatial resolution, which collects light that has been transmitted through or reflected from an object. The other is the output from a high spatial-resolution scanning photodetector array, which collects light that has not interacted with that object. It is defined as "ghost" imaging because of nonlocality, which means neither detector alone can yield an image. However, recent studies and theories showed that classical correlations can be implemented for ghost imaging [3]. For example, the pseudo-thermal light is extensively used in the ghost imaging field [2]. Even if the preparation of the light source is easier, collecting large quantities of images is still impractical due to imaging equipment and cost. So a sophisticated ghost imaging simulation system is significant for generating many synthetic images as training data.

© Springer Nature Singapore Pte Ltd. 2018
Y. Wang et al. (Eds.): IGTA 2018, CCIS 875, pp. 586–595, 2018.
https://doi.org/10.1007/978-981-13-1702-6_58

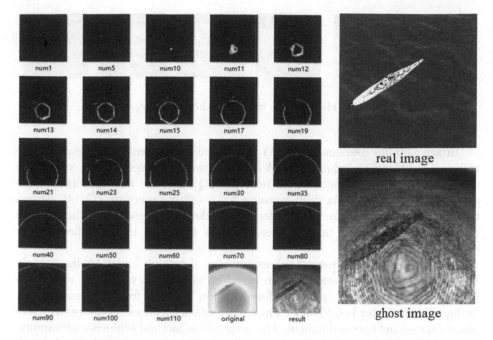

Fig. 1. The ghost image is simulated from the real scene and consists of a set of time slices which represent the different distances.

Ghost imaging has a strong anti-interference ability because the photodetector is invariant to ambient interference and any interference from any single path will be offset by the correlated algorithm. Based on the unique imaging principles, the ghost images have stronger anti-noise ability than traditional images. A ghost image consists of a set of time slices and every slice represent the optical reflection from the different distance (Fig. 1). So it can be regarded as a depth image containing 3D information of objects. Nonetheless, the color and texture features are missing and there are also problems with low visibility and resolution in ghost data. Hence, the application of object detection and quality assessment for ghost images is challenging.

For the detection task of RGB images, the traditional progress on visual recognition tasks is based mainly on the feature like SIFT [16] and HOG [4], which is extracted manually. However, the manual methods have gradually been replaced by well-performing methods relied on convolutional neural networks (CNNs) [10,20]. The R-CNN approaches [7,8,17] are the mainstream object detector for region proposals. Ghost images are similar to depth images, which are widely used for computer vision [9,11]. The depth channel is usually treated as the supplementary information, with which there are different fusion strategies to optimize the results. The usual approach is early fusion [15], score fusion, and late fusion [6].

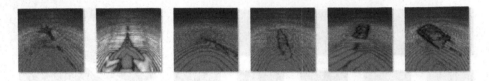

Fig. 2. The example images in the ghost dataset.

Image Quality Assessment (IQA) is a hot area of research in the computer vision. Traditional techniques of IQA for RGB can be divided into the subjective method and objective method. No-reference IQA has the most practical value and recent blind IQA via deep learning has worked superiorly [12,14]. Nevertheless, these methods are independent of the detection process. Without a real image for reference, we use No-reference IQA for ghost images relied on the detection result.

In this paper, we present a ghost imaging detection and IQA framework. First, we design a simulation system based on ghost data to imitate real imaging procedure. Then we applied different fusion methods for detection network extended from faster R-CNN [17]. The two inputs of this network are respectively ghost images and encoded images. The early fusion method achieved outstanding performance. We also proposed reliable criteria of no-reference IQA relied on the detection network. Several experiments are designed to validate the effectiveness of our approaches.

2   Detection and IQA Framework

Figure 3 shows our detection and IQA framework. The goal of the detection is to provide the bounding boxes with class labels of the objects for ghost images. The key part of this framework is the preparation of materials in simulation system as the input of the CNN, and the choice of an appropriate fusion strategy is also vital for the high accuracy of the detection. The IQA score is calculated directly related to the output of detection network in test.

2.1   Materials

Because of the lack of real ghost data, ghost images should be simulated from synthetic 3D scenes. We designed a simulation system (Fig. 3) for the preparation of materials. The first step is to create 3D scene automatically. We present 4 typical objects (categories): tank, plane, destroyer and carrier and 3 different scenes: airstrip, coast, and sea. From the various combination of the objects, the scenes, and the varied viewpoints, we render the depth image based on the distance from the object.

The input of the ghost imaging simulation process is the synthetic depth image. There are some critical parameters in this system, which determines the quality of the image and simulation speed. The threshold of background noise

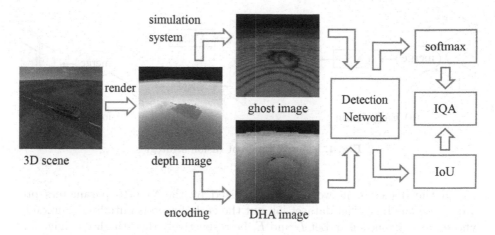

Fig. 3. The diagram of the detection and IQA framework.

n is a crucial factor for the measure of the noise in random reconstruction. We use nonlinear reconstruction algorithm to render a large number of ghost images with $n = 0.2$. The ghost images are reconstructed from time slices rendered from the depth images, so the ghost images only contain depth information in which the value of pixels represents the distance scale (Fig. 1).

The ghost dataset (Fig. 2) is simulated automatically with the annotation of location and category as ground truth, The limitations of correlation calculation process result in low image resolution with the size $128 \times 128 \times 3$. The pixel points of ghost images are incomplete, and there is information loss and disturb signal, so we proposed a feature encoded image call DHA (the new map of ghost containing three channels: density, height, and angle with gravity) as the additional input of the dual-branch network.

2.2 Detection Networks

The basic network of the fusion network (Fig. 3) is extended from faster R-CNN [17] with VGG16 architecture [19] as the convolutional layer. The network successively contains 5 convolutional layers, RPN layer, ROI pooling layer and 3 fully connected layers. The last layer $fc8$ is the softmax layer as the classification results with predicted bounding boxes.

We first train the single branch network for ghost images. On the contrast, the fusion network is of dual-branch architecture with different fused points in different fusion strategies. As early fusion (Fig. 4 (a)) we merge the pair of ghost images and encoded images in the data layer. We concatenate the two data into a $128 \times 128 \times 6$ input. As late fusion (Fig. 4 (b)) we merge the two branches after $fc7$, and these branches share the proposals. Although later point represents deeper characteristic with more implied semantic information, it doesn't always utilize complete feature more effectively.

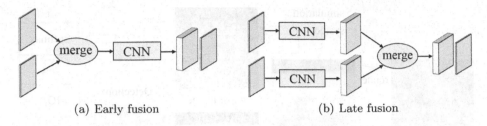

(a) Early fusion   (b) Late fusion

Fig. 4. The two different fusion strategies.

All the detection networks are initialized by the VGG16 parameters pre-trained on the ImageNet dataset [5], but the early fusion is initialized randomly, whose data channels is 6. Let I_i and E_i be respectively the i-th ghost image and DHA image. For N image pairs, y_i denotes the image label for ground truth. The fusion network is trained by two-stage strategy. First, we train the two branches individually. Let $r_I(I_i; \alpha_I)$ for ghost images be the representation before $fc7$ with α_I denoting the parameters of the network. Similarly, $r_E(E_i; \alpha_E)$ is applied to DHA images. We trained the single branch for ghost images through minimizing the loss

$$\min_{W_I, \alpha_I} \sum_{i=1}^{N} L(\text{softmax}(W_I r_I(I_i; \alpha_I)), y_i) \tag{1}$$

where W_I are the weights of the softmax layer and the loss L is the negative log likelihood. For DHA images, the process is the same. Second, we keep the parameters before fusion point and transfer them to the corresponding fusion networks. And then we fine-tune the fusion network analogously. We define $c(I_i, E_i)$ as the concatenation of two branches and replace I with F for fusion network and optimize all parameters to minimize the loss

$$\min_{W_F, \alpha_F} \sum_{i=1}^{N} L(\text{softmax}(W_F r_F(c(I_i, E_i); \alpha_F)), y_i) \tag{2}$$

2.3 Quality Assessment

Usually, the objective IQA measures the image quality according to the quantitative indicators or parameters given by the model, and is currently the research focus in the field of IQA. Traditional IQA criteria such as Peak Signal-to-Noise Ratio (PSNR) and Mean Square Error (MSE) are the most widely used for many years with their low computational complexity and clear physical meaning.

Due to the lack of reference to the original real image in the simulation module, traditional reference IQA cannot be applied. Proceeding from the object detection process, a non-reference IQA for ghost images are given. Image quality greatly affects the performance of detection. Theoretically, the higher score of IQA results in the higher accuracy of the detection, presenting the higher score of the corresponding category of the object and the higher intersection-over-union (IoU) overlap between the proposal and the ground truth. Since the detection performance indirectly reflects the image quality, the IQA criteria can be calculated in combination with detection process parameters. Let $p_F(I_i)$ be the proposals and g_i be the ground truth of image I_i, The non-reference IQA criteria score function is defined as follows

$$Q(I_i, y_i, g_i) = \mathrm{softmax}^k(W_F r_F(c(I_i, E_i); \alpha_F)) \times \mathrm{overlap}(p_F(I_i), g_i) \qquad (3)$$

where $\mathrm{softmax}^k(W_F r_F(c(I_i, E_i); \alpha_F))$ is the k-element of the output of $fc8$ and $\mathrm{overlap}(p_F(I_i), g_i)$ is the IoU. In the test process, The IQA score is calculated simultaneously as the product of the two parameters (Fig. 3). For low-quality images, one of these parameters may score higher, but the final product will be lower. The criteria consider both detection performance and recognition performance. Some contrast test will be designed to validate the reliability.

3   Experiments

For the network training process, we use the publicly available Caffe framework [13]. We evaluated our detection networks and IQA criteria on ghost dataset which consists of 2009 ghost images belonging to 4 different categories. The scale of the input of networks is resized to $400 \times 400 \times 3$. All the networks are trained for 80000 iterations with multi-step learning policy.

3.1   Detection Network

We tested various detection networks using different fusion strategies, including single branch network, late fusion network, and early fusion network. The single branch is based on faster R-CNN to train both ghost images and DHA images individually. Its parameters are transformed to fusion network, then two branches of which are trained simultaneously. Table 1 shows that the fusion network performed better than the single branch, and the accuracy of early fusion is higher than other networks in all categories. For low-resolution ghost images, the loss of the information in deep feature is more serious and the fusion at data layer is often more useful.

Table 1. Detection (AP%) on ghost dataset using varied networks.

Network	Input	Tank	Plane	Destr.	Carr.	mAP
Single branch	Ghost	97.7	94.8	75.0	94.8	90.6
Single branch	DHA	95.3	96.3	74.3	91.9	89.4
Late fusion	Ghost-DHA	95.9	96.4	80.5	94.3	91.8
Early fusion	Ghost-DHA	**97.8**	**99.3**	**84.4**	**95.1**	**94.2**

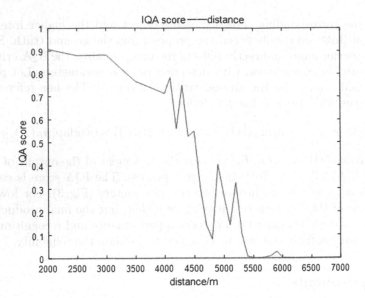

Fig. 5. IQA score as a function of the distance.

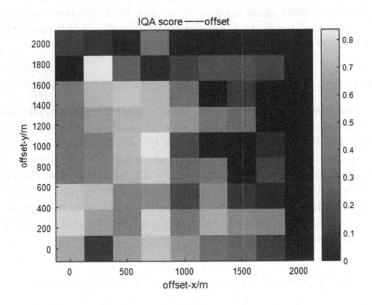

Fig. 6. IQA score as a function of the offset.

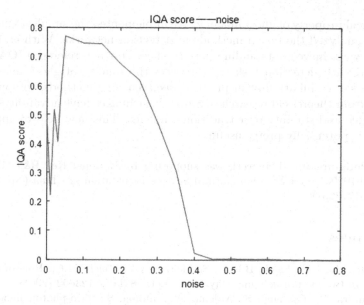

Fig. 7. IQA score as a function of the noise.

3.2   IQA Criteria

Intuitively, the ghost image quality depends mainly on the distance of the viewpoint, the offset from the center of the object in both x and y dimension, and the threshold of background noise n set in the simulation system. In order to verify the reliability of the IQA criteria, three groups of comparative experiments were conducted on the above three factors. We sampled images in uniform distribution within the scale of every factor. The experimental results are shown in Figs. 5, 6 and 7.

Figure 5 shows that the farther the distance is, the lower the IQA score is, but they are not nonlinear interaction. When the distance is greater than around 4500m, the score will drop sharply. Figure 6 shows that when the offset is large, the IQA score trends toward low. At a moderate offset, if the x and y values are more similar, the score is likely higher. The object near the border is more difficult to detect. Figure 7 shows that if the noise threshold is between 0.05 and 0.2, the image can maintain good quality. When the noise threshold is too low or too high, the score drops seriously. Overall, Our IQA method and criteria have the merits of simple calculation, high reliability, and strong correlation with object detection.

4   Conclusion

The framework we proposed in this paper is the application of ghost images for some typical tasks. We mainly focus on the object detection and IQA relied on the physical property of ghost imaging. We implemented the simulation technologies and analyzed the fusion methods in detection networks. With early fusion strategy, we achieved outstanding performance. Our non-reference IQA criteria correlated with detection task truly reflects the quality of ghost images. Our work is a successful attempt inspired by deep learning methods, to apply ghost imaging from theoretical researches. Since ghost images have advantages of anti-interference and stability over traditional images, This new field of application research is potentially pretty useful.

Acknowledgements. This work was supported by National Key R&D Plan (No. 2016YFB0100901) and National Natural Science Foundation of China (No. 61171113 and No. 61773231).

References

1. Abouraddy, A.F., Saleh, B.E.A., Sergienko, A.V., Teich, M.C.: Role of entanglement in two-photon imaging. Phys. Rev. Lett. **87**(12), 123602 (2001)
2. Alejandra, V., Giuliano, S., Milena, D., Yanhua, S.: Two-photon imaging with thermal light. Phys. Rev. Lett. **94**(6), 063601 (2005)
3. Bennink, R.S., Bentley, S.J., Boyd, R.W.: "Two-photon" coincidence imaging with a classical source. Phys. Rev. Lett. **89**(11), 113601 (2002)
4. Dalal, N., Triggs, B.: Histograms of oriented gradients for human detection. In: 2005 IEEE Computer Society Conference on Computer Vision and Pattern Recognition, CVPR 2005, pp. 886–893 (2005)
5. Deng, J., Dong, W., Socher, R., Li, L.J., Li, K., Li, F.F.: Imagenet: A large-scale hierarchical image database. In: 2009 IEEE Conference on Computer Vision and Pattern Recognition, CVPR 2009, pp. 248–255 (2009)
6. Eitel, A., Springenberg, J.T., Spinello, L., Riedmiller, M., Burgard, W.: Multimodal deep learning for robust RGB-D object recognition, pp. 681–687 (2015)
7. Girshick, R.: Fast R-CNN. In: Computer Science (2015)
8. Girshick, R., Donahue, J., Darrell, T., Malik, J.: Rich feature hierarchies for accurate object detection and semantic segmentation, pp. 580–587 (2013)
9. Gupta, S., Girshick, R., Arbeláez, P., Malik, J.: Learning rich features from RGB-D images for object detection and segmentation. In: Fleet, D., Pajdla, T., Schiele, B., Tuytelaars, T. (eds.) ECCV 2014. LNCS, vol. 8695, pp. 345–360. Springer, Cham (2014). https://doi.org/10.1007/978-3-319-10584-0_23
10. He, K., Zhang, X., Ren, S., Sun, J.: Delving deep into rectifiers: Surpassing human-level performance on imagenet classification, pp. 1026–1034 (2015)
11. Hoffman, J., Gupta, S., Jian, L., Guadarrama, S., Darrell, T.: Cross-modal adaptation for RGB-D detection. In: IEEE International Conference on Robotics and Automation, pp. 5032–5039 (2016)
12. Hou, W., Gao, X., Tao, D., Li, X.: Blind image quality assessment via deep learning. IEEE Trans. Neural Networks Learn. Syst. **26**(6), 1275–1286 (2017)
13. Jia, Y., et al.: Caffe: Convolutional architecture for fast feature embedding, pp. 675–678 (2014)
14. Kang, L., Ye, P., Li, Y., Doermann, D.: Convolutional neural networks for no-reference image quality assessment. In: Computer Vision and Pattern Recognition, pp. 1733–1740 (2014)

15. Long, J., Shelhamer, E., Darrell, T.: Fully convolutional networks for semantic segmentation. In: Computer Vision and Pattern Recognition, pp. 3431–3440 (2015)
16. Lowe, D.G.: Distinctive image features from scale-invariant keypoints. Int. J. Comput. Vision 60(2), 91–110 (2004)
17. Ren, S., He, K., Girshick, R., Sun, J.: Faster R-CNN: towards real-time object detection with region proposal networks. IEEE Trans. Pattern Anal. Mach. Intell. 39(6), 1137–1149 (2017)
18. Shapiro, J.H., Boyd, R.W.: The physics of ghost imaging. Quantum Inf. Process. 11(4), 949–993 (2012)
19. Simonyan, K., Zisserman, A.: Very deep convolutional networks for large-scale image recognition. Computer Science (2014)
20. Taigman, Y., Yang, M., Ranzato, M., Wolf, L.: Deepface: closing the gap to human-level performance in face verification. In: Computer Vision and Pattern Recognition, pp. 1701–1708 (2014)

An Effective and Efficient Dehazing Method of Single Input Image

Fu-Qiang Han, Zhan-Li Sun[✉], and Ya-Min Wang

School of Electrical Engineering and Automation, Anhui University, Hefei, China
zhlsun2006@126.com

Abstract. The quality of an image may be degraded seriously when it is captured in a foggy weather condition. In this paper, an effective and efficient dehazing method is proposed for a single input image by combining the dark channel prior information and a low-light image enhancement model. First, the dark channel is derived via two minimum operations. After estimating the atmospheric light, the transmission is initialized according to the property of aerial perspective. In terms of the atmospheric light, a bound constraint is computed further to refine the transmission. Finally, a high-quality image is obtained via the haze image model. Experimental results demonstrate the effectiveness and efficiency of the proposed method.

Keywords: Image dehazing · Transmission estimation
Dark channel prior

1 Introduction

In a hazed, fogy or smoking weather condition, the visibility of a captured image may be degraded seriously by the turbid medium, such as particle, water droplet, etc. For the degraded images, some important information, eg. contrast, edge, texture, may be lost to a certain degree. Such information is usually very important for many image processing techniques. Specifically, haze removal is a obviously under-constrained problem when the input is a single haze image. Nowadays, how to design an effective haze removal model is still an intractable problem in computer vision.

So far, many methods have been reported for the haze removal. By means of local atmospheric light estimation, a single-image based dehazing framework is proposed in [1] to remove haze artifacts from images. The proposed approach

Z.-L. Sun—The work was supported by a grant from National Natural Science Foundation of China (No. 61370109), a key project of support program for outstanding young talents of Anhui province university (No. gxyqZD2016013), a grant of science and technology program to strengthen police force (No. 1604d0802019), and a grant for academic and technical leaders and candidates of Anhui province (No. 2016H090).

© Springer Nature Singapore Pte Ltd. 2018
Y. Wang et al. (Eds.): IGTA 2018, CCIS 875, pp. 596–604, 2018.
https://doi.org/10.1007/978-981-13-1702-6_59

can avoid adverse effects caused by the error in estimating the global atmospheric light. In [2], the convolutional neural network is utilized to estimate a medium transmission map for an input hazy image. In [3], an effective dehazing method is proposed by utilizing the difference-structure-preservation prior. In [4], a spatial-temporal coherence optimization is proposed for haze removal of unmanned aerial vehicle aerial video. An efficient regularization method is explored in [5] by enforcing the inherent boundary constraint on the transmission function.

Recently, dark channel prior has become a useful information to remove haze. As a pioneer work, the dark channel prior is explored to optimize the computation of transmission map [6]. In [7], a high-speed refinement method is proposed to address the halo effects based on the gain intervention. A haze-removal method is proposed in [8] to restore hazy images by means of the sky segmentation and the dark channel prior. In order to avoid the color distortion, an improved algorithm is proposed for image haze removal based on dark channel priority [9]. In [10], the transmission map is refined by the dark channel prior method and Fast Fourier Transform.

In this paper, an effective and efficient dehazing method is proposed for a single input image by combining the dark channel prior information and a low-light image enhancement model. First, the dark channel is derived via two minimum operations. After estimating the atmospheric light, the transmission is initialized according to the property of aerial perspective. Considering the effectiveness of boundary constraint in [9], a bound constraint is computed further to refine the transmission. Finally, a haze removal image is obtained in terms of the haze image model.

The remainder of the paper is organized as follows. In Sect. 2, we present our proposed algorithm. Experimental results and related discussions are given in Sect. 3, and concluding remarks are presented in Sect. 4.

2 Methodology

The proposed method is constituted of three main components, i.e., estimating the initial transmission, computing the refined transmission, and recovering the scene reflection.

2.1 Estimating the Initial Transmission

Given a single hazy input image I, we first compute the dark channel J via two minimum operations [6], i.e.,

$$J = \min_{y \in \Omega(x)} (\min_{c \in \{r,g,b\}} I^c(y)) \tag{1}$$

where J_c is a color channel of J and $\Omega(x)$ is a local patch centered at x. After obtaining the dark channel J, the pixel locations are found for the top 0.1% brightest pixels. For the input image I, the pixels corresponding these locations are selected as the atmospheric light A. Then, the initial transmission $\tilde{t}(x)$ can be given by [6],

$$\tilde{t}(x) = 1 - \omega \min_{y \in \Omega(x)} \left(\min_{c \in \{r,g,b\}} \frac{I^c(y)}{A^c} \right), \tag{2}$$

where ω is a constant parameter to keep a very small amount of haze for the distant objects.

2.2   Computing the Refined Transmission

Consider that the scene radiance of a given image is always bounded, the following boundary constraint can be enforced on the transmission $\tilde{t}(x)$, i.e.,

$$0 \leq \tilde{t}_b(x) \leq \tilde{t}(x) \leq 1, \tag{3}$$

where the lower bound $t_b(x)$ can be given by [5],

$$t_b(x) = \min \left\{ \max_{c \in \{r,g,b\}} \left(\frac{A^c - I^c(x)}{A^c - C_0^c}, \frac{A^c - I^c(x)}{A^c - C_1^c} \right), 1 \right\}, \tag{4}$$

where I^c, A^c, C_0^c and C_1^c are the color channels of I, A, C_0 and C_1, respectively. After obtaining the bounded $\tilde{T}(x)$, the refined transmission $T(x)$ can be obtained via the following model [11],

$$\min_T \sum_x \left((T(x) - \tilde{T}(x))^2 + \mu \sum_{d \in \{h,\nu\}} \frac{W_d(x)(\nabla_d T(x))^2}{\left| \nabla_d \tilde{T}(x) \right| + \varepsilon} \right), \tag{5}$$

where the weight can be computed as,

$$W_d = \frac{K_\sigma(x,y)}{\left| \sum_{y \in \omega(x)} K_\sigma(x,y) \nabla_d \tilde{T}(y) \right| + \epsilon}, d \in \{h,\nu\}, \tag{6}$$

where $K_\sigma(x,y)$ is expressed as a distance weighting, which is made of a gaussian kernel with variance σ.

2.3   Recovering the Scene Reflection

After obtaining the global atmospheric light A and the refined transmission $T(x)$, the scene reflection J can be given by [6],

$$J(x) = \frac{I(x) - A}{\max(T(x), 0.1)} + A, \tag{7}$$

where the constant 0.1 is used to increase the exposure of the scene radiance.

3   Experimental Data and Set-Up

To validate effectiveness of the proposed method, a typcial image is used in our experiments. In our experiments, the patch sizes are set as 3×3 and 15×15 to deal with the initial transmission estimation and the boundary transmission estimation respectively. Other parameters are set as $\mu = 0.15$, $C_0 = (30, 30, 30)^T$, $C_1 = (300, 300, 300)^T$. Figure 1 shows an example of haze removal procedure.

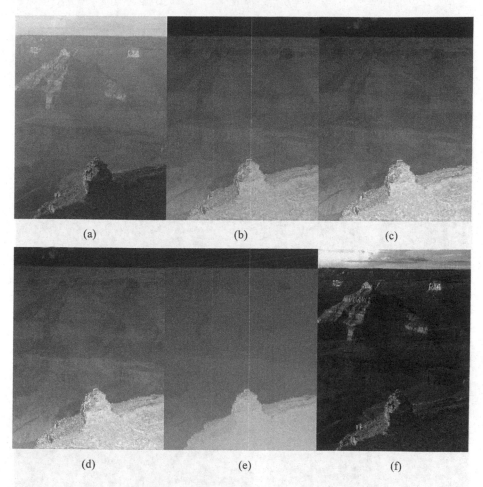

Fig. 1. An example of haze removal procedure. (a) input hazy image, (b) the initial transmission map, (c) the boundary constraint, (d) the transmission map with the boundary constraint, (e) the transmission map with depth map refinement, (f) the scene reflection image.

3.1   Qualitative Comparison

Figures 2, 3 and 4 show the output images after Haze removal via He's method, Guo's method, and our proposed method to estimate the initial transmittance,

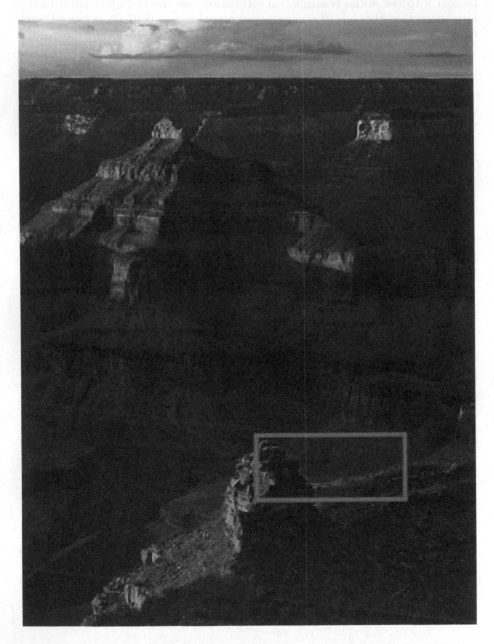

Fig. 2. The output image after Haze removal by He's method.

Fig. 3. The output image after Haze removal by Guo's method.

respectively. From the marked image patch, we can see that the edge is better preserved for our proposed method. Moreover, for the proposed method, the marked image patch is not as dark as other two methods.

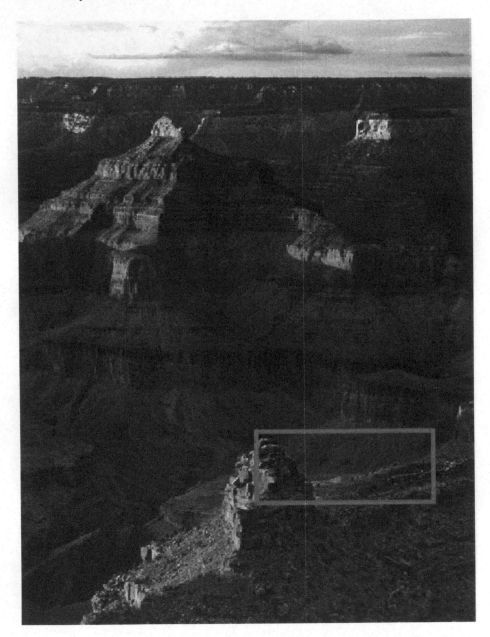

Fig. 4. The output image after Haze removal by our method.

3.2 Quantitative Comparison

In order to quantitatively compare different methods, Table 1 shows the experimental results of two performance indices, structural similarity index (SSIM)

Table 1. The experimental comparisons of different dehazing methods.

	FSIM	SSIM	TIME
He	0.9805	0.9866	48.146
Guo	0.6821	0.0032	7.339
Our	0.9824	0.9887	3.342

[12], feature-similarity index (FSIM), and [13]. Moreover, the computation times of different methods are also presented in Table 1. From Table 1, we can see that the performances of He's method and our proposed method are obviously better than that of Guo's method. Moreover, it can be seen that the proposed method has a better performance than He's method. Although the improvement is not so significantly, we can see that the computation time of the proposed method is obviously less than that of He's method. Thus, the proposed method is more efficient than other methods.

4 Conclusion

In this paper, an effective dehazing method is proposed for a single input image by combining the dark channel prior information and a low-light image enhancement model. Experimental results demonstrated the effectiveness and efficiency of the proposed method.

References

1. Sun, W., Wang, H., Sun, C.H., Guo, B.L., Jia, W.Y., Sun, M.G.: Fast single image haze removal via local atmospheric light veil estimation. Comput. Electr. Eng. **46**(C), 371–383 (2015)
2. Cai, B., Xu, X.M., Jia, K., Qing, C.M., Tao, D.C.: DehazeNet: an end-to-end system for single image haze removal. IEEE Trans. Image Process. **25**(11), 5178–5198 (2016)
3. He, L.Y., Zhao, J.Z., Zheng, N.N., Bi, D.Y.: Haze removal using the difference-structure-preservation prior. IEEE Trans. Image Process. **26**(3), 1063–1075 (2017)
4. Zhao, X.T., Ding, W.R., Liu, C.H., Li, H.G.: Haze removal for UAV aerial video based on optimization of spatial-temporal coherence. IET Image Process. **12**(1), 88–97 (2017)
5. Meng, G.F., Wang, Y., Duan, J.Y., Xiang, S.M., Pan, C.H.: Efficient image dehazing with boundary constraint and contextual regularization. In: IEEE International Conference on Computer Vision, pp. 617–624(2014)
6. He, K., Sun, J., Tang, X.: Single image haze removal using dark channel prior. In: IEEE Conference on Computer Vision and Pattern Recognition, vol. 33, no. 12, 1956–1963 (2009), pp. 3271–3282 (2013)
7. Chen, B.H., Huang, S.C., Cheng, F.: A high-efficiency and high-speed gain intervention refinement filter for haze removal. J. Disp. Technol. **12**(7), 753–759 (2016)

8. Liu, W., Chen, X.Q., Chu, X.M., Wu, Y.R., Lv, J.W.: Haze removal for a single inland waterway image using sky segmentation and dark channel prior. IET Image Process. **10**(12), 996–1006 (2017)

9. Huang, C.Q., Yang, D., Zhang, R.L., Wang, L., Zhou, L.H.: Improved algorithm for image haze removal based on dark channel priority. Comput. Electr. Eng. (2017, in press). https://doi.org/10.1016/j.compeleceng.2017.09.018

10. Kumari, A., Sahoo, S.K.: Real time visibility enhancement for single image haze removal. Proc. Comput. Sci. **54**, 501–507 (2015)

11. Guo, X.J.: LIME: low-light image enhancement via illumination map estimation. IEEE Trans. Image Process. **26**(2), 982–993 (2017)

12. Wang, Z., Bovik, A.C., Sheikh, H.R., Simoncelli, E.P.: Image quality assessment: from error visibility to structural similarity. IEEE Trans. Image Process. **13**(4), 600–612 (2004)

13. Zhang, D.: FSIM: a feature similarity index for image quality assessment. IEEE Trans. Image Process. **20**(8), 2378 (2011)

Study on User-Generated 3D Gestures for Video Conferencing System with See-Through Head Mounted Display

Guangchuan Li[1,2], Yue Liu[1,2(✉)], Yongtian Wang[1,2], and Rempel David[3]

[1] Beijing Engineering Research Center of Mixed Reality and Advanced Display, School of Optics and Photonics, Beijing Institute of Technology, Beijing 100081, China
lgc0106gogo@163.com, {liuyue,wyt}@bit.edu.cn
[2] AICFVE of Beijing Film Academy, 4, Xitucheng Rd, Haidian, Beijing 100088, China
[3] University of California, Berkeley, USA
david.rempel@ucsf.edu

Abstract. As video conferencing systems transition to using head-mounted displays (HMD), non-contacting (3D) hand gestures are likely to replace conventional input devices by providing more efficient interactions with less cost. This paper presents the design of an experimental video conferencing system with optical see-through HMD, Leap Motion hand tracker, and RGB cameras. Both the skeleton-based dynamic hand gesture recognition and ergonomic-based gesture lexicon design were studied. The proposed gesture recognition algorithm fused hand shape and hand direction feature and used Temporal Pyramid to obtain a high dimension feature and predicted the gesture classification through linear SVM machine learning. Subjects (N = 16) self-generated different hand gestures for 25 different tasks related to video conferencing and object manipulation and rated gestures on ease of making the gesture, match to the command, and arm fatigue. Based on these outcomes, a gesture lexicon is proposed for controlling a video conferencing system and for manipulating virtual objects.

Keywords: 3D gestures · Gesture recognition · Video conferencing system
Optical see-through HMD

1 Introduction

Touch 2D gestures were widely used in our daily life as the interaction interface with smartphones or pads [1, 2], and this interaction paradigm has influenced the operating habits of users. However, when using a HMD, there is no device for users to input with 2D gestures and interacting with such touch devices would be problematic. Researcher has been involved in designing new interaction pattern [3] for HMD. With a traditional video conferencing system, it will be difficult to use tele-controllers as interaction devices to manipulate virtual objects. The combination of visualizing virtual objects with real objects using Optical see-through HMD provides user with a personalized experience. Contactless 3D hand gestures used as interactive input in Augmented Reality (AR), and virtual Reality (VR) have been studied in [4]. The development of computer

© Springer Nature Singapore Pte Ltd. 2018
Y. Wang et al. (Eds.): IGTA 2018, CCIS 875, pp. 605–615, 2018.
https://doi.org/10.1007/978-981-13-1702-6_60

vision technology for hand posture capture, especially the emergence of commercial depth cameras such as Leap Motion and Microsoft Kinect etc., have allowed researchers to explore the design of 3D gesture for touchless human computer interaction (HCI), as well as algorithms for dynamic and static hand gesture recognition [5–7].

This paper presents the design of an experimental system with Optical see-through HMD, Leap Motion hand tracker, and RGB camera, which is used to elicit the user to design 3D hand gestures for a video conferencing system and virtual object manipulation. The video conferencing system is developed by Unity3d and is rendered on Optical see-through HMD which can combine real environment with virtual objects. In the experiment, subjects are asked to design gesture for 25 different tasks or commands, and subjects can "see" their virtual reconstructed skeleton hands provided by Leap Motion through Optical see-through HMD, which can help them to improve their designs. After experiment is over, subjects will be asked to complete a questionnaire to rate or rank the gestures on preference, match to command, ease of performing the gesture, and arm fatigue. The whole experiment is recorded by the web camera so that experimenter can analyze the user-generated gestures in details and grouped gestures.

Evaluating the 3D gesture lexicon from the point of recognition performance, a new framework is proposed in this study to recognize gestures. In the framework, fused features are used to fully describe 3D gesture, Temporal Pyramid (TP) extracts the temporal information from gesture sequence and Linear SVM [8] is used to classify the gestures.

Contribution: (1) This paper presents a gesture lexicon for control of a video conferencing system and for manipulation of virtual object with the use of Optical see-through HMD. (2) A new framework for 3D dynamic hand gesture is proposed. (3) Experimental findings show that the interaction paradigm based on touch devices have changed human interactive habits.

2 Related Work

Prior research on the design of 3D hand gestures has led to various lexicons based on whether the gestures are suitable and comfortable for signaling common computer commands.

Wobbrock et al. [9] propose an approach to design tabletop 2D gestures that relied on eliciting gestures from non-technical users by first portraying the proposed effect. The study doesn't consider postural risks for fatigue for gesture selection. Pereira et al. [10] present a framework for developing a 3D hand gesture lexicon for common HCI tasks that incorporates previously used subject ratings plus a new investigator rating of hand posture for estimating arm fatigue, without considering the gesture recognition performance with existing gesture recognition algorithms.

Shotton et al. [11] present a new method quickly and accurately predict 3D body joint angles from a single depth image, without considering temporal information. Nai et al. [7] propose a set of fast-computable depth features for static hand posture classification from a depth image. Smedt et al. [12] propose a new skeleton-based approach for 3D hand gesture recognition and exploit the geometric shape of the hand to extract an effective descriptor.

In addition, Rempel et al. [13] find that high discomfort is associated with hand gestures requiring a flexed wrist, discordant adjacent fingers, or extended fingers, in the design of hand gestures. Lin et al. [14] focus on evaluating parameters for 3D hand gesture design.

3   Methods

In this study, an experimental system based on Optical see-through HMD was developed for eliciting user to generate self-defined 3D gestures and a new framework was proposed for recognizing 3D dynamic hand gesture lexicon. In the experiment, subjects wore the Optical see-through HMD and generated their own hand gestures within the work the range of the Leap Motion detection for specific tasks (*zoom in/out* the scene, *rotate* the model, *volume up* etc.) which are of great importance in video conferencing system. Subjects had three choices to design gestures for one task without limitation of time and hand count. When subjects finished designing gestures for all tasks, subjects would be asked to complete a questionnaire to rate and rank the gestures they designed on various outcome measures, such as match to command and arm fatigue. According to the questionnaire and the data from analysis of user-generated gestures, a 3D gesture lexicon was proposed for video conferencing system and for manipulating virtual object. A framework for gesture recognition which could be used to recognize gesture lexicon, enabling that designing a new interaction paradigm-based 3D gesture lexicon which can improve the interaction efficiency.

3.1   Experiment Design for User-Generated Gestures

The main work of the experiment includes selecting tasks or commands, developing virtual video conferencing, designing questionnaire, and evaluating gestures. The tasks or commands were selected for controlling video conferencing system and for manipulating a virtual object, part of which were from manual of ZTE (A Chinese telecommunication company). Table 1 shows all the tasks selected in the study. Tasks 2–7 are used for adjusting the camera parameters, and tasks 8–11 are for setting system parameters. Task 12 is used to hang up the phone call. Task 13 is designed for superimposing a virtual model on the screen of video conferencing system, and task 14–25 are designed for manipulating virtual object.

The setup of experiment platform is shown in Fig. 1. Subjects sat in a chair, in front of a desk, and used Leap Motion and Optical see-through HMD. The Optical see-through HMD was developed by Beijing Institute of Technology with resolution of 1920×1080 and an adjustable inter-pupillary distance to meet subjects' requirements. RGB camera were used for recording the whole experiment's process, positioned to view in front of the subjects. Depth sensor, Leap Motion were used to provide the virtual hand as feedback to subjects and indicated whether the hand posture of subject could be reconstructed accurately.

Table 1. 25 tasks or commands for video conference system

Task	Task
1. Answer the call request	14. Move model left
2. Rotate camera left	15. Move model right
3. Rotate camera right	16. Select single model
4. Rotate camera up	17. Cancel selecting single model
5. Rotate camera down	18. Enlarge the model
6. Zoom in the scene	19. Shrink the model
7. Zoom out the scene	20. Add label to the model
8. Show the menu	21. Remove label from the model
9. Hide the menu	22. Rotate model left
10. Volume up	23. Rotate model right
11. Volume down	24. Rotate model up
12. Hang up the call	25. Rotate model down
13. Switch input channel	

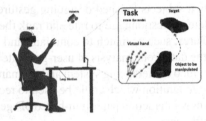

Fig. 1. The system setup with task "rotate the model" as an example.

Two virtual scenes were rendered by Unity3d on Optical see-through HMD showed in Fig. 2. The first scene was used to elicit the users to generate gestures for task 1–13, the retained scene for task 14–25. Before experiment started, every task was explained with written instructions and simulating experiment on the Optical see-through HMD until subjects fully understood their work and knew how to finish the task. During the experiment, there was no time limit for subjects designing gesture, and subjects were encouraged to think out aloud while designing gestures. When subjects finished designing the gesture for specific task, they would be asked to perform the gesture within the detection range of the Leap Motion. The time from when the task displayed to when the subject's hands moving out of the work range of depth sensor was recorded as the

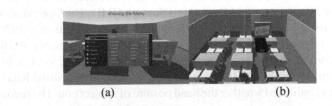

(a)   (b)

Fig. 2. (a) Is the scene for task 1–13, (b) is the scene for task 14–25.

response time. After subjects finished designing gestures for all tasks, they were asked to complete a questionnaire to rate or rank the self-generated gestures and explain why they designed such gesture for the task.

Subjects ranked or rated their gestures on four dimensions, preference, match, ease, and fatigue using the Likert scale (0 = low to 5 = high). Subjects ranked their most preferred gesture for a task on two statements: "the gesture is easy to perform" and "the gesture is good matched for the task". Fatigue (0 = comfortable to 5 = uncomfortable) was used to evaluate fatigue of the upper body, elbow, and wrist.

After all subjects finished the experiment, user-generated gestures were analyzed and were categorized according to the principle, gestures with same posture and same motion trajectories classified same one group.

3.2   Framework for 3D Dynamic Hand Gesture Recognition

A new framework for recognizing 3D dynamic hand gesture was proposed in this study showed in Fig. 3. In this study, various features based on the curvature of the hand contour, on the convex hull of the hand shape, and on the hand palm motion trajectory were used to fully extract hand features.

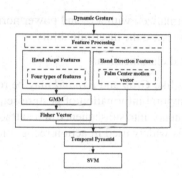

Fig. 3. Framework for gesture recognition

Hand Shape Features
Features used for describing hand skeleton data captured by Leap Motion detector were proposed in [15], which includes information of *Finger angels, Fingertip distances, Fingertip elevations, and Fingertip 3D positions.*

A. Histogram of hand directions

Motion trajectory information is of great importance to some gestures like *swipe gesture.* This paper computed the feature, Histogram of Hand Direction (HoHD) to extract the information of trajectory. HoHD feature was introduced in [12] in detail.

B. Fisher vector representation

Fisher Vector (FV) encodes the additional information of the distribution of the features. The process of figuring out FV includes fitting models to the features, encoding the derivative of log-likelihood of models with respect to its parameters. K-component Gaussian Mixture Model with parameters $\lambda = \{\pi_k, \mu_k, \sigma_k\}_{[1 \leq k \leq K]}$ is always selected for FV, where, π_k, μ_k and σ_k are respectively the prior weight, mean and covariance. After the GMM training process finished, the new sequence described by T_{seq} can be modeled as follow:

$$p(T_{seq}|\lambda) = \prod_{j=1}^{N} \sum_{k=1}^{K} \pi_k p(T_j|\lambda_k) \tag{1}$$

FV can be computed in the formula of Eq. (2).

$$\vartheta_\lambda^{T_{seq}} = \frac{1}{N} \nabla_\lambda \log p(T_{seq}|\lambda) \tag{2}$$

The item 1/N is used for removing the influence of the sequence size. Through concatenating the $\vartheta_\lambda^{T_{seq}}$, final FV feature is showed in Eq. (3).

$$\Phi(T_{T_{seq}}) = \{\vartheta_{u_k}^{T_{seq}}, \vartheta_{\sigma_k}^{T_{seq}}\}_{[1 \leq k \leq K]} \tag{3}$$

The final FV is also normalized with a $l2$ and power normalization to decrease the sparseness of the FV and increase the discriminability.

C. Temporal modelling and classification

Some inversed gestures like *Grab* and *Expand* may be recognized as same gesture because of ignoring the temporal information of gesture sequence. Temporal Pyramid (TP) could separate the sequence into subsequence and extract the temporal information from sub-sequence which is widely used in action recognition [16] and dynamic hand gesture recognition.

D. Dataset

The dataset [17] includes 8 types of dynamic hand gestures, *Grab, Expand, Swipe Right, Swipe Left, Tap, Pinch, Clockwise and Counter Clockwise*. Each gesture is performed by 10 times by 10 participants with Leap Motion, resulting 800 sequences.

4 Results

4.1 The Selection for Gesture Lexicon

The selection of a final lexicon was primarily based on popularity with adjustment for fatigue and recognition performance. To decrease the user cognitive load, some gestures were used to signal more than one command-based context. Some gestures with the highest popularity were abandoned due to poor recognition performance, little differentiation from other gesture, and fatigue risk. Only 23 gestures were generated more than twice by the subjects, which would be analyzed further. Subjects sometimes designed same gestures for different tasks, so 23 gestures associated with 25 tasks generated 60 different gesture-task combinations. For the final selection, 10 groups of gestures illustrated in Fig. 4 were assigned for 25 tasks as shown in Table 2. All gestures were performed by the right hand.

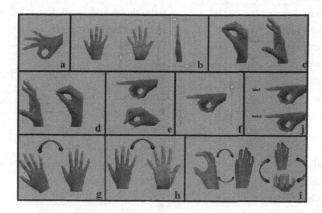

Fig. 4. Ten groups of gestures for 25 tasks

The most popular gesture for task *"Answer the call request"* was *"Both hands open towards the desk and move away from each other"*. The *"Okay"* gesture was chosen because it's easy to recognize and widely used in our daily life.

The most popular gesture for task, *"Rotate the camera right"*, was *"Right hand palm towards right and move right"*. However, this posture with angle of forearm pronation from neutral up to 90° caused high fatigue risk, so the selected gesture for this task was *"Right hand palm left and move right"*.

The popular gesture for tasks *"Zoom in the scene"* and *"Shrink the model"* were *"Grab"*, and the gesture for tasks *"Zoom out the scene"*, and *"Enlarge the model"* were *"Expand"* which could be distinguished according to the context, so the gestures *"Grab"* and *"Expand"* were used for two commands.

The popular gesture for task *"Switch the channel"* was *"Palm down and move right"*, which was disambiguated from gesture for task *"Rotate the camera right"*. Gesture *"Palm down rotated to palm up"* was selected for this task. In [10], the gesture selected for task *"Next"* was *"Palm down rotated to Palm up"*, whose purpose was the same as *"Switch the channel"*.

The most popular gesture for task *"Add label to model"* was *"point model and tap in"*, which was the same gesture for task *"Pick the single model"*. The gesture *"Point the label then point the model"* was chosen for the task. When hand posture was detected same as gesture group *j*, users can use hand to collide with virtual object and trigger the corresponding functions like modifying virtual object property of color, size and transparent, etc.

To compare our findings with prior studies in [9, 10], the same parameter, agreement score was used to evaluate our experiment. Response time was recorded by the virtual video conferencing system. The relationship between average response time for tasks and the agreement scores shows in Fig. 5.

Table 2. Final proposed gestures for tasks and the popularity score.

Task	Group	Gesture	Popularity
Answer the call request	a	Okay posture	3
Rotate the camera up	b	Palm up and move up	7
Rotate the camera down	b	Palm down and move down	7
Rotate the camera left	b	Palm left and move left	8
Rotate the camera right	b	Palm right and move right	8
Zoom in the scene	c	Grab	4
Zoom out the scene	d	Expand	4
Show the menu	e	Point and tap in	4
Hide the menu	e	Point and tap in	3
Volume up	f	Point in and move up	6
Volume down	f	Point in and move down	6
Hang up the call	g	Waving gestures toward camera	2
Switch the channel	h	Palm down rotated to palm up	1
Translate the whole model left	b	Palm left and move left	9
Translate the whole model right	b	Palm right and move right	9
Pick the single model	e	Point and tap in	8
Cancel picking single model	e	Point and tap in	2
Enlarge the model	d	Expand	6
Shrink the model	c	Grab	6
Add label to model	j	Point the screen and tap in	5
Remove label from model	b	Palm down and move left	4
Rotate the model left	i	Grasp and rotate to the	7
Rotate the model right	i	Grasp and rotate to the	7
Rotate the model up	i	Grasp and rotate to the	6
Rotate the model down	i	Grasp and rotate to the	6

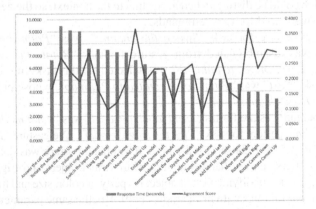

Fig. 5. Response time (orange bar) and agreement score for each task (blue solid line) (Color figure online)

4.2   Experimental Results with Different Shapes

To evaluate the performance of the proposed framework for dynamic hand gesture recognition. Hand shape features were concatenated into a vector with size = 19. The vectors were used to train a GMM of K = 20 clusters, resulting a FV with size = 760. The layer of TP was assigned to 3. Final size of feature extracted from hand sequence is 4848.

The average recognition accuracy of the dataset [17] can reach 90.0%, and the confusion matrix is illustrated in Fig. 6.

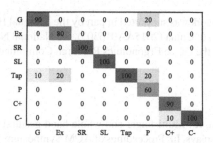

	G	Ex	SR	SL	Tap	P	C+	C-
G	90	0	0	0	0	20	0	0
Ex	0	80	0	0	0	0	0	0
SR	0	0	100	0	0	0	0	0
SL	0	0	0	100	0	0	0	0
Tap	10	20	0	0	100	20	0	0
P	0	0	0	0	0	60	0	0
C+	0	0	0	0	0	0	90	0
C-	0	0	0	0	0	0	10	100

Fig. 6. The confusion matrix of the proposed approach for dataset [17]

5   Discussion and Conclusion

5.1   Discussion

A 3D gesture lexicon was developed for 25 tasks used in video conferencing and for manipulating virtual object, and a new framework for dynamic hand gesture recognition was proposed in this paper.

Interestingly, subjects selected the same gestures in three choices for 320 gesture-tasks of all 400 gesture-tasks. In task *"Rotate the camera left"*, more than one subject pointed with index finger at the screen and moved the finger to the right. Subjects explained that it was the habitual manipulation in device-based touch-screen. So, when designing interaction paradigm for 3D gestures, paradigm based 2D gestures should be referred.

The average response time for the first gesture proposed by the subjects and the average agreement score had a weak inverse correlation ($r = -.161$), which was different from the results in [9, 10]. The difference might be caused by the experiment setup in this study, subjects were involved in the experiment, feeling of embodiment in the virtual video conferencing system with Optical see-through HMD. The feeling of embodiment encourages the users to use habitual gesture, and subjects also explained that they tried to finish designing gestures as soon as possible during the experiment.

5.2   Conclusion

There are some limitations in this study. First, the subjects were from Beijing, China. Subjects from other districts or cultures may propose a different lexicon. Second, whether the gesture lexicon could improve the interaction efficiency or meet users' needs still need to be investigated.

This paper presents a 3D gesture lexicon and a framework for 3D dynamic hand gesture. The experiment design and evaluation for user-defined gestures could be referred by other researchers with HMD.

Acknowledgment. This work was supported in part by the National High Technology Research and Development Program of China (2015AA016303), the National Natural Science Foundation of China (61631010), and the Office Ergonomics Research Committee.

References

1. Wu, M., Balakrishnan, R.: Multi-finger and whole hand gestural interaction techniques for multi-user tabletop displays. In: Proceedings of ACM Symposium on User Interface Software and Technology, pp. 193–202 (2003)
2. Ramadan, A., Hemeda, H., Sarhan, A.: Touch-input based continuous authentication using gesture-level and session-level features. In: IEEE Information Technology, Electronics and Mobile Communication Conference, pp. 222–229 (2017)
3. Şen, F., Díaz, L., Horttana, T.: A novel gesture-based interface for a VR simulation: re-discovering Vrouw Maria. In: International Conference on Virtual Systems and Multimedia, pp. 323–330 (2013)
4. Dardas, N.H., Alhaj, M.: Hand gesture interaction with a 3D virtual environment. In: JCM Conference on Innovation in Computing & Engineering Machinery (2011)
5. Kurakin, A., Zhang, Z., Liu, Z.: A real time system for dynamic hand gesture recognition with a depth sensor. In: Signal Processing Conference, pp. 1975–1979 (2012)
6. Zhang, J., Zhou, W., Xie, C., Pu, J., Li, H.: Chinese sign language recognition with adaptive HMM. In: IEEE International Conference on Multimedia and Expo, pp. 1–6 (2016)
7. Nai, W., Liu, Y., Rempel, D., Wang, Y.: Fast hand posture classification using depth features extracted from random line segments. Pattern Recognit. **65**, 1–10 (2016)
8. Chang, C.C., Lin, C.J.: LIBSVM: a library for support vector machines. ACM (2011)
9. Wobbrock, J.O., Morris, M.R., Wilson, A.D.: User-defined gestures for surface computing. In: SIGCHI Conference on Human Factors in Computing Systems, pp. 1083–1092 (2009)
10. Pereira, A., Wachs, J.P., Park, K., Rempel, D.: A user-developed 3-D hand gesture set for human-computer interaction. Hum. Factors **57**, 607 (2015)
11. Shotton, J., et al.: Real-time human pose recognition in parts from single depth images. In: Computer Vision and Pattern Recognition, pp. 1297–1304 (2011)
12. Smedt, Q.D., Wannous, H., Vandeborre, J.P.: Skeleton-based dynamic hand gesture recognition. In: Computer Vision and Pattern Recognition Workshops, pp. 1206–1214 (2016)
13. Rempel, D., Camilleri, M.J., Lee, D.L.: The design of hand gestures for human–computer interaction: lessons from sign language interpreters ☆. Int. J. Hum.-Comput. Stud. **72**, 728–735 (2014)
14. Lin, W., Du, L., Harris-Adamson, C., Barr, A., Rempel, D.: Design of hand gestures for manipulating objects in virtual reality. In: Kurosu, M. (ed.) HCI 2017. LNCS, vol. 10271, pp. 584–592. Springer, Cham (2017). https://doi.org/10.1007/978-3-319-58071-5_44

15. Marin, G., Dominio, F., Zanuttigh, P.: Hand gesture recognition with jointly calibrated Leap Motion and depth sensor. Multimed. Tools Appl. **75**, 1–25 (2016)
16. Evangelidis, G., Singh, G., Horaud, R.: Skeletal quads: human action recognition using joint quadruples. In: International Conference on Pattern Recognition, pp. 4513–4518 (2014)
17. [EB/OL]. http://download.csdn.net/download/lee_gc/10153572

A Novel Exhibition Case Description Method
of Virtual Computer-Aided Design

Xinyue Wang[2], Xue Gao[2], and Yue Liu[1,2(✉)]

[1] Beijing Engineering Research Center of Mixed Reality and Advanced Display, Beijing, China
[2] School of Optoelectronics, Beijing Institute of Technology, Beijing 100081, China
1464677442@qq.com, gao30703@126.com, liuyue@bit.edu.cn

Abstract. In a museum a large number of cultural, historical or scientific objects are kept and shown to the public. As people's requirements for culture become increasingly urgent, to offer visitors a better user experience attracts more attentions, which places greater demands on the abilities of museum's exhibition designers. However, during the exhibition design process of traditional museums, exhibition designers have difficulties in reusing and referring to the previous design cases. This paper presents a case description method which can be applied to exhibition design of museums. The case-based reasoning (CBR) method is introduced to retrieve and obtain similar cases, which are then provided to the designers for reference. These cases are described from three aspects, which are exhibition information, exhibits and exhibition halls. The case information retrieval based on floor plans of museum exhibition hall is realized by image processing and feature extraction. The experimental results show that the proposed method can help exhibition designers retrieve effective and accurate design cases for reference.

Keywords: Case-based reasoning · Museum exhibition design
Levenshtein distance · Image processing · Feature extraction

1 Introduction

Nowadays museums have many functions, such as collection, protection, exhibition, research and so on. They are public educational places for citizen to provide art, culture and science [1]. In the process of traditional museum exhibition design, it is difficult for designers to realize the reference and reuse of past design cases. With the development of economy, the demand for user experience of museums is being increased, which sets higher requirements for the skills of museum exhibition designers.

In recent years, various researchers have presented different aided design methods of museum exhibition. Weber et al. [2] put forward a method in which the house building design was represented by a single case. They divided the house into four categories: floor, unit, zone and room. Ayzenshtadt et al. [3] proposed an architectural design method based on case attribute value, in which the architectural design case was described as the form of semantic fingerprint [4]. Sabri et al. [5] focused on a similar case retrieval system based on network. Langenhan et al. [4, 6] proposed a visual query language for drawing

© Springer Nature Singapore Pte Ltd. 2018
Y. Wang et al. (Eds.): IGTA 2018, CCIS 875, pp. 616–625, 2018.
https://doi.org/10.1007/978-981-13-1702-6_61

sketches based on semantics. They defined four meanings of the input graphics to transform the graphic language of the building plane into the form of characters. Ahmed et al. [7, 8] presented an automatic analysis method to detect the feature of the building plan. Through the information segmentation [9], structural analysis and semantic analysis, every room in the house could be distinguished and endowed with corresponding function (for example: toilet, bedroom, living room, etc.). The method of information segmentation is mainly about the segmentation of text and graphics [10, 11], the separation of the outer contour, and the elimination of noise. The approach of structural analysis is mainly based on SURF (Speeded-Up Robust Features) algorithm to detect the door of a house and separate it from different rooms. As for semantic analysis, it aims to give different functions to each room by detecting and identifying the text in the graph. At present, the researches on the analysis of building plan and the methods of graphic matching are more sophisticated. Researchers can effectively transform the graphic language into digital or character language and achieve the retrieval and matching of architectural design through graphic segmentation, feature extraction and structural analysis. However, these methods haven't been applied to the field of museum exhibition design.

This paper presents a case description method applied to museum exhibition design. In order to help the museum exhibition designers to refer and reuse the previous design cases and improve the efficiency of the exhibition design, we present a solution to retrieve similar cases by case-based reasoning and describe the exhibition scheme from three aspects, which are exhibition, exhibits and exhibition hall. Case information retrieval based on museum exhibition plan is realized through image processing and feature extraction.

2 Design Method with Case-Based Reasoning

Case based reasoning analysis (CBR) is an important machine learning method [13]. In order to find a solution of a new problem, we should first search for similar problems in the existing exhibition database, extract the solution from the past similar problems, take it as the starting point to solve the actual problem, and obtain the solution of the new problem by adaptable modification [14]. When a new problem is generated, the similarity retrieval is carried out on the previous cases, and the most similar case is directly output as the solution of the new problem. As a result, the CBR method does not require prior knowledge.

In 1994, Aamodt et al. [15] proposed that the implementation process of CBR are divided in following four steps:

(1) Retrieve: The system compares the similarity between the previous cases according to the problem and draws the most similar case to the problem when a new problem comes into being.
(2) Reuse: The system matches the retrieved case solution to the target problem. This process may need to adjust the solution to adapt to the new situation.
(3) Revise: Mapping the solution to the target situation, testing the new solution in the actual situation, and modifying the solution when necessary.
(4) Retain: Finally, the new case will be stored after the solution has been successfully adapted to the target problem (Fig. 1).

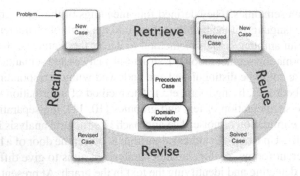

Fig. 1. The procedure of CBR.

3   The Creation of the Case of Museum Exhibition

The core part of the museum exhibition aided design system based on CBR is the description of exhibition design scheme, and the transformation of the graphical data information into semantic information in the exhibition scheme is the basis for the following case retrieval.

3.1   The Model Structure of a Case

We describe the design of museum exhibition through three concepts: exhibition, exhibits and exhibition hall, each of which is described respectively according to their attributes. These concepts and attributes constitute a case of exhibition design, which is stored in XML file.

Exhibition: It mainly describes the basic information of exhibition, including name, theme, and location. Exhibition theme is the first attribute of exhibition concept, which will occupy a larger weight in case retrieval process.

Exhibits: The exhibits are illustrated into nine aspects, age, area, texture, shape, function, quality, quantity, value and source. Among them, quantity, texture, function and shape of the exhibits are the primary attributes of the concepts. Age, area as well as quality are the secondary attributes, whereas value and source are the thirdly attributes.

Exhibition Hall: It mainly includes geometric and structural features of exhibition hall, including the information of wall, door, inflection point, showcase, acreage, compactness and approximate rectangle.

3.2   Extraction of Concepts and Attributes

It is not difficult to get the information of both exhibition and exhibits since they are mostly expressed in the form of string. On the contrary, the information of exhibition hall is generally stored in graphics. Graphic features should be first extracted, and then converted into the form of digital character. In this paper a feature extraction method of museum exhibition plan is introduced by referring to the methods of Mace [16] and Ahmed [7, 8] which is shown in Fig. 2.

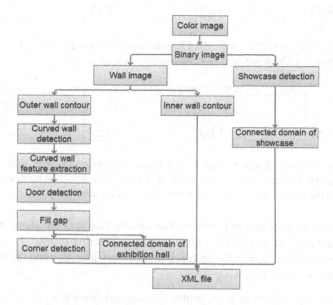

Fig. 2. The procedure of feature extraction method.

Given a plan as input, we first convert the original colour image to binary image. Then we perform closed operation of binary image, applying a 7 * 7 mask to extract the wall contour in the image, which contains outer wall contour and inner wall contour. Information such as text description is removed simultaneously. For outer wall contour, it is important to get the size information. And for inner wall contour, we focus on construction information.

In consideration that the outline of certain exhibition hall is not a straight line, we propose a method to detect curved wall of exhibition hall. If there is a curved wall, we first calculate the connected domain, then store the location information as well as geometric parameters in XML file. Otherwise no feature extraction is performed.

Different from the ordinary connecting rooms, museum exhibition hall is basically connected directly through the "door". Therefore, we extract the "door" from the exhibition plan, which helps us to analyse structural characteristics of exhibition hall. The wall image was subtracted from the binary image and a difference image was performed a closed operation with 4 * 4 mask. Finally, we get the "door" image.

We fill the gap in the "door" position of the wall image to facilitate the analysis of the overall structure. The proposed method counts the gap as a rectangle, the length of the rectangle is the distance between the door frames of the detected "door", and the width is the thickness of the wall. We then dilate the wall outline by using a small kernel to avoid too many invalid inflection points. The Harris inflection point detection method is adopted and a threshold is set, when the inflection point is less than the threshold, it is judged to be not an inflection point, otherwise it is judged to be an inflection point as shown in Figs. 3 and 4.

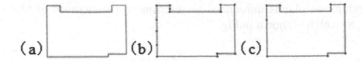

Fig. 3. (a) The original wall contour. (b) The inflection point obtained by using Harris corner detection method. (c) The result after removing excess inflection points.

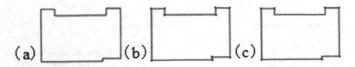

Fig. 4. Inflection point detected after an expansion operation. (a) The wall contour after expansion. (b) The turning point obtained by using Harris corner detection method. (c) The result after removing the excess inflection point (there is no invalid inflection point).

The small difference in the pixels on the straight line and the sharp pixels on the curve will cause inaccuracy of the inflection point detection results. As a result, after detecting the inflection point in the image, it is necessary to screen and delete the invalid inflection point with the following steps:

(1) Removing the inflection point which is detected from the curved wall: In wall images, if the inflection point is detected on the curved wall, it is considered to be an invalid inflection point and should be deleted (Fig. 5).

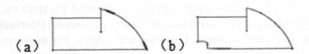

Fig. 5. Removing the inflection point which is detected from the curved wall. (a) The picture which is to delete the test results before. (b) The test result after the inflection point is deleted.

(2) Removing the inflection point with a similar position: As shown in Fig. 6, we calculate the distance between any two inflection points. If the distance is less than a threshold (which is set as 100 pixels), one of the inflection points is deleted.

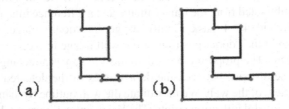

Fig. 6. Removing the inflection point with a similar position. (a) The picture which is to delete the test results before. (b) The test result after the inflection point is deleted.

(3) Removing the similar inflection point on the same line: If the two inflection points are on the same line and the distance between the two points is less than the threshold, one of the two points is deleted (Fig. 7).

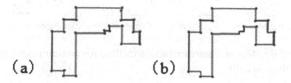

(a)   (b)

Fig. 7. Removing the similar inflection point on the same line. (a) The picture which is to delete the test results before. (b) The test result after the inflection point is deleted.

The inflection point information, location information, the concavity and convexity of the inflection point are stored in the XML file.

After filling the gap of the exhibition hall, we first calculate the connected area of the whole exhibition hall, absolute area and absolute circumference, then calculate the relative area, the relative circumference, the compactness of the exhibition hall.

Finally, we collect information of the display cabinet. In binary image, we perform closed operation to get the sign of the display cabinet, detect the connected area and calculate the relative parameters. The number, location information and the area information of the displayed cabinet are stored in the XML file.

The feature extraction method of the museum exhibition hall in this paper is run in the MATLAB software, which can effectively extract the features of the museum exhibition hall. The extracted features will be stored in XML file, and each exhibition hall plan corresponds to XML file. We collect information of the extracted features, the corresponding description of exhibition information and exhibits information as a complete case, which will serve as reference and basis for case retrieval and output (Figs. 8 and 9).

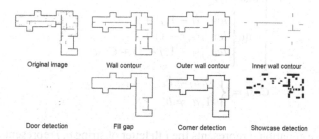

Original image   Wall contour   Outer wall contour   Inner wall contour

Door detection   Fill gap   Corner detection   Showcase detection

Fig. 8. Experimental results of feature extraction method for museum exhibition hall (exhibition hall does not contain curved wall).

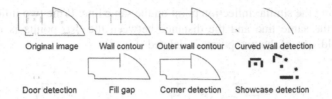

Fig. 9. Experimental results of feature extraction method for museum exhibition plan (including curved wall of exhibition hall).

3.3 Retrieval Matching of Case

The method of similarity measurement proposed in this paper mainly aims at measuring the attributes of concepts. We use the principle of Levenshtein distance to calculate the similarity relation between two strings and use the nearest neighbor algorithm to calculate the similarity relationship between two digital attributes. We set different weights for the attributes of different levels. The weight value of the first level attribute is 0.7, second level attribute is 0.2, and the third attribute is 0.1. By weighting sum of the similarity relation of all the attributes in the case, we draw the conclusion that the most similar case is the output of the result.

Levenshtein distance [17] is a measure method of the difference between two strings, which is the smallest number of single character editors (inserts, deletes, or substitutions) needed to change one string into another string. Generally speaking, the smaller the Levenshtein distance, the greater the similarity between the two strings.

For two strings a and b, the length of them are represented as $|a|$ and $|b|$, their Levenshtein distance is:

$$lev_{a,b}(i,j) = \begin{cases} \max(i,j) \\ \min \begin{cases} lev_{a,b}(i-1,j)+1 \\ lev_{a,b}(i,j-1)+1 \\ lev_{a,b}(i-1,j-1)+Cost \end{cases} \end{cases} \tag{1}$$

$$Cost = \begin{cases} 0, a_i = b_j \\ 1, a_i \neq b_j \end{cases}$$

In the above equation, i represents the i th letter of string a, j represents the j th letter of string b, $lev_{a,b}(i,j)$ represents the Levenshtein distance between a_i and b_j.

The similarity is:

$$Similarity_{a,b} = \frac{\max(m,n) - Levenshtein_{a,b}}{\max(m,n)} \tag{2}$$

in which m is the length of the string a, n is the length of the string b, and $Levenshtein_{a,b}$ is the Levenshtein distance between the strings. The data types of attributes include numbers, strings, arrays, and so on. Therefore, this paper uses the Levenshtein distance to calculate the similarity relationship between two strings and uses the nearest neighbor algorithm to calculate the similarity relationship between two numbers or arrays attributes. Finally, the similarity of all the attributes obtained is weighted to represent the similarity between the two cases.

4   Results and Analysis

In order to test the validity and rationality of the automatic extraction method for the feature of the exhibition hall, a comparative experiment is designed. In the experiment, the user can retrieve similar exhibition hall by inputting a plane map of the museum exhibition hall (Experiment A1–A20) or drawing a simple exhibition hall plane sketch (Experiment B1–B20). Table 1 shows part of the experimental results.

Table 1. Partial experimental result

Number	Retrieval image	Case image and similarity degree	Number	Retrieval image	Case image and similarity degree
A1		0.933	B1		0.848
A2		0.986	B2		0.853
A3		0.993	B3		0.835
A4		0.967	B4		0.844
A5		0.998	B5		0.724

As shown in Table 1, the system can retrieve a more similar exhibition hall case when an image is input or the exhibition hall is drawn. The retrieval results are very consistent with the geometric structure of the query image. Therefore, the automatic extraction method of the graphic feature for museum exhibition hall is more effective and more accurate, which proves the potential of the application of the automatic extraction method of plane map feature to the virtual museum exhibition aided design system.

5   Conclusion

We present a description method of exhibition case which is applied to the museum. We describe the museum exhibition design scheme through three concepts, which are exhibition, exhibits and exhibition hall. Besides that, we present a feature extraction method based on the plane map of museum exhibition hall. The conversion of graphic information into semantic information can help to realize the case. In order to help the museum designers to make reference and reuse of the previous design cases, we also propose a solution to retrieve similar cases by CBR, and the users can retrieve and reuse the similar cases directly according to the requirements of the design exhibition, which improving the efficiency of the design process.

The experimental results show that the automatic extraction method of the graphic feature for the museum exhibition hall is more effective and more accurate. It is reasonable to apply the automatic extraction method to the virtual museum exhibition aided design system.

Acknowledgments. This work has been supported by the National Technology Support Program of China (Grant No. 2015BAK01B05).

References

1. Chunxia, Y.: The integration and expansion of the functions for the museum. Technol. Pioneers **2**, 202 (2013)
2. Weber, M., Liwicki, M., Dengel, A.: a.SCAtch - a sketch-based retrieval for architectural floor plans. In: 2010 International Conference on Frontiers in Handwriting Recognition (ICFHR), pp. 289–294. IEEE (2010)
3. Ayzenshtadt, V., Langenhan, C., Bukhari, S.S., et al.: Distributed domain model for the case-based retrieval of architectural building designs. In: Proceedings of the 20th UK Workshop on Case-Based Reasoning, UK Workshop on Case-Based Reasoning (UKCBR-2015), Located at SGAI International Conference on Artificial Intelligence, pp. 15–17, December 2015
4. Langenhan, C., Petzold, F.: The fingerprint of architecture-sketch-based design methods for researching building layouts through the semantic fingerprinting of floor plans. Int. Electron. Sci.-Educ. J.: Architect. Mod. Inf. Technol. **4**, 13 (2010)
5. Sabri, Q.U., Bayer, J., Ayzenshtadt, V., et al.: Semantic pattern-based retrieval of architectural floor plans with case-based and graph-based searching techniques and their evaluation and visualization. In: ICPRAM, pp. 50–60 (2017)
6. Langenhan, C., Weber, M., Liwicki, M., et al.: Sketch-based methods for researching building layouts through the semantic fingerprint of architecture. In: Computer-Aided Architectural Design Futures (2011)
7. Ahmed, S., Weber, M., Liwicki, M., et al.: Automatic analysis and sketch-based retrieval of architectural floor plans. Pattern Recogn. Lett. **35**, 91–100 (2014)
8. Ahmed, S., Liwicki, M., Weber, M., et al.: Improved automatic analysis of architectural floor plans. In: 2011 International Conference on Document Analysis and Recognition (ICDAR), pp. 864–869. IEEE (2011)
9. Ahmed, S., Weber, M., Liwicki, M., et al.: Text/graphics segmentation in architectural floor plans. In: 2011 International Conference on Document Analysis and Recognition (ICDAR), pp. 734–738. IEEE (2011)
10. Tombre, K., Tabbone, S., Pélissier, L., Lamiroy, B., Dosch, P.: Text/graphics separation revisited. In: Lopresti, D., Hu, J., Kashi, R. (eds.) DAS 2002. LNCS, vol. 2423, pp. 200–211. Springer, Heidelberg (2002). https://doi.org/10.1007/3-540-45869-7_24
11. Fletcher, L.A., Kasturi, R.: A robust algorithm for text string separation from mixed text/graphics images. IEEE Trans. Pattern Anal. Mach. Intell. **10**(6), 910–918 (1988)

12. Bay, H., Ess, A., Tuytelaars, T., et al.: Speeded-up robust features (SURF). Comput. Vis. Image Underst. **110**(3), 346–359 (2008)
13. Shanlin, Y., Zhiwei, N.: Machine learning and intelligent decision support system, Beijing, Science Edition (2004)
14. Jian, C., Zhe, T., Zhenxing, L.: A review and analysis of case-based reasoning research. In: 2015 International Conference on Intelligent Transportation, Big Data and Smart City (ICITBS), pp. 51–55. IEEE (2015)
15. Aamodt, A., Plaza, E.: Case-based reasoning: foundational issues, methodological variations, and system approaches. AI Commun. **7**(1), 39–59 (1994)
16. Macé, S., Locteau, H., Valveny, E., et al.: A system to detect rooms in architectural floor plan images. In: Proceedings of the 9th IAPR International Workshop on Document Analysis Systems, pp. 167–174. ACM (2010)
17. Bin, C., Jianwei, Y., Huirui, C.: Process retrieval method based on Levenshtein distance. Comput. Integr. Manuf. Syst. (CIMS) **18**(8), 1766–1773 (2012)

An Automatical Camera Calibration Method Based on Coded Ring Markers

Yulan Chang[✉] and Hongmei Li

National Engineering Laboratory for Intelligent Video Analysis and Application,
First Research Institution of the Ministry of Public Security of PRC,
Beijing, China
yulan_chang@163.com

Abstract. In this work, an automatical camera calibration method based on coded ring markers is proposed, which is easy to operate and greatly improve automaticity of camera calibration. In this method, we firstly describe a calibration target, which consists of three coded ring markers and a planar pattern. In calibration, the ring markers are recognized and decoded, and then the center coordinates are sorted according to the coded values of the markers. Finally, the intrinsic parameters of the camera can be obtained with these sorted markers. Experimental results demonstrate the accuracy of the method.

Keywords: Camera calibration · Coded ring marker · Automaticity

1 Introduction

Camera calibration is a primary step for extracting metric information between the 3-D object coordinates and the image coordinates. According to the dimension of the used calibration object, the camera calibration can be classified as calibration based on 0D object [1–4], calibration based on 1D object [5–8], calibration based on 2D object [9–12], and calibration based on 3D object [13, 14].

Calibration Based on 0D Object. Techniques in this category do not use any physical calibration objects and can be considered as self-calibration because only correspondences of image points are involved. Just by rotating and translating a camera in a static scene, the camera's intrinsic parameters can be obtained by using image information alone. Therefore, if images are taken by the same camera with fixed intrinsic parameters, correspondences between three images are sufficient to recover both the intrinsic and extrinsic parameters which allow us to reconstruct 3-D structure up to a similarity. While this approach is very flexible and automatic, it has not yet matured. Because there are many parameters to estimate and the process of calculation is very complicated, we cannot always obtain reliable results.

Calibration Based on 1D Object. For filling the missing dimension in calibration, Zhang [7] proposed a calibration technique using 1D objects in 2004, and showed that the intrinsic parameters can be determined from images of a 1D calibration object rotating around a known fixed point if the calibration object has three or more known points. Wu, et al. [8] showed that the 1D calibration object of a rotating segment

© Springer Nature Singapore Pte Ltd. 2018
Y. Wang et al. (Eds.): IGTA 2018, CCIS 875, pp. 626–634, 2018.
https://doi.org/10.1007/978-981-13-1702-6_62

around a fixed point in Zhang's setup is in essence equivalent to a 2D rectangular calibration object with unknown sides and they proved further that the 1D apparatus could move within some planes. However, the marker fitting is prone to be affected by shadows in the method.

Calibration Based on 2D Object. Techniques in this category require to observe a planar pattern with a few different orientations [9]. The setup is easier for camera calibration, but the corner sorting is not automatic, it needs to remember the direction of the pattern or add markers on the pattern. For example, Zhao, et al. [12] designed an improved chessboard pattern and proposed an automatic corner detection and sorting algorithm. In the method, four rectangular boundaries are added to filter the complex background, and a double-triangle mark was used to determine the original point of the corner so as to adapt to the rotation of the pattern. However, for the application in large field of view measurement, a large calibration target in the field is needed to be observed by all the cameras, which is challenging for manufacturing and moving, and the markers are difficult to identify.

Calibration Based on 3D Object. Techniques in this category are required to observe a calibration object whose geometry in 3D space is known with good precision [13, 14]. Calibration can be done efficiently. However, the calibration object is often very expensive, and a good three-dimensional coordinate is established previously. In addition, the involved circle sorting is more complex than the 2D plane-based calibration.

To improve the automaticity of camera calibration, we proposed a novel model based on coded ring markers in this paper. Before calibrating, we firstly describe a calibration target, which consists of three coded ring markers and a planar pattern. For further to verify the accuracy of the coding mark point matching and make the computing process more convenient, the distance between the third marker and second marker is designed to be two times between second marker and first marker. Based on the previous research [15, 16], the markers can be decoded, and then the center coordinates of these encoded markers can be sorted according to the coded number, so that the corresponding points in each camera can be matched automatically. Finally, the intrinsic parameters of the camera can be obtained with these sorted markers, thereby achieving a fully automatic calibration function. Compared to the conventional calibration methods [9–11], the proposed one doesn't need complex sorting process, and it is also applicable for large field of view measurement. An experiment demonstrates that the accuracy of the method is similar with the method of Zhang's chessboard calibration.

The remaining of this paper is organized as follows. A brief introduction to the theory of camera calibration is presented in Sect. 2. Section 3 details the proposed camera calibration model. Section 4 describes the principle of calibration. Section 5 provides the results on both computer simulations and real data. Conclusions are given in Sect. 6.

2 Preliminaries

The coordinate of a point M in the 3D space is represented by $[X, Y, Z]^T$, and its projected point on the camera image plane is denoted by m with coordinate $[x, y]^T$. Their coordinates in homogeneous coordinate system are $\overline{M} = [X, Y, Z, 1]^T$ and $\overline{m} = [x, y, 1]^T$. A camera is usually modeled by a pinhole, then a 3D point M is projected to its image point m by

$$s\overline{m} = K[R\,t]\overline{M} \tag{1}$$

Where, s is a scale factor, $[R\,t]$ is the extrinsic matrix with $R = [r_1\,r_2\,r_3]$, t being the rotation and translation matrices from the world coordinate system to the camera coordinate system, and K is the intrinsic matrix, which is given by

$$K = \begin{bmatrix} \alpha & \gamma & u_0 \\ 0 & \beta & v_0 \\ 0 & 0 & 1 \end{bmatrix} \tag{2}$$

Where (u_0, v_0) is coordinate of the principal point, α, β are the scale factors for the x and y axes in the image, and γ is the parameter describing the skew of the two image axes.

Without loss of generality, we assume that $Z = 0$, then the formula (1) can be expressed as

$$s\begin{bmatrix} u \\ v \\ 1 \end{bmatrix} = K[r_1\,r_2\,r_3\,t]\begin{bmatrix} X \\ Y \\ 0 \\ 1 \end{bmatrix} = K[r_1\,r_2\,t]\begin{bmatrix} X \\ Y \\ 1 \end{bmatrix} \tag{3}$$

Then the relationship between m and M can be expressed by a homography H as follows

$$s\overline{m} = H\overline{M}, \quad H = [h_1, h_2, h_3] = K[r_1\,r_2\,t] \tag{4}$$

and we have

$$r_1 = K^{-1}h_1, r_2 = K^{-1}h_2 \tag{5}$$

As the rotation vector are mutually orthogonal, i.e.,

$$r_1^T r_2 = 0 \tag{6}$$

based on the formula (5) and formula (6), we have

$$h_1^T K^{-T} K^{-1} h_2 = 0 \tag{7}$$

In addition, the length of the rotation vector is equal, so

$$\|r_1\| = \|r_2\| \tag{8}$$

i.e.,

$$r_1^T r_1 = r_2^T r_2 \tag{9}$$

then we can obtain

$$h_1^T K^{-T} K^{-1} h_1 = h_2^T K^{-T} K^{-1} h_2 \tag{10}$$

Letting

$$B = K^{-T} K^{-1} = \begin{bmatrix} B_{11} & B_{12} & B_{13} \\ B_{12} & B_{22} & B_{23} \\ B_{13} & B_{23} & B_{33} \end{bmatrix}$$

$$= \begin{bmatrix} \frac{1}{\alpha^2} & -\frac{\gamma}{\alpha^2 \beta} & \frac{v_0 \gamma - u_0 \beta}{\alpha^2 \beta} \\ -\frac{\gamma}{\alpha^2 \beta} & \frac{\gamma^2}{\alpha^2 \beta^2} + \frac{1}{\beta^2} & -\frac{\gamma(v_0\gamma - u_0\beta)}{\alpha^2 \beta^2} - \frac{v_0}{\beta^2} \\ \frac{v_0 \gamma - u_0 \beta}{\alpha^2 \beta} & -\frac{\gamma(v_0\gamma - u_0\beta)}{\alpha^2 \beta^2} - \frac{v_0}{\beta^2} & \frac{(v_0\gamma - u_0\beta)^2}{\alpha^2 \beta^2} + \frac{v_0^2}{\beta^2} + 1 \end{bmatrix} \tag{11}$$

we can get

$$\alpha = \sqrt{\left(B_{33} - [B_{13}^2 + c_x(B_{12}B_{13} - B_{11}B_{23})]/B_{11}\right)/B_{11}}$$

$$\beta = \sqrt{\left(B_{33} - [B_{13}^2 + c_x(B_{12}B_{13} - B_{11}B_{23})]/B_{11}\right)B_{11}/\left(B_{11}B_{12} - B_{12}^2\right)}$$

$$\mu_0 = -B_{13}\alpha^2/\left(B_{33} - [B_{13}^2 + c_x(B_{12}B_{13} - B_{11}B_{23})]/B_{11}\right) \tag{12}$$

$$v_0 = (B_{12}B_{13} - B_{11}B_{23})/\left(B_{11}B_{22} - B_{12}^2\right)$$

$$\gamma = -B_{12}\alpha^2\beta$$

So the five intrinsic parameters of the camera can be obtained with the above formula.

3 The Improved Geometric Model

A new calibration target is presented in this paper, which allows a camera to be automatically calibrated. In this method, three coded ring markers are stuck on a planar pattern, as is shown in Fig. 1(a). For verifying the method applies to all coding mark points, we choose two coding mark points No. 146, and No. 147, which is difficult to distinguish, and another coded ring markers is No. 131. For further to verify the accuracy of the coding mark point matching and make the computing process more convenient, the distance between No. 146 marker and No. 131 marker is 10 cm, and the distance between No. 131 marker and No. 147 marker is 20 cm. The coded ring image consists of the black region and the white region. At the center of the ring marker is a white circle, embraced by a black ring and a white ring, each of which is divided into twelve parts, as shown in Fig. 1(b). The white area represents a binary 1, and the black area represents a binary 0. The principle of marker coding is as follows: we clockwise read the value from an arbitrary position, and twelve binary numbers can be obtained from twelve arbitrary positions, then the code of the ring marker is the minimum binary number.

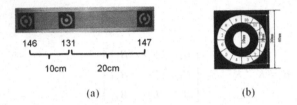

(a)   (b)

Fig. 1. (a) The proposed target. (b) The coded ring marker.

4   The Theory of Decoding

4.1   Identify the Coded Ring Marker

For accurately identifying the coded ring marker, we need to segment the image firstly. Image Edge Detection methods typically used are Sobel operator, Roberts operator, Prewitt operator, Canny operator and Kirsch operator. Since the environment of experiment is complex, this paper selects Canny operator to extract the edge. Canny operator has the characteristics of producing a single pixel edge and noise-insensitive. Figure 2 is the result of Fig. 1(a) with the Canny edge extracting.

Fig. 2. The Canny edge extraction of Fig. 1(a).

At the center of the coded ring marker is a circle, but in the actual, because of the lighting and the angle of the video camera, we usually obtain an ellipse. So, we employ the generalized least squares for ellipse fitting to get the center coordinate [15, 17–19]. An ellipse can be represented by

$$f(x, y) = x^2 + Axy + By^2 + Cx + Dy + E = 0 \tag{13}$$

Assuming we have N points $(N \geq 6)$, the objective function is

$$F(A, B, C, D, E) = \sum_{i=1}^{N} f^2(x_i, y_i) \tag{14}$$

Letting $\frac{\partial F}{\partial A} = \frac{\partial F}{\partial B} = \frac{\partial F}{\partial C} = \frac{\partial F}{\partial D} = \frac{\partial F}{\partial E} = 0$, we can work out the values of A, B, C, D, E.

The generalized least squares can find a set of parameters to minimize the distance between the data points and the ellipse where the distance measurements can be geometric distance or algebraic distance.

Geometric distance indicates the nearest distance from a point to the curve, which is the normal distance. For a point $P_i(x_i, y_i)$ in the plane, the algebraic distance is $f(x_i, y_i)$, and the geometric distance is:

$$d_{min}^{(i)} = \sqrt{(x_i - x)^2 + (y_i - y)^2} \tag{15}$$

As the geometric distance has the character of geometric invariant, we choose the geometry distance to evaluate the fitting error.

Since the angle between the target and the camera may be relatively large, we choose the ALPC (Affine LOG Polar Coordinate) method [15] to decode the coded ring markers. ALPC combines affine transformation with logarithmic coordinate transformation. Assume that the center of the transformation is (x_0, y_0). The ALPC transform for (x, y) can be represented as.

$$x' = M \log \sqrt{\left(\begin{array}{c} ((x - x_0) \cos \theta + (y - y_0) \sin \theta)^2 \\ + \frac{a^2}{b^2} ((-x + x_0) \sin \theta + (y - y_0) \cos \theta)^2 \end{array} \right)} \tag{16}$$

$$y' = \arctan \left(\frac{a((-x + x_0) \sin \theta + (y - y_0) \cos \theta)}{b((x - x_0) \cos \theta + (y - y_0) \sin \theta)} \right) \tag{17}$$

Where, the center of the transformation is the center of the ellipse, a/b is the ratio of long axis and short axis, and θ is the inclination of the concentric ellipse. To better show the feature of the image, we amplify the image with magnification(M) 20 in this paper. Figure 3(b) shows the parallel lines of the ALPC transform of concentric ellipses.

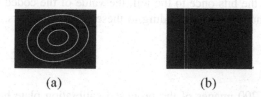

(a)   (b)

Fig. 3. ALPC transformation of Concentric ellipses. (a) Concentric ellipses. (b) Parallel lines after ALPC.

After ALPC transformation, the parallel lines from top to bottom clockwise corresponds to the concentric ellipses, so we do not need to rotate and split the concentric ellipses, and the decoding is more simple and accurate. The images for No. 146, No. 131, and No. 147 after ALPC transformation are shown in Fig. 4.

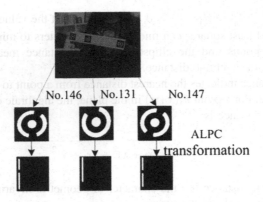

No.146   No.131   No.147

ALPC
transformation

Fig. 4. ALPC transformation of No. 146, No. 131, and No. 147

4.2   Decode the Coded Ring Marker

Decoding the coded ring marker is a key step to ensure the image matching accuracy. For the coded ring markers after the ALPC transformation, some black and white blocks are neatly arranged in the image, and we call it coded map. We can get the number of pixels in the black and white segments through scanning the coded map. Suppose there are M segments in a coded map, the number of pixels in each segment is stored in an array $P[M]$, and the information of the corresponding coded block is stored in the array $Flag[M]$. Where, $Flag[i] = 0$ represents that it is black in the ith segment, and $Flag[i] = 1$ represents that it is white in the ith segment. $P[i]$ is the number of pixels in the ith segment. As the coded map is a loop map, if $Flag[M-1] = Flag[0]$, we can combine the number of pixels in the head segment and tail segment, i.e., $P[0] = P[M-1] + P[0]$. After the merging operation, the coded value in the ith segment consists of n_i 1 or 0 in the array $P[M]$; if $Flag[i] = 1$, the coded value in the ith segment consists of n_i 1, and if $Flag[i] = 0$, the coded value in the ith segment consists of n_i 0, where $n_i = INT\left(\frac{12P[i]}{height} + 0.5\right)$, and *height* is the number of the pixel in the vertical direction. Finally, we can get the number of 0 or 1 in every segment. Read binary counter from any position, and we can get twelve bit binary number by rotating the bits once to the left, the value of the coded ring marker is the minimum decimal number corresponding to these binary numbers.

5   Experiment

In this experiment, 200 images of the proposed calibration plate have been collected from different angles with the two cameras. Because of the noise in the environment, we choose the generalized least squares for ellipse fitting [15] to obtain the center coordinates of all the ellipses, and then the coded markers can be decoded with the method in [15], the center coordinates of the coded ring markers are sorted according to the coded value of the coded ring markers. Finally, the intrinsic parameters of the camera can be obtained with these sorted markers. The intrinsic parameters of the two cameras are calculated and shown in Tables 1 and 2.

Table 1. The intrinsic parameters of the 1st camera.

	α	β	u_0	v_0	γ
The chessboard pattern	3001.589	2999.681	638.488	512.363	−0.003
The proposed target	2990.473	2986.431	599.159	520.944	−1.22
Relative error	0.37%	0.441%	1.31%	0.286%	0.04%

Table 2. The intrinsic parameters of the 2nd camera.

	α	β	u_0	v_0	γ
The chessboard pattern	2999.852	3000.997	628.305	515.921	0.001
The proposed target	3000.225	2995.75	622.282	526.768	1.34
Relative error	0.012%	0.174%	0.2%	0.361%	0.045%

The first row of the tables shows the results with the chessboard calibration, and the second row of the tables shows the results of the proposed target. The relative error (α is the benchmark, such as, the relative error of β is calculated by formula $|\beta_1 - \beta_2|/\alpha$) of calibration results are shown in the third row. As it can be seen from the above two tables, the relative error of the calibration results are below 2%.

6 Conclusion

In this paper, we proposed an automatical camera calibration method based on the coded ring markers. In contrast to the existing techniques, the proposed method has the advantages as follows:

(1) Simple design, easy operation, suitable for wide area calibration, and cost effective: Compared to the existing calibration targets, the proposed camera calibration method only need to stick three coded markers on a planar, and the calibration can be carried out by waving it in the space. When we lengthen the proposed target, it is also suitable for the wide area calibration, and the cost is still lower.
(2) Fully automatic calibration: The center coordinates of the coded markers can have been sorted in the code of the coded marker, which does not need complex sorting algorithm, thereby fully automatic camera calibration can be realized.

References

1. Svoboda, T., Martinec, D., Pajdla, T.: A convenient multicamera self-calibration for virtual environments. Teleop. Virt. **14**, 407–422 (2005)
2. Xiang, Z.Y., Sun, B., Dai, X.: The camera itself as a calibration pattern: a novel self-calibration method for non-central catadioptric cameras. Sensors **12**, 7299–7317 (2012)
3. Hartley, R.I.: An algorithm for self-calibration from several views. In: IEEE Computer Vision Pattern Recognition, pp. 908–912 (1994)
4. Wang, D.D., et al.: Stage error calibration for coordinates measuring machines based on self-calibration algorithm. Preci. Eng. **41**, 86–95 (2015)
5. Wang, L., Wu, F.C.: Multi-camera calibration based on 1D calibration object. Acta Autom. Sinica. **33**, 225–231 (2007)
6. Mitchelson, J., Hilton, A.: Wand-based multiple camera studio calibration. Tech. Rep. 41–49 (2003)
7. Zhang, Z.Y.: Camera calibration with one-dimensional objects. IEEE Trans. Pattern Anal. Mach. Intell. **26**, 892–899 (2004)
8. Wu, F.C., Hu, Z.Y., Zhu, H.J.: Camera calibration with moving one-dimensional objects. Pattern Recogn. **38**, 755–765 (2005)
9. Zhang, Z.Y.: A flexible new technique for camera calibration. IEEE Trans. Pattern Anal. Mach. Intell. **22**, 1330–1334 (2000)
10. Xia, R.B., Liu, W.J., Zhao, J.B., Xu, J.T.: Fully automatic camera calibration method based on circular markers. Chin. J. Sci. Inst. **30**, 368–373 (2009)
11. Lei, Z., Liu, X.J., Lu, W.L., Lei, Z.L., Chen, L.Z., Zhou, L.P.: A new calibration method of the projector in structured light measurement technology. Proc. CIRP **27**, 303–308 (2015)
12. Zhao, B., Zhou, J.: Automatic detection and sorting of corners by improved chessboard pattern. Opt. Precis. Eng. **23**, 237–244 (2015)
13. Heikkilä, J.: Geometric camera calibration using circular control points. IEEE Trans. Pattern Anal. Mach. Intell. **22**, 1066–1077 (2000)
14. Tsai, R., Lenz, R.K.: A technique for fully autonomous and efficient 3D robotics hand/eye calibration. IEEE Trans. **5**, 345–358 (1989)
15. Song, L.M., Chen, C.M., Chen, Z., Qin, M.C., Li, D.P.: Detection and recognition of cyclic coded targets. Opt. Precis. Eng. **21**, 3239–3247 (2013)
16. Huang, Z.R., Xi, J.T., Yu, Y.G., Guo, Q.H., Song, L.M.: Improved geometrical model of fringe projection profilometry. Opt. Express **22**, 32220–32232 (2014)
17. Meng, B., Cong, W.X., Xi, Y., Wang, G.: Image reconstruction for X-ray K-edge imaging with a photon counting detector. In: Proceedings of the SPIE, vol. 9212 (2014)
18. Meng, B., Cong, W.X., Xi, Y., Man, B.D., Wang, G.: Energy window optimization for X-ray K-edge tomographic imaging. IEEE Trans. Biomed. Eng. **63**(8), 1623–1630 (2016)
19. Meng, B., Cong, W.X., Xi, Y., Man, B.D., Yang, J., Wang, G.: Model and reconstruction of a K-edge contrast agent distribution with an X-ray photon-counting detector. Opt. Express **25**, 9378–9392 (2017)

A Survey on Dynamic Hand Gesture Recognition Using Kinect Device

Aamrah Ikram and Yue Liu[✉]

School of Optics and Photonics, Beijing Institute of Technology,
Beijing 100081, China
aamrahikram@yahoo.com, liuyue@bit.edu.cn

Abstract. In Human Computer Interface (HCI) technology, Hand Gestures Recognition (HGR) is a diverse field. In Dynamic Hand gesture recognition (DHGR), an unprecedented work has been done over few decades and it is still growing day by day. HGR has been extensively used in other scopes like biomedical, gaming and entertainment, research and monitoring etc. Because of its versatile utility, HGR is getting popular among the people, as it is making HCI more efficient, natural and user friendly. For the purpose of accurate segmentation and tracking a controller free and fascinating device, Kinect was introduced. In this paper Kinect based algorithms are discussed and addressed. Algorithms for DHGR are compared and particularly focused on Hidden Markov Model (HMM) and Support Vector Machine (SVM). At the end, it is observed that recognition accuracy improved significantly with Kinect device due to its good interactive features, efficiency and accuracy.

Keywords: Kinect device · Hidden Markov Model · Support Vector Machine
Gesture recognition · Human computer interaction

1 Introduction

Hand gestures interaction is common in our daily life and is one of the most feasible approach when interacting with computers. Now a-days user can interact with computers without any remote tool. Which is quite similar to the interaction between deaf and normal people in the real world. Therefore, significant research has been performed in universities and more and more interaction applications are developed in many different fields such as games, smart TV, medical equipment, robot controller, and so on [1].

There have been many techniques to recognize the hand gestures such as the glove based technique [1, 2]. Mechanical gloves are designed to measure the arm angles and spatial orientation [3]. The users need to wear it while making gestures to secure more precise results, which confines user's freedom. The current state-of-the-art vision-based method focuses on tracking the bare hand and recognizing hand gestures without the

This work has been supported by the National Key R&D Program of China (No. 2016YFB1001502) and National Science Foundation of China (61631010).

© Springer Nature Singapore Pte Ltd. 2018
Y. Wang et al. (Eds.): IGTA 2018, CCIS 875, pp. 635–646, 2018.
https://doi.org/10.1007/978-981-13-1702-6_63

help of any markers or gloves [4]. Such depth cameras as ASUS Xtion PRO and PMD Technologies CamCube, are used to improve the efficiency of hand tracking. However, vision-based recognition of hand gestures is an extremely challenging task because the same gesture varies in shape, trajectory and duration, even for the same person and the vision-based hand gesture system also needs to meet the requirements including real-time performance accuracy and robustness [4].

Certain approaches adopted machine learning algorithms to measure the hand movement. The geometric conversion of hand can be transformed into a feature vector such as centroid, area, Euclidian area among centroid and the initial points of the hand image [5]. However, three dimensional depth information cannot be handled by single camera, for this purpose a high performance depth camera was required.

In this paper we have compared the HGR algorithms based on Kinect based and addressed the best results in details. This survey is particularly depending DHGR. Section 2 outlines the previous researches related to HGR. In Sect. 3 different algorithms and the experimental results are presented in detail, HMM and SVM algorithms are particularly addressed. Finally, in Sect. 4 experimental results and future work are discussed.

2 Related Work

Significant models have been projected for HGR in the existing literature. It was a challenge to adopt RGB camera only under environmental limitations. The vulnerability of shaded spots and human body texture at the back end is not an easy task to deal with. However, now HGR is more vital and fast-tracked by Kinect depth cameras. Microsoft Kinect is able to catch the depth information with relatively high resolution.

Three dimensional Hand/Arm gesticulation setup was proposed by Caputo et al. [6], in which high definition and depth detector were settled to take the initial information. Kinect sensor is not able to take the image from more than one-meter distance as quality and resolution will be affected. To solve this issue, a web camera was connected to the device with the resolution of 1920×1080. To speed up the HGR process it is necessary to minimize the area of captured image.

Truong and Nguyen et al. in 2015 showed an easy HGR terminology that is also dependent on Kinect [7]. The initial step was to extract the applied breakpoints on hand sensed by NITE 2 library given by Prime Sense. The next step was to study the characteristic vector along with the number of gesticulation fingers.

Chen and Luo et al., in 2015 introduced a real-time strategy for HGR with Kinect, which involved gesticulation sorting, information handling, hand localization and scheme instruction [7]. In this approach, Kinect device took the three-dimension motion of hand movement by considering only two states that were opened and closed. Then hand localization was spotted by SVM. With the help of proposed method, the recognition rate of ten Arabic numbers (0 to 9) and twenty-six alphabetic characters were 95.42%.

In [8] Shihab Shahriar Hazari and Asaduzzaman, used Kinect device to capture the hand gesticulation. Different users performed a single gesture in a different way. To differentiated between these minor changes an efficient smart system was needed. An algorithm was designed that can interpret the training and translation state gestures. Hypothetical results of these experiments were 80% to translate the gesticulation of 12 distinct words performed by different persons successfully.

3 Existing Algorithms for Dynamic Hand Gesture Recognition Using Kinect

3.1 Dynamic Hand Gesture Recognition Using SVM

A real-time DHGR technique using Kinect sensor has been proposed along with hand tracking system [9]. SVM is used for the gesture identification, these results were executed by taking a database of 0 to 9 Arabic letters. A mean recognition rate 95.42% can be observed through the results made with this experimental setup.

3.1.1 Hand Localization and Hand Contour Identification

This can be realized by using Kinect sensor along with the computer and contains three main steps; gesture localization, input data execution and gesture identification as shown in Fig. 1. Two main states were defined for the hand localization; Fig. 2 shows the experimenter's hand trajectory in green color when the motion starts and the mark became red when the motion stops.

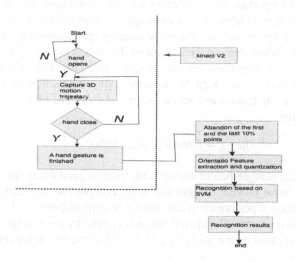

Fig. 1. System block diagram

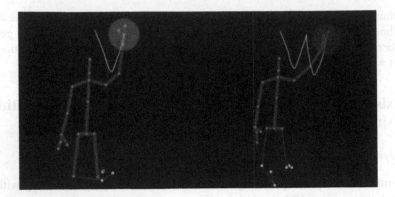

Fig. 2. Gesture localization with different colors (Color figure online)

Once the hand closes and opens again the new gesture is started captured through Kinect. P is sequential gesture and T is points in which every sequence has three points as mentioned in Eq. 1.

$$P = (p_1; p_2; \ldots; p_T); pi = (x_i; y_i; z_I) \qquad (1)$$

3.1.2 Input Data Execution and Image Processing

One of the most important job is filtering for data execution and image processing, because the starting and ending part of the sequence is useless as it consists of irregular vibrations of hand due to shaking. These meaningless parts should be eliminated before further execution. When dealing with Dynamic HGR it is necessary to study the shape of hand, localization, origin and velocity at same time [10]. The orientation feature of the arc tan value is measured with the movement of 2 points in trajectory. To achieve high accuracy rate of feature extraction, all the vectors are filtered according to the following equation.

$$fil_{angle} = filter(fil_b; fil_a; angle); \qquad (2)$$

In which fil_{angle} is angle before and after filtering, fil_a and fil_b are two components of the filter. To achieve precise recognition, filter components are adjusted differently. Vector Quantization is performed to convert the orientated code words to determine the direction of feature vectors. This quantization is created by presenting code words from one to twenty and dividing it equally by 20^0. This discrete vector will be an input to the SVM system.

3.1.3 Implementation of SVM Algorithm

SVM algorithm is the most preferably used algorithm, based on the VC dimension (Vapnik Chervonenkis dimension) theory of statistical learning. The SVM classifier works to study different data values in examples and classifies the data according to these data types. This algorithm creates a training section stored in a database. The database helps to distinguish between samples and decides in which category the sample lies.

Different classifiers have been utilized to categories the samples but a unique classifier is the nearest one to the hyper plane. This line creates a margin line between different types of samples and maximizes the distance between different classes as shown in Fig. 3.

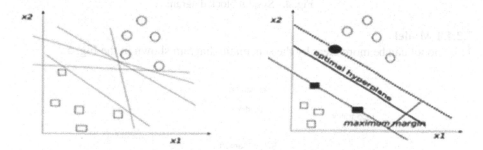

Fig. 3. SVM algorithm classifier

In this proposed method a database system has been implemented. The present gesture is compared with the previous one and closely matched gesture has taken as output from the database. All components are accurately categorized; *200* samples have stored in database as training values of gestures. At testing point each gesture is recognized with the help of eighty training samples.

3.2 Dynamic HGR Using HMM

The algorithm presented here is about dynamic hand trajectory identification done with Kinect device [11]. To achieve high rate of accuracy for gesture identification, HMM model has applied. Experimental results showed that output of gesture recognition rate has improved by this algorithm.

3.2.1 Identification of Gesticulation Trail
Flow of proposed method includes four main steps. As defined bellow and shown in the Fig. 4.

1. Design a model for gesture.
2. Analysis of received model.
3. Identification.
4. Response of System.

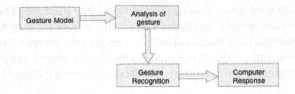

Fig. 4. System block diagram

3.2.1.1 Model
This model can be more clear by the schematic diagram shown in the Fig. 5.

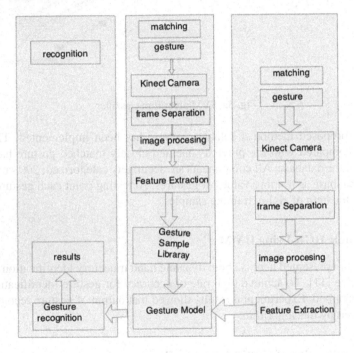

Fig. 5. Gesture localization with different color.

The initial step is frame separation after receiving an input through Kinect camera. Then smoothing process has performed to achieve exact coordinates of hand points to execute it for feature vectors. The trained feature figures are stored into HMM. Once the training process has finished, again input will be taken in similar way. The input data has stored in library, so that gesture identification can be obtained by using HMM. According to the system control, image detection has been performed on the basis of obtained results.

3.2.1.2 Hidden State Variables Distribution
This step is actually about smoothing, which has obtained by applying filter on hidden variables. Errors are generated because of surrounding noise and interference, that might

cause an unstable palm node. To obtain a stable image, spatial filter is utilized. Kinect has the ability to detect the palm coordinates. Therefore, smoothing process is necessary to be applied by Hands Generator.

3.2.1.3 Required Data Collection

A Gesture Starting and Ending Points

a. **Relative Statics:** If $r = 2$, it means that palm nodes moved in a small area, taken as stationary, whereas r is defining the radius.
b. **Start of the valid point:** If the relative static point number is exceeding by a factor N and $N = 15$ in this method. Therefore, it will be defined as start of valid point.
c. **End of the valid point:** When a valid point input is taken and whole gesture has received the valid point supposed to be ended. For more understating see the Fig. 5.

B Components for Data Selection

The data has been collected in the form of "up, down, left, right" and characters "S", "O", "E" seven kinds of gesture trajectory that define style. Each style has 30 training sample; eight other styles (seven defines and a non-defined gesture). Undefined gestures are some random gestures but one can easily distinguish between both gesticulation types. Figure 6(a) and (b), is depicting a trajectory which has followed (by map (above and below) verified by MATLAB figure) by the collected samples.

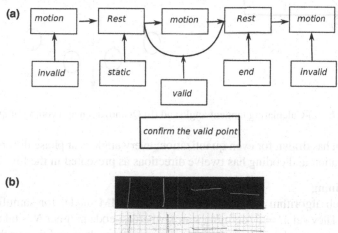

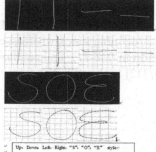

Fig. 6. (a) Collection of valid data. (b) Gesture validation and acquisition

3.2.1.4 Extraction of Feature Values

An important task is to find the trajectory feature values. Final success can only be achieved by studying the pattern of feature vectors whether it will pass or fail. This can only be observed by tangent angle, according to coordinate distance trajectory of gesture. Here they have presented an equation:

$$\theta = \frac{arctan\left(y_{t+1} - y_t\right)}{x_{t+1} - x_t}$$

(3)

In above equation, t is point of the palm moment having coordinates (x_t, y_t), these coordinates will change to x_{t+1}, y_{t+1} at some moment $t + 1$ as shown in the Fig. 7a.

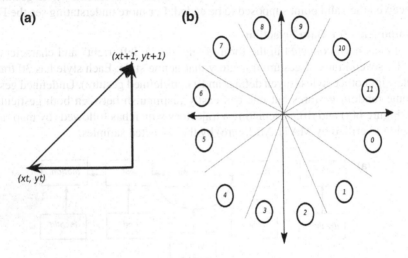

Fig. 7. (a) Calculating tangent angle and (b) Quantization and coding of angle

A pattern has drawn for even quantization; every angle is at phase difference of $\pi/6$. The quantization and coding has twelve directions as presented in the Fig. 7b.

3.2.1.5 Training

Baum-Weltch algorithm has used to trained the HMM model for sampling of each coordinate. They set $M = 5$ (defining state), whereas, code number N is taken to 12 (so that feature vector value is from 0 to 11). Training flow chart and first probability that is $\pi = (1.0\ 0.0\ 0.0\ 0.0\ 0.0\ 0.0)$ [12] is shown in Fig. 8.

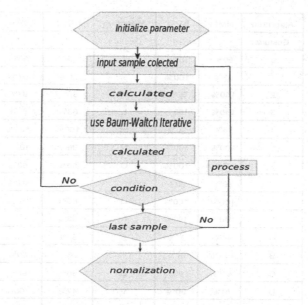

Fig. 8. Flow chart of purposed method using DHMM

4 Experimental Results and Discussion

In this section, a comparison is made for SVM [9] and HMM [11] to analysis which algorithm is best for Dynamic HGR. Different experiments has carried out to rate the results of these two proposed Kinect based algorithms. In case of Dynamic SVM algorithm the experimental data includes twenty-six alphabetical letters and ten Arabic numbers. For the same data they have used the HMM to evaluate the relative results. Figure 9 shows HMM and SVM recognition rate comparison that is 82.86% and 95.42% respectively.

Algorithm	HMM	SVM	Algorithm	HMM	SVM
Gesture	"	"	Gesture	"	"
0	60%	97%	I	100%	93%
1	67%	100%	J	70%	97%
2	100%	90%	K	86%	97%
3	100%	100%	L	83%	87%
4	96%	96%	M	100%	100%
5	100%	100%	N	96%	100%
6	27%	100%	O	50%	60%
7	90%	90%	P	60%	97%
8	100%	100%	Q	60%	97%
9	100%	100%	R	93%	90%
A	96%	97%	S	60%	100%
B	100%	97%	T	96%	80%
C	47%	100%	U	96%	96%
D	70%	90%	V	47%	100%
E	90%	90%	W	83%	97%
F	87%	100%	X	83%	97%
G	100%	100%	Y	100%	100%
H	100%	100%	Z	100%	100%
Average Rate				82.86%	95.42%
t				42.63s	1.02s

Fig. 9. Recognition rate with SVM in comparison with HMM.

In contrast with HMM, SVM showed more real-time results for these data types. However, in the case of HMM, forward and backward algorithms used to specify the data samples. In an array of the program, real time trajectory coordinates have saved. Than backward probability is estimated with the help of HMM. Figure 10 shows the extracted results of HMM, whereas 80% average recognition rate has observed from other algorithms [13]. Although, many applications can use these results in several ways like; keyboard control through gestures and photo editing etc.

kinds / style result	Traditional test	Sample test			Real-time test		
Gestures	Recognition rate	Total sample	correct	Recognition rate	Total sample	correct	Recognition rate
←	---	15	15	100%	3PX15	44	97.78%
→	---	15	15	100%	3PX15	45	100%
↑	---	15	15	100%	3PX15	45	100%
↓	---	15	15	100%	3PX15	45	100%
 ς	88%	15	14	93.33%	3PX15	40	88.89%
 Q	76%	15	14	93.33%	3PX15	44	97.79%
 ε	80%	15	15	100%	3PX15	43	95.56%
Non-defined	---	15	13	86.67%	3PX15	39	86.67%

Fig. 10. Recognition Results Using HMM

5   Conclusion

This article is an overview of gesture recognition systems for DHGR using Kinect, and focuses on the gesture recognition algorithm based on SVM and HMM. SVM operates with the help of training data stored in the backend database. DHGR based on Kinect sensor is proposed to utilize the recognition algorithm of SVM. First, Kinect device capture the image, which samples 3D motion trajectories of the hand gesture. Secondly, all gesture sequences are used to extract orientation feature and then filtered and quantized has been performed respectively. Finally, the experimental results showed efficiency of proposed method. On the other hand, HMM based DHGR has time invariance, automatic segmentation and classification advantages. In this case, they put forward a Kinect based DHGR and used the palm node which has defined by Kinect device. The results showed that final recognition rate has improved as compared to other traditional algorithms. These algorithms can be further enhanced to reduce the rate of error and to increase the average data recognition rate. Whereas, recognition data rate can be enhanced by implementing some other state-of-art algorithms like Convolution Neural Networks (CNNN) and Recurrent Neural Networks (RNN) for these data types.

References

1. Shrivastava, R.: A hidden Markov model based dynamic hand gesture recognition system using OpenCV. In: 2013 IEEE 3rd International Advance Computing Conference (IACC). IEEE (2013)
2. Ren, Z., Meng, J., Yuan, J.: Depth camera based hand gesture recognition and its applications in human-computer-interaction. In: 2011 8th International Conference on Information, Communications and Signal Processing (ICICS). IEEE (2011)
3. Liu, K., et al.: Fusion of inertial and depth sensor data for robust hand gesture recognition. IEEE Sens. J. **14**(6), 1898–1903 (2014)
4. Tan, W., Wu, C., Zhao, S., Li, J.: Dynamic hand gesture recognition using motion trajectories and key frames. In: 2nd (ICACC) (2010)
5. Lamberti, L., Camastra, F.: Real-time hand gesture recognition using a color glove. In: Maino, G., Foresti, G.L. (eds.) ICIAP 2011. LNCS, vol. 6978, pp. 365–373. Springer, Heidelberg (2011). https://doi.org/10.1007/978-3-642-24085-0_38
6. Caputo, M., Denker, K., Dums, B., Umlauf, G.: 3D Hand gesture recognition based on sensor fusion of commodity hardware. In: Mensch and Computer, vol. 2012, pp. 293–302 (2012)
7. Vinh, T.Q., Tri, N.T.: Hand gesture recognition based on depth image using kinect sensor. In: 2015 2nd National Foundation for Science and Technology Development Conference on Information and Computer Science (2015)
8. Hazari, S.S., Asaduzzaman: Designing a sign language translation system using kinect motion sensor device. In: International Conference on Electrical, Computer and Communication Engineering (ECCE), Coxs Bazar, Bangladesh, 16–18 February 2017
9. Chen, Y., Luo, B.: A real-time dynamic hand gesture recognition system using kinect sensor. In: Proceedings of the 2015 IEEE Conference on Robotics and Biomimetics, Zhuhai, China, 6–9 December 2015
10. Wang, X., Xia, M., Cai, H., Gao, Y., Cattani, C.: Hidden-Markov-models- based dynamic hand gesture recognition. Math. Prob. Eng. **2012**, 1–10 (2012)
11. Wang, Y., Yang, C., Wu, X.: Kinect based dynamic hand gesture recognition algorithm research. In: 2012 4th International Conference on Intelligent Human-Machine Systems and Cybernetics (2012)
12. Roccetti, M., Marfia, G., Semeraro, A.: Playing into the wild: a gesture-based interface for gaming in public spaces. J. Vis. Commun. Image Represent. **23**(3), 426–440 (2012)
13. GNU General Public License. "OpenNIUser Guide", pp. 6–9 (2011)

Collaborative Simulation Method for Research of Armored Equipment Battle Damaged

Jun-qing Huang[✉], Wei Zhang, Wei Liu, and Tuan Wang

Training Center, Army Armored Military Academy, Beijing, China
tigerhjq@126.com, zhangwei@126.com, liuwei@126.com,
wangtuan@126.com

Abstract. The collaborative simulation method was used to guide simulation research of armored equipment battle damaged included many realm complicated technology. Entity models of armored equipment were established base on basal function part of armored equipment partitioned and high precision entity model platform used. Numerical models of ammunition power were established base on explicit dynamic finite element analyzing program. Basal data of armored equipment battle damaged research by numerical analysis. Base on entity models of armored equipment and characteristic of ammunition damaged element, the result of armored equipment battle damaged was confirmed base on mutual effect of ammunition and armored equipment analyzed and the rule of armored equipment part damaged applied. By practice, the method of armored equipment battle damaged simulation based on collaborative simulation is feasible and operational, it can be used to research armored equipment battle damaged.

Keywords: Collaborative simulation · Armored equipment · Battle damaged

1 Introduction

With the development of simulation technology, simulation technology had gradually developed from single subject without collaboration into multi-disciplinary and inter-disciplinary collaborative simulation facing the complex engineering. For complex armored equipment battle damaged simulation environment, in order to complete and refine armored equipment battle damaged simulation model, it came down to machinery, mechanics and other fields or subjects. It was impossible by simple simulation means to solve such complex technological problems related to multi-fields.

Nowadays, CAD software based on three dimensional entity modeling technique and CAE software based on finite element technique had been increasingly mature, and had been widely used in designing and analyzing mechanical product. While professional software of different subject areas furnishes effective analysis tools for simulation focused differently. CAD software lay particular emphasis on 3D entity designing, however, its analysis ability was weak. CAE software engineering analysis ability was impressive while it was weak in modeling. The characteristics somehow made the functions of software were not to be given to the full. Develop collaborative simulation could bring the advantages of different software into simulation environment of

© Springer Nature Singapore Pte Ltd. 2018
Y. Wang et al. (Eds.): IGTA 2018, CCIS 875, pp. 647–656, 2018.
https://doi.org/10.1007/978-981-13-1702-6_64

armored equipment battle damage, deeply and specifically analysis the impact of multiple factors at complex battlefield environment, it made it possible to reflect equipment battle damage circumstance roundly and faithfully.

The basic train of thought to study equipment battle damage based on collaborative simulation first was to establish solid model of equipment, and on this basis establish material model of protective armored equipment. Then analysis armored equipment damage effect by finite element method aiming at different attack factors, to generate a table for mapping attack factors to equipment damage components. As thus, in armored equipment system counterwork simulation, according to specific damage event parameters, it was able to get sensible equipment damage components and equipment damage degree and provide these damage dates to damage effect of armored equipment system counterwork simulation environment, then simulation precision could be improved.

2   Equipment Solid Models

Equipment battle damage analysis needed to establish descriptive model of equipment. With the development of computer simulation technology, by combination of equipment battle damage analysis technology and computer application technology, it generated high resolution solid model for describing equipment. In other words, by modeling three-dimensional entity based on equipment components, established functional relation between different components and systems. It integrally described geometrical, structural and functional information of equipment, laying the foundation for the high resolution assess of equipment battle damage. To establish equipment solid model that meet the conditions of equipment battle damage analysis, firstly it needed to ensure the basic functional components of armored equipment, then established equipment solid model by using solid modeling tool.

2.1   Ensure the Basic Functional Components of Armored Equipment

The basic function of armored equipment was functions that essential for armored equipment to accomplish current tasks. By using system diagram and functional block diagram, analyzed each subsystem, module and component one by one from top to down to ensure which were the components that accomplish basic function. For example, according to operational mission, it was able to be divided into fire-power, mobility, protection, communication capacity. According to the principle of dividing basic functional components, analyze comprehensively from scope and granularity to ensure the basic functional components of a type of crawler-type IFV. As shown in Table 1.

2.2   Establish Equipment Solid Models

According to the certain basic functional components of armored equipment, by using high resolution armored equipment solid model building platform, equipment solid model could be established. There were different build platforms such as WORK-BENCH, SOLIWORKS, LS-DYNA to establish high resolution equipment solid model. They integrated CAD and CAE technology, with abundant model interface,

Table 1. Basic functional unit of the armored equipment

System	Basic functional unit	System	Basic functional unit
Engine	Engine body	Lubrication system	Oil pump
	Cylinder head		Oil filter
	...		...
Engine fuel system	Fuel injection pump	Cooling system	Water pump
	Oil atomizer		Water radiator
	Fuel delivery pipe		Water inlet and outlet pipe
	Fuel delivery pump	The exhaust and the pressurization system	Manifold
	Fuel filter		Air cleaner
	Oil tank		Electric dust extraction pump
...	...	...	...

tolerant materials and structural analysis functions. It could provide high resolution model data for equipment battle analysis. The cooperation environment of ANSYS/WORKBENCH was shown in Fig. 1. Figure 2 was 3D solid model of a type tank inside and outside components, built on ANSYS/WORKBENCH platform, which was divided based on trim size and basic functional components (Some had been simplified reasonably).

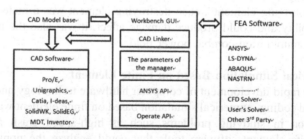

Fig. 1. The collaborative simulation environment base on ANSYS-Workbench program

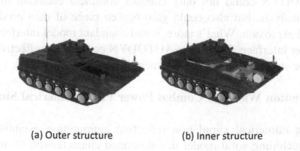

(a) Outer structure   (b) Inner structure

Fig. 2. Three-dimensional entity model of the tank

3   Equipment Damage Analysis Based on Finite Element

Equipment damage analysis based on finite element mainly used nonlinear dynamic analysis program based on finite element, established numerical modeling of ammunition combat power field, by numerical analysis, gained basic data for equipment damage analysis; with the goal of structuring equipment solid model, by analyzing interaction between ammunition and target, established intersection spatial relation between ammunition and target, according to characteristic of ammunition damage element, integrated equipment components damage criterion, to ensure equipment components damage degree, thus providing basic data for damage effect analysis in armored equipment system combat simulation environment.

3.1   Ammunition Warhead Combat Power Field Numerical Simulation Analysis

Ammunition warhead combat power field numerical simulation analysis was to establish numerical simulation modeling of ammunition warhead by analyzing knock-on effect and penetration effect of ammunition, then gained simulation result of ammunition combat power field (fragment, jet flow quality, direction, shape, speed, kinetic energy, impulse) by dynamic analysis based on finite element, it provided necessary basic data for equipment damage analysis.

3.1.1   Ammunition Warhead Combat Power Field

Ammunition warhead combat power field was a collection of all of the elements that could damage target inside or around the target by ammunition warhead. Each element was called "destroying element", each destroying element was a material carrier that had damage ability and could produce damage affect, it was also the minimum component unit of ammunition combat power field.

3.1.2   Numerical Simulation Based on Finite Element

Along with the rapid development of computer hardware technology and the advent of large-scale fluid coding, numerical simulation based on finite element was becoming an effective method in studying problems such as high-speed crash and explosion. Nowadays, finite element software tools that could analyze the nonlinear establish impact dynamics mainly included ANSYS/DYNA, ESIA and AUTODYN. Among the software, AUTODYN could not only conduct nonlinear establish impact dynamics finite element analysis, but also could gain broken piece of data producing by high-speed crash and explosion. What's more, it had abundant model interface and favorable human-computer interface. Therefore, AUTODYN could be an effective finite element analysis tool for studying armored equipment battle damage.

3.1.3   Ammunition Warhead Combat Power Field Numerical Simulation Analysis

By establishing numerical simulation reflecting ammunition establish and material characteristic, including solid model that described characteristic of ammunition warhead and material model that reflected material characteristic, with boundary condition

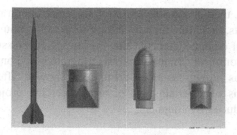

Fig. 3. The entity model of typical ammunition warhead

set, by numerical analysis based on AUTODYN finite element analysis tool, then it was able to get numerical simulation data of ammunition combat power field.

(1) Numerical analysis model

To gain the numerical simulation result of ammunition warhead combat power field, it was necessary to establish reasonable numerical analysis model of ammunition warhead, including definition of unit type, establish size, material parameter, contacting type and so on.

(1) Solid model

To be able to show forming process of combat power field and condition of damage element directly during ammunition combat power field numerical simulation analysis, it was necessary to establish solid model of ammunition warhead that including composition and establish, definition of unit type, mesh model. According to requirement to ammunition's tactical function and its structure characteristic, using ANSYS/WORKBENCH modeling tool, established solid model of ammunition warhead. Figure 3 was a solid model of a type ammunition warhead.

(2) Material model

Material model was a kind of model that describes characteristic and condition of materials, it could reflect condition and function of material. It mainly described by constitutive equations and state equations.

Constitutive equations reflected bias response of materials, it was connected with strain, strain rate and inner energy. In finite element dynamic analysis, it reflected constitutive relation of material mainly by intensity model that could describe nonlinear elastic-plastic response of objects. Nowadays, intensity models that used in dynamic analysis program included Johnson-Cook model, Steinberg-Guinan model and so on. State equations were relations that were related to pressure, density and thermodynamic parameters, reflecting volume features of material. Equations that conducted ammunition damage dynamic analysis mainly included Linear, JWL state equation.

(2) Ammunition warhead combat power field numerical simulation

According to solid model and material model that established for ammunition warhead, integrated boundary conditions that were set, by nonlinear dynamic analysis based on finite element, the continuum to solve discrete into a finite number of units, then it was able to obtain the ammunition power field numerical simulation results, including the formation process of ammunition power field, the characteristics of damage element, like speed, power, pressure, etc. The analysis process by the nonlinear dynamic analysis program based on finite element named AUTODYN was shown as Fig. 4. Figure 5 showed after the finite element dynamic analysis of a certain type of armor-piercing projectile penetrating the target plate produced by fragment.

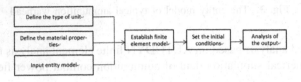

Fig. 4. The analytical process of AUTODYN program

Fig. 5. The fragments state after the armour-piercing warhead penetration the steel target

3.2   Computing Equipment Damage Components

3.2.1   Armored Equipment Vulnerability Analysis

Vulnerability for armored equipment, mainly for ammunition analysis of armored equipment produced by different damage element tourism by the target geometry, structure, function and related features. Usually, penetrator, play sunder armor class anti-armor ammunition was the main play of the armored equipment damage; they were heavily dependent on projectile or jet after breakdown equipment protective armor to produce a large number of broken piece of equipment damage internal components. The capacity of armored equipment protective armor against the breakdown by penetrator, sunder armor ejection flow and its related factors such as material, structure, thickness and inclination.

3.2.2   Intersection Space Relationship Analysis of Ammo and Target

Visual simulation platform was adopted to establish the intersection spatial relations of ammo and target. Joined ammunition mutilate metadata(fragment space coordinate, azimuth angle, etc.), equipment physical model into the visual simulation platform, using its intersection behavior module, through the simulation analysis it was able to obtain mutilate element killing rays formation and fellowship with parts of the visualization process, as well as the intersection parts statistics. This kind of platform included VEGA, CRY, VIRTOOLS, etc. Figure 6 showed how killing rays based on VIRTOOLS form and process of solving the intersection armored equipment parts.

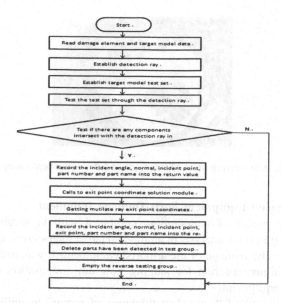

Fig. 6. The Solution flow of radial forming and intersecting with the target

As ammunition power field simulation and the intersection simulation of mutilate element and target was conducted by two different simulation platform, and there was no collaborative simulation interface to conduct data interaction between them, however, they could be associated with programming languages (such as C, C++, DELPHI language, etc.) to realize interface and was able to conduct file operation, it made it possible to realize the collaborative simulation by programming language and shared data files between the indirect way. Table 2 showed the text file of the intersecting collaborative simulation interface of ammunition power field and mutilate element with the target achieved by C langue.

Figure 7 showed the intersection simulation results of fragments and the inner car when the protective armor of penetrator breakdown through intersecting collaborative simulation of ammunition power field and the mutilate element with the target.

Table 2. The alternant document used in collaborative simulation environment

File name	Instructions
OldLine.txt	The file is for virtools reading data, record the ballistic trajectory of the end trajectory of ammunition
position.txt	The file is for virtools reading data, according to the content of the file, virtools configure tanks automatically, they are position and angle information of tanks
tank.txt	The file is for virtools reading data, when it is 1, virtools read the position and angle information in file named position_tank.txt

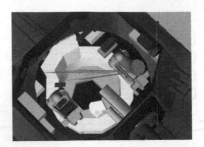

Fig. 7. Intersecting state of fragment and the equipment inner parts

3.2.3   The Armored Equipment Parts Damage Judgment

According to the power of ammunition, combined with vulnerability of armored equipment, and through the analysis of ammo and target intersection spatial relations, it was able to ensure the damage of the armored equipment. It was necessary to specify the appropriate failure criterion for judging how did ammunition mutilate element damage armored equipment.

Adopted the theory of "equivalent thickness of armor" to unified evaluation of different structure and different materials or remaining parts against fragment jet collision damage. "Equivalent thickness of armor" was a variety of different materials, different structure parts according to the density of the material and components of geometric parameters of the equivalent to the corresponding equivalent thickness of armored steel. "Equivalent thickness of armor" could be conversed through the formula below:

$$h_d = \frac{r}{7.85} \times h$$

In the formula, r was the original material density, h was geometric thickness of components structure.

Usually, the kinetic energy or specific kinetic energy of the fragment was used to measure the ability to damage. Specific kinetic energy of weight pieces could be calculated through the formula below.

$$e = m^{1/3}v^2/k$$

In the formula, m was weight of fragment, v was speed of fragment, k was form factor of fragment.

Under the condition of knowing specific kinetic energy of killing fragment and equivalent thickness of target components armor, it was able to judge the degree that the weight fragment damaged the components. For homogeneous armor steel, the specific kinetic energy of the average consumption per mm thickness fragment was 470 J/cm^2, according to the equivalent thickness (h) of components, it was able to determine the specific kinetic energy of components consumption fragment was

470 X h, by comparing specific kinetic energy of fragment with that of components consumption, it was able to judge component damaged or not.

$$e_s = e_p - e_b$$

In the formula, e_s was surplus specific kinetic energy, e_p was fragment specific kinetic energy, e_b was specific kinetic energy of components consumption fragment. Judgment method as follows:

If $e_s > 0$, component damaged, after calculating the residual wear energy into a component under the ray direction.

If $e_s = 0$, component damaged, turn to next fragment killing rays.

If $e_s < 0$, component doesn't damaged, turn to next fragment killing rays.

To analysis damage components, it was necessary to one by one in the direction of each fragment killer ray to determine each component damage.

3.2.4   The Equipment Damage Components Database

Through the equipment damage simulation analysis that based on finite element, built equipment damage components database. Database was made up of a number of ammunition damage efficiency data table and an index table, as shown in Fig. 8, it was mainly to provide basic data support system of armored equipment simulation.

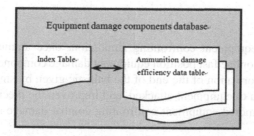

Fig. 8. The Database composing of equipment damage components

Ammunition damage efficiency data table divided according to ammunition and equipment model, and each table in the combination of the ammunition and equipment with other tables didn't overlap. To facilitate the query, unifying ammunition damage efficiency data table named "XX (ammunition) to XX (equipment) of ammunition damage efficiency data tables". These tables all used components structure level description. Table 3 showed through the numerical simulation analysis, the damage components circumstance a certain type of penetrator produced after conducting penetration to the tank.

Index table was used to quickly locate ammunition damage efficiency data tables that need to be query. Its data structures contained three fields, including "Ammunition Name", "Equipment Name" and "Table Name", among them, the "Ammunition Name" and "Equipment Name" was index entries, the "Table Name" was a pointer. While

Table 3. The datasheet of armour-piercing warhead damage the tank

Impact point (m)	Speed (m/s)	Incidence angle (°)	Damage component
(−0.41, 1.96, 0.49)	1500	10	Elevator, Car battery, Rotating lose play machine, Instrument panel
(−0.41, 1.96, 0.49)	1500	20	Rotating lose play machine, Driver micro night-vision goggles, Combination switch box
(−0.41, 1.96, 0.49)	1500	30	Motor expanding machine, Motor expanding machine control box, Turret seat, Commander radio, Distribution of electrical box, Gun control box
(−0.41, 1.96, 0.49)	...	...	...
...	...	...	...

querying the table, it was necessary to match the keywords in the name of the ammunition and equipment with ammo and target names of combat simulation, the same keyword matching success, then finding that records, according to the record pointer of the "table" could be classified as the corresponding ammunition damage efficiency data tables.

4 Conclusion

In the process of equipment confronting simulation, once ammunition damaged to equipment, it could online fast position equipment damage components database tables, according to the information of the end of the ballistic given by simulation, fast online queries damage data of equipment attacked, and improved the precision and credibility of the system of armored equipment confronting combat damage simulation.

References

1. Budiansky, B., O'connell, R.J.: Elastic moduli of a cracked solid. Int. J. Solids Struct. **12**, 81–97 (1976)
2. Grady, D.E., Kipp, M.E.: Continuum modeling of explosive fracture in oil shale. Int. J. Rock Mech. Min. Sci. **17**, 147–157 (1980)
3. Karless, H.E.V.: Computer simulation of shaped charge jet fragmentation. In: 19th International Symposium of Ballistics, Interlaken, Switzerland (2001)
4. Blache, A., Weimann, K.: Shaped charge with jetting projectile for extended targets. In: 17th International Symposium on Ballistics, Midrand, South Africa (1998)
5. Wu, Y.: The Research on Cumulative Penetrator Detonating the Shelled Explosive on the High Range. Nanjing Institute of Technology, Nanjing (2007)

Author Index

Ahmad, Mubashir 536
Ai, Danni 536
Ai, Mingjing 114

Bao, Xiuguo 192
Bian, Huiwen 302
Bu, Qirong 442

Cao, Tingrong 22
Cao, Youxia 506
Chang, Yulan 626
Che, Manqiang 471
Che, Wujun 483
Chen, Hao 330
Chen, Lei 319
Chen, Lijiang 45
Cui, Lei 442
Cui, Zhenchao 98

Dai, Lin 11
David, Rempel 605
Deng, Siqi 70
Ding, Jianwei 411, 421, 461
Ding, Wei-long 1
Dou, Wentao 45
Du, Longfei 135
Du, Minghan 451

Fan, Yachun 432
Fang, Han 546
Feng, Jun 442

Gao, Fei 238
Gao, Ke 192
Gao, Xue 616
Guan, Qiuyu 281
Guo, Dongqiao 106, 124
Guo, Zhengkun 272
Guo, Zihui 252

Han, Fu-Qiang 596
Hao, Shuang 546
He, Qili 88

Hu, Guozhen 252
Hu, Nan 586
Hu, Youcheng 292
Hua, Wenqiang 88
Huang, Jun-qing 647
Huang, Kun 566
Huang, Lin 292
Huang, Xin 201

Ikram, Aamrah 635

Jia, Xibin 380
Jiang, Bo 506
Jiang, Sicong 390
Jiang, Yiran 546
Jiang, Zhiguo 310, 546

Kang, Houliang 146, 157
Kang, Xuejing 252, 263

Le, Chao 578
Li, Chenglong 359, 494, 517
Li, Chunxiao 228
Li, Feng 114
Li, Guandong 238
Li, Guangchuan 605
Li, Hongmei 626
Li, Jin 80
Li, Lihua 22
Li, Lin 494
Li, Miao 319
Li, Naimin 98
Li, Ruikun 281
Li, Xu 212
Li, Yun 212, 272
Li, Zhaoxi 180
Liang, Geng 135
Liang, Xinyan 517
Liao, Keliang 88
Liu, Dunge 330
Liu, Jie 403
Liu, Jing 370
Liu, Junyu 281

Liu, Sa   292
Liu, Shan   556, 566
Liu, Wei   647
Liu, Xiaobo   390
Liu, Yang   281
Liu, Yue   451, 605, 616, 635
Liu, Yunfeng   380
Lu, Ling   22
Luo, Bin   359, 506
Luo, Dening   168
Luo, Lin-feng   1
Luo, Xiaoyan   70, 527
Luo, Xuanshu   252
Luo, Zhaohui   80

Ma, Huimin   578, 586
Ma, Yanxin   341
Ma, Yunpeng   359
Mao, Xia   45
Meng, Cai   180
Meng-jie, Jin   1
Ming, Anlong   263

Nie, Guangyu   451
Nie, Shanlan   310

Pan, Yuting   57
Peng, Yanhong   302
Peng, Yuxin   201

Qadri, Syed Furqan   536
Qi, Jing   98
Qiu, Feng   390
Qiu, Xiaohui   135
Qu, Zhenshen   281

Shao, Xuehui   586
Shen, Fang   370
Sheng, Weifan   88
Shi, Guowei   212, 272
Shi, Peng   349
Shi, Shufeng   349
Shi, Tianyang   330
Shi, Weifeng   442
Shi, Xiaofeng   70, 527
Shi, Zhenwei   330
Shu, Chang   403
Shui, Wuyang   432
Song, Xuedong   403

Song, Yong   212, 272
Sun, Pengfei   263
Sun, Zhan-Li   596

Tang, Jin   359, 494
Tang, Rui   556
Tang, Wenzhong   192
Tu, ZhengZheng   494

Wan, Yuan   57
Wan, Zang-xin   1
Wang, Dongdong   390
Wang, Guizhao   359
Wang, Hongyu   442
Wang, Jie   88
Wang, Jingxian   319
Wang, Lei   22
Wang, Liangjun   302
Wang, Mingkai   238
Wang, Pengrui   483
Wang, Rong   411, 421, 461
Wang, Runling   471
Wang, Tuan   647
Wang, Wenli   22
Wang, Xiaopei   380
Wang, Xin   135
Wang, Xinyue   616
Wang, Ya-Min   596
Wang, Yigang   220
Wang, Yongtian   451, 536, 605
Wei, Quanmao   310
Wei, Xiaodong   106, 124
Weng, Dongdong   106, 124
Wu, Peng   370
Wu, Xi   330
Wu, Yifan   442
Wu, Zeye   483
Wu, Zizhao   220

Xia, Zhenghuan   330
Xiao, Gang   98
Xiao, Yang   341
Xiao, Yujie   380
Xie, Fengying   403
Xing, Wanli   35
Xiong, Changzhen   471
Xiong, Longye   292
Xu, Yan   1

Yang, Changhui   292
Yang, Dawei   380
Yang, Jian   536
Yang, Junli   546
Yang, Wenzhu   98
Yang, Xin   212
Yang, Yang   302
Yang, Yifan   35, 80
Yang, Yuting   146, 157
Yang, Zhenghan   380
Yao, Chao   263
Yin, Congli   432
Yuan, Qingxi   88
Yuan, Yuan   319

Zeng, Jing   228
Zeng, Lanling   302
Zeng, WeiHui   319
Zhang, Chunju   238
Zhang, Fengjun   135, 228
Zhang, Haopeng   310, 546
Zhang, Hong   35, 80
Zhang, Huan   180
Zhang, Jian   319
Zhang, Jianing   390
Zhang, Jianwei   168
Zhang, Jun   341
Zhang, Junhao   57
Zhang, Mingdong   192

Zhang, Tong   411
Zhang, Wei   647
Zhang, Xiaofeng   421
Zhang, Xiaohong   35
Zhang, Xueying   238
Zhang, Yuan   506
Zhang, Yunhui   220
Zhang, Yunzhou   390
Zhang, Yuxin   281
Zhang, Zeyu   80
Zhang, Zichun   517
Zhao, Shangnan   212, 272
Zhao, Yufei   212, 272
Zhao, Yushan   349
Zheng, Aihua   359
Zheng, Aiyu   114
Zheng, Longshuai   228
Zhou, Hongning   135
Zhou, Jinglin   461
Zhou, Liangyu   527
Zhou, Min   341
Zhou, Mingquan   432
Zhou, Zhiping   220
Zhu, Peiping   88
Zhu, Zhongzhu   88
Zou, Jiancheng   471
Zu, Yueran   192
Zuo, Chun   228
Zuo, Qing   11